Handbook of Ontologies for Business Interaction

Peter Rittgen
University College of Borås, Sweden

INFORMATION SCIENCE REFERENCE

Hershey · New York

Acquisitions Editor:	Kristin Klinger
Development Editor:	Kristin Roth
Senior Managing Editor:	Jennifer Neidig
Managing Editor:	Sara Reed
Copy Editor:	Jeannie Porter
Typesetter:	Amanda Appicello
Cover Design:	Lisa Tosheff
Printed at:	Yurchak Printing Inc.

Published in the United States of America by
Information Science Reference (an imprint of IGI Global)
701 E. Chocolate Avenue, Suite 200
Hershey PA 17033
Tel: 717-533-8845
Fax: 717-533-8661
E-mail: cust@igi-global.com
Web site: http://www.igi-global.com/reference

and in the United Kingdom by
Information Science Reference (an imprint of IGI Global)
3 Henrietta Street
Covent Garden
London WC2E 8LU
Tel: 44 20 7240 0856
Fax: 44 20 7379 0609
Web site: http://www.eurospanonline.com

Library of Congress Cataloging-in-Publication Data

Handbook of ontologies for business interaction / Peter Rittgen, editor.
   p. cm.
  Summary: "This book documents high-quality research addressing ontological issues relevant to the modeling of enterprises and information systems in general, and business processes in particular covering both static and dynamic aspects of structural concepts. It provides reference content to researchers, practitioners, and scholars in the fields of language design, information systems, enterprise modeling, artificial intelligence, and the Semantic Web"--Provided by publisher.
  Includes bibliographical references and index.
  ISBN-13: 978-1-59904-660-0 (hardcover)
  ISBN-13: 978-1-59904-662-4 (ebook)
  1. Business enterprises--Computer networks. 2. Ontologies (Information retrieval) 3. Knowledge representation (Information theory) 4. Conceptual structures (Information theory) 5. Semantic Web. I. Rittgen, Peter, 1964-
  HD30.37.H365 2008
  658.4'038011--dc22
                2007023438

British Cataloguing in Publication Data
A Cataloguing in Publication record for this book is available from the British Library.

Table of Contents

Section I
Ontological Foundations

Section II
General Domain Ontologies for Business Interaction

Section III
Specialized Domain Ontologies

Section IV
Building Business Interaction Ontologies

Section V
Applying Ontologies in a Business Context

Section VI
Ontology Management

Detailed Table of Contents

Section I
Ontological Foundations

Chapter I

This chapter shows the importance of semantic technologies for the future of computing and the role that ontologies play in that context. It delivers a compact introduction into a wide field and helps the reader in developing a better appreciation of the remaining chapters that highlight particular aspects in greater detail.

Chapter II

This chapter shows how Aristotelian ontologies can be realized with the Web ontology language (OWL). The authors argue for the benefits of the Aristotelian approach to ontological modeling and discuss a detailed example of an OWL representation of such an ontology. They also deliver a number of reasons indicating advantages of an epistemological approach over the commonly used object-oriented approach in the area of domain knowledge engineering.

Chapter III

In this chapter the authors take a realist stance in approaching business ontologies with the aim of turning them into a more faithful representation of the targeted portion of reality. They suggest realism-based ontologies as the foundation, in particular basic formal ontology and granular partition theory, to describe the generic aspects of corporate memories. Referent tracking is used to capture the specific aspects, such as keeping track of each individual business entity.

Section II
General Domain Ontologies for Business Interaction

Chapter IV

This chapter is a good example of the framework approach to a general domain ontology of business. The authors' framework is called content ontology design patterns (CODePs) where the constituents are described by modular, interoperable ontologies, for example, for descriptions and situations and plans. These CODePs can be used to reconstruct existing business modeling languages in terms of a common formal context.

Chapter V

This chapter takes a completely different approach towards a domain ontology for business interaction. Instead of following a line of philosophical reasoning, the authors take their point of departure in experiences from action research projects and generalize them into a theory called business action theory. This theory in turn is grounded in a general, albeit informal, ontology of the social realm, socio-instrumental pragmatism, where the focus is on social (inter)action that is mediated by artifacts.

Chapter VI

This chapter starts from the same ontology as the previous chapter but aims at a different goal: formalizing the existing framework of socio-instrumental pragmatism by concretizing and refining the basic constituents, for example, actors, actions, and objects, and by providing an axiomatization in the form of associations between the constituents. The authors thus arrive at a meta-model that they apply to the reconstruction of an existing business modeling language to demonstrate the generality and descriptive power of the meta-model.

Chapter VII

In this chapter the authors start from the assumption that self-awareness is an important prerequisite for business action, both human and organizational. But while self-awareness comes as a natural ingredient with human beings, it has to be developed and maintained in the case of organizations. To support this endeavour, the authors suggest an architecture and an ontology as a high-level business modeling framework. This framework combines social, organizational, and psychological theories with enterprise modeling approaches.

Chapter VIII

In this chapter, the authors aim at supporting the communication between business and IT experts at the requirements stage of an information systems development project. Their approach is supposed to facilitate the creation of a specific enterprise model that captures knowledge about the organization and its processes and that can be used to build an agent-oriented requirements specification of the information system to be built and the organizational environment in which it operates. To this end they develop an integrated meta-model or ontology of an enterprise in general that includes concepts from the managerial and information systems domains. These general concepts are instantiated with concrete entities from the particular organization.

Section III
Specialized Domain Ontologies

Chapter IX

This chapter introduces a basic ontology of ICT management that comprises the concepts policy, project, assets and evaluation. The authors then go on to refine this core ontology by studying the possible contributions that some of the major organizational theories can make: stakeholder theory, theory of fit, theory of behavioral integration, agency theory, transaction cost theory, and theory of images of organization.

Chapter X

This chapter provides a specialized domain ontology for the memory of an organization. The development of this ontology follows a five-step process, two of which are elaborated in the chapter: analysis and structuring, and evaluation. The former addresses the classification of concepts derived from the literature and how they are mapped to ontological constructs. The results of this step are then validated in the evaluation step by assessing the conceptual coverage of the ontology.

Chapter XI

In this chapter the authors start by identifying the interface between organizations and their information systems as the primary source of security risks. In order to address security issues, we therefore have to model the information systems together with their organizational environment. The authors provide a modeling language for this purpose that comprises a number of relevant concepts based on permission, delegation, and trust, and their Datalog semantics.

In this chapter the authors present a method for eliciting knowledge for the design of a corporate intranet within a government agency to solve knowledge management-related issues, for example, work duplication, document location, and accessing tacit expertise. The method combines soft systems methodology, causal cognitive mapping, and brainstorming to create a knowledge ontology using UML class diagrams. It is suitable for understanding nonroutine but rigorous knowledge and making it accessible to the designers of solutions.

This chapter focuses on the integration of business processes at the interface between partners in a value chain or network. This integration is tedious because partners not only differ in the way they organize their processes but also in the languages they speak. This chapter attempts to solve the integration of diverging vocabularies by enriching the process modeling language of Petri nets with the Web ontology language (OWL).

This chapter applies ontology to a model-driven approach to business analysis and transformation. It relates business processes and components on one hand to IT solutions and capabilities on the other hand at different stages of the transformation. This is done by semantic models that show potential causes of problems during transformation and help with the identification of possible solutions. The authors also present a corresponding ontology management system that can be used in model-driven business transformation.

This chapter suggests a framework for information organization that is formalized as a reference model. This framework captures the specifics (e.g., dynamics and uncertainty) and functional requirements (e.g., information standardization and problem-orientation) of a supply chain which is interpreted as a managerial, dynamic, complex, and open system. It comprises an information modeling language that captures different aspects of the information system support for supply chains: a system taxonomy, a problem taxonomy, Ontology, and ontology-driven information system.

This chapter describes the use of ontologies for personalized and situation-aware information and service supply of mobile users in different application domains. This is supported by a modular application ontology that is composed of upper-level ontologies for location and time and of domain-specific ontologies. This application ontology is used as a semantic reference model for a matching description of demands and offers in a service-oriented architecture.

This chapter addresses issues associated with the overflow of information and the demand for semantic processing on the Web. The authors propose a semantic-based formal framework (ADP) that makes use of existing technologies to create and retrieve knowledge. Effectiveness is achieved by reusing and extending existing knowledge. The authors claim that the approach can also be used for organizational memories and knowledge management.

In this chapter the authors study a case from the banking industry where they evaluate strategic partnerships with the help of the so-called e3value ontology. The principle idea behind this approach is to model partnerships as networks for the mutual exchange of business values. It has been extended to cover investment arrangements and outsourcing, which are relevant for strategic partnerships.

This chapter investigates the support that ontologies can provide to manage business partner relations in large business communities. In such communities the task of building and maintaining a large number of relations becomes too complex to be handled by individual organizations or a central network manager. The paper suggests an appropriate ICT infrastructure as a solution where ontologies offer support for communication processes and complex interactions of business entities in collaborative spaces.

Section VI
Ontology Management

Chapter XX

One aspect of ontology management is that of making ontologies dynamic, that is, providing a context-aware access to them. This chapter takes up that issue. The basic idea is to provide users with information that is meaningful in their current work context. This is achieved by generating views on ontologies which applications can use to query highly specialized knowledge bases.

Chapter XXI

This chapter views business networks as networks of service agents that describe their services in service descriptions. As each such description, and likewise each service request, is written in the light of the particular agent's ontology, semantic inconsistencies arise that lead to undetected matches or wrongly assumed matches between offers and requests. To solve this issue the authors introduce a compatibility vector system, based on schema-based ontology-merging, to determine and maintain ontology compatibility and to help with the identification of suitable business partners.

Chapter XXII

This chapter deals with an issue that arises in the creation of large ontologies, which are often built by merging smaller existing ontologies from relevant domains. Much of this work had to be done manually so far. The authors of this final chapter propose an automatic method for this task that can handle inconsistencies, redundancies, and different granularities of information.

Foreword

This book can be regarded as philosophical in talking about ontologies for business interaction, but, as I will argue, it is a rather practical book as well, impacting effectiveness in business interaction and information systems design. First I will just say a few words about myself so that you get an idea of this person advising you to spend time with this book.

To be honest, I myself do not talk so much about ontology because the classical concept of ontology refers to an idea that we can know about the basic structure, relations, and functions of the world: the ontology. In connection to that, we assumedly can also use clever strategies to reach this knowledge, epistemologies.

My thesis is that we all have different views of the world around us and that these views are partly manifested in language to describe, reflect, and act in the world. As humans we can also codesign such views and agree upon them as "views in action," making it possible for us to both communicate and act in new ways. Implementing these views in computer applications reinforces the power of human action many times. That is why it is so important to reflect upon the process of finding and using the best possible views or ontologies. And that is what the book is about.

In the book there are discussions that range from high-level ontologies that cover the whole idea of business and business development to specific areas and application domains. Inspired by that, I would like to take a "high-level" example to show the importance of this book.

We can use different ontologies on what constitutes a living human being. The two most well-known ontologies are hearth death and brain death. If we use the brain death ontology, it will open up a whole new business area with new options, dilemmas, and problems for a lot of people.

We can also be sure that the brain death ontology will evolve over time. We want to be absolutely sure that a person who has been declared dead will not become alive again, but we also want to make use of all the possibilities regarding transplantation and research that arise when a person is dead. Therefore, specialized domain ontologies are developed for different types of transplantations.

In all these cases, the ontology serves as the basis for the development of instruments and routines that include computing resources to a high degree. In other words, the ontology is the fundament that allows us to both communicate in the domain of specialized transplantations and to develop computer applications supporting successful transplantations.

This was a top-level general example of life and death. But the same principles do apply in all businesses and organizations. Ontologies are the backbone of new innovations and services, as many of the articles in this book describe.

As some of the chapters indicate, there is an even more important aspect of ontologies that has to be mentioned. In most cases the suggested solutions manifested as computer applications and work routines will not serve the intended outcome if the people involved are not involved in the process. Often we talk about this challenge as user participation or requirements management but, as you can see by reading this book, ontologies play a fundamental role even in this context.

Let us go back to the transplantation case. If people cannot trust the acting ontology, they will not sign agreements for transplantation and the whole idea will fail. It is, therefore, important that the ontology is translated into ordinary language so that people can have a chance to feel safe with the acting ontology.

This challenge is very fundamental and causes a lot of problems in development projects in many organizations and businesses. In this book we can find clues to successfully handling this challenge with the help of metaphors. That is the art of using existing languages when discussing new phenomena. This is an advanced task but of crucial importance if new ontologies are going to have positive impact on human life. This book gives some advice in this direction and my estimation is that we will find a lot more research about this in the future. May be it will not just be a question of life and death for business ideas but also for civilizations.

Olov Forsgren
University College of Borås, Sweden

Preface

MOTIVATION

Even the well-disposed reader might ask the question: Why should we concern ourselves with ontologies for business interaction? The answers to this question are many-fold. For one, a renewed interest in ontologies has only recently been fueled by the efforts around the Semantic Web and Web 2.0 (Shadbolt, Hall, & Berners-Lee, 2006) where ontologies are a core technology. But the involvement of ontologies in today's business world goes deeper than that. This is witnessed by the vast amount of literature on enterprise engineering (Davenport & Short, 1990; Fox, Gruninger, & Zhan, 1994; Gustas & Gustiene, 2004; Jochem, 2002) and enterprise modeling (Barrios & Nurcan, 2004; Fox, 1994; Fox, Barbuceanu, & Gruninger, 1996; Fox, Barbuceanu, Gruninger, & Lin, 1998; Fox & Gruninger, 1998; Gruninger & Fox, 1996; Jureta & Faulkner, 2005; Liles & Presley, 1996; Shinkawa & Matsumoto, 2001). These disciplines are at the heart of many information systems projects and ontologies play a central role even there (Dietz, 2006; Dietz & Habing, 2004; Fox, Barbuceanu, & Gruninger, 1996; Fox, Barbuceanu, & Gruninger et al., 1998; Guarino, 1998; Jackson, 2004; Kof, 2004; Opdahl & Henderson-Sellers, 2002; Uschold, King, Moralee, & Zorgios, 1998; Wand & Weber, 1989; Weber, 1997).

But business interaction is a wide field and building ontologies for it is not a straightforward endeavor. There is not a unique vocabulary or terminology that we can use as a starting point but rather a multitude of languages that differ from industry to industry, from functional unit to functional unit, from organization to organization, and even from person to person. This makes it impossible to devise "the" business ontology. In order to cope with the intrinsic complexity of this task, ontology levels have been suggested.

ONTOLOGY LEVELS

Ontologies are typically divided into foundational (or top-level), domain, and application ontologies (Bugaite & Vasilecas, 2005). Foundational ontologies cover the most general categories that can be expected to be common to all domains, such as "individuals" vs. "universals" or "substantials" vs. "moments." They are, therefore, domain-independent. Domain ontologies are tailored for a specific area of human activity, for example, medicine, electrical engineering, biology, or business. Application ontologies further restrict attention to a particular activity in a domain, for example, the diagnosis of lung diseases in medicine or a computer-based order handling system in business. Figure 1 shows the level architecture and names a few examples on each level.

It can be argued, though, whether three levels of ontology are adequate to cover the whole breadth of ontological endeavors. In the business domain, for example, we can identify any number of dimensions that justify further ontological levels. Let us consider a few examples. We distinguish between private-sector and public-sector organizations. Each organization belongs to some industry (banking, car manufacturing, retail, etc.) and it is divided into functional units such as procurement, production, marketing, sales, and so on. Along the hierarchy we have the strategic, tactical, and operational levels. In addition to these we might also consider a level below the application domain level, the personal level that takes

Figure 1. Ontology levels

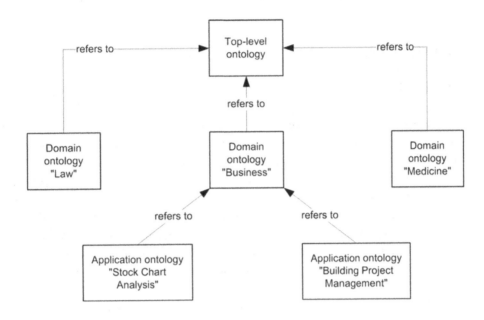

into account, for example, the way in which an individual uses a particular information system for a particular task which is often different from the way others use the same system for the same or a similar task (Carmichael, Kay, & Kummerfeld, 2004; Dieng & Hug, 1998; Haase, Hotho, Schmidt-Thieme, & Sure, 2005; Huhns & Stephens, 1999).

Domain-Level Ontologies

The diversity of phenomena along all these dimensions makes it difficult to find an adequate level of abstraction that fits the whole business domain. In organizational theory, a number of metaphors have been suggested to understand and explain organizational behavior at a high level of abstraction. Metaphors establish a link between a source field and a target field and explain phenomena in the target field in terms of the source field. For organizational theory as a target field the following source fields have been proposed: the machine metaphor (Scott, 1997), living systems (biology) (Kendall & Kendall, 1993), open systems (Flood, 2005), the brain metaphor (Gareth, 1997), learning systems (Senge, 1990), social networks (Davern, 1997), complex adaptive systems (Anderson, 1999), autopoietic social systems (Luhmann, 1990), and so on. Using a metaphor implies a shift of domain. Existing ontologies for the source domain can, therefore, be transferred to the business domain.

But metaphors also imply some severe restrictions. By viewing organizations as, for example, living systems, we fail to capture those parts of organizational behavior that are not found in biology. Established approaches to a business ontology draw therefore on a number of different related theories to develop a richer picture of the domain. Theoretical contributions can come from communication theories, for example, Speech Act Theory (Austin, 1962; Searle, 1969, 1979) and Theory of Communicative Action (Habermas, 1984); social theories, for example, actor network theory (Law, 1992; Walsham, 1997) or structuration theory (Giddens, 1984); economic theories, for example, agency theory (Jensen & Meckling, 1976; Ross, 1973) or transaction cost economics (Coase, 1937; Klein, Crawford, & Alchian, 1978; Williamson, 1975, 1981, 1985); and others.

Examples of existing approaches to a general ontology of the business domain are found in Dietz (2006), Fox, Barbuceanu, and Gruninger et al. (1998), Fox and Gruninger (1998), Goldkuhl (2002, 2005), Goldkuhl and Lind (2004b), and Uschold et al. (1998).

Application-Level Ontologies

As such a general ontology of the business domain cannot be used directly in any concrete business application. It is therefore necessary to have at least one more level, the application ontology. Some researchers suggest additional levels, for example, task ontologies (Guarino, 1998). But instead of introducing a multitude of levels, we propose to interpret all these levels as different domain ontologies because most of the interesting problems already occur in the presence of a second level. So we just abstract from complexity levels that do not contribute to our discussion. We do not argue that a reduction to three levels is indeed sufficient. According to this definition, a domain ontology can be task-specific, company-specific, and so forth.

When we take a look at the application-ontology level we discover that the idea of having a separate ontology for every application is fraught with a severe problem, as many individuals and organizations make use of several applications within the context of a single task or business process. Let us consider two of the solutions that have been proposed to solve this problem. The first one, a bottom-up approach, aims at integrating the affected application ontologies, each of which could have been developed independently, to derive a higher-level domain ontology for the task or the specific organization. An example of this is given in Corbett (2003).

The second solution is top-down. It assumes the existence of a library of ontologies that is used to build an application ontology (e.g., on the task level) by re-using existing domain ontologies (e.g., on the business process level). Systems that support this are called ontology library systems. Examples of such systems are WebOnto (Domingue, 1998), Ontolingua (Farquhar, Fikes, & Rice, 1997), and SHOE (Heflin & Hendler, 2000).

THE STRUCTURE OF THE BOOK

The structure of the book roughly follows the ontology levels stipulated above in the first three sections. We have decided, though, to drop the (unqualified) term domain ontology and the problematic term task/application ontology and rather speak of general vs. specialized domain ontologies instead. The remaining sections then deal with the development, use, and management of such ontologies. In a *Handbook of Ontologies for Business Interaction*, there is naturally a strong focus on domain issues as witnessed by the eight chapters in sections two and three. But domain issues also have considerable impact on the design of a foundational ontology. Evidence of this is given in Chapter III, where the authors identify problems in the business domain that call for the introduction of a unique object identifier already on the foundational level. We have therefore introduced a section that is devoted to ontological foundations. In the following, we give an overview of each section's content.

Ontological Foundations

This section provides an introduction to ontologies and addresses foundational issues. The first chapter, *Overview of Semantic Technologies*, is written by Anne Cregan. It shows the importance of Semantic Technologies for the future of computing and the role that ontologies play in that context. It delivers a compact introduction into a wide field and helps the reader in developing a better appreciation of the remaining chapters that highlight particular aspects in greater detail.

The second chapter is authored by Marcus Spies and Christophe Roche and is titled *Aristotelian Ontologies and OWL Modeling*. It shows how Aristotelian ontologies can be realized with the Web ontology language (OWL). The authors argue for the benefits of the Aristotelian approach to ontological modeling and discuss a detailed example of an OWL representation of such an ontology. They also deliver a number of reasons indicating advantages of an epistemological approach over the commonly used object-oriented approach in the area of domain knowledge engineering.

The third chapter by Werner Ceusters and Barry Smith, *Referent Tracking for Corporate Memories*, concludes this section. The authors take a realist stance in approaching business ontologies with the aim of turning them into a more faithful representation of the targeted portion of reality. They suggest realism-based ontologies as the foundation, in particular, basic formal ontology and granular partition theory, to describe the generic aspects of corporate memories. Referent tracking is used to capture the specific aspects, such as keeping track of each individual business entity.

After the foundational issues relevant for business interaction have been discussed thoroughly in the first section, we proceed to the domain level in sections two and three. Section two discusses domain ontologies on a general level, that is, not restricted to a specific task or application within the business domain. The third section then takes up solutions that are more specialized, that is, directed towards a specific business issue such as security.

General Domain Ontologies for Business Interaction

General domain ontologies try to capture the business domain in its breadth. This means that they claim to address all the essential constituents of enterprises and their behavior. As a consequence, these approaches do not cover any particular issue or constituent at a greater level of detail. They can rather be seen as frameworks that outline the contours of the business world. Such a framework can be used as a frame of reference by more specialized ontologies to fill it with content. The first chapter in this section, Chapter IV in the book, is a good example of this approach: *Ontology Design for Interaction in a Reasonable Enterprise* by Aldo Gangemi and Valentina Presutti. Their framework is called content ontology design patterns (CODePs) where the constituents are described by modular, interoperable ontologies, for example, for descriptions and situations and plans. These CODePs can be used to reconstruct existing business modeling languages in terms of a common formal context.

Chapter V, *Grounding Business Interaction Models: Socio-Instrumental Pragmatism as a Theoretical Foundation*, by Göran Goldkuhl and Mikael Lind, takes a completely different approach towards a domain ontology for business interaction. Instead of following a line of philosophical reasoning the authors take their point of departure in experiences from action research projects and generalize them into a theory called business action theory. This theory, in turn, is grounded in a general, albeit informal ontology of the social realm, socio-instrumental pragmatism, where the focus is on social (inter)action that is mediated by artifacts.

Chapter VI, *Towards a Meta-model for Socio-Instrumental Pragmatism*, is authored by Peter Rittgen. It starts from the same ontology as the previous chapter but aims at a different goal: formalizing the existing framework of socio-instrumental pragmatism by concretizing and refining the basic constituents, for example, actors, actions, and objects, and by providing an axiomatization in the form of associations between the constituents. The author thus arrives at a metamodel that he applies to the reconstruction of an existing business modeling language to demonstrate the generality and descriptive power of the meta-model.

Chapter VII, *Towards Organizational Self-Awareness: An Initial Architecture and Ontology*, is written by the team of Marielba Zacarias, Rodrigo Magalhães, Artur Caetano, H. Sofia Pinto, and José Tribolet. They start from the assumption that self-awareness is an important prerequisite for business action, both human and organizational. But while self-awareness comes as a natural ingredient with human beings it has to be developed and maintained in the case of organizations. To support this endeavor the authors suggest an architecture and an ontology as a high-level business modeling framework. This framework combines social, organizational, and psychological theories with enterprise modeling approaches.

Chapter VIII, *An Agent-Oriented Enterprise Model for Early Requirements Engineering*, by Ivan J. Jureta, Stéphane Faulkner, and Manuel Kolp, concludes this section. The authors aim at supporting the communication between business and IT experts at the requirements stage of an information systems development project. Their approach is supposed to facilitate the creation of a specific enterprise model that captures knowledge about the organization and its processes and that can be used to build an agent-oriented requirements specification of the information system to be built and the organizational environment in which it operates. To this end they develop an integrated metamodel or ontology of an enterprise in general that includes concepts from the managerial and information systems domains. These general concepts are instantiated with concrete entities from the particular organization.

The ontologies for business interaction contained in this section target the whole business. The following section addresses specific business activities such as ICT management, or particular aspects of business such as security and organizational memory.

Specialized Domain Ontologies for Business Interaction

The first chapter in this section, Chapter IX in the book, is written by Roy Gelbard and Abraham Carmeli. Its title is *Towards an Ontology of ICT Management: Integration of Organizational Theories and ICT Core Constructs*. It introduces a basic ontology of ICT management that comprises the concepts policy, project, assets and evaluation. The authors then go on to refine this core ontology by studying the possible contributions that some of the major organizational theories can make: stakeholder theory, theory of fit, theory of behavioral integration, agency theory, transaction cost theory, and theory of images of organization.

Chapter X, *KnowledgeEco: An Ontology of Organizational Memory*, is authored by Hadas Weinberger, Dov Te'eni, and Ariel J. Frank. It provides a specialized domain ontology for the memory of an organization. The development of this ontology follows a five-step process, two steps of which are elaborated in the chapter: analysis and structuring, and evaluation. The former addresses the classification of concepts derived from the literature and how they are mapped to ontological constructs. The results of this step are then validated in the evaluation step by assessing the conceptual coverage of the ontology.

Chapter XI, *An Ontology for Secure Socio-Technical Systems*, is written by Fabio Massacci, John Mylopoulos, and Nicola Zannone. The authors start by identifying the interface between organizations and their information systems as the primary source of security risks. In order to address security issues we therefore have to model the information systems together with their organizational environment. The authors provide a modeling language for this purpose that comprises a number of relevant concepts based on permission, delegation, and trust, and their Datalog semantics.

Chapter XI concludes this section and also the first half of the book and addresses the foundational and domain levels. The remaining sections deal with development, application, and management of business interaction ontologies. The next section, Section IV: Building Business Interaction Ontologies, shows how a concrete instance of an ontology can be created and filled with content.

Building Business Interaction Ontologies

This section contains two chapters that deal with the development of particular ontologies. The first one, Chapter XII in the book, is written by Paul Jackson and Ray Webster: Linking *Ontological Conceptions and Mapping Business Life Worlds*. The authors present a method for eliciting knowledge for the design of a corporate intranet within a government agency to solve knowledge management-related issues, for example, work duplication, document location, and accessing tacit expertise. The method combines soft systems methodology, causal cognitive mapping, and brainstorming to create a knowledge ontology using UML class diagrams. It is suitable for understanding nonroutine but rigorous knowledge and making it accessible to the designers of solutions.

Chapter XIII, *Modeling Semantic Business Process Models*, is authored by Agnes Koschmider and Andreas Oberweis. It focuses on the integration of business processes at the interface between partners in a value chain or network. This integration is tedious because partners do not only differ in the way they organize their processes but also in the languages they speak. This chapter attempts to solve the integration of diverging vocabularies by enriching the process modeling language of Petri nets with the Web ontology language (OWL).

Applying Ontologies in a Business Context

Section V subsumes five chapters that apply ontologies in a specific business context, for example, in the form of a case study in a particular company or a number of cases studies in an industry. The first chapter in this section, Chapter XIV in the book, is written by Juhnyoung Lee. Its title is *Ontologies for Model-Driven Business Transformation*. This chapter applies ontology to a model-driven approach to business analysis and transformation. It relates business processes and components on the one hand to IT solutions and capabilities on the other hand at different stages of the transformation. This is done by semantic models that show potential causes of problems during transformation and help with the identification of possible solutions. The authors also present a corresponding ontology management system that can be used in model-driven business transformation.

Chapter XV, *Ontology as Information System Support for Supply Chain Management*, is by Charu Chandra. It suggests a framework for information organization that is formalized as a reference model. This framework captures the specifics (e.g., dynamics and uncertainty) and functional requirements (e.g., information standardization and problem-orientation) of a supply chain which is interpreted as a managerial, dynamic, complex, and open system. It comprises an information modeling language that captures different aspects of the information system support for supply chains: a system taxonomy, a problem taxonomy, ontology, and ontology-driven information system.

Chapter XVI, *Matching Dynamic Demands of Mobile Users with Dynamic Service Offers* by Bernhard Holtkamp, Rüdiger Gartmann, Norbert Weißenberg, and Manfred Wojciechowski, describes the use of ontologies for personalized and situation-aware information and service supply of mobile users in different application domains. This is supported by a modular application ontology that is composed of upper-level ontologies for location and time and of domain-specific ontologies. This application ontology is used as a semantic reference model for a matching description of demands and offers in a service-oriented architecture.

Chapter XVII, *Knowledge Management Support for Enterprise Distributed Systems*, is written by Yun-Heh Chen-Burger, and Yannis Kalfoglou. It addresses issues associated with the overflow of information and the demand for semantic processing on the Web. The authors propose a semantic-based formal framework (ADP) that makes use of existing technologies to create and retrieve knowledge. Effectiveness is achieved by reusing and extending existing knowledge. The authors claim that the approach can also be used for organizational memories and knowledge management.

Chapter XVIII is jointly written by Carol Kort and Jaap Gordijn. It is titled *Modeling Strategic Partnerships Using the e3value Ontology: A Field Study in the Banking Industry*. The authors study a case from the banking industry where they evaluate strategic partnerships with the help of the so-called *e3value* ontology. The principle idea behind this approach is to model partnerships as networks for the mutual exchange of business values. It has been extended to cover investment arrangements and outsourcing which are relevant for strategic partnerships.

Chapter XIX, the final chapter of this section, is authored by Peter Weiß, *Towards Adaptive Business Networks: Business Partner Management with Ontologies*. The chapter investigates the support that ontologies can provide to manage business partner relations in large business communities. In such communities the task of building and maintaining a large number of relations becomes too complex to be handled by individual organizations or a central network manager. The chapter suggests an appropriate ICT infrastructure as a solution where ontologies offer support for communication processes and complex interactions of business entities in collaborative spaces.

Ontology Management

The first five sections of this book discussed how ontologies can be designed and deployed. The final section, Section VI, explores how they can be managed. One aspect of management is that of making ontologies dynamic, that is, providing a context-aware access to them. Chapter XX, *POVOO: Process Oriented Views On Ontologies Supporting Business Interaction*, by Eva Gahleitner and Wolfram Wöß, takes up this issue. The basic idea is to provide users with information that is meaningful in their current work context. This is achieved by generating views on ontologies which applications can use to query highly specialized knowledge bases.

Chapter XXI, *Ontology-Based Partner Selection in Business Interaction*, by Jingshan Huang, Jiangbo Dang, and Michael N. Huhns, views business networks as networks of service agents that describe their services in service descriptions. As each such description, and likewise each service request, is written in the light of the particular agent's ontology, semantic inconsistencies arise that lead to undetected matches or wrongly assumed matches between offers and requests. To solve this issue the authors introduce a compatibility vector system, based on schema-based ontology-merging, to determine and maintain ontology compatibility and to help with the identification of suitable business partners.

Chapter XXII, *A Language and Algorithm for Automatic Merging of Ontologies*, by Alma-Delia Cuevas-Rasgado and Adolfo Guzman-Arenas, deals with an issue that arises in the creation of large ontologies, which are often built by merging smaller existing ontologies from relevant domains. Much of this work had to be done manually so far. The authors of this final chapter propose an automatic method for this task that can handle inconsistencies, redundancies, and different granularities of information.

Peter Rittgen
University College of Borås, Sweden

REFERENCES

Anderson, P. (1999). Complexity theory and organization science. *Organization Science, 10*(3), 216-232.

Austin, J.L. (1962). *How to do things with words*. Oxford: Oxford University Press.

Barrios, J., & Nurcan, S. (2004, June 7-11). Model driven architectures for enterprise information systems. In A. Persson & J. Stirna (Eds.), *Advanced Information Systems Engineering, 16th International Conference, CAiSE 2004, Riga, Latvia, Proceedings* (pp. 3-19). Berlin, Germany: Springer.

Bugaite, D., & Vasilecas, O. (2005). *Framework on application domain ontology transformation into set of business rules*. Paper presented at the International Conference on Computer Systems and Technologies - CompSysTech' 2005.

Carmichael, D.J., Kay, J., & Kummerfeld, B. (2004). Personal ontologies for feature selection in intelligent environment visualizations. In J. Baus, C. Kray, & R. Porzel (Eds.), *Artificial intelligence in mobile systems* (pp. 44-51). Saarbrücken, Germany: Universität des Saarlandes.

Coase, R.H. (1937). The nature of the firm. *Economica, 4*, 386-405.

Corbett, D. (2003, October 28-31). Comparing and merging ontologies: A concept type hierarchy approach. In N. Zhong, Z.W. Ras, S. Tsumoto, & E. Suzuki (Eds.), *Foundations of Intelligent Systems, 14th International Symposium, ISMIS 2003, Maebashi City, Japan* (pp. 75-82). Berlin: Springer.

Davenport, T.H., & Short, J.E. (1990). The new industrial engineering: Information technology and business process redesign. *Sloan Management Review, 32*(5), 554-571.

Davern, M. (1997). Social networks and economic sociology. A proposed research agenda for a more complete social science. *American Journal of Economics and Sociology, 56*(3), 287-301.

Dieng, R., & Hug, S. (1998). Comparison of <<personal ontologies>> represented through conceptual graphs. In H. Prade (Ed.), *ECAI 98. 13th European Conference on Artificial Intelligence* (pp. 341-345). New York: John Wiley & Sons.

Dietz, J.L.G. (2006). *Enterprise ontology: Theory and methodology*. Heidelberg, Germany: Springer.

Dietz, J.L.G., & Habing, N. (2004, October 25-29). A meta ontology for organizations. In R. Meersman, Z. Tari, A. Corsaro, P. Herrero, M.S. Pérez, M. Radenkovic, et al. (Eds.), *On the move to meaningful Internet systems 2004: OTM 2004 Workshops. OTM Confederated International Workshops and Posters, GADA, JTRES, MIOS, WORM, WOSE, PhDS, and INTEROP 2004,* Agia Napa, Cyprus (Vol. 3292, pp. 533-543). Berlin, Germany: Springer.

Domingue, J. (1998, April 18-23). Tadzebao and Webonto: Discussing, browsing, and editing on the Web. In B. Gaines & M. Musen (Eds.), *Proceedings of the 11ᵗʰ Knowledge Acquisition for Knowledge-Based Systems Workshop,* Banff, Canada.

Farquhar, A., Fikes, R., & Rice, J. (1997). The ontolingua server: Tools for collaborative ontology construction. *International Journal of Human Computer Studies, 46,* 707-728.

Flood, R.L. (2005). Unleashing the "open system" metaphor. *Systemic Practice and Action Research, 1*(3), 313-318.

Fox, M.S. (1994). Issues in enterprise modeling. In S.Y. Nof (Ed.), *Information and collaboration models of integration.* Dordrecht: Kluwer.

Fox, M.S., Barbuceanu, M., & Gruninger, M. (1996). An organization ontology for enterprise modeling: Preliminary concepts for linking structure and behavior. *Computers in Industry, 29,* 123-134.

Fox, M.S., Barbuceanu, M., Gruninger, M., & Lin, J. (1998). An organization ontology for enterprise modeling. In M. Prietula, K. Carley & L. Gasser (Eds.), *Simulating organizations: Computational models of institutions and groups* (pp. 131-152). Menlo Park, CA: AAAI/MIT Press.

Fox, M.S., & Gruninger, M. (1998). Enterprise modeling. *AI Magazine, 19*(3), 109-121.

Fox, M.S., Gruninger, M., & Zhan, Y. (1994). Enterprise engineering: An information systems perspective. In L. Burke & J. Jackman (Eds.), *3ʳᵈ Industrial Engineering Research Conference Proceedings* (pp. 461-466). Norcross, GA: Institute of Industrial Engineers.

Gareth, M. (1997). *Images of organization.* London: Sage.

Giddens, A. (1984). *The constitution of society. Outline of the theory of structuration.* Cambridge: Polity Press.

Goldkuhl, G. (2002, April 29-30). *Anchoring scientific abstractions – Ontological and linguistic determination following socio-instrumental pragmatism.* Paper presented at the European Conference on Research Methods in Business and Management (ECRM 2002), Reading.

Goldkuhl, G. (2005). *Socio-instrumental pragmatism: A theoretical synthesis for pragmatic conceptualization in information systems.* Paper presented at the 3ʳᵈ International Conference on Action in Language, Organizations and Information Systems (ALOIS), University of Limerick.

Goldkuhl, G., & Lind, M. (2004a, June 14-16). *Developing e-interactions – A framework for business capabilities and exchanges.* Paper presented at the 12ᵗʰ European Conference on Information Systems, Turku, Finland.

Goldkuhl, G., & Lind, M. (2004b). *The generics of business interaction: Emphasizing dynamic features through the BAT model.* Paper presented at the 9ᵗʰ International Working Conference on the Language-Action Perspective on Communication Modeling, Rutgers University.

Gruninger, M., & Fox, M. S. (1996). The logic of enterprise modeling. In P. Bernus & L. Nemes (Eds.), *Modeling and methodologies for enterprise integration.* London: Chapman & Hall.

Guarino, N. (1998). Formal ontology and information systems. In *Proceedings of the First International Conference on Formal Ontology in Information Systems (FOIS'98)* (pp. 3-15). Amsterdam: IOS Press.

Gustas, R., & Gustiene, P. (2004). Towards the enterprise engineering approach for information system modeling across organizational and technical boundaries. In *Enterprise information systems V* (pp. 204-215). Amsterdam: Kluwer Academic.

Haase, P., Hotho, A., Schmidt-Thieme, L., & Sure, Y. (2005). Collaborative and usage-driven evolution of personal ontologies. In A. Gómez-Pérez & J. Euzenat (Eds.), *Proceedings of the 2nd European Semantic Web Conference,* Heraklion, Greece (Vol. 3532, pp. 486-499). Heidelberg, Germany: Springer.

Habermas, J. (1984). *The theory of communicative action 1 - Reason and the rationalization of society.* Boston: Beacon Press.

Heflin, J., & Hendler, J. (2000). Dynamic ontologies on the Web. In *Proceedings of the Seventeenth National Conference on Artificial Intelligence (AAAI-2000)* (pp. 443-449). Menlo Park, CA: AAAI/MIT Press.

Huhns, M.N., & Stephens, L.M. (1999). Personal ontologies. *IEEE Internet Computing, 3*(5), 85-87.

Jackson, P. (2004). *Ontology and business: Creating structure for storing and accessing organisational knowledge on intranets.* Paper presented at the 13th European Conference on Information Systems, the European IS Profession in the Global Networking Environment, ECIS 2004, Turku, Finland.

Jensen, M.C., & Meckling, W.H. (1976). Theory of the firm: Managerial behavior, agency costs and ownership structure. *Journal of Financial Economics, 3*, 305-360.

Jochem, R. (2002). Enterprise engineering - The basis for successful planning of e-business. In L.M. Camarinha-Matos (Ed.), *Collaborative business ecosystems and virtual enterprises* (pp. 19-26). Amsterdam: Kluwer Academic.

Jureta, I., & Faulkner, S. (2005, October 24-28). An agent-oriented meta-model for enterprise modeling. In J. Akoka, S.W. Liddle, I.-Y. Song, M. Bertolotto, I. Comyn-Wattiau, S. Si-Said Cherfi, et al. (Eds.), *Perspectives in Conceptual Modeling, ER 2005 Workshops AOIS, BP-UML, CoMoGIS, eCOMO, and QoIS* (pp. 151-161). Berlin: Springer.

Kendall, J.E., & Kendall, K.E. (1993). Metaphors and methodologies: Living beyond the systems machine. *MIS Quarterly, 17*(2), 149-171.

Klein, B., Crawford, R., & Alchian, A. (1978). Vertical integration, appropriable rents, and the competitive contracting process. *Journal of Law and Economics 21*, 297-326.

Kof, L. (2004). Using application domain ontology to construct an initial system model. In M. Hamza (Ed.), *IASTED International Conference on Software Engineering* (pp. 18-23). Calgary, Canada: ACTA Press.

Law, J. (1992). Notes on the theory of the actor-network: Ordering, strategy and heterogeneity. *Systemic Practice and Action Research, 5*(4), 379-393.

Liles, D.H., & Presley, A.R. (1996). Enterprise modeling within an enterprise engineering framework. In J.M. Charnes, D.J. Morrice, D.T. Brunner, & J.J. Swain (Eds.), *Proceedings of the 28th Winter Simulation Conference* (pp. 993-999). New York: ACM.

Luhmann, N. (1990). The autopoiesis of social systems. In N. Luhmann (Ed.), *Essays on self-reference* (pp. 1-21). New York: Columbia University Press.

Opdahl, A.L., & Henderson-Sellers, B. (2002). Ontological evaluation of the UML using the Bunge-Wand-Weber Model. *Software and Systems Modeling, 1*(1), 43-67.

Ross, S. (1973). The economic theory of agency: The principal's problem. *American Economic Review, 63*(2), 134-139.

Scott, A. (1997). Modernity's machine metaphor. *The British Journal of Sociology, 48*(4), 561-575.

Searle, J.R. (1969). *Speech acts - An essay in the philosophy of language*. London: Cambridge University Press.

Searle, J.R. (1979). *Expression and meaning. Studies in the theory of speech acts*. London: Cambridge University Press.

Senge, P.M. (1990). *The fifth discipline. The art and practice of the learning organization*. New York: Doubleday.

Shadbolt, N., Hall, W., & Berners-Lee, T. (2006). The Semantic Web revisited. *IEEE Intelligent Systems, 21*(3), 96-101.

Shinkawa, Y., & Matsumoto, M. J. (2001). Identifying the structure of business processes for comprehensive enterprise modeling. *IEICE Transactions on Information and Systems, 84-D*(2), 239-248.

Uschold, M., King, M., Moralee, S., & Zorgios, Y. (1998). The enterprise ontology. *Knowledge Engineering Review, 13*(1), 31-89.

Verharen, E. (1997). *A language-action perspective on the design of cooperative information agents*. Tilburg: Katholieke Universiteit Brabant.

Walsham, G. (1997). Actor-network theory: Current status and future prospects. In A.S. Lee, J. Liebenau, & J.I. Degross (Eds.), *Information systems and qualitative research*. London: Chapman & Hall.

Wand, Y., & Weber, R. (1989). An ontological evaluation of systems analysis and design methods. In E.D. Falkenberg & P. Lindgreen (Eds.), *Information systems concepts: An in-depth analysis* (pp. 79-107). Amsterdam: North-Holland.

Weber, R. (1997). *Ontological foundations of information systems*. Melbourne, Australia: Coopers & Lybrand and the Accounting Association of Australia and New Zealand.

Williamson, O.E. (1975). *Markets and hierarchies*. New York: Free Press.

Williamson, O.E. (1981). The modern corporation: Origins, evolution, attributes. *Journal of Economic Literature, 19*, 1537-1568.

Williamson, O.E. (1985). *The economic institutions of capitalism*. New York: Free Press.

Acknowledgment

The editors would like to acknowledge the help of all involved in the collation and review process of the book, without whose support the project could not have been completed. A further special note of thanks goes to the staff at IGI Global, whose contributions throughout the whole process from inception of the initial idea to final publication have been invaluable. Deep appreciation and gratitude is due the University College of Borås for providing a unique research and teaching environment that stimulated and supported this year-long project.

Most of the authors of chapters included in this book also served as referees for articles written by other authors. Thanks go to all those who provided constructive and comprehensive reviews. However, some of the reviewers must be mentioned as their reviews set the benchmark. Reviewers who provided the most comprehensive, critical, and constructive comments include: Alma-Delia Cuevas-Rasgado of the Instituto Politécnico Nacional in Mexico City, Hadas Weinberger of the Holon Institute of Technology in Israel, Marielba Zacarias of the University of Algarve in Portugal, and Maurizio Ferraris of the University of Torino in Italy.

Special thanks go to the publishing team at IGI Global. In particular to Kristin Roth, who continuously prodded via e-mail to keep the project on schedule and to Mehdi Khosrow-Pour, whose enthusiasm motivated me to initially accept his invitation for taking on this project.

Special thanks also goes to my colleagues at University College of Borås who gave me many new insights and provided inspiring thoughts while enduring my lack of understanding. And last but not least, I am grateful to my colleague, Mikael Lind, for his unfailing support and encouragement during the months it took to give birth to this book.

In closing, I wish to thank all of the authors for their insights and excellent contributions to this book. I also want to thank all of the people who assisted me in the reviewing process. Finally, I want to thank my partner for her love and support throughout this project.

Peter Rittgen, PhD
Borås, Sweden
June 2007

Section I
Ontological Foundations

Chapter I
Overview of Semantic Technologies

Anne M. Cregan
National ICT, Australia
University of New South Wales, Australia

ABSTRACT

Semantic technologies are a new wave of computing, using explicit representation of meaning to enable data interoperability and more powerful and flexible information services and transactions. At the core of semantic technologies are ontologies, which capture meaning explicitly and may be used to manipulate and reason over information via its semantics. Unlike traditional data schemas or models, ontologies are capable of representing far more complex relations, may be linked directly to the data they describe, and have a formal logical semantics, facilitating automated deductive reasoning. This chapter introduces the vision of semantic technologies, and provides an overview of the approach and the techniques developed to date. It provides both an executive summary and an orienting framework for reading more technical material.

INTRODUCING THE VISION

I have a dream for the Web [in which computers] become capable of analysing all the data on the Web—the content, links, and transactions between people and computers. A "Semantic Web," which should make this possible, has yet to emerge, but when it does, the day-to-day mechanisms of trade, bureaucracy and our daily lives will be handled by machines talking to machines. The "intelligent agents" people have *touted for ages will finally materialize. (Berners-Lee & Fischetti, 1999, p. 169)*

Technology visionaries like Sir Tim-Berners Lee, the inventor of the World Wide Web, have long dreamed of such a seamless information technology platform (Berners-Lee & Fischetti, 1999) to support distributed business and government and personal interactions, as well as other information-based activities like research, learning, and entertainment. The benefits of sharing and using knowledge seamlessly, globally, and on demand hold great promise for the future of economics, government, health, the environment, and all areas of human life. Semantic technologies, which are designed to process information at the level of its meaning, hold the key for delivering this vision.

The amount of worldwide digital data generated annually is now measured in exabytes (10^{18} bytes), (Lyman, & Varian, 2003) providing access to unprecedented amounts of information. While methods and technologies to store data and retrieve it reliably and securely over distributed environments are well-developed and generally highly effective, the ready availability of vast amounts of data is, in itself, not enough. Each data store is designed within its own organization or business unit for a specific purpose, and the resulting vocabularies, data formats, data structures, data value relationships, and application processing vary considerably from one system to another. Faced with information overload and a spectrum of incompatibility, most organizations are experiencing a constant struggle to find, assemble, and reconcile even a portion of the potentially relevant and useful data, even within the enterprise itself, and the potential benefits of leveraging the knowledge implicit in this data are largely untapped.

Semantic Technologies are a new wave of computing (Niemann, Morris, Riofrio, & Carnes, 2005) that enable one system to make use of the information resident in another system, without making fundamental changes to the systems themselves or to the way the organization operates. In the same way that a universal power adaptor enables an Australian appliance to be plugged into a PowerPoint in Europe, the U.S., or Asia without the need to change the local power grid, semantic technologies enable semantic interoperability for IT systems with different data structures, formats, and vocabularies, without changing the core systems themselves. By providing more effective ways to connect systems, applications, and data, greater capabilities like intelligent search, automated reasoning, intelligent agents, and adaptive computing become possible, and the potential to leverage existing information for far greater benefits becomes realizable.

HARNESSING SEMANTICS

Typically, each IT system reflects the unique missions, work flows, and vocabularies of its own organization. Differences in syntax, structure, and the concepts used for representation prevent the interoperability of information across systems and organizations. Whilst middleware and data exchange standards like XML (Bray, Paoli, Sperberg-McQueen, Maler, & Yergeau, 2006) address some of the problems, they provide only a partial solution. The main obstacle in achieving efficient and seamless system integration is the lack of effective methods for capturing, resolving, and using meaning, a field referred to as "semantics."

To date, information processing has been primarily at the syntactic or symbol-processing level, whilst the semantic level—the level of the *meaning* of the information—has been relatively inaccessible to machine processes. The knowledge of exactly what the data means resides in the mind of the database architect, system designer, or business analyst, or, if made explicit, in a document or diagram produced by these people. Such documentation is not in an executable form and without a direct function in the live system it quickly becomes out of date. On the other side of the coin, the understanding of the needs and wants of the information consumer resides in their mind, and traditionally there has been no way for them to represent this directly or to match their needs with the system.

Semantic technologies provide the capability to handle information on the basis of its meaning, or semantics. The core idea of semantic technologies is to use logical languages to make the structure and meaning of data explicit, and to attach this information directly to the data, so that at run-time, automated procedures can determine whether and how to align information across systems. By enabling this "semantic interoperability" across systems, a linked virtual data structure is created, where the relevant data can be searched, queried, and reasoned over across multiple native data stores based on its common meaning.

KEY STRATEGIES OF SEMANTIC TECHNOLOGIES

The goals of semantic technologies are twofold: firstly, to make distributed, disparate data sources semantically interoperable so that data can be retrieved and aligned automatically and dynamically on demand, and secondly, to provide techniques and tools to enable machines to intelligently search, query, reason, and act over that data.

Semantic technologies capitalize on the availability of data in sharable, processable electronic form. Some of these forms (e.g., databases and XML documents) contain structured data, and some contain less structured or unstructured data (e.g., text documents and Web pages). Semantic technologies can work with data in any form, providing it can be directly electronically linked into an ontology through some form of unique identifier. Ontologies are explicit, machine-readable specifications of the structure and meaning of data concepts, enabling automated processes to map and reconcile the data into a conceptually cohesive whole for searching and intelligent processing over the virtual data store created.

The key strategies used by semantic technologies are:

- Tagging physical data with metadata describing the data. Metadata is unlimited, in the sense that it can describe anything about the data. Additionally, because it links directly to the data it is about, the tag provides a handle for data identification and retrieval.
- Metadata tags are organized into logical structures called ontologies, which capture the logical and conceptual relationships between the tags, and provide a semantic map overarching the data.
- Aligning and mapping ontologies produces a semantic map over all the data sources, creating semantic interoperability, and providing the possibility for coordinated and seamless searching, querying, and processing over the virtual data structure.

Figure 1. Semantic technologies overview

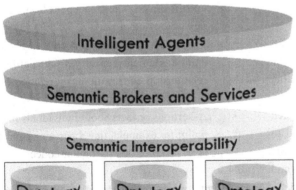

Intelligent Agents:
Compose and use Semantic Brokers and Services to perform complex tasks on behalf of the user

Semantic Brokers and Services:
Use semantic interoperability as a platform for searching, processing and analysing data across multiple data sources

Semantic Interoperability:
Mappings between ontologies provide a cohesive virtual view over the distributed data stores

Ontologies:
Logical Conceptual Structures which organise metadata according to semantic principles

MetaData:
Descriptions of what the data is, virtually linked to the physical data it refers to

Data Stores:
Structured, Semi-Structured and UnStructured distributed Physical Data Stores from different business units or organizations

- As ontologies are underpinned by formal logics, they support automated reasoning over the amassed data. Semantic interoperability thus provides a basis for semantic brokers and semantic services. Intelligent agents then may compose these services to perform more complex tasks on behalf of the user.

As shown in Figure 1, each level builds successively upon the previous one, while emphasizing the decoupling of data from applications for greater reuse and modularity.

Data

Rather than replacing existing database technology, semantic technologies allow data to continue to physically reside in its native environment, while providing improved access to the data via a conceptual virtual layer. By making the meaning of the data explicit, it may be harvested more easily for new uses. The data simply needs to be linked to a metadata tag via some form of unique identifier. For World Wide Web resources, unique resource identifiers (URIs) perform this function.

Metadata

Metadata is data about data. XML, for instance, is a common standard used to attach metadata tags to raw data. Metadata can be used to capture anything at all about data: its format, syntax, structure, semantics, pragmatics, or any other relevant aspect. Metadata about format and syntax can be used to guide processes which physically link and retrieve the data, while metadata about the data's structure and meaning can guide semantic alignment of the data. Pragmatic metadata can be used to capture information about how the data can be used in action. Semantic Technologies represent metadata in a form suited to logical manipulation, and are thus a tool which may be applied in any or all of these scenarios. As ontologies support the co-existence of multiple kinds

of meta-data over the same data, there is no limit to the kind or amount of metadata that may be used to describe and organize the same information. Complex relationships within and between the various metadata can be harnessed and used for knowledge processing.

Ontologies

Ontologies are the key component of semantic technologies, whether for the Semantic Web or other applications. The word was borrowed from philosophy, but as applied to Semantic Technologies, it is commonly defined as "the specification of a conceptualization" (Gruber, 1993), and may be thought of as an explicit conceptual model representing some domain of interest.

Ontologies organize metadata tags, capturing the logical and conceptual relationships between them, and electronically linking each tag directly to the data or resource it represents. Typically ontologies describe the individuals, concepts, and relationships that are relevant for conceptualizing some real-world domain. The kind of knowledge they capture include:

- The concepts of the domain, and relations between the concepts such as broader, narrower, and disjointed. These set up the basic terminology of the domain.
- Properties that relate concepts to each other and to data fields, specifying the nature of the relationship, constraints on the relationship, and ranges for data values.
- Assertions or facts about individuals in the domain; for example, that a particular individual is an instance of a particular concept.

Ontologies are closely related to existing data modeling methodologies, but enable more explicit, richer descriptions, with more emphasis on the multiplicity of relationships and on precise formulation of logical constraints. One of the key principles of semantic technologies is to decouple information from applications, so that it can be redistributed and re-used by other applications, both inside and outside the enterprise. Whilst current methodologies implicitly reference logical relationships, ontologies capture these explicitly, decouple them from the application, and make them available for machine processing.

For instance, a coded application procedure may make use of the programmer's knowledge about the way years, months, weeks, days, and hours are related in order to process temporal data, without actually making this knowledge explicit in a way that can be reused by other applications, or redeployed for unforseen purposes. In contrast, an ontology captures such knowledge explicitly, removing the need for it to be coded in at the application level, making the knowledge available for automated reasoning, and supporting reuse by other applications. As ontologies are the key enabler for semantic technologies, they are examined in depth in the section titled "Exploring Ontologies."

Semantic Interoperability

Mapping and aligning ontologies provides a cohesive semantic view of multiple data sources, enabling searching, querying, and reasoning across them as though they were a single data store. Mechanisms for one ontology to import and use another at run time are provided, as well as tools for the semantic alignment of ontologies. Aligned ontologies are connected via explicit mapping of the entities in one ontology via semantic relationships to entities in the other ontology. Such alignment can be human-mediated or semi-automated, using heuristics and matching algorithms.

Semantic Brokers and Services

Semantic brokers and services take advantage of semantic data interoperability to provide intelligent search and other reasoning-based services over the interlinked data. The use of ontologies supports model-driven applications to access and process executable models of the domain.

Intelligent Agents

Finally, intelligent agents can use semantic brokers to find and compose services to undertake complex tasks on behalf of users. The modularity of data, logic, and application supports the composition and redeployment of each element for new and innovative uses.

APPLICATIONS AND BENEFITS

The innovations that semantic technologies offer simplify the process of achieving interoperability between data sources, paving the way for vastly improved searching, querying, and reasoning over the amassed data.

The semantic interoperability community of practice (SiCoP) forecasts that in the near term, semantic technologies will deliver the capabilities of information integration and interoperability, intelligent search, and semantic Web services, and in the longer-term, will deliver model-driven applications, adaptive autonomic computing, and intelligent reasoning (Niemann et al., 2005). Each of these applications brings its own specific benefits.

Information Integration and Interoperability

Typically, an organization needs to work with and reconcile multiple data sources, including disparate systems within the enterprise or between different organizational systems in the supply chain, across an industry, between government organizations, or on the Web. The ability to seamlessly integrate these into a cohesive whole for search, querying, retrieval, and reasoning is clearly of great benefit. When business units or parts of the supply chain are not currently connected, or when a corporate merger takes place, the ability to connect data at a virtual semantic level, rather than having to physically merge it, is a powerful means to expedite operational efficiency and effectiveness.

Semantic technologies reduce the cost and effort involved in integrating or aligning heterogeneous data sources by obviating the need for system architects to perform pairwise mappings between each and every system in order to achieve interoperability. Using semantic technologies to appropriately represent the data at a meta-level, each system may only need to be mapped once to achieve interoperability with other systems. Having data mediation take place at the meta-level, based on explicit logical representation and automated inferencing, thus reduces the time and cost involved in achieving system interoperability.

Intelligent Search

Most search capabilities are currently based on string matching, and make limited use of conceptual relations like synonyms and contextual information, let alone more complex semantic relations. As a result, most searches deliver only a subset of the available relevant data and a large amount of irrelevant data. Sifting through search results to find the accurate "hits" is time-consuming and tedious. Additionally, the relevant data sources may not present the data in a way that is easily processable for the intended usage, so significant effort is needed to adapt the data into the right format, structure, terminology, measurement units, currency, and so on. In contrast, Intelligent search, combined with interoperability capabilities, enable searches to be conceptual-driven. Context-sensitive, preference-driven searching can be performed across combined data sources to find all the relevant information, and, additionally, the approach supports flexibility in specifying the form results should take, with retrieved data automatically transforming accordingly.

Semantic Web Services

The World Wide Web has an existing suite of Web service standards based on universal description discovery and integration (UDDI), Web services description language (WSDL), and simple object access protocol (SOAP), and Semantic Web services combine these with a Web ontology language service specification (OWL-S), according to the OWL Services Coalition (2004). OWL-S provides a core set of constructs for describing the properties and capabilities of a Web service. Itself an ontology, it enables better discovery of relevant Web services and a more flexible framework for composing and using them.

Model-Driven Applications

Model-driven applications enable software applications to directly access and process actionable models of a domain. These models explicitly capture the entities, logical relationships, and business rules of the domain. By separating logic and business rules from applications, they can be maintained centrally and explicitly. When domain logic such as business rules change, the domain model can be updated with the new logic and the change automatically flows through to the relevant applications. This enables software developers to produce software applications to support and execute business processes more quickly and easily. Less code maintenance is required and the business is able to be more responsive to changes in the business environment.

Adaptive and Autonomic Computing

Adaptive and autonomic computing capabilities enable applications to diagnose and forecast system problems and system administration needs. The use of self-diagnostics and support for complex systems planning are helpful for system administrators, and allow them to maintain reliable systems with less cost and effort involved.

Intelligent Reasoning

The ability to reason effectively over a virtual data store using meaning directly is clearly very powerful, and creates all kinds of new possibilities in terms of what machines can do for us and for business. Ontologies currently provide a formal logical semantics to enable automated reasoning over the amassed data. Whilst traditional databases already have an underlying logical base supporting their existing functionality, which ensures, for instance, that querying is sound and complete, ontologies enable more sophisticated reasoning techniques to be used while still ensuring the fidelity of the results. Some of these techniques require greater processing power than databases typically use, and work is proceeding on optimization algorithms to ensure response time is not compromised. In the future, as reasoning tasks become more intelligent, techniques for probabilistic and other kinds of reasoning are likely to appear. Safeguards are required to ensure reasoning is conducted correctly and transparently with the ability to provide accountability, including human-understandable explanations and justifications for any conclusions reached.

CASE STUDY: U.S. FEDERAL GOVERNMENT

Semantic Technologies have extensive applications for interoperability, integration, capability reuse, accountability, and policy governance within and across government agencies (Hodgson & Allemang, 2006). The U.S. Federal Government has made use of semantic technologies to improve cost-effectiveness and service quality across the U.S. Federal Government agencies, as described in detail in Allemang, Hodgson, and Polikoff (2005) and outlined below.

Federal Enterprise Architecture Reference Models

In the U.S. in 2004, a federal enterprise architecture (FEA) designed by the U.S. Office of Management and Budget (OMB) to facilitate cross-agency analysis and identify duplicative investments, gaps, and opportunities across U.S. Federal Agencies was released. The framework for providing these benefits comprised five reference models relating to performance, business, services, technology, and data. These models were conceived by researching and assembling the current practices of the various government agencies

with a view to each agency aligning its architecture to a common reference model, enabling architects in other agencies to more readily understand architectural components and to identify possibilities for collaboration and re-use. The specific goals of the FEA architecture framework included:

- Elimination of investments in redundant IT capabilities, business processes, and capital assets
- Identification of common business functions across agencies and reuse of business processes, data, and IT-components for time and cost savings
- A simpler way for agencies to determine whether potential new IT investments were duplicating efforts of other agencies, eliminating unnecessary expenditure
- A means for agencies to evolve the FEA business reference model as their needs and situations changed

These goals had the potential to save the U.S. Federal Government many millions of dollars annually, while significantly improving the quality and effectiveness of government services.

Formalizing the FEA Reference Models Using Ontologies

The reference models of the FEA were written in natural language and presented as PDF files. Whilst they could be read by anyone, the alignment process could not be implemented or verified without significant subjective interpretation, which is prone to ambiguity and errors. Creating formal representations of the reference models provides objective criteria for conformance. However, the reference models were exceedingly complex and could not be represented by simple lists and hierarchies. Luckily, by early 2004, the OWL (Web ontology language) standard (Smith, Welty, & McGuinness, 2004) had been formally recommended by the World Wide Web Consortium (W3C), the Web's governing body. By using OWL ontologies, it was possible to fully capture the models formally, ensure the conformance and logical consistency of implementations, and provide a basis for combining the implementations of different agencies into a unified whole.

The work of creating the ontologies was performed by TopQuadrant Consultants over a 3 month period. By creating a set of OWL ontologies to cover the five reference models, plus bridging and reference ontologies, they were able to create an ontology-based system to support an automated advisor to answer questions such as:

- Who is using which business systems to do what?
- Who is using what technologies and products to do what?
- What systems and business processes will be affected if we upgrade a software package?
- What technologies are supporting a given business process?
- Where are components being re-used or where could they be re-used?
- What are the technology choices for a needed component?
- How is our agency architecture aligned with the FEA?

An ontology graph was produced, which captured the rich relationships connecting the concepts stated across the five FEA reference models. These relationships provided a basis for understanding and reasoning over the overall model. Some of the resulting benefits included:

- Answering the listed questions through use of model querying and automated reasoning. For instance, automated graph traversal reasoning was used to infer "line-of-sight" between different enterprise entities.
- Context-specific information: a "capabilities advisor", using a semantic engine to advise different stakeholders on the capabilities available or in development to support the FEA and the U.S.

presidents' e-government initiatives, was able to provide project-specific guidance for preparing business cases, ensuring project compliance with the FEA, knowledge of related initiatives and possible duplication, and candidate federal, state, and local partners for the project.

- Ability to dynamically generate cross-reference tables showing multidimensional agency relationships and capabilities, through use of a "model-browser" directly linked to the relevant data, ensuring an up-to-date view over all information gathered directly from the information source.

EXPLORING ONTOLOGIES

Broadly speaking, an ontology is any specification of a conceptualization, and, in this broad sense, can include virtually any kind of model or representation, including taxonomies, entity-relationship diagrams, flowcharts, and so on. In recent years, ontologies have drawn from the disciplines of artificial intelligence, particularly knowledge representation & reasoning, and formal logics, evolving the ability to represent more complex relationships supported by an underlying formal semantics. This section explores those capabilities. The Semantic Web ontology language (OWL) is currently the most well-developed language for building ontologies, and the examples and descriptions used may be taken to reflect OWL unless stated otherwise. Please note, however, that OWL is not confined to use on the Web: being XML-based it may be implemented as widely as XML itself.

Expressing Knowledge

The typical constructs used by ontologies include classes (also known as concepts), instances (or individuals), and properties (or relations), which have a complex set of possible roles, interrelationships, and constraints.

Instances correspond to individual things that have associated properties, whilst classes are various

Figure 2. Typical ontology constructs

groupings over those things and properties are the connections between them. Figure 2 shows an example of an ontology illustrating these notions.

- *Classes* contain *instances*, for example, the class `Female` contains specific individual `Mary Smith`.
- *Classes* are typically related to each other by *subclass* relations, meaning that the instances in one class are a subset of another; for example, `Male` is a subclass of `Human`. Subclasses inherit the properties of all their superclasses; for example, if `Engineer` is a *subclass* of `Technical Profession`, and `Technical Profession` is a *subclass* of `Occupation`, then `Engineer` inherits all the properties of both `Technical Profession` and `Occupation`. This entails that instances of subclasses are automatically classified as instances of the classes above, for example, if `John Smith` is a `Male`, he is automatically an *instance* of the class `Human` also, inheriting any properties of `Human`.
- There can be distinct sets of class-subclass hierarchies that overlap; that is, ontologies are not just a tree (hierarchy) but a graph. For instance, `Engineer` can be a subclass of *both* `Technical Profession` and of `Person`.
- *Classes* may be *disjoint* from each other, that is, have no instances in common. For example, the

class `Person` may have subclasses `Male` and `Female` defined to be disjoint from each other, so that no `Person` may be an instance of both `Male` and `Female`. A set of subclasses may also give complete coverage of the class they belong to—for instance, it can be specified that the two classes `Male` and `Female` completely cover the class `Person`, so that every `Person` must be an instance of either `Male` or `Female`; there can be no `Person` who is neither `Male` nor `Female`.

- *Classes* may have *properties* which connect them to specific literal values or individuals; for example, a `Person` may have a specific age which is a non-negative integer and have a specific relationship to other individuals. For example, a `Person` can be a familial relative of another `Person`. While the property is defined on the class, note that it applies to the individuals in the class, rather than to the class itself—that is, it is each individual `Person` who has an age value, not the class `Person` itself.
- *Properties* may have specific *domains* and *ranges*. For example, "husband of" is a property with domain `Male` and range `Female`. This means that the `Husband Of` property may *only* apply to an individual who is an instance of the class `Male` and may only connect that individual to an individual who is an instance of the class `Female`.

Figure 3. Example ontology

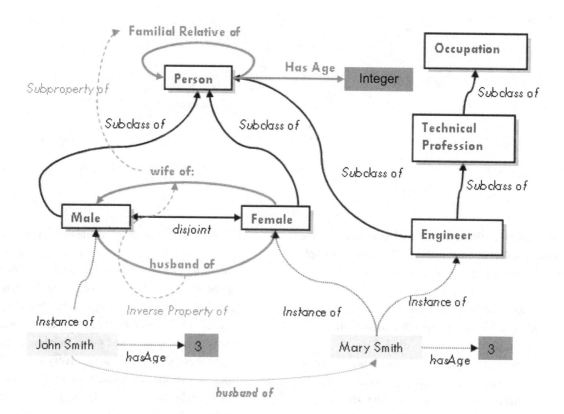

- *Cardinalities* and other property characteristics like *subproperty of*, *transitivity*, being the *inverse* of another property, and so on may be specified. For instance, Has Age is given a *cardinality* of exactly one: a Person has exactly one age. Has Husband would have a cardinality of maximum one: a Female may have no more than one husband, but may have no husband. Has Wife is the inverse property of Husband Of: if a certain Male is the husband of a Female, then that Female is the wife of the Male. Has Husband is also a *subproperty of* Familial Relative Of, and thus inherits from and specializes this property.

In building an ontology, there are potentially many design decisions in choosing how to represent the domain to be made to ensure the ontology will best suit the stated purpose. More than one model may be considered to be "correct", but usually some designs will provide the desired functionality more readily than others. As experience and understanding develops, ontology engineering is emerging as a research area and profession in its own right.

Components

Ontologies may be understood in terms of language, structure and content components. While closely intertwined, each component performs a separate and distinct function.

Figure 4. Ontology components

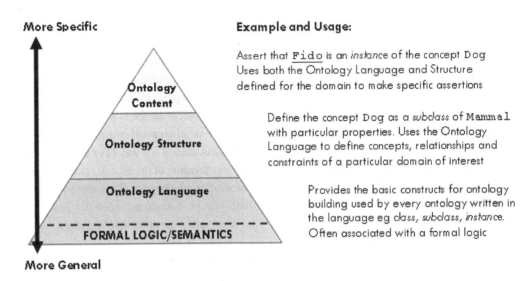

Ontology Language

The ontology language provides the fundamental modeling constructs for building specific ontologies. It includes language constructs relating to classes, properties, instances, and other formal constructs reflecting the various interrelationships and constraints these may have. Grammatical rules specify how these may be combined. Every ontology written in the ontology language uses these constructs, independently of the domain being modelled.

The particular language used is chosen by the ontology builder for its ease of use, expressivity, logical properties, and tool support. OWL is a very expressive ontology language, based on a kind of formal logic known as description logics. Several subspecies or "flavors" of OWL with different expressive and logical properties are available (OWL-Full, OWL-DL, and OWL-Lite). OWL essentially extends the constructs of the resource description framework (RDF) and RDF-schema.

Ontology Model Structure

Using the ontology language, a model is built to represent information about a domain of interest. This structure is like a template or stencil, specifying the concepts and the logical relationships and constraints they must satisfy in every specific case. For instance, the example in Figure 3 defines classes Person, Male, and Female and their relationships. In description logics, this part of the ontology is referred to as the T-box, as it is where the terminology is defined.

Ontology model structure is usually static in real-time processing (excepting the provisions for automated merging and importation between ontologies), but ontology authors or owners may choose to adapt and extend it as often as they wish, usually in a way that is backwards compatible with previous versions of the ontology, unless the entire conceptualization is radically changed. Ontologies for business are likely to be reasonably shallow and relatively static, whereas ones describing intricate research domains like medical science may need progressive clarifications, extensions, and revisions as the underlying understanding of the research area evolves and the conceptual model changes.

Ontology Content

Ontology Content pertains to the object level of the ontology, corresponding to specific facts, individuals, and data values populating the ontology model structure. In the example in Figure 3, this would include specific individuals like `John Smith`, his gender, age, and relationships. In description logics this is referred to as the A-box, as it is where assertions are made. Ontology content reflects and conforms to the ontology model structure, for example, when `John Smith` is asserted to be `Male`, he is automatically a `Person`, because `Male` has been defined as a subclass of `Person` at the structural (terminological) level.

Depending on the tools that are used to construct and edit the ontology, in some cases it will not be possible to insert inconsistent or nonconformant data, and in others errors will automatically be identified. For instance, an attempt to assert that `John Smith` is both `Male` and `Female` will either not be permitted or will be flagged as an error, if the ontological structure has specified that these two classes must be disjoint, and, therefore, can have no instances in common.

In some ontology languages, the structure and content level are not kept separate: for instance, in OWL-Full, a class may also be an instance, while OWL-DL and OWL-Lite do not allow this. While it gives more freedom of expression, this has ramifications for its inferencing capabilities, as the underlying logic is no longer tractable. In contrast, the OWL-DL and OWL-Lite flavors of OWL are well-behaved in every respect.

Features of Ontologies

Virtual Structures

An ontology is a virtual conceptual structure over distributed physical resources, dynamically linking multiple data sources. Elements of the ontology language, model structure, and content can physically reside anywhere: the ontology language may reside in a W3C namespace, linked in by its URI, the ontology structure can live on an analyst's desktop in another namespace, and the data can live in a corporate data base. For instance, John Smith's age may reside in a human resources database, while the ontology contains a unique identifier providing a direct link to this data. All that is needed is a way of uniquely specifying the address/location of the data or resource, via a URI or some other mechanism. This approach ensures that data can be maintained centrally and applications always access the current information.

Ability to Import, Merge, and Align at Run-time

Additionally, ontologies can import and build on other ontologies, providing the ability to reuse and extend ontologies. This can occur at the design phase, but can also occur at run-time, merged based on matching URIs or identifiers: if two data resources have the same URI, they are assumed to be the same, and a combined ontology structure is generated on this basis. There are also language constructs within ontology languages to explicitly specify that one information resource is the same as another, even though they may have different identifiers, for example, synonymous concepts in different ontologies.

Connection to Formal Logics

Typically, ontology languages are designed to have what is called a "formal semantics," which give inference rules for drawing valid conclusions from an existing knowledge base. This ensures that starting from a knowledge base that includes only propositions that are true, and following only the specified rules of inference to deduce more propositions, will be guaranteed to generate only statements which are also deductively true. Under certain circumstances, this process can also be guaranteed to produce every possible logical conclusion (RDF and the OWL-Lite and OWL-DL subspecies of OWL have this property).

OWL has a description logic formal semantics, where description logics are a well-behaved fragment of first order logic. The ontology engineer has some choice in selecting a suitable underlying description logic via the language used to build the ontology. This choice should optimize the relative expressiveness and inferencing capabilities, as in any formal logic there is a tradeoff between logical expressivity (freedom in what can be stated) and decidability (the ability to determine, using a terminating procedure, whether a proposition is or is not a valid inference).

Inferencing with Reasoning Engines

Inferencing over ontologies based on formal logics can be automated using reasoning engines, the implications being:

- Two or more ontologies can be joined automatically to create a logically consistent, combined, interconnected framework. Given the nodes to be matched, the ontologies organize themselves to form a cohesive whole that is logically consistent across all the component ontologies.
- Implicit knowledge can be generated automatically from the knowledge representation; that is, it is possible to generate statements which must be true, given what has been asserted, even though it has not itself been explicitly asserted. Because ontologies have an underlying logical basis, they can be used with automated reasoners to derive new information which is implicit in the ontology but not explicitly represented. From the example in Figure 3, it can be determined that if `John Smith` is the husband of `Mary Smith`, then `Mary Smith` is the wife of `John Smith`, because husband of and wife of are inverse properties, thus it is a logical necessity. Similarly, if `Mary Smith` is the wife of `John Smith`, she is not anyone else's wife because of the cardinality constraint on the wife of property, and furthermore, `John Smith` must be `Male` due to the range constraint.

- Combining multiple ontologies into a consistent logical framework gives the potential to generate logical conclusions that could not be made from any component ontology alone.
- The data described by ontologies may be queried in a large variety of different and novel ways. Automated inference procedures can deduce the answers, even though they are not specifically asserted in the knowledge base, simply because they can be logically derived from the ontology's specification of logical relationships and constraints. This optimizes re-use, and enables data to be used in novel ways unanticipated by the data owners or even by the ontology designers.

Rules

It is a matter for debate whether rules are part of or separate from ontologies, and depends on the specific language used and the logical constructs it supports. Generally speaking, rules can be used alongside ontologies as a cohesive whole, providing additional logical constraints above and beyond what is represented in the ontology as logical axioms. This can be useful for making business rules explicit, providing the ability to apply different sets of business rules to the same ontology and its data.

Tools

Ontologies need to be supported with tools for viewing, editing, querying, and alignment. Because ontologies are often inherently complex, ontology editors often provide multiple views over the ontology. Display may be either text-based, graphical, or a combination of both, and editors will usually offer a variety of views from different perspectives, for example, by properties, classes, individuals, and so on.

Annotation

Ontology languages provide the means to annotate elements of an ontology with descriptive text, directly linked to those elements.

Figure 5. Screenshots from the Protégé ontology editing tool developed by Stanford Medical Informatics (Free, open source software available at http://protege.stanford.edu/)

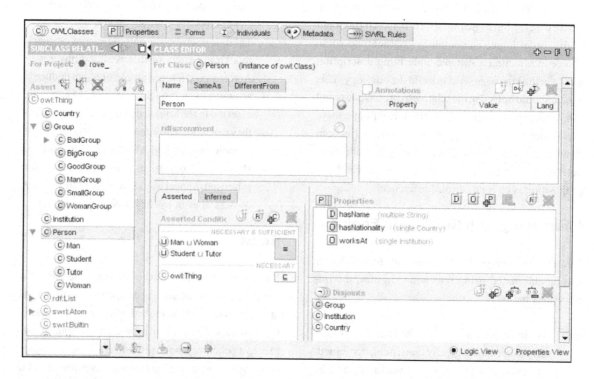

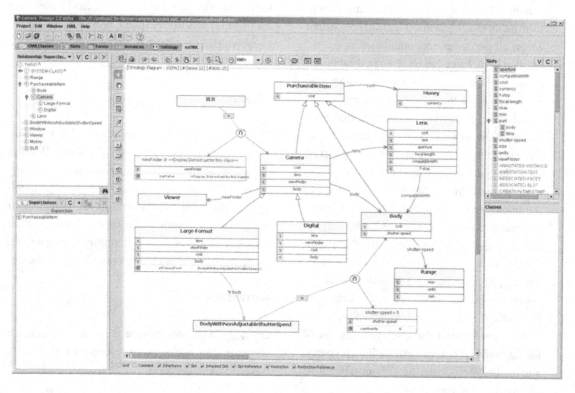

Ontologies vs. Other Data Structures and Models

Ontologies are generally compatible with other methods, and rather than replacing them, leverage their value. A brief comparison of the key differences between ontologies and other technologies follows.

Ontologies vs. Data Models

While a data model may be the outcome of a conceptual analysis and provides the design for a database, the data model itself is not directly linked to the data, whereas an ontology is an explicit map of data, directly linked to the data. Updating a data model, such as an entity-relationship diagram, does not automatically generate new knowledge about instance data or adapt the way the data links to other data sources but updating an ontology can potentially do so. Data models are not as expressive as ontologies: ontology languages are richer and treat relationships as "first-class" constructs. Data models can usually be constructed as simple ontologies in a straightforward manner.

Ontologies vs. Unified Modeling Language (UML)

UML is a specific modeling language, and compared to current ontology languages, it provides more constructs because it is intended not only for data modeling, but for modeling processes, use cases, and so on. However, it is not linked directly or dynamically to the data and does not support automated reasoning. Work is proceeding on a formal semantics for UML, a UML standard notation for ontologies, and executable capabilities, and it is likely that a convergence between ontologies and UML will be reached at some point. In the short-term, a tool for importing UML data models directly to an ontology editor is certainly feasible.

Ontologies vs. Databases

While data can be stored within an ontology, ontology tools are generally not optimized to do this, and for performance reasons it is not be advisable unless working with a very small data set. Some data base vendors such as Oracle now support some aspects of semantic technologies in conjunction with more traditional data base technology. Rather than replacing databases, ontologies are best used in conjunction with then to providing a conceptual virtual view over the data, enabling interoperability and leveraging its value.

Ontologies vs. Taxonomies

Taxonomies and ontologies are related, but whereas a taxonomy has a tree structure, ontologies have a graph structure due to their ability to support multiple inheritance and to link via properties. Also, ontologies have a much richer ability to capture relationships than the basic taxonomical "is-a" relation. Taxonomies may be viewed as very simple ontologies.

Ontologies vs. Expert Systems

Ontologies may be considered as weak expert systems, in the sense that they make knowledge explicit, can use rules, and support deductive capabilities. However, ontologies are currently more geared to capturing knowledge than to decision making per se. Intelligent agents using ontologies may, in the future, incorporate some of the capabilities envisioned for expert xystems.

THE SEMANTIC WEB

Semantic Technologies and the Semantic Web

While "semantic technologies" is an umbrella term encompassing all those technologies that seek to explicitly specify, harness, and exploit meaning for automated processing, the Semantic Web is a specific application of this idea to the World Wide Web. The World Wide Web Consortium (W3C), in collaborative association with many researchers and other organizations, has developed a suite of complementary technologies which together comprise the "Semantic Web." In one sense, the Semantic Web is narrower than semantic technologies generally, as not all semantic technologies necessarily make use of the W3C-endorsed recommendations. However, in scope, the Semantic Web is broader and probably more challenging than any other application, as it potentially interlinks data across the breadth and depth of the entire Web, and needs to handle the constant ebb and flow of available data sources across an unlimited and constantly evolving subject domain. The Semantic Web thus has to be more robust, or less brittle, than any other application of semantic technologies, as any brittleness is likely to produce cracks very quickly in such a demanding environment.

Idea

"The Semantic Web is an extension of the existing Web in which information is given well-defined meaning,

better enabling computers and people to work in cooperation" (Berners-Lee, Hendler, & Lassila, 2001).

The Semantic Web coalesced as a specific vision for the World Wide Web in 1998, initiated by Berners-Lee himself (Berners-Lee, 1998). However, many of the principles on which semantic technologies are based pre-date the Web itself, coming from diverse areas such as artificial intelligence, formal logics, database theory, information modeling, and library science. The Semantic Web has been an effective catalyst to crystallize the efforts of many research and industry groups into a cohesive and coordinated effort, and currently represents the most highly developed and complete approach for delivering Semantic Technology. The Semantic Web suite of standards is not confined for use only on the Web: it is equally applicable to enterprise systems for organizing internal data or across private data networks coordinating information between multiple participants.

Figure 6. Semantic Web "layer cake" (Berners-Lee & Swick, 2006)

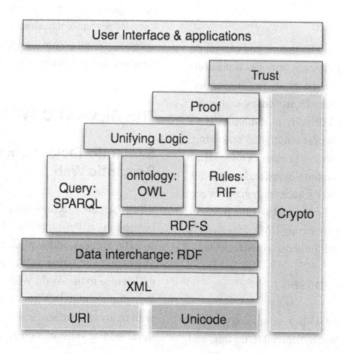

Table 1. Description and status of Semantic Web 'layer cake' elements, as of August 2007

Element	Description
Unicode	The basic character set encoding (pre-existing). **Status: Operational**
URI Universal Resource Locator	Provides a mechanism for uniquely identifying and locating current and future resources on the Web. **Status: Operational**
XML Extensible MarkUp Language	XML provides a syntax for structuring data and tagging it, without specifying or constraining the structure or tags.
	XML Schema is a language for restricting the structure of XML documents. **Status: Operational**
RDF Resource Description Framework and **RDF-S** RDF Schema	RDF is a simple data model for referring to objects (known in RDF as resources) and specifying how they are related. An RDF-based model can be represented in XML syntax. RDF Schema is a vocabulary for describing properties and classes of RDF resources with a semantics for generalization-hierarchies of such properties and classes. **Status: Operational; significant Database vendor support implemented**
OWL Web Ontology Language	OWL adds more vocabulary for describing properties and classes, such as relations between classes (e.g., disjointness), cardinality (e.g., "exactly one"), equality, richer typing of properties, characteristics of properties (e.g., symmetry), and enumerated classes. **Status: Operational; Further extensions in development**
RIF Rule Interchange Format	Certain kinds of logical constraints cannot be implemented by OWL alone. Rule languages provide a means to implement these and are potentially very useful for encoding business rules. RIF working group currently active at W3C, developing a framework for rule interchange. **Status: Candidates are under consideration, including SWRL and Rule-ML**
SPARQL RDF Query Language	Provides the ability to query RDF. Similar in nature to SQL, but SPARQL allows for a query to consist of triple patterns (for RDF triples), conjunctions, disjunctions, and optional patterns. **Status: Candidate Recommendation**
Unifying Logic	A logical framework providing Formal Semantics for inferencing. OWL currently has a Description Logic basis. **Status: DL Formal Semantics for OWL (2004); Horn Logics proposed for RIF; continuing evolution.**
Proof	Logical conclusions by themselves are not convincing. This layer provides justification of inferences made, giving logical grounds for inferences. **Status: In development**
Trust	Once a basis of logic and proof is set up, it leads to an environment of trust for conducting transactions. **Status: A social variable, to be engendered by the technologies in development, especially Proof and Cryto**
Crypto	Support privacy and security. **Status: In development**
User Interface and Applications	Provide the semantic technology to the user through appropriate user interfaces and applications. The W3C has emphasised the need for more well-designed UIs to encourage the spread of Semantic Technologies. **Status: Mechanisms to embed RDF in existning Web are in development.**

Relationship to the World Wide Web

The Web's governing body, the World Wide Web Consortium (W3C), believes the Web can only reach its full potential when data can be shared, processed, and used by automated tools as well as people, and furthermore can be used by programs that have been designed independently of each other and the original data sources. The Semantic Web does not replace the existing Web, but builds on it, enabling better interoperability and further capabilities. While the existing Web focuses on uniquely identifying resources (URIs), displaying information using HTML, and publishing documents online, the Semantic Web focuses on data and interlinking it, ultimately supporting intelligent Web services/agents.

Semantic Web Components

The Semantic Web is comprised of several layers, summarized by Tim Berners-Lee's now famous "Semantic Web Layer Cake" shown in Figure 6, which has been revised several times since it first appeared.

The lower layers are already well-established Web standards used in the existing Web (URI, Unicode, XML), while the higher layers are specific to the Semantic Web, and build on the platform provided by the existing technologies. Table 1 contains a brief description of each element and its current status. Full details may be found by following the links at the W3C's Web site (www.w3.org).

ISSUES AND CHALLENGES

Semantic technologies range from being emergent to being quite well-developed and mature. Many of the key issues are social, rather than technological. The exposition in this chapter has concentrated on the vision of semantic technologies. While key technical components have been delivered, widespread adoption requires addressing several issues.

Large-Scale Semantic Markup of Existing Data

Semantic Technologies rely on data owners to semantically markup their data and, to date, there is no way to automate the process. There is an element of critical mass here: if only a few sources are marked up, not as much value is delivered. However, the benefits of sharing data effectively among even a few sources can be quite considerable. Whether it becomes universal remains to be seen, but key players in the IT industry are starting to embracing Semantic Technologies. The successful and widespread adoption of bottom-up tagging in Web 2.0 applications such as FlickR and del.icio.us has shown the potential of the approach and the willingness of participants to do tagging to support virtual communities. While existing tagging is essentially unorganized, Semantic Technologies can provide structure, logic, and reasoning to make tagging far more powerful.

Large Scale Data Manipulation and Querying

Tools and techniques for supporting large scale applications need further development. While ORACLE and other vendors currently support RDF triple stores, further integration with existing database technologies is needed. Some semantic techniques and algorithms need further optimization to ensure computing resources can adequately support them.

Ontology Building by NonExperts

A new initiative known as Sydney OWL Syntax helps nonlogicians to build ontologies by offering the option of using a simple English syntax for building and reading ontologies, instead of having to use formal logical or XML-based notations (Cregan, Schwitter, & Meyer, 2007). This is to be supported by a guided interface.

Standards and Methods for Resolving Meaning

Interoperability relies on representing data explicitly and mapping it with other representations. However, it is not always obvious whether it is appropriate for the elements of different ontologies to be mapped to each other and the constructs currently available in ontology languages for mapping them are somewhat limited. The ideal scenario would include a more descriptive mapping for data transformations and mediation without human intervention. One approach is to gather stakeholders to jointly develop ontologies for a domain, for use as a common standard. It is not imperative that everyone use the standard, only that they map their own ontology to it as a kind of "lingua franca". This avoids the need for pairwise mappings of every ontology needed for interoperability, as each can simply be mapped once to the common standard.

On the other hand, in order to truly automate the resolution of meaning in a way that is dynamic and adaptable, it is necessary to have a solid understanding of the underlying theory of semantics—not just formal semantics, but cognitive semantics, situated meaning, the identification of semantic primitives, and symbol grounding strategies. Work on upper level ontologies fits in this space, as well as the author's own work on symbol grounding for the Semantic Web (Cregan, 2007).

Dealing with Incomplete, Uncertain, and Probabilistic Data

Real world data tends to be imperfect and is not always suited to deductive reasoning. A W3C incubator group [URW3] has formed to investigate bridging the gap between the reasoning capabilities currently provided by Semantic Web technologies and what is needed to deal effectively with incomplete, uncertain, and probabilistic data.

Proof, Trust, and Security

The capability of accessing and dynamically lining data must be balanced with appropriate measures to handle who can access what data at what level, ensuring privacy, security, and the protection of digital rights. Challenges also include ensuring that intelligent agents will be accountable for their actions and able to provide useful and understandable explanations of the chain of reasoning underlying their decisions.

CONCLUSION

While there are issues and challenges to be addressed and further developments in the pipeline, semantic technologies are already sufficiently developed to be applied in real-world scenarios, as shown by the case study, to achieve interoperability and other benefits. Looking to the future, Semantic Technologies hold great promise for delivering more intelligent information services enabling much more effective support for finding, analyzing, and using knowledge, hopefully leading to the emergence of what might be called "pragmatic technologies" which use this knowledge as a basis for effective, informed, automated action.

ACKNOWLEDGMENT

NICTA is funded by the Australia Government's Department of Communications, Information, and Technology and the Arts and the Australian Research Council through Backing Australia's Ability and the ICT Center of Excellence program. It is supported by its members the Australian National University, University of NSW, ACT Government, NSW Government, and affiliate partner University of Sydney.

REFERENCES

Allemang, D., Hodgson, R. & Polikoff, I. (2005). *Federal reference model ontologies (FEA-RMO), version 1.1.* TopQuadrant. Retrieved June 6, 2007, from http://www.topquadrant.com/documents/TQFEARMO.pdf

Berners-Lee, T. (1998, October). *Semantic Web roadmap* (W3C Draft 14). Retrieved June 6, 2007, from http://www.w3.org/ DesignIssues/Semantic.html

Berners-Lee, T., & Fischetti, M. (1999). *Weaving the Web.* San Francisco: Harper.

Berners-Lee, T., Hendler, J., & Lassila, O. (2001, May). The Semantic Web. *Scientific American.*

Berners-Lee, T., & Swick, R. (2006). *Semantic Web development final technical report* (Tech. Rep. No. AFRL-IF-RS-TR-2006-294). Retrieved from http://www.scribd.com/doc/122258/semantic-web-development-2006

Bray, T., Paoli, J., Sperberg-McQueen, C.M., Maler, E., & Yergeau, F. (Eds.). (2006, August 16). *Extensible markup language (XML) 1.0 (4ᵗʰ ed.)* (W3C Recommendation). Retrieved June 6, 2007, from http://www.w3.org/XML/Core/#Publications

Cregan, A.M. (2007). Symbol grounding for the Semantic Web (2007). In *Proceedings of ESWC07* (pp. 429-442). Retrieved June 6, 2007, from http://www.eswc2007.org/

Cregan, A.M., Schwitter, S., & Meyer, T. (2007). *Sydney OWL syntax - Towards a controlled natural language syntax for OWL 1.1.* Retrieved June 6, 2007, from http://www.ics.mq.edu.au/~rolfs/sos

Gruber, T.R. (1993). A translation approach to portable ontologies. *Knowledge Acquisition, 5*(2), 199-220.

Hodgson, R., & Allemang, D. (2006). *Semantic technologies for e-government* (SiCoP Working document). Retrieved June 6, 2007, from colab.cim3.net/file/work/SICoP/2006-02-09/Proposals/RHodgson.pdf

Lyman, P., & Varian, H.R. (2003). *How much information 2003?* Retrieved June 6, 2007, from http://www.sims.berkeley.edu/how-much-info-2003

Niemann, B., Morris, R.F., Riofrio, H.J., & Carnes, E. (Eds.). (2005). *Introducing semantic technologies & the semantic Web* (SICoP White Paper Series Module 1). Retrieved June 6, 2007, from http://colab.cim3.net/file/work/SICoP/WhitePaper/

OWL Services Coalition (2004). *OWL:S semantic markup for Web services* (W3C Draft). Retrieved June 6, 2007, from at http://www.daml.org/services/owl-s/1.0/owl-s.pdf

Smith, M.K., Welty, C., & McGuinness, D.L (Eds.). (2004, February 10). *OWL Web ontology language guide* (W3C Recommendation). Retrieved June 6, 2007, from http://www.w3.org/TR/2004/REC-owl-guide-20040210/. Latest version available at http://www.w3.org/TR/owl-guide/

Chapter II
Aristotelian Ontologies and OWL Modeling

Marcus Spies
Innsbruck University, Austria

Christophe Roche
Université de Savoie, France

ABSTRACT

This chapter shows how the Aristotelian or epistemological approach to ontologies can be understood in the framework of recent domain ontology modeling languages like the Web ontology language (OWL). After a short introduction to the specific properties of the Aristotelian approach to ontological modelling, we discuss one detailed example of a reformulation of such an ontology with OWL. In the final discussion, we give some indications concerning the differences in applying an epistemological vs. a more common object oriented approach to domain knowledge engineering in practice.

INTRODUCTION

More and more industrial applications rely on communication between interacting components or actors like people in global teams, cooperating organizations, and collaborating software systems. In recent years, buzzwords like *on-demand business* (coined by IBM) have marked the increasing importance of dynamic composition of services for global offerings of products and services.

For business interactions involving mostly or at least partially human communication, a general necessity related to the high degrees of business interaction interoperability needed in modern service-based businesses is *common understanding* between agents participating in the interaction—understanding here taken in a very broad sense of the word (excluding mere translation issues between natural languages, however). If all agents use their own description conventions for business objects and relationships with proprietary terms and meanings, cooperation or collaboration becomes extremely difficult. As a consequence, without a semantic level of shared understanding, only very limited interoperability on the business level can be reached.

The most promising way to address the problem of common understanding, that is, a representation of agreed knowledge of actors from different partners to be used for business interaction, is to define *formal ontologies*, understood as an agreed vocabulary of common terms and meanings shared by a group of interaction participants. In recent years, the Web ontology language (OWL) has become one de facto standard for formal ontologies. Beyond supporting development of editors for ontology building, OWL is XML-serializable and therefore allows ontologies to be shared and to be represented using an interchangeable format (Smith, Welty, Volz, and McGuinness, 2003; Bechhofer et al.,2004). OWL can be used in three dialects, one of which can be made equivalent to various dialects of description logic (Baader, Calvanese, McGuinness, Nardi, & Patel-Schneider, 2003).

From a domain specific point of view, logic oriented ontology languages with interchangeable formats like OWL do not provide sufficiently precise guidelines for ontology-building from expert knowledge. A prominent case in point is the gene ontology, as Smith (2004) has shown. Being one example of a real world ontology used for enabling data interchange and data mining across heterogeneous representation standards in the life sciences laboratories of different countries and different expertise, this ontology lacks some fundamental semantic properties that are necessary to ensure consistency and correctness of logical inferences. These problems relate to issues like the distinction of sub/superclasses from that of a part/whole relationship. For details, see Smith (2004) and further references mentioned there. Relating to domain semantics, they cannot be discovered by offering mere description logic based ontology representation language.

For business interactions involving computer systems, Web services have allowed an unprecedented level of interoperability (Zimmermann, Tomlinson,

& Peuser, 2003). The Web services protocol stack contains WSDL as a common language for service interface and implementation descriptions. This enables the necessary degree of common understanding in many cases. However, if services are to be composed on the basis of textual or other semantic description criteria, the interface definition is not sufficient to establish interoperability. Therefore, research into semantic Web services has proposed additional description languages. To be more specific, there are many categorization systems for business entities and business services that can be used as descriptors in UDDI (Bellwood et al., 2004). These categorizations are only a first step towards an encompassing semantic layer on top of the Web services protocol stack. OWL-S (The OWL Services Coalition, 2003) embeds service categories in service profiles that comprise input/output relations, preconditions, and effects, as well. The Web services modeling ontology WSMO (Fensel et al., 2006), proposes several metaconcepts for semantic Web services modeling, among which *goals, capabilities, and mediators* are the most prevailing. Both OWL-S and WSMO rely on *ontologies* providing agreed concepts and relationships within an interaction domain. The semantic layer defined in this way can be extended to provide semantic descriptions of business processes like those modeled in the business process execution language (BPEL). Using semantic frameworks for description of real services and their interactions can enable shared understanding on the business and on the technical level. This can be accomplished by suitably annotating Web service definitions with related business goals and by implementing mediation components that allow identification of partner services fitting a given semantic description and plug them into a given service.

In the present chapter, we will focus on ontologies for at least partially human driven business interactions. A general answer to the problem of defining languages suitable for establishing common understanding could be searched by looking at theories of concepts and definitions like in Margolis (1999), which, due to being rooted either in the analysis of natural language semantics or of philosophical theories of meaning, provide meaningful constraints to business or service concepts and relations beyond those of mere first order logic or description logic. More specifically, we will focus on Aristotelian definition theory and its implications for ontology engineering.

The Aristotelian approach is based on the *specific differentiation* principle which focuses on differences between concepts. This theory distinguishes itself from description logic (Baader et al., 2003) by restricting classes in an interpretation that can correspond to meaningful concepts. A concept, according to Aristotle, is always defined by taking its next superconcept (or *genus*) and a defining property (*difference*) whose interpretation intersects with the superconcept class to give the subconcept class. Qualities like size or color cannot define a concept. Intersections or unions of classes interpreting a concept are usually not corresponding to concepts themselves—a sharp difference to description logic, where this is allowed in many dialects (Baader et al.). While Aristotle's view can be reconstructed using modern extensional first order logic (Berg, 1983), it restricts the way concepts may be formed much more than description logic in all its variants.

A more detailed description of the Aristotelian approach will be given. Since this approach allows us to construct classes from concepts of *natural kinds*, we argue that it greatly simplifies building a *consensual* ontology in accordance with knowledge of domain experts. See Roche (2000), which is in line with the work in Smith (2004).

In the present chapter, we will outline some of the central assumptions and consequences of the Aristotelian approach to conceptualization of a domain and building a suitable ontology. The main goal is, then, to show how we can translate Aristotelian ontologies in OWL. We will show that simple restrictions of the usage of OWL allow us to comply with the Aristotelian approach.

APPROACHES TO DOMAIN ONTOLOGIES

There are at least three traditional lines of research in which structures related to domain ontologies are built without reference to modern formal ontological methods as they are implemented in OWL tools.

Classification and taxonomy analysis has been used in biology since Linnés taxonomies. For a general overview, see Diderot (1755) and Foucault (1966), using systems of characterizing properties to define general classes (*genera*) and their specifications (*species*). Today, several methods of statistically-based cluster analysis (not assuming apriori known classes) and classification analysis (assuming apriori known classes) are used for data mining purposes. For an example, see Ester and Sander (2000).

Terminology construction is defining concepts based on *delimiting a characteristic which is an essential characteristic used for distinguishing a concept from related concepts* (Depecker et al., 2001).

Formal conceptual systems is an analysis of matrices of class properties into a conceptual lattice (Ganter & Wille, 1996). In the simplest case, the properties considered are binary and can be viewed as essential characteristic in the sense of ISO-1087.

There is still other work related to conceptual modeling, notably the theory of structural elements in UML 2 (Object Management Group, 2005), however, we will not explicitly determine the relationship of the present work to it.

The common denominator of the aforementioned lines of research is an approach to domain modeling going back to Aristotle, which we will quote following Berg (1983) and one of his best known commentators, Porphyry (1975), and refered to as Aristotelian ontological approach or simply Aristotelian ontology (where it should be noted that Aristotle's own concept of ontology was not instantiable to modeling single application domains). We will call this method alternatively epistemological, since it is derived from an approach of *theory of knowledge* rather than modeling in terms of concepts and roles of description logic (Baader et al., 2003).

ARISTOTELIAN ONTOLOGIES

Aristotelian or epistemological ontologies construct a domain of entities by a sequence of definitions. Definitions, according to the famous formulation of Aristotle, proceed by stating the *genus proximum* and the *differentia specifica*. In this way, a concept tree is built by successive definitions of species from genders (*genera*), where defined species are used as genders for subspecies until a set of leaf species is reached. The concept tree corresponding to an Aristotelian approach is usually binary, since the very notion of difference in its traditional philosophical sense allows only dichotomous alternatives (like being an eternal being or a temporal being). An axiomatic reconstruction of Aristotelian definition theory on the basis of careful examination of all related writings by the philosopher has been given by Berg (1983), who also discusses exceptions to the strict tree structure of a definitional hierarchy.

In order to appreciate this approach, it is important to point out the distinction between *defining* and *describing* properties. Defining properties or differences are assumed to be essential predicates of a class, while properties or accidental attributes may, in general, apply to different individuals of a class in different degrees or not at all. For instance, a car can be described as having four seats (an object property); however, this does not contribute to the definition of a car, since a car-like vehicle with any number of seats greater than one still would commonly be called a car. Specific differences (or delimiting characteristics, in the parlance of terminology standards) are always defining—and therefore must be distinguished from properties or accidental attributes. A frequently used subset of describing properties are *qualities* like size (Berg, 1983). Defining properties or *differentiae* always delineate the extension of a *species* qua intersection with the extension of its closest *genus*. A *differentia*

can be reused in various definitions of a conceptual hierarchy (examples of this follow).

There appear to be some principal hurdles in applying Aristotelian ontologies to practical domain modeling tasks:

- It has been discussed in the literature on concepts that often delimiting characteristics or specific differences are not readily available (Margolis, 1999). There are many examples indicating that the specific difference approach is not applicable without additional conventions.

- In Depecker et al. (2001), a distinction is made between specialization and comprehension (or part-of) hierarchies. While this distinction is important in practice, Aristotelian ontologies are based on the substance category rather than on the part-of relationship between objects. In practical solutions, part-of relationships may be used for expressing specific differences.

- Some problems arise if a defining difference of a concept is a relationship, for example, defining mother as a woman that has a child, a standard example in description logic, according to Baader et al. (2003). Here, the defining difference is not an *essential* predicate of the *definiendum*. In this case, the rigid Aristotelian approach would require not considering mother as a concept in its own right. Being a mother should be considered as a role in the sense of UML, according to the Object Management Group (2005)—that is, some individuals of the class of women implement the interface (in UML parlance) of giving birth to a child, and so forth, but that does not define a class (or a concept).

- Multiple inheritance can be realized implicitly by classifying an individual according to several ontologies or conceptual systems. So, in the Aristotelian view, concepts themselves may not have multiple generalizations, but individuals may be members of several classes (like you do not have multiple class inheritance in Java, but objects may realize several interfaces belonging to different hierarchies).

Aristotelian ontologies in our understanding are relative to a state of knowledge and a perspective of analysis. As an example, take the definition of men and women in an ontology of living beings. In this ontology, age is an attribute, since it is not a defining difference for either concept. However, in an ontology of beings in general, including eternal beings, having an age is a defining property of the non-eternal beings.

ARISTOTELIAN ONTOLOGIES FROM A LOGICAL POINT OF VIEW

Let us consider the definition approach according to Aristotelian logic in more detail. Let $C_0, \ldots, C_m$ be concepts, that is, generic notions (*genera*), and let $D_1, \ldots, D_n$ be unary predicates representing specific differences. Then, an epistemological ontology seems to be expressible for concepts $C_0, \ldots, C_m$ as follows:

$$(\forall x)C_0(x) \tag{1}$$

$$(\forall x) \quad (C_1(x) \Longleftrightarrow C_0(x) \wedge D_1(x)) \tag{2}$$

$$(\forall x) \quad (C_2(x) \Longleftrightarrow C_0(x) \wedge \neg D_1(x)) \tag{3}$$

$$(\forall x) \quad (C_3(x) \Longleftrightarrow C_1(x) \wedge D_2(x)) \tag{4}$$

Here, C_0 would be the root concept (like *thing* in OWL), and, in a full binary hierarchy, each of C_k, $k \geq 1$ would have C_j as *genus proximum* where $j = \lfloor k/2 \rfloor - (k+1) \bmod 2$. Note that in applications some of the concepts at different depths of the binary hierarchy will become leaf concepts.

A further property of the Aristotelian or epistemological ontology is that non-leaf concepts should correspond to abstract classes (in practice, not all of them do). Abstract classes in the OO sense appear as non-leaf nodes in the epistemological ontology (OO: object oriented systems). See, for example, Gamma, Helm, Johnson, and Vlissides (1995). Abstract classes may be unnamed (anonymous) in an Aristotelian ontology since in the domain of discourse targeted by

the ontology there is no generally accepted name for the corresponding concept.

However, the set of formulae given above does not adequately capture the intended ontological meaning of definition by specific differences. The basic tenet of classical definition theory is that a specific difference is not applicable further up (towards C_0 in the conceptual hierarchy. E.g., the difference of *can fly* (yes or no) is not applicable to things in general. However, a straightforward representation with first order logic and unary predicates is not capable of representing this constraint due to the *tertium non datur* principle. One could only state that for individuals in, say, C_1, tautologically $D_2(x) \vee \neg D_2(x)$ holds. Instead, we need to assume some form of sorts in the individuals in order to express, for example, that $D_2(x)$ is not applicable to objects in $C_1(x)$ or $C_2(x)$. This corresponds to defining class hierarchies in OO modeling. Classes under some specific definition in such a hierarchy actually are assumed to be interpreted within some subuniverse of individuals.

Thus, in a standard first order logic framework with unary predicates only the notion of applicability of a predicate to an individual would lead to contradictions. One way to express the notion of predicate applicability is to use Hintikkas state descriptions. In the Hintikka (1974) formalization of state descriptions, a state is an exhaustive set of existence or nonexistence statements with respect to a finite set of predicates. If all predicates are unary, this corresponds to a list of possible worlds in analogy to propositional calculus. If n-ary predicates are allowed, applicability can be expressed as existence of related objects. For example, the predicate of fluidness is not applicable to human beings because they are no simple substances. In a suitable state description, a simple substance would be described as aggregate having one state (fluid, solid, or gaseous), while human beings would lack such a relationship to an individual of class aggregate state. As another example consider the notion of mortality. It is reasonable to postulate that only living beings or God can be mortal or immortal, while an molecule or a rock can neither be called mortal nor immortal—the predicate of mortality is not applicable to simple substances. Again, this can be modeled by n-ary predicates in state descriptions. In this case we might say living beings have a slot (binary relationship) indicating their mortality, while molecules or rocks do not have such a slot. Note that this construction seems close to a dichotomous predicate; however, we are able again to express applicability, which would have been impossible without the slot in a state description. For the formulae reflecting these considerations, see Hintikka (1974) and Spies (2004).

Therefore, an Aristotelian ontology is not just a sequence of binary partitions of some universe, it is deeply related to object oriented modeling and domain ontology modeling. This led us to asking how an Aristotelian ontology might be represented in a domain ontology modeling language like OWL.

APPROACHES TO SIMULATING ARISTOTELIAN ONTOLOGIES IN OWL

In order to examine the differences between an epistemological and a description-based approach to ontological modeling of application domains, an epistemological ontology that has been created by Roche (2000) for basic classes in machine processing

of substances containing metal has been recast in OWL with the Stanford University Protégé ontology editor. For reference, we include in Figure 1 the ontology as formulated with the OCW editor of Condillac Research Group of Université de Savoie (Roche, 2000).

In this section, the principal assumptions of a working representation of an Aristotelian ontology in OWL are explained. For introduction to OWL, see Smith et al. (2003); for a reference, see Bechhofer et al. (2004). This approach has been tested on the machining ontology using Protégé 3.2 of Stanford University (http://protege.stanford.edu).

The main requirements of such an approach are:

- Concepts of an Aristotelian ontology must appear as classes in an OWL ontology.
- Classes in the OWL ontology should be related by subclass relationships according to the Aristotelian ontology.
- Non-leaf classes in the Aristotelian ontology correspond to abstract classes in an OWL model, for example, to classes without individuals. Non-leaf classes may be named or anonymous in an Aristotelian ontology.
- Leaf classes in the Aristotelian ontology must correspond to concrete or real classes in an OWL model, that is, to classes that may have

Figure 1. The machine processing Aristotelian ontology of Condillac Research Group

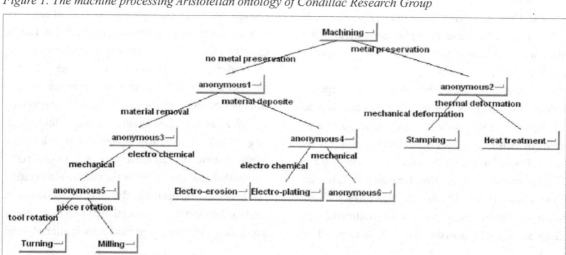

individuals. There are applications, however, where even leaf classes are anonymous from a terminology point of view.

- A definition is the conjunction of specific differences along the path from the root class of the representing class hierarchy to the given real or abstract class. This should be modeled via inheritance and become visible in appropriate Protégé 3.2 browsers.

As a matter of fact, these requirements do not suffice to give a unique translation of an Aristotelian ontology into an OWL ontology. We will examine three possible representations in turn.

Representing Specific Differences as Individuals

In this approach, an Aristotelian ontology is formulated in OWL by mapping subclass relationships as such into the OWL class hierarchy. Anonymous subclasses are named arbitrarily (in our example we chose strings representing the current nodes predecessor path). Specific differences are represented as individuals of an additional class called Difference.

Each class in the class hierarchy has an object property with domain in the root class machining and range in class Difference called specificDifference. The individual values of this object property are inherited through the class hierarchy.

Additionally, couples of opposite differences are defined by using another object property of the class Difference, which we call CoupleOfOppositeDifferences. This property is used to identify the opposite specific difference of any given specific difference.

For an example, see Figure 2.

Representing Specific Differences as Datatype Properties

In this approach, an Aristotelian ontology is formulated in OWL by mapping—like in the previous approach—subclass relationships into the OWL class hierarchy. Anonymous subclasses are again named arbitrarily. Specific differences, however, are now represented as boolean-valued datatype properties. No additional class called difference is necessary.

Each class in the class hierarchy is attributed the specific difference according to its position in the Aristotelian ontology hierarchy. Specific differences

Figure 2. The class hierarchy of Université de Savoie machining ontology together with a display of inherited differences and the specific difference piece rotation for the class milling, according to the representation of differences as individuals, which appear as values of an object property of a class

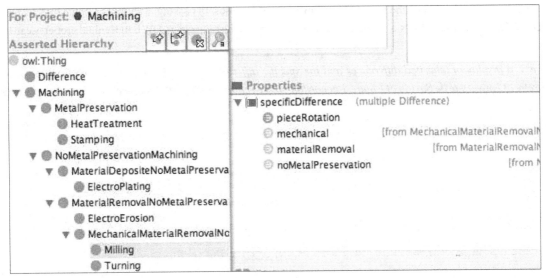

of gender classes apply to any species class automatically via inheritance.

In OWL DL, the description logic variant of OWL (Baader et al., 2003), it is necessary to specify for each class both the positive and the negative specific difference.

This approach is illustrated for the machine processing ontology in Figure 3.

Representing Specific Differences as Object Property Classes

In this approach, an Aristotelian ontology is formulated in OWL by mapping—like in the previous approaches—subclass relationships into the OWL class hierarchy. Anonymous subclasses are again named arbitrarily. Specific differences are represented as property subclasses of an abstract property class called difference. The subclass structure obtained this way is isomorphic to the subclass hierarchy; however, note that different nodes in the property subclass may correspond to precisely the same property subclass.

In the first approach reported above, specific differences were modeled as individuals. In the second approach, differences in the Aristotelian sense were modeled as individual properties. In the present approach, specific differences are modeled as property classes, instances, or individuals of which can be properties of individuals of a concrete species. So, in a way, this is a synthesis of the two previous approaches. This synthesis allows a more convenient

expression of species properties corresponding to specific differences.

Thus, specific differences in the Aristotelian sense are modeled in the present approach as relationship classes or, in OWL parlance, object property classes that can be individualized for a concrete species. Technically, the object property classes are ordinary subclasses of a general subclass of the object property OWL-class and are consequently endowed with domain and range (the general object property subclass in our model was called *difference* again.)

To illustrate this by an example, saying that a bird is a vertebrate animal that has wings would translate to the class of birds being characterized by a hasWings property class. The domain and range of this hasWings property class are unspecified, since we are here at an abstract class level, and, at this point in our defining hierarchy, the mere difference of having wings vs. not having them is what constitutes the delimiting characteristic.

Then, traversing our ontology down to leaf species or concrete classes, there must be an individual property derived from hasWings that actually applies to the domain of a given bird species. A reasonable individual property would be hasFeatheredWings. The individual property of having feathered wings then applies to any instance of a specific bird species, and the form, color, and so on, of these feathered wings can be described by adding further suitable object properties. In passing, it should be noted that, technically, the range of an OWL individual property can be

Figure 3. A display of inherited differences and the specific difference piece rotation for milling from the class hierarchy of Université de Savoie of Figure 1 according to the representation of differences as boolean properties of a class

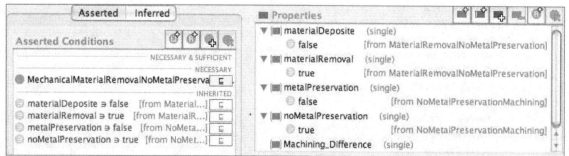

another property class, like anatomic or biophysical features.

Thus, in this approach, each leaf class in the class hierarchy has an object property with domain in its own class and range in a related class—here, for the sake of simplicity, we introduce only one related class, that of material. This object property is an individual of the property class modeling the specific difference applicable. The specific differences and their corresponding individual object properties are again inherited through the class hierarchy.

An important consequence of this approach to modeling epistemological ontologies with OWL concerns the multiple appearance of a specific difference in an ontology. In general, specific differences are not restricted to appearing only once in a class hierarchy. As for the property class of hasWings, it is well known that it is a specific difference for a subclass of invertebrates, as well. The same holds true for the corresponding object property class that represents this specific difference. In the present approach we can reuse the specific difference of having wings and just give it another instance for the insects' wings that allows to describe their anatomy and physiology at any desired detail. For example, our specific difference object property class hasWings can be instantiated to hasHummingWings to be applied to the class of honey bees.

Technically, multiple appearance of a specific difference in an ontology presupposes multiple inheritance of object property classes representing specific differences. In OWL, multiple inheritance is allowed for any subclass system (be it in the property or the class hierarchy). However, Aristotelian ontologies share the assumption of many modern object oriented programming systems in that they require single inheritance for the genders and species hierarchy. Thus, in the present modeling approach, the object property classes do not form a single-inheritance hierarchy, while the gender and species classes do. For a similar distinction between singly inheriting classes and a multiply inheriting hierarchy of properties, see Gamma et al. (1995), where the multiply inheriting hierarchy is referred to as type system.

In the mechanical production ontology of the Savoie University (Roche, 2000), it is the difference between electrochemical and mechanical substance change that appears both in the substance adding and in the substance removal branch of the class tree. From a statistical point of view, one might be tempted to describe such a situation as cross-classification. Note, however, that other subclasses of substance adding vs. removal evolve in the class tree without repeating distinctive features.

The application of the present modeling will now be illustrated in the context of the example ontology from Roche (2000). First, we show the class tree in OWL (see Figure 4). It should be noted that we introduced a second root class, Material, that serves as abstract domain of the specific differences in mechanical production. Basically, this amounts to defining a general object on which each mechanical production method operates. Of course, in other examples, none such reified relation domain may be necessary, while in others, more than a single additional abstract class will be required. Additionally, we depict the hierarchy of object properties used for the defining differences in the mechanical production ontology (see Figure 5).

As discussed before, real differences between individuals belonging to concrete classes are modeled as individuals belonging to some subclass of the class of difference object properties. Using this approach in Protégé will lead to all applicable individual properties (or property individuals) being offered in the individuals tab of the main interface menu. So, finally, we illustrate the use of these constructions by a screen shot that shows how individual properties evolve proceeding through the object hierarchy, see Figure 6.

It should be noted that OWL editors will need to be enabled at the OWL-full level (instead of mere description logic) in order to work with this approach. The DL analogy to subclasses are subproperties in OWL. With subproperties, however, Aristotelian difference systems can not be represented, because assigning subproperties to a class implies inheriting all property values of higher (or super-) properties. This would make reusing a difference in different branches of the conceptual hierarchy impossible. It should be noted, however, that in all practically relevant cases we never iterate instantiation of property classes, therefore, there is no risk of undecidability of reasoning, as it can occur with OWL-full ontologies in general.

To sum up, in this approach we ontological differences as finite hierarchy of metaclasses. They comprise a finite set of individual properties as members from which to generate a suitable conceptual model.

DISCUSSION AND CONCLUSION

In this chapter, we argue that it is reasonable for practical ontology engineering to follow an approach derived from the definition theory by Aristotle. Some of our suggestions serve as an ontology design guideline in application projects in the manufacturing and human resource domains using the ontology editor by the Condillac research group at Savoie University. Our argument here, however, goes beyond these results

in suggesting several methods for implementing the Aristotelian approach in the most commonly used ontology modeling language, namely OWL.

What is still missing is systematically gained empirical evidence of the practical implications of ontology editing using Aristotelian theory. However, the approaches outlined correspond exactly to design options in applications, like, for example, in building an ontology representation of taxonomies from the extensible business reporting language (for example, XBRL, see http://www.xbrl.org). The EU project MUSING (MUlty Industry Semantic based Next Generation Business Intelligence, see http://www.musing-project.eu) is building an integrated decision support platform which contains, among many other components, ontology representations for XBRL balance sheet data and metadata, regional economic indicators, and statistical models of their dependencies and predictive value for specific business decisions. In this highly demanding context, ontologies must satisfy functional requirements (integration into business applications) and still must remain understandable and

Figures 4, 5. The Protégé 3.2 class and property class hierarchies for the mechanical production ontology example

Figure 4.

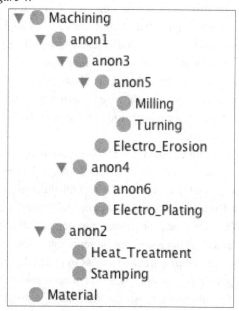

Figure 5.

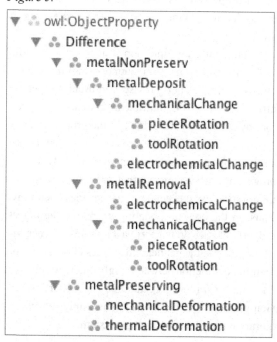

maintainable by domain experts. It appears that the Aristotelian approach outlined in the present chapter helps in fulfilling both requirements. More details on the experiences and methodologies from MUSING will be presented in subsequent publications.

To put our approach in perspective from a more philosophical point of view, it should be mentioned that the OWL approach to object modeling is, by far, not unique. For instance, Stroustrup (2003) explicitly rejected an approach reminding of ontologies in the description logic sense for his design of the C++ standard library STL. Therefore, one should be cautious in declaring any approach as generally recommendable because it is based on logic. Certainly, with the advent of a definition of concepts as functions in Frege (1973), the Aristotelian definition theory has lost some of its intuitive attractiveness. We have shown why in the first part of this chapter: It is by far not obvious how to model applicability of differences to individuals without assuming a sorted domain (i.e., by postulating domain properties that the ontology is about to introduce ...). However, as it was shown, the Aristotelian theory can elegantly be retrieved by the very means of the leading modern domain ontology languages, with a little help taken from Hintikkas' (1974) concept of state descriptions. Whether OO-flavored or epistemologically-flavored ontological modeling is applied in practice can, therefore, be

decided on practical reasons alone.

There are at least three conclusions to be drawn from the results of the present chapter:

• Constructing a terminology the Aristotelian methodology provides a useful guideline because it forces us to distinguish defining features from accidental attributes. As an example, take the modeling decision in XML Schema to put information into an element item or an attribute item which is sometimes considered as an arbitrary choice. An element information item corresponds to a constituent of an entity, like an object property in OWL, while attribute information item corresponds to a property or even an accidental attribute in the Aristotelian approach. It should be helpful to think in these terms borrowed from a long philosophical tradition when working on practical modeling tasks.

• Another point is that the negation of a concept in an extensional sense often does not lead to another concept—this is similar to the situation in object oriented or entity relationship modeling. The negation of a class (defined by inverting the defining and non-defining features) is in most cases not itself a class (or a relational table or ...). Since most description logic dialects treat nega-

Figure 6. Protégé 3.2 property individuals inherited and specific to one concept (here sheet metal working)

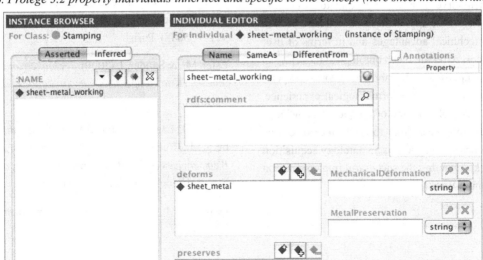

tion as an operation applicable to any concept, this can lead to model elements that would be considered meaningless in an Aristotelian approach. Again, considering this approach will lead to a very careful use of description logic syntax in real projects.

- The same holds true of concept union and concept intersection. According to the Aristotelian approach, a union of concepts is only a concept if it leads to the immediate generic predecessor in the generalization tree, otherwise such a union simply has no conceptual meaning. This is similar to the approach in conceptual lattices. For details, see Ganter and Wille (1996). It seems that a conceptual space does have a more constrained structure than a set-theoretic approach of concept definition by standard set-theoretic operations of complementation, intersection, and union can express. This structure may be not fully expressible by the Aristotelian approach to ontologies, but at least this approach gives an indication of how to build practically useful models.

A recommendation from these conclusions would be to design ontology editing tools that allow for ontology modeling with target language OWL along any of the three epistemologically founded approaches outlined in the present chapter. Such implementations would then serve as a starting point to evaluating the usability of the approaches outlined here both in terms of technical advantages and in terms of user experiences. After all, much ontological modeling in practice is supposed to be performed by domain experts with comparatively little formal logical experience. It seems desirable that the often quoted knowledge acquistion bottleneck from the old times of expert systems does not reappear as an ontology acquisition bottleneck impacting the successful implementation of a semantic Web.

ACKNOWLEDGMENT

The authors are indebted to Barry Smith for fruitful discussions during a workshop at IFOMIS in May, 2006, and, in particular, for the reference to the work by Jan Berg.

REFERENCES

Baader, F., Calvanese, D., McGuinness, D., Nardi, D., & Patel-Schneider, P. (Eds.). (2003). *The description logic handbook*. Cambridge: Cambridge University Press.

Bechhofer, S., van Harmelen, F., Hendler, J., Horrocks, I., McGuinness, D., Patel-Schneider, P., et al. (2004, February). *OWL Web ontology language reference*.

Bellwood, T., Capell, S., Clement, L., Colgrave, J., Dovey, M.J., Feygin, D., et al. (2004). *UDDI version 3.0.2* (Technical Report). OASIS.

Berg, J. (1983). Aristotle's theory of definition. In *Atti del convegno internazionale di storie della logica*. San Gimignano.

Depecker, M., et al. (2001). *Travaux terminologiques – Vocabulaire (ISO-1087)* (Tech. Rep.). Association Française de Normalisation.

Diderot, D. (1755). Encyclopédie ou dictionnaire raisonné des sciences, des arts et des métiers. In (Vol. V, p. 635648). Paris.

Ester, M., & Sander, J. (2000). *Techniken und Anwendungen [Knowledge discovery in databases]*. Berlin: Springer.

Fensel, D., Lausen, H., Polleres, A., de Bruijn, J., Stollberg, M., Roman, D., et al. (2006). *Enabling semantic Web services – The Web service modeling ontology*. Berlin, Heidelberg, Germany: Springer.

Foucault, M. (1966). *Les mots et les choses*. Paris: Gallimard.

Frege, G. (1973). Funktion und Begriff. In G. Patzig (Ed.), *Funktion, Begriff, Bedeutung* (pp. 18-39). Göttingen: Vandenhoeck und Ruprecht.

Gamma, E., Helm, R., Johnson, R., & Vlissides, J. (1995). *Design patterns – Elements of reusable object-oriented software.* Boston: Addison Wesley Professional Computing Series.

Ganter, B., & Wille, R. (1996). *Formale begriffsanalyse.* Berlin: Springer.

Hintikka, J. (1974). *Knowledge and the known.* Dordrecht: D. Reidel Publishing Company.

Margolis, E. (1999). *Concepts: Core readings.* Cambridge: Cambridge University Press.

Object Management Group. (2005). *Unified modeling language superstructure* (Tech. Rep.). OMG (Object Management Group).

OWL Services Coalition. (2003, December). *OWL-S: Semantic markup for Web services.*

Porphyry. (1975). *Isagoge (transl. e. warren).* Toronto: Pontifical Institute of Mediaeval Sciences.

Roche, C. (2000). Corporate ontologies and concurrent engineering. *Journal of Materials Processing Technology, 107,* 187-193.

Smith, B. (2004). The logic of biological classification and the foundations of biomedical ontology. In D. Westerstahl (Ed.), *Invited papers from the 10th International Conference in Logic Methodology and Philosophy of Science.* North Holland: Elsevier.

Smith, M., Welty, C., Volz, R., & McGuinness, D. (2003, August). *OWL Web ontology language guide.*

Spies, M. (2004). *Einführung in die Logik—Werkzeuge für Wissensrepräsentation und Wissensmanagement.* Heidelberg, Berlin, Germany: Spektrum Akademischer Verlag.

Stroustrup, B. (2003). *Die C++ Programmiersprache.* München: Addison Wesley.

Zimmermann, O., Tomlinson, M., & Peuser, S. (2003). *Perspectives on Web services.* Berlin: Springer.

Chapter III
Referent Tracking for Corporate Memories

Werner Ceusters
New York State Center of Excellence in Bioinformatics and Life Sciences, USA

Barry Smith
University of Buffalo, USA

ABSTRACT

For corporate memory and enterprise ontology systems to be maximally useful, they must be freed from certain barriers placed around them by traditional knowledge management paradigms. This means, above all, that they must mirror more faithfully those portions of reality which are salient to the workings of the enterprise, including the changes that occur with the passage of time. The purpose of this chapter is to demonstrate how theories based on philosophical realism can contribute to this objective. We discuss how realism-based ontologies (capturing what is generic) combined with referent tracking (capturing what is specific) can play a key role in building the robust and useful corporate memories of the future.

INTRODUCTION

Corporate memories (CM) are information systems designed to keep track of the history and evolution of an enterprise with the goal of using lessons learned from past experiences to enhance the performance of the business transactions in the future. A well-designed CM should contain data about both the enterprise and the environment in which it operates.

The former, traditionally embodied in what is referred to as an *enterprise model*, consists of data about the organizational structure and operating procedures of the enterprise, its mission and strategic objectives, its staff, their skills and competences, the products and services the company is able to deliver, and, most importantly, data about projects or business transactions brought to a successful (or unsuccessful) end. The latter, the CM's *environment model*, includes data about prospects and clients, competitors and partners, applicable laws and regulations, and techniques and methodologies proposed by outsiders to complement the results of research carried out within the company itself.

For understandable reasons, CM technology is standardly approached from a backward-looking perspective, employing passive knowledge management techniques with the prime goal of making legacy electronic documents more easily accessible. To this end, such documents are manually or semi-automatically annotated with tags that reformulate words or relevant phrases in a document in a more structured and standardized manner (e.g., occurrences of the words *car*, *van*, *bus*, and so forth, are all tagged with the compound *motor vehicle*), or with meta-tags that add additional context to phrases or paragraphs (e.g., *important, motivation, marketing, outsourced operations,* and so forth). When these meta-tags are organized in a structure that reflects more or less the way the enterprise itself is structured, they form what is referred to as "enterprise ontologies".

CM applications can also, however, be used for the development of more proactive, forward-looking systems in which data that reflect changes in either the organization or its environment are able to trigger warnings indicating business opportunities for the enterprise or imminent hazards to its proper functioning. To achieve these goals, CM applications must be freed from certain barriers placed around them by traditional knowledge management paradigms. This means, above all, that they must be required to mirror more faithfully those portions of reality which are salient to the workings of the enterprise, including changes that occur with the passage of time. It is especially in the domain of health care that work on such proactive technologies is most advanced. The purpose of this chapter is to demonstrate how the proposals to create proactive systems based on electronic health care record systems can be generalized in such a way as to achieve analogous objectives in the area of enterprise ontologies and corporate memories.

BACKGROUND

Corporate Memories

The word "corporate memory", including its quasi-synonym "organizational memory," is interchangeably used to denote distinct though related entities. Originally, the term referred to a specific type of "collective memory" found in organizations and groups, primarily commercial enterprises, and which, according to social and behavioral scientists descending from Durkheim, is something supra-individual which cannot be reduced to the memories in the minds of single individuals (Wexler, 2002). Collective memory so conceived typically comprehends various kinds of information about (1) external contacts, (2) internal know-how, (3) the types of authority and influence exerted not only by company owners but also employee associations, (4) the behavior of customers, (5) operational rule sets and routines, and (6) implementation strategies for company operations that determine how the information about all of these things should interact with the company's primary business (Beckett, 2000). With the advance of computer science, corporate memories became conceived as computer systems which embody a company's entire stock of knowledge assets, including accumulated know-how (skills), and make the latter available to enhance the efficiency and effectiveness of knowledge-intensive work processes (Kühn & Abecker, 1997).

How to build corporate memory systems is a research topic in its own right, since any such system has to be able to communicate with the majority of computer systems already installed in the company and to re-use the information they contain. Since this involves issues of semantic interoperability, it is no surprise that ontologies have become essential components of corporate memory systems, contributing to a wide variety of tasks. Most prominent, however, are the ontologies that describe organizational aspects of the enterprise, and are therefore called *enterprise ontologies*. This includes ontologies that are designed to deliver background knowledge in applications for electronic business interactions (Haller & Oren, 2006).

Enterprise Ontologies

Where corporate memories capture primarily what is *specific* for an enterprise, such as information about its employees, projects, business rules, contracts, and so forth, enterprise ontologies capture primarily what is *generic*. The first ontologies of this sort were developed in the course of The Enterprise Project in the United Kingdom (Stader, 1996) and the TOVE project in Toronto, Canada (Fox, 1992).

One of the outcomes of the Enterprise project was The Enterprise Ontology, which is described by its authors as a collection of terms and definitions relevant to business enterprises (Uschold, King, Moralee, & Zorgios, 1998). Approximately 90 terms are defined, grouped in five clusters labeled *activity, organization, strategy, marketing,* and *time.*

Of more recent date is the REA enterprise ontology (Geerts & McCarthy, 2002), whose acronym derives from the primary components of the framework's original domain: (economic) resources, events, and agents, and which is based on the REA accounting model (McCarthy, 1982).

The purpose of the *multi metamodel process ontology* (m3po) is to incorporate and unify the different currently existing workflow metamodels and reference models and to provide the representational resources for extracting what are called *choreographies* from internal business processes (Haller & Oren, 2006) in such a way as to capture the various sorts of relationships that obtain between participants in business interactions.

WHY ARE SUCH SYSTEMS NOT IN USE?

Despite the massive interest in and research activities directed towards both corporate memories and enter-

prise ontologies, reports on success stories are limited to unverifiable marketing claims or mere speculations. This is, for instance, witnessed by Rosenthal, Manola, and Seligman's (2001, p. 1) statement that:

... many initiatives, governmental and commercial, have pursued the grand vision of "transparent access"—making all data available to all consumers (users and applications), in a way the consumer can interpret, anywhere and at any time. Among large-scale enterprises, success stories in achieving such visions seem rare or nonexistent ...

or by papers such as Hill (2006), of which the title *Service Taxonomy and Service Ontologies Deliver Success to Enterprise SOA* does indeed imply the existence of actual success even though no evidence is provided in the actual paper.

As pointed out in the literature, there are several reasons for this. In Partridge and Stefanova (2001), for instance, it is argued that neither the TOVE nor the enterprise ontology meets the criteria of clear characterization and domain coverage, and that the problem cannot be compensated for by merging them because they do not share a common view of what an organization is. This provided the motivation to develop a new ontology: the Core Enterprise Ontology (Bertolazzi, Krusich, & Missikoff, 2001), but when this system was analyzed by other scholars, then it too was found not to meet certain crucial requirements, which again led to the creation of a new artifact (Osterwalder, Lagha, & Pigneur, 2002), and so on, ad infinitum.

Our research on the (generally low) quality of ontologies has demonstrated that the main reason for failure of ontology projects is the adoption of a methodology rooted in traditional expert-systems-based approaches to knowledge representation and therefore centered around the representation of *concepts* or *conceptualizations* (Smith, Ceusters, & Temmerman, 2005). The problem with this approach is that, by focusing on the semi-idealized concepts (ideas, meanings, knowledge) in the minds of divergent groups of semi-idealized experts, it does not take into account the concrete reality by which such putative experts are engaged in their day-to-day activities. This is because concepts in the minds of experts are always in one way or another simplifications of the reality to which they are intended to correspond. Representations of concepts in computer systems add a further level of simplification (and thus a further removal from reality) by imposing the restrictions of expressivity needed to guarantee computational tractability of the systems which result. Indeed, when knowledge engineers and information analysts proceed by first defining "concepts" and "relationships" and only then connecting these to bodies of data deriving in turn from some area of concrete reality, then they have things precisely the wrong way around. What they should be doing is finding a way to allow the concrete real-world entities to which given systems relate, and about which large amounts of data are typically already on hand, to determine the analysis from the very start and to serve as anchor for this analysis and for the workings of the system in every stage thereafter. Viewing reality always in terms of semi-idealized conceptual surrogates has given rise to several so-called "ontologies" in which these surrogates themselves, rather than reality, have become the objects of study, so that the quality of one ontology is gauged by the degree to which it conforms to a second ontology (Goossenaerts & Pelletier, 2003). Focusing on reality directly, in contrast, can provide an independent benchmark for the correctness of ontologies, and thus allow systematic measures of quality resting on investigation of the ways in which changes introduced in successive versions of an ontology relate to changes in the reality towards which it is directed (Ceusters & Smith, 2006a). Such measures are indispensable if we are to initiate an evolutionary path towards improvement in ontologies of the sort that we have in other empirical domains.

The predominant focus on conceptualizations which deviate in substantial ways from the structures found in reality applies also to ontologies developed in the context of enterprise engineering. Huhns and Stephens (2002), for instance, describes a methodology under which a multiplicity of ontology fragments, encapsulating the semantics employed by several independent parties, can be related together automatically without the use of any single global ontology. Inspection of the examples provided, however, reveals that the resulting unifications contain many erroneous associations. Interestingly, Huhns and Stephens do not consider this to be problematic. Indeed, they assert that a:

... consensus ontology is perhaps the most useful for information retrieval by humans, because it represents the way most people view the world and its information. For example, if most people wrongly believe that crocodiles are a kind of mammal, then most people would find it easier to locate information about crocodiles if it were located in a mammals grouping, rather than where it factually belonged. (Huhns & Stephens, p. 89)

If ontologies are ever to become useful in mission-critical domains like business or medicine, however, then they must be built on the basis of an approach which maximizes the degree to which entities *are* located where they factually belong—and this means an approach that is resolutely grounded in reality. Ontologies which are intended to be used more specifically in the context of enterprise engineering and corporate memory systems must be able to reflect not only how our perceptions and beliefs about reality change in the course of time but also how reality itself changes, and to reflect how the former are related to the latter. If, for the purposes of a given ontology application, it is judged relevant that many people believe that crocodiles are mammals, then this fact should indeed be represented; but it should be represented as a *false belief*, rather than being incorporated into an ontology as a fact on a par with all others.

In the following sections, we describe how to achieve these ends in such a way as to obtain a level of sophistication in ontology development that is able to draw a clear distinction between reality and the conceptualizations thereof on the part of managers, employers, and customers and the business interactions in which they engage.

ONTOLOGIES AND FAITHFULNESS TO REALITY

Basic Formal Ontology

The core of our proposal is basic formal ontology (BFO), a framework that is designed to serve as basis for the creation of high-quality shared ontologies especially in the domain of natural science. BFO embraces a methodology which is realist, fallibilist, perspectivalist, and adequatist (Grenon, Smith, & Goldberg, 2004). It holds, in other words, (1) that reality and its constituents exist independently of our (linguistic, conceptual, theoretical, cultural) representations thereof; (2) that our theories and classifications can be subject to revision; (3) that there exists a plurality of alternative, equally legitimate perspectives on reality; and (4) that these alternative views are not reducible to any single basic view.

BFO subdivides reality according to a number of basic dichotomies. First, it distinguishes *particulars* from *universals*; the former are entities such as Microsoft Corporation or the specific contract #17896 Microsoft signed with the University of Ohio in 1999; the latter are entities, such as *company* and *contract*, which have the former as their instances. Both universals and instances are restricted to what exists (or existed) in reality, and are thus different from classes and instances as referred to in ontologies adhering to a concept-based view (Smith, 2004). On the concept-based view, "employees of Microsoft Inc." would be perceived as designating a concept; according to BFO this phrase, as used at some specific time, designates a particular, namely the specific collection of persons who are employees of Microsoft Corporation at that time. Whereas under the concept-based view any specific Microsoft employee would be an *instance* of some putative corresponding concept, he or she would be a *member* of the collection under BFO.

Second, BFO distinguishes, within the realm of particulars, between *continuants* and *occurrents*. Continuants are those entities, such as Microsoft and its current CEO, that endure continuously through a period of time while undergoing changes of various sorts. Occurrents *are* such changes; they are entities which unfold in time through their successive temporal parts or phases—thus they are the entities otherwise called "processes," "actions," "events."

The difference between occurrents and continuants is crucial, and any ontology neglecting this distinction is not capable of dealing with changes over time in an appropriate way. While, for instance, a continuant particular may become an instance of distinct universals over time (Bill Gates was once an instance of *child*, later an instance of *adult*; his societal role was once an instance of *student*, later of *CEO*), occurrents cannot undergo such changes because occurrents *are* changes.

Third, there is the distinction between *dependent* and *independent* entities, where each dependent entity is defined as being such that it cannot exist without some independent entity which is its bearer. A contract, for example, cannot exist without contracting organizations or persons, and the process of signing a contract cannot exist without some person who signs. Persons themselves, in contrast, are independent: as soon as they exist, they do not depend on the existence of something else in the given sense, although, of course, their coming into existence did depend on other independent entities, for example, their parents. The utility of introducing this distinction into an ontology becomes obvious when the ontology is used to annotate data in a repository: when a particular is annotated as being an instance of a dependent entity, then there must be other particulars, perhaps yet unknown to the person who performs this annotation, on which that entity depends. In cases of this sort, the ontology becomes a valuable resource for formalizing business rules and database integrity constraints (Hay & Healy, 2000).

Fourth, there is the distinction between *fiat* and *bona fide* entities, which is based on the opposition between bona fide (or physical) and fiat boundaries, the latter being exemplified especially by boundaries—such as the boundary of Utah, or of the 20th century—introduced via human demarcation (Smith & Varzi, 1997). Fiat boundaries are overwhelmingly present in the realm of social entities, where they delineate for example markets, market segments, marketing regions, and serve in establishing what is an employee, a minor, a family member for purposes of health insurance coverage, and so forth.

BFO also distinguishes three major families of relations between the entities just sketched: (1) <p, p>–relations, obtaining between particular and particular (for example, Steve Ballmer being the CEO of Microsoft); (2) <p, u>-relations, obtaining between particular and universal (for example, Steve Ballmer being an instance of the universal *person*); and (3) <u, u>-relations, obtaining between universal and universal (for example, *software company* being a subkind of *company*) (Smith, Ceusters, Klagges, et al., 2005). The importance of this distinction is exemplified by the fact that relationships such as parthood have distinct properties at the particular and at the universal levels, and that ignoring these distinctions has led to a number of erroneous representations of relations (Donnelly, Bittner, & Rosse, 2006). These distinctions can be handled also in regular concept-based ontologies, but they have thus far characteristically been ignored – not least because concept-based ontologies very often reflect an unsure understanding of the distinction between an instance and a universal.

Granular Partition Theory

The second element of our proposal is granular partition theory, a highly general framework for understanding the ways in which, when cataloguing, classifying, mapping, or inventoring a certain *portion of reality* (POR), human beings and other cognitive agents divide up or partition this reality at one or more levels of granularity (Bittner & Smith, 2003). The resultant partitions are composed of *partition units* (analogous to the cells in a grid) and the theory provides a formal account of the different ways in which such units can correspond, or fail to correspond, to the entities in reality towards which they are directed. The theory takes account, for example, of the degree to which a partition represents the mereological structure of the domain onto which it is projected, and also of the degree of completeness with which a partition represents this domain.

Drawing on this framework, we have proposed a calculus for use in quality assurance of complex representations created for clinical or research purposes in the context of both ontology evolution (Ceusters & Smith, 2006a) and ontology mapping (Ceusters, 2006). The calculus is based on a distinction between three levels (Smith, Kusnierczyk, Schober, & Ceusters, 2006):

1. The level of reality (for example, on the side of a specific enterprise, its employees, managers, etc.)
2. The cognitive representations of this reality (for example, as embodied in observations and interpretations on the part of sales personnel or business analysts)
3. The publicly accessible concretizations of these representations in artefacts of various sorts, of which ontologies and corporate memories are specific examples

The representations on levels 2 and 3 are composed in hierarchical fashion out of modular sub-representations built ultimately out of smallest modules called *representational units*, whereby:

1. Each module is assumed to be veridical, that is, to conform to some relevant POR on the basis of our best current understanding (which may, of course, be based on errors)
2. Distinct modules may correspond to the same POR by presenting different though still veridical views or perspectives of this reality, for instance one and the same event may be described both as an event of buying and as an event of selling
3. What is to be represented by the modules in a representation depends on the purposes which that representation is designed to serve

Relevant portions of reality can include not only physical things (buildings, physical goods) but also mental acts and states (acts of valuation on the part of stockholders, states of willingness of potential customers to buy a certain good) and entities of many other types, including institutions, social roles, social relations of authority or ownership, and so forth.

THE REFERENT TRACKING PARADIGM

In ontologies and terminologies the representational units are terms from some natural or formal language and are assumed to refer to universals or defined classes (Smith et al., 2006); in corporate memories the representational units must refer also in robust and unambiguous fashion to enterprise-specific entities at the level of instances.

Referent tracking (RT) is a new approach to the handling of data about real world entities introduced in Ceusters and Smith (2006b). It allows instances in reality to serve as benchmark for the correctness of the ontologies used to describe them. The RT paradigm has been developed thus far to support the entry and retrieval of data in the electronic health record (EHR), where its purpose is to avoid the problems which arise when statements in an EHR refer to disorders, lesions, and other entities on the side of the patient by means of logically complex descriptive phrases such as "there is a fracture in the leg of patient X" or "there is a tumour in the lung of patient Y." These problems arise because the phrases in question employ generic terms in ways which may fail to identify the relevant instances unambiguously (John may have multiple fractures in his leg; or he may have fractured his leg twice at different times in his life). In Parsons and Wand (2000), it is argued that problems in schema integration, schema evolution, and interoperability of databases are precisely the consequence of ambiguities of this sort, which are deeply rooted in the erroneous assumption adhered to in many database design circles according to which entities can be referred to only as instances of prespecified classes. They make the case that this *assumption of inherent classification* violates philosophical and cognitive guidelines on classification.

Referent tracking avoids such ambiguities by introducing unique identifiers, called instance unique identifiers (IUIs), for each numerically distinct entity that exists in reality and that is referred to in statements in a record. Currently the items uniquely identified for EHR purposes are restricted to entities such as patients, care providers, buildings, machines, and so forth. The referent tracking paradigm expands this list beyond the current range to include also fractures, polyps, seizures, and a vast variety of other clinically salient real-world instances in all the categories distinguished by the BFO ontology.

In the context of corporate memories, analogously, IUIs would be assigned not merely to the various organizations and persons relevant to the enterprise (companies, employees, customers, and so forth) but also to contracts, applicable laws, meetings, all sorts of business transactions, accidents in manufacturing facilities, deliveries, and so forth. It would include also various types of failures, absences, and other putative negative entities, although these call for special treatment (Ceusters, Elkin, & Smith, 2006). For many entities, unique identifiers will exist already in the various information systems of a large corporation. Our proposal is that these identifiers should be consolidated into a single corporate memory store, where they will constitute an evolving dynamic map of the corporation and of all events and processes with which the corporation is involved.

The following requirements have to be addressed if the paradigm of referent tracking is to be given concrete form in a referent tracking system (RTS) able to serve the needs of an enterprise: (1) a mechanism for generating IUIs that are guaranteed to be unique strings; (2) a procedure for deciding which particulars should receive IUIs; (3) protocols for determining whether or not a particular has already been assigned a IUI (each particular should receive maximally one IUI); (4) rules governing the processing of IUIs in information systems, including rules concerning the syntax and semantics of statements containing IUIs; (5) methods for determining the truth values of propositions that are expressed through descriptions in which IUIs are employed; (6) methods for correcting errors in the assignment of IUIs, and for investigating the results of assigning alternative IUIs to problematic cases; and (7) methods for taking account of changes in the reality to which IUIs get assigned, for example when particulars change their qualities or when they merge or split.

With respect to (1), IUIs are to be assigned to particulars directly, and thus independently of the universals of which they are instances and of any ontology describing such universals. A strategy consisting of assigning unique IDs to representational units within each ontology, and then adding prefixes to these IDs to denote the particulars which instantiate them, would not work because particulars can be instances of universals denoted in several ontologies. Moreover, particulars may change over time and so instantiate different universals, or the classification status may change or a given particular may change as errors in a data resource are corrected. The goal of referent tracking is, we recall, to provide a means by which instances in reality can serve as benchmark for the correctness of ontologies. If ontologies themselves are used to generate the referent tracking IDs, then this goal will be defeated from the start.

An RTS can be set up in isolation, for instance, within a single department of a large company. Clearly, however, the referent tracking paradigm will serve its purpose most optimally when used in a distributed, collaborative environment such as a large company with several offices dispersed over a wide area. One and the same customer is often served by a variety of departments within a single enterprise, many of them working in different settings, and each of these settings may use its own separate information system. These systems contain different data, but these data often provide information about the same particulars. Under the current state of affairs, it is very hard, if not impossible, to query these data in such a way that, for a given particular, all information available can be retrieved. With the right sort of distributed RTS, such retrieval becomes in very many cases a trivial matter and this even on a meta-company level. It could, for instance, give considerable added value to services of the kind delivered by a business information service company such as Factiva, which uses a four step automated and manual process to ensure that everything falling under the coverage of its 12,000 information sources is correctly categorized. Customers can receive the data either as an XML feed or a Web service for integration into their corporate intranets, or their CRM or competitive-intelligence systems (Drew, 2006).

Services of a Referent Tracking System

An RTS should offer at least three services: (1) generation of unique identifiers to be used as IUIs, (2) management of the IUIs generated, and (3) provision of access to the IUIs stored.

As to (1), several schemes for generating strings that are guaranteed to be unique are already in use. If RTS services would be offered by a player external to a specific organization, it might be beneficial that this player not only registers IUIs but also certifies the uniqueness of the strings to be used within a given IUI-repository and guarantees that the assignments claimed to have been made by given authors were indeed made by those authors. Persons assigning IUIs, who will typically play a variety of other roles within the enterprise, will themselves be identified by IUIs, which will enable them to be identified automatically in these several roles and enable also cross-links between the corresponding different groups of entities (including other persons) with which they have to deal.

Service (2) involves what we shall refer to as the *IUI-repository*, whose purpose is to keep track of the identifiers assigned to already existing entities, or reserved for entities that are expected to come into existence in the future. It will do this in such a way that (i) each IUI represents exactly one particular, and (ii) no particular is referred to by more than one IUI. These two requirements are not easy to fulfil, since both depend on the ability and willingness of users to provide accurate information. This, however, introduces no problems different in principle from those already faced by the users of existing systems when called upon to provide information of a non-trivial and occasionally sensitive sort about individuals.

Service (3), here called the referent tracking database (RTDB), should provide access to the information entered into a given corporate memory about the particulars referred to in the IUI-repository. Where the IUI repository is an inventory of concrete entities that have been acknowledged to exist, and, consequently, of what IDs to use if one wants to refer to them, the RTDB is an inventory of descriptions concerning the features of and interrelations between these entities and of the ways in which they change in the course of time. The RTDB, too, does not need to be set up as a single central database but can rely on any paradigm for distributed storage.

The role of the RTDB is to keep track not only of the features and interrelations of given particulars as they change through time but also of the assertions that have been made about such particulars, including those assertions that have been shown to be false (stored, for example, for the purposes of providing an audit trail). The RTDB also helps users to determine whether a particular they encounter for the first time has been registered already in the IUI-repository or whether a new IUI must be created for use in new descriptions. To be sure, this places some additional burden on the person who has to enter the information; but, given that cases such as this are likely to be of high salience, the time perceived as being lost at this stage will likely be recovered when searching for information thereafter.

Applying BFO and Referent Tracking to Corporate Memories

For the remainder of this chapter, we will provide examples of how the theories and paradigms described above can be used to detect and solve a number of problems and inconsistencies that we (and others) encountered in studying the literature on enterprise engineering and corporate memories.

Quite common is the inclusion of representational units in an ontology that do not have a counterpart in reality. This happens at the level both of relationships and of the entities which serve as their relata. Consider the difference between the "Sale" and "Have-Capability" relationships as defined in the enterprise ontology (Uschold et al., 1998). A "Sale" is (acceptably)

defined as "a relationship constituting an agreement between two Legal Entities to exchange a Product for a Sale Price," (p. 44) in keeping with the enterprise ontology's treatment of relationships as entities in their own right that can thus be instantiated. Two instances of legal entity thus enter into a single instance of the "Sale" relationship. The "Have-Capability" relationship, on the other hand, is defined as "a relationship between a Person and an Activity denoting that the Person is able to perform the Activity." (p. 47). The first problem here is the confusion of use and mention: relationships themselves do not "denote"; this is the task of the corresponding denoting expressions. But more importantly, being able to engage in an activity does not require that any instance of such an activity exists. Under BFO, properties of this sort would be represented correspondingly as falling within the realm of realizable entities (such as powers, functions, dispositions, orders, plans, algorithms, recipes), in order to do justice to the fact that the existence of a capability does not imply the existence of any realization of this capability (IFOMIS, 2006).

The use-mention confusion—which is common not only among enterprise ontology developers—confuses the level of reality with the level of our representations thereof. Many data dictionaries suffer from this confusion. The *ACORD Data Dictionary for Global Insurance Industry*, for example, which is used to assist in automating business interactions between insurers and clients (ACORD, 2005), defines a building as "a construction that normally has a roof and wall." "Air conditioning", however, it defines as "information necessary to describe a given type of air conditioning in a building." Consistency in providing definitions would dictate that "entity" is used in such a way that it refers always either to *information about* something in reality, or to *that something in reality* itself. ACORD, however, provides a problematic mishmash, in which *buildings*, for example, would contain *information about air conditioning* as parts.

The same confusion is found in Goossenaerts and Pelletier (2003); the latter correctly argues that the Enterprise and TOVE ontologies do not emphasize the distinction between things and their changes on the one hand and conceptual entities on the other, drawing their analysis from the work of Bunge (1977) and specifically from its application in the Bunge-Wand-Weber model in the domain of information systems (Wand, Storey, & Weber, 1999). This analysis led them to develop participative simulation environment for integral manufacturing renewal ontology (PSIM), which was inspired also by earlier work conducted in the European Research Project CIMOSA (AMICE-Consortium, 1989) and from Peircean semiotics (Hoopes, 1991). The result, however, is not without its own dramatic mysteries and misinterpretations. Thus we read that the PSIM Ontology distinguishes three main categories: Activity, Object, and Information (element), whereby an "Information (element)" is defined as "a characteristic of either an object or activity or information, which is used to constrain directly or indirectly the involvement of an object in an activity" (Goossenaerts & Pelletier, 2003, p. 45). PSIM then classifies as information elements not only "the time needed to perform an activity" and "how an activity has to be performed", but also "how the enterprise is organized", "the way the responsibilities are distributed among the enterprise", and even "the weight of a piece of material". Weight, for BFO, is a dependent continuant that depends on the material object of which it is the weight, and this independently of whether or not a cognitive being has any sort of information about the matter. Confusions of this sort are a direct result of the concept orientation in ontology.

This concept orientation leads quite often also to a blurring of the distinction between instantiation and subtyping. Where in BFO *instantiation* is a relationship between a particular and a universal, *subtyping* is a quite different relationship holding between one universal and another. Nothing which is an instance can itself have instances, while something that is a subtype can itself have other subtypes. As is correctly recognized in Uschold et al. (1998), the distinction between a type of entity, and a particular entity of a certain type, that is, an instance, is not consistently made when using natural language. This does not, however, mean that it is acceptable that the authors

of the Enterprise Ontology "intentionally blurred this distinction" in the informal description of their ontology (Uschold et al., 1998, p. 35). And when the methodological work underlying the core enterprise ontology allows John Doe to be an instance of "consumer," and "consumer" to be an instance of "entity" (Bertolazzi et al., 2001), the result is a mistake that is impermissible in any serious ontology work.

Note that it is not just natural language that blurs the mentioned distinction: traditional database design paradigms exhibit the same type of confusion, as do some ontology authoring environments such as Cyc (Foxvog, 2005). A table about cars may contain "instances" such as "Volkswagen" or "Audi." Under a realist paradigm, such a representation can only be the result of a sloppy analysis in which a *car brand* is mistaken for a *car*.

Even more unfortunate are the views adhered to by (Noy & McGuinness, 2001) who claim that "individual instances are the most specific concepts in an ontology" (p. 18), or that "deciding whether a particular concept is a class in an ontology or an individual instance depends on what the potential applications of the ontology are" (p. 18). As an example, for an expert system intended to give advice on what types of wine pair best with certain types of food, it may not matter whether a specific brand of Elsasser Riesling is represented in the system by means of a class or an instance. But if the latter option is chosen, and this system needs to be used in interactions with restaurants or wine merchants who would like to link their inventory to that expert system, then it will lead to problems if what is a class for the former, is an instance for the latter.

The rigorous identification schemes proposed by the Referent Tracking paradigm are an important first step in doing away with such confusions, and they have been proposed in this capacity for example in solving problems related to digital rights management (Ceusters & Smith, in press). That they can help, too, in the specific case of enterprise engineering is witnessed by a recent case study exploring the possible complementarity of the demo engineering methodology for organizations (DEMO) and the object role modeling (ORM) paradigm (Dietz & Halpin, 2004). DEMO enables the business processes of organizations to be modeled independently of how these processes are implemented, thereby focusing on the communication acts that take place between human actors in the organization. ORM enables business information to be modeled in terms of *fact types* as well as the business rules that constrain how the fact types may be populated for any given state of the information system and how derived facts may be inferred from other facts. One important feature of ORM is its requirement for the inclusion of at least one identification scheme for each entity type, which functions as an identity criterion for instances of that type. Because of this requirement, data use cases, that is, samples of information, can be used to seed an initial model. However, if ORM is to be used for the purposes of building an ontology rather than a database schema, then developers should pay attention to the fact that several records in a database may refer to the same entity in reality. This is certainly the case, for example, when databases maintained in originally distinct organizations are merged because of a company takeover.

CONCLUSION

For a company to anticipate and manage change for the future, to design appropriate strategies that will create business value for customers, and to improve profitability in current and new markets, its activities must be based on a synoptic view of its present business environment as a complex dynamic whole comprehending the activities, resources, markets, customers, products, services, regulations, and costs associated with the enterprise. Such an overview, the key to strategic intelligence, is cultivated, for example, through the methods used to improve the capabilities of the company's managers and workers to learn about changes in the business or industry environment that are summarized in Marchand, Davenport, and Dixon (2000). Corporate memories are crucial to building

and sustaining such strategic intelligence, and we believe that ontologies *combined with referent tracking* can play a key role in building the robust and useful corporate memories of the future. Ontology is in essence a philosophical discipline that seeks to capture high-grade terminological knowledge that can provide a sound basis for data schemas and data dictionaries such as are employed by large organizations. The development of ontologies as artifacts for use in computer systems has, unfortunately, been too often conducted in a way that ignores reality. The referent tracking paradigm, by bringing reality back into business, can solve this problem and thereby save businesses from the "conceptual models" of their IT personnel.

REFERENCES

ACORD. (2005). Data dictionary for global insurance industry. Retrieved June 8, 2007, from http://www.acord.org/dataDictionary/dataDictionary.htm

AMICE-Consortium. (1989). *Open system architecture for CIM, research reports of ESPRIT project 688* (Vol. 1). Berlin: Springer Verlag.

Beckett, R.C. (2000). A characterization of corporate memory as a knowledge system. *Journal of Knowledge Management, 4*(4), 311-319.

Bertolazzi, P., Krusich, C., & Missikoff, M. (2001). *An approach to the definition of a core enterprise ontology: CEO.* Paper presented at the OES-SEO 2001 International Workshop on Open Enterprise Solutions: Systems, Experiences, and Organizations.

Bittner, T., & Smith, B. (2003). A theory of granular partitions. In M. Duckham, M.F. Goodchild & M.F. Worboy (Eds.), *Foundations of geographic information science* (pp. 117-151). London: Taylor & Francis Books.

Bunge, M. (1977). *Treatise on basic philosophy, ontology I: The furniture of the world* (Vol. 3). Boston: Reidel.

Ceusters, W. (2006). Towards a realism-based metric for quality assurance in ontology matching. In B. Bennett & C. Fellbaum (Eds.), *Formal ontology in information systems* (pp. 321-332). Amsterdam: IOS Press.

Ceusters, W., Elkin, P., & Smith, B. (2006). Referent tracking: The problem of negative findings. In A. Hasman, R. Haux, J.v.d. Lei, E.D. Clercq, & F. Roger-France (Eds.), *Studies in Health Technology and Informatics. Ubiquity: Technologies for Better Health in Aging Societies. Proceedings of MIE2006* (Vol. 124, pp. 741-746). Amsterdam: IOS Press.

Ceusters, W., & Smith, B. (2006a). A realism-based approach to the evolution of biomedical ontologies. In *Proceedings of AMIA 2006* (pp. 121-125).

Ceusters, W., & Smith, B. (2006b). Strategies for referent tracking in electronic health records. *Journal of Biomedical Informatics, 39*(3), 362-378.

Ceusters, W., & Smith, B. (2007). Referent tracking for digital rights management. *International Journal of Metadata, Semantics and Ontologies, 2*(1),45-53.

Dietz, J.L.G., & Halpin, T.A. (2004). Using DEMO and ORM in concert: A case study. *Advanced Topics in Database Research, 3*, 218-236.

Donnelly, M., Bittner, T., & Rosse, C. (2006). A formal theory for spatial representation and reasoning in biomedical ontologies. *Artificial Intelligence in Medicine, 36*(1), 1-27.

Drew, R. (2006, March 20). In Google's shadow. *Computerworld.* Retrieved August 23, 2007 from http://www.computerworld.com/softwaretopics/software/story/0,10801,109613,00.html

Fox, M.S. (1992). *The TOVE project: Towards a common-sense model of the enterprise* (Tech. Rep.). Enterprise Integration Laboratory.

Foxvog, D. (2005). Instances of instances modeled via higher-order classes. In *Proceedings of the Workshop on Foundational Aspects of Ontologies (FOnt 2005)* (pp. 46-54).

Geerts, G., & McCarthy, W.E. (2002). An ontological analysis of the primitives of the extended-REA enterprise information architecture. *The International Journal of Accounting Information Systems, 3*, 1-16.

Goossenaerts, J., & Pelletier, C. (2003). Ontology and enterprise modeling. Retrieved June 8, 2007, from http://is.tm.tue.nl/staff/jgoossenaerts/4PublicPdf/PSIM%20book%20ch%205%20Ontol&EM.pdf

Grenon, P., Smith, B., & Goldberg, L. (2004). Bio-dynamic ontology: Applying BFO in the biomedical domain. In D.M. Pisanelli (Ed.), *Ontologies in medicine* (pp. 20-38). Amsterdam: IOS Press.

Haller, A., & Oren, E. (2006). A process ontology to represent semantics of different process and choreography meta-models. Retrieved June 8, 2007, from http://www.m3pe.org/deliverables/process-ontology.pdf

Hay, D., & Healy, K.A. (2000). *Defining business rules ~ what are they really?* (Final Report No. Revision 1.3). The Business Rule Group.

Hill, M. (2006). Service taxonomy and service ontologies deliver success to enterprise SOA. *Service Oriented Architecture Webservices Journal, 6.* Retrieved June 8, 2007, from http://webservices.sys-con.com/read/175385.htm

Hoopes, J. (1991). *Peirce ON SIGNS. Writings on semiotic by Charles Sanders Peirce.* Chapel Hill and London: The University of North Carolina Press

Huhns, M.N., & Stephens, L.M. (2002). Semantic bridging of independent enterprise ontologies. In K. Kosanke (Ed.), *Enterprise inter- and intra-organizational integration: Building international consensus* (pp. 83-90). Boston: Kluwer Academic Publishers.

IFOMIS. (2006, December). Basic formal ontology. Retrieved June 8, 2007, from http://www.ifomis.uni-saarland.de/bfo/

Kühn, O., & Abecker, A. (1997). Corporate memories for knowledge management in industrial practice: Prospects and challenges. *Journal of Universal Computer*

Science, 3(8), 929-954.

Marchand, D.A., Davenport, T.H., & Dixon, T. (2000). *Financial times – Mastering information management, complete MBA companion in information management*. London: FT Prentice Hall.

McCarthy, W.E. (1982). The REA accounting model: A generalized framework for accounting systems in a shared data environment. *The Accounting Review, LVII* (3), 554-578.

Noy, N.F., & McGuinness, D.L. (2001). *Ontology development 101: A guide to creating your first ontology* (No. KSL-01-05). Stanford Knowledge Systems Laboratory.

Osterwalder, A., Lagha, S.B., & Pigneur, Y. (2002). *An ontology for developing e-business models*. Paper presented at the IFIP DSIAge 2002.

Parsons, J., & Wand, Y. (2000). Emancipating instances from the tyranny of classes in information modeling. *ACM Transactions on Database Systems, 25*(2), 228-268.

Partridge, C., & Stefanova, M. (2001). A synthesis of state of the art enterprise ontologies - work in progress. Retrieved June 8, 2007, from http://citeseer.ist.psu.edu/632089.html

Rosenthal, A., Manola, F., & Seligman, L. (2001). Getting data to applications – why we fail – Part 1: Common fallacies. *The Mitre Information Technology Advisor, 1*(10), 1-2.

Smith, B. (2004). Beyond concepts: Ontology as reality representation. In *Proceedings of the 3rd International Conference on Formal Ontology in Information Systems (FOIS 2004)* (pp. 73-84). Amsterdam: IOS Press.

Smith, B., Ceusters, W., Klagges, B., Köhler, J., Kumar, A., Lomax, J., et al. (2005). Relations in biomedical ontologies. *Genome Biology, 6*(5), R46.

Smith, B., Ceusters, W., & Temmerman, R. (2005). Wüsteria. In R. Engelbrecht, A. Geissbuhler, C. Lovis, & G. Mihalas (Eds.), *Connecting medical informatics and bio-informatics. Medical informatics Europe 2005* (pp. 647-652). Amsterdam: IOS Press.

Smith, B., Kusnierczyk, W., Schober, D., & Ceusters, W. (2006). *Towards a reference terminology for ontology research and development in the biomedical domain*. Paper presented at the KR-MED 2006, Biomedical Ontology in Action. Retrieved June 8, 2007, from http://ontology.buffalo.edu/bfo/Terminology_for_Ontologies.pdf

Smith, B., & Varzi, A.C. (1997). Fiat and bona fide boundaries: Towards on ontology of spatially extended objects. In *Lecture Notes In Computer Science* (Vol. 1329, pp. 103-119). London: Springer Verlag.

Stader, J. (1996). *Results of the enterprise project*. Paper presented at the 16th Annual Conference of the British Computer Society Specialist Group on Expert Systems.

Uschold, M., King, M., Moralee, S., & Zorgios, Y. (1998). The enterprise ontology. *The Knowledge Engineering Review, 13*(1), 31-89.

Wand, Y., Storey, V., & Weber, R. (1999). An ontological analysis of the relationship construct in conceptual modeling. *ACM Transactions on Database Systems, 24*(4), 494-528.

Wexler, M.N. (2002). Organizational memory and intellectual capital. *Journal of Intellectual Capital, 3*(4), 393-415.

Section II
General Domain Ontologies for Business Interaction

Chapter IV
Ontology Design for Interaction in a Reasonable Enterprise

Aldo Gangemi
ISTC-CNR, Rome

Valentina Presutti
ISTC-CNR, Rome

ABSTRACT

In this chapter we show a simple example of how different but complementary approaches to enterprise business interaction modeling (e.g., business process management, business objects, e-services, workflow management systems, etc.) can be reengineered and integrated within a same formal context. Our method is based on content ontology design patterns (CODePs), which provide a conceptual tool to build content modularly, and to describe an enterprise and its interactions in the same domain of discourse as its social and informational contexts. The objectives of our method include: (1) encoding the requirements from the communities of practice involved in business interactions; (2) reengineering and integrating existing languages and ontologies for business interaction; (3) creating a formal infrastructure to represent the dependencies between enterprises, social interaction and practices, legal regulations, and the physical world. As a result, entities like organizations, roles, social relationships, material resources, information objects, workflows, events, and so forth, are represented according to a set of modular, interoperable ontologies.

INTRODUCTION

Ontologies, intended as logical theories suitable to represent a domain of discourse, are the backbone of semantic technologies, including the Semantic Web.

Domains of discourse may include entities conceived in the physical, social, or cognitive worlds: minerals, proteins, elevators, food, persons, organizations, human activities, legal norms, commercial transactions, recipes, ideas, mathematical entities, data, and so forth.

While there exist ontologies and logical theories/languages for enterprises and business objects, no conceptual framework has been developed so far which holds together the very different and heterogeneous entities involved in business interaction: organizations, roles, social relationships, communities, material resources, information objects, workflows, regulations, events, and so forth.

In order to "hold together" those entities, we need to define appropriate relations and axioms that govern their possible interactions. For example, what are the relations, and the restrictions on their use, between:

- An organization and the agents that act for it?
- Two persons who play two interdependent roles in a team?
- A contract and the workflows to define, sign, and enact it?
- The information from a text and its realizations, for example, in a file?
- A community and its members?
- An agent and an action that must be performed in order to achieve a task defined within a workflow?

The previous list includes just an excerpt of the many relations that underlie business interactions, and none of them is really specific of the business world. What is actually specific in business interaction should then result from the complex of those relations and their composition in real-world contexts. For example, even a basic business interaction, like two employees exchanging e-mails about an order, includes at least one organization, one team, one (maybe explicit) workflow, two roles, one task, one communication situation, the related information flowing in that situation, two text messages, and two agents performing a communication action.

One may wonder why we need all those types of entities in order to describe the ordinary fact of two employees who are exchanging e-mails about an order. The answer is straightforward: the relations between those entities distinguish two employees from any two humans, a team from a scattered collection of humans, a sequence of goal-oriented actions from a set of nonintentional, accidental events, an organized community from a set whatsoever of agents. Those distinctions are acquired by cognitive agents during a lifelong learning, but in most cases are not available to information systems.

That said, one can still wonder why information systems need to go into that detail, instead of simply providing good communication channels and applications. This second question requires a more articulated answer, which will be given in the "roadmap" section of this chapter. The basic assumption here is that current organizations and enterprises are too complex for any management team to be governed without accessing the crucial, sensible knowledge of their community and the related processes. Selection and analysis of such information requires a move from information to knowledge processing. The main difference between information and knowledge is that the second allows inferences to be made, so that much more information, and in more flexible ways, is eventually available, not only to the management team, but to the entire community associated to an organization or enterprise.

Inferences do not only include traditional, deterministic logical inferences, but also probabilistic reasoning on unstructured text corpora, images, social networks, partial data sets, and so forth. While reasoning support for ontologies usually rests on deterministic logical inferences, it can be used to put together the heterogeneous data coming from those inferential processes, and to present appropriate *views* to a community whose members act for an enterprise. In other words, independently on the kind of inferential process required to gather new information from existing knowledge, the integration of that new information requires a common framework in order to assist rational agents in taking decisions and extracting relevant knowledge for a task.

Our objective in this chapter is to introduce methods and practices to formally describe that common framework, including enterprise-related entities, their identity, structure, functions, social relationships, and interaction aspects.

On one hand, we aim to reuse existing work, presented here in a (necessarily incomplete) small-scale roadmap (see the section titled Roadmap). On the other hand, we describe and exemplify a method to exploit "reference ontologies" in the form of *ontology design patterns* (see the section entitled Patterns), which help reengineering and integrating existing work. Our choice is motivated by an assumption of *liberality* with reference to different methods, ontologies, approaches, and so forth. The rationale of our liberality assumption is simple: most approaches are usually task-oriented and tasks cannot be standardized without a negotiation. Ontology engineers should then take for granted the need to reengineer existing patterns and models and then act in order to integrate them into ontologies that can be applied to realistic cases. Valuability of existing models should be judged against a variety of criteria. For a comprehensive framework to ontology evaluation, selection, and reengineering, see Gangemi, Catenacci, Ciaramita, and Lehmann (2006).

Besides the liberality assumption, we summarize here a set of specific assumptions that underlie our approach to modeling the enterprise business interaction domain. They are based on previous experiences in ontology engineering projects (Gangemi, Fisseha, Keizer, Pettman, & Taconet, 2004; Gangemi, Pisanelli, & Steve, 2001; Gangemi, Sagri, & Tiscornia, 2005), as well as on good practices from ontology engineering (Gangemi & Mika, 2003; Masolo, Vieu et al., 2004; Noy & Rector, 2005).

- **Transparency:** An enterprise can be understood both as an aggregate of persons and resources and as a legal person supposed to interact with other social entities. In most legal systems, enterprises have legal existence independently from the agents and facilities that allow them to take action in societies. But agents should not be left unaware of the reasons and objectives that govern the social action of an enterprise.

- **Informational dependency:** No enterprise can exist without information, not only because information allows business interaction, it lies at the very beginning as a social creation act, for example, when a company is founded according to the laws of a certain legal system and specific legal actions are required. With respect to that, an enterprise is a virtual entity, that is, it does not exist in nature. Paradoxically, being virtual makes enterprises much more effective as they only have to plan their behavior according to legal constraints, and those constraints react only to the available information about enterprises, and not to the laws of nature.

- **Social dependency:** The way an enterprise is described substantially influences (i.e., changes) the way it shows its wise in the social environment, and consequently the impact it has on markets and societies in general. Being solely dependent on information makes enterprises able to tune their behavior on the actual information that is conveyed, possibly to a selected part of the community that acts for them or is affected by their behavior. Hence, the behavior of the agents acting for enterprises must be carefully reconstructed in the context of the social/legal rights and duties of a certain community. That careful reconstruction is rarely made and exploited to the advantage of the entire community.

- **Knowledge-based control:** An infrastructure for the management of information flows is crucial, and not just as a set of communication means to be used by executives, employees, customers, and so forth, but primarily as a formal description of the origin, structure, functions, and evolution of an enterprise. The level of information flow awareness, as required by business interactions between agents as well as between agents and enterprises, calls for appropriate formal frameworks that can master different kinds of knowledge and their effective integration.

- **Ontology-based community awareness:** Ontology engineering and Semantic Web technologies can help in working out such formal description by providing models that allow designers to describe an enterprise environment in the same domain of discourse as the other social entities. The resulting formal model could then be compared to other models describing a society, a social network of a community, a set of regulations or policies, a legal system, economic theories, and so forth.

Our assumptions are motivated by a rationale in which enterprises exist as *reasonable* entities in the social lifecycle, especially now, when organizations and corporations are sometimes considered *abnormal* entities that tend to impair the lifecycle of individual human persons. In this sense, a formal model of an enterprise should be able to make its ethical behavior emerge through the analysis of its logical behavior. Although we are agnostic on what specific behavior is best to a given context, we are nonetheless convinced that a formal analysis, aided by automatic reasoning capabilities, can assist the decision-making process on those behaviors effectively.

In this chapter we show a simple example of how several and sometimes complementary approaches to enterprise business modeling (e.g., business process management, business objects, e-services, workflow management systems, etc.) can contribute data within a same formal context. The example applies a conceptual framework that captures a substantial amount of the primitives that are expected to integrate data coming from those different modeling approaches.

Our method is based on content ontology design patterns (CODePs) (Gangemi, 2005), which provide a tool to build content modularly and to describe an enterprise in the same domain of discourse as that used to describe social contexts.

The rest of the chapter is organized as follows: in the Roadmap section we present a small-scale roadmap of the related work, in the Patterns section we describe two highly-reusable CODePs taken from descriptions and situations(D&S), and plan ontology (PO) (*The description and situation ontology,* 2006; *The plan ontology,* 2006), while in the Example section we exemplify our method by means of a simple merging case. Finally, the Conclusion section recaps on the chapter's content.

A SMALL-SCALE ROADMAP OF ENTERPRISE MODELING

There is a huge literature on business modeling and a substantial one also for the ontological approaches to those models. Since this chapter concentrates on a practical example of how ontology engineering and design principles can be applied to business interaction, only a small roadmap to the literature is presented here.

Business modeling studies span from sociological observations to computational-oriented solutions, which we summarize briefly in this section.

Since Taylor's time, many attempts at describing the structure, management, and production process of enterprises and their business have been conducted. The aim of these studies, conceived from different perspectives, has been to govern the behavior and impact of an enterprise within society. Taylorist (Taylor, 1964) and antiTaylorist theories deal with "teamworking" models and aim to maximize business profit through the instantiation of such models. For example, in Pruijt (2002), different views and divergences in the applications of such theories are reported. The author concludes that there is not a unique way to achieve the desired goal because it depends on several factors.

With reference to socio-economic studies, enterprise business can be placed in the context of a "knowledge-based economy", which is defined as an economy where knowledge is the most important productive factor (Rooney, Joseph, Mandeville, & Hearn, 2003). In such an economy, the exchange of information, which is the glue between business interactions, is the primary economic interaction (Metcalfe & Saviotti, 1991).

Business interaction copes with heterogeneous entities and the business domain is characterized by a fast-changing environment (Uschold, King, Moralee, & Zorgios, 1998). Its evolution depends on a wide range of social, economical, and technological objects, events, and relationships among them. Enterprise governance must take in consideration such complexity in order to undertake its goals. This view requires a move from information-centric to knowledge-centric approaches.

Knowledge arises from social relations, language, culture, people and societies, and depends on its situation and enactment (Rooney, 2005). According to (Smith, 1995), knowledge "must be considered in its social context and a large part of the social context of knowledge is global". These suggestions coming from economic studies are not trivially transferable into practical methods and tools for the knowledge society. The most productive intellectual assets that are moving forward the vision of a knowledge society are currently the notion of knowledge as information that a system can reason about, and the formal semantic methods that allow to represent and reason on knowledge. These frameworks are nonetheless only an infrastructure, while the problem of representing and reasoning on social context, the local/global issue, and the encoding of the relationships between social relations, language, theories, people, and so forth, are still at a very preliminary stage of investigation.

In the context of information technology, business modeling has been the focus of a huge effort, which has concentrated on providing designers with languages, methods, and techniques conceived in order to support the modeling of typical business problems and solutions. The most relevant are listed here:

- Data model patterns (Hay, 1996; Marco & Jennings, 2004; Silverston, 2001) are modeling solutions for domain-oriented typical scenarios, defined and presented by means of Entity-Relationship (E/R) diagrams (Chen, 2002).
- Workflow patterns (Van Der Aalst, Ter Hofstede, Kiepuszewski, & Barros, 2003) describe primitive and complex structures for representing recurring configurations within a workflow.
- Software-engineering-driven techniques, for example, Petri Nets (Keen & Lakos, 1994) are a formal, graphical, executable technique for the specification and analysis of concurrent, discrete-event dynamic systems

- Unified modeling language (UML) (OMG, 2004) is an object-oriented visual notation for the design of software systems. Different diagram types (class, activity, sequence, use-case, etc.) optimize different generic design patterns.[1]
- Business process management notation (BPMN) (White, 2006) has been defined by an OMG (OMG, 2006a) standard. It is a graphical notation for coordinating the steps and the message flows within a business process.
- Event-driven process chain (EPC) (Mendling, Neumann, & Nuttgens, 2005) is a method using ordered graphs of events and functions. EPC is used for modeling, analyzing, and redesigning business processes.
- Structure, mechanisms, and policies (SMP) (Perry & Kaiser, 1991), is a model for software development environments (SDE). SMP is relevant to business interaction because it identifies four classes of SDE, based on sociological metaphors: individual, family, city, and state (IFCS taxonomy). IFCS taxonomy suggests typical patterns of interaction, and issues (coordination, cooperation, commonality), to be considered in the design of tools supporting them.

Several technologies coming from the Web science domain are relevant:

- ebXML (Kim, 2002) is a set of XML-based specification supporting business processes, core data components, collaboration protocol agreements, messaging, registries, and repositories.
- Web service choreography (http://www.w3.org/TR/ws-chor-reqs/) concerns the observable interactions of Web services with their users. (Bauer & Muller, 2004) applies model driven architecture (MDA) (OMG, 2006) to choreography. MDA is a way of defining specifications and developing applications based on a platform independent model.
- Business process execution language for Web Services (BPEL4WS) (Leymann & Roller,

2004) provides a language for the specification of business processes and business interaction protocols. It extends the Web services interaction model and enables it to support business transactions.

- Semantic Web services support, for example, Web service modeling ontology (WSMO) (Lausen & Polleres, 2005) provides formal languages to describe all relevant aspects of Web services. The main objective is to facilitate the discovery, composition, and invocation of electronic services over the Web.

These approaches contribute to many aspects of the business interaction domain by representing sensible information. They have proven suitable to the task they have been conceived for. On the other hand, they are closed to their specific task, so that possible relations to other approaches are not covered. Therefore, they are difficult to compare and evaluate. See Green and Rosemann (2002) for empirical evidence of such difficulty.

Despite their heterogeneity in both content and scope, each of these techniques and methods has been conceived with a (more or less explicit) conceptual model in mind, as shown, for example, in Green and Rosemann (2000). A homogeneous, formal expression of those conceptual models would promote interoperability among applications based on them and would provide a way to compare them for evaluation. Ontology-based techniques can provide formal models and best practices to undertake such an endeavor.

In several works (Green & Rosemann, 2000; Green & Rosemann, 2002; Wand & Weber, 1990) ontologies have been used as gold standards in order to evaluate conceptual modeling languages and for developing guidelines for their use. Popular examples of ontology-based techniques are the Bunge-Wand-Weber (BWW) ontology (Wang & Zhu, 2004), and the unified foundational ontology (UFO) (Guizzardi & Wagner, 2004), which is based on foundational ontologies like DOLCE (Gangemi, Guarino, Masolo, & Oltramari, 2003; Masolo, Gangemi, Guarino, Oltramari, & Schneider, 2004), and GFO-GOL (Degen, Heller, Herre,

& Smith, 2001), which also shows how UFO can be used to evaluate the suitability of business modeling methods. It uses an example involving the enterprise ontology (EO) (Uschold et al., 1998). The core ontology of services (Oberle, 2006; Oberle, Mika, Gangemi, & Sabou, 2004), and the plan ontology (PO) are other examples of ontologies relevant for modeling business interactions.

However, even in these proposals the modeled elements are those strictly related to the business domain or to its typical tasks, either at a generic (e.g., services or plans), or specific (e.g., enterprise roles) level.

Ontologies can be used for more challenging tasks than evaluation. For example, they can support interoperability among applications and more precise encoding of requirements coming from the communities of practice involved in business interactions.

To that purpose, a more comprehensive modeling framework is needed, which allows creating relations between the different types of entities involved. This need, evidenced by our quick overview of information technology approaches, nicely pairs to the needs coming from socio-economic studies, which also address the problem of relating organizations, interaction patterns, social relationships, and the mutual dependency between an enterprise and its community.

While a complete account of social knowledge is, of course, impossible, in this chapter we propose a way to create useful shortcuts to express complex knowledge and to organize it in a unique domain of discourse. Our aim is to show how ontologies can be used most profitably in the business interaction domain, when a unified conceptual framework allows a comprehensive design of domain entities.

A SELECTION OF PATTERNS

A content ontology design pattern (CODeP) (Gangemi, 2005) is a fragment of an existing ontology that is relevant because it is widely reusable (e.g., the *Time interval relations* pattern), or because it is well-suited or central to a specific domain of interest (e.g., an *Invoicing* pattern in a business transaction domain), or because it solves a recurring modeling problem (e.g., a domain-independent *Relation reification* pattern). CODePs are a viable alternative to large and complex foundational or core ontologies, as well as to repositories of informal modeling patterns that cannot be easily composed or reused because of the difficulty of encoding them in a unique reasoning framework.

Typically, CODePs are quite small (usually smaller than 10 classes), richly axiomatized (most classes have more than one association with the others), and close to the human expertise (they typically emerge from reasoning patterns developed by experts). Formally, CODePs are theories that include invariant structures against some specific transformations ("vocabulary morphisms") that can occur across a variety of domain patterns. Notably, many abstract patterns have similarities to so-called *frames* from cognitive linguistics (Baker, Fillmore, & Lowe, 1998). A formal theory of CODePs is still under development, but Clark, Thompson, and Porter (2000) and Gangemi (2005) have laid down some of its foundations.

As noticed by Ambler, Nalbone, and Vizdos (2005) an "anti-pattern" in enterprise business modeling is "being real-world disconnected." The CODeP-based approach presented here allows designers of business information systems to perform modeling within the same domain of discourse as that of social environments like legal systems, economics theories, and social relationships.

In this section we show two CODePs resulted very useful for enterprise business modeling that avoids that anti-pattern: *Basic Description and Situation*, and *Plans*. They are taken from the following OWL ontologies:

- Extended descriptions and situations (ExtendedDnS) (D&S)
- Plans (PO)

In the next subsections, we describe their general form, while in the next section we exemplify how they can be specialized for the enterprise business domain in order to harmonize existing data model patterns, workflow patterns, as well as business language constructs.

Following a common practice in business modeling, CODePs are presented here as UML class diagrams, but we use UML with an OWL profile, because the ontologies we refer to are expressed in OWL (OWL, 2004). For example, in the OWL profile, *UML class* maps to *OWL class*, *UML generalization* maps to *OWL subclass axiom*, UML *association* maps to *OWL object property restriction*, *UML attribute* maps to *OWL datatype property restriction*, *UML object* maps to *OWL individual*, and *UML instantiation association* maps to *rdf:type* (the instance of relation used in OWL).

The Basic Description and Situation Pattern

Figure 1 depicts the general structure of the basic description and situation (DnS) CODeP.

The classes involved in this pattern are *description*, *concept*, *entity*, and *situation*. A *description* is a social object that represents a sharable conceptualization, hence it is dependent on some *agent* and must be communicable (i.e., expressed by means of *information objects*). Descriptions can be also seen as viewpoints on some *situation* (state of affairs or context). Descriptions typically *define* or *use concepts*, and the association *Usage* captures this part of the pattern by relating concepts to viewpoints or descriptions in which a concept is defined or used.

Descriptions can be *satisfied* by *situations* as expressed by the association *Satisfaction*. A specific situation has to satisfy a description, and satisfaction is guaranteed by the fact that a situation is a *setting for* some specific *entities*, as described by the association *Setting*. Those entities are *classified by* at least one concept *used by* the description that the situation satisfies. The association *Classification* captures this part of the pattern. Finally, the association *Specialization* between concepts is used to specify concept taxonomies, for example, reifications of *UML generalizations*.

Figure 1. The DnS CODeP

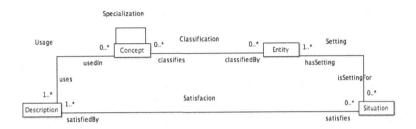

The DnS CODeP is extracted from the ExtendedDnS ontology. For a comprehensive discussion and explanation, the reader can refer to Gangemi and Mika (2003) and Masolo, Vieu, et al. (2004), and for the complete ontology, see (D&S). ExtendedDnS also takes into account:

- Social agents
- Collectives or communities which these agents are members of
- Information objects by which a description is expressed
- Time-spans characterizing the situations

However, an appropriate description and exemplification of all patterns that can be extracted from ExtendedDnS and used in business modeling would require too much space, therefore we refer to the literature for the complete picture. For the sake of this chapter, we provide anyway a simplified, first-order-logic explanation of the *DnS Maximal Relation* (DMR) (Gangemi & Catenacci, 2006), a logical structure that is used as a generic design pattern to represent ontologies about social reality (the former UML diagram for ExtendedDnS is (logically) a projection[2] of DMR. A toy use case is also provided, in order to strengthen the reader's intuition.

DMR has the following structure:

$$DnS(a, k, s, t, i, d, c_{1...n}, e_{1...n}) \rightarrow$$
$$A(a) \wedge K(k) \wedge S(s) \wedge T(t) \wedge I(i) \wedge D(d) \wedge C(c_1), ..., C(c_n) \wedge E(e_1), ..., E(e_n)$$

A can be read as *Social agent*, *K* as *Collection*, *S* as *Situation*, *T* as *Time interval*, *I* as *Information object*, *D* as *Description*, *C* as *Concept*, and *E* as *Entity*. Intuitively, the *DnS* relation says, for example, that *a social agent (a), as a member of a community (k), singles out a situation (s) at a certain time (t), by using information (i) whose meaning is a descriptive relation (d) that assigns concepts (c_{1...n}) to entities (e_{1...n}) within that situation.*

The DnS maximal relation is complex, but its expressivity is able to catch the social context surrounding the process of knowledge extraction and sharing. For example, a local situation of two employees exchanging e-mails about an order can be represented analytically as follows:

DnSSupervisor#134ACME_CommunityE-mailThread#13092008
Time#13092008LogMessage#13092008ACME_EmailWorkflow
{OrderManagerShippingCoordinatoremailMessageOrder}
{MarkSean{email_texts}EngineOrder#02062008}

The relationship formally states that a supervisor from the ACME company community has been able to verify an e-mail thread on September 13, 2008, as evidenced by a log message whose meaning is based on the ACME workflow for e-mails, which assigns the concepts: Order Manager, Shipping Coordinator, e-mail Message, and Order, to the agents, information, and resources involved in the e-mail thread situation, that is, Mark (as order Manager), Sean (as Shipping Coordinator), some e-mail texts (as e-mail Message), and an order for an engine (as Order).

This toy example illustrates the scope of DMR. The same pattern can be applied, for example, to represent team coordination situations, financial performance indicators, contract execution, social interaction data extracted from social network analysis, and so forth.

Projections of the pattern can help focusing on specific aspects of social interaction, for example, a social relationship situation can be represented by means of the following projection of DMR:

$SocRl(s, t, a_{1...n}, k)$

SocRl states that a social relationship situation s at time t includes a set of agents ($a_{1...n}$) from a collective (k). This projection only uses the s, t, and $e_{1...n}$ arguments of DMR, where entities are agents and collectives. In practice, DMR allows to talk about how agents and communities become aware of some situation, and at the same time, to talk about agents and communities within those situations. For example, in the previous example, the supervisor #134 is the agent that becomes aware of the e-mail thread, while Mark and Sean are the agents within that thread situation.

In the next section, we will concentrate on smaller projections of DMR, like *DnS* CODeP, in order to keep the complexity of our presentation under control.

The Plans Pattern

In this section we are going to describe the *Plans* CODeP (PO), a specialization of the DnS CODeP. This pattern is useful to describe procedures in contexts such as the enterprise business domain.

Figure 2 depicts the general structure of the pattern. *Plan* is actually more complex, but we present here a simplified version of it (although complete with main elements).

A *plan* is characterized as a *method* for executing or performing a procedure or a stage of a procedure. It must *use* at least one *role played by* an agent, and at least one *task*. It might also use *parameters*, whose values are taken from appropriate *regions* (e.g., spatial, temporal, or physical values). Finally, a plan has always a *goal* as a *proper part*, and can also have regulations or other descriptions as parts.

Figure 2. The plans CODeP

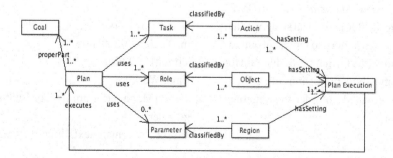

Figure 3. Generalization of plan elements

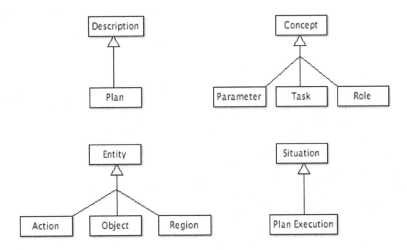

Figure 4. Conditions and sequences in plan

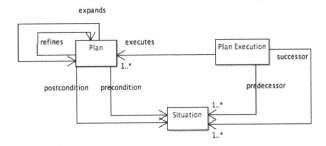

The definition of *plan* characterizes its conceptual aspects.

A plan can be satisfied by a *plan execution*, which provides the setting for entities like *actions* (classified by a given task), *objects* (classified by roles), and *regions* (classified by parameters). Figure 3 depicts how *Plan* classes specialize *DnS* classes.

Plans can be *refined* or *expanded* by other plans, and they can have *pre-* and *post-conditions* for their execution. Furthermore, a plan execution can be part of a sequence. These aspects provide a further characterization of *Plan*. Figure 4 shows the relations *precondition, postcondition, successor, predecessor, refines*, and *expands*. Situations can be a precondition for the execution of a plan when they are assumed as required predecessors to its execution. Analogously, a situation is a post-condition for the execution of a plan when it is assumed as a required successor to that execution.

Figure 5. Relations between concepts of plan

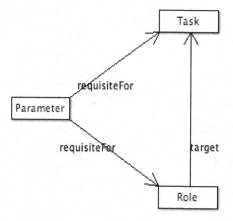

Figure 6. Plan tasks taxonomy

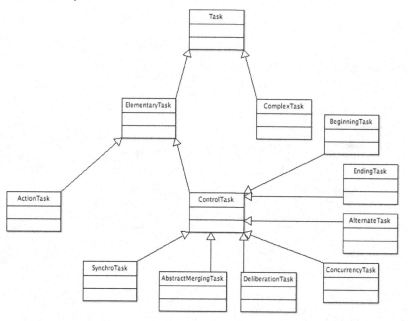

Figure 5 shows that tasks are assigned to (they are *target* of) some role played by an agent. Tasks can be complex and ordered according to an abstract *successor* relation. Tasks are organized in a taxonomy. Figure 6 depicts some of them; for the full taxonomy, see The Plan Ontology.

A task is *complex* when it has at least two other tasks as components, or *elementary* when it is atomic within a certain plan model. Elementary tasks can be either action task or control task. Action tasks rep-

resent the activities to be accomplished during plan execution, while control tasks represent the control activities supporting the execution. This list includes some classes of control tasks from (PO):

- **Beginning task:** A control task that is predecessor to all tasks defined in the plan
- **Ending task:** A control task that has no successor tasks defined in the plan

- **Alternate task:** A task branched to exactly two tasks, not executable in parallel. It is a specialization of the case task, which can be branched to a set of tasks not executable concurrently
- **Deliberation task:** A task representing the decision taken after a case task execution
- **Concurrency task:** A task branched to a set of tasks executable concurrently
- **Synchro task:** Represents a merging activity, consisting in waiting for the execution of all (except the optional ones) tasks that are direct successor to a concurrent task
- **Abstract merging task:** A formal merging that is never executed and is used to indicate the closing of the branches of a case task

AN EXAMPLE IN BUSINESS MODELING

In order to show an example application of our approach, we describe a possible use case scenario for a generic enterprise. In particular, from Hay (1996), we take a data model pattern named *Kinds of Contracts (KoC)* and from (Sales order), we take the description of the *Sales Order Process (SOP)*. We use a UML class diagram for KoC and UML use case and activity diagrams for SOP. We also highlight the workflow

patterns used within the activity diagram, by reusing the patterns from Van Der Aalst et al. (2003). After presenting the scenario, we describe an integrated scenario ontology by specializing a set of suitable CODePs so that the scenario gets redescribed in a unified domain of discourse.

The Scenario

Figure 7 depicts the data model pattern *Kinds of Contracts (KoC)*, as it is defined in Hay (1996).

KoC models *contracts* set up between two parties that can be either persons or organizations, while each possible party can be on one or the other "side" of a contract. The subject of the contract can be assets, asset types, services, or activities. The goods involved in the contract are represented by the class line item, that is, they can be bought via a certain line item. One or more line items compose the contract. The pattern also considers the case of dealing with services and their execution (i.e., activities).

The classes from KoC can be associated to a workflow for a given enterprise. Typically, the information about flows is not embedded within data model patterns, while it is usually expressed by means of other formalism (e.g., UML activity diagram). This practice can be enhanced by ontology-based model representation, because it allows designers to describe

Figure 7. Kinds of contracts data model pattern

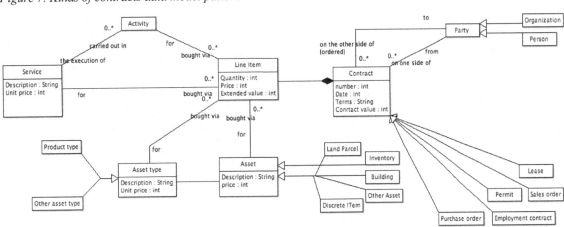

both data models and flows. The advantage of a unique formalism is the creation of a common domain of interpretation for data modeling, querying, mining, as well as for integrating and mapping elements of heterogeneous models.

As an example, from IBM WebSphere Web site (Sales order), we take the description of so-called *Sales Order Processing (SOP)*, which is, as it is stated there, "a core process in any business." Sales order (SOP) is described as a set of tasks, performed by different actors in different possible sequences, that is, workflows. The focus of SOP is on system requirements, and the description of the intended meaning of the elements in SOP diagram is provided solely as English comments. SOP uses diagrams and other notations which deal with system specifications based on those requirements. Although system specification is an interesting domain to be represented in ontologies, as shown in Oberle (2006), Oberle et al. (2004), Rosengard and Ursu, (2004), in this context we focus on models for enterprise business and production processes instead of software system models. Therefore, SOP workflow is reengineered here by using traditional UML use case (Figure 8) and activity (Figure 9) diagrams.

Figure 8 represents the SOP use case. SOP involves three actors: customer, customer service representative

(CSR), and back office system (BOS), and seven use cases, describing that an *order* has to be requested, forwarded, and fulfilled. Other cases describe conditions that must be verified: check for reliability of customer, availability of goods, product configuration, order recording.

Figure 9 shows a workflow for SOP. *Customer* initiates a *request* for certain products that a company manufactures or distributes. *CSR records* the request. In this scenario, before going on, *CSR checks for customer reliability*, and *if check result is positive*, then the *availability of goods is verified*, otherwise *the order is rejected* and the process *finishes*. If the order is accepted and *goods are not available*, then it is needed to *place an order to the appropriate supplier.* On the other hand, *if goods are already available* the *order is sent to BOS*, which is in charge of *configuring products* in order to meet customer's needs, and to *fulfill the order.*

This workflow is a simple example and it does not cover all possible workflow structures that might be needed for a full-fledged case. In Van Der Aalst et al. (2003), a thorough collection of structures needed for representing from basic to complex workflows, called *workflow patterns*, is presented. Each business modeling language covers to some degree a set of those

Figure 8. Sales order use case

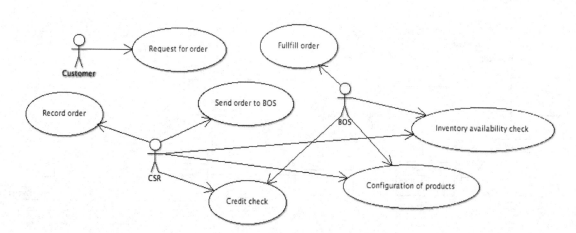

Figure 9. Sales order process possible workflow

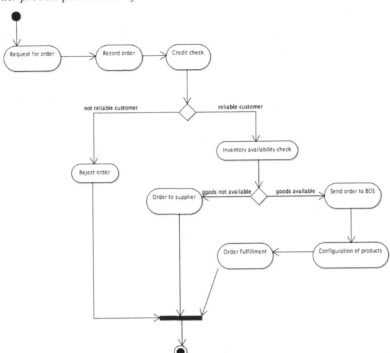

patterns. With CODePs-based modeling, it is possible to gather the desired expressivity, based on specific enterprise domain needs. For example, in order to describe the workflow of Figure 9 we have used the following workflow patterns (Van Der Aalst et al.):

- **Sequence:** An activity in a workflow process is enabled after the completion of another activity in the same process
- **Exclusive choice:** A point in the workflow process where, based on a decision or workflow control data, one of several branches is chosen
- **Simple merge:** A point in the workflow process where two or more alternative branches come together without synchronization. It is assumed that none of the alternative branches is ever executed in parallel

In Figure 9, these patterns are represented respectively by a directed arrow, a diamond, and a bar.

The scenario we have built includes an enterprise whose business consists in selling and/or buying products (either artifacts or services). The sales order process is managed by means of a defined workflow, and is regulated by a contract, one of many possible kinds of contracts. The scenario is split into parts observed from different perspectives.

In this subsection, we have used natural language and UML class, use case, and activity diagram notation. In the next subsection, we show how to use suitable CODePs in order to describe the scenario within a unique domain of discourse, and by using only one formalism. We proceed by specializing the generic CODePs from the "patterns" section to the domain of interest, that is, enterprise business interaction.

The Workflow Ontology

Figure 10 shows a UML object diagram, which describes the workflow from Figure 9 as an instantiation/specialization of the *Plans* CODeP. Each UML object maps to an OWL individual, and, according to the UML notation for object diagrams, the name of an individual is followed by the name of its class, and a colon separates the two names. For the sake of readability, Figure 10 contains only a few examples of the *uses* and *target* relations. The reader can infer the others by observing the types of individuals.

Sales order process is a *plan*, which uses three *roles*: *Customer, CSR*, and *BOS*, and a set of tasks: *Request For Order, Credit Check*, and so forth. Roles, according to *Plans* pattern, *target* some *tasks*. Task sequences are represented by the relation *successor*.

In this workflow, two *AlternateTask* occurrences have been *used*: *Credit Check* and *Inventory Availability Check*. Each of them has its corresponding pair of *DeliberationTask*: *Reliable Customer* vs. *Non-reliable Customer* for the former, and *Goods Available* vs. *Goods Not Available* for the latter. They also have their *AbstractMergingTask*, that is, *Credit Check Abstract Merge* and *Inventory Availability Check Abstract Merge*, respectively. The pairs of *AlternateTask* and

Figure 10. Sales order process CODeP-based description

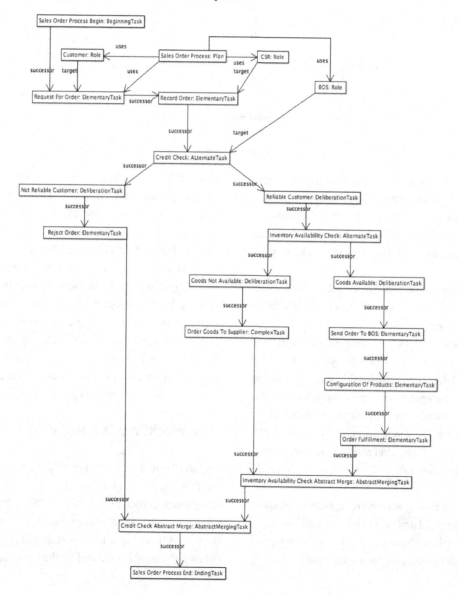

Figure 11. Kind of contracts classes after integration to plans

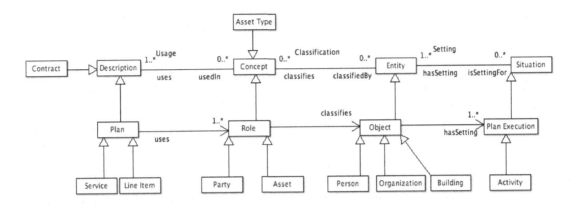

Figure 12. Kind of contracts ontology

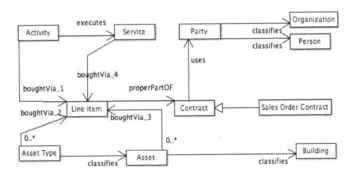

DeliberationTask occurrences correspond to "exclusive choices", while *AbstractMergingTask* occurrences corresponds to "Simple merges" as defined in Van Der Aalst, Ter Hofstede, Kiepuszewski, and Barros (2003). *Sales Order Process Begin* is a *BeginningTask* while the *Sales Order Process End* is an *EndingTask*, as they describe respectively the start and the end of the workflow.

The Contract Ontology

In this subsection we show the reengineering of the data model pattern *Kind of Contracts (KoC)* presented in Figure 7, by means of the CODePs presented in the "patterns" section. The example shows how we can combine the same expressivity of ad-hoc languages (e.g., entity-relationship, UML) with the additional value of expressing all aspects in the same domain of discourse. As a first step, we define KoC classes as OWL classes in terms of *DnS* and *Plans* CODePs. The result of the alignment of KoC to *Plans* is depicted in Figure 11.

Contract is a subclass of *Description*, while *Service* and *Line Item* are subclasses of *Plan*. *Party* and *Asset* are subclasses of *Role*, *Asset Type* is a subclass of *Concept*, and *Person*, *Organization*, and *Building* are subclasses of *Object*. Finally, *Activity* is a subclass of *Plan Execution*. Notice that in Figure 7 *Activity* is related to *Service* through an association labeled as *execution of*. This is in line with the mapping of those entities to *Plans* CODeP.

Figure 12 shows the relations between *KoC* classes after alignment to *Plans*.

The following rationales have led to the reengineering of *KoC* into the ontology.

- In the original model, composition/aggregation associations are used, but they are far too ambiguous, as shown in Guizzardi (2005), then we use here the *properPartOf* relation, as defined in DOLCE (Gangemi et al., 2003; Masolo, Gangemi, et al., 2004). In the resulting ontology, a *Contract* has a *Line Item* as a proper part.

- In the original model, *Contract* is agreed *from* a *Party* to another; "from" is too generic as a reasonable relation name, then we propose its super-relation from *DnS*, that is, *uses*.

- The generalizations between *organization/person* and *party*, as well as between *building* (or other objects) and *asset* are "non-rigid" (Guarino & Welty, 2002), because, for example, persons are not always parties and buildings are not always assets. Therefore, based on *DnS*, we transform those generalizations into *classifies* relations.

- *Person* or *Organization* instances can play the role of *Party* in a *Contract*, that is, *Party* classifies *Person* and *Organization*.

- The *Line Item* of a *Contract* may deal with one or more among *Asset*, *Asset Type*, *Service*, or *Activity*.

- *Asset* is classified by an *Asset Type*, for example, a car which is of a specific brand and model.

- *Activity* is the execution of a *Service*, for example, the reparation of my car is the execution of a specific workflow (i.e., plan) for fixing that problem.

- Originally, *Asset*, *Asset Type*, *Activity*, and *Service* are all associated to *Line Item* through the

Figure 13. The unified KoC/SOP ontology. Arrows with dashed line represent the rdf:type relation that holds between an individual and its class.

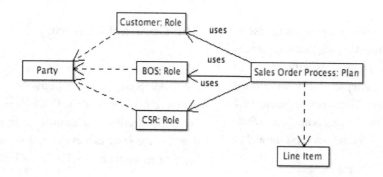

"bought via" association. Since those classes are all disjoint in the reference ontology of our CODePs, and a best practice in ontology engineering is to provide different relations for disjoint domains, the original association results to have different meanings that, both legally and commercially, imply different practices and regulations. Consequently, we have numbered the four associations according to the class associated with *Line Item*. Each numbered association can then be formalized as a subproperty of (i.e., owl:subPropertyOf) the *involves* property that composes the uses and classifies properties from *DnS*.

A Unified Model

In this subsection, we describe the integration of KoC with SOP in a CODeP-based unified model. Figure 10 contains the model of a SOP workflow based on *Plans*, while Figures 11 and 12 contain the KoC ontology after the reengineering of its data model pattern, based on *DnS*. The integration is required, for example, in an enterprise that wants to endorse the SOP workflow to work out sales orders, and the KoC contract datamodel to regulate their sales order contracts. Figure 13 depicts the main relations that allow us to obtain an integrated model, and to describe the scenario as a whole. The integration is simple because we can directly conceive SOP workflow as an instance of KoC *Line Item* class, and the roles used by SOP as instances of the class that includes the roles expected to be used by a *Line Item* instance. For space reasons, we show here neither the complete reengineered and integrated scenario, nor an example within a real enterprise, but the OWL code for both the scenario and application examples are contained in the repository of CODePs for the NeOn project (NeOn) that we are building at http://www.loa-cnr.it/codeps/.

CONCLUSION

We have presented models and methods to represent and reason on enterprises, their communities, and the related business interactions. The main components we have presented are: ontologies, content ontology design patterns, and a conceptual framework that allows an integrated representation of the entities involved in business interaction within and across enterprises and their context. Such entities: organizations, roles, social relationships, communities, material resources, information objects, workflows, regulations, events, and so forth, are in fact assumed as elements from a unique logical domain.

We have introduced some objectives of our conceptual framework: (1) encoding the requirements from the communities of practice involved in business interactions; (2) comparing, reengineering, and integrating existing languages and ontologies for business interaction; and (3) creating a formal infrastructure to represent the dependencies between enterprises, social interaction and practices, legal regulations, and the physical world.

Existing socio-economic studies and information science solutions do not provide any such conceptual framework, be it theoretical, formalized, or implemented. Nonetheless, they provide many partial solutions that can be aligned, reused, or integrated by means of a unified formal infrastructure like the one we envisage in this chapter. The examples provided are intended as guidelines to apply formal languages and reusable components for business interaction ontologies.

Ongoing work within the EU FP6 NeOn project is developing Semantic Web support for storing, matching, and composing ontology design patterns, and correlating design patterns with ontology learning patterns.

ACKNOWLEDGMENT

We are grateful to the members of the NeOn consortium who contributed to the NeOn vision being funded by the European Commission 6th IST Framework Program. Further information on NeOn is available on http://www.neon-project.org.

REFERENCES

Ambler, S.W., Nalbone, J., & Vizdos, M.J. (2005, February). *The enterprise unified process: Extending the rational unified process.* Prentice Hall.

Baker, C.F., Fillmore, C.J., & Lowe, J.B. (1998). The Berkeley FrameNet project. In C. Boitet & P. Whitelock (Eds.), *Proceedings of the 36th Annual Meeting of the Association for Computational Linguistics* (pp. 86-90). San Francisco: Morgan Kaufmann Publishers.

Bauer, B., & Muller, J.P. (2004). MDA applied: From sequence diagrams to Web service choreography. In N. Koch, P. Fraternali, & M. Wirsing (Eds.), *Icwe* (Vol. 3140, p. 132-136). Springer.

Chen, P. (2002). Entity-relationship modeling: Historical events, future trends, and lessons learned. In *Software pioneers: Contributions to software engineering* (pp. 296-310). Springer-Verlag New York.

Clark, P., Thompson, J., & Porter, B. (2000). Knowledge patterns. In A.G. Cohn, F. Giunchiglia, & B. Selman (Eds.), *KR2000: Principles of Knowledge Representation and Reasoning* (pp. 591-600). San Francisco: Morgan Kaufmann.

Degen, W., Heller, B., Herre, H., & Smith, B. (2001, October). GOL: Towards an axiomatized upper level ontology. In B. Smith & N. Guarino (Eds.), *Proceedings of FOIS01* (pp. 34-46). Ogunquit, ME: ACM Press.

The description and situation ontology. (2006, June) Retrieved June 9, 2007, from http://www.loa-cnr.it/ontologies/ExtendedDnS.owl

Gangemi, A. (2005). Ontology design patterns for Semantic Web content. In M. Musen et al. (Eds.), *Proceedings of the Fourth International Semantic Web Conference* (pp. 262-276). Galway, Ireland: Springer.

Gangemi A., & Catenacci C. (2006). *A constructive ontology of descriptions and situations* (Tech. Rep. ISTC-CNR). Retrieved June 9, 2007, from http://www.loa-cnr.it/TR/ConstructiveDnS.pdf

Gangemi, A., Catenacci, C., Ciaramita, M., & Lehmann, J. (2006). Modeling ontology evaluation and validation. In *Proceedings of the Third European Semantic Web Conference* (p. 140-154). Springer.

Gangemi, A., Fisseha, F., Keizer, J., Pettman, I., & Taconet, M. (2004). *A core ontology of fishery and its use in the fishery ontology service project.* Paper presented at the First International Workshop on Core Ontologies at EKAW Conference, CEUR-WS (Vol. 118).

Gangemi, A., Guarino, N., Masolo, C., & Oltramari, A. (2003). Sweetening wordnet with DOLCE. *AI Magazine, 24*(3), 13-24.

Gangemi, A., & Mika, P. (2003). Understanding the Semantic Web through descriptions and situations. In *Proceedings of ODBASE03 Conference* (pp. 689-706). Springer.

Gangemi, A., Pisanelli, D.M., & Steve, G. (2001). An ontological framework to represent norm dynamics. In R. Winkels (Ed.), *Jurix Conference, Workshop on Legal Ontologies.* Retrieved September 6, 2007 from http://www.lri.jur.uva.nl/jurix2001/papers/gangemi.pdf

Gangemi, A., Sagri, M.T., & Tiscornia, D. (2005). A constructive framework for legal ontologies. *Law and the Semantic Web, LNCS, 3369,* 97-124.

Green, P.F., & Rosemann, M. (2000). Integrated process modeling: An ontological evaluation. *Information Systems, 25,* 73-87.

Green, P.F., & Rosemann, M. (2002). Usefulness of the BWW ontological models as a core theory of information systems. In *Proceedings of Information Systems Foundations: Building the Theoretical Base,* Canberra, Australia (pp. 147-164).

Guarino, N., & Welty, C.A. (2002). Evaluating ontological decisions with OntoClean. *Communications of the ACM, 45*(2), 61-65.

Guizzardi, G. (2005). *Ontological foundations for structural conceptual models* (Doctoral dissertation, University of Twente, Enschede, The Netherlands, Enschede). Retrieved June 9, 2007, from http://eprints.eemcs.utwente.nl/7146/

Guizzardi, G., & Wagner, G. (2004). A unified foundational ontology and some applications of it in business modeling. *CAISE Workshops, 3,* 129-143.

Hay, D.C. (1996). *Data model patterns.* Dorset House Publishing.

Keen, C., & Lakos, C. (1994). Information systems modeling using LOOPN++, an object oriented Petri net scheme. In *Proceedings of the 4th International Working Conference on Dynamic Modeling and Information Systems* (pp. 31-52). Noordwijkerhout, The Netherlands: Delft University Press.

Kim, H. (2002). Conceptual modeling and specification generation for b2b business process based on ebxml. *SIGMOD Record, 31*(1), 37-42.

Lausen, H., & Polleres, A. (2005, June). Web service modeling ontology. Retrieved June 9, 2007, from http://www.w3.org/Submission/WSMO/

Leymann, F., & Roller, D. (2006). Modeling business processes with BPEL4WS. *Information Systems and E-Business Management, 4*(3), 265-284.

Marco, D., & Jennings, M. (2004). *Universal meta data models.* Wiley Computer Publishing.

Masolo, C., Gangemi, A., Guarino, N., Oltramari, A., & Schneider, L. (2004). Wonderweb EU project deliverable D18: The wonderweb library of foundational ontologies. Retrieved June 9, 2007, from http://wonderweb.semanticweb.org/deliverables/documents/D18.pdf

Masolo, C., Vieu, L., Bottazzi, E., Catenacci, C., Ferrario, R., Gangemi, A., et al. (2004). Social roles and their descriptions. In D. Dubois, C.A. Welty, & M.-A. Williams (Eds.), *Proceedings of KR2004 Conference* (p. 267-277). AAAI Press.

Mendling, J., Neumann, G., & Nuttgens, M. (2005). Yet another event-driven process chain. Modeling Workflow Patterns with yEPCs. *Business Process Management, 1*(1) 428-433.

Metcalfe, J., & Saviotti, P. (Eds.). (1991). *Evolutionary theories of economic and technological change.* Harwood.

NeOn. (2006, May) *EU project home page.* Retrieved June 9, 2007, from http://neon-project.org

Noy N., & Rector A. (2005). Defining n-ary relations on the Semantic Web: Use with individuals (Tech. Rep. W3C). Retrieved June 9, 2007, from http://www.w3.org/TR/swbp-n-aryRelations/

Oberle, D. (2006). *Semantic management of middleware* (Vol. I). New York: Springer.

Oberle, D., Mika, P., Gangemi, A., & Sabou, M. (2004). Foundations for service ontologies: Aligning OWL-S to DOLCE. In *Proceedings of the World Wide Web Conference (WWW2004)* (pp. 563-572).

Object Management Group (OMG). (2004). *Unified modeling language specification: Version 2, revised final adopted specification (ptc/04-10-02).* OMG.

Object Management Group (OMG). (2006). *Model-driven architecture (MDA) specifications.*

OWL Web ontology language family of specifications. (2004). Retrieved June 9, 2007, from http://www.w3.org/2004/OWL

Perry, D.E., & Kaiser, G.E. (1991, March). Models of software development environments. *IEEE Transaction on Software Engineering, 17*(3), 283-295.

The plan ontology. (2006, July) Retrieved June 9, 2007, from http://www.loa-cnr.it/ontologies/Plans.owl

Pruijt, H. (2002). Neo-Tayloristic and anti-Tayloristic models of team-working. In *ISA World Congress of Sociology, Research Committee 26.* Rotterdam. Retrieved September 06, 2007 from http://www.eur.nl/fsw/staff/homepages/pruijt/papers/working/

Rooney, D. (2005). Knowledge, economy, technology and society: The politics of discourse. *Telematics and Informatics, 22,* 405-422.

Rooney, D., Joseph, R., Mandeville, T., & Hearn, G. (2003). *Public policy and the knowledge economy: Foundations and frameworks (new horizons in public policy).* Edward Elgar Publishing.

Rosengard, J.-M., & Ursu, M.(2004). Ontological representations of software patterns. *Lecture Notes in Computer Science, 3215,* 31.

Sales order processing collaboration template. (2005). Retrieved June 9, 2007, from http://publib.boulder.ibm.com/infocenter/wbihelp/v6rxmx/index.jsp? -topic=/com.ibm.wbi_order_management.doc/doc/collaboration_temp-lates/ct_salesorderprocessing.htm

Silverston, L. (2001). *Data model resource book.* Wiley Computer Publishing.

Smith, K. (1995). Interactions in knowledge systems: Foundations, policy, implications and empirical methods. *Science Technology Industry (STI) Review, 1995*(16), 70-102.

Taylor, F.W. (1964). Shop management. In F.W. Taylor (Ed.), *Scientific management: Shop management, the principles of scientific management, and the testimony before the Special House Committee.* London: Harper and Row.

Uschold, M., King, M., Moralee, S., & Zorgios, Y. (1998). The enterprise ontology. *Knowledge Engineering Review, 13*(1), 31-89.

Van Der Aalst, W., Ter Hofstede, A., Kiepuszewski, B., & Barros, A. (2003). Workflow patterns. *Distributed and Parallel Databases, 14,* 5-51.

Wand, Y., & Weber, R. (1990). Mario BungeOs ontology as a formal foundation for information systems concepts. In P. Weingartner & G. J. W. Dorn (Eds.), *Studies on Mario Bunge's treatise* (pp. 123-150). Atlanta: Rodopi.

Wang, L., & Zhu, G. (2004). Developing an xml schema of BWW ontologies for Semantic Web. In *Proceedings of the International Symposium on Parallel Architectures, Algorithms and Networks* (ISPAN'04) (pp. 220-225).

White, S. (2006). Business process modeling notation (BPMN), OMG final adopted specification. Retrieved June 9, 2007, from http://www.bpmn.org

ENDNOTES

[1] An agreed-upon semantics for UML is not yet available. For example, it is a user decision to employ a class to describe domain entities or application data elements; it is also left to users to distinguish states, activities, and processes.

[2] A projection of a relation is a part of it, which keeps the relative position of arguments, and is implicitly dependent on the complete relation. For example, given the relation *eats*(*agent,food*) can be a projection of the complete relation *eats*(*agent,food,tool*).

Chapter V
Grounding Business Interaction Models:
Socio-Instrumental Pragmatism as a Theoretical Foundation

Göran Goldkuhl
Linköping University, Sweden, & Jönköping International Business School, Sweden

Mikael Lind
University College of Borås, Sweden, & Linköping University, Sweden

ABSTRACT

In the information systems field there exist several theories for guiding the evaluation and design of information systems. These theories need to be transparent and harmonious. In this chapter, business action theory (BAT) as a domain ontology for business interaction and business processes is clarified by elaborating on socio-instrumental pragmatism (SIP) as a base ontology. SIP is an eclectic theory synthesizing several pragmatic theories from reference disciplines outside the IS area. One purpose of SIP is to enable seamless theorizing in the IS area. In this chapter we put forward the foundations of BAT and SIP which are then followed by grounding BAT in SIP. This grounding means that there will be an ontological clarification of BAT by specifying the social action and interaction character of business interaction.

INTRODUCTION

Business action theory (BAT) is an ontology and a practical theory for business interaction and business processes. During the last 10 years we have been working actively to continually improve business action theory. This knowledge evolution process can be characterized as empirically-driven theory development. The goal has been to create an empirically, internally, and theoretically grounded theory for business interaction. Today, BAT has the epistemological status of a multigrounded theory (Goldkuhl & Cronholm, 2003; Lind & Goldkuhl, 2006). In this chapter we will further ground BAT as a business domain ontology in a higher level domain ontology (Guarino, 1998) for the distinction between different types of ontologies.

The basic characteristics of a practical theory have earlier been elaborated by Cronen (1995, 2001) and Craig and Tracy (1995). Cronen (1995, p. 231) describes practical theories in the following way:

They are developed in order to make human life better. They provide ways of joining in social action so as to promote (a) socially useful description, explanation, critique, and change in situated human action; and (b) emergence of new abilities for all parties involved.

Practical theories should help us to see things, aspects, properties, and relations which otherwise would be missed (Cronen, 2001). The constituents of a practical theory have lately been elaborated by Goldkuhl (2006). Goldkuhl emphasizes conceptualizations, patterns, normative criteria, design principles, and models as (partially overlapping) such constituents of a practical theory. BAT is today regarded as a practical theory since all these constituents have been elaborated. For further elaboration, see Goldkuhl (1996), Lind and Goldkuhl (2003), and Goldkuhl and Lind (2004). The choice for us focusing on BAT is based on our good experiences in adopting BAT in practical situations and due to shortcomings in other theories for business interaction (Goldkuhl, 2006).

The notion of ontology is in this chapter was conceived as a particular system of categories accounting for a certain vision of the world (Guarino, 1998). Essential in the conception of ontology is conceptualization, which can be made on more or less formal foundations. According to Gruber (1993), an ontology is to be conceived as a specification of a representational vocabulary for a shared domain of discourse—definitions of classes, relations, functions, and other objects.

Guarino (1998) claims that an ontology is a logical theory accounting for the intended meaning of a formal vocabulary, but not necessarily that the formal vocabulary is to be a part of a logical language, as, for example, it may be a protocol of communication between agents. Different conceptualizations of the world thus need to be included in the ontology. BAT as a practical theory is based on a pragmatic paradigm that sees scientific knowledge as means to improve human practices (Dewey, 1938). This also means a special interest in social actions constituting the world. See, for example, Goldkuhl (2005a), building on Mead (1938). The characteristics of a practical theory and requirements to put upon the domain-dependent ontology as BAT thus strongly overlap.

The starting point for the development of BAT was when Goldkuhl (1996), at the first language action perspective for communication modeling (LAP) conference, criticized the action workflow model of Medina-Mora, Winograd, Flores, and Flores (1992) for being asymmetric. See Goldkuhl (1996) for the complete criticism. An alternative to the action workflow model was presented which was the first version of the BAT model. This model emphasized business interaction as an exchange process with mutual commitments, fulfilments, and satisfaction. Both action workflow and BAT were founded in the language-action perspective (Winograd & Flores, 1986). This means that there were many theoretical affinities between the two models. There were, however, also substantial differences.

The BAT-model has since then been applied in many action research projects concerning codesign of business processes and IT (e.g., Axelsson, Goldkuhl, & Melin, 2000; Goldkuhl & Melin, 2001). Due to experiences from these applications of the model, it was continually redeveloped (Goldkuhl, 1998; Goldkuhl & Lind, 2004). Some essential characteristics of the BAT-model are that (see the section on BAT for a more thorough description) it emphasizes:

• Business interaction between customer and supplier as two actor roles; supplier and customer

- A number of different exchanges, constituted by communicative and/or material acts organized as patterns of initiatives and responses
- The continual development of business relations and business capabilities
- The acknowledgement of other parties in the value transformation context
- The recurrence between several following business transactions
- The difference between interaction with the potential and the particular customer

The BAT-model originated within the language-action perspective with its basis in speech act theory (e.g., Searle, 1969; Habermas, 1984). However, from the start there was a criticism towards a narrow focus on only speech acts in business interaction (Goldkuhl, 1996). The fulfilments phase in the BAT model as a *value exchange* have been emphasized from its inception. There have been other kinds of deviation from a pure LAP orientation. The use of predefined communication patterns has been criticized by Goldkuhl (2003).

The BAT-model is built on several foundational concepts as roles, phases, and actions. One important attempt to clarify the BAT ontology was made in Lind and Goldkuhl (2003) where five conceptual layers were described. These layers were (from bottom to top): business act, action pair, exchange, business transaction, and transaction group. Through this work the need to ground this ontology not only in LAP was obvious. Other social action theories were used as basis.

Parallel to the development of BAT was the evolution of socio-instrumental pragmatism (SIP) as a foundational and progenitive theory for several practical theories in the IS area (Goldkuhl, 2002; Goldkuhl & Ågerfalk, 2002). By progenitive, we mean that SIP gives a theoretical grounding to other theories. SIP is in this chapter regarded as a domain ontology on a higher level than BAT; a base ontology since it describes general social domain concepts, which are independent of a particular problem or domain. For some ontology-researchers SIP would probably be regarded as a social domain ontology. Due to the need to

distinguish beween BAT as a business domain ontology (Guarino, 1998) from SIP as a social domain ontology, we characterize SIP as a base (domain) ontology. Goldkuhl and Röstlinger (2003) made an articulation of SIP as foundational basis for workpractice theory (Goldkuhl & Röstlinger, 2003), information systems actability theory (Goldkuhl & Ågerfalk, 2002), and sociopragmatic communication theory (Goldkuhl, 2005b) besides BAT. SIP is an eclectic theory synthesizing several pragmatic theories from reference disciplines outside the IS area (Goldkuhl, 2005a). One purpose of SIP is to enable seamless theorizing in the IS area (Goldkuhl, 2005).

Although important steps have been taking by Goldkuhl and Röstlinger (2003a) and Lind and Goldkuhl (2003) in grounding the BAT model in socio-instrumental pragmatism, much work remains. The purpose of this chapter is to clarify BAT as a business interaction ontology (business interaction as the domain) by elaborating on SIP as a base ontology for such clarification. Different concepts of business interaction will be grounded in foundational concepts of social interaction as they come through in socio-instrumental pragmatism. This will lead to three types of theoretical contributions (ontology clarifications):

- Clarification of business interaction concepts in the BAT-model
- Clarification of social interaction concepts within socio-instrumental pragmatism
- Conceptual grounding of the BAT-model in socio-instrumental pragmatism (conceptual relating)

After this introduction, a more thorough description of the BAT-model will follow. This description also includes, for the purpose of putting the BAT-model on the scene of contemporary concepts, relationships towards other similar concepts will be explicated. Following this description we will put forward the foundations of the socio-instrumental pragmatism as the base ontology used in this chapter. After these two foundational parts of this chapter, different business interaction phenomena according to BAT will be grounded in socio-instrumental pragmatism. The chapter will conclude with some highlights from this grounding.

BUSINESS ACTION THEORY

Overview of the BAT Model

The BAT-model is a phase-model describing a generic business interaction logic (Goldkuhl, 1998). BAT describes customer—supplier interaction. Business interaction should be understood as the performance of business acts (Lind & Goldkuhl, 2003). A vital aspect here is that a business act can be both a so-called speech act (a communicative act) and a material act. Thus business interaction is not restricted to communication but also comprises vital material acts as the exchange of products vs. money.

The BAT-model is a generic framework for business dyads. Being a generic framework means that it covers different types of business interaction as B2B (business-to-business) and B2C (business-to-con-

Figure 1. Levels of business interaction (Goldkuhl & Lind, 2004)

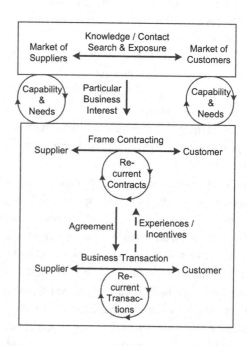

Figure 2. The business transaction (Goldkuhl & Lind, 2004)

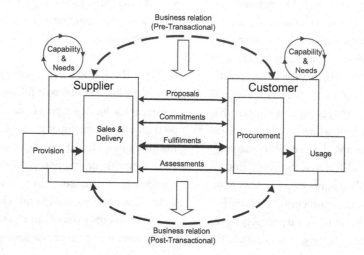

sumer). It also covers different types of products, both goods and services and both standard and tailor-made products. The application scope of the model is to be used for evaluation, modeling, and design of business interaction. In the current version of BAT (Goldkuhl & Lind, 2004), two levels of business interaction are distinguished: the market level and the dyadic level (see Figure 1). On the market level, suppliers and customers search for knowledge and contacts concerning the correspondent party. The interaction on this level is, according to BAT, driven by a *general business interest* of both suppliers and customers.

When a contact is established between a particular supplier and a particular customer, the general business interest is turned into a particular business interest. The business interaction moves to the dyadic level where business transactions take place. According to the BAT-model a business transaction consists of four phases: (1) proposal phase, (2) commitments phase, (3) fulfilments, and (4) assessments phase (Figure 2). Each phase consists of exchanges of a particular character, for example, the first phase consists of exchanges of proposals.

The BAT-model is characterized as a comprehensive framework (Goldkuhl & Lind, 2004) that sees business action as a building block, emphasizes the exchange character of business interaction, adopts a symmetric view on business parties and their interaction, and acknowledges both communicative, material, and financial interaction.

Essential Concepts

The BAT-model is based upon the *business action* as the basic unit of analysis. Conditions for and results of business actions are *action objects* that could be of communicative and/or material character. The notion of business acts builds upon the notion of social action. Performing social actions—either communicative or material—introduces *relations* between two *actors in roles* (supplier and customer). The performance of a communicative action (like a business order) introduces clearly certain relations between sender and recipient (Habermas, 1984). Based upon the generic

model of social action (see the next section) a business act is defined as "performance of a communicative and/or material act by someone aimed towards someone else" (Lind & Goldkuhl, 2003, p. 335). Business acts are often multifunctional. One example of multifunctionality is that the order both represents a *request* to the supplier to deliver something and a *commitment* of paying for the delivery corresponding to the order. Another example of multifunctionality is that a delivery of a product can both be a change of place of some material stuff and a fulfilment of a request and a promise.

The interactivity in the BAT-model is constituted by grouping two business acts into an action pair. The basis for grouping business acts into an action pair is that one business act functions as a trigger for another act, which will have the function of a response. Action pairs are patterns of triggers and responses. One example in business interaction is an order as the trigger and an order confirmation as the response of that trigger. By issuing an order the interventionist (i.e., the customer) expect the recipient (i.e., the supplier) to respond in a certain way: by confirming the order, by negotiating, or by turning the order away. Action relations between the actors are created through such an interaction.

One or several action pairs, that is, patterns of action pairs, constitute exchanges between actors. An exchange means that *one actor gives something in return for something given by another actor*. Exchanges are, however, not only related to exchange of value (such as physical goods in return for money)—exchange is related to different kinds of communicative as well as material business acts. As indicated in the description of the BAT-model, exchanges are of different types (such as proposals, commitments, values, and assessments). Exchanges constitute the core of business interaction. Each type of exchange distinguishes a *business phase*.

Several exchanges together constitute a *business transaction*. There is a certain logic of interaction between the supplier and customer when doing business. This logic is the pattern covered by the business transaction (Axelsson et al., 2000; Goldkuhl, 1998).

A business transaction has different *states* (in the social and material world) where the initial state is that the customer has a need and the supplier has a corresponding ability. The interaction between the two parties is determined by their *dispositions,* such as capabilities, business interests, and needs. By going through a number of *phases* consisting of exchanges the goal is to arrive at a state where both supplier and customer have satisfied (parts of) their needs. Patterns of exchanges, covering different phases, between the two roles continually evolve relations between the two business parties.

BAT in Relation to Other Business Interaction Frameworks

Within the language/action (L/A) community there is an interest for business interaction. The strength of the language/action perspective is that it is based on the idea that communication is not just transfer of information. When you communicate you also act (Searle, 1969). Actions are performed, including building commitments and agreements between business parties. Agreements are to be regarded as the backbone of L/A approaches. Both agreements on what to do and agreements on performed actions are accentuated. Such emphasis on agreements causes a division of the communication process into three or four phases.

Action workflow (AW) (Medina-Mora et al., 1992) and DEMO (Dietz, 1999) are two frameworks founded in the language/action tradition. Although valuable features exist in these frameworks, certain limitations also exist. The interactive character is not fully developed. See Goldkuhl and Lind (2004) for further explanation of this criticism. As a reaction towards these deficiencies, the BAT-model was introduced (Goldkuhl, 1996, 1998; Goldkuhl & Lind, 2004; Lind & Goldkuhl, 2003). The BAT-model has been applied in different studies (e.g., Axelsson et al., 2000; Goldkuhl & Melin, 2001; Lind, 2002).

As mentioned in the introduction, there is a need for comprehensive frameworks covering business interaction. The BAT-model is claimed to be one. An-other promising attempt to create such comprehensive framework has been made by Weigand and van den Heuvel (1998) in which metapatterns for electronic commerce is proposed. This framework is built on the idea to integrate different L/A-oriented approaches, such as DEMO, action workflow, and BAT for business modeling.

Originally outside the language/action tradition, Schmid and Lindemann (1998) have presented a reference model for electronic markets that in later works (Lechner & Schmid, 2000) has been expanded to a more general framework—a media reference model (MRM). A comparison of BAT and MRM has been made in Petersson and Lind (2005).

SOCIO-INSTRUMENTAL PRAGMATISM

Social Action

Socio-instrumental pragmatism (SIP) is a foundational theory (base ontology) specifically aimed for studies concerning information systems (e.g., Goldkuhl, 2002, 2005a; Goldkuhl & Röstlinger, 2003). It is an eclectic synthesis based on several action-theoretic frameworks form reference disciplines, like, for example, philosophy, linguistics, sociology, psychology, and organization theory. It is based on foundational pragmatic insights leading to action as a core concept. Herbert Blumer, one of the founders of symbolic interactionism, claims that

... the essence of society lies in an ongoing process of action—not in a posited structure of relations. Without action, any structure of relations between people is meaningless. To be understood, a society must be seen and grasped in terms of the action that comprises it. (Blumer, 1969, p. 71)

The social world is created and recreated through human actions. This means that most actions are of social character. The great sociologist Max Weber has made a classical definition of social action: "That action will be called *social* which in its meaning as intended by the actor or actors, takes account of the behaviour of others and is thereby oriented in its course" (Weber, 1978, p. 4). Our interpretation of this definition is that a social action (performed by an actor) has *social grounds* ("takes account of the behaviour of others") and *social purposes* ("thereby oriented in its course").

From this follows the basic idea in SIP that (most) actions are directed towards other humans. There are addressees of most actions. When we, as human actors, create or change some material object, there may be addressees for this action object. When we say something, there are definitely addressees for these communicative actions. In SIP, there is a basic model of social action (Figure 3). This model consists of two actors. One actor is conducting an intervening action (a communicative action or a material action) directed towards the addressee. The addressee performs a receiving action, that is, the receipt of a material object or the interpretation of a message. The intervening actor is the focused actor in the model. This actor has social grounds for the action. The actor pre-assesses external and internal grounds in a deliberative phase before

the intervening action. After intervention, the actor postassesses the result and the effects. This builds on a continuity model of actions with a division into three stages: (1) pre-assessment, (2) intervention, (3) post-assessment (Goldkuhl, 2004). Originally, this builds on Mead's (1938) four stage model of human action: impulse, perception, manipulation, and consummation. In SIP these stages have been renamed and the first two stages have been integrated into one.

In SIP, the action is seen as knowledgeable. The actor uses her knowledge in order to make a difference in the external world (Dewey, 1931). The actor is seen as purposeful with abilities to reflect and deliberate before intervention (Dewey, 1931; von Wright, 1971). The SIP model of human action also builds on an important difference between result and effect (von Wright, 1971). The result is what the actor produces, that is, the direct result of the action. The result is what lies in the range and control of the actor. Effects are what arise as consequences of the performed action.

Social action takes place in a temporal and spatial context. We can distinguish between an intratemporality and an intertemporality of an action. With intratemporality we delimit to the actor (an intra-

Figure 3. Socio-instrumental action: A basic model (Goldkuhl, 2005a)

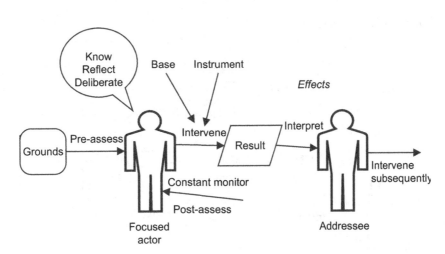

actor characterization). This means the phasing of pre-assessment, intervention and postassessment described above. The intertemporality emphasises the actor interacting with other actors: In this case we follow the division of (1) social grounds for action, (2) the (interventive) action, and (3) the social effects of action.

The SIP model also acknowledges that human actions often are mediated through the use of some instrument (e.g., Vygotsky, 1962). Instruments are mediational means for human action with enabling and constraining functions for the actor. Many actions can be seen as transformation of objects. A base object is transformed into a result object (Goldkuhl & Röstlinger, 2003).

Social Interaction and Relations

As every model, Figure 3 is a simplification. It describes a one-way action from the focused actor to the addressee. There is no explicit interaction depicted in this model. Within the social grounds, there may be an implicit interactional component. There may be, for example, a request of some action from the addressee actor in the figure. This basic social action model is therefore complemented with a social interaction model (Figure 4). In this model the interactive nature of social life is more explicitly depicted. The interaction model describes two related actions. One action is an initiative for the subsequent action, which is seen as a response to the first. The response action can then function as an initiative for subsequent responsive actions. The concepts of initiative and response is fetched from the concept adjacency pair in conversation analysis (Sacks, 1992) and later refined in dialogue theory (e.g., Linell, 1998). Goldkuhl (2005a, 2005b) describes the integration and use of these concepts in socio-instrumental pragmatism.

Another important aspect of social interaction is also depicted in Figure 4. Social actions imply relational changes between actors. When one actor says something or does something else directed to an addressee, certain social relations between the actors are established. For example, when an actor is posing a question, expectations are arisen that an answer or some other adequate response will follow. SIP builds on communication theories where this kind of relational changes are emphasized; speech act theory/communicative action theory (Habermas, 1984; Searle, 1969) and conversation analysis (Sacks, 1992). Some scholars (e.g., Linell, 1998) conceive these theories as contradictory. In SIP, these theories are

Figure 4. Interactivity in social actions (Goldkuhl, 2005a)

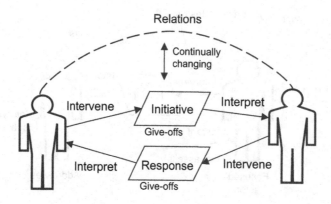

conceived as complementary. Goldkuhl (2003, 2005b) has described how aspects from speech act theory and conversation analysis are integrated into one congruent communication model founded in SIP.

What is a social relation? What does it mean? Where do social relations exist? In order to discuss this matter, we need to use the concepts of a focused actor ("ego") and another actor ("alter"). Relations exist as ego's apprehension of the alter and vice versa. In order to succeed in social interaction, parts of these relational apprehensions need to be intersubjective and not only intrasubjective (these concepts will be further discussed). Different emotions concerning each other may be personal and thus intrasubjective. However, in order to conduct a business conversation in a mutually understandable and coordinated way, different relations between ego and alter need to be intersubjective to a sufficient degree. If ego asks for a product price, then expectations are raised for some answer from alter. After this question has been posed, both parties are usually aware of the expectations for a proper response (Heritage, 1984). Otherwise there will be a breakdown in the communication. Every "move" in the social interplay of a conversation introduces new relations and changes old ones. A communicative action is usually both a response to previous actions

and an initiative to subsequent actions. This means that a certain action may change earlier relations and introduce new ones. This is described in Table 1 and Table 2.

Table 1 describes the different types of relational development that occur from ego action. The table both pinpoints the ego action in relation to alter action as well as ego actions as response (to earlier actions) and projection (for future actions). As stated, an ego action has, as an initiative, connections to future actions. In a communicative act, there are often projections of possible future actions (Goldkuhl, 2005b). An ego action gives *expectations* for future alter actions. A request is a typical example; the request gives expectations for some future alter actions. An ego action may not only have connections to alter future actions, but also to ego coming actions. A promise is a typical example of introducing *commitments* for future actions (Searle, 1969). An ego action has, as a response, connections to earlier actions. This relational aspect of an ego action means that it is a reply to alter's earlier action and the kind of expectations which are raised in this alter actions. We call this relational aspect *replication*. One example of this is ego's answer to an earlier posed question by alter. An ego action may not only have connections to alter previous actions, but also to ego

Table 1. Relational development through ego action

	Responded (earlier actions)	**Projected (future actions)**
Ego actions (focused actor)	Fulfilment of or deviation to ego action	Commitment of ego
Alter actions (other actor)	Replication to alter action	Expectation on alter

Table 2. Relational development through alter action

	Responded (earlier actions)	**Projected (future actions)**
Ego actor	Experiences of ego actions	Expectation on ego
Alter actor	Experiences of alter actions	Commitment of alter

own actions. Ego may have done some commitment in a previous action (e.g., a promise), and the present ego action may be in accordance or not to this commitment. Being in accordance, the ego action is a *fulfilment* and if not, it will be a *deviation*.

Table 1 described the relational meanings of an ego action. Table 2 describes the relational meanings of an alter action. Here we use the postassessment perspective explicitly. The situation described is when ego makes a (post-)assessment of alter's conducted action. What relational changes may occur after alter's action? If there are any action projections made in alter action, relational changes of commitment or expectations may occur. If alter requests something to be done by ego, then an expectation (towards ego) is introduced. If alter promises to do something, commitments for future actions are introduced. What alter does can also be assessed in relation to ego previous actions and alter previous actions. If alter replies to a

question earlier posed by ego, then different kinds of experiences may arise. If alter gives a proper answer then ego may conclude that alter seems to be knowledgeable person. If the answer does not seem to be adequate or correct, then ego's experiences of alter as knowledgeable may diminish. Or ego may reflect upon ego's question (earlier action), that it was not so properly formulated. This follows the principle of action reflexivity described by, for example, Giddens (1984). All actions have repercussions back on the actor himself. Table 1 and Table 2 have been introduced here as an important refinement of SIP and will be used when performing a SIP analysis of business actions.

Realms of the World

With socio-instrumental pragmatism comes also a division into different realms of the world. Goldkuhl

Figure 5. Different realms of the world (Goldkuhl, 2002)

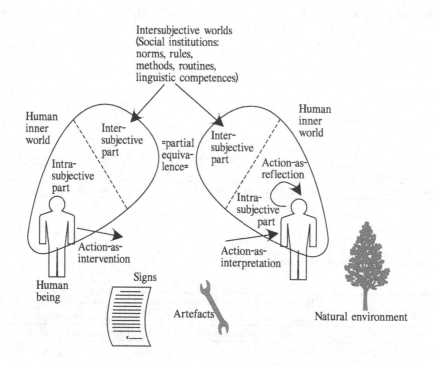

(2002) has made a principal division into different ontological categories (realms). These are depicted in Figure 5. The different ontological categories are the humans, their inner worlds, their actions, and the external world consisting of signs, material artefacts, and nature. Actions are subclassed into three types: (1) Intervening actions, that is, making changes in the external world, (2) interpreting actions, that is, making sense of the external world, and (3) reflective action, that is, making internal changes through thought processes. This follows the division made by Schutz (1970) in overt actions (intervention) and covert actions (interpretation and reflection). Signs and material artefacts are created or changed through intervening actions.

Human inner world is divided into an intrasubjective part and an intersubjective part. The intersubjective part is knowledge that is shared with fellow-actors, for example norms, rules, linguistic competence and methods. This intersubjective part is known under different labels as, for example, social institutions (Berger & Luckmann, 1966; Scott, 1995), structure (Giddens, 1984), and culture (Duranti, 1997).

The SIP consists of some basic ontological building blocks as described in Figure 5. More complex phenomena are built from these elements. One very important phenomenon of complex nature in business interaction is organizations. An organization (a company), acting as a supplier or as a customer is of prime interest for business interaction models. What is an organization in a SIP view? Goldkuhl and Röstlinger (2003) has presented such an ontological clarification based on socio-instrumental pragmatism. "An organization exists as an agreement (a communicative fact) between the principals and other parts of the society. Through such constitutive actions, an organization is given a formal authority to act" (Goldkuhl & Röstlinger, 2003, p. 157). An organization is the result of constituting communicative acts between its principals and legal authorities. As such it is an intersubjective phenomenon depending on formal communicative acts. In a continual existence an organization must comprise different resources; financial and material resources and employed humans and their knowledge.

In SIP, organizations are seen as actors (Goldkuhl and Röstlinger, 2003; Taylor & Van Every, 2000). They can, however, not act by themselves. Organizations act through their human agents and sometimes also through artificial agents, like IT systems. Organizational agents (like employees) act as representatives of the organization.

GROUNDING BUSINESS INTERACTION ACCORDING TO BAT IN SOCIO-INSTRUMENTAL PRAGMATISM

Socio-instrumental pragmatism has contributed to sharpen BAT in several respects. Lind and Goldkuhl (2003) and Goldkuhl and Röstlinger (2003) are two important earlier contributions. Further ontological clarifications are needed in order to specify the social action and interaction character of business interaction. This will be shown below.

BAT is a theory and model for business interaction. It is built from some basic concepts as

- Actors in roles (supplier and customer) can be a human actor or an organization
- Business actions (e.g., offering, ordering, delivering, and complaining) with corresponding action objects of communicative (e.g., offer, order, complaint) or material (e.g., goods) character
- Business phases consisting of actions concerning similar type of exchange (i.e., meaningful action aggregates)
- Business transactions consisting of actions within business phases from proposal to assessment (i.e., meaningful action aggregates)
- Relations between business parties which continually change through the business transaction (i.e., changes in the intersubjective world); a certain role plays the business agreement established in phase 2 and resolved in later phases
- Actor dispositions, which are preconditions for interactive business actions; for example, capabilities (of human and artefact character),

business interests, and needs (human inner world and often expressed in signs)

Every generic business action described in the BAT-model is a social action and can be described in accordance with the generic model of social action (Figure 3). One actor (business party) conducts an action (e.g., offering) directed towards the other actor. An action object (e.g., an offer) is created/presented to the other actor. This other actor receives the action object and interprets it. Through this interpretation subsequent actions can be performed (e.g., ordering). This means that business actions are performed as a social interplay. One action functions as an initiative to another action, which is a response to the first action.

We will below perform a social action analysis of some generic business acts from the four business phases. In this analysis, we use concepts and perspectives from SIP. This will lead to contextual definitions of business actions emphasizing their social interaction character. When clarifying the business actions, the performing actor and the addressee must, of course, be described. This is done together with stating the *action direction* (from intervening actor to addressee). *Social grounds* for the action are also important for describing the action. The actor should not be seen as a social marionette just functioning in a stimulus-response

Table 3. Characterization of actions in proposal phase

Action	Action direction	Social grounds	Deliberation	Action modus	Propositional contents
Inquiry	Customer → Supplier	Knowledge about possible suppliers	Needs for product; exploration desire	Product question (information seeking)	Needs → products? Product → product details, delivery terms?
Invitation to tender	Customer → Supplier	Limited knowledge about suppliers	Needs for product; desire for (alternative) tenders	Purchase interest	Type of product, desired commercial terms
Offer	Supplier → Customer	Knowledge about possible customers and their needs	Desire to make a competitive offer	Sales offer (proposal)	Product, product characteristics
(Counter) Bid	Customer → Supplier	Knowledge about suppliers and their products and offers	Precise product needs, business consideration	Purchase proposal	Product, product characteristics, commercial terms

Table 4. Relational characterization of offer

	Responded (earlier actions)	Projected (future actions)
Supplier actions (focused actor)	-	Commitment to sell in accordance with given offer
Customer actions (other actor)	Replication to inquiries, tender, invitations, counterbids	Expectation to order product

fashion. The actor has capabilities for *deliberation* before action. SIP is based on speech act theory (e.g., Searle, 1969) with the important differentiation into illocutionary force (here called *action modus*) and *propositional contents*. The focused action's relations to future actions are important. They are, however, not described in this type of table. This aspect is instead described in special relational tables below, based on the principal Table 1 above.

The social action analysis of some of the generic business actions are thus a step towards *defining* key concepts and intentionally *relating* them to each other within the domain ontology (BAT). Relations between different concepts are to some extent elaborated on by using tables. An important task in ontology declaration is to make intentional relations (cf. Guarino, 1998) explicit. This task has been initiated in our former work (e.g., Lind & Goldkuhl, 2003). The more explicit definitions put forward in this chapter should be seen as a further extension of this work.

In Table 3, we have described four types of actions from the proposal phase. Offer is the typical action of a supplier in this phase. We have described three types of customer actions: inquiry, invitation to tender, and counter bid. Table 3 is followed by Table 4, in which we have made a relational characterization of the offer action based on the relational development through the supplier's actions.

Contractual Phase

The second phase in the BAT-model is the commitments phase. In this phase the business parties arrive at a business contract. The two main actions in this phase are the customer ordering and the supplier confirming. These two actions are characterized in Tables 5-7. We have also described the supplier's invoicing as an action in this phase (Table 5). It might be seen as disputable. In the first BAT-model (Goldkuhl, 1996), it was described as part of the fulfilment phase. We have classified the invoicing to be part of the contract phase since these actions are concerned with directives for the exchange of value in the fulfilment phase. The order is a directive for delivery. The invoice is a corresponding directive for payment. Table 6 covers the relational characterization of the order action performed by the customer (as the ego). In Table 7, the relational characterization of the delivery confirmation action.

Fulfilment Phase

The main actions in the fulfilment phase are the delivery and the payment. These actions of exchange of value are mainly material and not communicative. Therefore we have left out the column "propositional contents" in Table 8.

Table 5. Characterization of actions in contract phase

Action	Action direction	Social grounds	Deliberation	Action modus	Propositional contents
Order	Customer → Supplier	Given offers	Evaluation of offers vs. needs	Purchase order	Product, no of items, commercial terms
Delivery confirmation	Supplier → Customer	Order	Checking delivery possibilities	Delivery promise	Product, no of items, delivery terms
Invoice	Supplier → Customer	Delivery agreement, planned or conducted delivery	Appropriate time for payment	Payment directive	Delivery, payment amount, payment details

Table 6. Relational characterization of order

	Responded (earlier actions)	Projected (future actions)
Customer actions (focused actor)	Fulfilment of expressed purchase desire	Commitment to pay for future delivery
Supplier actions (other actor)	Replication to offer	Expectation to confirm and deliver products in accordance with order

Table 7. Relational characterization of delivery confirmation

	Responded (earlier actions)	Projected (future actions)
Supplier actions (focused actor)	Fulfilment of given offer	Commitment to deliver products
Customer actions (other actor)	Replication to order; acknowledging the order leading to an establishment of a contract	Expectation to pay for delivered products

Table 8. Characterization of actions in fulfilment phase

Action	Action direction	Social grounds	Deliberation	Action modus
Delivery	Supplier → Customer	Business contract (order + confirmation)	Time for delivery	Product provision
Payment	Customer → Supplier	Business contract (order + confirmation), invoice, possibly conducted delivery	Time for payment	Money transfer

Assessment Phase

The assessment phase can consist of positive and negative assessments. The two negative assessments, complaint and reminder to pay, are described in Table 9. A relational characterization of the complaint action is made in Table 10.

CONCLUSION

The purpose of this chapter has been to clarify BAT as business interaction ontology (a domain ontology). For this purpose socio-instrumental pragmatism (SIP) has been used as a base ontology. SIP uses social action as the core concept. A social action, which can be communicative and/or material, means that the action is

Table 9. Characterization of actions in assessment phase

Action	Action direction	Social grounds	Deliberation	Action modus	Propositional contents
Complaint	Customer → Supplier	Delivered products	Discontent with product use	Express of discontent, request for improved product	Product, product deficiencies
Reminder to pay	Supplier → Customer	Delivered products, absent/ unsatisfying payment	Discontent with payment	Claim for payment	Delivery, absent payment

Table 10. Relational characterization of delivery of deficient products (grounds for complaint) from customer viewpoint

	Responded (earlier actions)	Projected (future actions)
Customer (ego actor)	Experiences (ego actions): Could have chosen a better supplier	Expectation to customer: To give feedback concerning product use
Supplier (alter actor)	Experiences (alter actions): Unreliable supplier	Commitment of supplier: Products should be useful

conducted and directed towards another actor. Social actions have social grounds and social purposes. To act towards another actor in patterns of interaction implies relational changes between the actors. Every move in a social interplay introduces new relations and changes old ones. It is thus important to consider several adjacent (social) actions, communicative as well as material, in patterns of interactive acts between the two (or several) parties. The BAT-model empha-sizes phases and interaction patterns for establishing expectations, fulfilment of, as well as evaluation of fulfilled expectations.

In order to clarify BAT as business interaction ontology we have in this chapter made SIP-based social action analyses of the four business phases constituting the BAT-model. This has been done by stating action direction, social grounds, deliberation, action modus, and propositional content for essential business acts within each of the four business phases. For each of the main actions in each business phase, relational characterizations has also been made. In order to make such characterization, we have, in this chapter, introduced the notion of ego as the focused actor and alter as the other actor. In the social interplay the two actor roles, supplier and customer, alternate between being an ego or an alter. In each phase of the business interaction sequence possible business actions are determined ego's response to earlier actions and projected actions towards the alter.

This analysis has led to a more explicit grounding of the BAT-model in SIP as an ontological foundation. The BAT-model and SIP co-exist in the same socio-pragmatic "family" of theories with SIP on a more foundational level. This pursued analysis has also implied a further sharpening of some social interaction concepts within socio-instrumental pragmatism. The typologies of different kinds of relations in social interaction are such a theoretical result.

The work reported in this chapter is to seen as a further step towards a practical theory. SIP is a foundational ontology building on social action. It can thus now be claimed that BAT has been further grounded in *general* social action concepts. This work also means that BAT, as a practical theory, now should be seen as a more congruent domain ontology—at least within the four phases of the BAT-model focused in this chapter.

BAT is intended to be used as a pragmatic instrument for understanding business interaction. It is a comprehensive framework to be used for several purposes. It can be used as a conceptual instrument when *evaluating* existing business interaction. The framework can also be used for *modeling* and *designing* business interactions. It reminds the designers about different dynamic features of business interaction as exchanges, recurrence, evolvement of business relations, and capabilities. It can give structure in the design process and be a basis for the important design of business actions and the allocation of actions to different agents (human agents and IT artefacts). Development of IT-support for business interaction is to be seen as a basic development of business capability.

The work reported in this chapter is to be seen as a rather informal metamodel (based on text and tables) pinpointing some key concepts in the BAT-model. An important step in the future is to make a more formalized metamodel based on the insights derived from grounding BAT in SIP, covering all key concepts in BAT.

Another step in future ontological clarification of the BAT-model is to investigate the relations between different business phases (initiatives and responses as the glue between different phases) as well as looking into different types of dyadic interactions. This is an important task since the logic of business

interaction is conceived as establishing expectations (which is performed in two of the phases), fulfilling these established expectations and finally assessing the fulfilment. It is, therefore, important to highlight these relations since the actions in the latter phases are responses to earlier performed business actions. We also acknowledge a need to explicitly ground the differentiation between market-based interaction and dyadic interaction in the SIP ontology.

REFERENCES

Axelsson, K., Goldkuhl G., & Melin U. (2000). Using business action theory for dyadic analysis. In *The 10th Nordic Workshop on Interorganizational Research* (pp. 18-20/8). Trondheim.

Berger, P.L., & Luckmann T. (1966). *The social construction of reality.* Garden City: Doubleday & Co.

Blumer, H. (1969). *Symbolic interactionism: Perspective and method.* Berkeley, CA: University of California Press.

Craig, R.T., & Tracy, K. (1995). Grounded practical theory: The case of intellectual discussion. *Communication Theory, 5*(3), 248-272.

Cronen, V. (1995). Practical theory and the tasks ahead for social approaches to communication. In W. Leeds-Hurwitz (Ed.), *Social approaches to communication* (pp. 217-242). New York: Guildford Press.

Cronen, V. (2001). Practical theory, practical art, and the pragmatic-systemic account of inquiry. *Communication Theory, 11*(1), 14-35.

Dewey, J. (1931). *Philosophy and civilization.* New York: Minton, Balch & Co.

Dewey, J. (1938). *Logic: The theory of inquiry.* New York: Henry Holt.

Dietz, J.L.G. (1999). Understanding and modeling business processes with DEMO. In *The 18th International Conference on Conceptual Modeling (ER'99)*, Paris.

Duranti, A. (1997). *Linguistic anthropology.* Cambridge: Cambridge University Press.

Giddens, A. (1984). *The constitution of society. Outline of the theory of structuration.* Cambridge: Polity Press.

Goldkuhl, G. (1996). Generic business frameworks and action modeling. In *The First International Workshop on the Language/Action Perspective on Communication Modeling* (pp. 24-39). Oisterwijk, The Netherlands.

Goldkuhl, G. (1998). The six phases of business processes – business communication and the exchange of value. In *The 12th Biennial ITS (ITS'98) conference – Beyond convergence*, Stockholm.

Goldkuhl, G. (2002) Anchoring scientific abstractions – Ontological and linguistic determination following socio-instrumental pragmatism. In *European Conference on Research Methods in Business*, Reading.

Goldkuhl, G. (2003). Conversational analysis as a theoretical foundation for language action approaches? In *The 8th Intl Working Conference on the Language Action Perspective (LAP2003)* (pp. 51-69). Tilburg.

Goldkuhl, G. (2004). The socio-pragmatics of organizational knowledge: An inquiry of managing eldercare knowledge. In *The First Scandinavian Workshop on e-Government*, Örebro University.

Goldkuhl, G. (2005a). Socio-instrumental pragmatism: A theoretical synthesis for pragmatic conceptualization in information systems. In *The 3rd Intl Conf on Action in Language, Organizations and Information Systems (ALOIS)* (pp. 148-165), University of Limerick.

Goldkuhl, G. (2005b). The many facets of communication – A socio-pragmatic conceptualization for information systems studies. In *Workshop on Communication and Coordination in Business Processes* (pp. 1-16). Kiruna.

Goldkuhl, G. (2006). What does it mean to serve the citizen? Towards a practical theory on public e-services founded in socio-instrumental pragmatism. In *International Workshop on E-services in Public Administration* (pp. 27-47). Borås.

Goldkuhl, G., & Ågerfalk, P.J. (2002). Actability: A way to understand information systems pragmatics. In K. Liu, et al. (Eds.), *Coordination and communication using signs: Studies in organizational semiotics—2* (pp. 85-113). Boston: Kluwer Academic Publishers.

Goldkuhl, G., & Cronholm, S. (2003). Multi-grounded theory—adding theoretical grounding to grounded theory. In *The 2nd European Conference on Research Methods in Business and Management (ECRM 2003)*, Reading.

Goldkuhl, G., & Lind, M. (2004). Developing e-interactions—A framework for business capabilities and exchanges. In *The 12th European Conference on Information Systems*, Turkku, Finland.

Goldkuhl, G., & Melin, U. (2001). Relationship management vs. business transactions: Business interaction as design of business interaction. In *The 10th International Annual IPSERA Conference*, Jönköping International Business School.

Goldkuhl, G., & Röstlinger, A. (2003). Towards an integral understanding of organizations and information systems: Convergence of three theories. In H.W.M. Gazendam, R.J. Jorna & R.S. Cijsouw (Eds.), *Dynamics and change in organizations. Studies in organizational semiotics* (pp. 132-162). Boston: Kluwer.

Gruber, T.R. (1993). A translation approach to portable ontology specifications. *Knowledge Acquisition, 5,* 199-220

Guarino, N. (1998). Formal ontology and information systems. In *Proceedings of FOIS'98*, Trento, Italy.

Habermas, J. (1984). *The theory of communicative action 1.* Beacon Press.

Heritage, J. (1984). *Garfinkel and ethnomethodology.* Cambridge: Polity Press.

Lechner, U., & Schmid, B.F. (2000). Communities and media – Towards a reconstruction of communities on media. In E. Sprague (Ed.), *Hawaiian Int. Conf. on System Sciences (HICSS'00).* IEEE Press.

Lind, M. (2002). Dividing businesses into processes – foundations for modeling essentials. In K. Liu, R.J. Clarke, P.B. Andersen, & R.K. Stamper (Eds.), *Organizational semiotics—Evolving a science of information systems*, IFIP TC8/WG8.1 (pp. 211-230). Kluwer Academic Publisher.

Lind, M., & Goldkuhl, G. (2003). The constituents of business interaction—generic layered patterns. *Data & Knowledge Engineering, 47,* 327-348.

Lind, M., & Goldkuhl, G. (2006). How to develop a multi-grounded theory: The evolution of a business process theory. *Australian Journal of Information Systems (AJIS), 13*(2), 68-85.

Linell, P. (1998). *Approaching dialogue. Talk, interaction and contexts in dialogical perspectives.* Amsterdam: John Benjamins.

Mead, G.H. (1938). *Philosophy of the act.* Chicago: University of Chicago Press.

Medina-Mora, R., Winograd, T., Flores, R., & Flores, F. (1992). The action workflow approach to workflow management technology. In J. Turner & R. Kraut (Eds.), *Proceedings of the Conference on Computer-Supported Cooperative Work, CSCW'92* (pp. 281-288). ACM Press: New York.

Petersson, J., & Lind, M. (2005). Towards the concept of business action media: Frameworks for business interaction in an electronic market place setting. In *Proceedings of the 3rd Intl Conf on Action in Language, Organizations and Information Systems (ALOIS)* (pp. 85-113), University of Limerick.

Sacks, H. (1992). *Lectures on conversation.* Oxford: Blackwell.

Schmid, B.F., & Lindemann, M.A. (1998). Elements of a reference model for electronic markets. In *31st Hawaii Int. Conf. on System Science (HICSS'98).*

Schutz, A. (1970). *On phenomenology and social relations.* Chicago: University of Chicago Press.

Scott, W.R. (1995). *Institutions and organizations.* Thousand Oaks, CA: Sage.

Searle, J.R. (1969). *Speech acts. An essay in the philosophy of language.* London: Cambridge University Press.

Von Wright, G.H. (1971). *Explanation and understanding.* London: Routledge & Kegan Paul.

Vygotsky, L.S. (1962). *Thought and language.* Cambridge: MIT Press.

Weber, M. (1978). *Economy and society.* Berkeley, CA: University of California Press.

Weigand, H., & van den Heuvel, W.-J. (1998). Meta-patterns for electronic commerce transactions based on FLBC. In *31st Annual Hawaii International Conference on System Sciences* (pp. 261-270).

Winograd, T., & Flores, F. (1986). *Understanding computers and cognition: A new foundation for design.* Norwood: Ablex.

Chapter VI
Towards a Meta-Model for Socio-Instrumental Pragmatism

Peter Rittgen
University College of Borås, Sweden

ABSTRACT

We claim that a general conceptual framework for the IS field should provide some kind of common upper-level ontology to describe and explain artifact-mediated social interaction. Such an ontology, socio-instrumental pragmatism (SIP), has been suggested. Our aim is to refine and formalize this ontology by providing a meta-model in the form of a unified modeling language (UML) class diagram. We discuss the implications of such a model as well as its relation to other ontologies. The meta-model is validated by using it in the evaluation of an existing

INTRODUCTION

The rise in the use of information systems (IS) is undeniable, and every day IS become a more important part of organizations. But far from being perfect, the design and implementation of IS in organizations is still a very problematic task that is often fraught with failure (Ågerfalk & Goldkuhl, 2006). There is a need for a better understanding of IS, organizations, and their relation to come up with a framework capable of integrating these two concepts. For the past two decades, theories of communication have been imported into the IS field and the language action perspective

(LAP) has been proposed as a way to understand IS and organizations based on communication (Goldkuhl, 1982; Winograd & Flores, 1986). Later on, an ontology to capture the social world was proposed and described in Goldkuhl (2001), Goldkuhl, Röstlinger, and Braf (2001), Goldkuhl (2005), and Goldkuhl and Ågerfalk (2002). This ontology was named "socio-instrumental pragmatism" since it aims at human actions which are supported by instruments and performed within the social world (Goldkuhl, 2002). Socio-instrumental pragmatism (SIP) presents a generic framework which allows for the analysis of the social world. Within this world there are six ontological categories:

1. Humans
2. Human inner worlds
3. Human Actions
4. Signs
5. Artifacts
6. Natural objects

Since SIP was intended as a generic framework which can serve as a base to analyze the social world, it is not aimed exclusively at the IS field. We think that a meta-model based on the SIP ontology but with a focus on the IS field is needed. This meta-model has its foundations in both LAP and SIP and presents a model that will allow us to view organizations and IS together with a focus on actions.

The model consists of the basic categories actions, actors, and objects. In addition to this we also consider other important aspects of organizations that are related to their functioning.

TOWARDS A META-MODEL SOCIO-INSTRUMENTAL PRAGMATISM

As mentioned before, there is a need for a framework that allows us to describe social systems in a clearer and more thorough way. Our work is based on the SIP ontology. Within the SIP ontology there are six ontological categories (Goldkuhl, 2002):

- **Humans** are the most important participants in the social world described by the SIP ontology; they act in the world based on meanings and perceptions that they derive from the world.
- **Human inner world** represents the knowledge that a human being has acquired over time about themselves and the external world; this inner world is intended to be seen as part of the human being.
- **Human actions** also form a part of the human being; they can be overt, which means that the actions are intended to intervene in the external world, thus trying to change something about it.

And they can be covert when they are aimed to change some human being's inner world; covert actions try to change knowledge that is present in the human inner world.

- **Signs** are the result of communicative actions; for instance, when write a note saying, "I will be at the store", the writing of the note is by itself a communicative action but the note created is a sign which will mean something to the person that will read it.
- **Artifacts** are things which are not symbolic and not natural but which are material and artificially created. Examples of artifacts are cars, clothes, a knife, and so forth. The difference between signs and artifacts is that while signs are intended to mean something to someone (symbolic), artifacts perform material actions. For instance, a human might use a knife (artifact) to cut some carrots, that is, artifacts are needed to perform material actions.
- **Natural environment** are the objects present in the environment that are not artificially created by humans (e.g., trees).

Figure 1 shows the different realms of the world according to the SIP ontology.

META-MODEL

Our model is divided into three main categories:

- Actions
- Actors
- Objects

Although we do not see Agent as a category; we do acknowledge the importance of agency and describe it as a special element in the model.

Actors

Actors are the main entities in our model, and they can perform either as locutor or addressee within the

Figure 1. Realms of the world within the SIP ontology (Goldkuhl, 2002)

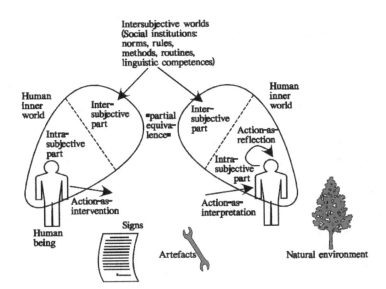

communicative context. When actors perform actions that are directed towards another actor we speak of social actions. They can be performed either in a human-human relation or in a human-artifact-human relation. When performing as locutor the actor is trying to change some aspect of the world by means of his/her actions. For instance, when a person pays the phone bill she is trying to avoid the interruption of her phone service. When performing as addressee the actor receives and interprets an action directed to him and can act himself as a consequence of that action. Taking our example the addressee will be the phone company, which at the moment of receiving the payment will not make any attempt to interrupt the customer's phone service.

Besides locutor and addressee we can distinguish between organizational actors and human actors. The former is an actor that performs as an agent on behalf of the organization, the latter performs an action on behalf of herself.

Objects

An object may be physical or conceptual and it may be formed by other objects or related to them, but every object is unique (Embley, Kurts, & Woodfield, 1994). Under the object category we have artificial and natural objects. Artificial are those that are created by human beings; natural objects are those created by nature and found in the environment. Among the artificial objects, we have artifacts (material objects) and signs (can be material or immaterial). Artifacts are created to extend actors' capabilities. An artifact is seen as a tool. Signs on the other hand are not tools but messages in a static phase waiting to be interpreted by actors or artifacts. A message can take either a physical form (a written text) or a non-physical form (an utterance) (Goldkuhl, 2002).

We can distinguish between four different types of artifacts: static, dynamic, automated, and multi-level. Static artifacts are those that cannot perform any operation by themselves, for example, a stone, a knife, or an axe. Dynamic objects are those capable of performing some operations by themselves but they need constant control by a human being to function properly, for example a car or a drill. Automated artifacts are those that can operate entirely by themselves and only need to be started by an actor. Here we can mention a washing machine as an example (Goldkuhl & Ågerfalk, 2005).

Multi-level artifacts are those that have a mix of capabilities and can perform either as static, dynamic, or automated artifacts depending on the circumstances. Multi-level artifacts have an important property which is the capability of creating and interpreting signs. They lack consciousness and are ruled by a predefined set of instructions that serve as a guide to perform the predefined actions they do. IT systems are an example of multilevel artifacts. Signs can be created either by human beings or artifacts, and every sign can be interpreted by human beings only, by artifacts only, or by both (Goldkuhl, 2005). A written note is a sign, an utterance performed by an actor is another example of a sign as well as a ticket printed by a system in an electronic store.

Actions

The objective of human actions is to change something in the world. They can be communicative or material. The main difference between these two types of actions lies in the fact that communicative actions are intended to change knowledge. Knowledge is implicitly meaningful to someone; and knowledge handling is an exclusive characteristic of actors within an IS. On the other hand, material actions are aimed at material conditions and aspects of the world which are meaningful to someone. They are intended to change something physical among the external world. Winograd and Flores (1984) stated that language is prior to consciousness and we might add that consciousness is prior to actions performed by actors. As a human characteristic, knowledge can be learned through actions, either communicative actions (for instance,

a conversation) or material actions (e.g., when studying an object). Knowledge is the result of the actor's interpretation of both communicative and material actions, and it can be acquired in a social context (from other actors transferring knowledge, for example, in a classroom) or in a non-social context (a person reading a book on her own) (Goldkuhl, 2001).

We can divide actions into i-actions (intervening actions) and r-actions (receiving actions). I-actions are those intended to make a change in the external world, for example, the action of opening a window is intended to change a particular aspect of the external world (the window will move from closed to open). R-actions are those executed covertly, for example when two people are going out and person A tells B "It's cold outside" (communicative i-action). Then person B listens and interprets the message (r-action) and maybe after that person B will take a jacket on the way out (material i-action) (Goldkuhl, 2001). Among i-actions and r-actions we have indefinite and predefined actions.

Indefinite actions are those performed by humans and we call them indefinite since it is not certain how they will be performed by the actor. The same action can vary from actor to actor. When two employees are ordered to clean a shelf, they will both do it but not in the same way; one can do it better or faster than the other one. Indefinite actions can be either r-actions or i-actions. On the other hand we have predefined actions which are performed by artifacts. These actions will always be performed in the same way following previously programmed instructions (Goldkuhl, 2005). Predefined actions are i-actions, since they are intended to change an aspect of the external world. Among indefinite and predefined actions we find both communicative and material actions.

Both types of actions are aimed at changing an aspect of the world surrounding the actor or artifact but we can see communicative actions as a two-phase action (at least) where the actor A performs a communicative action that is intended to change an aspect of the world but is directed toward another actor or artefact B in the first phase. In the second phase B (if

A was successful) executes the action that A desired. Although material, the last action can sometimes be performed without an initial communicative action.

Organizational actions can be either internal or external, and material or communicative. Material and communicative actions within organizations form patterns. Although human beings perform the actions within organizations, we can say that an organization can act. An organizational action has human origins and purposes and is done through humans, by humans, or by artifacts that act on behalf of the organization (Goldkuhl et al., 2001). We will consider organizational actions that constitute an interaction of two or more elements from the organization (actors or artifacts) within an organizational context. We can say that a worker at a clothing factory using a sewing machine to manufacture clothes is performing an organizational action. He is acting to perform an organizational objective (to produce clothes). But, for instance, a man on a farm that goes to the forest to chop wood using an axe, although using an artifact to perform the action, is not performing an organizational action since there is no organizational purpose if he merely burns the wood to warm up his house.

When performing actions by means or with the help of IT systems, we can distinguish between three different types of actions: interactive, automatic, and consequential actions. Interactive actions are supported by and performed through IS and they consist of one or more elementary interactions. Elementary interactions (e-actions) consist of three phases: a user action, an IT system action, and a user interpretation (Goldkuhl, 2001). Let us take the example of an online bank transfer done by the user online. The user will initially introduce his username and password to access the bank system (phase 1), after this the IT system will check in the database if the information is correct and if it is it will grant access to the user and display a welcome screen (phase 2). The welcome screen is interpreted, and the user now knows that he can start his transaction. This is the end of the elementary interaction. Later on the user inputs the data to make the bank transfer, such as account number, amount

to be transferred, and so forth (phase 1 of a second e-interaction), and so on.

Automatic actions are performed by IT systems that produce messages for the actors or other systems. They are done entirely without human intervention. Let us take the banking system again: after logging on, a message pops up in telling the customer that the due date for the credit card payment is very close. The system will execute this operation by itself and present it to the user.

Consequential actions are those performed as a consequence of a message. Taking the bank example again, when the customer sees that his payment is due he might proceed to execute the payment, or he might decide not to do it and wait for the final day.

Based on these types of IS actions, IS are seen as information action systems. This perspective is called actability. Actability is supposed to reinforce the concept of usability within the IS framework and focuses on action and communication. IS actability is the information system's ability to perform actions, and to permit, promote, and facilitate the performance of actions by users, either by means of the system or based on information provided by it in a business context (Sjöström & Goldkuhl, 2002). An IS is said to be actable when it has the following characteristics (Cronholm & Goldkuhl, 2005):

- Clear action repertoire
- Good communication satisfaction
- Easy to navigate interface
- Action transparency
- Clear feedback
- Easy access to action log
- Personalized information
- Familiar vocabulary
- Good support for business actions
- Capability to understand different communicative intentions

The components of the IS are the IT system, the actor, and the e-action. IT systems are social systems that are technically implemented and have an action memory which stores the past actions and some future actions. Actors can play the role of communicator, performer, or interpreter in the IS.

Agents

Agents are a special type of object; we can position agents between objects and actors. They are created by actors, and perform actions to help them complete their tasks. They can be seen as servants of actors, but they have a level of communicative capabilities that allow them to act as communicative mediators, and they are also capable of creating signs for the actors or other agents to interpret. Agents have a transformative capability, a property that human beings have as well. The difference between agents and human beings lies in the fact that human beings can perform both socially aware actions (such as a conversation) and nonsocially aware actions (such as a blink) while agents can only execute the latter (Rose & Jones, 2004).

IT systems can perform as agents, but describing an IT system can be a very tricky task due to the versatility that these artifacts have. An IT system can either be seen as a static artifact (e.g., when we are reading an e-mail), it can be seen as an automated artifact (e.g., a payroll system from a bank that executes the payments for the employees automatically every 15 days), and it can be a dynamic artifact (e.g., a sales system used by a sales person in an electronics store) (Goldkuhl & Ågerfalk, 2005). In all three cases there is a common denominator: communication. In the first case the IT system is acting as an intermediate device between the sender and the receiver of the e-mail. In the second case it can also be seen as a communicative mediator between the employer and the employee, that is, by executing the payments it communicates to the employees that their employer is paying them. In the third case the system acts also as a communicative device between the salesperson and the customer. The IT system gives information about the products to the salesperson which is transmitted to the customers and it also prints a ticket of the sale which is taken by the customer. This ticket communicates to the customer what she bought and how much it cost. The IT system

in this case executes other tasks which may turn into communicative actions. It decreases the inventory of the article sold and if the article inventory is low it will communicate to the inventory manager that the article is running out.

Communication is seen as a kind of action that IT systems can perform and by doing so they become communication mediators. IT systems as well as actors have the capability to create signs and process them (in the case of the IT system) and to interpret them (in the case of actors) (Goldkuhl, 2001). The relation between the signs and the interpreters/processors of them is called pragmatics. Messages are a product of communication and are also an important prerequisite of it. Within IS pragmatics, actions are divided into those that occur within the sign transfer and consequential actions that are performed in response to the transferred sign (Goldkuhl & Ågerfalk, 2002).

Organizational Actions

Roughly, we can say that within an organization every actor acts to fulfil organizational objectives; hence, they are agents helping to accomplish organizational actions. Let us take the example of an electronics store. A customer (C) comes into the store and the following dialog with the salesperson (S) develops.

(S): "May I help you?"
(C): "Yes, I would like to buy some batteries."
(S): "Which type of batteries do you want?"
(C): "Rechargeable AA batteries please."
(S): "We have X and Y brands."
(C): "I would like X."
(S) passes the batteries over the bar code reader and says "$10, please."
(C) pays.
(S) completes the sale in the system and hands the receipt to the customer.

When we analyze this business interaction according to our meta-model we arrive at the results shown in Table 1. We will see organizational actions as those actions performed to fulfill an organizational objective.

Table 1. Sales process for an electronic store

Actor	Action	Type of action	Details
Salesperson	Utterance: May I help you?	Communicative i-action	S performs an i-action
Customer	Utterance: Yes I would like to buy some batteries	R-action; followed by a Communicative i-action	C interprets the utterance performed by S (r-action) and makes an utterance (i-action)
Salesperson	Utterance: Which type of batteries?	R-action; followed by a Communicative i-action	SP interprets the utterance performed by C (r-action) and makes an utterance (i-action)
Customer	Utterance; Rechargeable AA batteries please	R-action; followed by a Communicative i-action	C interprets the utterance performed by S (r-action) and makes an utterance (i-action)
Salesperson	Take the batteries and pass them through the bar code reader	R-action; followed by an Interactive i-action	S interprets the utterance performed by C (r-action) and performs an interactive i-action
IS (Agent)	Reads bar code and gets the information for the product from database	Automatic action	IT system performs an automatic action and displays articles details on the screen
Salesperson	Gets information of product and tell it to the customer	R-action; followed by a Consequential i-action	S interprets the message on the screen (r-action) and makes an utterance (i-action), telling the customer about the details
Customer	Pays for the batteries	R-action; followed by a Material action	C interprets the message of S and performs a material action (payment)
Salesperson	Receives payment and give receipt	R-action; followed by an Interactive i-action; followed by an Automatic action; Material action	S receives the payment and closes the sale in the IT system, IT system executes the automatic actions of modifying the inventory and printing the receipt, S hands the receipt to C (material action)

In Table 1, this objective is to sell batteries. We can also notice that many of the actions are multi-functional, that is, one "surface" action corresponds to a number of implied, "hidden" actions. When the salesperson asks for the type of batteries, he performs an implicit r-action by correctly interpreting the request "I would like to buy some batteries". At the same time he also responds appropriately by performing the i-action of asking for the type of batteries.

As a result of the contemplations in the previous sections we have developed a meta-model (see Figure 2) that covers the most important aspects of socio-instrumental pragmatism as discussed in the relevant literature. Technically the meta-model takes the form of a UML class diagram with generalization/specialization and association.

OTHER ONTOLOGIES

In the literature, we can find a number of competing ontologies that are also potential candidates for a general conceptual framework for the IS field. We look at three of them and discuss their role in such a framework and their relation to SIP.

Social Roles

This theory emphasizes the importance of social roles among the social concepts. Social roles are concepts that can be played by certain entities when they interact with other entities. Examples of social roles are money, professor, and president. The premises behind roles are (Masolo et al., 2004):

Figure 2. Meta-model of SIP

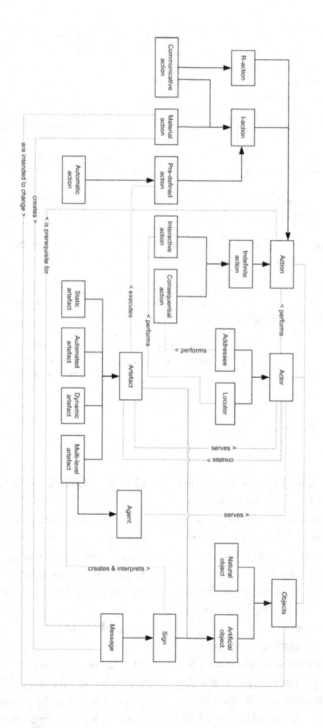

- Roles are properties and can be predicated of different entities. This means that different entities can play the same role.
- Roles are anti-rigid; this aspect regards the temporal nature of the relation between roles and their players.
- Roles have a relational nature, being properties, and they have different types of dependencies to other roles/entities. Notional, identificational, and definitional dependence are some of them.
- Roles are linked to contexts; roles are described as determined by external factors (context).

But as mentioned by Masolo et al. (2004), social roles theory "makes use of a simplified ontology, and therefore only partially characterizes social entities." (p. 5). With the social roles framework we can only partially describe social aspects. We can get a good description of social actors (a professor, a president, an employee) and objects, but we cannot get a description for other important aspects of social concepts such as actions. Another point to highlight is the fact that there is no explicit distinction between actors and objects, since they are both seen as endurants with the difference that objects lack intentionality.

Intentional Collectives

Collections are seen as social objects which depend on member entities and concepts. Several types of collections are distinguished: simple collections (e.g., a collection of stamps), organized collections can be conceived as characterized roles played by members of the collection and that relate among them through social objects. For instance, in a collection of senators, although all of the members have the same role (senator), one of them can be the president of the economic commission, another one can be the secretary of the agricultural commission, and yet another one can be the vice-president of the senate.

Collectives are considered to be something more than collections (Bottazzi, Catenacci, Gangemi, & Lehmann, 2006). Collectives are built around the concepts of intentionality, agent, and plan, the latter being the most important concept within collectives. Intentionality can be seen as the feature by which agents are directed to something. An agent is considered to be intentional and it is oriented towards producing results. An agent function is also to conceive plans. By plan we refer to a description that represents an action schema. Another concept described within the framework of this theory is that of a task, which is a course that is mostly used to sequence activities or other processes that are under the control of a planner. Collectives are a collection of agents. In collectives roles are played by agents and they actively participate in plans and roles.

This theory presents a more detailed conception of social concepts based on social roles. We can find some similarities with our perspective:

- Tasks represent actions within our perspective
- Agents represent actors within our perspective
- Plans can be seen as organizational objectives that lead to the execution of organizational actions

Actor Network Theory

The actor network theory (ANT) describes a world containing both human and nonhuman entities but at the same time it makes no difference in the importance of the elements within the network. Instead of separating the social from the technical, ANT analyzes the world in a sociotechnical manner by arguing that a merely technical or a merely social relation is not possible. Instead of actors, the term actant is used in ANT which can be used to refer either to human or nonhuman elements within the network. ANT's objective is not to analyze the nature and features of the entities in the network, but to study the relations that compound the network, the mechanics of power between the elements, and how the network relations are built (Tatnall & Gilding, 1999).

The ANT approach appears as radical, and the main issue with it is the symmetry between humans, non-human objects, and natural objects. Within our model, the distinction between all these elements is very important in order to understand the functioning and communication within organizations.

For the ANT theorists, the elements of the network relay and prolong collective actions, and no element is considered as the source of the actions. Therefore, instead of being actions, they are seen as events. As we can see, events can be mapped to organizational actions within our perspective. Organizational actions are collective actions performed by one or more actors, agents, or artifacts within organizational boundaries and with a common goal. Thus, events are described in the same way as being collective actions that have no source but that are performed by the actants of the network (McLean & Hassard, 2004).

EVALUATING A BUSINESS MODELING LANGUAGE

To validate the completeness and correctness of the meta-model, we investigated an existing business modeling language. We have chosen the language of SIMM (situation-adaptable work and information systems modeling method), Goldkuhl (1996), because we have considerable experience with this language in action research projects. The analysis proceeded in the following way. First we have extracted the constituting concepts from the diagrams. The diagrams are: collaboration graph, interaction graph, process graph, and action graph. These concepts can be found in the left column of Table 2.

In the second step, we have related the concepts of SIMM to the categories of SIP as formalized in the meta-model. For this step we have thoroughly analyzed the documentation of SIMM (Röstlinger & Goldkuhl, 2006). The result of this step is presented in the middle column of Table 2. The right column contains a textual description of the respective concept.

In the third step, we have analyzed the table to identify deficiencies of the meta-model and the language SIMM. We found that all business concepts of SIMM could be captured accurately by some category of the meta-model. Only concepts originating from a different domain (knowledge) or belonging to general upper-level ontology (time and place) could not be represented.

On the other hand, we discovered some minor shortcomings of SIMM. One is that of construct (or concept) overload where one concept takes on different meanings in different contexts and is therefore mapped to several ontological categories. An example of that is *Initialization*, which can be both an actor and an object/sign.

Another issue is that of construct (or concept) redundancy where one and the same ontological category can be expressed by several concepts of the modeling language. An example of this are *directly related actions* and *Indirectly related actions*. Both concepts cannot be distinguished ontologically which can be seen as a case of over-specification from the point of view of the ontology. In the latter it is not considered to be relevant whether actions follow each other immediately or not.

CONCLUSION

We started our chapter with the assumption that socio-instrumental pragmatism might contribute towards the development of a general conceptual framework for the IS field. We then set out to capture both the breadth and depth of the SIP literature with a suitable meta-model. This process consisted of uncovering the central concepts and their (often implicit) relations and making them explicit in a clear and concise way. We did this with the help of a UML class diagram, a modeling language which is well established and documented and can therefore be expected to support the communication of and about the meta-model among a large group of IS researchers.

We are well aware of the fact that such a meta-model is not, and cannot be, the ultimate solution to a general conceptual framework for the IS field. But we think that it can stimulate a fruitful discussion about the vital components of such a framework. We do not know of any other meta-models that cover the breadth of IT-mediated social action with similar stringency.

Table 2. Mapping SIMM concepts to meta-model categories

SIMM concept	Related SIP concept	Comment
Activity/action	Action	Describes what is done and by whom (executor); this is complemented by place, time, and instrument of execution
Actor	Actor	Person, group of persons, role, organizational unit
Alternative actions	Action (with conditional sub-actions, # = 1)	One of two or more actions/action sequences is carried out
Alternative prerequisites/ results	Object (with conditional sub-objects, # = 1)	One of two or more objects is required for or the result of an action
Artifact	Artifact	Artificial system that performs actions automatically, for example, an IT system
Being	Actor/object	Human being or animal
Cancellation	Object/sign	The action is canceled when a certain object is present or at a certain time
Closed information	Sign	Information that can only be interpreted with the help of some instrument
Collaboration object	Object	Information, material
Combined actions	Action (with concurrently ordered sub-actions)	Two or more actions/action sequences are carried out
Combined or alternative actions	Action (with conditional sub-actions, # > 0)	One or more of two or more actions/action sequences is carried out
Combined or alternative prerequisites/results	Object (with conditional sub-objects, # > 0)	Two or more objects are required for or the result of an action
Combined prerequisites/ results	Object (with sub-objects)	Two or more objects are required for or the result of an action
Composite action	Action	A number of actions that is carried out together
Composite executor/unit	Actor/artifact	Several executors that together form a named unit for execution
Composite process	Action	A number of processes that are combined to a meaningful unit
Condition	Sign	Condition for prerequisite, result or action
Conditional action	Action (conditional)	Action that is carried out or not depending on some condition
Customer	Actor	A special role of actor as the final receiver of a product
Data storage	Artifact	Place to store closed information
Directly related actions	Action (with sequentially ordered sub-actions)	Actions that are immediately follow each other
End	Sign	End of process
Executor	Actor/artifact	Performer of an interactive action
Executor	Actor/artifact	Performer of an action in a process
Executor	Actor/artifact	Person, group of persons, role, organizational unit or artifact
Independency relation	Action (without effect)	Control flow between actions
Independent actions	Action (with sequentially ordered sub-actions)	Sequential actions that have no causal relation
Indirectly related actions	Action (with sequentially ordered sub-actions)	Actions that follow each other but not immediately
Information	Sign	Messages that can be interpreted directly by human beings

Table 2. continued

SIMM concept	Related SIP concept	Comment
Information relation	Communicative action	Flow of information between executors/units
Information relation	Communicative action	Flow of information between actions
Information storage	Artifact	Place to store information/messages
Initialization	Actor	Actor that starts a mutually interactive action
Initialization	Object/sign	An action is started when a certain prerequisite becomes available or at a certain time
Instrument	Object/artifact	A tool that is used in an action
Interaction partner	Actor/Artifact	Executor/unit that performs interactive actions
Interaction sequence	(Ordered) actions	A number of actions that is ordered in time
Interactive action	Action	An action that the sender directs towards the receiver
Knowledge	(refers to an ontology of the mind)	Internal state of the mind
Marked actor	Actor	A focused actor
Marked collaboration object	Object	A focused collaboration object
Marked interaction partner	Actor/artifact	A focused interaction partner
Marked process	Action	A focused process
Material	Object	Material objects that can be accompanied by information
Material relation	Material action	Flow of material between executors/units or between actions
Material storage	Artifact	Place to store material that can be accompanied by information
Mutually interactive action	Action	Two or more interactive actions that follow an initiative/response pattern
Non-object	Object	Hypothetical object
Parallel actions	Action (with concurrently ordered sub-actions)	Actions that are performed concurrently
Place	(refers to an upper-level ontology)	Describes where an action is performed
Prerequisite	Object	Action object that is required for an action
Process	Action	A number of actions with a common goal
Process object	Object	Product/result of a process that is useful for the customer or order that initiates a process
Producer	Actor/artifact	Executor/unit that produces and directs information and/or material for/towards the receiver
Receiver	Actor/artifact	Executor/unit that receives and uses information and/or material
Result	Object	Product of the executed activity/action
Reused process	Action	A process that occurs in different places in the process graph
Sequential actions	Action (with sequentially ordered sub-actions)	Actions that follow one after the other
Start	Sign	Start of process
Time	(refers to an upper-level ontology)	Point in time for execution of an action
Variants	Action (with conditional sub-actions)	One action is chosen from a number of alternatives

REFERENCES

Ågerfalk, P., Goldkuhl, G., Fitzgerald, B., Bannon, L. (2006). Reflecting on action in language, organizations and information systems. *European Journal of Information Systems, 15*(1), 4-8.

Bottazzi, E., Catenacci, C., Gangemi, A., & Lehmann, J. (2006). From collective intentionality to intentional collectives: An ontological perspective. *Journal of Cognitive Systems Research, Special Issue on Collective Intentionality, 7*(2-3), 192-208.

Cronholm, S., & Goldkuhl, G. (2002). *Actability at a glance.* Sweden.

Embley, D., Kurtz, B., & Woodfield, S. (1994). *Object oriented system analysis: A model-driven approach.* NJ: Prentice Hall.

Goldkuhl, G. (1996). Generic business frameworks and action modeling. In F. Dignum, J. Dietz, E. Verharen, & H. Weigand (Eds.), *Proceedings of the First International Workshop on Communication Modeling, Electronic Workshops in Computing* (pp. 1-15). Berlin, Germany: Springer.

Goldkuhl, G. (2001). Communicative vs. material actions: Instrumentality, sociality and comprehensibility. In *Proceedings of the The Language-Action perspective on communication modeling 2001* (pp. 1-20).

Goldkuhl, G. (2002). Anchoring scientific abstractions: Ontological and linguistic determination following socio-instrumental pragmatism. In *Proceedings of the European Conference on Research Methods in Business and Management Studies (ECRM 2002)* (pp. 1-11). Reading, UK: MCIL.

Goldkuhl, G. (2005). Socio-instrumental pragmatism: A theoretical synthesis for pragmatic conceptualization in information systems. In *Proceedings of the Action in Language, Organizations and Information Systems (ALOIS 2005)* (pp. 148-165). Limerick, Ireland.

Goldkuhl, G., & Ågerfalk, P. (2002). *Actability: A way to understand information systems pragmatics.* Sweden.

Goldkuhl, G., & Ågerfalk, P. (2005, July-September). IT artefacts as socio-pragmatic instruments: Reconciling the pragmatic, semiotic, and technical. *International Journal of Technology and Human Interaction, 1*(3) 29-43.

Goldkuhl G. & Lyytinen K. (1982). A language action view of information systems. In C. Ross & M. Ginzberg (Eds), *Proceedings of the Third International Conference on Information Systems*, (pp. 13-31). Ann Arbor, Michigan.

Goldkuhl G., Röstlinger, A., & Braf, E. (2001, July). Organizations as practice systems – Integrating knowledge, signs and artefacts and action. In *Proceedings of the IFIP 8,1 Working Conference Organizational Semiotics: Evolving a Science of Information Systems* (pp. 1-15). Montreal.

Masolo, C., Vieu, L., Bottazzi, E., Catenacci, C., Ferrario, R., & Gangemi, A., et al. (2004). Social roles and their descriptions. In *Ninth International Conference on the Principles of Knowledge Representation and Reasoning* (pp. 1-11). Whistler, Canada.

McLean, C., & Hassard, J. (2004) Symmetrical absence/symmetrical absurdity: Critical notes on the production of actor-network accounts. *Journal of Management Studies, 41*(3), 493-519.

Rose, J., & Jones, M. (2004). *The double dance of agency: A socio-theoretic account of how machines and human interact.* Denmark.

Röstlinger, A., & Goldkuhl G. (2006). Grafnotation för SIMM metodkomponenter. Linköping University, Linköping, Sweden. Retrieved June 10, 2007, from http://www.vits.org/publikationer/dokument/547.pdf

Sjöström, J., & Goldkuhl G. (2002, June). Information systems as instruments for communication – refining the actability concept. In *Proceedings of the 5th International Workshop on Organizational Semiotics* (pp. 1-21). Delft.

Tatnall, A., & Gilding, A. (1999). Actor-network theory and information systems research. In *Proceedings of the 10th Australian Conference on Information Systems* (pp. 955-966).

Winograd, T., & Flores, F. (1986). *Understanding computers and cognition: A new foundation for design.* Ablex, Norwood.

Chapter VII
Towards Organizational Self-Awareness:
An Initial Architecture and Ontology

Marielba Zacarias
INESC/INOV, Portugal

Rodrigo Magalhães
University of Lisbon, Portugal

Artur Caetano
University of Lisbon, Portugal

H. Sofia Pinto
University of Lisbon, Portugal

José Tribolet
University of Lisbon, Portugal

ABSTRACT

Human beings are, by nature, self-aware beings. This capacity lets us know who we are, how we do things, and what we (and others) are doing at any particular moment. In organizations, self-awareness is an essential prerequisite for effective action, decision-making, and learning processes. However, it must be built and maintained by continuous interactions among their members. This chapter lays out the foundations of a comprehensive high-level modeling framework as a means for enhancing organizational self-awareness. The modeling framework encompasses an architecture and ontology, which puts together human, social, and organizational approaches with modeling frameworks coming from the computer sciences and IS/IT fields. The proposed approach is illustrated with two example applications which use the finer-grained concepts of the framework. An analysis of the implications of this approach and issues to be addressed is provided.

INTRODUCTION

The challenge of today's organizations is to develop capabilities of continuous sensing, learning, and adjusting to the dynamics of their environments (Magalhães, 2004). An essential requirement of these capabilities entails developing organizations' self-awareness. Human consciousness gives subjects the capacity of self-awareness. Self-aware beings know who they are, how they do things, and what they (and others) are doing at any particular moment. Whereas this capacity is innate in individuals, *organizational self-awareness* must be built and maintained by continuous interactions among their members.

From our point of view, enterprise models are an essential communication tool in supporting and enhancing organizations' self-awareness. Organizational modeling has a long tradition in organizational and management sciences. In these fields, the main goal is to provide ways of thinking about the organization and to produce management principles and theories based on these ways of thinking. These models, described in natural language and with a high level of abstraction, are limited to human use and lead to different interpretations. The information systems (IS) and artificial intelligence (AI) fields have also addressed organizational modeling activities. These models are commonly referred as enterprise architectures (EA) or enterprise ontologies. They have been mainly used as communication tools (Shekkerman, 2004) to facilitate the design and implementation of business applications. Consequently, both EA and enterprise ontologies are described using more formal syntax and semantics, enabling its processing by automated agents and reducing inconsistent interpretations. However, these enterprise representations are restricted to concerns relevant for participants and stakeholders of systems development. Moreover, most of these representations are based on static, mechanistic, and deterministic views of the organization.

Modeling the organization for its self-awareness is a more challenging task. It requires integrating approaches coming from organizational and IS fields, to capture: (1) an organization's structural and dynamic aspects, (2) routines and decision-making processes, and (3) its formal and informal sides. Moreover, it entails capturing an organization's evolution. All these aspects must be captured from different viewpoints and levels of details. Means for mapping between different aspects, viewpoints, and levels of details must also be provided.

A first step in achieving this end is the definition of a conceptual framework to address the aforementioned issues. Departing from an ontological position that regards organizations as complex and adaptive sociotechnical systems, in this chapter we describe and illustrate a three-layered architecture which encompasses a set of different, but inter-related concepts. This basic architecture can be applied at several levels of detail of the organization and aims at providing a comprehensive and semiformal modeling framework, which enables a complementary usage of approaches of the IS field and organizational sciences.

The remaining portions of this chapter are structured as follows; the second section describes the theoretical background supporting the proposed framework, followed by sections summarizing related work on agent and enterprise modeling, describing the framework, and summarizing two examples applications illustrating the finer-grained concepts of the framework. In the final two sections, we give our conclusions and future directions.

THEORETICAL BACKGROUND

Organizations as Resultant of the Agency-Structure Duality

The approach proposed in this chapter is based on a view of organization as a sociotechnical entity, which self-realizes in the permanent action and interaction of its component parts. This view of organization is the outcome of a number of intellectual influences, namely organizational constructionism (Giddens, 1984), autopoiesis (Maturana & Varela, 1980), organizational intelligence (March, 1999), *organizational complexity* (Tsoukas, 2005), and organizational evolution (Aldrich & Ruef, 2006). In this chapter, we focus on the organization as the resultant of the actions of individual and social agents.

Agency is an essential notion of social theory. Human action is more than a mere combination of acts. Human beings have the capacity to understand what they do (Giddens, 1984). These reflexive capacities are (a) largely carried tacitly and (b) embedded in the flow of day-to-day activities. A social actor is "an organizational entity" whose interactions are simultaneously enabled and constrained by the environments of the firm, its members, and its industry (Lamb & Kling, 2003). *Structure* is another important notion emerged from social theory. According to Giddens (1984), it comprises rules and resources. Rules are generic procedures of action applied in reproduction of social practices. Resources are the media through which power is exercised. Resources may be *allocative* or authoritative. *Allocative* resources include information, objects, goods or material phenomena, and capabilities to allocate or transform them. Authoritative resources include soft competencies and social resources such as power relationships.

The notions of *agency* and *structure* are the cornerstones of structuration theory (Giddens, 1984). This theory suggests a recurrent duality between agency and structure. For Giddens, social action makes up what he calls the system, that is, the observable patterns of events and behavior. Social systems comprise the situated activities of human agents, reproduced across time and space. Structure refers to the unobservable rules and resources used to generate the system. Structure is saved as memory traces and is recursively implicated in social systems. Structuration is the process of producing and reproducing social structures through the daily activity of social actors.

Refining Organizational Agency: A Complex, Adaptive Framework

Our conception of organization includes considering it a result of an evolution process. Axelrod and Cohen (2000) have taken the principles of evolution and have put together a truly innovative framework

for organizational analysis, which allows refining the notion of organizational action. We summarize below the essential concepts of this framework:

- Agents are collections of properties that include location and capabilities. Agents interact with artifacts and other agents. Agents can respond to what happens around them and can do things more or less purposefully; thus, agents have goals. Agents can be not only persons but also families, businesses, countries, or computer programs.

- Artifacts are objects with properties such as location or capabilities. Agents interact with other agents and/or artifacts. An artifact has "affordances" (features evoking certain behavior from agents). However, they do not have purposes of their own or reproduction capabilities.

- Strategies are ways of an agent of responding to its surroundings and pursuing its goals. A strategy is a conditional action pattern that indicates what to do in which circumstances.

- Success measures are "scores" used by an agent or by a designer to define how well an agent or strategy is doing.

- Populations are collection of agents, or, in some situations, collections of strategies.

- Systems are larger collections, including one or more populations of agents and possibly also artifacts.

- Designers are agents that introduce new agents, artifacts, or strategies into the world.

- Adaptation takes place when a selection process leads to improvement according to some measure of success. Adaptations for some agents may not be for others. Moreover, adaptations of agents do not necessarily leads to an adaptation of the system

- Selection involves the change processes triggered by success measures.

- Variety defines the diversity of types within a population or system. Variety is driven by change processes. Variety is a central requirement to adaptation.

- Interactions address the question of who or what should interact with who or what and when. Interactions make a complex adaptive system come alive. Interactions give rise to events and develop an unfolding history.

- Interaction patterns define the recurring regularities of contact among types within a system. These patterns are neither random nor completely structured. Interaction patterns are determined by two kinds of factors; proximity and activation. *Proximity* determines how agents become likely to interact. *Activation* determines the sequencing of their activities. Activation groups together many different processes that affect the timing of agent activity.

Human Activity and Consciousness

In order to be fully understood, agency must be regarded at collective and individual levels. Whereas structuration theory and Axelrod and Cohen's (2000) framework explain the formation and evolution of societies, activity theory (AT) is a psychological theory which analyzes the formation and evolution of individual and collective activities, and its relationship with human consciousness.

Leont'ev (1974) has described an activity as being composed of *subjects, object, actions,* and *operations*. *Actions* are conscious, goal-directed processes that must be undertaken to fulfill the object. *Operations* are actions that become unconscious with practice. The *subjects* involved comprise multiple individuals and/or subgroups who share the same general object of activity and who construct themselves as distinct from other groups. This model was later extended to include *social rules,* that is, regulations, norms, and conventions constraining actions and interactions within the activity system; *community,* that is, activity stakeholders and *division of labor,* that is, horizontal division of tasks and vertical division of power and status (Engeström, Miettinen, & Punamäki, 2005).

Activity constituents may change in time according to a set of key principles. The first principle assumes that events should not be analyzed in isolation but

as result of *developments* over time. Another key principle is *mediation* by tools and signs. Tools and signs are artifacts that shape the way human beings interact with reality. The principle of *object-orientation* (different from object-oriented programming) is one of the most important principles of AT. Every motive is an object that drives activity execution and coordination. AT also differentiates between internal (mental) and external activities. *Internalization* is the transformation of external activities into internal ones. *Externalization* transforms internal activities into external ones.

According to Leont'ev (1977), consciousness is the basis of all human activity. Activity theorists argue that consciousness is not a mere set of discrete disembodied cognitive acts. For AT, having human consciousness means to be part of a web of social activities and to live and act in a culturally elaborated environment populated by a wealth of tools, including language (Nardi, 1998). In other words, consciousness is an individual and social phenomenon that both influences and is influenced by human activities.

Organizational Consciousness and Self-Awareness

The notion of consciousness of activity and structuration theories can be refined further in search of the intellectual foundations for a new construct that has been labeled as organizational consciousness (Magalhães & Tribolet, in press). Such a refinement can be found in the teaching of Weick (1995) about sense-making in organizations. Sense-making is defined as structuring unknown contexts and/or actions and assigning them with meaning. Sense-making is distinguished from other explanatory processes such as understanding or interpreting by the following characteristics; the process of sense-making is (1) social, (2) grounded on identity construction, (3) retrospective, (4) focused on extracted cues, (5) ongoing, (6) driven by plausibility rather than accuracy, and (7) enactive. The seven properties of sense-making affect the initial sense that a person develops of a situation and strongly influences how this perception is developed for future action. In other words, sense-making lies at the foundation of the consciousness that organizational agents develop of the organization as a whole and of their place in it. Sense-making and organizational consciousness are closely related notions. However, these are rather abstract notions comprising several capacities including perception, memory, reasoning, association, and awareness among others.

In this work, we narrow our focus and refer to a more specific and operational capacity given by consciousness; self-awareness. Organizational self-awareness has an individual and an organizational dimension. The individual dimension refers to the capacity that individual members of the organization have of answering questions such as: *Who am I in this organization?, How are things done here?, What is the organization—as a whole—doing now?* The organizational dimension refers to the combination of human or automated agents, resources, and procedures that provides organizations with the necessary intelligence for dealing with questions such as: *Who are my members?, How do they do things?, What are they doing now?* An organization is self-aware when these two dimensions are aligned. In practice, achieving this alignment has proved to be neither straightforward nor easy. Despite the existence of several IS/IT providing already some degree of self-awareness, it is partial, frequently inconsistent or outdated. It is precisely in supporting a dynamic alignment between organizations and its agents where we envision the value of enterprise representations and tools.

Summary

Summing up, the objective of the architecture and ontology proposed in this chapter is to enhance organizational self-awareness (OSA). Such an objective has three implications. One implication concerns our own understanding of organizations and OSA. In this chapter, we summarized three theories that consistently regard organizations as complex, adaptive systems in which the formation and evolution of individual and organizational behavior are inter-dependent processes. Departing from this ontological position, we have defined OSA as being simultaneously an individual and collective phenomenon that must be supported by a continuous communication among organizational agents.

The second implication points to the very specific need of the modeling framework itself. According to Weick (2001), some organizational conditions seem to hinder sense-making, and, thus, OSA, while others seem to enhance it. If we were able to represent, communicate, and discuss organizational conditions through appropriate enterprise representations, we would be able to improve OSA on the drawing board, so to speak. This would not be restricted to IS development and implementation; it can also involve an organization's design issues. However, this entails the definition of models enabling organizations to answer the required questions about the organization and its members.

The third implication points to the ways of using IS/IT in building and updating these representations to support OSA. Current organizational dynamics require a continuous updating of enterprise representations. Hence, it is necessary to devise appropriate data collection and analysis mechanisms facilitating the depiction of up-to-date representations.

RELATED WORK

Enterprise Architectures: The CEO Framework

Structuration theory, AT, and the Axelrod and Cohen (2000) Framework provide approaches consistent with the complexity paradigm of organizations. Nonetheless, these approaches are described in natural language and with a high level of abstraction. Hence, they are limited to human use and lead to different interpretations.

There are several EA providing frameworks to model organizations. Since their essential function is to facilitate communication between IS/IT stakeholders, they are described using more formal syntax and semantics. Most EA frameworks enable to model organizations in terms of two essential concepts; activities and entities or resources. These two concepts are combined in several ways to depict different perspectives or viewpoints. The most commonly depicted enterprise perspectives are the process, information, application, and technology perspectives (Schekkerman, 2004).

The CEO framework is a conceptual EA modeling framework put forward by the Center for Organizational Engineering (Sousa, Caetano, Vasconcelos, Pereira, & Tribolet, 2006). This framework extends the two essential concepts to three: (1) entities, (2) activities, and (3) roles. Entities are the relevant things that compose an organization. Entities have a distinct, separate existence (concrete or abstract) and are identified with *nouns*. An entity can be a person, machine, place, concept, or event. There is no presumption that an entity is animate. An animate entity is able to exhibit active behavior.

Activities describe what organizations do and are identified with *verbs*. Activities are an abstraction representing how a number of entities collaborate through roles to produce a specific outcome. Since the same entity may play several roles and the same role may be played by several entities, the inclusion of the concept of role fosters reuse and enables more efficient representations.

Roles represent the observable behavior or an entity in the scope of a specific collaboration context. Roles aim at separating the different concerns that arise from collaborations between the entities fulfilling an activity. Roles are organized in role models that how roles relate to each other. Roles join together verbs and nouns and form organizational predicates.

Based on these three fundamental concepts, the CEO framework defines a set of role types (resource, actor, observable state, organizational units, business vision, mission, goal, and strategy) and proposes five architectural perspectives: (1) organizational, (2) business, (3) information, (4) application, and (5) technology, each one comprising a different subset of role types.

Enterprise Ontologies

Enterprise ontologies have also provided formal or semiformal models of organizations, along with richer agent models. Two well known *enterprise ontologies* are the enterprise ontology (EO) proposed by Uschold (1996) and the organization ontology of the TOVE project (Fox, Barbuceanu, Gruninger, & Lin, 1998). EO proposes a set of activity, organization, strategy, marketing, and time-related concepts. The TOVE ontology is composed of an activity/time terminology and an organizational terminology. The concepts of *activity, resource, goal, agent, role, group or teams, divisions,* or *organizational units* are common to these ontologies.

The paradigm shift in multi-agent systems (MAS) design from agent-centered to organization-centered approaches has motivated the creation of ontologies comprising several social and organizational concepts, which include single-agent, two-agent, group, and organizational level concepts (Ferber, Gutknecht, & Fabien, 2003). The concepts of *agent, role, interaction pattern, communication, group and group structure, organization, organization structure,* and *organizational rule* can be found in several ontologies proposed in agent oriented software engineering (AOSE) such as MaSE, Gaia, ALAADIN, among others (Bernon, Cossentino, Gleizes, Turci, & Zambonelli, 2004; Mao & Yu, 2004).

Most of the previous approaches assume that systems to be developed are closed and static. Other methodologies are dealing with extensions to support the modeling of open and dynamic systems. At a single-agent level, Odell (2003) addresses the formalization of temporal aspects of role assignment. The Opera framework for multi-agent systems (Dignum, 2003) defines four structures (communicative, social, interaction, and normative) and two models (social and interaction). Whereas structures describe generic organizational characteristics, models describe organization's particular characteristics given specific agent populations. The separation of structures from models allows representing agent interactions in a way that (1) is independent from the agent internal architectures, (2) distinguishes organizational characteristics from agent goals, (3) creates links between organizational structures and agent populations, and (4) allows the adaptation of interaction patterns to the characteristics of specific populations.

Limitations of Current Enterprise Representations in Supporting OSA

Most existing enterprise representations are created as a means for systems design and implementation. Their purpose is to facilitate the elaboration of systems specifications. Consequently, these ontologies are designed to answer questions related to how activities are performed, who performs these activities, and which resources are required. Supporting OSA means to enhance a shared understanding of the organization's structure and dynamics. Rather than supporting systems engineering in the organization, we point at facilitating a "reverse engineering" of the organization.

An effective support to OSA does require generic models of its activities, resources, and their interrelationships, but it is not enough. Frequently, organizations need to know how specific agents, not generic roles, accomplish their work. It is also necessary to have reasonable estimates of what organizational agents are doing at particular moments. Finally, it is important to provide means of evaluating how work practices evolve in time. More specifically, it is necessary to answer questions such as:

- Which roles play Agent X?
- How does Agent X perform activity Y? Which rules follows?
- Which Agents interact more frequently?
- How does Agent X interact with Agent Y? Which interaction rules govern Group G?
- At a particular time interval t:
  - o   What role plays Agent X? Which activity(ies) performs? Which resource(s) uses?

- o   With which agents interacts?
- o   Which event(s) trigger Agent X's role?
- o   Which rules govern how Agent X manages his different roles, activities, and resources?

Most enterprise representations do not allow capturing the particularities of individual agents and their interactions. Opera (Dignum, 2003) makes this possible through a separate modeling of structures and models. However, it focuses on modeling organizations and agent populations rather than individual agents. Moreover, it regards agent's internal architecture independent from organizational characteristics. We do not share this basic assumption. Our theoretical background points to the need of using a single, integrated approach to capture the architecture of individual and collective organizational agents.

Current representations are also not situated in time. Hence, time-related questions cannot be answered. Other requirements required for OSA not currently addressed are:

- Reality of organizations where agent interactions are subject to several unexpected events, changes, or contingencies.
- *Organizational agents* form several aggregates, which are typically described in terms of their components. The emergent properties of these aggregates are commonly disregarded.
- No means for capturing organizational change are provided. When changes take place, whole new representations must be depicted.

Agent Cognitive Architectures

Developing enterprise models and architectures capable of addressing the previous questions need not only to acknowledge organizational complexity. Agent themselves are complex entities that possess several cognitive capabilities.

These capabilities have been modeled and implemented in cognitive architectures. Cognitive modeling is the characteristic research methodology of cognitive science, resulting in theories that are formulated as computer programs (Strube, 2005). A cognitive model is a theoretically grounded and empirically guided specification of the mental representations and processes involved in a given cognitive function. Many cognitive models haven been developed in the past decade to investigate different aspects of cognition; attention and multitasking, judgment and choice in decision-making, and skill acquisition in dynamic situations (Gonzalez, 2002).

Cognitive models are blueprints of cognitive architectures. A cognitive architecture is a theoretical structure and set of mechanisms for human cognition, within which models for specific tasks and phenomena can be constructed (Kieras & Meyer, 1997). According to Sloman (2002), a typical cognitive architecture has the following components: (1) a perception box at the left, (2) a (motor) action box at the right, and (3) three internal layers connecting those two boxes. These internal layers are the reactive, deliberative, and reflective layers.

Reactive mechanisms are highly parallel and respond automatically to triggering conditions. This layer operates in very short intervals. The particular configuration of the reactive layer might be set by outputs from the deliberative and reflective layers, so that the reflexive (as distinct from reflective) behavior of the overall system may well depend on both context and past experience. Deliberative mechanisms can do "what if" reasoning, considering possible futures. This layer corresponds to planning, scheduling, and decision-making. This layer, which operates on longer intervals, decides what actions to take based on predictions of what effects they will have on the world. Reflective mechanisms monitor, evaluate, and, to some extent, redirect processes in the other layers. This layer is able to monitor the overall performance of the complete system and reconfigure the deliberative and reactive layers, so that performance improves. This layer does not need to operate in real-time in any sense.

THE PROPOSED FRAMEWORK

On the basis of the background summarized in the previous sections, we propose a three-layered architecture, each one comprising a different set of concepts.

Fundamental Concepts of the Ontology

This framework is based on the same fundamental concepts of the CEO framework: activities, entities, and roles. In this framework we distinguish two kinds of entities: *resources* and *agents*.

- *Activities* describe what organizations do. Activities are identified with *verbs*.
  Examples: sell, hire, write.
- *Entities (Resources)* are the things relevant for the operation of the organization and are identified with *nouns*. In this framework, *entities* are synonym of organizational resources. *Resources* can be persons, machines, places, concepts, or capabilities. Resources may be physical or abstract, inanimate or animate, technical or social. Examples: book, employee, paper, programming skill.
- Joining together organizational verbs (activities) and nouns (resources) we form *organizational predicates*.
  Examples: sell book, hire employee, write paper. Organizational predicates provide a more complete specification of what the organization does.
- *Agents* are regarded as physical and animate resources with special capabilities that enable them to (1) perform, coordinate, and change activities, (2) provide, consume, manage, and change resources, and (3) monitor, coordinate, and change their own activity and the activity of other agents. The agent concept enables to make explicit and represent the physical and active part of organizations. Agents may be human (per-

sons, dyads groups, and whole organizations), automated, or semi-automated. Automated and semi-automated agents are machines or human-machine combinations exhibiting some essential features defined by Odell (2000). Agent are *autonomous, interactive, adaptive, proactive, rational, unpredictable* (capable of non-deterministic behavior), and *coordinative* (agent are capable of coordinating themselves, as well as other agents). Agents are identified with *nouns.* However, agents are not part of organizational predicates. Rather, they are the subject of these predicates.

Examples: Selling Department, Prof. Smith, Book Recommender Agent. Agents possess a set of capabilities, enabled by skills (know-how) or knowledge (know-what).

- Joining together agents (nouns), activities (verbs), and resources (nouns), we form organizational sentences, that is, we define what the organization does and who does it. Examples: Selling Department sells books, Professor Smith writes paper, Book Recommender Agent suggest books.

- The agent-resource duality. As aforementioned, agents are a special kind of resource.

Nonetheless, agency is a capability, a potential behavior not always exhibited. Entities such as *Prof. Smith, Planning Group,* or the *book recommender system*, may also behave as plain resources. In this case, they are not the subject of the sentence. Rather, they are part of the predicate. For example, in the sentence *Human Resource Dept.* hires *Prof. Smith,* the agent is the *Human Resource Dept* and *Prof. Smith*, a passive resource.

- *Roles* define the observable behavior of an entity in the scope of particular interaction contexts. Agents play several roles and interact with other agents through these roles. This definition shares the four key features defined in Massolo et al. (2004): (1) roles are properties, (2) roles are temporal (3) roles have a relational nature, and (4) roles are linked to particular contexts.

- *Contexts* define agent roles. Linking roles to contexts requires clarifying what context is. In this framework, the notion of context integrates computer sciences, cognitive, and social approaches to context (for more details how these three approaches are integrated, see Zacarias, Pinto, & Tribolet, 2006). Context here is regarded as network of interacting agents playing related

Figure 1. Fundamental concepts

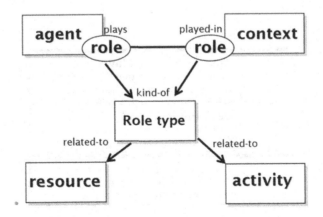

to specific activities and resources. It also reflects the state of participating agents and their interactions and the set of rules governing agent interactions. Figure 1 depicts the fundamental concepts of the framework and their inter-relationships. Agents play specific roles in specific contexts. Roles are related to some activity or resource.

Agent Role Set. Based on the fundamental concepts defined, we describe *organizational agents* in terms of a set of essential, resource, and activity-related roles (depicted in Figure 2). Agent essential roles define agent main generic capabilities (acting, self-coordinating, and learning). The essential roles of self-coordination and learning operate on the agent itself. Acting roles operate on activities or resources. Resource-related roles include resource producer or consumer, resource manager, and resource designer roles. Activity-related roles include activity performer, activity coordinator, and activity designer roles.

Agent Architecture. Drawing on Axelrod and Cohen's (2000) framework and the generic architecture of cognitive systems, we define an agent architecture

Figure 2. Agent basic role set

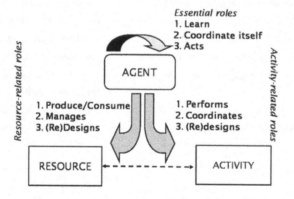

Figure 3. Agent architecture

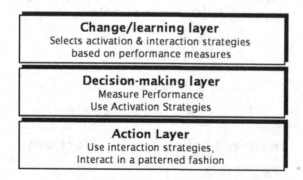

integrated by three interdependent layers: (1) action, (2) decision-making, and (3) change/learn. Figure 3 depicts these three layers.

1. **Action:** This layer addresses agent reactive, predefined behaviors. Drawing on Axelrod and Cohen (2000), agents in complex, adaptive systems interact in a recurrent, patterned fashion. Agents possess a collection of strategies. In this framework, strategies are analogous to patterns. In this layer, we seek to capture agent interaction strategies.

2. **Decision-making:** This layer addresses agent performance measuring and deliberation processes controlling its interactions. In this layer, we aim at providing a dynamic, state-based representation of agents and capturing the events provoking state changes. Axelrod and Cohen's (2000) framework define activation as the processes affecting agent timing and activity sequencing. Thus, we define these processes as activation strategies. Activation strategies are rules defining when to use specific interaction strategies. In this layer, we aim at capturing agent activation strategies.

3. **Change/learning:** This layer addresses agent reflective behavior, that is, it aims at capturing how activation and interaction strategies change

in time, based on performance measures of these strategies. Whereas changes take place when new strategies arise, learning only occurs when new or redesigned strategies improve the performance of the previous strategies.

The three layers are inter-related (see Figure 4). Agents decide what to do according to activation strategies given by its deliberation capabilities. They also interact according to interaction strategies defined by his reflective and learning capabilities. Agents change their strategies upon interactions not handled by his reactive or deliberative mechanisms, based on performance measures attributed to their strategies. Performance measures are mostly subjective and tacit. However, they may be inferred through the proliferation, reduction, or elimination of strategies.

Basic Architecture and Ontology

In this framework, organizations are modeled as a network of interactions between autonomous resource and activity-related agents. Figure 5 depicts the model basic architecture and related concepts. Both resource and activity-related agents and their interactions are modeled on the basis of the agent three-layered architecture depicted in Figure 3.

Layers and Agent Roles. Resource-related agents provide and/or consume resources at the action layer, manage resources (including themselves) at the decision-making layer, and design (or redesign resources, including themselves) at the change/learn layer. Analogously, activity-related agents perform activities at the action layer, coordinate activities at the decision-making layer, and design (or redesign activities) at the change layer.

1. The action layer captures the interaction strategies (patterns) between activity performers and resource provider or consumer agents. Interaction strategies vary according to specific contexts. Interaction strategies recurrent sequences or flows of valid interaction and resource types.

Figure 4. Relation between the layers

2. The decision-making layer captures the activation strategies (rules) used by agents as resource managers or activity coordinators. Rules are triggered by events. Rules invoke particular a context, along with its associated action-layer role (resource provider/consumer, activity performer) and strategies. When several rules are triggered simultaneously, the agent selects one according to higher-order rules.

3. The change/learn layer addresses interactions between activity and resource designer agents. This layer aims at capturing (re)design of interaction and activation strategies of resource managers, producer, and consumers, as well as activity coordinators and performers. This layer comprises mostly emergent behavior. Thus, we do not address the modeling of this layer. Rather, we will focus on detecting changes of the previous layers.

Mediating Artifacts. Artifacts have typically been defined as objects made, used, or modified by people. We define artifacts as resources made, modified, or used by agents. Hence, mediating artifacts are resources that support and constrain agent interactions.

Contexts. Agent interactions are supported and constrained by a particular set of contexts. We define (interaction) contexts as the network of mediating artifacts used in agent interactions. The kind of mediating artifact used varies according the layer.

1. At the action layer, the mediating artifacts are (a) the expected interaction types and (b) resource types exchanged. Each interaction types is related to a specific set of resources.

2. The mediating artifacts in this layer are commitments between activity and resource-related agents. Commitments are related to the notions of pledge, promise, agreement, or contract. According to speech act theory (Searle, 1978), interactions produce, modify, reschedule, or cancel commitments. Commitments reflect the state of interactions. Each specific interaction type is related to a set of possible commitments.

3. At the change/learn layer, resource and activity (re)design is on one side, both constrained and supported by current interaction rules of

Figure 5. Model basic architecture and ontology of each layer

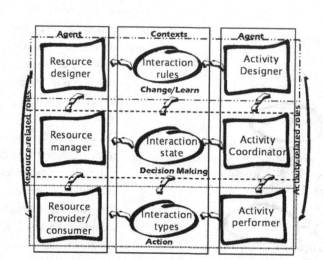

the corresponding activities and resources. On the other side, activity and resource (re)design may trigger changes on corresponding activity-resource interaction rules. According to Giddens (1984), these rules govern interaction patterns and most of them are unobservable and tacit. However, some of them can be inferred from observable interaction patterns and expressed through informal or formal languages.

Architectural Layers and OSA. Figure 6 depicts the concepts used at the action and decision-making layers and the relation between them. Complexity of agent behavior is captured in separate layers, each using different concepts and roles. Identifying all the roles agent play at each layer contributes to OSA in answering the questions related to the identity of *organizational agents*. In the action layer, agents are regarded as actors employing a set predefined interaction pattern. Interaction patterns are flows of interactions types that use or produce specific kinds of resources. In terms of OSA, the action layer representations describe how the organizations and its agents do things. The decision-making layer captures agent deliberation processes such as planning or scheduling. Events (actual interactions) update agent commitments, which

trigger agent activation rules. This may cause agents to decide the activation in a different context. An explicit modeling of this layer allows answering time-related questions of organizational agents.

Applying the Basic Architecture at Several Levels of Detail

In the present framework, we regard organizations as complex, adaptive, socio-technical systems created and maintained by the interactions among their agents. According to systems theory, systems are organized in hierarchies where systems may be agents of larger systems. Thus, organizations are also agents of broader organizational systems that can be modeled using the proposed agent architecture. Figure 7 depicts this idea. Figure 7 also illustrates the fact that agent and system interactions are always mediated by contexts.

The basic concepts and inter-relationships depicted in Figure 5 can be recursively applied for several organizational levels of detail (see Figure 8). On one side, human agents are typically studied at an individual, inter-personal, group, and organizational levels. On the other side, business processes are commonly analyzed and designed at process, activity, and task levels. Whereas processes are typically related to orga-

Figure 6. Ontology details for the first two layers

Figure 7. Agent and systems (organizations)

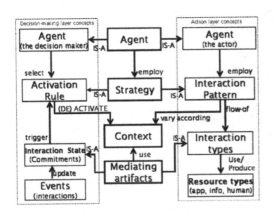

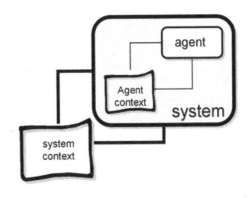

nizations or organizational units, activities are related to groups and tasks are more related to individual or interpersonal levels.

Although the same basic ontology is present in all levels, each level uses a different universe of discourse, that is, a different set of nouns, verbs, attributes, state variables, and rules. Verbs and nouns used in defining processes, resources, and their corresponding contexts (e.g., sell *vehicles*) are different for those defining activities (e.g., develop sells application), tasks (e.g., elaborate *sales report*) or actions (e.g., update *sales document*). At the action level, a distinction is made between communicative and noncommunicative actions. Communicative actions (also named as interactions) are sentences with an indirect object (ask *John a question*), which represent an agent (individuals) working as resources for the agent performing the interaction.

The kind of agent (subject of predicates) also depends on the level of detail addressed; at the individual and interpersonal layers subjects are persons (e.g.,

Prof. Smith), at the group layer subjects are formal or informal teams such as sections in departments or task forces (e.g., *Application Maintenance Team*). At the organizational level, subjects may be organizational units or whole organizations (e.g., *Marketing Unit*). Though corresponding nouns and verbs of different levels are interrelated, tracing these relationships throughout all levels of detail is not straightforward.

Interactions at all levels are mediated by contexts. However, the nature of the mediating artifacts composing each context varies according the layer. For instance, commitments within personal action contexts commitments refer to to-do lists. In interpersonal contexts, they mean interpersonal commitments. In group-level contexts, they mean formal or informal agreements. Finally, in organization-level contexts, commitments refer to interorganizational contracts. Interaction types, rules, and state variables of different granularity can be also found in all organizational levels.

Figure 8. Basic architecture and concepts at different levels of detail

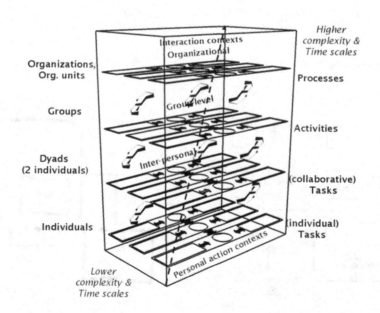

Complexity increases with higher organizational levels of detail (Magalhães, 2004). Moreover, the separation of time scales is characteristic of complex systems (Axelrod & Cohen, 2000). Hence, there is an increase of complexity and a separation of time scales along two axes. For the same agent, complexity and time scale increase from the action to the learn/change layer. The other axis is related to the level of detail of the organization. Processes are more complex and operate at higher time scales than activities and tasks. Also, finer-grained resources (e.g., individual competencies) are less complex and they change more frequently than coarse-grained resources (e.g., organization's competencies).

EXAMPLE APPLICATIONS

In this section we discuss two example applications of the framework. These examples illustrate how the framework can be used at the individual and interpersonal levels. Uses of the applications at higher levels will be explored in future work.

Modeling Human Multitasking at Work

Modeling and supporting multitasking behavior at work has been acknowledged as an important issue in the design of task and project management tools and there are several works addressing this issue (Czerswinski, Horvitz, & Wilhite, 2004; Wild, Johnson, & Johnson, 2004). Organizational activities have been modeled with a variety of concepts such as tasks, interactions, roles, actors, goals, and resources. Whereas these concepts enable modeling behavior inside activities, they do not capture activity or task-switching patterns. Modeling multitasking means capturing the scheduling heuristics we use in switching among independent, unrelated tasks. It does not address how things are done, but when they are done.

Thus, in terms of our framework, it requires modeling the decision-making layer of agents. This means capturing events and commitments as well as agent activation rules. Particularly, it means how to discover the activation rules used by agents in managing themselves. In other words, when modeling multitasking, we model agents as resource managers, where the resource managed is the agent itself. We proposed an ontology and an approach to capture and model multitasking behavior based on these concepts in Zacarias et al. (2006). The benefits of this ontology are illustrated with a case study where a software development team was observed during three weeks. Here we show how the framework concepts were used in this particular application.

Multitasking behavior was discovered from action and interaction logs (events). At the action layer, personal action contexts (bottom of Figure 8) define log groupings of similar types of actions, interactions, and resources of a single task performer.

Figure 9 illustrates a personal action context (data collection for mail application) of Alexandre, an individual from our case study. This context example is composed of:

- **Task performer:** Alexandre.
- **Resource providers:** Mariana, Cards Application Responsible, Cards Data Owner, Mail Application User.
- **Actions/interactions:** ask, answer, request, analyze, send. These interactions use the following resources:
  o   Information items: example mail records, mail template, mail application documentation, cards application responsible name, cards availability, cards data
  o   Applications: Microsoft Word, Excel®
  o   Skills/Knowledge: analysis skills, office application skills, cards application knowledge, programming skills, mail application requirements knowledge, mediation skills. Analysis and office application skills belong to Alexandre. Remaining skills belong to the resource providers

Figure 9. Personal action contexts: an example

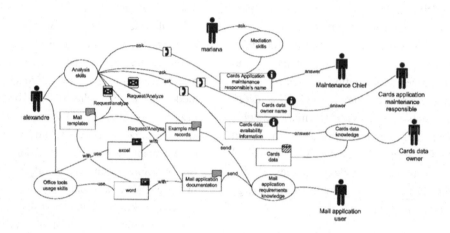

Table 1. Some personal action contexts (case study examples)

Person Name	Context ID	Context Name
Alexandre	*a1*	Data Collection for Mail Application
	a3	Evictions Web Service Problem
	a5	Carla's Support (Web Serv & Mail App)
Carla	*c1*	Common Services Application Programmin
	c2	Programming support (Mail & Suppliers Ap
	c3	Team Meetings
Mariana	*m1*	Project Management Reports and Meetings
	m011	Cards Information Collection
	m6	Evictions Web Service Problem
	m8	Suppliers Application Programming

At the decision-making layer, each action or interaction is regarded as an event related to specific commitments. Grouping events around their corresponding contexts allows detecting context switches. Table 1 shows some personal action contexts of three subjects: Alexandre, Carla and Mariana (the team leader). Context switches were registered, along with the event triggering each switch. In terms of our framework, personal scheduling heuristics are context activation rules. These heuristics were discovered from recurrent context switches.

Figure 10. Context switches of Mariana

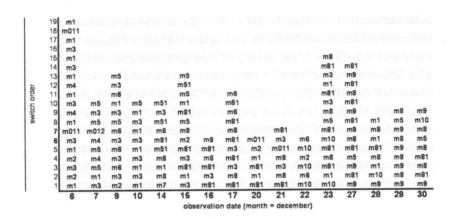

Table 2. Some personal scheduling (activation) rules of Mariana

Rule	Trigger (event)	Trigger (commitment)		Activate Context
1	meeting accepted	ellaborate project list	m1	project reports and meetings
2	Dept. Head's request	ellaborate project status report	m1	project reports and meetings
		provide information of the		
3	Alexandre's request	cards application	m011	cards information collection
4	CG team informs test failure	resume tests	m3	Integration tests
5	Catarina's request	perform message maintenance	m9	message maintenance

Mariana (the team leader) handled a total of 14 contexts along the observation period. Figure 10 depicts the context switching behavior of Mariana along the observation period among these contexts. Table 2 shows the personal heuristics discovered from this behavior.

Adding a Human Perspective to EA

Human resources in EA are commonly represented through hierarchies of organizational units, which are linked to activities or processes. Current EA do not show the relationship between particular individuals or groups and organizational activities and resources. Adding a human perspective to EA entails determining how each organizational member is related to activities and resources. In other words, it requires identifying both activity and resource-related roles of all members of the organization. The dynamics of current work environments constantly changes how individuals and groups relate to organizational activities and other resources. Hence, it is necessary to depict time-based relations of individuals vs. activities and resources. Including time as an explicit variable allows us to see how the work of individuals and groups evolve in time.

The proposed framework facilitates these representations in several ways. First, events register agent actions/interactions in time, belonging to different contexts. Activities and resources are identified analyzing interaction types and patterns found in agent contexts. Separating agent activity and resource-related roles facilitates tracing agent relations with activities and resources. In this application, concepts from both the action and decision-making layers are used.

Figures 11-12 illustrate these ideas using data collected in the first application. Figure 11 depicts time-based representations of Mariana's interaction

Figure 11. Mariana's tasks along the observation period

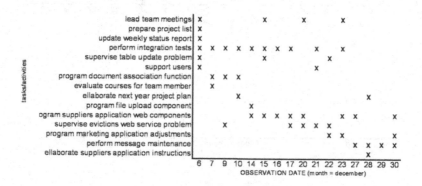

Figure 12. Resources provided (P) or consumed (C) by Mariana

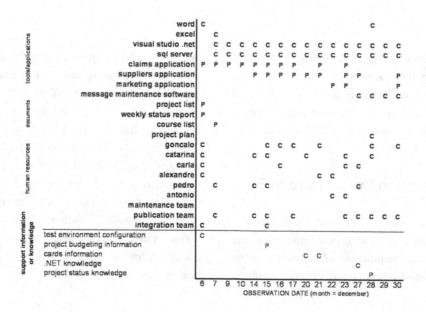

with tasks or activities along several days. Figure 12 depicts Mariana's interactions with several kinds of resources along the same period. Left-aligned, bold resource names represent resources used or produced by Mariana within their core tasks (tasks in Figure 11). Right-aligned names represent resources used and produced in contexts different from the execution of core tasks. Since these resources are shared when people play supporting and frequently informal roles, the interaction with these resources is not captured when we model tasks or activities.

CONCLUSION

Organizational self-awareness is a prerequisite for effective action, decision-making, and learning in organizations. Due to the dynamics of current environments, the development of this capacity entails a continuous communication effort among organizational agents. Enterprise models have proved to be effective communication tools; however, it is necessary to explore appropriate representations for the purpose of enhancing organizational self-awareness.

This work lays out the foundations of a comprehensive high-level modeling framework for an integrated modeling of resource and activity perspectives of individuals and groups within their organizations. The modeling framework provides an "architected" ontology, which puts together human and social approaches to organizations with modeling approaches coming from the computer sciences field.

FUTURE WORK

The present work represents a first step in this effort. Many more issues remain to be addressed. The framework itself requires further development. More formal and detailed representations must be explored. These representations will vary according the requirements and complexity of each layer and level of detail. Since the action layer captures agent deterministic aspects, several ontology languages are able to model this layer.

At the decision-making layer, we seek a dynamic, state-based view of organizational agents and their interactions. In this layer, we will model agents as non-deterministic state machines. The change/layer is the most complex layer since it must address mostly emergent behavior. Hence, we do not address the modeling of this layer. Rather, we will focus in detecting changes in the other two layers.

The example applications described in this chapter illustrate applications of the finer-grained concepts of the framework. However, additional case studies addressing varying layers and levels of detail should be conducted to test the full benefits of this framework. This will require using methodologies from both computer and organizational sciences.

Another issue to be addressed is related the third implication of our proposal: exploring and testing ways of using IS/IT in acquiring and updating enterprise representations. Creating representations for the finer-grained levels entails analyzing high volumes of fast-changing, frequently unstructured data. We are currently researching semi-automatic mechanisms for capturing, structuring, and analyzing action and interaction logs, as well as personal and interpersonal contexts.

REFERENCES

Aldrich, H.E., & Ruef, M. (2006). *Organizations evolving*. London: Sage.

Axelrod, R., & Cohen, M. (2000). *Harnessing complexity: Organizational implications of a scientific frontier*. New York: Basic Books.

Bernon, C., Cossentino, M., Gleizes, M.P., Turci, P., & Zambonelli, F. (2004). A study of some multi-agent meta-models. In J. Odell, P. Giorgini, & J. Muller (Eds.), *Springer LCNS 3382, Agent-Oriented Software Engineering (AOSE), 5th International Workshop* (pp. 62-77). Berlin, Germany: Springer-Verlag.

Czerwinski, M., Horvitz, E., & Wilhite, S. (2004). A diary study of task switching and interruptions. In E.

Dysktra-Erickson & M. Tscheligi (Eds.), *Proceedings of the SIGCHI Conference on Human Factors in Computing Systems* (pp. 175-182). New York: ACM Press.

Dignum, V. (2004). *A model for organizational interaction: Based on agents, founded in logic.* Doctoral dissertation, SIKS Dissertation Series No. 2004-1, Utrecht University, Netherlands.

Engeström, Y., Miettinen, R., & Punamäki, R.L. (Eds.). (2005). *Perspectives on activity theory.* New York: Cambridge University Press.

Ferber, J., Gutknecht, O., & Fabien, M. (2003). From agents to organizations: An organizational view of multi-agent systems. In J. Odell, P. Giorgini, & J. Muller (Eds.), *Springer LCNS 2935, Agent-Oriented Software Engineering (AOSE) 4th International Workshop* (pp. 214-230). Germany: Springer-Verlag.

Fox, M.S., Barbuceanu, M., Gruninger, M., & Lin, J. (1998). An organization ontology for enterprise modeling. In M. Prietula, K. Carley, & L. Gasser (Eds.), *Simulating organizations: Computational models of institutions and groups* (pp. 131-152). Menlo Park, CA: AAAI/MIT Press.

Giddens, A. (1984). *The constitution of society: Outline of the theory of structuration.* Cambridge, UK: Polity Press.

Gonzalez, C. (2002). The role of cognitive modeling in enhancing dynamic decisions. In B. Bel & I. Marlien (Eds.), *Twenty-fourth annual meeting of the cognitive science society* (pp. 187-198). Fairfax, VA: Laurence Erlbaum Association.

Kieras, D., & Meyer, D. (1997). An overview of the epic architecture for cognition and performance with application to human-computer interaction. *Human-Computer Interaction, 12*, 391-438.

Lamb, R., & Kling, R. (2003). Reconceptualizing users as social actors in information systems research. *MIS Quarterly, 27*(2), 197-235.

Leont'ev, A. (1974). The problem of activity in psychology. *Soviet Psychology, 13*(2), 4-33.

Leont'ev, A. (1977). Activity and consciousness. In *Philosophy in the USSR, Problems of dialectical materialism.* Moscow: Progress Publishers. Retrieved from http://www.marxists.org/archive/leontev/works/1977/leon1977.htm

Magalhães, R. (2004). *Organizational knowledge and technology.* Cheltenham, UK: Edgar Elgar.

Magalhães, R., & Tribolet, J. (in press). Engenharia Organizacional: das partes ao todo e do todo às partes na dialéctica entre pessoas e sistemas. In Costa S., Vieria L & Rodriges J., *Ventos de Mudança.* Brazil: Fundo de Cultura.

Mao, X., & Yu, E. (2004) Organizational and social concepts in agent oriented software engineering. In J. Odell, P. Giorgini, & J. Muller (Eds.), *Springer LCNS 3382. Agent-Oriented Software Engineering (AOSE) 5th International Workshop* (pp. 1-15). Berlin: Springer-Verlag.

March, J.G. (1999). *The pursuit of organizational intelligence.* Malden, MA: Blackwell Publishers.

Massolo, C., Vieu, L., Bottazzi, E., Catenacci, C., Ferrario, R., Gangemi, A., et al. (2004, June). Social roles and their descriptions. In D. Dubois, C. Welty, & M. Williams (Eds), *Principles of Knowledge Representation and Reasoning: Proceedings of the Ninth International Conference KR2004* (pp. 267-277). Menlo Park, CA: AAAI Press.

Maturana, H.R., & Varela, F.J. (1980). *Autopoiesis and cognition: The realization of the living.* Dordrecht, Holland: D. Reidel Publishing.

Nardi, B.A. (1998). Concepts of cognition and consciousness: Four voices. *Journal of Computer Documentation, 22*(1), 31-48

Odell, J. (2000). Agents: Technology and usage (Part 1) (Executive Report, Vol. 3, No. 4). Retrieved June 11, 2007, from http://www.jamesodell.com/publications.html

Odell, J., Van Dyke, Parunak H., Brueckner, S., & Sauter, J.A. (2003). Temporal aspects of dynamic role assignment. In J. Odell, P. Giorgini, & J. Muller (Eds.), *Springer LCNS 2935. Agent-Oriented Software Engineering (AOSE) 4th International Workshop* (pp. 201-213). Berlin: Springer-Verlag.

Schekkerman, J. (2004). *How to survive in the jungle of enterprise architecture frameworks.* Victoria, Canada: Trafford.

Searle, J. (1978). Austin on locutionary and illocutionary acts. *The Philosophical Review, 77,* 405-442.

Sloman, A. (2002). Architecture-based conceptions of mind. In P. Gardenfors, K. Kijania-Placek, & J. Wolenski (Eds.), *Scope of logic, methodology, and philosophy of science* (Vol II), Synthese Library Vol. 316 (pp. 403-427). Dordrecht: Kluwer Publishers.

Sousa, P., Caetano, A., Vasconcelos, A., Pereira, C., & Tribolet, J. (2006). Enterprise architecture modeling with the unified modeling language 2.0. In P. Ritten (Ed.), *Enterprise modeling and computing with UML* (pp. 69-92). Hershey, PA: IRM Press.

Strube, G. (2005). Cognitive modeling: Research logic in cognitive science. Retrieved June 11, 2007, from http://cognition.iig.uni-freiburg.de/team/members/strube/iesbsmod.pdf

Tsoukas, H. (2005). *Complex knowledge.* Oxford: Oxford University Press.

Uschold, M. (1996, December). *Building ontologies: Towards a unified methodology.* Paper presented at the16th Annual Conference of the British Computer Society Specialist Group on Expert Systems, Cambridge, UK.

Weick, K.E. (1995). *Sensemaking in organizations.* Beverly Hills, CA: Sage.

Weick, K.E. (2001). *Making sense of the organization.* Malden, MA: Blackwell Publishing.

Wild, P.J., Johnson, P., & Johnson, H. (2004). Towards a composite modeling approach for multitasking. In S. Pavel & P. Palanque (Eds.), *Proceedings of the 3rd International Workshop on Task Models and Diagrams for User Interface Design TAMODIA '04* (pp. 17-24). New York: ACM

Zacarias, M., Pinto, H.S., & Tribolet, J. (2006). *Discovering multitasking behavior at work: A context-based ontology.* In K. Coninx, K. Luyten, & K. Schneider (Eds.), *Springer LCNS 4385, Task Models and Diagrams for User Interface Design* (pp. 292-307). Berlin: Springer-Verlag.

Chapter VIII
An Agent–Oriented Enterprise Model for Early Requirements Engineering

Ivan J. Jureta
University of Namur, Belgium

Stéphane Faulkner
University of Namur, Belgium

Manuel Kolp
Université Catholique de Louvain, Belgium

ABSTRACT

This chapter introduces an agent-oriented enterprise model for conducting enterprise modeling during the early stages of information system requirements engineering. The enterprise model integrates a set of concepts and relationships that the analyst instantiates when building a model of the part of the organization in which the future information system will operate. The aim is to allow the analyst to produce an enterprise model which captures knowledge about an organization and its business processes, and which can be used to build an agent-oriented requirements specification of the future system and of its organizational environment. Compared to similar models, the present one integrates concepts and relationships allowing the analyst to capture the relevant intrinsic characteristics, such as autonomy and intentionality of human and software agents that are to participate in the future system.

INTRODUCTION

Business analysts and IT managers increasingly recognize that the ability to correctly and often extensively specify and analyze early requirements about an information system (IS) is critical for gaining organizational acceptance of the future system and achieving a close match between the expected and observed quality thereof. Within the requirements engineering (RE) effort which initiates and subsequently guides the development and deployment of any IS within an organization, *early* RE is its first step, focusing on the representation and analysis of the organizational environment before the future system is introduced, dealing with the definition of desired behaviors and qualities of the future system that would fit this environment, and finally anticipating the effects that its introduction is likely to have on the performance of the organization. In order to analyze such organizational environments, it is necessary to understand the objectives, organizational processes, roles, and interdependencies of different stakeholders. Although errors and misunderstandings at this level are frequent and costly, early RE is usually done informally.

In this chapter, we propose to address this issue by suggesting a precisely and formally defined enterprise model to facilitate the modeling and analysis of early requirements for IS. This enterprise model allows the representation of the structures, organizational processes, resources, actors, work roles, behaviors, goals, and constraints of the organizational setting in which the future IS will function. It can be both descriptive and definitional, that is, spanning what is and what should be. One of its key characteristics is its support for the agent software engineering paradigm which allows developers to handle the life cycle of complex, distributed, and open systems required to offer open and dynamic capabilities in the latest generation of enterprise IS (see, e.g., Castro, Kolp, & Mylopoulos, 2002). By instantiating the concepts and relationships provided in the enterprise model, the analyst can:

- Analyze the current organizational structure and business processes in order to reveal problems and opportunities
- Evaluate and compare alternative organizational processes and structures
- Achieve common understanding and agreement between stakeholders (e.g., managers, owners, workers, etc.) about different aspects of the organization

- Build a database along the structure of the enterprise model for use in collecting, managing, and reusing the knowledge available in the organization

The proposed enterprise model draws on research in RE frameworks (e.g., Dardenne, van Lamsweerde, & Ficklas, 1993; Yu, 1994), management theory found to be relevant for enterprise modeling (e.g., Brickley, Smith, & Zimmerman, 2001; Johnson & Scholes, 2002; Simon, 1976; Uschold, King, Moralee, & Zorgios, 1997), and agent-oriented software engineering (e.g., Castro et al., 2002). It aims to reduce the semantic gap between enterprise and requirements representations, providing a conceptual foundation for modeling organizational IS. Through agent-orientation, our proposal advances current research results towards an integrative approach to the representation of human and organizational issues found relevant to the RE of organizational IS, all in the aim of arriving at a better understanding of the setting in which the IS will be used.

The following section motivates the use of the agent paradigm to model and design IS. The following sections gives an overview of related works, introduce the enterprise model, define and discuss all elements of the enterprise model, and, to increase precision, specify using the Z specification language. The final section summarizes the results and points to further work.

AGENT-ORIENTATION IN ENTERPRISE MODELS FOR MODERN ORGANIZATIONAL IS

The characteristics and expectations of new application areas for the enterprise such as electronic and mobile commerce, supply-chain management, peer-to-peer computing, or Web services are deeply affecting IS engineering. Most of the IS designed for these application areas are now concurrent and distributed. They tend to be open and adaptable in that they exist in a changing organizational and operational environment where new components can be added, modified, or removed at any time.

Given these new needs, many researchers (e.g., Castro et al., 2002; Yu, 1994; Zambonelli, Jennings, & Wooldridge, 2003) have suggested and discussed novel paradigms that would enable more appropriate conceptualization, design, and implementation systems that can operate efficiently and effectively in such circumstances. The paradigm of agent orientation is being increasingly applied when the aim is to design complex yet flexible organizational IS that adapt to the changing operating conditions of modern organizations. Such systems are composed of *agents*, that is, open, modular, interoperable, and self-contained components, commonly characterized as intelligent, in that they may be autonomous, proactive, and exhibit some degree of learning and adaptation to operating environment conditions.

Agent orientation does not represent a radical departure from current software and IS engineering thinking; instead, legacy system can be incorporated in agent systems under limited cost. The cited benefits of agent orientation, along with the broad range of potential applications, lead to the conclusion that agent orientation does have the capacity to succeed as mainstream software and IS engineering paradigm.

It appears relevant to enrich concepts and relationships employed in enterprise modeling with those appropriate for representing information proper to an agent-oriented perspective. Following the established results in agent-oriented software engineering (e.g., Jennings, 2000; Yu, 1994, 2001; Zambonelli et al., 2003) modeling constructs are introduced to enable the representation of autonomy, intentionality, sociality, identity, and boundary, of human and/or software agents. In the paragraph below, the terms in italics refer to concepts or relationships in the agent-oriented enterprise model proposed in the remainder of the chapter.

Actors are autonomous as their behavior is not prescribed and varies according to their *dependencies, personal goals,* and *capabilities.* They are intentional since they base their *actions* and *plans* on *beliefs* about the environment, as well as on *goals* they have to achieve. Being autonomous, actors can exhibit cooperative behavior, resulting from similar *goals* and/or reciprocal *dependencies* concerning *organizational roles* they assume. The *dependencies* can either be direct or mediated by other *organizational roles. Actors* can have competing goals which lead to conflicts that may result from competing use of resources. *Actors* have varying power and interest in the ways in which *organizational goals* contribute to their *personal goals.* Boundary and identity are closely related to power and interest of actors. We model variations in boundary and identity as resulting from changes in power and interest since these vary with respect to the modifications in the roles an actor assumes and the dependencies involving these roles. *Actors* can act according to their self-interest, as they have *personal goals* to achieve. They have varying degrees of motivation to assume *organizational roles,* according to the degree of *contribution* to *personal goals* these roles have in achieving *organizational goals. Actors* apply *plans* according to the rationale described in terms of *personal goals, organizational goals,* and *capabilities.* The rationale of our *actors* is not perfect, but bounded (Simon, 1976, 1979), as they can act based on *beliefs* that are incomplete and/or inconsistent with reality.

RELATED WORK

The discussion is organized around five types of frameworks for enterprise modeling relevant to the results presented in this chapter. There is no clear distinction of enterprise modeling from requirements elicitation since their objective is similar: to improve the organization through the representation of knowledge about its main constituents, processes, purpose, and so forth. In addition, most frameworks that are clearly intended for RE involve the modeling of the organizational context in which the future IS will be implemented. The relevant modeling frameworks are distinguished on the basis of their main modeling concepts and their overall purpose. Methodological issues related to how the modeling elements are instantiated are not considered herein.

Activity-Oriented Models

The various business process modeling techniques fall into activity-oriented modeling (for an overview, see, e.g., Kettinger, Teng, & Guha, 1997).

Activity-based frameworks such Activity Diagrams, DFDs, and IDEF0 (see, e.g., Elmagarmid & Du, 1998; Kamath, Dalal, Chaugule, Sivaraman, & Kolarik, 2003; Mentzas, Halaris, & Kavadias, 2001; Sheth, van der Aalst, & Arpinar, 1999) describe enterprise's business processes as sets of activities. Strong emphasis is put on the activities that take place, the order of activity invocation, invocation conditions, activity synchronization, and information flows. Workflows have received considerable attention in the literature (for an extensive overview, see zur Muehlen, 2002).

In the generic business process modeling (BPM) approach employed in (Kettinger et al., 1997) to evaluate a range of available BPM techniques, BPM proceeds through stages, starting, broadly, from the identification of a business process to change, process redesign, towards change management to move in reality to the new process structure, and the monitoring and evaluation of the performance of the new process. The variety of techniques that can be applied (e.g., brainstorming, visioning, force field analysis, Delphi technique, business systems planning, critical success factors, and so forth—more than 50 techniques are cited in Kettinger) and their usually informal presentation makes it particularly difficult to elaborate on the comparison with the enterprise model introduced herein. It can, nevertheless, be argued that the enterprise model here has a double interest for the researchers and the practitioners of BPM. First, it indicates that establishing sound conceptual bases is necessary for ensuring that the methodology that can later be constructed is grounded in well-understood foundations. Basing a methodology on informal grounds can only entail difficulties in its use for lack of clarity and precision

is bound to increase the cost of applying it within realistic settings: different people will understand and use it differently, making cooperation difficult. Second, this chapter in itself indicates how the definition of conceptual foundations can be performed.

In activity-oriented models, agents have been treated mostly as a computational paradigm, with focus on the design and implementation of agent systems. Compared to our enterprise model, they do not incorporate social metaphors for agent systems and there is a limited treatment of inconsistencies.

Ontology-Driven Approaches to Enterprise Modeling

Ontological modeling is concerned with capturing the relevant entities of a domain in an ontology using an ontology-specification language based on a small set of basic, domain-independent ontological categories (Guizzardi, Herre, & Wagner, 2002). The ontology is used to share common understanding of the structure of information among people or software agents, to enable reuse of domain knowledge, to analyze domain knowledge, and so on.

The aim of the TOVE project (Fox & Grüninger, 1997) is the creation of enterprise ontology for creating deductive enterprise models. Such enterprise models build onto generic enterprise models by adding axioms expressed in first-order logic and a deduction engine, so that the model integrates some degree of deductive capability. Deductive enterprise models can be used for extracting information about the organization using "common-sense" queries that require limited deduction in order to support functions such as accounting, forecasting, and so forth.

The enterprise ontology (Uschold et al., 1997) defines the ontology used in the Enterprise Project (Stader, 1996; Uschold & Grüninger, 1996). The overall aim of the project is to improve and, where necessary, replace existing modeling methods with a framework for integrating methods and tools which are appropriate to enterprise modeling and the management of change. The project resulted in a toolset which is used to modeling processes, supporting agent development, matching agents with process tasks, and communicating among people and software.

The main difference of our framework from both Tove and the Enterprise Project is that they are not oriented towards RE. Tove intends to create a computable model of the organization by using axioms defined in first-order logic and a deduction engine. Our aim is closer to engineering software than creating computable enterprise models. Tove does not treat potential inconsistencies in processes, has limited support for process modeling (Koubarakis & Plexousakis, 2002), and does not treat the strategic dimension of agent interactions (i.e., it does not integrate dependency relationships). Inconsistencies are not treated in the Enterprise Ontology. In addition, our model provides more specific specialization of goals which is particularly useful in the context of open systems with self-interested agents. Even though the aim of our model is different to some extent, these frameworks have served as a source of inspiration for providing clear and unambiguous definitions of the terminology used in our enterprise model.

Goal-Driven Modeling

Goal-based modeling focuses on goals that the IS should achieve within an organization. The concept of goal has been argued easy to understand and can be used at different activities of the RE process (Kavakli, 1999).

The KAOS framework for RE (Dardenne et al., 1993) provides a specification language, an elaboration method, and meta-level knowledge used for guidance while the method is applied (van Lamsweerde, Darimont, & Letier, 1998). The KAOS specification language provides constructs for capturing the various types of concepts that appear during requirements elaboration. The elaboration method describes steps (i.e., goal elaboration, object capture, operation capture, etc.) that may be followed to systematically elaborate KAOS specifications. Finally, the meta-level knowledge provides domain-independent concepts that can be used for guidance and validation in the elaboration process.

Enterprise knowledge development (EKD), Kavakli and Loucopoulos (1999), is used primarily in modeling of business processes of an enterprise. Through goal-orientation, it advocates a closer alignment between intentional and operational aspects of the organization and links reengineering efforts to strategic business objectives. EKD describes a business enterprise as a network of related business processes which collaboratively realise business goals.

Other goal-based approaches have also been proposed. Kavakli (1999) provides an extensive discussion of a number of other approaches.

Actors appear in EKD without explicit treatment of their autonomy and sociality (Yu, 2001). In KAOS, actors (i.e., agents) interact with each other nonintentionally, which reduces the benefits of using them as modeling constructs. They are considered as specialization of objects. In our approach, actors are considered clearly as autonomous and social entities which exhibit intentional behavior. As noted in Koubarakis and Plexousakis (2002), an important limitation of EKD is the lack of formal support for its conceptual models meaning that formal specification of the IS cannot be derived without considerable additional effort. While KAOS relies on an elaborated formalism, it does not integrate social concepts for multi-agent systems, such as organizational role, group, organization, and so forth. Consequently, it does not benefit from the advantages of such concepts. Our framework integrates such social metaphors since they aid in dealing with system complexity. They are also easy to understand by developers and users and stakeholders, and help to reduce the concept distance between the systems in the "real world" and models that are developed on the basis of these concepts (Mao & Yu, 2004).

Strategy maps proposed in management literature (Kaplan & Norton, 2000, 2004) can also be categorized as goal-driven modeling: a strategy map is a diagram built to indicate how an organization creates value. Strategic objectives are related through cause and effect relationships with each other, and this within the four balanced scorecard perspectives (i.e., financial, customer, internal, and learning and growth perspective). Compared to the enterprise model proposed herein, a strategy map can be argued to feature only goals and cause and effect relationships as modeling primitives. As such, it is of very limited use in the RE of organizational IS. The enterprise model herein does not integrate causal relationships per se, but the contribution relationships. This kind of relationships is weaker, but more realistic knowing the complexity of organizational environments and the difficulty in precisely understanding causal links therein.

Role-Driven Modeling

Roles seem to be a suitable concept for the development of agent-oriented IS, in particular for the engineering of interactions between agents (Cabri, Ferrari, Leonardi, & Zambonelli, 2004). Roles are used to abstractly model the participants of the organization, without considering their specific characteristics. Roles promote the organizational view of the IS, which helps in understanding the main functions of the system and can be translated in and agent-based design model.

Gaia (Zambonelli et al., 2003) is a methodology for agent-oriented analysis and design. The Gaia process consists in orderly constructing a series of models aimed at describing both the macro (societal) aspects and the micro (intra-agent) aspects of a multi-agent system, generally conceived as an organized society of individuals (i.e., a computational organization of autonomous entities) (Cernuzzi, Juan, Sterling, & Zambonelli, 2004). Roles are specified in terms of permissions (which express the resources available to it, that is, what a role can or cannot use), responsibilities (which specify the expected behavior of the role), and protocols and activities (which specify interactions involving the role). Gaia integrates the concepts of organizational rule, which is used to specify the responsibilities of the entire agent organization. Organizational structure of the IS is defined through a role model that defines the topology of interaction patterns and the control regime of organization activities (Zambonelli et al., 2003).

A number of other role-based approaches have been proposed, such as Aalaadin, Kendall, RoleEP, TRUCE, and ROPE. A comprehensive overview and critique of these is provided in Cabri et al. (2004, Ferber and Gutknecht (1998), and Ferber, Gutknecht, and Michel (2003).

Compared to Gaia, our model integrates the possibility of competitive behavior that may lead to conflicts, resulting from the pursuit of actor's personal goals. In a recent paper, Cabri et al. (2004) affirm the need for treating roles as concepts in order to fully exploit the advantages of the concept at analysis, design, and implementation phases. In general, when compared to Gaia, Aalaadin, Kendall, RoleEP, TRUCE, and ROPE, our model is conceptually closer to users, clients, and domain experts, while remaining usable to software architects, software developers, and development tools.

Agent-Driven Modeling

Most of the discussed frameworks in this section incorporate the concept of agent. However, a truly agent-base framework must consider an agent as its basic concept, both in the requirements elicitation and subsequent steps of the requirements and software engineering process. Currently there seems to be only *i** (Yu, 1994, 2001) and TROPOS which are truly agent-based.

The *i** modeling framework (Yu, 1994) has been proposed for business process modeling and reengineering. Processes in which IS are used are viewed as social systems populated by intentional actors which cooperate to achieve goals. The framework provides two types of dependency models: a strategic dependency model used for describing processes as networks of strategic dependencies among actors, and the strategic rationale model used to describe each actor's reasoning in the process, as well as to explore alternative process structures. In this context, agent-based approaches provide significant advantages: agents are autonomous, intentional, social, and so forth. Yu (1994) which is of particular importance for the development of open distributed IS in which change is ongoing.

Tropos (Castro et al., 2002) uses *i** in its early requirements phase of the software development process. One of the significant differences between Tropos and the other methodologies (such as, e.g., Gaia) is its strong focus on early requirements analysis where the domain stakeholders and their intentions are identified and analyzed.

Our enterprise model makes it possible to combine the strengths of *i** notably in terms of strategic dependency analysis among the process' organizational roles, with the analysis of the realization of the process as a series actions; *i** includes neither concepts such as group or organization, nor conflicts, which limits its expressivity. As Tropos uses *i** during early requirements, these same limitations are present.

Figure 1. The agent-oriented enterprise model

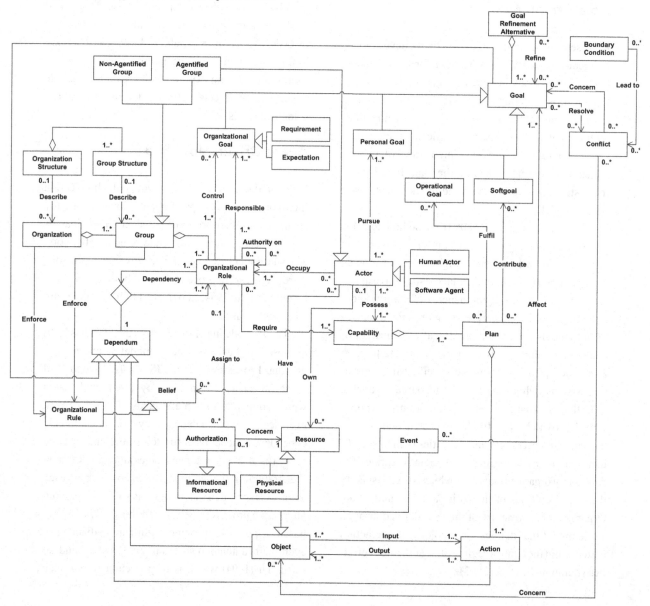

OVERVIEW OF THE ENTERPRISE MODEL

The proposed enterprise model is built with a set of primitives common to business management (that are comprehensible to clients, users, domain experts) and system development (that are comprehensible to system analysts and developers). The set of primitives and their relationships are represented in Figure 1 using the UML (Bennett, McRobb, & Farmer, 2002) notation. The rest of this section overviews the enterprise model from the point of view of business managers (the management perspective) and of systems developers (the information-system perspective). It also presents and discusses the different kinds of primitive used to describe the enterprise model.

The Management Perspective

Our enterprise model provides common concepts used to describe strategic, behavioral, and informational aspects of an organization. *Goals* represent the purposes of the organization and of its processes. They are the responsibility of *Organizational Roles* which are defined as *Groups* formed in the *Organization* for structural and/or functional reasons (i.e., to establish a clear hierarchy and/or to accomplish specific, non-recurrent business projects). *Organizational* and *Group Structure* describe the internal structure of the *Organization* and of its *Groups* in terms of strategic *Dependencies* that influence the interactions among their members. *Organizational Rules* are enforced at the organizational and group levels, defining policies and constraining the behavior of *Actors* so that the expression of their self-interest (expressed with *Personal Goals*) does not limit the performance of the organization. *Actors* occupy *Organizational Roles* if they possess the required *Capabilities*. Actors discharge the responsibilities assigned through organizational roles by executing *Actions*. Actions accomplished sequentially or in parallel, specify how processes are structured. *Events* affect the goals of the organization making it responsive to changes in its internal or external environment.

The Information-System Perspective

Our enterprise model also provides widely-used concepts for specifying the architecture of agent-oriented IS. *Software Agents* are the components of the IS. They act according to their *Beliefs*, *Goals* and *Capabilities*. *Beliefs* represent their information about the environment in which they exist. *Goals* determine the desired states of the environment. *Capabilities*, *Plans,* and *Actions* represent the intentional state of an agent, that is, means for satisfying its external and internal stimuli. *Objects* are non-intentional entities that are manipulated by agents and/or that influence their behavior, and that are significant for the organization. *Organizational Roles* provide the building blocks for agent social systems and the requirements by which agents interact. Each agent is related to other agents by the roles that it occupies and according to the responsibilities that these roles assume. When related organizational roles are assembled, agent *Groups* can be created, according, for example, to a specific and reusable (patterned) group structure. Groups can be characterized as single agents (i.e., "agentified") to benefit from synergies in capabilities of its member agents. An *Organization* of agents can be seen as a framework which is open and dynamic, integrating cooperative and self-interested agents (i.e., those pursuing also *Personal Goals*). The *Group* and *Organization* concepts aid in increasing the modularity of the system and in managing its complexity. *Organizational Rules* are applicable to agent organizations and govern the running of the whole multi-agent system, expressing how the organization is expected to work.

Kinds of Primitives

The enterprise model uses different kinds of primitives: concepts (*Goal*, *Actor*, *Object*, etc.), relationships (*possess*, *require*, *pursue*, etc.), attributes (*Power*, *Interest*, *Motivation*, etc.), and constraints (e.g., "*an actor occupies a position if and only if that actor possesses all the capabilities required to occupy it*").

Concepts represent abstractions of real-world entities significant to model the "inner" and "outer" aspects of an IS. Relationships define interaction among concepts. Attributes describe significant properties of concepts. Finally, constraints impose restrictions upon concepts, relationships, and attributes.

For consistency, any primitive of the enterprise model has two mandatory attributes:

- *Name*, which allows unambiguous reference to the instance of the concept;
- *Description*, which is a precise and unambiguous description of the corresponding instance of the concept. The description should contain sufficient information and be precise so that, if required, a formal specification can be derived for use in requirements specifications for a future IS.

Figure 1 shows only concepts and relationships. Attributes and constraints are specified using the Z state-based specification language (Bowen, 1996; Spivey, 1992). We use Z as it provides sufficient modularity, abstraction, and expressiveness to describe in a consistent, unified, and structured way an agent-oriented IS and the wider context in which it is used. It has a pragmatic approach to specifications by allowing a clear transition between specification and implementation of software (Bowen, 1996; Faulkner, 2004). In addition, it is widely accepted in the software development industry and has been used in large-scale projects.

In the following sections, we provide definitions of primitives and discuss their relevance for enterprise modeling and early RE. For clarity, we have subdivided the enterprise model into five sub-models:

- Organizational submodel, describing the organization in terms of the actors, their organizational roles, groups that they constitute, and their responsibilities and capabilities
- Goals submodel, describing enterprise and business process purposes, that is, what the actors are trying to achieve and why

- Conflict submodel, representing inconsistencies in the business process
- Process submodel, describing how actors achieve or intend to achieve goals
- Objects submodel, describing non-intentional entities and assumptions about the environment of the organization and the business processes

ORGANIZATIONAL SUBMODEL

The organizational submodel is presented in Figure 2. It is used to specify the *Groups* in which *Actors* coexist and interact, by *occupying* diverse *Organizational Roles*. Each *Actor occupies* one or more *Organizational Roles* according to the *Capabilities* that are *required* by these roles, and that the *Actor possesses*. The following subsections provide details on each of the elements of the sub-model.

Actor

Figure 3 shows the Z formal specification of the *Actor* concept. The first part of the specification represents the definition of types. A given type defines a finite set of items. The *Actor* specification first defines the type Name (which represents the *Name* attribute) by writing [Name]. Such a declaration introduces the set of all names, without making assumptions about the type (i.e., whether the name is a string of characters and numbers, or only characters, etc.). Note that the type Actor_Type is defined as being either a Human_Actor or Software_Agent. Defining types in such way indicates either that further detail about the type would not add significant descriptive power to the specification or that a more elaborate internal representation is not required.

More complex and structured types are defined with schemas. A schema groups a collection of related declarations and predicates into a separate namespace or scope. The schema in Figure 3 is entitled *Actor* and is partitioned by a horizontal line into two sections: the declaration section above the line and the predicate section below the line. The declaration section introduces a set of named, typed variable declarations.

Figure 2. Organizational submodel

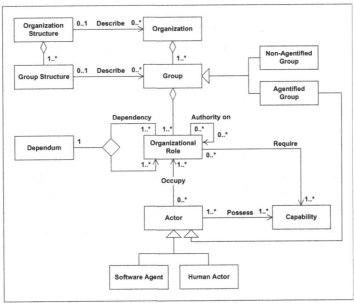

Figure 3. Formal specification of the Actor concept

[Name]
[Informal_Definition]
[Actor_Type]:= Human_Actor | Software_Agent

[Organizational_Role]

[Goal]

[Interest_Value]
[Power_Value]

___

Actor

___

name: *Name*
description: *Informal_Definition*
isa: *Actor_Type*
occupy: set *Organizational_Role*
possess: set *Capability*
has: set *Belief*
own: set *Resource*
pursue: set *Goal*
interest: *Interest_Value*
power: *Power_Value*

___

(c1)   (occupy ≠ ∅) ∧ (possess ≠ ∅) ∧ (pursue ≠ ∅)

(c2)   (∀ act: *Actor*) act.isa = Human_Actor ⇒ act.interest ≠ ∅ ∧ act.power ≠ ∅

___

The predicate section of the schema provides predicates that constrain values of the variables, that is, predicates are used to represent constraints. In order to clarify the Z formal specifications of the concepts, we will refer in the text to specific Z schema predicates by using identifiers placed left of the schema in the form for example, "(c1)" to refer to predicate, that is, constraint (c1) of the schema.

An *Actor* is either a *Human Actor* or a *Software Agent*. A *Human Actor* is used to represent any person, group of people, organizational units, or other organizations that are significant to the organization, that is, that have an influence on its resources, its goals, and so forth. A *Software Agent* represents a software component of the multi-agent IS for which the requirements are being specified.

Whenever an *Actor* enters the system, its *Capabilities* must be known (c1) so that it can *occupy* at least one *Organizational Role*. There can be no *Actor* in the system that does not *occupy* at least one role, since the *Organizational Role* defines the purpose of the *Actor* in the *Organization*, through the responsibilities it carries.

A *Human Actor* is characterized with two specific attributes (c2): *Interest* and *Power* (Johnson & Scholes, 2002). *Interest* is the degree of satisfaction of an actor to see *Organizational Goals* positively contributing to its *Personal Goals*. *Power* is the degree to which the actor is able to modify the objectives of the organization or its business processes through its *Capabilities*. For instance, when automating a business process, the values of *Interest* and *Power* attributes of *Human Actors* change: in the new configuration of the process, some actors will gain decision power while maintaining the same level of interest; others that previously benefited from high power in the initial process structure might become less powerful. It is crucial to take these changes into account when eliciting software requirements. It may lead otherwise to introducing *Goals* not identified during the initial requirements analysis, and/or changing the priority of already specified *Goals*. *Interest* and *Power* help to find *Human Actors* that will play a crucial role in the software-to-be.

Organizational Role

An *Organizational Role* is an abstract characterization of expected behavior of an *Actor* within some specified context of the organization. An *Actor* can *occupy* multiple roles, and a role can be *occupied* by multiple *Actors*.

The concept of *Organizational Role* is important to abstractly model the agents in an agent system and helpful to manage system complexity without considering the concrete details of agents. Roles enable the separation between different functionalities of software agents (e.g., mobility from collaboration), or between different phases of the development process (e.g., functions in the design from methods in the implementation). Figure 4 shows the Z formal specification of the *Organizational Role* concept.

Each *Organizational Role* requires a set of *Capabilities* to fulfill or contribute to *Organizational Goals* for which it is *responsible*. An *Actor* can *occupy* the *Organizational Role* only if it *possesses* the required *Capabilities* (c4)[1]. In addition to entering *Organizational Roles*, *Actors* should be able to leave roles at runtime. The attribute *Leave Condition* is used to specify the *Belief* that has to be true in order for the *Actor* to leave the *Organizational Role* (c5).

Organizational Roles are *responsible* for *Organizational Goals* (c6) and can *control* their *fulfillment*. In case an *Organizational Goal* has been fulfilled, the *Actor*, occupying the *Organizational Role* which *controls* that *Goal*, executes a *Plan* in which an *Action* outputs a new *Belief* to mark the goal fulfillment (c7). This control procedure requires that a single *Actor* can never occupy distinct *Organizational Roles* that are *responsible* of and *control* the fulfillment of the *Organizational Goal* (c8).

Organizational Roles can have different levels of authority. Consequently, an *Organizational Role* can have *authority on* other *Organizational Roles*. The *authority on* relationship specifies the hierarchical structure of the organization. For instance, in the context of multi-agent systems, it can be used to define security policies that differ according to authority attributed to software agents.

Figure 4. Formal specification of the organizational role concept

[Goal_Control_Status]:= Fulfilled | Unfulfilled
[Belief]

Organizational Role

---

name: *Name*
description: *Informal_Definition*
require: set *Capability*
leave_condition: set *Belief*
responsible: set *Goal*
control: set (*Organizational_Goal, Goal_Control_Status*)
authority_on: set *Organizational_Role*

(c3) (require $\neq \varnothing$) $\wedge$ (leave_condition $\neq \varnothing$) $\wedge$ (responsible $\neq \varnothing$)

(c4) ($\forall$ act: *Actor*; r: *Organizational_Role*) r $\in$ act.occupy $\Rightarrow$ r.require $\subset$ act. possess
//An Actor *act* that occupies the Organizational Role *r* possesses the Capabilities required by the Organizational Role *r*.//

(c5) ($\forall$ act: *Actor*; r: *Organizational_Role*)
      act.has $\subset$ r.leave_condition $\Rightarrow$ r $\notin$ act.occupy
//If the Leave Condition is true, than the Actor *act* no longer occupies the Organizational Role *r*.//

(c6) ($\forall$ r: *Organizational_Role*; g: *Goal*)
      g $\in$ r.responsible $\Rightarrow$ g.sec_isa = Organizational_Goal
//If Organizational Role *r* is responsible of Goal *g*, then *g* is an Organizational Goal.//

(c7)
($\forall$ r: *Organizational_Role*; g: *Goal*)
(g.prim_isa = Operational_Goal $\wedge$ g.sec_isa = Organizational_Goal $\wedge$
g $\in$ r.control $\wedge$ g.status = Fulfilled)
$\Rightarrow$ ($\exists$ b!: *Belief*) (g.status = Fulfilled) $\in$ b.term $\wedge$ (g, Fulfilled) $\in$ r.control)
//If an Organizational Operational Goal *g* is fulfilled, then the Organizational Role *r* which controls the fulfillment of *g* outputs a new Belief *b* which indicates that the Goal *g* has been fulfilled.//

(c8) ($\forall$ r_1, r_2: *Organizational_Role*; g: *Goal;* a_1, a_2: *Actor*) (g.sec_isa = Organizational_Goal $\wedge$ g $\in$ r_1.responsible $\wedge$ g $\in$ r_2.control $\wedge$ $r_1 \neq r_2 \wedge r_1 \in$ act. occupy $\wedge$ $r_2 \in$ act.occupy) $\Rightarrow$ $a_1 \neq a_2$
//There can be no Actor *a* which occupies both the Organizational Role r_1 which is responsible for Organizational Goal *g*, and the Organizational Role r_2 which controls the fulfilment of Organizational Goal *g*.//

Figure 5. Formal specification of the capability concept

[Cap_Atom]:= Plan | Capability
[Cap_Availability]:= Available | Unavailable

Capability

---

name: *Name*
description: *Informal_Definition*
composed_of: set *Cap_Atom*
availability: *Cap_Availability*

(c9)   composed_of $\neq \varnothing$

(c10)

($\forall$ cap: *Capability*)
$\exists$ act: *Actor;* cap $\in$ act.possess $\Rightarrow$ cap.availability = available
//If there is some Actor *act* that possesses Capability *cap,* then *cap* is
available.//

Capability

A *Capability* specifies the behaviors that *Organizational Roles* should have in order to be responsible for or to control their *Organizational Goals.* An *Actor possesses Capabilities.* The formal specification in Figure 5 shows that a *Capability* can be structured as a set of *Plans* and/or other *Capabilities.* This increases system modularity as libraries of capabilities can be built up and then combined to provide complex functionalities.

When exploring possible alternative business processes or organizational structures, newly identified *Organizational Roles* can *require Capabilities* that no *Actor possess.* These *Capabilities* have to be confronted to those available in the organization (*Capabilities* that the *Actors possess,* see (c10)), in order to evaluate the proposed alternatives with respect to the current *Roles* and the way they use existing *Capabilities.* This is significant to determine which and how proposed *Ca-*

pabilities and *Roles* will be finally introduced through the system-to-be. The availability of a *Capability* is formally expressed through the *availability* attribute, as indicated in the *Capability* schema.

Group and Group Structure

A *Group* is an aggregation of *Organizational Roles.* Each *Organizational Role* is part of one or more groups. In its most basic form, the *Group* is only a way to tag a set of *Roles.* In a more developed form, in conjunction with the *Actor* definition, groups can be used for partitioning the organization and organizing actors with some common goals together.

Groups are formed or dissolved according to the states of the environment described in their *Formation Condition* and *Dissolution Condition* attributes. For example, a group can be formed if some specific goal has not yet been achieved, and may be dissolved as soon as the goal has been achieved. Whenever a

Figure 6. Formal specification of the group concept

[Group_Structure]
[Group_Type]:= Agentified_Group | Non-Agentified_Group
[Organizational_Rule]

Group

---

name: *Name*
description: *Informal_Definition*
isa: *Group_Type*
composed_of: set *Organizational_Roles*
formation_condition: set *Belief*
access_condition: set {*Capability, Belief*}
dissolution_condition: set *Belief*
described_by: *Group_Structure*
enforce: set *Organizational_Rule*

(c11) $(\text{composed\_of} \neq \varnothing) \wedge (\text{access\_condition} \neq \varnothing)$

(c12)   ($\forall$ act: *Actor*; r: *Organizational_Role*; gr:*Group*; sb: *Organizational_Rule*)
$r \in \text{act.occupy} \wedge r \in \text{gr.composed\_of} \wedge \text{sb} \in \text{gr.enforce} \Rightarrow \text{sb} \in \text{act.has}$
//If an Actor *act* occupies an Organizational Role *r* which composes the Group *gr* and if Organizational Rule *sb* is enforced by *gr*, then *act* has *sb*.//

(c13) $\exists$ r: *Organizational_Role* $\wedge$ ($\neg\exists$ act: *Actor* | r $\in$ act.occupy) $\wedge$
($\exists$ act$_1$,...,act$_n$: *Actor* | r.require $\subset$ act$_1$.possess $\cup$ ... $\cup$ act$_n$.possess)
$\Rightarrow \exists$ gr!: *Group* (rl$_1$!,..., rl$_n$!: *Organizational_Role* $\wedge$ rl$_1$ $\cup$ act$_1$.occupy $\wedge$ ... $\wedge$
rl$_n$ $\cup$ act$_n$.occupy) $\wedge$ gr.composed_of = {rl$_1$,...,rl$_n$} $\wedge$ agentify_group(gr)
//If there is no single Actor *act* which can occupy the Organizational Role *r*, and if there is a set of Actors *act$_1$,...,act$_n$* which together do possess the capabilities required to occupy *r*, then a Group *gr* is formed, as composed of this set of Organizational Roles *rl$_1$,...,rl$_n$*, attributed to Actors *act$_1$,...,act$_n$*. Group *gr* is agentified.//

Group is formed, a series of *Organizational Roles* will be added to it. The *Access Condition* specifies diverse criteria for granting access to an *Organizational Role* to a *Group*. For example, an *Organizational Role* can be granted access to the *Group* if it *possesses* the *Capabilities* required and not available to the *Group*. Another example is the constitution of a *Group* con-

taining only similar *Organizational Roles*.

Whenever an *Actor* becomes a member of a *Group*, it must conform to the constraints for the *Group*. The *Group* thus *enforces* a set of *Organizational Rules* upon every *Actor* that is its member (c12).

The constraint (c13) is used for the agentification of a group. Its use will be clarified in the next subsection.

Figure 7. Axiomatic description of the agentify group function

$$\text{agentify\_group: } Group \rightarrow Actor$$

(c14)

$(\forall \ i = 1,\ldots,n \ act_i: Actor; \ j = 1,\ldots,m \ r_j: Organizational\_Role; \ gr: Group)$
$\exists \ r_j \in act_i.\text{occupy} \land gr.\text{composed\_of} = \{r_1,\ldots,r_m\}$
$\text{agentify\_group}(gr) = (gr.\text{isa} = \text{Agentified\_Group} \land$
$actr! \mid actr.\text{possess} = act_1.\text{possess} \cup \ldots \cup act_n.\text{possess})$
//A Group *gr* is agentified into an Actor *actr* that possesses all the
Capabilities that individual Actors composing the Group *gr* possess.//

Agentified and Nonagentified Groups

An *Agentified Group* posses all the features that any *Actor* might have (Odell, Nodine, & Levy, 2004). Such a group can be considered by other *Actors* in the organization as a single *Actor*. This pushes further the modularity and encapsulation principles in the organization. It facilitates interaction between groups and between a group and individual actors, by establishing standard interaction points for each group.

An *Agentified Group* can occupy an *Organizational Role*, and have all features that are associated with it. This makes it possible to combine the individual capabilities of an actor in order to constitute more complex actors which can occupy highly important roles in the organization. Figure 7 is an axiomatic description of the *agentify_group* function, used to agentify a group. It indicates that the *Actor* formed by agentifying a *Group* possesses all the *Capabilities* that the individual *Actors* composing the *Group* possess (c14). This function has been used in the constraint (c13) to agentify a group formed in order to fulfil responsibilities associated with an organizational role still unoccupied by a single actor can be fulfilled.

A *Nonagentified Group* is any group that is formed for purposes such as intragroup synergies or to parti-

tion the organization. When an actor wishes to interact with such group, it must interact directly with one of its members, that is, actors which occupy organizational roles that compose the group.

Group Structure

A *Group* can be established according to a specific *Group Structure*. The *Group Structure* is the abstract description of a *Group* in terms of *Organizational Roles* that compose it and *Dependencies* that exist among these *Organizational Roles*. Its aim is to define generic structures that can be reused in the formation of groups.

The *Composed Of* attribute in Figure 8 explicitly identifies the set of roles that compose the *Group Structure*. On the basis of identified *Organizational Roles*, the *Dependencies* among them can be derived. They define the *Internal Structure* of the group (c16). A *Dependency* among *Organizational Roles* exists when some of these roles depend on the other ones to provide a *Dependum*, which can be an *Object*, a *Goal*, or an *Action*.

In the simplest case, the *Group Structure* will specify only the *Organizational Roles* which compose the group (c15). That means that a *Group Structure* might be instantiated in a partial form in the actual

Figure 8. Formal specification of the group structure concept

[Dependum]
[Dependency]:=
      (set Organizational_Role) × Dependum × (set Organizational_
Role)

Group Structure

---

name: *Name*
description: *Informal_Definition*
composed_of: set *Organizational_Role*
internal_structure: set *Dependency*

(c15)   composed_of ≠ ∅

     ($\forall$ gs: *Group_Structure*; d: *Dependency*; r_1, r_2: *Organizational_Role* $\wedge$ $r_1 \neq r_2$

(c16) $\wedge$

     dpd: *Dependum*) $\{r_1, r_2\} \in d \wedge (d \equiv r_1 \times dpd \times r_2) \wedge \{r_1, r_2\} \in$ gs.composed_of
           $\Rightarrow$ d $\in$ gs.internal_structure
     //If Organizational Role r_1 depends on r_2 and if they both compose the Goal
     Structure *gs*, then the Dependency *d* among these Organizational Roles
     defines the Internal Structure of the *Group Structure*.//

---

moment: group dynamics might imply that not all roles defined in the group structure will be present at a given moment.

Organization and Organization Structure

An *Organization* is a collection of *Groups* that have certain relationships to one another and take part in systematic institutionalized patterns of interactions with other *Groups*. This concept specifies the macro organization information needed to describe the *Organization structure* and the *Organizational Rules* that must be satisfied by all *Groups* in the organization. The main differences between *Group* and *Organization* concepts are:

- An *Organization* cannot be agentified.
- An *Organization* cannot be part of another *Organization*. An *Agentified Group* can be part of another *Group*, by playing some *Organizational Role* in that other *Group*.

Relationships among *Groups* that compose an *Organization* are determined by *Dependency* relationships among their component *Groups*. In order to enable open and dynamic systems, it is not necessary to specify a priori the *Dependencies* in a *Group*. However, this is necessary when defining *Organizational Structures* as discussed.

Actors that enter the *Organization* must have adequate *Capabilities* and *Beliefs*, as specified in the *Access Condition* attribute in Figure 9. For example, it can be used to forbid entry to actors that have beliefs which are contradictory to some organizational goals in order to avoid conflicts in the organization.

As for *Groups*, an *Organization* can be an instance of a specific *Organizational Structure*. The *Organizational Structure* provides an abstract description of the architecture of an *Organization*. As discussed above, the structure of an *Organization* can be entirely specified as a set of *Groups* and inter-group *Dependencies*, as shown in Figure 10.

Figure 9. Formal specification of the organization concept

[Organizational_Structure]

Organization

name: *Name*
description: *Informal_Definition*
composed_of: set *Groups*
access_condition: set {*Capability, Belief*}
described_by: *Organizational_Structure*
enforce: set *Organizational_Rule*

(c17)   (composed_of $\neq \emptyset$) $\wedge$ (access_condition $\neq \emptyset$)

(c18)   ($\forall$ gr:*Group*; org: *Organization*; sb: *Organizational_Rule*)
gr $\in$ org.composed_of $\wedge$ sb $\in$ org.enforce $\Rightarrow$ sb $\in$ gr.enforce
//A Organizational Rule *sb* that is enforced in the Organization *org* is
enforced in every Group *gr* that compose *org*.//

Figure 10. Formal specification of the organizational structure concept

Organizational Structure

name: *Name*
description: *Informal_Definition*
composed_of: set *Group*
internal_structure: set *Dependency*

(c19)   composed_of $\neq \emptyset$

Further analogy with *Group Structure* can be made as the intention with *Organizational Structure* is to use it to define generic reusable organizational structures. In this respect, work on organizational patterns (Kolp, Giorgini, & Mylopoulos, 2003) in the context of TROPOS can be reused here.

Dependum and Dependency

It has been widely accepted (see the literature on *i**; for example, Liu & Yu, 2004; Yu, 1994, 2001) that the representation of dependencies among members of an organization makes it possible to provide a better

Figure 11. Formal specification of the dependum concept

[Dependum_Type]:= Organizational_Goal | Object | Action

Dependum

---

name: *Name*
description: *Informal_Definition*
type: *Dependum_Type*
depender: set *Organizational_Role*
Dependee: set *Organizational_Role*

(c20) $(type \neq \varnothing) \land (depender \neq \varnothing) \land (dependee \neq \varnothing)$

(c21) $(\forall d: Dependency;\ dpd: Dependum;\ r_1, r_2: Organizational\_Role)$
$r_1 \neq r_2 \land (d \equiv r_1 \times dpd \times r_2) \Rightarrow (depender = r_2 \land dependee = r_1)$

(c22) $(\forall d: Dependency;\ dpd: Dependum;\ r_1, r_2: Organizational\_Role)\ r_1 \neq r_2 \land$
$(d \equiv r_1 \times dpd \times r_2) \land (dpd.type = Authorization) \Rightarrow r_1 \in r_2.authority\_on$
//If the Dependum is an Authorization, then Dependee r_2 has authority on
Depender r_1.//

(c23) $(\forall obj: Object;\ a_1, a_2: Actor;\ cap_1, cap_2: Capability;\ pl_1, pl_2: Plan;\ actn_1, actn_2:$
$Action;\ r_1, r_2: Organizational\_Role)$
$(a_1 \neq a_2 \land cap_1 \neq cap_2 \land pl_1 \neq pl_2 \land actn_1 \neq actn_2 \land$
$(actn_1 \in pl_1.composed\_of \land pl_1 \in cap_1.composed\_of \land cap_1 \in a_1.possess) \land$
$(actn_2 \in pl_2.composed\_of \land pl_2 \in cap_2.composed\_of \land cap_2 \in a_2.possess) \land$
$obj \in actn_1.postcondition \land obj \in actn_2.input \land r_1 \in a_1.occupy \land r_2 \in$
$a_2.occupy \land \{r_1, r_2\} \notin \{a_1.occupy \cap a_2.occupy\}) \Leftrightarrow (\exists dm: Dependum \land$
$dm.type = Object \land dm.name = obj.name \land dm.depender = r_2 \land dm.dependee$
$= r_1)$
//Suppose that there are two different Actors a_1 and a_2 that respectively occupy
two different Organizational Roles r_1 and r_2. These Actors possess respectively
two different Capabilities cap_1 and cap_2, which respectively contain distinct
Plans pl_1 and pl_2. These plans enable them to execute respectively the distinct
Actions $actn_1$ and $actn_2$. If Action *actn₁* has Object *obj* in its postcondition,
and Action *actn₂* outputs *obj*, then Organizational Role r_2 depends on the
Organizational Role r_1 to provide the Object *obj*.//

---

understanding of its strategic and social dimensions. Indeed, members of the organization are involved in numerous interactions; as they have limited capabilities and limited access to resources, they will depend on one another in order to realize their responsibilities.

The *Dependency* relationship was defined in Figure 8 as involving *Organizational Roles* that depend on other *Organizational Roles* for a *Dependum*. A *Dependum* can be an *Organizational Goal*, an *Object*, or an *Action*. In a *Dependency*, the *Organizational Role* that expects the *Dependum* is called the depender, while the *Organizational Role* that is expected to supply the *Dependum* is called the dependee (c21). We define the following dependency types:

- **Organizatonal-Goal dependency:** The depender depends on the dependee to fulfill and/or contribute to an Organizational Goal
- **Action dependency:** The depender depends on the dependee to accomplish some specific Action
- **Object dependency:** The depender depends on the dependee for the availability of an Object

Object dependency allows us to represent any specialization of the *Object* concept as a *Dependum*. For example, an *Organizational Role* r_1 might *depend* on another *Organizational Role* r_2 for an *Authorization*. This has implications on the *authority on* relationship, as this dependency means that r_2 must have *authority on* r_1 (c22).

The constraint (c23) in Figure 11 shows that the existence of an *Object Dependum* among *Organizational Roles* has implications on the *Input* and *Postcondition* of *Actions* accomplished by *Actors* that *occupy* these *Organizational Roles*. This constraint provides a mapping rule between *depend* and *input/output* relationships. Its interest (c23) is twofold:

- If we know *Object* dependencies exist among several organizational roles, we can derive the activity diagram and the collaboration diagram (such as the ones in UML) without difficulties:

actions that are related by dependencies (through their respective inputs/outputs) can be either sequential or parallel, which is sufficient to define the activity diagram.

- If we know the sequence of activities in a process, we can derive the dependencies among roles that participate in the realization of the process. Dependencies can then be analyzed for vulnerabilities and alternative process structures can be evaluated.

Constraint (c23) makes it possible to combine the strengths of the *i** dependency representation with the analysis of the realization of the process as a series of sequential and/or parallel actions that can be realized using, for example, UML activity and collaboration diagrams or scenario-based approaches.

GOALS SUBMODEL

The aim of the Goals submodel illustrated in Figure 12 is to explicitly show the purpose of the process that is being modeled. It allows us to describe the actual or desired state of the process in terms of the goals that it should satisfy. The process is then analyzed according to its performance in the fulfillment and contribution of goals and modified so that its performance is improved.

Figure 12. Goals and conflicts submodels

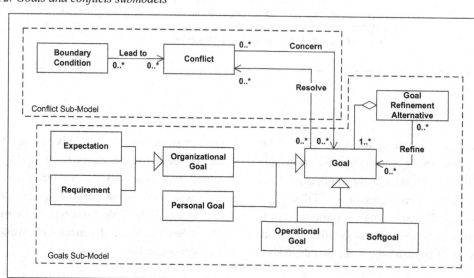

- Goals have been recognized as an essential component of the RE process. See van Lamsweerde (2001) for an overview. They are used in a number of RE frameworks: for example, *i** (Yu, 1994), KAOS (Dardenne et al., 1993), NFR (Chung, Nixon, Yu, & Mylopoulos, 2000). In management, their importance has been recognized in frameworks such as management by objectives, the balanced scorecard (Kaplan & Norton, 2000) and enterprise knowledge development (Kavakli & Loucopoulos, 1999).

Goal

A *Goal* describes a desired or undesired state of the environment. The environment is the context where actors live and interact with other actors. A state of the environment is described through the states of *Objects* (*Beliefs, Resources,* etc.).

In addition to standard attributes, a *Goal* is characterized by the optional *Priority* attribute (van Lamsweerde, 2000), which specifies the extent to which the goal is optional or mandatory. The values and the measurement of priority are domain specific.

To support qualitative and formal reasoning about goals, we classify them along two axes: *Operational Goals vs. Softgoals* and *Organizational Goals vs. Personal Goals.* In addition, we use patterns to specify the temporal behavior of *Goals.* These classifications are treated in more detail in the following sections.

Operational Goal vs. Softgoal

An *Operational Goal* describes a desired or undesired state of the environment that can be achieved by applying *Plans.* An *Operational Goal* has been *fulfilled* if the state of the environment described by the *Operational Goal* has been achieved by a Plan. An *Operational Goal* has *State* and *Status* optional attributes (see Figure 13). *State* describes the state of the environment in which the *Operational Goal* is fulfilled (c25). *Status* indicates whether the *State* of the *Operational Goal* has been achieved, that is, whether the *Goal* has been fulfilled or not (c26).

A *Softgoal* also describes a desired or undesired state of environment, but its fulfil criteria (i.e., how achieve the desired state) may not be formally specified. A consequence of this is that *Plans* that are otherwise applied to *fulfil Operational Goals* can only *contribute* (positively or negatively) to *Softgoals.* For example, "increase customer satisfaction", "implement a flexible IS", "improve productivity of the workforce", are *Softgoals.*

Organizational Goal vs. Personal Goal

An *Organizational Goal* describes the state of the environment that should be achieved by cooperative and coordinated behavior of *Actors.* An *Organizational Goal* is either a *Requirement* or an *Expectation* (c27). A *Requirement* is an *Organizational Goal* under the responsibility of an *Organizational Role occupied* by a *Software Agent* (c28). An *Expectation* is an *Organizational Goal* under the responsibility of an *Organizational Role occupied* by a *Human Actor* (c29). This distinction between a requirement of the IS and the expectation of its human users contributes to the successful accomplishment of a process that generally involves interaction among them.

Organizational Goals can solve *Conflicts* (c30) by specifying the state of the environment in which the *Conflicts* cannot be true.

A *Personal Goal* describes the state of the environment that an *Actor pursues* individually (i.e., without cooperative and coordinated behavior). It can require competitive behavior with other *Actors.*

We distinguish what is expected from the participation of the *Actor* in the process (through the *Organizational Role* it *occupies*), from what the *Actor* expects from its participation in the process (*fulfilment* of or *contribution* to its *Personal Goals*). In reality, consistency between the *Organizational Goals* and *Personal Goals* is not necessarily ensured. Consequently, it is important to reason about *Conflicts* that may arise between *Personal* and *Organizational Goals,* as well as about the degree to which an *Organizational Goal* assists in the pursuit of *Personal Goals.* We use

Figure 13. Formal specification of the goal concept

[Primary_Goal_Type]:= Operational_Goal | Softgoal

[Secondary_Goal_Type]:= Organizational_Goal | Personal_Goal

[Org_Goal_Type]:= Requirement | Expectation

[Goal_Pattern]:= Achieve | Cease | Maintain | Avoid

[Object]:= Resource | Authorization | Belief | Event

[Goal_Status]:= Fulfilled | Unfulfilled

[Refinment_Alternative]
[Priority_Value]
[Conflict]

Goal

---

name: *Name*
description: *Informal_Definition*
prim_isa: *Primary_Goal_Type*
sec_isa: *Secondary_Goal_Type*
org_isa: *Org_Goal_Type*
pattern: *Goal_Pattern*
state: set *Object*
status: *Goal_Status*
refined_by: set *Refinement_Alternative*
priority: *Priority_Value*
resolve: set *Conflict*

(c24) $(\text{prim\_isa} \neq \varnothing) \wedge (\text{sec\_isa} \neq \varnothing) \wedge (\text{pattern} \neq \varnothing)$

(c25) $(\forall\, g\!: Goal)\ g.\text{prim\_isa} = \text{Operational\_Goal} \Rightarrow g.\text{state} \neq \varnothing$
//If Goal g is an Operational Goal, then g must have a specified state, that is, the environment in which g is fulfilled must be specified as a set of Objects.//

(c26) $(\forall\, g\!: Goal)\ g.\text{prim\_isa} = \text{Operational\_Goal} \wedge \exists\, \text{oset} = \{ob_1,\dots,ob_n\!: Object\} \wedge g.\text{state} \subseteq \text{oset} \Rightarrow g.\text{status} = \text{Fulfilled}$
//If there is a set of Objects *oset*, such that the state of Goal g is a subset of *oset*, then g is fulfilled.//

(c27) $(\forall\, g\!: Goal)\ g.\text{sec\_isa} = \text{Organizational\_Goal} \Leftrightarrow g.\text{org\_isa} \neq \varnothing$
//If the Goal g that is an Organizational Goal, then g must be either a Requirement or an Expectation.//

(c28) $(\forall\, g\!: Goal;\ r\!: Organizational\_Role;\ act\!: Actor)$
$(g.\text{sec\_isa} = \text{Organizational\_Goal} \wedge r \in act.\text{occupy} \wedge g \in r.\text{responsible} \wedge act.\text{isa} = \text{Software\_Agent}) \Rightarrow g.\text{org\_isa} = \text{Requirement}$
//An Organizational Goal g is a Requirement, if there is some Software Agent Actor *act* which occupies the Organizational Role r which in turn is responsible for g.//

(c29) $(\forall\, g\!: Goal;\ r\!: Organizational\_Role;\ act\!: Actor)$
$(g.\text{sec\_isa} = \text{Organizational\_Goal} \wedge r \in act.\text{occupy} \wedge g \in r.\text{responsible} \wedge act.\text{isa} = \text{Human\_Actor}) \Rightarrow g.\text{org\_isa} = \text{Expectation}$
//An Organizational Goal g is an Expectation, if there is a Human Actor *act* which occupies an Organizational Role r which in turn is responsible for g.//

(c30) $(\forall\, g\!: Goal)\ g.\text{sec\_isa} \neq \text{Organizational\_Goal} \Rightarrow g.\text{resolve} = \varnothing$
//If Goal g is not an Organizational Goal, then g cannot resolve Conflicts.//

Figure 14. Formal specification of the goal refinement alternative concept

[Status_Value]:= Complete | Incomplete

Goal Refinement Alternative

---

name: *Name*
description: *Informal_Definition*
contains: set *Goal*
status: *Status_Value*

(c31)   contains $\neq \varnothing$

(c32)   ($\forall$ gra: *Goal_Refinement_Alternative*; $g_1,\dots,g_n$: *Goal*; g_k: *Goal*)
($\wedge_{1\leq i\leq n}g_i$.prim_isa = Operational_Goal) $\wedge$ g_k.prim_isa = Operational_Goal $\wedge$
gra.contains = $\{g_1,\dots,g_n\}$ $\wedge$ $g_k \notin \{g_1,\dots,g_n\}$ $\wedge$ gra $\in g_k$.refined_by $\wedge$ ($\wedge_{1\leq i\leq n}g_i$.
status = Fulfilled) $\Rightarrow$ gra.status = Complete
//If some Goal Refinement Alternative *gra* composed of Operational Goals
$g_1,\dots,g_n$ refines Operational Goal g_k and if all Goals $g_1,\dots,g_n$ are fulfilled, then
Goal Refinement Alternative *gra* is complete.//

---

fulfil and *contribute* relationships to show how *Plans* *fulfil* and *contribute* to both *Personal Goals* that the *Actor pursues* and *Organizational Goals* for which its *Organizational Roles* are *responsible*.

Temporal Behavior of Goals

A behavioral pattern is associated to each *Goal*. The possible patterns are: *achieve, cease, maintain,* and *avoid* (Dardenne et al., 1993). For example, organizations tend to *avoid* "conflict of interest" (*Softgoal*) and *achieve* "replenish stock" (*Operational Goal*). When we associate a pattern to a *Goal*, we restrict the possible behavior of the *Actors* concerning the *Goal*: *achieve* and *cease* generate behavior, *maintain* and *avoid* restrict behavior.

Goal Refinement Alternative

Refining a goal consists in identifying a set of subgoals that, when achieved, imply that the refined goal has been achieved. As a goal can often be refined into alternative sets of goals that may lead to its achievement, we introduce *Goal Refinement Alternative* in order to better organize goal refinement information, which is significant when evaluating alternative process structures. Each set of alternatives is identified through goal refinement and represented as a *Goal Refinement Alternative*.

A *Goal Refinement Alternative* contains a set of *Goals* (c31). Its *Status* indicates whether the alternative is sufficient or not (i.e., complete or incomplete) to *fulfil* the *refined Operational Goal* (c32).

Figure 15. Formal specification of the conflict concept

[Boundary_Condition]
[Conflict_Type]:= Object_Inconsistency | Divergence | Obstacle
[Criticality_Value]
[Likelihood_Value]

Conflict

---

name: *Name*
description: *Informal_Definition*
concern: set *Object* $\cup$ set *Goal* $\cup$ set *Boundary_Condition*
isa: *Conflict_Type*
criticality: *Criticality_Value*
likelihood: *Likelihood_Value*

(c33)   concern $\neq \varnothing$

(c34) $(\forall\ obj_1,\ldots,obj_n\colon Object)\ \neg\exists(\wedge_{1\leq i\leq n}obj_i)\wedge(\neg\exists\ obj_i\ |\ \neg\exists(\wedge_{j\neq i}obj_j))$
$\Rightarrow \exists cfl\colon Conflict \wedge cfl.concern = \{obj_1,\ldots,obj_n\}\wedge cfl.isa = Object\_$ Inconsistency
//If there is a set of Objects $obj_1,\ldots,obj_n$ which is minimal – that is, there is no Object obj_i such that its elimination from the set results in maintaining the inconsistency – and if it is impossible that all *Objects* in the set be true together, then there is an Object Inconsistency Conflict *cfl* which concerns the set of Objects $obj_1,\ldots,obj_n$.//

(c35)

(c36) $(\forall g_1,\ldots,g_m\colon Goal;\ cfl\colon Conflict)\ \forall i=1,\ldots,m\ g_i.state \subseteq cfl.concern\wedge\forall i\neq j\ g_i\neq g_j$
$\Rightarrow cfl.concern == cfl.concern \cup \{g_1,\ldots,g_m\}$
//If there is a set of different Goals $g_1,\ldots,g_m$ such that the set of Objects that defines the state of each Goal g_i of the set is a subset of Objects that are concerned by Conflict *cfl*, then the Conflict concerns also the set of Goals $g_1,\ldots,g_m$.//

(c37) $(\forall\ bc\colon Boundary\ Condition;\ cfl\colon Conflict)\ bc \in cfl.concern \Rightarrow (\exists\ g\colon Goal \wedge$
$g.prim\_isa = Operational\_Goal \wedge g.sec\_isa = Organizational\_Goal \wedge$
$(g.status = Fulfilled \Rightarrow \neg bc) \wedge cfl \in g.resolve)$
//For any Conflict *cfl* which contains a Boundary Condition *bc* exists an Operational Organizational Goal *g* which, when fulfilled, resolves Conflict *cfl*, by eliminating the Boundary Condition *bc*.//

$(\forall\ g\colon Goal;\ gra_1\colon Goal\_Refinement\_Alternative;\ cfl\colon Conflict)$
$(g.refined\_by = gra_1 \wedge gra_1.status = Complete \wedge cfl.concern = gra_1.contains)$
$\Rightarrow (\exists\ gra_2\colon Goal\_Refinement\_Alternative \wedge g.refined\_by = gra_2 \wedge$
$cfl.concern \neq gra_2.contains)$
//Whenever a Goal Refinement Alternative gra_1 of Goal *g* generates Conflict *cfl*, there exists another Goal Refinement Alternative gra_2 of Goal *g* which does not generate Conflict *cfl*.//

CONFLICT SUBMODEL

Identification and resolution of inconsistencies is a necessary condition for successful development of a system. From the management perspective, the representation of *Conflicts* makes them clearly visible to stakeholders, serving as a basis for the negotiation among stakeholders that would lead to the introduction of *Organizational Goals* that *resolve Conflicts*. The conflicts sub-model is shown in Figure 12.

Conflict

The *Conflict* concept represents inconsistencies that may exist in a business process and/or in the system to build. *Conflicts* may result from *Goals* that cannot be concurrently *fulfilled* and/or *contributed* to (e.g., when a *Goal* is *fulfilled* and/or *contributed* to, other *Goals* cannot be *fulfilled* and/or *contributed* to), and/or from inconsistencies among *Objects* (e.g., *Beliefs* that cannot be true in the same state of the environment, *Resources* that are concurrently *input* into several *Actions*).

The *concern* relationship identifies the *Objects, Goals,* and *Boundary Conditions* that are involved in the *Conflict*.

In addition to standard attributes, we further characterize *Conflict* with a degree of *Criticality* (which describes the severity of consequences of the *Conflict*), and *Likelihood* (which describes how likely the *Conflict* occurrences are). Their values are domain-specific.

Taking inspiration from the work on inconsistencies in the context of the KAOS framework (Dardenne et al., 1993; Spivey, 1992; van Lamsweerde, 1998) we consider three types of *Conflict*: *Object Inconsistency* (which exists whenever several *Objects* cannot be considered true together (c34)), *Divergence* (existing whenever a set of *Objects* and a *Boundary Condition* cannot hold true together (c38)), and *Obstruction* (which is a particular case of divergence where a single *Object* and a single *Boundary Condition* cannot be true together (c39)).

After *Conflicts* have been identified, diverse methods for their resolution can be applied. See, for example, van Lamsweerde et al. (1998). In the *Conflict* schema, we provide two resolution methods. When a *Boundary Condition* is source of *Conflict*, we can introduce some *Operational Organizational Goal* which eliminates the possibility of the *Boundary Condition* being true after such *Goal* has been fulfilled (c36). In case a *Goal Refinement Alternative* is a source of *Conflict*, we can substitute that alternative with another one which does not lead to *Conflict* (c37).

The constraint (c35) is used to derive goals that are concerned by the conflict from objects that have already been identified as being involved in the conflict, since goals are specified as sets of objects that describe the desired state of the environment.

Boundary Condition

A *Boundary Condition leads to Conflict*. We use this concept to represent specific circumstances (in terms of conditions specified on *Objects*) which make *Goals* and/or *Objects* conflicting. Consequently, in situations other than those described in a *Boundary Condition*, the *Conflict* does not exist. The *state* of the *Boundary Condition* specifies the circumstances under which the *Conflict* exists.

PROCESS SUBMODEL

The process submodel describes how goals of the organization are achieved through transformation of objects. To fulfil and contribute to goals, actors apply *Plans*. *Plans* are composed of *Actions*, which realize the transformation of inputs into outputs, according to their specific internal procedures.

Action

An *Action* is a transformation of an *input Objects* to an *output Objects*. It has the following mandatory attributes:

Figure 16. Formal specification of the boundary condition concept

---

Boundary Condition

---

name: *Name*
description: *Informal_Definition*
state: set *Object*

(c38)   ($\forall$ obj$_1$,..., obj$_n$: *Object*; bc: *Boundary_Condition*)
$\neg\exists((\wedge_{1\leq i\leq n}\text{obj}_i) \wedge \text{bc}) \wedge \exists((\wedge_{1\leq i\leq n}\text{obj}_i) \wedge \neg\text{bc}) \wedge (\neg\exists \text{ obj}_i \mid \neg\exists((\wedge_{j\neq i}\text{obj}_j) \wedge \text{bc})))$
$\Rightarrow \exists$ cfl: *Conflict* $\wedge$ cfl.concern = {obj$_1$,..., obj$_n$, bc} $\wedge$ cfl.isa = Divergence
//If there is a set of Objects *obj$_1$...., obj$_n$* which is minimal – that is, there is
no Object obj$_i$ such that its elimination from the set results in maintaining the
inconsistency – and for which there is a Boundary Condition *bc* such that both
the set of Objects and the Boundary Condition can never be true together, then
there is a Divergence Conflict *cfl* which concerns the set of Objects *obj$_1$...,
obj$_n$* and the Boundary Condition *bc.//*

(c39)   ($\forall$ obj: *Object*; bc: *Boundary_Condition*) $\neg\exists(\text{obj} \wedge \text{bc}) \wedge \exists(\text{obj} \wedge \neg\text{bc})$
$\Rightarrow \exists$ cfl: *Conflict* $\wedge$ cfl.concern = {obj, bc} $\wedge$ cfl.isa = Obstruction
//If there is an Object *obj* and a Boundary Condition *bc* such that *obj* and
bc cannot be true together, then there is an Obstruction Conflict *cfl* which
concerns the Object *obj* and the Boundary Condition *cfl.//*

Figure 17. Process and object submodels

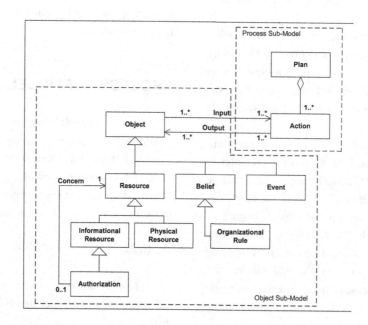

Figure 18. Formal specification of the action concept

[Action_Outcome]:= Succeeded | Failed

[Cost_Value]
[Duration_Value]

Action

---

name: *Name*
description: *Informal_Definition*

precondition: set *Object*
trigger: set *Object*
postcondition: set *Object*
contingency: set *Object*
status: *Action_Outcome*

input: set *Object*
output: set *Object*

precedent: set *Action*
concurrent: set *Action*
alternative: set *Action*

cost: *Cost_Value*
duration: *Duration_Value*

(c40) $(\text{trigger} \neq \varnothing) \wedge (\text{postcondition} \neq \varnothing)$

(c41) $(\forall\ a:\ Action)$
$\exists\ obj_1,\ldots,obj_n:\ Object \wedge \{obj_1,\ldots,obj_n\} = a.\text{postcondition} \Rightarrow a.\text{status} = \text{Succeeded}$
//If the set of Objects *{obj₁,...,objₙ}* is the postcondition of an Action *a*, and if this set exists, then the Action *a* has succeded. Otherwise, the Action *a* has failed.//

(c42) $(\forall\ a:\ Action \wedge obj:\ Object)$
$obj \in a.\text{input} \Leftrightarrow obj \in a.\text{precondition} \cup a.\text{trigger}$
//Any Object *obj* that is input into Action *a* is in the precondition or trigger of that Action.//

(c43) $(\forall\ a:\ Action \wedge obj:\ Object)$
$obj \in a.\text{output} \Leftrightarrow obj \in a.\text{postcondition} \cup a.\text{contingency}$
//Any Object *obj* that is output from Action *a* is in the postcondition of that Action.//

(c44) $(\forall\ a_1, a_2:\ Action;\ obj:\ Object)$
$obj \in a_1.\text{input} \wedge obj \in a_2.\text{output} \Rightarrow (a_2 \in a_1.\text{precedent})$
//If Action *a₂* outputs Object *obj* and *obj* is input into Action *a₁* then Action *a₂* precedes Action *a₁*.//

(c45) $(\forall\ a_1, a_2:\ Action)$
$a_1.\text{trigger} = a_2.\text{trigger} \Rightarrow a_2 \in a_1.\text{concurrent} \wedge a_1 \in a_2.\text{concurrent}$
//Any two Actions *a₁* and *a₂* that have identical triggers are concurrent.//

(c46) $(\forall\ a_1, a_2:\ Action;\ obj:\ Object)\ obj \in a_1.\text{output} \wedge obj \in a_2.\text{output}$
$\Rightarrow ((a_2 \in a_1.\text{alternative}) \wedge (a_1 \in a_2.\text{alternative}))$
//Any two Actions *a₁* and *a₂* that can both output the same Object *obj* are alternative to one another.//

- *Precondition*, describes the necessary *Objects* (*Beliefs*, *Resources*, etc.) required by the *input* in order to apply the *Action*.
- *Trigger* describes the sufficient *Objects* required by the *input* in order to apply the *Action*.
- *Postcondition* describes the *Objects* being *output* after the *Action* has succeeded.
- *Contingency* describes the *Objects* being *output* after the *Action* has failed.

Precondition differs from *Trigger* in the sense that an *Action* may be applied when the *Precondition* holds, whereas it must be applied when the *Trigger* holds (e.g., a stock-trading agent might sell some company's stock if it starts to fall, but must sell it if it falls under some threshold value).

Whenever an *Action* has been applied, its *Status* attribute indicates if it has succeeded (c41), resulting in either *Postcondition* or *Contingency* being achieved.

Figure 19. Formal specification of the plan concept

[Plan_Outcome]:= Succeeded | Failed

Plan

name: *Name*
description: *Informal_Definition*
composed_of: seq *Action*
fulfil: set *Goal*
contribute: set *Goal*
status: *Plan_Outcome*

(c47)   composed_of $\neq \varnothing$

(c48) $(\forall$ pl: *Plan* $\wedge$ g: *Goal*) g $\in$ pl.fulfill $\Rightarrow$ g.prim_isa $\neq$ Softgoal
//If a Goal g can be fulfilled, then g is not a Softgoal.//

(c49) $(\forall$ pl: *Plan* $\wedge$ g: *Goal*) g $\in$ pl.contribute_to $\Rightarrow$ g.prim_isa $\neq$ Operational_Goal
//If Plan pl contributes to Goal g, then g is not an Operational Goal.//

(c50) $(\forall$ pl: *Plan*) $\forall$ $a_1,...,a_n$: *Action* $\wedge$ $\langle a_1,...,a_n \rangle$ = pl.composed_of $\wedge$ $\wedge_{1 \leq i \leq n} a_i$.status = Succeeded $\Rightarrow$ pl.status = Succeeded
//If some Plan pl is composed of a sequence of Actions $\langle a_1,...,a_n \rangle$ and if each of the Actions in the sequence has been succeeded, then the Plan pl has succeeded.//

(c51) $(\forall$pl: *Plan*) $\forall$ $a_1,...,a_n$: *Action* $\wedge$ $\langle a_1,...,a_n \rangle$ = pl.composed_of $\wedge$ $\exists$ $a_i \in \langle a_1,...,a_n \rangle$ $\wedge$
a_i.status = Failed $\Rightarrow$ pl.status = Failed $\wedge$ $\exists$ objcont! = {$obj_1,...,obj_m$: *Object*} $\wedge$
objcont = a_i.contingency
//If some Action a_i which is in the sequence of Actions that compose Plan pl has failed, then the Plan pl has failed and the Action a_i outputs the set of Objects *objcont*, which belong to its contingency meta-attribute.//

Relations between *Actions* can be explicitly modeled by using the optional attributes *Precedent*, *Concurrent*, and *Alternative*. Respectively, *Actions* can be accomplished sequentially (when an *Action* precedes some other *Action* (c44)), concurrently (when they are accomplished in parallel (c45)), and can be alternative to one another (when they output identical *Objects* (c46)). This is of particular interest since activity diagrams, such as those in, for example, UML (Bennett et al., 2002), can be derived directly from the model.

An *Action* may also be described using the following optional attributes: *Cost* (which specifies the material cost of applying the *Action*), and *Duration* (which specifies time necessary to apply the *Action*). These attributes can be used to evaluate each alternative in terms of cost and time necessary to fulfil *Goal or* achieve a process, which helps in alternative selection when specific budget and performance constraints apply.

Plan

A *Plan* represents a way of doing something (e.g., a sequence of *Actions*). It can *fulfil* and/or *contribute*

to a *Goal*. An *Actor* selects *Plans* according to the *Goals* that it pursues and *Beliefs* that it *follows*. An *Actor* can select only among *Plans* which compose the *Capabilities* that it *possesses*.

When a *Plan* is applied, each of the *Actions* that compose it can either succeed or fail. Consequently, we say that a *Plan* has succeeded only if all *Actions* that compose it have succeeded (c50). When a *Plan* has failed, the *Action* of that *Plan* which has failed *outputs* the set of *Objects* specified in its *Contingency* attribute (c51).

OBJECT SUBMODEL

The object submodel describes the *Objects* in the environment relevant for the process and the organization. An *Object* is a nonintentional entity of interest for the organization or involved in its business processes. *Objects* can be *input* and *output* of *Actions*. An *Object* can be a *Resource*, a *Belief*, or an *Event*. Contrary to *Actors*, *Objects* exhibit neither intentional nor social behavior.

Figure 20. Formal specification of the resource concept

```
[Resource_Type]:= Informational_Resource | Physical_Resource
[Relevance_Value]
[Information_Quality_Value]
```

_____
Resource
_____

name: *Name*
description: *Informal_Definition*
isa: *Resource_Type*
state: *Belief*
relevance: *Relevance_Value*
information_quality: *Information_Quality_Value*

_____

(c52)   isa ≠ ∅

Resource

A *Resource* is an *Object* that can be used or consumed during the performance of an *Action*.

Resources can be owned by actors and can be assigned to organizational roles. As the characteristics of a resource can change with its utilization and/or with time, the *state* of a resource is used to specify how and when changes occur. The *state* of the resource is specified as a *Belief* concerning the resource.

Usually the resources are needed when organizational roles intend to fulfil and/or contribute to organizational goals. They are often rare and used by a number of organizational roles. The exchange of rights to use resources is done through *Authorizations*: whenever an organizational role requires the resource, it must receive the authorization to use it from the organizational role occupied by the owner of the resource.

We distinguish *Informational Resources* from *Physical Resources*. An *Informational Resource* is a piece of data or information used as *input* in or produced as *output* by one or more *Actions*. We can characterize an *Informational Resource* with two optional attributes:

- *Relevance* describes the degree to which the informational resource aids the *Action*.
- *Information Quality* describes the quality of the informational resource in terms of domain-specific quality criteria.

A *Physical Resource* is a tangible *Resource* used as *input* in *Actions* or produced by them as *output*. We do not propose specific attributes for *Physical Resources* as they are domain-specific (e.g., different sets of attributes would be used to describe resources used in steel industry than those used in pharmaceuticals).

Authorization

An *Authorization* is a specific type of *Informational Resource*. It is assigned to *Organizational Roles* and enables them to use the *Resource* that it *concerns*. It

Figure 21. Formal specification of the authorization concept

Authorization

---

name: *Name*
description: *Informal_Definition*
assigned_to: *Organizational_Role*
concern: *Resource*
valid until: *Belief*

(c53) $(assigned\_to \neq \emptyset) \wedge (concern \neq \emptyset)$

(c54) $(\forall$ act: *Actor*; res: *Resource*) res $\in$ act.own
$\Rightarrow \exists$ actn: *Action* , pl: *Plan* , cap: *Capability* , azn: *Authorization* $|$
(azn $\in$ actn.postcondition $\wedge$ actn $\in$ pl.composed_of $\wedge$ pl $\in$ cap.composed_of
$\wedge$
cap $\in$ act.possess)
//If an Actor *act* owns the Resource *r*, then *act* is capable of executing an
Action *actn* that has an Authorization *azn* as postcondition.//

---

is similar to the concept of permission in Gaia (Zambonelli et al., 2003) since:

- It identifies the resources that can legitimately be used to carry out a role as it is *assigned to* organizational roles.
- It states the resource limits within which a role must operate, since an authorization has limited validity: it "expires" as soon as the belief specified in its *Valid Until* attribute becomes true. An authorization may last until, for example, the resource has been consumed to a certain level or up to some point in time.

As indicated in Figure 3, an *Actor* may own a resource, and that resource may be required by other actors in order to fulfil their responsibilities. Consequently, the owner of the resource must be capable of providing authorizations to organizational roles that

require the execution of actions that use or consume that resource (c54).

Belief

A *Belief* corresponds to true or false information that an actor carries about the environment in which it exists. The environment is described through *Terms* which are variables or functions defined over other *Terms*. A *Term* can be an *Object, Actor, Organizational Role, Group,* or *Organization*.

A *Belief* is specified either as an *Atomic Belief,* a negated *Atomic Belief,* a series of *Atomic Beliefs* connected using logic connectives, or an *Atomic Belief* characterized with a temporal pattern. We use the following temporal patterns (van Lamsweerde et al., 1998): ○ (in the next state), ● (in the previous state), ◊ (some time in the future), ◆ (some time in the past), □ (always in the future), ■ (always in the past), W (always in the future unless), and U (always in the future until).

Figure 22. Formal specification of the belief concept

```
[Term]:= Function(Term,…)
        | Object
        | Actor
        | Organizational_Role
        | Group
        | Organization
```

Atomic Belief
_____

name: *Name*
description: *Informal_Definition*
Terms: seq *Term*
_____

```
[Belief]:=        Atomic_Belief
        | ¬ Atomic_Belief
        | Atomic_Belief Connective Atomic_Belief
        | Temporal_Pattern Atomic_Belief
[Connective]:= ∧ | ∨ | ⇒
[Temporal_Pattern]:= ○ | ● | ◊ | ◆ | □ | ■ | W | U
```

Figure 23. Formal specification of the event concept

[Affect]:= Add | Remove | Modify

Event

name: *Name*
description: *Informal_Definition*
affect: set (*Affect*, *Goal*)

(c55) affect ≠ ∅

Organizational Rule

Organizational Rules are a specific type of *Belief* which defines global constraints in the group or organization. They govern interactions among actors and specify how the group or the organization is supposed to work.

Organizational rules are of particular importance in the context of open systems. They constrain the behavior of self-interested actors as they make it possible to distinguish legitimate from illegitimate expression of self-interest (Zambonelli et al., 2003).

Organizational rules are enforced both in groups and in the entire organizations. As indicated in (c18), an organizational rule specified for the organization is enforced in every group of the organization.

Event

An *Event* is a change of *Goals*. It is either *output* of an *Action*, or exogenous to the organization, resulting from an action not accomplished by actors in the organization (e.g., for a company, a change in the currency exchange rate is such an *Event*). An *Event* *affects Goals*, by dynamically adding, removing, or modifying them.

CONCLUSION

Modeling the organizational and operational context within which a software system will eventually operate has been recognized as an important element of the engineering process (e.g., Kolp et al., 2003). Such models are usually founded on primitive concepts such as those of *actor* and *goal* (e.g., Yu, 1994). Unfortunately, no specific enterprise modeling framework really exists for engineering modern corporate IS. This chapter proposes an integrated agent-oriented enterprise model for enterprise modeling. Moreover, our approach differs primarily in the fact that it is founded on ideas from within RE frameworks, management theory concepts found to be relevant for enterprise modeling, and agent-oriented software engineering.

We have only discussed here the concepts that we consider the most relevant at this stage of our research. Further classification of, for instance, goals is possible and can be introduced optionally into the enterprise model. For example, goals could be classified into further goal categories such as Accuracy, Security, Performance, and so forth. We also intend to define a strategy to guide enterprise modeling using our model as well as define a modeling tool à la Rational Rose to visually represent the concepts.

REFERENCES

Bennett, S., McRobb, S., & Farmer, R. (2002). *Object-oriented systems analysis and design using UML*. McGraw-Hill International.

Bowen, J. (1996). *Formal specification and documentation using Z: A case study approach*. Thomson Publishing.

Briand, L., Melo, W., Seaman, C., & Basili, V. (1995). Characterizing and assessing a large-scale software maintenance organization. In *Proceedings of the 17th International Conference on Software Engineering*, Seattle, WA.

Brickley, J.A., Smith, C.W., & Zimmerman, J.L. (2001). *Managerial economics and organization architecture*. McGraw-Hill Irwin.

Cabri, G., Ferrari, L., Leonardi, L., & Zambonelli, F. (2004). Role-based approaches for agent development. In *Proceedings of the International Workshop on Agent-Oriented Software Engineering (AOSE)*.

Castro, J., Kolp, M., & Mylopoulos, J. (2002). Towards requirements-driven information systems engineering: The tropos project. *Information Systems, 27*.

Cernuzzi, L., Juan, T., Sterling, L., & Zambonelli, F. (2004). The Gaia methodology: Basic concepts and extensions. *Methodologies and Software Engineering for Agent Systems*. Kluwer.

Chung, L.K., Nixon, B.A., Yu, E., & Mylopoulos, J. (2000). *Non-functional requirements in software engineering*. Kluwer Publishing.

Dardenne, A., van Lamsweerde, A., & Ficklas, S. (1993). Goal-directed requirements acquisition. *Sciences of Computer Programming, 20*, 3-50.

Elmagarmid, A., & Du, W. (1998). Workflow management: State of the art versus state of the products. In *Workflow Management Systems and Interoperability*. Heidelberg, Germany: Springer.

Faulkner, S. (2004). *An architectural framework for describing BDI-multi-agent information systems*. PhD Thesis, University of Louvain.

Faulkner, S., Kolp, M., Coyette, A., & Tung Do, T. (2004). Agent-oriented design of e-commerce system architecture. In *Proceedings of the 6th International Conference in Enterprise Information Systems Engineering*, Porto.

Ferber, J., & Gutknecht, O. (1998). A meta-model for the analysis and design of organizations in multi-agent systems. In *Proceedings of the Third International Conference on Multi-Agent Systems*.

Ferber, J., Gutknecht, O., & Michel, F. (2003). From agents to organizations: An organizational view of multi-agent systems. In *Proceedings of the International Workshop on Agent-Oriented Software Engineering (AOSE)*.

Fox, M.S., & Grüninger, M. (1997). On ontologies and enterprise modeling. In *Proceedings of the International Conference on Enterprise Integration Modeling Technology*. Springer-Verlag.

Guizzardi, G., Herre, H., & Wagner, G. (2002). On the general ontological foundations of conceptual modeling. In *Proceedings of the 21st International Conference on Conceptual Modeling (ER 2002)*. Berlin, Germany: Springer-Verlag.

Jennings, N.R. (2000). On agent-based software engineering. *Artificial Intelligence, 117*, 277-296.

Johnson, G., & Scholes, K. (2002). *Exploring corporate strategy, text and cases*. Prentice Hall.

Kamath, M., Dalal, N.P., Chaugule, A., Sivaraman, E., & Kolarik, W.J. (2003). A review of enterprise process modeling techniques. In V. Prabhu, S. Kumara, & M. Kamath (Eds.), *Scalable enterprise systems: An introduction to recent advances*. Boston: Kluwer Academic Publishers.

Kaplan, S., & Norton, P. (2000). *The strategy-focused organization*. Harvard Business School Press.

Kaplan, R.S., & Norton, D.P. (2004). *Strategy maps: Converting intangible assets into tangible outcomes.* Boston: Harvard Business School Press.

Kavakli, E. (1999). *Goal-driven requirements engineering: Modeling and guidance.* PhD Thesis, University of Manchester.

Kavakli, V., & Loucopoulos, P. (1999). Goal-driven business process analysis application in electricity deregulation. *Information Systems, 24,* 187-207.

Kettinger, W.J., Teng, J.T.C., & Guha, S. (1997). Business process change: A study of methodologies, techniques, and tools. *MIS Quarterly.*

Kolp, M., Giorgini, P., & Mylopoulos, J. (2003). Organizational patterns for early requirements analysis. In *Proceedings of the 15th International Conference on Advanced Information Systems Engineering (CAiSE'03),* Velden, Austria.

Koubarakis, M., & Plexousakis, D. (2002). A formal framework for business process modeling and design. *Information Systems, 27,* 299-319.

Liu, L., & Yu, E. (2004). Designing information systems in social context: A goal and scenario modeling approach. *Information Systems, 29,* 187-203.

Mao, X., & Yu, E. (2004). Organizational and social concepts in agent oriented software engineering. In *Proceedings of the International Workshop on Agent-Oriented Software Engineering (AOSE).*

Mentzas, G., Halaris, C., & Kavadias, S. (2001). Modeling business processes with workflow systems: An evaluation of alternative approaches. *International Journal of Information Management, 21,* 123-135.

Odell, J., Nodine, M., & Levy, R. (2004). A metamodel for agents, roles, and groups. In *Agent-oriented software engineering V* (pp. 78-92). Springer.

Sheth, A.P., van der Aalst, W., & Arpinar, I.B. (1999). Processes driving the networked economy. *IEEE Concurrency, 7,* 18-31.

Simon, H.A. (1976). *Administrative behavior: A study of decision-making processes in administrative organization.* New York: The Free Press.

Simon, H.A. (1979). Rational decision making in business organizations. *The American Economic Review, 69*(4), 493-513.

Spivey, J.M. (1992). *The Z notation: A reference manual* (2nd ed.). Prentice Hall International.

Stader, J. (1996). Results of the enterprise project. In *Proceedings of Expert Systems '96, the 16th Annual Conference of the British Computer Society Specialist Group on Expert Systems,* Cambridge, UK.

Uschold, M., & Grüninger, M. (1996). Ontologies: Principles, methods and applications. *Knowledge Engineering Review, 11*(2).

Uschold, M., King, M., Moralee, S., & Zorgios, Y. (1997). *The enterprise ontology.* The University of Edinburgh: AIAI.

van Lamsweerde, A. (2000). Requirements engineering in the year 00: A research perspective. In *Proceedings of the 22nd International Conference on Software Engineering,* Limerick, Ireland (pp. 5-19). ACM.

van Lamsweerde, A. (2001). Goal-oriented requirements engineering: A guided tour. In *Proceedings RE'01, 5th IEEE International Symposium on Requirements Engineering,* Toronto, Canada (pp. 249-263).

van Lamsweerde, A., Darimont, R., & Letier, E. (1998). Managing conflicts in goal-oriented requirements engineering. *IEEE Transactions on Software Engineering, Special Issue on Managing Inconsistency in Software Development.*

Yu, E. (1994). *Modeling strategic relationships for process reengineering.* PhD Thesis, Department of Computer Science, University of Toronto.

Yu, E. (2001). Agent-oriented modeling: Software vs. the world. In *Proceedings of the International Workshop on Agent-Oriented Software Engineering (AOSE).* Springer Verlag.

Zambonelli, F., Jennings, N.R., & Wooldridge, M. (2003). Developing multiagent systems: The Gaia methodology. *ACM Trans. Softw. Eng. Methodol, 12*(3), 317-370.

zur Muehlen, M. (2002). *Workflow-based process controlling.* Berlin, Germany: Logos Verlag.

ENDNOTE

[1]   To clarify the formal specifications, we embed the comments on predicates between two "//" signs.

Section III
Specialized Domain Ontologies

Chapter IX
Toward an Ontology of ICT Management:
Integration of Organizational Theories and ICT Core Constructs

Roy Gelbard
Bar-Ilan University, Israel

Abraham Carmeli
Bar-Ilan University, Israel

ABSTRACT

As an emergent field of research and practice, the management of information and communication technologies (ICT) offers complex challenges, such as how to structure and organize the accumulated body of knowledge as well as the need to orchestrate and encapsulate theoretical perspectives and methodologies. As in any emergent field, the ICT management (ICTM) body of knowledge has mostly expanded through diverse theoretical lenses. It also has to overcome concept redundancy and ambiguity in order to gain insights that are more than "old wine in new bottles." In this chapter, we focus on two main issues. First, we strive to achieve a holistic perspective of ICTM. Second, we explore the way in which organizational theories can contribute to a better understanding of this holistic perspective. For this, we introduce an ontology that describes four ICTM core constructs—policy, project, assets, and evaluation—and their interrelationships. We discuss each one of these constructs in light of six common organizational theories.

INTRODUCTION

As an emergent field of research and practice, the management of information and communication technologies (ICT) offers complex challenges. One of these challenges is how to structure and organize the accumulated body of knowledge as well as the need to orchestrate and encapsulate theoretical perspectives and methodologies. This is one of the key drivers for scholars' growing interest in the ontology of the field (e.g., Guarino, 1998; Kayed & Colomb, 2005; Kitchenham et al., 1999). ICT ontologies range from terminological representations (Kitchenham et al., 1999) to mathematical representations (Antoniou & Kehagias, 2000).

System analysis is considered the first step in any endeavor to develop an information system. Therefore, a domain analysis is required in order to construct an ontological management approach for ICT (ICTM) (i.e., this is the domain ontology). According to Antoniou and Kehagias (2000),

... an ontology defines the terminology of a domain: it describes the constructs that constitute the domain, and the relationships between those constructs. Every information system uses its own ontology, either implicitly or explicitly. As applications become increasingly complex, we can observe a trend towards the explicit representation and management of ontologies.

As in any emergent field of research, the body of knowledge in our field has mostly expanded through diverse theoretical lenses. Although diversity is valuable for any evolved field, it also poses the key challenge of overcoming concept redundancy and ambiguity. As Gregor (2002) indicated, there has been little discussion of what ICT theory constitutes. Moreover, the field has been criticized for (1) its lack of focus and cohesion, and (2) the fact that it often offers insights that are nothing more than "old wine in new bottles".

A review of the literature also reveals that although there is a common agreement about the supporting role of ICT underlying the organizational/functional activities (i.e., human resources, accounting, finance, manufacturing, sales, and marketing) at all levels (strategic, tactical, and operational levels), these management concepts have rarely been applied regarding information technology (IT) departments or discussed thoroughly in ICT textbooks (*cf.* Laudon & Laudon, 2004).

Figure 1. Adding the "ICT Sector" to the classic management pyramid

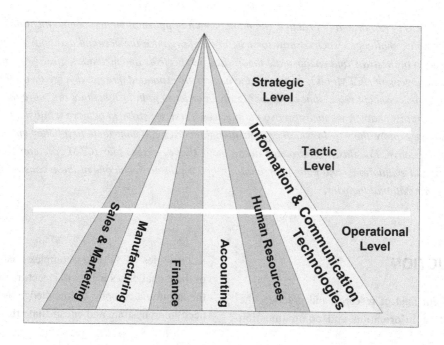

Specifically, the organizational pyramid commonly lacks a specific functional area representing ICT. Hence, in the same manner that human resource management is an independently functioning area, it is also of importance to view ICT as an individual sector in the classic management pyramid. Figure 1 illustrates this proposed structure.

As such, the ontology construction of ICTM should take into account organizational theories that are applied with regard to other functional areas. Furthermore, the ICT functional area is to be supported by meta information systems in the same manner that other functional areas are being supported by different kinds of ICT (e.g., ERP, CRM, billing, finance, and BI).

In this study, we focus on two main issues. First, we strive to achieve a holistic perspective of ICTM. Second, we explore the way in which organizational theories can contribute to a better understanding of this holistic perspective of ICTM. The other aspect of supportive Meta information systems for the ICT sector is analyzed and prototyped in a separate technical-oriented research. In an attempt to structure the knowledge of unorganized and scattered observations in the field, we introduce integrated enterprise ICTM ontology. This ontology describes four core constructs—policy, project, assets, and evaluation—and their interrelationships. We discuss each one of these constructs in light of various organizational theories. Integrating those organizational theories into the field of ICTM may serve to illuminate insights in a more explicit manner.

The chapter is structured as follows: The first section defines four core constructs dominating the activities of ICT management: policy, projects, assets, and evaluation. The next section presents the essence and applications of the following six organizational theories as they relate to ICTM issues: the stakeholder theory, the theory of fit, the behavioral integration theory, the agency theory, the transaction cost theory, and the images of organizations theory. The four core constructs are discussed according to these organizational theories. Discussion, limitations, and implications for future researches are discussed in the fourth section.

DEFINING FOUR CORE CONSTRUCTS OF ICT MANAGEMENT

Consistent with previous ontology in ICT literature (Gregor, 2002), we first provide a descriptive theory, which is necessary for the development of other types of theories (i.e., understanding, predicting, explaining, designing, and acting). In addition, a clear construct definition, necessary when formulating a theory, is discussed. Finally, an interface between organizational theories and each one of the identified constructs is described.

Policy formulation is an iterative process of considering resources, activities, and choices. Scholars of the resource-based view suggest that resources are at the basis for the firm choices and competitive advantageous position (Barney, 1991; Grant, 1991; Peteraf, 1993). For industrial economists, however, choices should determine the preferable position within a particular industry. The order of resources and choices (which should be considered first) is not as important as the understanding that both interdependently determine the viability of the organization.

Compared to hardware assets, software assets are organization-specific in that they are being "tailored" to respond to the specific needs of the organization. This includes on-the-shelf products such as ERP are "tailored". The assessment of firm choices is done by measurable parameters and indicators that enable redirections of resources, processes, and entire policy. Policy implementation, as well as monitoring, evaluating, and deciding on corrective actions are included among the five tasks of strategic management (Thompson & Strickland, 2003).

Following generic frameworks of strategic management (e.g., Thompson & Strickland, 2003) and the resource-based perspective, we suggest the following four core elements that constitute ICT management:

Figure 2. ICT management core constructs

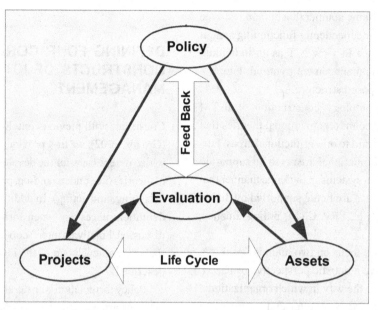

(1) strategy and policy, (2) ICT assets that serve as organization unique resources, (3) ICT projects, and (4) evaluation.

Practically, *ICT projects* refer to a framework in which ICT applications are developed and *ICT assets* concern with the software maintenance framework. The two additional constructs: *policy* and *evaluation*, together with *projects* and *assets*, form the four constructs underlining the ICTM ontology. *ICT policy* is viewed as ICT decision-making concerning the ways in which organizational goals and objectives are met (e.g., how to make the organizational products and services more visible and attractive to potential consumers). *ICT evaluation* is concerned with assessing the flexibility, agility, quality, efficiency, and effectiveness of both ICT processes and ICT outcomes.

ICT Projects

ICT projects are about the framework in which ICT applications are developed. Projects have a central role in ICT. This important role is demonstrated by the fact that major institutions in our field, PMI (PMBOK), SEI (CMM, CMMI), IEEE (IEEE Standards), UK CCTA (Prince), and ISO (ISO Standards) have extensively developed a substantial body of knowledge, methodologies, measures, and standards.

ICT Assets

The issue of ICT assets is concerned with the software maintenance framework. Delivered ICT Projects become ICT assets that are constantly maintained with regard to changes in time, platforms, geography, and

Figure 3. Multiple sources of software assets (Doublait, 1997)

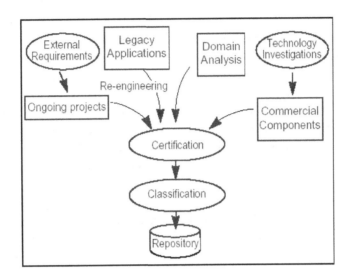

markets. However, as shown in Figure 3 (Doublait, 1997), ICT assets also derive from additional sources (see also, Bennett, 2000; Hordijk, 1999). ICT assets become a prominent subject of inquiry for which Kitchenham et al. (1999) have formulated a specific ontology.

ICT Policies

ICT policy is viewed as ICT decision-making concerning the ways in which organizational goals and objectives are met (e.g., how to make the organizational products and services more visible and attractive to potential consumers). Policy choices are an important element in management. It is clearly evident that policy choices have a role in determining the viability of an organization. Within the ICT context, it is argued that we could better understand ICT success and failure by directing more attention to ICT policy choices. This is crucial in light of the considerable failure rate of ICT systems.

ICT Evaluation

ICT evaluation is concerned with assessing the flexibility, agility, quality, efficiency, and effectiveness of both ICT processes and outcomes. The measurement of organizational performance is a difficult task for all kinds of organizations and their subunits. There are various approaches to evaluating performance (see Daft, 1995) such as (1) the goal model – measuring performance by examining the extent to which the real goals are achieved (Etzioni, 1964; Mohr, 1973; Perrow, 1970); (2) the system resource approach – evaluating performance with respect to the capacity to obtain critical resources (Yuchtman & Seashore, 1967); and (3) the constituency approach – assessing performance with regard to the extent to which constituencies' expectations are met (Connolly, Conlon, & Deutsch, 1980). In our context, the major institutions are involved in the development of ICT metrics by which ICT elements are assessed.

The ICTM Ontological Framework

The triangle in Figure 2 depicts the proposed constructs in our ICTM ontology. There are reciprocated feedback relationships between policy and evaluation and reciprocated life cycle relationships between assets and projects. In addition, the triangle consists of four currents: *Policy → Projects, Policy → Assets, Projects → Evaluation, and Assets → Evaluation.*

Feedback refers to the evaluating and re-evaluating of business policies according to metrics analysis, as well as the evaluating and re-evaluating of measures and metrics, according to emergent or revised policies. *Lifecycle* refers to an ongoing cycle in which a project becomes an asset, and an asset's maintenance and upgrading results in additional new projects. *Policy → Projects current* refers to the process by which business objectives define new projects. Business and ICT Policy determine project characteristics. *Policy → Assets current* refers to the process by which business objectives define operation policy concerning ICT assets. *Projects → Evaluations current* refers to projects that are measured as a multi-state process. *Assets → Evaluations current* refers to assets, which are measured by physical and usage characteristics: lifecycle costs, CPU, or other resource usage, such as manpower and time, among others.

ICTM AND ORGANIZATIONAL THEORIES

The purpose of this section is to explore the ways in which organizational theories contribute to the development and explanation of ICTM theories, as well as practical issues. To this end, we review and discuss six dominant organizational theories that can be used to categorize ICTM theories. The theories are presented briefly followed by specific applications for ICTM. These categorizations together with their key research questions are presented in Table 1.

The Stakeholder Theory

The stakeholder theory became of interest to organizational scientists and practitioners starting in the late 1970s when Connolly et al. (1980) and others took a constituent-based approach to studying organizational effectiveness. It was not, however, until Freeman's (1984) influential work, followed by an increased effort (see Donaldson & Preston, 1995), that the firm-based stakeholder theory became prominent in organizational science.

The stakeholder theory holds that the firm should be analyzed with regard to the firm's key interest constituents. Firm constituents (stakeholders) are individuals or groups that hold legitimate interests in the firm's activities. These constituents maintain relationships with the firm; they affect and are affected by its behaviors (Donaldson & Preston, 1995; Freeman, 1984; Savage, Nix, Whitehead, & Blair, 1991).

Since Freeman's (1984) work, scholars have drawn on stakeholder theory to explain, for example, variance in environmental commitment (Henriques & Sadorsky, 1999), and the influence of CEOs' perceptions of stakeholder attributes on stakeholder salience and firm performance (Agle, Mitchell, & Sonnenfeld, 1999).

Stakeholder Theory and ICT Management

The stakeholder theory and its application for each one of the ICTM core constructs are presented in Table 1. In the context of ICTM, stakeholders develop interests and maintain relationships with the firm and its ICT department in order to influence them. At the same time, the stakeholders can be influenced by the decisions and actions taken by the firm and its ICT department. Firm relations with stakeholders are established through the concept of service level agreements (SLA). SLA can be signed with external stakeholders, as well as with internal stakeholders. SLA can be defined and phrased in a formal manner, but it may also be defined in informal ways. The wide concept of SLA also reflects norms and standards adopted by the firm, as well as firm priorities.

Formal SLA is measured by the ICT department as well as by an additional independent party. Bonus and penalties are paid according to SLA measurements. In the case of informal SLA, the "payment" is not made through monetary exchanges, but as a result of stakeholders' attitudes, expectations, and preferences, which have both short- and long- term effects.

The Theory of Fit

In recent years, we have witnessed a revival of viewing organizations as complex systems that are composed of periphery (non-core) and core elements that interact directly and indirectly with one another (Levinthal, 1997; Porter, 1996; Rivkin, 2000; Rivkin & Siggelkow, 2003; Siggelkow, 2002a, 2002b). This view can be traced back to the early writings of Chandler (1962) who linked organization's strategy and structure, Khandwalla (1973), who made the case that effective design means consistency among choices, Weick (1976), who suggested that organizations are both loose (autonomous) and coupled (interdependent) systems, and Miller and Friesen (1984), who argued that organizations are complex entities composed of closely interrelated elements, among others. More recent studies include Porter (1996), who mapped the system of activities of firms such as Southwest Airline to demonstrate the role of mutually reinforced activities in competitive advantage creation, Nadler and Tushman (1997), who argued that the alignment of key or major elements has a role in enhancing organizational performance, Rivkin (2000), who made the case that complex strategies are internally aligned to pose barriers against potential imitation efforts, and Siggelkow (2002a, 2002b), who used the in-depth qualitative analyses of two companies (the Vanguard Group and Liz Claiborne) in an attempt to explore fitness and change, that is, the theory of fit.

An effective system is organized around a system of elements (policies, resources, and activities) that interact with one another to create fitness (*cf.* Siggelkow, 2002a). This definition is built on the

concept that states that an organization should create a system of tightly interacted core elements that complement and strengthen one another. This system is an important source of competitive advantage (see also Levinthal, 1997; Porter, 1996; Rivkin, 2000; Siggelkow, 2002b).

Theory of Fit and ICT Management

Applications of the fit theory for each one of the ICTM core constructs are presented in Table 1. In the context of ICTM, the idea of fit and balance is an essential dogma. "Doing the right project" reflects balance considerations (tradeoffs) relating to: resources and functionality, risk and opportunity for advantage, recourses, and time to market. The complementary aspect of the phrase "Doing the project right" reflects maintainability, portability, scalability, reusability, and other balances, which will have major influences throughout the entire lifecycle of the ICT product-asset.

Fit and balances are also required when considering the right metrics by which the ICT department processes and products will be evaluated: What to measure? How to measure? What are the "side effects" of the measurement? What are the costs and benefits of the measurement?

Fit and balances are major issues in the creation of core competences within the ICT department. ICT departments have to decide how much effort to put into the development of in-house technological and methodological infrastructures. These infrastructures are needed in order to make software development and software maintenance more efficient, more agile, and more available (i.e., easy to share with other ICT members), as well as for constructing a methodology, which better fits the organization's specifications, and, therefore, is also more efficient and agile.

The Theory of Behavioral Integration

The theory of behavioral integration was developed by Hambrick (1994) to address the lack of research about the processes by which managerial elites manage their tasks and the need to open up the "black box" of demography research that left subjective concepts "unmeasured and the hypotheses untested" (Lawrence, 1997, p. 2; see also Hambrick, 1994; Pelled, Eisenhardt, & Xin, 1999; Pettigrew, 1992; Smith et al., 1994).

Behavioral integration is viewed as a "meta-construct" (Hambrick, 1994) that refers to interactions within the top management teams and encompasses elements of information sharing, collaboration, and joint decision-making (Hambrick). *Behavioral integration* is defined as "the degree to which the group engages in mutual and collaborative interaction" (Hambrick, p. 188). A well-designed and functioning team is behaviorally integrated. Such a team is characterized by a high degree of mutual and collective interactive processes through which it displays information exchange, collaborative behavior, and joint decision-making. These processes have implications for quality decisions and organizational functioning (see Carmeli & Schaubroeck, 2006; Hambrick, 1998). Behavioral integration can be applied in other units of analysis such as non-management work groups.

The Theory of Behavioral Integration and ICT Management

Applications of the behavioral integration theory for each one of the ICTM core constructs are presented in Table 1. Collaborative behavior, join decision-making, and information sharing are main constructs not only at the Top Management Team (TMT) level, but also at departmental levels, steering committees, project groups, and development teams. Collaboration behavior and information sharing are key issues for the creation and maintaining of ICT core competence. While fit and balances are required in order to decide how much effort to devote to the development of in-house technological and methodological infrastructures, collaboration behavior and information sharing are required in order to give life to those intentions and in order to make these infrastructures available and comprehensible; they should also be easy to assimilate, adapt, and be used by other members of the ICT department.

In the ICT domain, knowledge elicitation and knowledge sharing has a wide range of aspects and purposes, from the elicitation and sharing of knowledge regarding new tools, new technologies, and new methodologies to the "low" end of knowing how to use, how to operate and how to maintain existing assets, products, tools, methodologies, and so forth.

The Agency Theory

Agency theory addresses two key research issues concerning the principal-agent relationships. The first issue is concerned with the issue that arises when (1) the principal and agent pursue conflicting goals, and (2) the principal faces difficulties in fully monitoring the agent's actions. The second issue concerns risk sharing that arises from the principal and the agent's different attitudes about risk, and, by implication, their likelihood to take different decisions and actions (Eisenhardt, 1989). According to Eisenhardt (1989, p. 58), "Agency theory is directed at the ubiquitous agency relationship, in which one party (the principal) delegates work to another (the agent) who performs that work. Agency theory attempts to describe this relationship using the metaphor of a contract (Jensen & Meckling, 1976)."

Agency theorists view parties as self-interested actors who act to maximize their own benefits. Hence, governance mechanisms have a role in solving the agency problem through (1) outcome-based contracts that are effective in curbing agent opportunism, and (2) information systems by which the principal can verify that the agent does not deceive her or him, and make the agent realize that deceiving is not a real option (Eisenhardt, 1989).

The Agency Theory and ICT Management

Applications of the agency theory for each one of the ICTM core constructs are presented in Table 1. The agency theory gives a profound background to the walls and separations we establish within a system lifecycle, such as the separation between analysis and development phases and the separation between development and maintenance phases. These separations are required in order to avoid conflicting interests, contentions, and contrast. When the developer is also asked to make the analysis, the system analysis will probably be less challenged than a system analysis made by an independent entity. On the other hand, an independent entity may include functionality and features, which may not be cost effective. Therefore, not only balances should be made, but also a deep interest analysis, as recommended according to the agency theory.

The other side of these walls and separations is avoidance of duplications. How can duplications within analysis and design phases be avoided? How can knowledge transfer, capability transfer, and authorization transfer from the development group to the maintenance group can be avoided? How can corresponsibility among the separate groups be ensured?

Concerning the evaluation aspect, issues of modeling standards, reuse standards, coding standards, and QA standards can all be analyzed in light of the engineering aspect, for example, how do we ensure that the analysis model is satisfying, so there won't be any need for additional analysis during the design and the development phases? However, the "agency" caution aspect should also be considered, for example, Is our standard strict enough to lead us to the best choice among all the vendors/solution providers/integrators, who have submitted project proposals?

The Transaction Cost Theory

Transaction cost theory was introduced by Coase (1937) and is concerned with the provisional cost of goods or services obtained through the market rather than providing the goods or services from within the firm.

Transactions cost theorists view all individuals as self-interested and therefore opportunistic; hence, it is important to know with whom you are making a deal, how to obtain a bargain, and what information, bargaining and decisions, and control costs are involved

in a transaction. In essence, market relationships fail under opportunistic conditions (because individuals seek to benefit at the expense of others), asset specificity (because a specific asset is limited to a very narrow set of applications), uncertainty (because not all possible scenarios can be observed and put into a contract), and high frequency (because frequent transactions expose firms to holdup) (see also Williamson, 1975).

The Transaction Cost Theory and ICT Management

Applications of the transaction cost theory for each one of the ICTM core constructs are presented in Table 1. Issues of assets specificity, frequency, uncertainty, and opportunism, which are discussed in the transaction cost theories, are of much importance to ICT management. Traditional issues regarding projects' and assets' total cost of ownership (TCO), and return on investment (ROI) are at the core of transaction cost analysis. Furthermore, the transaction cost theory supports issues such as how to minimize voluntary HR turnovers, how to minimize headhunting, and how to minimize competition over HR. These issues are relevant not only at an organizational level but also at the project level, regardless if the project is an in-house project or developed by any integrator.

How can opportunism on the part of the maintenance group, whether it's an internal or an external group, be avoided? What is the *right* investment regarding QA efforts (i.e., the quality assurance budget) in order to minimize project uncertainty? How can the effectiveness of QA actions be measured? All these questions, as well, can be analyzed in light of the transaction cost theory.

Theory of Images of Organization

Images are powerful tools that shape the ways in which individuals perceive and interact with the world. Individuals' view of the world (people, places, issues) guides their decisions, behaviors, and actions (Morgan, 1986). Organizational images generally incorporate various constructs such as reputation, identity, and construed external image.

According to Fombrun (1996), organizational reputation is held by people inside and outside a company and consists of four interrelated characteristics: credibility, reliability, responsibility, and trustworthiness; however, there is a distinction between insiders' and outsiders' evaluative view of the organization's credibility, reliability, responsibility, and trustworthiness. As such, organizational reputation is concerned with outsiders' (people outside the organization) overall evaluative view of the organization's past and present actions and behaviors. An insider's (organizational members) overall view of what her or his organization represents and stands for is termed as perceived organizational identity (Dutton et al., 1994), while the set of beliefs insiders (organizational members) share about the things their organization represents and stands for is termed as an organization's identity (Albert & Whetten, 1985).

Organizations are concerned with establishing and sustaining a favorable reputation and self-image. Questions such as "What will happen to the organization's reputation and its units if we enter into a contract with a specific player?" and "How does the reputation we attribute to others guide our decisions and actions?" are very important in explaining how and why things are done. The way we believe outsiders think about and view our organizations (i.e., construed external image) shape our attitudes toward it (e.g., identification), which, in turn, results in intentions and actual behaviors (Dutton, Dukerich, & Harquail, 1994). Finally, the organization's identity also shapes patterns of behaviors.

Theory of Images of Organization and ICT Management

How do the images and reputation of others influence our ICT decisions? The reputations of vendors, integrators, outsourcers, and others along with images of technology may shape our view of the world and, thus, influence ICT decisions. Both the top management team and ICT management need to consider how best to choose a particular ICT project (or ask: How would choosing a particular solution for an ICT project affect the organization's identity and reputation?). System lifecycle can be also affected by images (buzzwords, wishful thinking, or technological promises). We may make a decision to upgrade or replace a system not only because of real limitations, but also because of promises and images of new technologies. In addition, ICT departments, suppliers, and integrators have to decide (1) what kind of standards to adopt (e.g., ISO, IEEE, or CMMI), and (2) what kind of project management methodology to adopt (e.g., PMI or Prince)? Applications of the theory of organization images for each one of the ICTM core constructs are presented in Table 2.

DISCUSSION

ICTM scholars face the challenges of overcoming concept redundancy and ambiguity and the need to offer more focused and cohesive insights that are more than "old wine in new bottles". This study was a first attempt to address these challenges by offering ontology of the ICTM field that describes four core constructs—policy, project, assets, and evaluation—and their interrelationships. In addition, the study illuminated how organizational theories contribute to the development and explanation of ICTM theories.

A review of the literature revealed that the classic organizational pyramid, presented in ICT textbooks, lacks a specific functional area delegated to ICT. It was argued that as a first step, the ICT sector should be added to the classical management pyramid. A case was made that as other functional areas (e.g., human resource management) are considered to be independent functional areas, scholars need to view ICT as an important component of the classic management pyramid and realize that the ICTM (the operational, tactical, and strategic levels of ICTM) should be supported by designated systems (i.e., meta information systems).

Table 1. Six blocks for each organization theory

Theory	Key Research and Practitioners Questions			
	Policy	Projects	Assets	Evaluation
1. **The Stakeholder Theory**	How and why do stakeholders affect decision-making on ICTM? How and why do the firm and its ICT department's decisions affect stakeholders? Penalty and rewards policy regarding formal and informal SLA. How should the SLA reflect firm priorities?	What types and features of ICT projects do stakeholders need? Why and how should they respond and balance different needs and expectations?	How do stakeholders expect a firm to maintain ICT assets (e.g., quality, effectiveness) and how should the firm and its ICT department respond to these needs? What are the right criteria for ICT's SLA (formal and informal SLA, for in-house and external users)?	What methods, measures, and standards should stakeholders expect a firm to use when evaluating the ICT/ICTM? How can the firm influence the methods and measures and meet the standards required by stakeholders? How can independent measurement be ensured?
2. **The Theory of Fit**	How can managerial choices create or destroy fit within a system and among its parts? How can fit between business objectives and ICT projects be ensured? Cost/Benefits of projects, assets, and measurements. How much effort should be invested in the development of in-house ICT infrastructures?	How do ICT projects augment and strengthen other ICT projects? How does complex interdependency influence, change, and sustain ICT projects? "Doing the Right Project" – Fit/Balances regarding: Resources/Functionality. Risk/Advantage Resources/Time to Market	How can fit among different types of ICT assets and infrastructures be created? What is the role of fit in creating complexity and flexibility in the management of ICT assets? "Doing the Product Right" – Fits of Maintainability, Portability, Scalability, Reusability.	How can complementarities in the evaluation approaches in ICTM be created? What to measure? How to measure? Measure's influence?
3. **The Theory of Behavioral Integration**	How do processes within a top management team (TMT) affect decision-making? How do processes within ICT group levels, steering committees, and project groups affect decision-making? How can conflict resolution mechanisms be created?	How does behavioral integration at TMT and ICT group levels and the interactions between them determine the success of ICT projects? How can information sharing and collaborative behavior concerning new tools, new technologies, and new methodologies be created?	How does behavioral integration at top management team and ICT group levels and the interactions between them determine the success of ICT assets? Information sharing and collaborative behavior concerning how to use, how to operate, and how to maintain existing assets, products, tools, and methodologies.	How can behaviorally integrated TMT and ICT groups create effective evaluation processes? Measures for knowledge elicitation, knowledge sharing, knowledge usability.

Table 1. continued

Theory	Key Research and Practitioners Questions			
	Policy	**Projects**	**Assets**	**Evaluation**
4. **The Agency Theory**	How do principal-agent relationships affect ICTM? What kinds of separations/ differentiations/distinctions are required? How can duplications be avoided without giving up required separations? How can coresponsibility among the different groups be ensured?	How do principal-agent relationships determine the success of ICT projects? How can maintenance considerations within analysis and development stages be ensured? How can duplications among analysis and design stages be avoided?	How do principal-agent relationships (TMT and ICT groups; owners and TMT/ ICT groups) determine the success of ICT assets? How can knowledge, capability, and authorization transfer from development group to the maintaining group be ensured?	How can evaluation systems reduce and curb principal/agent conflicts? Modeling standards. Reuse standards. Coding standards. QA standards.
5. **Transaction Cost Theory**	With whom and how can bargains be made? How can voluntary HR turnovers /headhunting and competition over HR be minimized? What are the real ROI and TCO of projects and assets?	How can asset specificities be created? How can HR turnover during lifetime be minimized? What is considered to be the right investment in QA in order to minimize project-product uncertainty?	How can difficulties such as opportunism, specificity, uncertainty, and high frequency in ICT assets be overcome? How can the opportunism of the maintenance group (whether it is an internal or an external group) be avoided?	How can an effective evaluation system to reduce transaction costs be created? How can real TCO be estimated and measured? How can QA effectiveness be measured?
6. **Theory of images of organization**	How can the reputations of others affect our decisions? How do organizational identity and construed external image shape our actions? How do images of the world shape our expectations?	How do the reputations of vendors, implementers, and technologies influence our decisions concerning ICT projects? How does choosing particular ICT projects affect the organization's identity and reputation?	How do outsourcers' reputations shape our management of ICT assets? How do analysts' and institutions' reputations shape ICT lifecycle?	How do the reputations of institutions that develop standards, evaluation criteria, and methodologies influence ICT assessment approach, adoption of QA standards, and adoption of project management methodologies?

The current study contributes to the ICTM field by offering a theoretical basis for ICTM ontology. It defined four constructs and an interface between organizational theories and each one of the identified constructs. Six key organizational theories and their implications for the field of ICTM were introduced. Clearly, there are many theories that were not discussed here that can be used to explain phenomena in the ICTM field. Further research should explore additional organizational theories (e.g., organization learning) and the way in which these theories contribute to the development and explanation of ICTM theories. Nevertheless, the theories presented in this study are a useful platform that raises many unresolved research questions. Using structures offered by this study can further develop the ICTM field. For example, we know that images of organizations and their products play a role in the management of ICT, but this point has received very little attention and has yet to be examined in a systematic way. The current study advanced the field by providing an ontology that described four core constructs and explained how organizational theories could be used to contribute to main subjects of inquiry in the field of ICTM.

The ontology this study offers is not without limitations. *Ontology* describes the constructs that constitute the domain and the relationships between those constructs. Our review of the literature resulted in a definition of four constructs. It may be that other constructs should be incorporated into this ontology. Clearly, the risk in doing so is concept redundancy. Hence, researchers first need to devote more effort towards reaching a common definition of which constructs constitute the ICTM domain. A second step would be to thoroughly explore the relationships between those constructs and the ways in which we build theories that are novel, interesting, and useful.

REFERENCES

Albert, S., & Whetten, D.A. (1985). Organizational identity. In L.L. Cummings & B.M. Staw (Eds.), *Research in organizational behavior, 7* (pp. 263-295). Greenwich, CT: JAI Press.

Antoniou, G., & Kehagias, A. (2000). A note on the refinement of ontologies. *International Journal of Intelligent Systems, 15*(7), 623-632.

Barney, J.B. (1991). Firm resources and sustained competitive advantage. *Journal of Management, 17*(1), 99-120.

Bennett, K.H., & Rajlich, V. (2000). Software maintenance and evolution: A roadmap. *ICSE - Future of SE Track*, 73-87.

Carmeli, A., & Schaubroeck, J. (2006). Top management team behavioral integration, decision quality, and organizational decline. *The Leadership Quarterly, 17*(5), 441-453.

Coase, R.H. (1937). The nature of the firm. *Economica, 4*, 386-405.

Connolly, T., Conlon, E.J., & Deutsch, S.J. (1980, April). Organizational effectiveness: A multiple-constituency approach. *Academy of Management Review, 5*(2), 211-217.

Daft, R.L. (1995). *Organization theory and design* (5th ed.). Minneapolis, MN: West Publishing.

Doublait, S. (1997). Standard reuse practices: Many myths vs. a reality. *Standard View, 5*(2), 84-91.

Dutton, J.E., Dukerich, J.M., & Harquail, C.V. (1994). Organizational images and member identification. *Administrative Science Quarterly, 39*, 239-263.

Eisenhardt, K.M. (1989). Agency theory: An assessment and review. *Academy of Management Review, 14*, 57-74.

Etzioni, A. (1964). *Modern organizations.* Englewood Cliffs, NJ: Prentice-Hall.

Fombrun, C.J. (1996). *Reputation: Realizing value from the corporate image.* Boston: Harvard Business School Press.

Grant, R.M. (1991). The resource-based theory of competitive advantage: Implications for strategy formulation. *California Management Review, 33,* 114-133.

Gregor, S. (2002). A theory of theories in information systems. In S. Gregor & D. Hart (Eds.), *Information systems foundations: Building the theoretical base* (pp. 1-20). Canberra, Australia: Australian National University.

Guarino, N. (1998). Formal ontology and information systems. In N. Guarino (Ed.), *Formal ontology in information systems* (pp. 3-15). Amsterdam: IOS Press.

Hambrick, D.C. (1994). Top management groups: A conceptual integration and reconsideration of the "team" label. In B.M. Staw & L.L. Cummings (Eds.), *Research in organizational behavior* (pp. 171-214). Greenwich, CT: JAI Press.

Hambrick, D.C. (1998). Corporate coherence and the top management team. In D.C. Hambrick, D.A. Nadler, & M.L. Tushman (Eds.), *Navigating change: How CEOs, top teams, and boards steer transformation* (pp. 123-140). Boston: Harvard Business School Press.

Hordijk, W., Linos, P., Molterer, S., Paech, B., & Salzmann, C. (1999). Maintainable systems with a business object approach. *Annals of Software Engineering, 9,* 273-292.

Jensen, M.C., & Meckling, W.H. (1976). Theory of the firm: Managerial behavior, agency costs, and ownership structure. *Journal of Financial Economics, 3,* 303-360.

Kayed, A., & Colomb, R.M. (2005). Using BWW model to evaluate building ontologies in CGs formalism. *Information Systems, 30*(5), 379-398.

Khandwalla, P.N. (1973). A viable and effective organizational designs of firms. *Academy of Management Journal, 16* (3), 481-495.

Kitchenham, B.A., Travassos, G.H., von Mayrhauser, A., Niessink, F., Schneidewind, N.F., Singer, J., et al.

(1999). *Journal of Software Maintenance: Research and Practice, 11*(6), 365-389.

Laudon K.C., & Laudon, J.P. (2004). *Management information systems: Managing the digital firm* (8th ed.). Upper Saddle River, NJ: Prentice-Hall.

Lawrence, B.S. (1997). The black box of organizational demography. *Organization Science, 8*(1), 1-22.

Levinthal, D.A. (1997). Adaptation on rugged landscapes. *Management Science, 43,* 934-950.

Mohr, L.B. (1973, June). The concept of organizational goal. *The American Political Science Review, 67*(2), 470-481.

Morgan, G. (1986). *Images of organization.* Newbury Park, CA: Sage Publications.

Nadler, D.A., & Tushman, M.L. (1997). *Competing by design: The power of organizational architecture.* New York: Oxford University Press.

Pelled, L.H., Eisenhardt, K.M., & Xin, K.R. (1999). Exploring the black box: An analysis of work group diversity, conflict and performance. *Administrative Science Quarterly, 44,* 1-28.

Perrow, C. (1970). *Organizational analysis: A sociological view.* Belmot, CA: Brook/Cole Publishing Company and London: Tavistock.

Peteraf, M.A. (1993). The cornerstones of competitive advantage: A resource-based view. *Strategic Management Journal, 14,* 179-191.

Pettigrew, A.M. (1992). On studying managerial elites. *Strategic Management Journal, 13,* 163-182.

Porter, M.E. (1996, November-December). What is strategy. *Harvard Business Review,* 61-78.

Rivkin, J.W. (2000). Imitation of complex strategies. *Management Science, 43,* 934-950.

Rivkin J.W., & Siggelkow N. (2003). Balancing search and stability: Interdependencies among elements of organizational design. *Management Science, 49*(3), 290-311.

Siggelkow, N. (2002a). Evolution toward fit. *Administrative Science Quarterly*, *47*(1), 125-159.

Siggelkow, N. (2002b). Misperceiving interactions among complements and substitutes: Organizational consequences. *Management Science*, *48*(7), 900-916.

Siggelkow, N. (2003). Change in the presence of fit: The rise, the fall, and the renaissance of Liz Claiborne. *Academy of Management Journal*, *44*(4), 838-857.

Smith, K.G., Smith, K.A., Olian, J.D., Sims, H.P., O'Bannon, D.P., & Scully, J.A. (1994). Top management team demography and process: The role of social integration and communication. *Administrative Science Quarterly*, *39*, 412-438.

Thompson, A.A., & Strickland, A.J. (2003). *Strategic management: Concepts and cases* (13th ed.). McGraw-Hill/Irwin.

Weick, K.E. (1976). Educational organizations as loosely coupled systems. *Administrative Science Quarterly*, *21*, 1-19.

Williamson, O. (1975). *Markets and hierarchies: Analysis and antitrust implications*. New York: Free Press.

Yuchtman, E., & Seashore, S.E. (1967). A system resource approach to organizational effectiveness. *American Sociological Review, 32*(6), 891-903.

Chapter X
KnowledgeEco:
An Ontology of Organizational Memory

Hadas Weinberger
Holon Institute of Technology, Israel

Dov Te'eni
Tel-Aviv University, Israel

Ariel J. Frank
Bar-Ilan University, Israel

ABSTRACT

This chapter presents KnowledgeEco, a domain ontology for organizational memory (OM). Based on extant theories of the domain, KnowledgeEco defines static and dynamic aspects of OM as a basis for formulating an evaluation framework, which can be used by organizations irrespective of their specific field. A key innovation in the KnowledgeEco ontology is the introduction of the concept of structural memory (SM). SM aggregates Type, which defines types of organizational memory, and Component, which aggregates Content (i.e., Knowledge Resource and Meta-Knowledge) and Means (i.e., Agent and Process) that manage the SM content. We demonstrate the considerations of ontology conceptualization in two stages of developing KnowledgeEco. The first is analysis and structuring of the ontology and the second is the assessment of its conceptual coverage. For researchers, KnowledgeEco provides a model that can be used in the evaluation of OM. For practitioners, the ontology offers a unified framework of objects and processes that need to be considered in the design of OM.

INTRODUCTION

This chapter presents KnowledgeEco, a domain ontology for organizational memory (OM). We base our ontology on the interdisciplinary literature on OM. The ontology includes static and dynamic aspects of OM. The first represents the concepts that compose an OM, and the latter represents a spectrum of tasks and challenges rooted in extant theories of the domain. The KnowledgeEco ontology covers theoretical and practical aspects, human and technology dimensions, as well as operational and strategic viewpoints.

Since "emphasis has shifted from static to an active interpretation of memory" (Maier, Hadrich, & Peinl, 2005, p. 33), OM is a critical aspect of implementing knowledge management in learning organizations (Alavi & Leidner, 2001; Argrys & Schon, 1978; Dieng, Corby, Gibon, & Ribiere, 1999; Jennex & Olfman, 2004; Lehner & Maier, 2000; Nevo & Wand, 2004; Wijnhoven, 1999). In their influential review, Walsh and Ungson (1991) observed that OM is designed to enable "stored information from an organization history that can be brought to bear on present decisions" (p. 61). Stein and Zwass (1995) extend this work by stressing the role of Information Systems (IS) as an integral part of OM. Other much cited publications refer to OM structure (Abecker, Bernardi, Hinkelman, Kuhn, & Sintek, 1998; Edington, Choi, Hensen, Raghu, & Vinze, 2004; Walsh & Ungson, 1991), OM processes (Davenport & Prusak, 1998; Dieng et al., 1999; Marcus, 2001; O'Leary, 1998), OM socialization tactics (Anand, Mantz, & Glick, 1998), and OM content (Holsapple & Joshi, 2004; Wijnhoven, 1998).

Fortunately, the literature of the OM domain is a rich resource, which takes into account its various perspectives. Unfortunately, the OM literature lacks a structured approach and also lacks a comprehensive framework for the evaluation of OM. Indeed, researchers have called for systematic, replicable, and theoretically-based evaluation of systems and practices for managing knowledge (King & Ko, 2001; Zhang & Zhao, 2006). The need for evaluation is obvious, particularly considering enterprise's current interest in domain-specific models that allow for representation of dynamic aspects. This implies the need to specify potential means and methods for evaluation; for instance, one that is based on a descriptive and prescriptive framework, thus providing a description of a domain and design guidelines (Frank, 2007).

In order to provide the IS community with a basis for a new management tool for OM, there is a need for an ontology and an evaluation methodology. Against this background, the goal set for this research is two-fold. On one hand we introduce KnowledgeEco ontology as a prescriptive and comprehensive representation of OM, and on the other hand we suggest KnowledgeEco as a road map that yields a methodology to inform OM design and guide its evaluation. Our treatment of OM creates a unified framework of the structure, content, and means, as well as behavioral and social constraints, to form an evaluation framework that specifies the characteristics of OM (Holsapple & Joshi, 2004), based on domain ontology. For researchers, the ontology provides a model that can be used in evaluation of OM and learning processes in organizations. For practitioners, it offers a unified perspective on concepts and processes that need be considered in the design of OM.

The KnowledgeEco ontology is a generic account of the entities and processes of the OM domain, as well as their relationships. A key innovation in our proposed ontology is the introduction of the concept of structural memory[1] (SM), which is an abstraction of several types of memory and includes diverse knowledge structures as well as the means required to manage the knowledge (Figure 1).

Our approach to developing KnowledgeEco follows the design science paradigm (Havner, March, Park, & Ram, 2004). March and Smith (1995) identified two design processes and four design artifacts specified by design-science research in IS. The processes are *build* and *evaluate*, and the artifacts are constructs, models, methods, and instantiations. Of the research activities outlined in this framework, this chapter covers *build* (i.e., this research is limited to building of a model, rather than an IT artifact) and *evaluate*, of an artifact, also using techniques mentioned by March and Smith. For the research outputs, this chapter is about a model (i.e., an ontology), which informs a methodology (i.e., for evaluation). The latter paves the way for instantiation of the model.

The next section describes the KnowledgeEco ontology. The section following outlines the ontology development methodology and presents the natural language analysis techniques applied to the ontology conceptualization and modeling. This is followed

Figure 1. KnowledgeEco: An upper-level view of the ontology

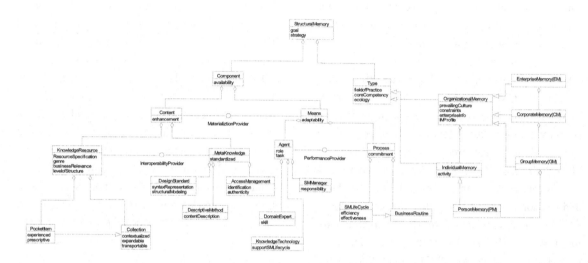

by a discussion of ontology assessment based on the completeness criteria and the relevance of KnowledgeEco to practice. The chapter concludes with a discussion of the theoretical and practical contributions to the field.

KNOWLEDGEECO: ONTOLOGY FOR THE DOMAIN OF OM

Ontologies have been shown to be effective in formalizing problems to create a coherent domain model (Gruber, 1995; Guarino, 1997). In IS, ontologies were applied for enterprise modeling (Uschold & Gruninger, 1996) and creation of business models (Osterwalder, Pigneur, & Tucci, 2005), for example, as a structural and conceptual part of a multiple perspective business interaction (Frank, 1999). In knowledge management, ontologies were applied in knowledge reuse (Abecker et al., 1998; Abecker, Bernardi, & van Elst, 2003; Edington et al., 2004; Wijenhoven, 2003), in specific domains (Abou-Zeid, 2005; Jurisica, Mylopoulos, & Yu, 2004), and as general-purpose, descriptive frameworks (Holsapple & Joshi, 2004).

Ontology development is the art of weaving together independent semantic networks into a unified structure (Frank, 1999; Uschold & Gruninger, 1996) for the goal of representing reality (Wand, Monarchi, Parsons, & Woo, 1995). Ontology developers aim at balancing the ontological cognitive and methodological aspects – the knowledge of the domain and its semantics (McGuiness, 2002; Weinberger & Frank, 2006). Usually this also entails a certain world view of the ontology developers (Fridman Noy & McGuiness, 2001).

Our ontology was developed using UML as a modeling language (Booch, Rumbaugh, & Jacobson, 1999), an OMG standard that is MOF (meta-object facility) compliant, whose underlying metamodel is thus appropriate for achieving integration not only across related domains, but also across various business and enterprise models. UML integrates notation and graphics conventions, which are a tribute to potential end-users in organizations. Herein we use several notational conventions. Class diagrams are used for representation of entities and relationships in the logical view and object diagrams for representation of processes, while in the use case view we employ use case diagrams. Class diagrams also use relationships (i.e., generalization and aggregation) and interface (i.e., indicated as a lollipop) notation.

KnowledgeEco in Detail

KnowledgeEco (Figure 1) is described with accompanying explanations that reflect the decision processes used in conceptualizing this ontology. The description of the ontology follows four core classes. We commence with the introduction of Structural Memory class, and the Type class, followed by introducing Component. Next we elaborate on issues related to processes and activities essential to the evolution of memory in organizations via the concept of SM Lifecycle.

Structural Memory and Type

SM, which is the top entity of the ontology, is defined thus: *SM is an abstract class that aggregates two interrelated classes: Type (Individual Memory and Organizational Memory) and Component (Content and Means) to enable organizational learning processes. Each Type is realized by a set of components.*

The attributes of the SM class are goal (i.e., a statement that defines the ideal outcomes expected from the SM) and strategy. The value assigned to each of these attributes (e.g., <set of goals>) enables a real world organization to express its unique value properties.

The aggregation relationship (Figure 1) indicates that both Type and Component are required in any SM. Type differentiates SMs that represent Individual Memory, (e.g., Person Memory), from those that represent Organizational Memory, (e.g., Group Memory). Component defines the SM Content and Means required for a particular Type.

Type enables different characterizations for individual and organizational memories (Ackerman, 1998; Walsh & Ungson, 1991). Type can represent the existence of diverse interpretations held by different actors as well as those shared explicitly by groups of actors (Anand et al., 1998; Nevo & Wand,

2004). Using the concrete subclasses of Type, we distinguish between the concepts of Group Memory, which serves an informal or formal group working on a common issue or project, Corporate Memory, which serves various actors across the organization, and Enterprise Memory, which serves actors across interrelated organizations. Our definition of Type denotes these observations:

Type is an abstract class used to define individual and organizational memory structures.

The attributes of Type are field of practice, core competency, and ecology. The attributes assigned to Organizational Memory refer to the plural aspect and include prevailing culture, constraints, IM profile, and other relevant enterprise information. The latter is usually described also by other ontologies dedicated to enterprise models (Uschold & Gruninger, 1996). Thus, Type can represent the existence and idiosyncrasies of multiple views (Boland, Tenkasi & Te'eni, 1994). Individual Memory is described using the activity attribute, which defines areas of interest in which it specializes.

Type underscores the importance of individual-organizational interaction, as emphasized throughout the literature (Argrys & Schon, 1978; Mullaholand, Zdeahal, Domingue, & Hatal, 2001; Orlikowski, 2002), which requires methods that enable knowledge diffusion and elaboration (King & Ko, 2001). For example, the method "transfer" denotes the possibility of individual-level memory becoming part of another SM through socialization and externalization, and the method "include" denotes the possibility of organizational-level memory evolving through combination and internalization (Nonaka & Takeuchi, 1995).

Component

Following Wijenhoven (1998), OM components can be classified as Content (i.e., Knowledge Resource and Meta-knowledge) and Means (i.e., Agent and Process). Any component should be made available to an actor; hence it has an attribute of availability. Our definition of Component denotes these observations.

Table 1. Attributes assigned to component and subclasses

Class	Attribute	Description
Component	availability <set-of keywords>	The communication mechanism by which a component can be reached by an agent.
Content	enhancement <text>	The contribution of content to the SM.
Knowledge Resource	resource Specification <set-of keywords>	A set of elements designed to describe Knowledge Resource at the metadata level (e.g., Dublin Core).
	genre <set-of genres>	The Knowledge Resource genre being either: (1) procedural (skill based), which usually is dynamic (also known as "know-how"), and (2) declarative (fact) knowledge which usually is static (also known as "know-what"). Declarative knowledge can be either semantic (established by cultural consensus) or episodic (experienced based).
	business Relevance <text>	classification of a Knowledge Resource according to specific business relevance (e.g., operating units, projects or actions).
	level of Structure <set-of keywords>	classification of a Knowledge Resource by its codification, i.e., highly structured (as in database), semi-structured (e.g., metadata plus free text), unstructured (free text) or tacit (in people minds).
Meta-Knowledge	standardized <set-of standards>	Standardization of applied meta-knowledge.
Pocket Item	experienced <text>	The origin of the pocket item.
	prescriptive <Boolean>	The context of pocket item use.
Collection	contextualized <key-words>	The semantics of the collection element. This is achieved using descriptive meta-knowledge.
	expandable <text>	Extension channels for the collection item. This is gained as consequence of sharing among peers.
	transportable <key-words>	The possible sharing mechanisms. This should be defined in accordance with users' preferences.
Means	adaptability <text>	Agents and processes should be able to modify, change, and fit their involvement according to changing SM goals.
Agent	role <set-of keywords>	The collection of responsibilities for an agent involved in SM lifecycle.
	task <text>	The collection of activities for an agent.
Process	commitment <text>	The nature of an activity for achieving a goal.

Component is an abstract class that aggregates two classes: Contents and Means of the SM to a unified view of the static and the dynamic aspects of SM.

The relative significance of these classes is reinforced by the semantics of their attributes. For instance, as indicated in Table 1 (i.e., Table 1[2] is a subset of classes and their attributes, which are dealt with in our text), attributes assigned to Knowledge Resource are designed to carry the information that is relevant for using, sharing and managing the specific resource—regardless of its kind. Accordingly, The intuitive aspect is a lead motive when specifying Pocket Item, while in the classification of Collection, the emphasis is on the added value gained through the manipulation of these products, such as following some kind of an intervention or manipulation (i.e., of a Domain Agent) denoting the assignment and deployment of metaknowledge to enable knowledge sharing and reuse.

Knowledge Resource details kinds that can be found in varied enterprises, such as Collection (e.g., Best Practice, FAQ, Lesson Learned, Publication, Guide) and Pocket Item (e.g., Heuristic, Idea, Story, Insight). Attributes assigned to Pocket Item uniquely emphasize its origin in individual tacit knowledge (e.g., experienced and prescriptive), whereas entities that are part of the Collection class are associated with explicit knowledge (e.g., contextualized, expandable, and transportable). As exhibited in the use of the generalization relationship, the unified view of these classes expresses an integrated view of knowledge.

Figure 1 also illustrates the relationships between entities that are part of Means, using the aggregation relationship. The three agents are SM Manager and Domain Expert (can be human or an intelligent agent), and Knowledge Technology, described using the role and task attributes. While the Domain Expert is uniquely identified using the skill attribute, the SM Manager was assigned the responsibility attribute. There are several typologies that address the classification of Knowledge Technology (O'Leary, 1998; Tiwana, 2001), which leads to the definition of three subclasses: Resource Discovery (e.g., data mining, data analysis, and search engines), Sharing and Collaboration (e.g., content management system, e-learning, and collaboration), and Knowledge Repository (e.g., document repository, online repository, and data warehouse), detailed in (Weinberger, 2004) as well as subclasses of other entities represented in Figure 1.

Interdependencies between subclasses are represented using the UML interface notation and three such interfaces are used in Component. The Interoperability-provider interface indicates that Knowledge Resource depends on Meta-Knowledge to encourage knowledge contextualization. Meta-Knowledge governs access management, structural design, and knowledge description. The Performance-provider interface indicates that Agent is designed to support the execution of Process. The Materialization-provider interface indicates the interrelation between the two aspects of Component: Content and Means, that is, where the latter supports the operation of the former.

The Dynamic Aspect: SM Lifecycle

We assume knowledge in organizations has to be represented as dynamic entities in the sense that knowledge continuously evolves in order to be useful, so as to support action and consequently increase performance (Ackerman, 1998; King, 2006; Lenhenr & Maier, 2000; Verkasalo & Lappalainen, 1998; Wijenhoven, 1998). The SM must therefore be designed to support evolution. Following Siemienuich and Sinclair (1999), and as elaborated in Te'eni and Weinberger (2000), we borrow the idea of systems development life cycle and adapt it to the specification of SM development and application. As the development of SM Means and the evolution of SM Content are intricately interwoven, we represent it all in a single SM Lifecycle, as part of the KnowledgeEco ontology.

SM Lifecycle (Figure 2) evolves from requirements specification to achieve specific goals that are important to the organization, and continues with analysis, design, and construction. The SM Lifecycle supports the stages of evolution and evaluation to support the

Figure 2. SM lifecycle in KnowledgeEco

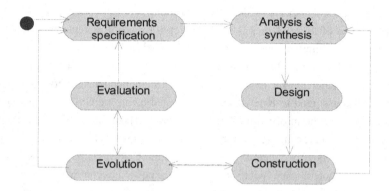

maintenance, growth, and adaptation of SM to both evolving knowledge and changing conditions, which are critical to the support of organizational learning. Evaluation of SM is important in order to control and guide evolution (Abecker et al., 1998; Ackerman, 1998). An inflexible SM repository will stifle knowledge development. Evaluation of SM is important in order to control and guide evolution (Abecker et al., 1998; Ackerman, 1998). SM Lifecycle is defined thus: *SM Lifecycle is an abstract class which defines the processes required for the development and evolvement of memory types in an organization.*

In our research we have not yet evaluated the impact of SM on organizational performance. Nevertheless, we believe that, whenever measured, the impact should be represented in the SM. We therefore note, but do not expand on, the SM Lifecycle attributes of efficiency and effectiveness. While the former attribute defines the appropriateness of SM Lifecycle to enabling execution of agent's tasks, the latter defines the usability of SM Lifecycle to organizational goals and strategy.

DEVELOPMENT METHODOLOGY

Ontologies include a detailed description of concepts that map into ontological constructs: entities, their instances, attributes, methods, and relationships among entities (Chandrasekaran, Josephson, & Benjamines, 1999; Fridman Noy & McGuiness, 2001). The completeness of an ontology is dependent on the correct mapping of ontological concepts to ontological constructs (Wand et al., 1995).

In recent years, several methodologies were reported for ontology development, sometimes with relation to a specific tool (Gomez-Perez, Fernandez, & Corcho, 2004). While the choice of a specification language depends on several factors, that is, is a function of relevancy, the use of multiple methodologies contributes to the research rigor (Palvia, Mao, Salam, & Soliman, 2003). In the approach taken here, several ontology development methodologies were compiled and applied to the KnowledgeEco research (Fernandez, Gomez-Perez, & Sierra, 1999; Gomez-Perez, Fernandez, & De Vincento, 1996; Uschold & Gruninger, 1996).

The KnowledgeEco ontology was developed in five iterative steps: (1) specification – following an initial framework; (2) knowledge acquisition – following an exhaustive, though maybe not always inclusive, literature review (Te'eni & Weinberger, 2000); (3) analysis and knowledge structuring – integrating natural language analysis techniques and software standards; (4) documentation – using UML diagrams, and semi-formal natural language description (i.e., using tables for the description of classes which comprise the ontology); and (5) assessment (Weinberger & Frank, 2006).

Using the classification introduced by (Palvia et al., 2003, p. 5), throughout the execution of these steps we used commentary and conceptual models, library research and literature analysis, as well as qualitative research.

In implementing these steps we adhered to three objectives:

1. Need for a prescriptive, rather than the common descriptive definition of entities and their interrelations (Holsapple & Joshi, 2004)
2. An integration of people and information systems in OM, as advocated by Stein and Zwass (1995) and demonstrated by Ackerman (1996)
3. A hierarchical representation of both static and dynamic aspects of OM. This is because memory in organizations evolves through a series of processes (Nonaka & Takeuchi, 1995; Stein & Zwass, 1995)

It is beyond the scope of this chapter (i.e., for lack of space), to fully describe the ontology engineering effort. We, however, specifically address two complementary processes: analysis and structuring, and evaluation. The former concerns the classification of the concepts acquired from the literature and their mapping to ontological constructs. The latter process tests the results of the former. Herein, we describe seven techniques that guide the ontology analyst confronting a need to represent a hierarchical concept tree based on natural language analysis. Each technique is discussed from the perspective of knowledge structuring and examples from the KnowledgeEco ontology are used to illustrate its application.

Managing Ontological Constructs

The ultimate goal for developing an ontology is to establish its pragmatics. To this end, the semantics of ontology representation should be considered alongside structural and syntactical constraints. Managing ontological constructs entails the analysis of the literature to form a glossary of terms, and, subsequently, the classification of the selected terms and their mapping to ontological constructs. This process is also referred to as conceptualization (Fernandez et al., 1999). We considered ontology design techniques suggested by Gruber (1995), as well as analysis techniques suggested by (Gomez-Perez, 1995; Guarino, 1997; Guarino, Carrara, & Giaretta, 1994), and an analysis methodology proposed by (Fernandez et al., 1999). We demonstrate the application of these techniques for the purpose of natural language analysis.

There are three steps in the conceptualization process applied for each technique. First, we deconstruct the analysis process, especially with respect to syntax (i.e., linguistic patterns and relationships), structure (i.e., how parts are related), and semantics (i.e., refers to aspects of meaning). Second and third, we identify the entities and map them to ontological constructs. Usually each of the techniques discussed here was used in response to a distinct representation goal, and in the context of other techniques. Table 2 introduces these seven techniques, in general, and particularly in view of their application in our case. In addition, examples from the KnowledgeEco ontology are used to illustrate its application.

The analysis process supports the iterative and incremental process of ontology conceptualization by suggesting various techniques to consider the syntax (e.g., *Differentiating between abstract and concrete concepts, and between objects and processes*, and *differentiating entities from attributes*), and the structure (e.g., *Management of hierarchies*) of the ontology, alongside its semantics (*Context-specific analysis of concepts*) for the purpose of establishing meaning through representation. Lastly, the technique of *Definition of attributes' value* allows for particular organizations to define their own goals and constraints (i.e., defined in the ontology as attributes) and set them as values of the defined attributes. This indicates that not only does the ontology represent the generic case of OM, it is also attentive to the individual organization business model (i.e., aiming at instantiation of the model).

Table 2. Natural language analysis techniques and their application

Technique	Application	Reference
1. Whole part and classified or non- classified concept distinction	This technique was used to identify upper-level ontological entities (Te'eni & Weinberger, 2000), and the identification and mapping of sub concepts, as well as the modeling of domain specific typologies (e.g., the classification of knowledge technology and meta-knowledge, for which the literature suggests a spectrum of classifications).	Guarino, 1997; Uschold & Gruninger, 1996
2. Observing related terms	This technique was used for negotiating the interdisciplinary literature of OM, which is prone to the use of concepts with alternate naming. Specifically it motivated higher-order classification distinctions, such as Type and subclasses.	Fernandez et al., 1999
3. Context specific analysis of concepts	Applying this technique motivated the coining of the SM concept and for associating conceptually related classes, such as Knowledge Resource and Meta-Knowledge, and Processes and Agents.	Frank, 1999; Fridman Noy & McGuiness, 2001; Guarino, 1997
4. Differentiating between abstract and concrete concepts, and between objects and processes	Applying this technique reinforced context-dependent observations, paving the way to modeling static and dynamic aspects and differentiating between common and individual phenomena.	Gruber, 1995; Gruninger & Fox, 1995
5. Managing classification hierarchy	This technique was used to establish coherency and avoid multiple inheritance while balancing other ontological distinctions.	Fridman Noy & McGuiness, 2001
6. Distinguishing between entities and attributes	Applying this technique serves to balance between the concepts, which are part of the ontological constructs and attributes for which organization specific values can be assigned.	Fernandez et al., 1999
7. Definition of attributes' value	An attribute value encourages relevancy of the ontology for practice. Here, different kinds of values are assigned to attributes, as guidelines for organizations.	Weinberger, 2004

Evaluation of Conceptual Coverage

Since we aim for organizations to utilize Knowledg-eEco as a management tool designed to guide OM design and evaluation, ontology evaluation should address its conceptual coverage (Gomez-Perez, 2003). Models, methods, and word constructs that are represented in a particular way should be evaluated using an appropriate method.

Much like the IS evaluation approach, Gomez-Perez (2003) draws a distinction between two main evaluation dimensions: content evaluation and ontology technology evaluation. Herein, we focus on the former one. Content evaluation is mostly appropriate for the evaluation of domain ontology (Fridman Noy & Hafner, 1997). The validation of KnowledgeEco ontology was focused on the assessment of conceptual coverage using the completeness criteria (Gomez-Perez, 1995). *Completeness* answers the question: "Does the ontology build a comprehensive description of the domain" (Fridman Noy & Hafner, p. 2). This is considering not only the elements (e.g., entities and relationships) of the ontology, but also the meaning they convey. On one hand, the validation process has to answer for the correctness of the classification, in terms of management of hierarchy and context specific analysis of concepts. On the other hand, through validation, one can assess the correctness of the classification with relation to the role of the ontology, that is, the representation of the domain.

To assess the completeness of KnowledgeEco, we follow a theoretical framework based on the one suggested by Zachman (1987) for evaluation of information systems. This framework combines two dimensions of representation. The first suggests different views of the system and the second distinguishes six foci of the system used to classify major characteristics of it depicted by six questions: What, How, Where, Who, When, and Why. Our treatment of the ontology evaluation process capitalizes on these six foci to assess the aim of obtaining representation of the domain, which answers the goals defined for the ontology. Particularly, it is intended to assess the mapping of concepts of previous theories to ontological constructs. Table 3

Table 3. Evaluation of completeness

Evaluation criteria	Focus	Question	Question	Representation
Completeness	Data	What	Has the ontology captured (i.e, represents as entities, attributes or methods) the major aspects of OM as described in the literaure?	A bidimensional view of Type and Component aggregated using the new concept of SM, as part of a classification which distinguishes between concrete and abstract levels.
	Function	How	Does the ontology represent processes referenced in previous theories of the domain?	Integrative representation of the static and dynamic view of OM to include an explicit representation of the SM Lifecycle.
	Network	Where	Does the ontology enable the interactions required for knowledge-intensive processes (i.e., a framework for networking)?	Using subclasses of Type, where for each individual- or organizational-level type there exists a dimension of Component. The realization of concrete level SMs facilitates the interaction between Types.
	People	Who	Does the ontology include a defintion of agents and roles assigned to these agents?	Defining agents whose responsibility is to perform a series of tasks. These tasks realize KM and organizational learning.
	Time	When	Does the ontology reflect the management of a sequence of events?	Iterative lifecycle schedules activities, which in turn are assigned to agents' methods.
	Motivation	Why	Does the ontology define the motivation to perfrom these tasks?	A spectrum of attributes allowing for the definition of an attribute value (i.e., allowing also for the definition of a goal specific to an instantiation of the ontology).

describes the six foci and the questions they posit, as well as the ontological deliverable established using each view, as also discussed below.

The *What* question is applied to the Data focus. Based on this technique, we note the significance of two higer-level ontological decisions: (1) the bi-dimensional view of Component and Type, and (2) the distinction between abstract and concrete ontological levels. The first paves the way for the representation of Component and subclasses for each SM Type, and the second denotes our wolrd view (i.e., differentiating between that which should exist in any organization, and its possible kinds).

The *How* question is applied to the Function focus. It is primarily reflected by the SM Lifecycle, designed to direct the enterprise towards a structured approach in the evolution and evaluation of OM. Also, this approach can form a basis for further study of exisiting theories of business interaction. Tied to the notion of the *Where* question that is applied to the Network focus, is the representation of Means, designed to realize the possibilities exhibited in the Function view.

The *Who* question is applied to the People focus. Its aim is to target lower ontological levels in order to establishe a more profound understanding of the former observations (e.g., the defintion of human and computerized agents and their role in realizing events declared as part of the dynamic view of the ontology). Complementary to the former is the Time focus examined using the *When* question. As part of the definition and representation of processes, the ontology further outlines the scheduling of events using the detailed description of each of the SM Lifecycle stages (Figure 2). Lastly, the *Why* question, which explores the Motivation focus, exposes that the ontology was desgined to define a spectrum of stategic goals, which motivate an OM.

RELEVANCE TO PRACTICE

From a design science perspective, the success of a model depends on its relevance to practice. Not only does KnowledgeEco introduce a model of the domain

of OM, there is in the ontology to inform the design of the KnowledgeEco ontology-based methodology, which can be used to evaluate existing OMs in organizations. For instance, mapping the OM of the individual organization based on KnowledgeEco (i.e., by comparison), can help to realize which entities are missing from the instantiated model. Moreover, to assess the significance of the missing entities, the evaluation framework was extended to suggest four evaluation rules (Table 4) based on the ontology semantics (Weinberger, Te`eni, & Frank, 2003, 2007).

The first rule, *SM strategy*, calls for use of the strategic perspective while negotiating the development and utilization of both SM dimensions (i.e., Component and Type). The second rule, *Sharing between SMs*, posits that there is complementary relationship between the individual- and the organizational-level SMs. This is to ensure the flow of knowledge through business interactions. The third rule, *Design of components*, addresses the reciprocal relationship, which exists between the two aspects of the Component dimension. The fourth rule, *Dynamic SM lifecycle*, is dedicated to the role of utilizing the dynamic aspect of SM through a series of activities – without addressing the dynamic aspect, a SM would be useless.

By applying these rules, organizations using KnowledgeEco methodology can significantly enhance the merit suggested by it, as part of aiming to consider and resolve business interaction challenges. Several examples can demonstrate this:

- An organization that encounters a problem of underdeveloped Content. Following KnowledgeEco ontology-based methodology, this might be understood as a result of either lack of Means (e.g., shortages of Domain Agent), or else shortage in strategy.
- An organization where the Means (e.g., Knowledge Technology Agent) do not meet the goals of the business processes. By using KnowledgeEco, the relevancy of the mapping of Types, or else the availability of appropriate Agents could be assessed to form decision guidelines.

Table 4. KnowledgeEco evaluation rules

Rule	Description
SM strategy	For every SM, there should be a strategy for developing and utilizing its components to achieve specified organizational goals.
Sharing between SMs	SM types should enable the sharing of knowledge from one to another. This rule is represented by the aggregation relationship between SM types and the methods for transfer-include that enable knowledge transfer.
Design of components	The SM Means should be designed to support effective utilization of the SM Content. This rule is represented in the SM by interfaces between Content and Means, and, furthermore, between those of Knowledge Resource and Meta-knowledge, and Process and Agent.
Dynamic SM lifecycle	The development and utilization of the SM should progress within a controlled lifecycle. The SM lifecycle should include (1) planning through requirements specification, analysis, and synthesis, and (2) development and control through design, implementation, evolution, and evaluation processes.

- Using KnowledgeEco, an organization could realize the role of organizational prevailing culture (i.e., an attribute assigned to Organizational Memory) and its influence on patterns of business interaction. Noteworthy, in a case where there is in this to create an obstacle to organizational goals.

By introducing these rules we meet also the second goal suggested – a framework to guide organizations in using the OM representation during evaluation.

SUMMARY AND CONCLUSION

Aiming to introduce a prescriptive representation of Organizational Memory (OM) which also suggests a framework for evaluation is a challenging task. However, achieving this goal is of substantial importance to organizations. This is for several reasons. It may change the way OM design is carried out, that is using the ontology as a reference model. It may motivate enterprise modeling initiatives to be more thorough

in the design of knowledge management solutions, thus fostering organizational learning. Moreover, this applies to organizations that need to obtain a model and a methodology, which can guide the design of an OM and the evaluation of existing OMs.

In this chapter we proposed the KnowledgeEco, a domain ontology for OM. In conceptualizing this ontology, which also corresponds to abstractions common in IS, we introduced the concept of Structural Memory that suggests a bidimensional view of OM as being a composite of Component and Type. The dynamic aspect of OM is represented in the ontology in an integrated way, alongside its static aspect. The value of this distinguishing and integrative view is with its viability in an enterprise setting striving for significant evolution. For instance, by motivating the effort needed to use KnowledgeEco.

From a design science perspective, this chapter covers two processes, *build* of a model, and *evaluate* of an artifact; and two outputs, model and method, while also referencing instantiations. The ontology was developed using UML, and, thus, it can be either easily integrated into any enterprise modeling activity or else translated to meet other specifications. Researchers can find its vocabulary compatible and its language interoperable for ease of integration with a spectrum of enterprise modeling initiatives.

Tied to the discussion of the ontology was the description of utilizing several natural language techniques to support an iterative decision process while mapping concepts of the domain to ontological constructs. This conceptualization emphasizes not only the compound nature of analysis and structuring, but also the need for explicit representation. This, in turn, calls for evaluation. To assess the conceptual coverage of the ontology, we used the completeness criteria following the Zachman (1987) framework for evaluation of information systems. In accordance with the suggested six foci, we assessed the mapping between the design decisions (i.e., concepts and constructs) and our objectives, as follows:

- The ontology is designed to include prominent OM concepts as part of a prescriptive ontological construct.
- Both people and information systems are identified as agents operating together to realize OM goals. This is not only because of the bidimensional view of Type and Component, but also through defining human and computerized agents as components.
- The hierarchical structure of the ontology includes the definition of a dynamic aspect, which is elaborated in the iterative SM Lifecycle.

Several suggestions can be made for meeting future trends. For researchers, KnowledgeEco can be used as a reference library of OM, based on which a theory of OM can be grounded. Practitioners working in an enterprise setting can apply the KnowledgeEco ontology described here to instruct business applications. Researchers and practitioners can use the ontology as a basis for further study of exisiting models of KM and OM, and for the intergration with other, related ontology development initiatives; for instance, as part of enterprise modeling initiatives.

Moreover, KnowledgeEco can be part of, or an extension of, an existing enterprise modeling attempt, irrespectively of its domain. We consider the ontology suggested here as a building block in a library of ontologies for business interaction. In this context, to ensure that an OM is evolving to meet strategic goals of the organization, we would suggest the use of KnowledgeEco as part of business interaction applications.

ACKNOWLEDGMENT

The chapter builds on the doctoral dissertation of the first author, which was supervised by the other two co-authors, carried out at the Department of Information Science, Bar-Ilan University, Israel. We would like to thank Professor I. Spiegler, Faculty of management, Tel-Aviv University, for his scholarly advice throughout this research, and Professor Dr. U. Frank, Chair of Information Systems and Enterprise Modeling at the University of Duisburg-Essen, Germany, for helpful discussions. We also thank the anonymous reviewers for their constructive comments.

REFERENCES

Abecker, A., Bernardi, A., Hinkelman, K., Kuhn, O., & Sintek, M. (1998). Toward a technology for organizational memories. *IEEE Intelligent Systems, 13*(3), 40-48.

Abecker, A., Bernardi, A., & van Elst, L. (2003). Agent technology for distributed organizational memories. In *Proceedings of the 5th International Conference on Enterprise Information Systems*.

Abou-Zeid, E.S. (2002). An ontology-based approach to inter-organizational knowledge transfer. *Journal of Global Information Technology Management, 5*(3).

Ackerman, M.S. (1998). Augmenting organizational memory: A field study of Answer Garden. *ACM Transactions on Information Systems, 16*(3), 203-224.

Alavi, M., & Leidner, D. (2001). Review: Knowledge management and knowledge management Systems: Conceptual foundations and research issues. *MIS Quarterly, 25*(1), 107-136.

Anand, V., Mantz, C.C., & Glick, W.H. (1998). An organizational memory approach to knowledge management. *The Academy of Management Review, 23(*4), 796-809.

Argrys, C., & Schon, D. (1978). *Organizational learning: A theory of action perspective*. Reading, MA: Addison Wesley.

Boland, R.J., Tenkasi, R.J., & Te'eni, D. (1994). Designing information technology to support distributed cognition. *Organizational Science, 5*(3), 456- 477.

Booch, G., Rumbaugh, J., & Jacobson, I. (1999). *The unified modeling language user guide*. Reading, MA: Addison-Wesley.

Chandrasekaran, B., Josephson, J.R., & Benjamines, R.V. (1999). What are ontologies, and why do we need them. *IEEE Intelligent Systems & Their Applications, 14*(1), 20-27.

Davenport, T., & Prusak L. (1998). *Working knowledge, how organizations manage what they know*. Boston, MA: Harvard Business School Press.

Dieng, R., Corby, O., Gibon, A., & Ribiere, M. (1999). Methods and tools for corporate knowledge management. *International Journal of Human-Computer Studies, 51*, 567-598.

Edginton, T., Choi, B., Hensen, K., Raghu, T.S., & Vinze, A. (2004). Adopting ontology to facilitate knowledge sharing. *Communications of the ACM, 47*(11).

Fernandez, M.L., Gomez-Perez, A., & Sierra, P. (1999). Building a chemical ontology using the methontology and the ontology design environment. *IEEE Intelligent Systems, 14*(1), 37-54.

Frank, U. (1999). Conceptual modeling as the core of the information systems discipline – Perspectives and epistemological challenges. In D.W. Haseman, D.

Nazareth & D. Goodhue (Eds.), *Proceedings of the AMCIS '99*. Milwaukee, WI: AIS.

Frank, U. (2007). Evaluation of reference models. In P. Fettke & P. Loos (Eds.), *Reference modeling for business systems analysis*. IGI Global.

Fridman Noy, N., & McGuiness, D. (2001). *Ontology development 101: A guide to creating your first ontology* (SMI technical report SMI-2001-0880).

Fridman Noy, N., & Hafner, C.D. (1997, Fall). The state of the art in ontology design. *AI Magazine*, 53-74.

Gomez-Perez, A. (1995). Some ideas and examples to evaluate ontologies. In *Proceeding of the 1995 Conference on Artificial Intelligence*, Los Angeles, CA.

Gomez-Perez, A. (2003). Ontology evaluation. In S. Staab & R. Studer (Eds.), *Handbook on ontologies*, Series on Handbooks in Information Systems. Berlin: Springer Verlag.

Gomez-Perez, A., Fernandez, M.L., & Corcho, O. (2004). *Ontological engineering*. Berlin: Springer.

Gomez-Perez, A., Fernandez, M.L., & De Vicento, A.J. (1996). Towards a method to conceptualize domain ontologies. In *Workshop on Ontological Engineering, ECAI*.

Gruber, T.R. (1995). Toward principles for the design of ontologies used for knowledge sharing. *International Journal of Human-Computer Studies, 43*, 907-928.

Gruninger, M., & Fox, M.S. (1995). Methodology for the design and evaluation of ontologies. In *IJCAI Workshop on Basic Ontological Issues in Knowledge Sharing*, Montreal, Canada.

Guarino, N. (1997). Understanding, building and using ontologies. *International Journal of Human-Computer Studies, 46*, 293-210.

Guarino, N., Carrara, M., & Giaretta, P. (1994). An ontology of meta-level categories. In *Proceedings of the Fourth International Conference on Knowledge Representation and Reasoning* (pp. 270-280). San Mateo: Morgan Kaufmann.

Havner, A.R., March, S.T., Park, J., & Ram, S. (2004). Design science in information system research. *MIS Quarterly, 28*(1), 75-105.

Holsapple, C.W., & Joshi, K.D. (2004). A formal knowledge management ontology: Conduct, activities, resources, and influences. *Journal of the American Society for Information Science and Technology, 55*(7), 593-612.

Jennex, M., & Olfman, L. (2004). Organizational memory. In C.W. Holsapple (Ed.), *Handbook on Knowledge Management, 1* (pp. 207-235). Berlin: Springer.

Jurisica, I., Mylopoulos, J., & Yu, E. (2004). Ontologies for knowledge management: An information system perspective. *Knowledge and Information Systems, 6*, 380-401.

Kayworth, T., & Leidner, D. (2004). Organizational culture as a knowledge resource. In C.W. Holsapple (Ed.), *Handbook on Knowledge Management 1* (pp. 235-252). Berlin: Springer.

King, W.R. (2006). The critical role of information processing in creating an effective knowledge organization. *Journal of Database Management, 17*(1), 1-15.

King, W.R., & Ko, D. (2001). Evaluating knowledge management and the learning organization: An information/knowledge value chain approach. *Communications of the Association for Information Systems, 5*(14).

Kulikoowski, C., (1990). Domain knowledge. In S.C. Shapiro (Ed.), *Encyclopedia of artificial intelligence,* Vol. 2. New York: Wiley.

Lehner, F., & Maier, R.K. (2000). How can organizational memory theories contribute to organizational memory systems? *Information Systems frontiers, 2*(3/2).

Leonard, D., & Swap, W. (2004). *Deep smarts. How to cultivate and transfer enduring business wisdom.* Boston: Harvard Business School Press.

Maier, R., Hadrich, T., & Peinl, R. (2005). *Enterprise knowledge infrastructure.* Berlin: Springer.

March, S.T., & Smith, G.F. (1995). Design and natural science research on information technology. *Decision Support Systems, 15*, 251-266.

Marcus, M.L. (2001). Toward a theory of knowledge reuse: Types of knowledge reuse situations and success factors. *Journal of Management Information Systems, 18*(1).

McGuiness, D.L. (2002). Ontologies come of age. In D. Fensel, J. Hendler et al. (Eds.), *Spinning the Semantic Web: Bridging the World Wide Web to its full potential.* MIT Press.

Mullaholand, P., Zdeahal, Z., Domingue, J., & Hatal, M. (2001). A methodological approach to supporting organizational learning. *International Journal of Human Computer Studies, 55*, 337-367.

Nevo, D., & Wand, Y. (2004). Organizational memory information systems: A transactive memory approach. *Decision Support Systems, 39*, 549-562.

Nonaka, H.T., & Takeuchi, H. (1995). *The knowledge-creating company, now Japanese companies create the dynamics of innovation.* New York: Oxford University Press.

O'Leary, D.E. (1998). Using AI in knowledge management knowledge bases and ontologies. *IEEE Intelligent Systems, 13*(3), 34-39.

Orlikowski, W.J. (2002). Knowing in practice: Enacting a collective capability in distributed organizing. *Organization Science, 13*(3), 249-273.

Osterwalder, A., Pigneur. Y., & Tucci, C.L. (2005). Clarifying business models: Origins, present and future of the concept. *Communication of the Association of the Association for Information Systems, 15*.

Palvia, P., Mao, E., Salam, A.F., & Soliman, K. (2003). Management information systems research: What's there in a methodology. *Communications of AIS, 11*(16).

Siemienuich, C.E., & Sinclair, M.A. (1999). Organizational aspects of knowledge lifecycle management in manufacturing. *International Journal of Human-Computer Studies, 51*, 517-547.

Stein, E.W., & Zwass, V. (1995). Actualizing organizational memory with information systems. *Information Systems Research, 6*(2), 85-117.

Te`eni, D., & Weinberger, H. (2000). System development of organizational memory: A literature survey. In M. Hansen, Bicheler, & H. Mahrer (Eds.), *Proceedings of the 2000 European Conference on Information Systems*, Vienna, Austria, (1) (pp. 219-227).

Tiwana, A., & Balasubramaniam, R. (2001, May-June). Integrating knowledge on the Web. *IEEE Internet Computing*.

Uschold, M., & Gruninger, M. (1996). Ontologies: Principles, methods and applications. *The Knowledge Engineering Review, 11*(2), 93-136.

Verkasalo, M., & Lappalainen P. (1998). A method of measuring the efficiency of the knowledge utilization process. *IEEE Transactions on Engineering Management, 45*(4), 414-423.

Walsh, P.J., & Ungson, G.R. (1991). Organizational memory. *Academy of Management Review, 16*(1), 57-91.

Wand, Y., Monarchi, D.E., Parsons, J., & Woo, C.C. (1995). Theoretical foundations for conceptual modeling in information systems development. *Decision Support Systems, 15*, 285-304.

Weinberger, H. (2004). *An evaluation model for structural memory using ontologies*. Unpublished PhD, Bar-Ilan University, Israel.

Weinberger, H., & Frank, J.A. (2006). Evaluating organizational memory: A three-layer model. In F. Lehner, H. Nosekabel & P. Kleinschmidt (Eds.), *Multikonferenz Wirtschaftsinformatik (MKWI) 2006*. Berlin: GITO-Verlag.

Weinberger, H., Te`eni, D., & Frank, J.A. (2003). Ontologies of organizational memory as a basis for evaluation. In *European Conference on Information Systems*. Naples, Italy.

Weinberger, H., Te`eni, D., & Frank, J.A. (2007). Ontology-based evaluation of organizational memory (Technical paper). Tel Aviv University, Faculty of Management.

Wijnhoven, F. (1998). Designing organizational memories: Concept and method. *Journal of Organizational Computing and Electronic Commerce, 8*(1), 29-55.

Winhoven, F., van der Belt, E., Verbriggen, E., & van der Vet, P. (2003). Internal data market services: An ontology-based architecture and its evaluation. *Information Science Journal, 6*.

Zachman, J.A. (1987). A framework for information system architecture. *IBM Systems Journal, 38*(2/3), 454-470.

Zhang, D., & Zhao, J.L. (2006). Knowledge management in organizations. *Journal of Database Management, 17*(1), 1-15.

ENDNOTES

[1] We use an uppercase first letter to designate class names.

[2] Organizations or individuals interested in a full description KnowledgeEco are invited to contact the first author.

Chapter XI
An Ontology for Secure Socio-Technical Systems[1]

Fabio Massacci
University of Trento, Italy

John Mylopoulos
University of Trento, Italy

Nicola Zannone
University of Trento, Italy

ABSTRACT

Security is often compromised by exploiting vulnerabilities in the interface between the organization and the information systems that support it. This reveals the necessity of modeling and analyzing information systems together with the organizational setting where they will operate. In this chapter we address this problem by presenting a modeling language tailored to analyze the problem of security at an organizational level. This language proposes a set of concepts founded on the notions of permission, delegation, and trust. The chapter also presents a semantics for these concepts, based on Datalog. A case study from the bank domain is employed to illustrate the proposed language.

INTRODUCTION

The last years have seen the emergence of standards for capturing security and privacy aspects of information systems (Ashley, Hada, Karjoth, Powers, & Schnuter, 2003; Cranor, Langheinrich, Marchiori, & Reagle, 2002; OASIS, 2005). Those standards provide language constructs but offer no methodological tool for actually making design decisions. In this setting, the inclusion of security features within the system design is usually done after the functional design phase. This is a critical issue since security services and related protection mechanisms have to be fitted into an existing design that might be not able to accommodate them.

It is generally accepted in the requirements engineering (RE) research community that system development requires models that represent the system-to-be along with its intended operational environment. This is even more important when the system has to meet security requirements, since security breaches often occur at an organizational level, rather than a technical one (Anderson, 1994). Even though there are mature methodologies for modeling and analyzing enterprises and their organizational structure, their focus is mostly on process and marketing aspects rather than security (AMICE Consortium, 1993; Bryce & Associates, 2006; Dignum, 2004; Hübner, Sichman, & Boissier, 2002; Stader, 1996; Yu, 1996).

Socio-technical system analysis has been proposed to overcome this issue (Emery & Trist, 1960). This approach aims at capturing the interactions between people and technology in workplaces. In this setting, security is the ability of the system to protect itself against deliberate misbehavior by actors of the organizations involved in the application scenario while still providing expected services when requested by benign actors. For instance, an actor may abuse his position within the organization to gain personal advantages (House of Lords, 1999; Michaely & Womack, 1999). Therefore, modeling and analyzing the organizational environment where the system will act is crucial for building secure systems. This allows designers to identify security mechanisms that can best protect the system, and their impacts on the system.

This chapter aims at analyzing the problem of modeling security at an organizational level. Based on such an analysis, we identify and formally define basic ontological primitives for modeling organizational and security concepts, paying particular attention to the security relevant social interaction within organizations.

To allow for a systematic design of security in organization, we have developed an agent-oriented requirements engineering methodology, Secure Tropos

(Giorgini, Massacci, Mylopoulos, & Zannone, 2006; Giorgini, Massacci, & Zannone, 2005), tailored to describe both the organizational environment of a system and the system itself. The methodology provides a requirements analysis process that drives system designers from the acquisition of the requirements model up to its verification and validation. One of its main features is the prominent role given to early requirements analysis phase that precedes a prescriptive requirements specification. The main advantage in having such a phase is that one can capture not only the "what" or the "how", but also "why" a software system is developed. Secure Tropos was originally based on the i* modeling framework (Yu, 1996). This framework has already been used to model and analyze security requirements (Liu, Yu, & Mylopoulos, 2003). In this work, security requirements are treated as nonfunctional requirements. This approach supports the representation of design decisions that can contribute to a security goal and the modeling of attackers (both internal and external) who prevent the fulfillment of goals.

However, our work revealed early on that the i* ontology needs to be extended in order to adequately model security because it lacks fundamental concepts needed in order to talk about security within an organization (Giorgini et al., 2006). To this end, we have proposed an enhanced ontology with three main notions, namely *ownership, delegation,* and *trust,* which together form the very foundation of all security concerns (Giorgini et al., 2005). Ownership is used to identify goals, tasks, and resources that an actor controls; delegation is used to model the transfer of entitlements and responsibilities between actors; finally, trust represents the belief of actors about the behavior of other actors (Mayer, Davis, & Schoorman, 1995; Rousseau, Sitkin, Burt, & Camerer, 1998). Once basic ontological primitives have been identified, we develop a comprehensive ontology tailored to model security at an organizational level. To this end, we provide an axiomatic characterization of their intended semantics using answer set programming (Leone et al., 2006). The proposed ontology is intended to serve as the basis for security-related domain ontologies. From an IT perspective, it can serve as a basis for specifying functional and security requirements.

The chapter is organized as follows. The next section reviews the current state-of-the-art in ontologies for organization and security modeling by presenting the issues in current proposals. The following sections introduce a bank scenario used as a running example to illustrate the application of the proposed ontology, introduce a set of primitive concepts for modeling security at organizational level, present an axiomatic theory of the identified primitives, show how the introduced concepts are enough to detect security vulnerabilities, and, finally, conclude with some directions for future work.

RELATED WORK

Several research communities have approached the problem of enterprise modeling and analysis and some of these have addressed issues of security. We discuss some of the more prominent approaches:

- **Enterprise engineering:** Organizational modeling of enterprises is often dealt with by enterprise engineering methodologies (AMICE Consortium, 1993; Bernus & Nemes, 1996; Bryce & Associates, 2006; Stader, 1996). Each methodology includes an ontology for modeling organizations, usually supported by a modeling environment and various analysis tools.
- **Multi-agent systems (MAS):** Efforts towards modeling organizations have also originated in the MAS community (Dignum, 2004; Hübner et al., 2002). These approaches propose to model multi-agent systems as organizational structures.
- **Semantic Web:** Ontologies constitute basic infrastructure for the Semantic Web. The idea underling Semantic Web proposals is to use shared vocabularies for describing entities of the domain and their inter-relationships (Masolo et al., 2004).

- **Security engineering:** One of main challenges of security is data protection. Resources must be protected against unauthorized access and/or tampering. This has spurred many researchers to define languages tailored to model privacy and access control policies (Ashley et al., 2003; Cranor et al., 2002; OASIS, 2005).

Enterprise engineering approaches tackle the issues of organizational analysis and modeling from an enterprise perspective. For instance, the Enterprise Project (Stader, 1996) aims to capture an enterprise-wide perspective of organizations. Such models are intended to drive enterprises in making strategic, tactical, and operational decisions. To achieve a high degree of integration, the Enterprise Project proposed the enterprise ontology (Uschold, King, Moralee, & Zorgios, 1998) which includes a set of terms often used to describe enterprises. This ontology focuses on organizational structure, strategy, activities, and processes, as well as marketing aspects. The enterprise engineering methodology (Bryce & Associates, 2006) provides a framework that allows the study of an organization and the development of an enterprise strategy synchronized with organizational goals. The methodology includes an ontology for specifying priorities within an organization, along with plans for implementing them.

The computer-integrated manufacturing open-system architecture (CIMOSA) (AMICE Consortium, 1993) aims at integrating enterprise operations by means of efficient information exchange within the enterprise. CIMOSA models enterprises using four perspectives: the *function view* describes the functional structure required to satisfy the objectives of an enterprise and related control structures; the *information view* describes the information required by each function; the *resource view* describes the resources and their relations to functional and control structures; and the *organization view* describes the responsibilities assigned to individuals for functional and control structures. The generalized enterprise reference architecture and methodology (GERAM) (Bernus & Nemes, 1996) defines a set of concepts for designing and maintaining enterprises during their entire life-history spanning from products to enterprise integration and strategic enterprise management. This framework identifies basic concepts used to describe the structure, content, and behavior of enterprises. Such concepts enable the modeling of the human component in an enterprise operation as well as the parts of business processes and their supporting technologies.

Among proposals from the multi-agent systems domain, OperA (Dignum, 2004) aims at designing models of organizations that support dynamic and autonomous interactions by focusing on agent societies. This proposal uses the agent paradigm to provide a natural way to view and characterize intelligent organizational systems. To model different roles, goals, and interactions within an organization, the framework adopts a 3-layer approach: the *organizational model* describes the intended behavior and overall structure of the society from the perspective of the organization in terms of roles, interactions, and social norms, the *social model* instantiates the organizational model with specific agents mapped to roles through a social contract, finally, the *interaction model* describes the society agents interactions by the means of interaction contracts. The OperA framework is supported by a language based on deontic temporal logic that provides a formal framework and integrated semantics at all three levels of society specification. MOISE+ (Hübner et al., 2002) focuses on the structure and functionalities of organizations, and the deontic relation between them to explain how an MAS achieves its purpose. Accordingly, the organizational specification is formed by a structural specification, a functional specification, and a deontic specification. The structural specification adopts the concepts of role, role relation, and groups to model the individual, social, and collective structural levels of organizations. The functional specification is based on the concepts of missions and global plans. The deontic specification then links the structural specification to functional specification in terms of permissions and obligations.

The Tropos methodology (Bresciani, Giorgini, Giunchiglia, Mylopoulos, & Perini, 2004) is an agent-oriented software engineering methodology intended to support all analysis and design activities in the software development process. The methodology consists of five phases, namely, early requirements, late requirements, architectural design, detailed design, and implementation. Early requirements aims at understanding the domain with its stakeholders and their individual and shared goals. Late requirements focuses on the elicitation of requirements for the system-to-be. Architectural design specifies the system architecture in terms of a set of interacting software agents. Detailed design is concerned with the specification of agent capabilities and interaction. Finally, implementation deals with the production of code from the detailed design specification. Tropos adopts the i* modeling language (Yu, 1996), which allows designers to model the organizational environment of a system and the system itself. This language offers primitive concepts such as actor, goal, plan, resource, as well as social dependency relationships between two actors. The modeling framework of i* includes strategic dependency models for describing the network of inter-dependencies among actors, as well as strategic rationale models for describing and supporting the reasoning of each actor vis-a-vis other actors.

Among proposals for Semantic Web, we note the descriptive ontology for linguistic and cognitive engineering (DOLCE) (Masolo et al., 2004). DOLCE aims to capture ontological categories that underlie natural language and human common sense. This ontology uses three main entities for modeling organizational settings: organizations, norms, and roles. Norms describe the structure and purposes of an organization by identifying its main concerns and the behavior of its agents. The link between agents and norms is represented in terms of roles.

In the realm of security and privacy modeling, we find sophisticated proposals such as XACML (OASIS, 2005), EPAL (Ashley et al., 2003), and P3P (Cranor et al., 2002). XACML is an OASIS standard supporting both an access control policy language and an access control decision language. XACML defines schemes for the specification of both context and access control policies. An EPAL policy is a set of privacy rules that includes a data user, an action, a data category, and a purpose with conditions and obligations. On the other hand, P3P aims at formalizing privacy statements that are published by an enterprise. Its goal is to define a machine-readable equivalent for the human readable privacy promises that are published as a privacy statement on a Web page. Unlike XACML and EPAL, P3P defines a global terminology that can be used to describe privacy policies for an enterprise. However, these standards do not address issues of design: the system administrator must manually decide which is the right policy to protect the information system he is responsible for. Moreover, these proposals do not provide facilities for modeling the structure of an organization together with organizational goals. Accordingly, it is not possible to verify whether a given policy is consistent with the functionalities of the system.

Requirements engineering usually treats security as a nonfunctional requirement (Chung, Nixon, Yu, & Mylopoulos, 2000). Nonfunctional requirements introduce quality characteristics, but they also represent constraints under which the system must operate (Sommerville, 2001). Although system designers have recognized the need to integrate most of the nonfunctional requirements, such as reliability and performance, into the software development process (Dardenne, van Lamsweerde, & Fickas, 1993), security requirements are identified after the definition of the functional design. This attitude may lead to generating serious design challenges that usually translate into software vulnerabilities or serious organizational blunders.

Security needs are generically expressed by organizational security policies. An organization defines high-level policies about security with respect to its strategic objectives and its organizational structure. Such policies have to be mapped to the specific functionalities of their information systems. Without an explicit model of the organization and the trust relationships among its components it can be result particularly complex to find the reasons that have motivated their introduction (Lampson, 2004). For instance, ignor-

ing trust concerns seriously affects the effectiveness of security measures imposed on a system. System designers may not introduce security measures since they may implicitly assume trust relationships among users that are in fact not there in the domain. Alternatively, system designers may introduce expensive mechanisms for protecting a trusted system that has not been perceived as such by designers.

The purpose of this chapter is to define a novel ontology supporting the integration of security and requirements engineering during early phases of system development. Such an ontology is intended to aid designers in understanding why security mechanisms such as authentication, access control, or back ups are necessary, and once they are selected, what are the trade-offs from the standpoint of corporate missions. Although there have been several proposals for modeling security features, what is still missing are models that focus on high-level security concerns without forcing designers to immediately get down to security mechanisms. For instance, Jürjens (2004) proposed UMLsec for modeling security related features such as confidentiality and access control. Basin, Doser, and Lodderstedt (2006) proposed an UML-based modeling language, SecureUML. Their approach is focused on modeling access control policies and integrating them into a model-driven software development process. McDermott and Fox (1999) adapt use cases to capture and analyze security requirements, and they call these abuse cases. An abuse case is an interaction between a system and one or more actors, where the results of the interaction are harmful to the system, or one of the stakeholders of the system. Guttorm and Opdahl (2005) define misuse cases, the converse of UML use cases, which describe uses that the system should not allow.

A RUNNING EXAMPLE

A major source of vulnerabilities is due to the presence of conflicts and loopholes at the interface between an IT system and its operational environment. Only by analyzing the system from an organizational perspective can designers identify appropriate security solutions.

An application domain where such issues are prominent is the banking domain. Banks, by their very nature, have to enforce security in the context of distributed control and responsibility, also evolving services and infrastructures. Protection measures, such as access control policies, separation of duties, auditing, non-repudiation action, digital signatures, all need to be considered and applied to comply with security and legal requirements besides functional requirements for a system-to-be.

In this chapter, we focus on a banking scenario and, more specifically, on loan process in the context of which activities take place and assignment of rights, roles, and tasks need to be carefully considered from a security perspective. In this scenario, we are going to emphasize the necessity of preventing frauds, preserving data integrity, and protecting customer privacy rights.

SI*: A LANGUAGE FOR SRE

The definition of a modeling language for designing secure socio-technical systems includes the definition of primitive concepts for modeling organizational and security concerns, as well as the logical formalization of such primitives. Our language, Si* (Secure i*), is based on the i* ontology (Yu, 1996), where specifications employ basic primitives such as "actor," "role," "goal," "task," "resource," and "social relationships between actors."

Actors and Their Specializations

An actor is an active entity that has strategic goals and performs actions to achieve them. Actors can be decomposed into subunits for modeling the internal structure of organizations. Complex social actors can be modeled using two types of subunits: agents and roles. An *agent* is an actor with concrete, physical manifestations. The term agent can be used to refer to human as well as software agents and organizations. A

Figure 1. Si* graphical representation of agents and roles

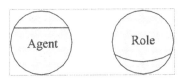

role is the abstract characterization of the behavior of a social actor within some specialized context. Figure 1 shows the graphical representation of actors and their specializations.

An agent is said to *play* a role. The play relation is similar in the intuition to the user-role assignment of the RBAC approach (Sandhu, Coyne, Feinstein, & Youman, 1996). According to such an approach, an agent inherits the properties of the roles he plays. Agents and roles can be further analyzed by decomposing them using the relation *is part of*. For instance, this relation can be used to identify the member of an organization as well as the subcomponents of a software agent.

Si* provides support for modeling role hierarchies based on the concepts of specialization and supervision. A role is a specialization of another if it refers to more specialized activities. In this setting, all specialized subroles inherit all properties of the generalized super-role. The basic idea underlying supervision is that, if a role supervises another role, the first is responsible for the behavior of the latter and has the capabilities to control and evaluate the latter's work. This concept is used to build the supervision hierarchy (Figure 3), whereas the specialization hierarchy is built using the ISA relation (Figure 2).

Example 1. The director of a bank is responsible for the correct delivery of the services offered by the bank itself. The director cannot perform all such services by himself, and so appoints managers and clerks (e.g., preprocessing clerks and postprocessing clerks) to perform some of the tasks he is responsible for. If

Figure 2. Specialization hierarchy

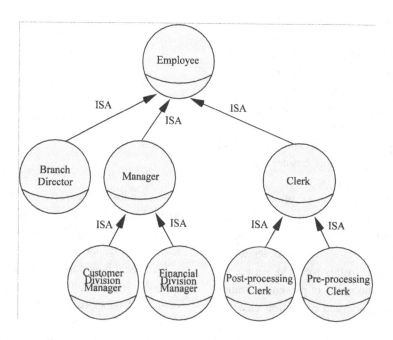

Figure 3. Supervision hierarchy

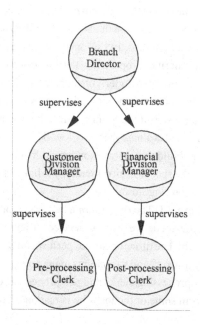

services are not provided in compliance with bank policies, he is personally liable. Thereby, the director has good reasons to check and evaluate the behavior of subordinate roles. Figures 2 and 3 represent the roles presented above and the relations between them.

Goals, Tasks, and Resources

A *goal* represents a strategic interest of an actor. Si*, as well as i*, differentiates between hard (only goals hereafter) and soft goals. The latter have no clear definition or criteria for deciding whether they are satisfied or not and are typically used to model nonfunctional requirements. According to Chung et al. (2000), the different nature of fulfillment is underlined by saying that goals are *satisfied*, while softgoals are *satisficed*.

Goals can be fulfilled by means of tasks or resources. A *task* represents a particular course of

Figure 4. Si* graphical representation of goal, softgoal, task, and resource

actions that produces a desired effect. A task can be executed in order to satisfy a goal or satisfice a softgoal. A *resource* represents a physical or an informational entity without intentionality. A resource can be consumed or produced by a task. Figure 4 depicts the graphical representation of goals, softgoals, tasks, and resources.

Si* is based on the idea of building a model of the system that is incrementally refined and extended. Goal modeling consists of refining goals and elicit-

Figure 5. Goal diagram

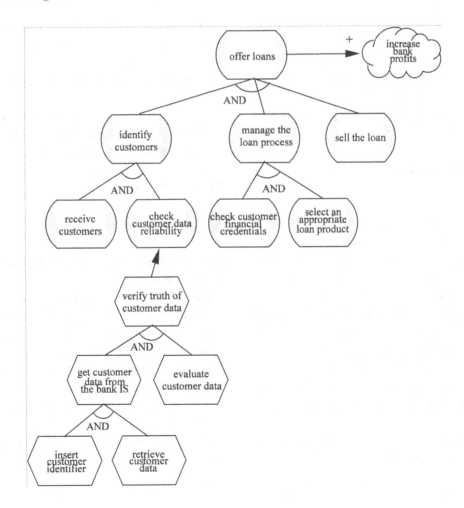

ing new social relationships among actors. Goals are analyzed from the perspective of single actors using three techniques, namely *AND/OR decomposition*, *contribution analysis*, and *means-end analysis*. AND/OR decomposition combines AND and OR refinements of a root goal into subgoals, modeling a finer goal structure. In essence, AND-decomposition is used to define the process for achieving a goal, while OR-decomposition defines alternatives for achieving a goal. Contribution analysis identifies goals and tasks that contribute positively or negatively in the fulfillment of the goal to be analyzed. Means-end analysis aims at identifying goals, softgoals, tasks, and resources that provide means for achieving a goal.

Example 2. One of the services offered by the bank is to offer loans. The provisioning of such a service contributes to increase bank profits. The bank AND-decomposes offer loans into identify customers, manage the loan process, sell the loan. These subgoals can be further decomposed until a plan to fulfill them is identified. For instance, getting customer data can be achieved by executing tasks insert customer identifier and retrieve customer data. Figure 5 shows the goal diagram derived applying goal analysis to offer loans.

Objectives, Entitlements, and Capabilities

The first intuition in modeling security aspects of information systems is to distinguish between actors who want access to a resource, fulfillment of a goal, or execution of a task, from actors who have the capabilities to do any of the above, and, last but not least, actors who are entitled to do any of the above. Essentially, every actor is defined along with a set of objectives, capabilities, and entitlements.

Objectives, entitlements, and capabilities of actors are modeled through relations between actors and services, namely *request*, *own*, and *provide*.

- **Request** indicates that an actor intends to achieve a goal, execute a task, or requires a resource.

- **Own** indicates that an actor is the legitimate "owner" of a goal, a task, or a resource. The basic idea is that an owner has full authority concerning access and disposition over his entitlements.

- **Provide** indicates that the actor has the capability to achieve a goal, execute a task, or deliver a resource.

The distinction between being entitled and providing allows us to model situations where the actor that has the capabilities to fulfill a goal is different from the one that has the permission to do it.

Example 3. According to data protection legislation, a customer is entitled to control the use of his personal data. The preprocessing clerk is appointed to identify customers. Thereby, he needs to access customer information to achieve his duties. However, he does not directly interact with the customer but he retrieves such data from the bank IT system. Thus, the bank should seek the consent of the customer for granting access to the customer's data to all employees assigned to him.

Relations *request*, *own*, and *provide* are graphically *represented* as edges between an actor and a service, labeled by **R, O,** and **P,** respectively.

Trust and Delegation

Si* supports the notion of *delegation* in order to model the transfer of entitlements and responsibilities from an actor to another. Thus, delegation is a ternary relation among two actors (the *delegator* and the *delegatee*) and a goal, task, or resource (the *delegatum*).

Example 4. A preprocessing clerk is interested in gathering customer data, for which he depends on the bank IT system. The customer delegates the permission to provide his data to the bank IT system on the condition that they are not disclosed to third parties.

In this scenario (Figure 6), there is a difference of relationship between the preprocessing clerk and the bank IT system and between the customer and the bank IT system. This difference is based on the type

Figure 6. Delegation

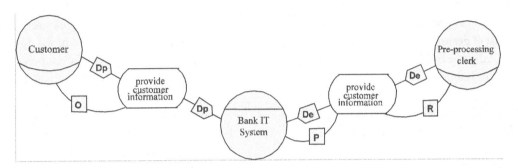

of delegation used in the two relationships. Thereby, we introduce a conceptual refinement of delegation that allows us to capture and model important security facets.

- **Delegation of execution** indicates that one actor delegates to other actors the responsibility to achieve a goal, execute a task, or deliver a resource. This would be matched, for instance, by a call to an external procedure. As a consequence, the delegatee is responsible for the achievement of the goal, execution of the task, or delivery of the resource.
- **Delegation of permission** indicates that one actor delegates to other actors the permission to achieve a goal, execute a task, or use a resource. This would be matched by issuing a delegation certificate, such as digital credential or a letter. As consequence, the delegatee is entitled to achieve the goal, execute the task, or use the resource.

In the graphical representation of Figure 6, we represent these relationships as edges respectively labeled **De** and **Dp**.

Example 5. The customer delegates the permission to the bank IT system to provide only information relevant for the required service. On the other hand, the pre-processing clerk, who wants customer data, delegates the execution of his goal to the bank

IT system. According to the preprocessing clerk, the bank IT system should provide the required information. He is not interested in what the bank IT system does with the customer consent, apart from getting his information. The clerk's major concern would be that tasks are delegated to people that can actually do them, whereas the customer would be concerned that his data are given to people who will not misuse the permissions they have acquired.

Further, we want to separate the concepts of trust and delegation, as we might need to model systems where some actors must delegate permission or execution to untrusted actors. Trust represents the willingness to accept vulnerability based on positive expectations about the behavior of another actor (Mayer et al,. 1995; Rousseau et al., 1998). It is related to belief in honesty, trustfulness, competence, and reliability (Castelfranchi & Falcone, 1998) and it is used to build collaboration between humans and organizations (Axelrod, 1984). Trust is an important aspect for making decisions on security since it allows to economize on information processing and protection mechanisms.

Similarly to delegation, we represent trust as a ternary relation among two actors (the *trustor and the trustee*) and a goal, a task, or a resource. The object around which the trust relationship centers is called *trustum*. Also in this case it is convenient to have a suitable distinction for trust in managing permission and trust in managing execution.

- **Trust of execution** indicates the belief of one actor that the trustee will achieve the goal, perform the task, or furnish the resource.
- **Trust of permission** indicates the belief of one actor that the trustee will not misuse the goal, task, or resource.

These relationships are graphically represented as edges respectively labeled **Te** and **Tp**.

A FORMAL ONTOLOGY

To define a formal semantics for the new primitives, we use the answer set programming (ASP) paradigm (Leone et al., 2006). The ASP paradigm is based on the concepts of facts and rules expressed as Horn clauses and evaluated using the stable model semantics.[2] Facts are atomic statements representing the extensional description of the system. Rules can be axioms or properties: axioms are used to complete the extensional description of the system, whereas properties correspond to integrity constraints and are used to verify requirements consistency.

Predicates

Our setting distinguishes two types of predicates: intentional and extensional. Extensional predicates (Table 1) correspond to the edges and circles drawn by the requirements engineer during the modeling phase and are used to formalize the intuitive description of the system. Intentional predicates (Table 2) are determined with the help of rules by the reasoning system.

Extensional Predicates

For an automatic and precise analysis of requirements, graphical diagrams need to be translated in formal specifications. This has spurred us to define an extensional predicate for each primitive concept. This set of predicates is presented and a summary is given in Table 1.

- **Type predicates:** The unary predicates *goal, task,* and *resource* are used respectively for identifying goals, tasks, and resources. For the sake of compactness, we will use the unary predicate *service* when it is not necessary to distinguish among goals, tasks, and resources. We shall use letters *S, G, T,* and *R* possibly with indexes as variables ranging over services, goals, tasks, and resources, respectively. The unary predicates *agent* and *role* are used respectively for identifying agents and roles. For sake of compactness, we introduce the unary predicate *actor* when is not necessary to distinguish among

Table 1. Extensional predicates

Type Predicates
service(Service:s)
goal(Goal:g)
task(Task:t)
resource(Resource:r)
actor(Actor:x)
agent(Agent:a)
role(Role:p)
Goal Analysis
AND_decomp(Service:s,Service:s1,Service:s2)
OR_decomp(Service:s,Service:s1,Service:s2)
pos_contribution(Service:s1,Service:s2)
neg_contribution(Service:s1,Service:s2)
means_end(Service:s1,Service:s2)
Association Relations
play(Agent:a,Role:p)
is_a(Role:p,Role:q)
supervise(Role:p,Role:q)
is_part_of(Actor:x,Actor:y)
Actor Properties
request(Actor:x,Service:s)
own(Actor:x,Service:s)
provide(Actor:x,Service:s)
Delegation and Trust
delegate(perm,x,y,s)
delegate(exec,x,y,s)
trust(perm,x,y,s)
trust(exec,x,y,s)

them. We shall use letters *X, Y,* and *Z* as variable to indicate generic actor, *A, B,* and *C* as variables to indicate agents, and *P, Q,* and *V* as variables to indicate roles.

- **Goal analysis:** Predicates *AND_decomp* and *OR_decomp* are used to model AND- and OR-decomposition, respectively. Predicates *pos_contribution* and *neg_contribution* are used to model positive and negative contribution, respectively. Finally, *means_end* states that a service provides means for achieving a goal with respect to the perspective of an actor.

- **Association relations:** Predicate *play* identifies the roles played by an agent. Predicate *is_a* is used to build specialization hierarchies, whereas *supervise* is used to build supervision hierarchies. Finally, *is_part_of* identifies the sub-components of an actor.

- **Actor properties:** Predicate *request* identifies the objectives of actors, *provide* the capabilities of actors, and *own* the legitimate owner of services.

- **Delegation and trust:** Predicates *delegate(perm,x,y,s)* and *delegate(exec,x,y,s)* correspond to delegation of permission and delegation of execution, respectively. Predicates *trust(perm,x,y,s)* and *trust(exec,x,y,s)* correspond to trust of permission and trust of execution, respectively.

Intentional Predicates

The intuitive description of the system is not sufficient for an accurate verification of the system (Giorgini et al., 2006). To derive the right conclusions, such a description is completed using rules. To distinguish the relations drawn by the requirements engineer from the ones derived by the system, we introduce a set of intentional predicates (Table 2). Next, we present such predicates.

- **Goal analysis:** These predicates identify the relations among services in terms of subparts. Predicates *subservice, OR_subservice,* and

AND_subservice respectively identifies a subservice, OR-subservice and AND-subservice of a service. More specific predicates should be introduced for goal, task, and resource decomposition.

- **Actor properties:** Predicate *aim* identifies direct and indirect objectives of actors and *has_perm* identifies direct and indirect entitlements of actors.

- **Trust:** Trust relations can be combined to build trust chains. In particular, *trustChain(perm,x,y,s)* and *trustChain(perm,x,y,s)* chains of trust of permission and trust of execution, respectively.

- **In charge and fulfill:** Predicate *in charge* identifies actors who take care of the final delivery of a service and *fulfill* identifies actors who are actually willing to deliver a service.

- **Confidence of execution:** This set of predicates is used to capture the notion of confidence from the requester's perspective. Predicate *can_satisfy* identifies actors who delegate their

Table 2. Intentional predicates

Goal Analysis
subservice(Service:s1, Service:s2)
AND_subservice(Service:s1, Service:s2)
OR_subservice(Service:s1, Service:s2)
Actor Properties
aim(Actor:x, Service:s)
has_perm(Actor:x, Service:s)
Trust
trustChain(perm, Actor:x, Actor:y, Service:s)
trustChain(exec, Actor:x, Actor:y, Service:s)
Confidence and Need-to-Know
in_charge(Actor:x, Service:s)
fulfill(Actor:x, Service:s)
can_satisfy(Actor:x, Service:s)
can_execute(Actor:x, Service:s)
confident(satisfy, Actor:x, Service:s)
confident(execute, Actor:x, Service:s)
confident(owner, Actor:x, Service:s)
need_to_have_perm(Actor:x, Service:s)

objectives to actors who have the capabilities to fulfill them. Predicate *can_execute* identifies actors who delegate their objectives to actors who will fulfill them. *Confident(satisfy,x,s)* identifies actors confident that a service can be satisfied. *Confident(execute,x,s)* identifies actors confident that a service will be fulfilled. This is the case if an actor knows that all delegations have been done to trusted actors and that the actor, who will ultimately deliver the service, has permission to do so.

- **Confidence of entitlements**: From the viewpoint of the owner, confidence means that the owner is confident that the permission that he has delegated will not be misused. Thereby, *confident(owner,x,s)* holds if an actor is confident that the permission on his entitlements is granted only to trusted actors.

- **Need-to-know**: Current privacy and data protection legislation requires that information is unavailable to actors except those who need legitimately to know (need-to-know principle). Essentially, this corresponds to the desire of owners to delegate permissions to providers only if the latter actually do need the permission. Predicate *need_to_have_perm* is used to capture this idea.

Axioms

This section describes the axioms that define the semantics underlying Si*. They are used to complete the extensional description of the system.[3]

Trust

Table 3 presents the axioms for propagating trust relations along chains and service refinement.

- *Trust* (T1-6) T1-2 are used to build trust chains for execution. T3 propagates trust relationships from a service to its parts. T4-5 are used to build trust chains for permission. T6 propagates trust along service refinements. If an actor trusts that another will not overstep the set of actions required to fulfill a part of a service, then the first can trust the last will not overstep the set of actions required to fulfill the service. Thereby, trust of permission flows bottom-up with respect to goal refinements.

Fulfillment, Confidence, and Need-to-Know

Tables 4 and 5 present the set of axioms for identifying entitlements and responsibilities of actors; also, actors who will fulfill services and actors who are confident that their objectives will be fulfilled and their entitlements will not be misused.

- *Aim* (AP1-3). AP1 states that if an actor requests a service fulfilled, he aims its fulfillment. AP2 states that if an actor requires a service delivered and delegates its execution to another actor, the service becomes an objective of the delegatee. Finally, AP3 propagates objectives through service refinement.

Table 3. Trust propagation

	Trust
T1	*trustChain(exec,X,Y,S)←trust(exec,X,Y,S)*
T2	*trustChain(exec,X,Y,S)←trust(exec,X,Z,S)∧ trustChain(exec,X,Y,S)*
T3	*trustChain(exec,X,Y,S1)←subservice(S,S1)∧ trustChain(exec,X,Y,S)*
T4	*trustChain(perm,X,Y,S)←trust(perm,X,Y,S)*
T5	*trustChain(perm,X,Y,S)←trust(perm,X,Z,S)∧ trustChain(perm,X,Y,S)*
T6	*trustChain(perm,X,Y,S)←subservice(S,S1)∧ trustChain(perm,X,Y,S1)*

Table 4. Entitlements and objectives transfer and fulfillment

Aims	
AP1	*aim(X,S)←request(X,S)*
AP2	*aim(X,S)←delegate(exec,Y,X,S)∧ aim(Y,S)*
AP3	*aim(X,S)←subservice(S1,S)∧ aim(Y,S)*
Has permission	
AP4	*has_perm(X,S)←own(X,S)*
AP5	*has_perm(X,S)←delegate(perm,Y,X,S)∧ has_perm(Y,S)*
AP6	*has_perm(X,S)←subservice(S1,S)∧ has_perm(Y,S)*
In charge	
AP7	*in_charge(X,S)←aim(X,S)∧ provide(X,S)*
Fulfill	
AP8	*fulfill(X,S)←in_charge(X,S)∧ has_perm(X,S)*
Can satisfy	
AP9	*can_satisfy(X,S)←in_charge(X,S)*
AP10	*can_satisfy(X,S)←delegate(exec,X,Y,S)∧ can_satisfy(Y,S)*
AP11	*can_satisfy(X,S)←OR_subservice(S1,S)∧ can_satisfy(X,S1)*
AP12	*can_satisfy(X,S)←AND_decomp(S,S1,S2)∧ can_satisfy(X,S1)∧ can_satisfy(X,S2)*
Can execute	
AP13	*can_execute(X,S)←fulfill(X,S)*
AP14	*can_execute(X,S)←delegate(exec,X,Y,S)∧ can_execute(Y,S)*
AP15	*can_execute(X,S)←OR_subservice(S1,S)∧ can_execute(X,S1)*
AP16	*can_execute(X,S)←AND_decomp(S,S1,S2)∧ can_execute(X,S1)∧ can_execute(X,S2)*

- *Has permission* (AP4-6). The owner of a service has full authority concerning access and disposition of it. Thus, AP4 states that if an actor owns a service, he is entitled to deliver it. AP5 states that if an actor is entitled to deliver a service and delegates the permission to another actor, the delegatee is entitled to deliver the service. Finally, AP6 propagates entitlements through service refinement.

- *In charge* (AP7). An actor will take charge of the fulfillment of a service if he has the capabilities to fulfill it and it belongs to his objectives.

- *Fulfill* (AP8). An actor will fulfill a service if he has taken charge of its fulfillment and has the permission to fulfill it.

- *Can satisfy* (AP9-12). An actor can satisfy his objectives if either he has taken charge of them (AP9) or has delegated them to someone who can satisfy them (AP10). Service decompositions are accounted for through axioms AP11-12. If an actor can satisfy at least one of the OR-subservices of a service, then he can satisfy the root service. Dual axiom holds for AND-decompositions.

- *Can execute* (AP13-16). These axioms are used to identify actors that actually can deliver a service by combining execution with permission. An actor can fulfill his objectives if either he will fulfill them directly (AP13) or has delegated its execution to someone who can execute them (AP14). Service decompositions are accounted for through axioms AP15-16. If an actor can execute at least one of the OR-subservices of a service, then he can execute the root service. Dual axiom holds for AND-decompositions.

Table 5. Confidence and need-to-know

Confident of satisfaction	
AP17	*confident(satisfy,X,S)←in_charge(X,S)*
AP18	*confident(satisfy,X,S)←delegate(exec,X,Y,S)∧ trustChain(exec,X,Y,S)∧ confident(satisfy,X,S)*
AP19	*confident(satisfy,X,S)←OR_subservice(S1,S)∧ confident(satisfy,X,S1)*
AP20	*confident(satisfy,X,S)←AND_decomp(S,S1,S2)∧ confident(satisfy,X,S1)∧ confident(satisfy,X,S1)*
Confident of execution	
AP21	*confident(execute,X,S)←fulfill(X,S)*
AP22	*confident(execute,X,S)←delegate(exec,X,Y,S)∧ trustChain(exec,X,Y,S)∧ confident(execute,X,S)*
AP23	*confident(execute,X,S)←OR_subservice(S1,S)∧ confident(execute,X,S1)*
AP24	*confident(execute,X,S)←AND_decomp(S,S1,S2)∧ confident(execute,X,S1)∧ confident(execute,X,S1)*
Confident of entitlements	
AP24	*confident(owner,X,S)←owns(X,S)∧ not diffident(X,S)*
AP26	*diffident(X,S)←delegate(exec,X,Y,S)∧ not trustChain(perm,X,Y,S)*
AP27	*diffident(X,S)←delegate(exec,X,Y,S)∧ diffident(X,S)*
AP28	*diffident(X,S)←subservice(S1,S)∧ diffident(X,S)*
Need to know	
AP29	*need_to_have_perm(X,S)←in_charge(X,S)*
AP30	*need_to_have_perm(X,S)←delegate(perm,X,Y,S)∧ not other_delegater(X,Y,S)∧ need_to_have_perm(Y,S)*
AP31	*other_delegater(X,Y,S)←delegate(perm,X,Y,S)∧ delegate(perm,Z,Y,S)∧ need_to_have_perm(Z,S)∧ X≠Z*

- *Confidence of satisfaction* (AP17-20). An actor is confident that its objectives will be satisfied if he takes care of them (AP17) or he has delegated their execution to trusted actors (AP18). Axioms AP19-20 specify how confidence of satisfaction is propagated upwards along service decomposition.

- *Confidence of execution* (AP21-24). An actor is confident to fulfill his objectives if he fulfills them by himself (AP21) or he has delegated their execution to trusted actors (AP22). Axioms AP23-24 propagate confidence of execution upwards along service decomposition.

- *Confidence of entitlements* (AP25-28). An owner is confident if there is no likely misuse of his permission. It can be seen that there is an intrinsic double negation in the statement. We model it using a predicate *diffident*. A delegating agent is diffident if the delegation is being done to an untrusted agent (AP26) or if the delegatee could be diffident himself (AP27). AP28 propagates diffidence upwards along service decomposition.

- *Need to Know* (AP29-31). These axioms defines the semantics of intentional predicates that are necessary to analyze *need-to-know* properties.

These axioms also capture the possibility of having alternate paths of permission delegations through predicate *other_delegater*. In this case the formal analysis will not yield one model but multiple models in which only one path of delegation is labeled by the need-to-have property and the others are not. Essentially, AP30-31 introduce nondeterminism, so they make search and verification harder.

ANALYSIS AND VERIFICATION

The suggested primitives were sufficient to deal with most of the security organizational requirements we encountered. For instance, it has been shown that Si* is able to cope with the complexity of a real ISO-17799-like case study (Massacci, Press, & Zannone, 2005). Security requirements are verified using *properties*. Such properties are defined in form of patterns that have to be checked. In ASP, they are represented as constraints that a good design should satisfy. If these features are not consistent, vulnerabilities may occur in the implementation of the system-to-be. Table 6 presents the basic set of properties.

- *Authorization* (Pro1-3). Pro1 is used to detect untrusted delegations of permission. Pro2 verifies whether an actor who delegates the permission to deliver a service is entitled to do it. Pro3 verifies that the owner of the service has to be confident to give the service only to trusted actors.
- *Availability* (Pro4-9). Pro4 is used to detect untrusted delegations of execution. Pro5-6 check to see whether actors can satisfy and execute the required services. Pro7-8 verify whether requesters are confident to satisfy and execute required services, respectively. Pro9 verifies whether actors have the permission necessary to perform their duties.
- *Privacy* (Pro10). Pro10 verifies that actors, who have the permission on a service actually need such permission.

CONCLUSION

This chapter has proposed an ontology intended to model security at an organizational level. The proposed concepts proved up to the challenge and revealed a number of pitfalls, especially when formal

Table 6. Security properties

Authorization	
Pro1	←delegate(perm,X,Y,S)∧ not trustChain(perm,X,Y,S)
Pro2	←delegate(perm,X,Y,S)∧ not has_perm(X,S)
Pro3	←own(X,S)∧ not confident(owner,X,S)
Availability	
Pro4	←delegate(exec,X,Y,S)∧ not trustChain(exec,X,Y,S)
Pro5	←request(X,S)∧ not can_satisfy(X,S)
Pro6	←request(X,S)∧ not can_execute(X,S)
Pro7	←request(X,S)∧ not confident(satisfy,X,S)
Pro8	←request(X,S)∧ not confident(execute,X,S)
Pro9	←need_to_have_perm(X,S)∧ not has_perm(X,S)
Privacy	
Pro10	←has_perm(X,S)∧ not need_to_have_perm(X,S)

analysis techniques were applied (Massacci & Zannone, 2006).

We are currently extending the ontology to capture behavioral aspects of the system. This extension has two implications. On one hand, it allows system designers to capture more sophisticated security properties. On the other hand, such concepts support the (semi-)automatic derivation of business processes from the requirements model.

Another direction under investigation involves the enrichment of the Si* ontology with concepts necessary for capturing privacy concerns. According to existing privacy legislations in many countries (e.g., the U.S. Privacy Act and the EU Privacy Directive), privacy is mainly maintained by controlling the usage of information. This requires that information be linked to the functional requirements of the original application. Following this trend, researchers have recently proposed frameworks for specifying and enforcing privacy policies. However, they do not support policy writers in the analysis of organizational requirements and leave them to manually define privacy policies. Our objective is to bridge the gap between the requirements analysis and policy specification by deriving privacy policies directly from the requirements model.

ACKNOWLEDGMENT

We thank Nicola Guarino and ISTC-CNR Laboratory for Applied Ontology in Trento for many useful discussions. This work was partly supported by the projects FIRB-TOCAI, IST-FP6-FET-IP-SENSORIA, IST-FP6-IP-SERENITY, and PAT-MOSTRO.

REFERENCES

AMICE Consortium. (1993). *Open system architecture for CIM*. Springer-Verlag.

Anderson, R. (1994). Why cryptosystems fail. *Communication of the ACM, 37*(11), 32-40.

Ashley, P., Hada, S., Karjoth, G., Powers, C., & Schunter, M. (2003). Enterprise privacy authorization language (EPAL 1.2). W3C Recommendation.

Axelrod, R. (1984). *The evolution of cooperation*. Basic Books.

Basin, D., Doser, J., & Lodderstedt, T. (2006). Model driven security: From UML models to access control infrastructures. *ACM Transactions on Software Engineering and Methodology, 15*(1), 39-91.

Bernus, P., & Nemes, L. (1996). A framework to define a generic enterprise reference architecture and methodology. *Computer Integrated Manufacturing Systems, 9*(3), 179-191.

Bresciani, P., Giorgini, P., Giunchiglia, F., Mylopoulos, J., & Perini, A. (2004). TROPOS: An agent-oriented software development methodology. *Autonomous Agents and Multi-Agent Systems, 8*(3), 203-236.

Bryce, M., & Associates. (2006). PRIDE-EEM enterprise engineering methodology. Retrieved June 15, 2007, from http://www.phmainstreet.com/mba/pride/eemeth.htm

Castelfranchi, C., & Falcone, R. (1998). Principles of trust for MAS: Cognitive anatomy, social importance, and quantification. In *International Conference on Multi-Agent Systems* (pp. 72-79). IEEE Press.

Chung, L.K., Nixon, B.A., Yu, E., & Mylopoulos, J. (2000). *Non-functional requirements in software engineering*. Kluwer Publishing.

Cranor, L., Langheinrich, M., Marchiori, M., & Reagle, J. (2002). The platform for privacy preferences 1.0 (P3P1.0) Specification. W3C Recommendation.

Dardenne, A., van Lamsweerde, A., & Fickas, S. (1993). Goal-directed requirements acquisition. *Science of Computer Programming, 20*, 3-50.

Dignum, V. (2004). *A model for organizational interaction: Based on agents, founded in logic*. PhD thesis, Universiteit Utrecht.

Emery, F.E., & Trist E.L. (1960). Socio-technical systems. In *Management Sciences: Models and Techniques*, Vol. 2 (pp. 83-97). Pergamon Press.

Giorgini, P., Massacci, F., Mylopoulos, J., & Zannone, N. (2006). Requirements engineering for trust management: Model, methodology, and reasoning. *International Journal of Information Security, 5*(4), 257-274.

Giorgini, P., Massacci, F., & Zannone, N. (2005). Security and trust requirements engineering. In *FOSAD III*, LNCS 3655 (pp. 237-272). Springer.

House of Lords. (1999). Prince Jefri Bolkiah vs. KPMG. 1 All ER 517. Retrieved June 15, 2007, from www.parliament.the-stationeryoffice.co.uk

Hübner, J.F., Sichman, J.S., & Boissier, O. (2002). A model for the structural, functional, and deontic specification of organizations in multiagent Systems. In *Brazilian symposium on artificial intelligence* (pp. 118-128). Springer.

Jürjens, J. (2004). *Secure systems development with UML*. Springer-Verlag.

Lampson, B.W. (2004). Computer security in the real world. *Computer, 37*(6), 37-46.

Leone, N., Pfeifer, G., Faber, W., Eiter, T., Gottlob, G., Perri, S., et al. (2006). The DLV system for knowledge representation and reasoning. *ACM Transactions on Computational Logic, 7*(3), 499-562.

Liu, L., Yu, E.S.K., & Mylopoulos, J. (2003). Security and privacy requirements analysis within a social setting. In *IEEE International Requirements Engineering Conference* (pp. 151-161). IEEE Press.

Masolo, C., Vieu, L., Bottazzi, E., Catenacci, C., Ferrario, R., Gangemi, A. et al. (2004). Social roles and their descriptions. In *Conference on the Principles of Knowledge Representation and Reasoning* (pp. 267-277). AAAI Press.

Massacci, F., Prest, M., & Zannone, N. (2005). Using a security requirements engineering methodology in practice: The compliance with the Italian data protection legislation. *Computer Standards & Interfaces, 27*(5), 445-455.

Massacci, F., & Zannone, N. (2006). *Detecting conflicts between functional and security requirements with secure tropos: John Rusnak and the Allied Irish Bank* (Tech. Rep. DIT-06-002). University of Trento.

Mayer, R.C., Davis, J.H. , & Schoorman, F.D. (1995). An integrative model of organizational trust. *Acad. Management Rev, 20*(3), 709-734.

McDermott, J., & Fox, C. (1999). Using abuse case models for security requirements analysis. In *Annual Computer Security Applications Conference* (pp. 55-66). IEEE Press.

Michaely, R., & Womack, K.L. (1999). Conflict of interest and the credibility of underwriter analyst recommendations. *Review of Financial Studies, 12*(4), 653-686.

OASIS. (2005). eXtensible access control markup language (XACML) Version 2.0. OASIS Standard. Retrieved June 15, 2007, from http://docs.oasis-open.org/xacml/2.0/access_control-xacml-2.0-core-spec-os.pdf

Rousseau, D.M., Sitkin, S.B., Burt, R.S., & Camerer, C. (1998). Not so different after all: A cross-discipline view of trust. *Acad. Management Rev., 23*(3), 393-404.

Sandhu, R.S., Coyne, E.J., Feinstein, H.L., & Youman, C.E. (1996). Role-based access control models. *Computer, 29*(2), 38-47.

Sindre, G., & Opdahl, A.L. (2005). Eliciting security requirements with misuse cases. *Requirements Engineering Journal, 10*(1), 34-44.

Sommerville, I. (2001). *Software engineering*. Addison-Wesley.

Stader, J. (1996). *Results of the enterprise project* (Tech. Rep. AIAI-TR-209). University of Edinburgh.

Uschold, M., King, M., Moralee, S., & Zorgios, Y. (1998). The enterprise ontology. *Knowledge Engineering Review, 13*(1), 31-89.

Yu, E. (1996). *Modeling strategic relationships for process reengineering.* PhD thesis, University of Toronto.

ENDNOTES

[1] Methodological aspects of this research have been addressed in (Giorgini et al., 2005; Giorgini et al., 2006).

[2] We assume that the reader is familiar with such concepts. Otherwise see (Leone et al., 2006) for a tutorial.

[3] We do not present here the axiomatization for the user-role assignment and goal analysis. We refer to (Giorgini et al., 2005) for it.

Section IV
Building Business Interaction Ontologies

Chapter XII
Linking Ontological Conceptions and Mapping Business Life Worlds

Paul Jackson
Edith Cowan University, Australia

Ray Webster
Murdoch University, Australia

ABSTRACT

This chapter describes a methodology developed to elicit knowledge for the design of a corporate Intranet within a government agency. This Intranet was intended to supply knowledge management systems solutions to various problems such as work duplication, document location, and accessing tacit expertise that was distributed across different office locations and departments. An inventory of the pertinent knowledge was required. We situate our discussion of this undertaking within the context of ontology and what it means for something to be a depiction of a socially constructed reality, a representation of the knowledge of a group. We developed a methodology combining soft systems methodology, causal cognitive mapping, and brainstorming to create a knowledge ontology using UML class diagrams. The methodology offers an effective approach for understanding nonroutine yet rigorous knowledge work and conveying relevant and contextual knowledge to the designers of solutions.

INTRODUCTION

This chapter describes an action research project which was intended to identify key knowledge resources within an organization and develop design solutions for the creation of Intranet knowledge portals. These portals should facilitate access to relevant knowledge and information for knowledge workers engaged in a variety of tasks and contexts within a government agency. From the beginning, we took the view that actionable knowledge to support or constrain decision making is far more than information in documents or computer databases. We also anticipated that the factors that influence decision-making extend beyond the instrumental, though tacit, knowledge we can obtain from experts via forums, conversations, or communities of practice. Heuristics, judgment calls, intuition, and ethical considerations are all constituent elements in the general mix of skill and expertise at the workplace. In order to identify as much of this "knowledge" as we could, we located ourselves within the tradition of social constructivism (Berger & Luckmann, 1967; Giddens, 1984; Schutz, 1972), examining the social reality of agents in work contexts and the objects within this reality which have a causative effect upon their actions.

Knowledge can be characterized as the sets of beliefs people use to interpret actions and events in the world. A shaman's knowledge of the spirit world allows him to interpret naturally occurring phenomena as portents or signs. Moral knowledge allows us to assess behavior as right or wrong, criminal or naughty, unethical or fair. The social constructivist paradigm abstains from any judgement about whether or not there are actually such "things" as "spirits" or "right and wrong". "What is 'real' to a Tibetan monk may not be 'real' to an American businessman" (Berger & Luckmann, 1967, p. 3). The realities of the shaman or the business manager are constructed by each of them within social groups over periods of time. For something to be objective, or real, does not necessarily mean that you can stub your toe on it. But it can certainly cause pain.

This then is the philosophical realm of ontology, the concern with what is real and what kinds of "things" exist. The Oxford English Dictionary says ontology is "The science or study of being; that department of metaphysics which relates to the being or essence of things, or to being in the abstract" (p. 824). The information systems design approach called "design ontology" attempts to capture, specify, and relate the constructs and elements within given domains

and create a "specification of a conceptualization" (Gruber, 1993). For computer scientists, "A specification of a representational vocabulary for a shared domain of discourse—definitions of classes, relations, functions, and other objects—is called an ontology" (Gruber, 1993, p. 199). Guarino (1998) refines this as "An ontology is a logical theory accounting for the intended meaning of a formal vocabulary, i.e., its ontological commitment to a particular conceptualization of the world" (p. 8). However, he also suggests that "Philosophy and linguistics play a fundamental role in analysing the structure of a given reality at a high level of generality and in formulating a clear and rigorous vocabulary" (Guarino, p. 3).

We have found that design "ontologies," which appear to offer comprehensive methods for the rigorous capture of shared conceptualizations, generally remain in the comfort zone of what can be written down. Using a single case study, we argue that any type of knowledge which is used for effective action should be considered in the design of a system. Design formalisms such as UML could be used to capture tacit, role-related, and value-oriented and relationship knowledge and therefore provide context in a rigorous, integrated form of representation for those other explicit items of knowledge which may be candidates for computerization or Intranet-based tools. This chapter shows a path to that formalism by linking process modeling, the soft systems methodology, and causal cognitive and issue mapping to elicit knowledge from staff in a government agency for the purpose of Intranet information design through ontologies.

We begin by discussing the notion that when we capture requirements for any form of information or knowledge management system, we are in fact capturing elements of a socially constructed domain of action. In order to specify a blueprint for any intended information system, designers need to understand this world, its salient elements, and the context within which these elements make sense. In order to capture such elements, we derive and utilize a contingent methodology based upon soft systems methods (Checkland & Scholes, 1990), causal cognitive mapping (Rughase, 2002), and brainstorming and then create a design ontology of the resulting elements using business processing mapping notation (Object Management Group, 2006) and UML class diagrams (Bennett, McRobb, & Farmer, 1999). The implications of the work are discussed before conclusions are drawn and future research considered.

CAPTURING KNOWLEDGE REQUIREMENTS FOR INFORMATION SYSTEMS

There are many formal analysis techniques notations to rigorously capture and document information systems requirements for the purposes of design. But in the messy world of nonroutine knowledge work, the interesting and important elements are often those which evade documentation. There is now a multiplicity of knowledge management solutions (such as yellow pages of expertise, bulletin boards, and multimedia) which can assist in managing access to all kinds of knowledge and expertise (Vail, 1999), so there may well be advantages in documenting the existence, if not the content, of those elements in our design formalisms. If we don't, we may be in danger of committing the error of looking under the lamp: although the light is brightest there, it is not where the most important gems are hidden. This chapter therefore concerns itself with the interface between that type of business activity which loosely calls itself "knowledge work" and that group of assorted technologies which can be referred to as "knowledge management systems." The key research challenge taken up here is to construct representations which will assist us in designing appropriate tools and management solutions to support the knowledge processes of creating, finding, sharing, and using knowledge to achieve good business outcomes. We contend that this knowledge, while not all propositional or itself amenable to computerization, is useful as contextualizing knowledge to designers of systems (in particular knowledge management systems), managers, and, finally, to users.

Research Area

The context of this chapter is that of managing knowledge in organizations—not just information, reports or transactional systems—but knowledge in all its gritty and inconvenient particularity (Davenport, 1997; Markus, 2001). Because Intranets and browser technology are becoming an almost ubiquitous medium for information and knowledge management tools (DTI, 2001; Gottschalk, 1999), this chapter has used a real life consulting case study to show how the information and knowledge needs of organizations can be analyzed by providing rigorous classifications of their knowledge as a basis for knowledge storage and access on Intranets (or as inputs to requirements gathering processes). The discussion space of "ontologies" is used in its philosophical as well as its technological sense to provide a platform of methods to try to provide a practical response based upon theory.

The general requirement confronting knowledge management is to identify, catalogue, and then provide access to organizational knowledge such that it can be easily stored, found, used, and enhanced (Boisot, 1998; Davenport & Prusak, 1998; Leonard-Barton, 1995; von Krogh & Roos, 1996). A core task is that of taking inventory of organizational memory and mapping these in some diagrammatic form to provide clarity and gain intellectual mastery over knowledge stocks and how they are related to each other (Hansen, Nohria, & Tierney, 1999; Nissen, Kamel, & Sengupta, 2000; Vail, 1999). The knowledge management solutions which build upon these maps include such technology as forums, databases, organizational "yellow pages", and knowledge bases (Alavi & Tiwana, 2002). Knowledge models can be used to match a business need to an identified knowledge repository via a knowledge management system.

Increasingly, Intranets are being used as a preferred mode of information management within organizations. In 6 out of 10 industrialized countries reported in a benchmarking report by the UK Department of Trade and Industry, 56% to 61% of businesses had a corporate intranet, the tendency being in all but one that the number of Intranets was growing (DTI, 2001). Microsoft has 3 million documents on its Intranet alone (Gilchrist, 2003). In order to maintain the integrity of information, while maximising its availability, forms of information storage, search, and selection are required which reduce the complexity of access and present responses to users, which are most likely to match the intent of a query posed by the user. This intent will be contingent upon context and work activity. Furthermore, if a user is navigating or browsing through an Intranet-enabled knowledge neighborhood, then signposts to catch the eye should be manufactured to a specification of *pragmatic serendipity*: creating a landscape within which fortuitous cognitive accidents can occur.

Ordering and Describing Knowledge Using Ontologies

Ontologies are a sophisticated method of knowledge representation and embody contextual, functional, and relational aspects of information or knowledge categories (Gilchrist, 2003; McGuinness, 2003). This has implications for the design of browser-enabled access to corporate content on Intranets: the more formal the specification, the greater the ability of technology to sort and mediate the access to the objects within categories (Berners-Lee, 1998; Maedche, Staab, Stojanovic, Studer, & Sure, 2003). Guarino (1998, p. 8) also says we can classify ontologies according to their accuracy: an ontology can get closer to the underlying conceptualization "by developing a richer axiomatization, and by adopting a richer domain and/or richer set of relevant conceptual relations."

If it is to be complete and correct, a design ontology of a domain of human activity should reflect the salient institutional features of the reality of the agents who act within that domain and contain the elements that determine the logic of social action. This would, for example, include any values or beliefs that influence decision making and action. Masolo et al. (2004) argue that extensions to ontologies are required for "representing collective intentions and mental attitudes

of communities of agents that create, maintain and accept descriptions" (p. 10). Designing knowledge technology solutions requires an appreciation not only of explicit, propositional knowledge (the "information requirements") but also of the tacit and behavioral knowledge which is used to effect work practice. Work practice is a language game (Wittgenstein, 1958) with a purpose, words, and rules, in which the players know the meanings of allowed expressions. The rules provide boundaries to the game, defining what a nonsensical behavior is or what constitutes good play. These moves (and the skills needed to make those moves) are not limited to what can be written down or articulated for the benefit of a designer of highly explicit computer systems. When requirements and design considerations are transcribed, they become decontextualized, alienated from their "language game." Meaning is lost, even though the words may appear to be clear. This context gives sense to language, actions, and roles and inhibits nonsensical moves. In the context of the language game in which propositional utterances make sense, the focus is not on the orthogonal correctness of a design, but "upon how well ways of doing things mirror the desires and needs of the users…a good design artefact…will support good moves within a specific design language game (Ehn, 1992, p. 121). Human action and decision-making is situated, contextual, and interpretive. An understanding of the work that is to be done with a computer tool is critical if appropriate and useful tools are to be developed and all forms of work involve significant amounts of tacit knowledge. We need to understand the knowledge requirements within the context of work and communicate these to designers if we are to develop appropriate technology solutions.

Eliciting Knowledge

Making sense of the business while requirements gathering for information or knowledge management solutions is usually done through some form of business analysis method and process mapping, which identifies work activities, and sequences, and other salient features such as the flows of information, key competencies, and roles and responsibilities. In our case study, we used the Soft Systems Methodology (Checkland & Scholes, 1990) as our initial elicitation methodology. Because we wanted to reveal as much of the knowledge which is required to execute business processes as possible, we introduced *cognitive mapping*. We hoped to derive not only the explicit knowledge prerequisites for work (those pieces of information which constitute the typical grist of information systems), but also derive the tacit knowledge and contextual information within work processes (Ambrosini & Bowman, 2002; Huff & Jenkins, 2002). A cognitive map is a representation of an individual's personal knowledge, of an individual's own experience (Rughase, 2002). A causal cognitive map is a type of cognitive map that uncovers those resources, including tacit routines, which are required for successful achievement of a goal. Causal cognitive maps are particularly useful in tacit knowledge mapping, as this enables us to focus on action and elicit knowledge that is context dependent.

Causal cognitive maps are generally developed by asking a series of questions geared towards uncovering what "causes success in the organization?" (Ambrosini & Bowman, 2002, p. 29). After preliminary interviews and document perusal to identify key constructs which support success, a workshop is generally held to explore each construct (Johnson & Johnson, 2002). A series of *"what causes that?"* questions are asked, and these causes are linked to the construct. This is continued, until no further constructs are suggested.

We have argued that the contextual and tacit factors which influence work performance need to be conveyed to designers of information systems solutions. We have also argued that the uses to which designers put requirements information is neither linear nor procedural; therefore, some innovations were introduced in this project, which address the tacitness of much knowledge work and the importance of informing designers of this tacit knowledge.

Causal mapping was performed to elicit knowledge objects, but from *subprocesses* within a process model. Each subprocess was identified and defined through

using the soft systems methodology. Cognitive mapping was performed upon each subprocess as a point of origin. The cognitive maps develop as tree structures, the process definition being the "trunk". The first concept (or branch) from the process tends to be the clustering concept (this was sometimes imposed *post hoc* by the facilitator).

Subsequent to completion of a cognitive map, workshop participants were asked to reflect upon the elements which had been identified as prerequisites for successful work and to annotate those with any *issues* or *hindrances* to the provision of those resources. In this way, the clustering of issues around groups of concepts was highly visible, highlighting deficiencies and breakdowns which required focus and resolution, possibly through a knowledge management system.

After the information had been elicited from staff, this was moved into a high-level blueprint for input to design for an Intranet system. In the case study discussed in the next section, it will be demonstrated that although there is an element of "black art," the cognitive map method of information capture assists the formulation of design models, in this case into UML.

Information Collection Overview

Figure 1 shows how data pertaining to information systems requirements can be collected in a way that reveals insights into the life-worlds of participants in particular work tasks.

1. The top level process model shows the generic tasks as they relate to the overall purpose of the organization. Each task stands for a life-world, in that the perspectives, meanings, and actions of participants in that process relate to the purpose of that process. Defining this process sets the boundaries and the context for knowledge elicitation, locating the protagonists within a role and a purposeful activity or language game.

2. The second level provides a more detailed set of tasks which need to be performed to achieve the goals of the higher level process. These tasks

Figure 1. The information collection method

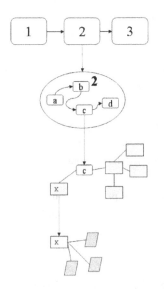

1. High Level Business Process Model provides activity, or "life world" delineation using OMG activity and sequence flow notation

2. Sub-Process Model provides greater detail on actions and uses SSM techniques (such as CATWOE) to gather further knowledge about work purposes.

3. Cognitive Map provides concepts, attributes and relationships which are mapped into the activity

4. Brainstorming issues provides insight to weak points, missing knowledge and identifies improvement potential for the activity

serve as more specific catalysts for triggering protagonists to realize what information, materials, or knowledge is required to get things done.

3. The third level identifies knowledge (tacit and explicit) which is used to achieve task objectives. No limits are set to the type of knowledge: it could be level of education, skill, relationship management, or even "gut feel". Some of this knowledge can be provided or facilitated by tools such as database applications, workflow systems, e-mail, bulletin-boards, skills databases, and so on.

4. The fourth level reveals issues and problems in the provision of the required knowledge: these issues, both individually and taken collectively, can be translated into specifications in the acquisition or development of solutions (for example, work procedure adaptation or technology).

METHODOLOGY

This research was conducted as a commercial, action research project (Baskerville, 2001; Kemmis & Mc-Taggart, 2000), fully funded by the client. The tools of information management such as process modeling and data modeling were used extensively within an overall knowledge management discovery context. The project was conducted by the first author of this chapter, currently a university researcher, who has 22 years experience in IT development and strategic consulting. The case study description and observation is therefore a combination of:

- Straightforward first-person reporting of organizational characteristics and information from corporate documentation and workshop outputs
- Collaborative learning and observations made and discussed with colleagues

- Observations of the protagonists who participated in the project and the effect of the innovations on their ability to contribute data to the
requirements gathering process
- Reflection in action and the use of a reflective
journal regarding the innovations in requirements gathering workshops and the usefulness of
the information in creating a high level design

The knowledge elicitation methodology, in particular the innovations mentioned, was not changed
during the execution of the project. This chapter has
been read and verified by the client project manager
and other participating managers, who agree with the
representation of the approach and the outcomes.

Case Study

The context of this chapter was the analysis of existing
knowledge for a small but highly visible public service
agency concerned with the sustainable development
and management of harvesting of natural resources.
The intent of the plan was to identify main areas of
knowledge and issues in the sharing and acquisition
of that knowledge and to propose initiatives for improvement.

The organization has about 400 employees. The
major activities of these employees are to develop
strategy and policy for the sustainable use of natural
resources, conduct research to ascertain the condition
of the environment and ascertain sustainable levels
of exploitation and harvesting, develop plans for the
management of those resources and instantiate those
in regulations and law, monitor users of the resource to
ensure they comply with the regulations, and prosecute
breaches of the regulations.

The following sections demonstrate how we moved
from the messy problem space of the business to the
solution space, an enterprise ontology diagram to be
used as a basis for designing an Intranet knowledge
portal.

The Corporate Process Model

The first exercise was to understand the nature of the
organization: its mission, key processes, and values.
These were gleaned in the first instance from the annual report and a series of strategic departmental plans,
which cascaded down from the overall corporate plan.
A workshop was conducted with senior management
in which the major knowledge objects, communities of
practice, and issues in knowledge management were
identified. A corporate process model was developed
(Figure 2), which presented the nine most important
business processes and their interactions. For each
process, interviews, and workshops were conducted
to identify the major activities and develop a second
level process model.

SSM and Cognitive Mapping

A soft systems "CATWOE" and cognitive mapping
workshops were conducted for each second level
process model. Each process step was defined to the
group as establishing the given context, for example,
the process "Prepare Policies and Plans" in Figure
2 establishes the work routine of consulting with
stakeholders, gathering research, environmental data,
and developing a management plan. Participants were
asked to identify all things which led to successful
completion of that work. This could be anything from
documents, previous experience, friendship, materials,
attitudes, or conditions such as time and space. These
were written on *yellow* post-it stickers and stuck on
the white board, fanning out from the process, which
had been drawn on the middle of the board. The post-
its were clustered together in meaningful collections
(see Figure 3).

The next step was to identify issues with the process
and information on the board. Participants were asked
to write inhibitors to the yellow post-its (the success
factors) on *green* post-its, which they then connected
to the appropriate point. What was gained from this
exercise therefore was a list of resources required to

Figure 2. High level enterprise process model

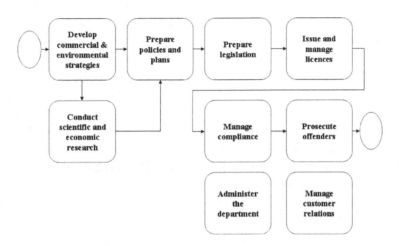

Figure 3. A subset of the knowledge elicitation for "prepare policies and plans"

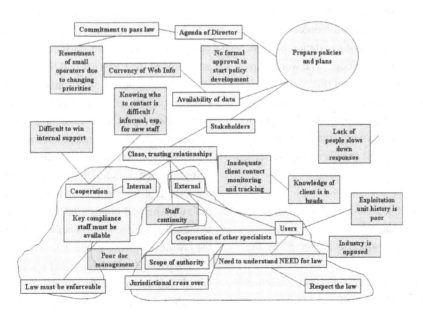

perform the task (giving a clear context) and a list of issues which inhibited good performance. For the purposes of ontological mapping, this provides us with (1) a domain (the process or sub-process), (2) elements in the domain (including issues), and (3) their relationship with each other.

An analysis of the clustering of the knowledge elements reveals insights into reality which may escape the "knowledge engineer" who is seeking explicit, rule-driven behavior. In Figure 3 the element of "close trusting relationships" with *stakeholders* is of central importance. The cooperation of other specialists is required as well as the involvement of the users of the natural resource which is to be harvested. Without understanding the need for the law, the users will not respect it and continue to over-utilize the resource in contravention of the law, thereby placing a greater burden upon control rather than voluntary compliance. So the law must be articulated and promulgated in a way that conveys why the law is important. Furthermore, the formulation of effective law includes understanding what is physically and realistically "enforceable" by compliance officers (a kind of policeman). This knowledge has previously not been included in the formulation of laws (compliance officers have not been involved), and as a consequence, complex and impractical regulations have been developed. Now compliance officers are involved in the law-formulation process, in order to introduce this knowledge. The workshops were able to capture and document this.

In Figure 3, therefore, certain types of knowledge are depicted which are critical to the development of policies and plans, but which would not find their way into a specification document or information system. These are:

1. How to maintain a good relationship with and involve all stakeholders
2. How to create law which is respected by the users of the resource
3. How to draft law which can be readily understood and implemented by compliance officers

These are sets of knowledge which determine the effectiveness of the policies and laws which are developed by policy development staff. So, therefore, they should be included in any design document which purports to represent important knowledge, even if that may not be amenable to codification in a database or document at some future time. In particular, any formalism which claims to represent phenomenological reality should have pointers to the existence of these prerequisite forms of knowledge.

The Ontology as Knowledge Map

A design ontology which reflects the important knowledge inputs to developing effective laws should reflect this stock of deep knowledge and form the basis for systems or procedures which are required to ensure it is used when appropriate. Even if it is not explicit knowledge, it must be acknowledged and mapped as it is of major importance, as should any decision making principles. These elements are in a sense "contextualising objects", they give additional information and meaning to the objects with which they are associated. So, for example, in Figure 4 (a subset of the resulting high-level ontology) there is a relationship depicted between "Laws" and "Stakeholders," showing that stakeholders submit information in the domain "Develop Policies and Plans" as input to Laws. Important attributes of the Laws are that they are respected (by users of the resource), well-founded (in science), and enforceable (by compliance officers). Therefore, the information inputs to Laws require an understanding of local conditions, an understanding of what can be realistically enforced, and an understanding of the actual science which defines quotas for sustainable harvesting of the resource. Knowledge management tools within a well-configured Intranet may give access to these knowledge holders at the appropriate point in the law development process.

The partial UML diagram in Figure 4 depicts a "life world" related to specific processes and was derived from the information elicited from the workshops and the organizational documentation.

Figure 4. Extract from an indicative high level ontology diagram

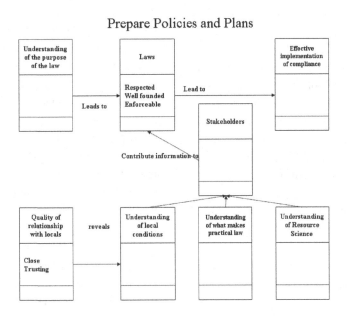

Prepare Policies and Plans

- **Domains:** The definition of domains was driven from two directions. First, natural domains were circumscribed by the corporate process models; then domains were derived from clusters of classes which appeared to be used in several processes, such as customer or location information.
- **Relationships:** Derived from the links instantiated in the cognitive maps. The annotation of these links, whether they were "of a kind" or associations, was done subsequent to the workshops based upon an analysis of the outputs and using other organizational documentation following standard data and object modeling techniques.
- **Classes:** The definition of classes, or the elements within the ontology, was a process of abstraction from the concepts raised in the cognitive

mapping workshops and deriving concepts from clusters where necessary (for example, "Relationships" and "External" and "Trust" were combined to be "Quality of Relationship").
- **Attributes:** It is also possible to annotate the classes with some preliminary attributes which also function as performance targets in some cases.

The UML diagram can be enriched over time with formalisms describing the rules and attributes of the respective classes, such that where appropriate, access and extraction of information can be automated through the intranet or Internet. This UML diagram is taken as the basis for further design work in preparing an intranet knowledge portal and understanding the social logic of the respective work activity systems.

THE KNOWLEDGE PORTAL

As suggested previously, a natural solution to the knowledge problem situations in the case study is provided by an Intranet knowledge portal (Collins, 2003; Mack, Ravin, & Byrd, 2001), which presents a consolidated suite of tools for finding, storing, and adding to information and providing tools for collaboration from a single workstation and using a consistent, intuitive user interface (Collins, 2003). Such a knowledge portal provides several components to assisting knowledge management:

- A single point of entry and consistent view of organizational information
- A common user interface
- An information search and access point for corporate information and knowledge

Corporate knowledge portals should be organized around work processes and job roles (Collins, 2003)

and provide a platform for maintaining organizational knowledge and building for the future. They can be core components of a knowledge creating organization and integrate KM tools in the broadest sense such as database applications, e-mail, organizational forums, and document management systems. The organization of knowledge within a portal must optimize the location of knowledge, either as digital content or a connection to a knowledge bearer. Classification of corporate knowledge is the first step to making knowledge accessible. The relationship and clustering between knowledge elements usually indicates domain boundaries as captured in our model: where there is high connection and tight coupling, there tends to be association with a type of activity. Search and indexing capability either within the context of a classification or from a corporate-wide level, simplify access to elements when volume and complexity of information transcend certain limits.

A draft portal has been developed from the ontology domains as part of the knowledge management

Figure 5. Intranet design schema

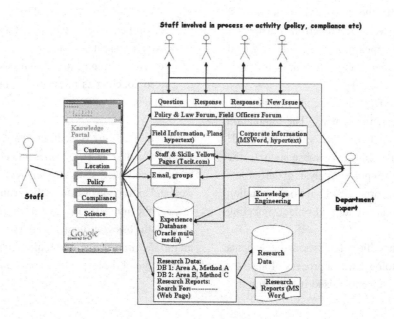

strategy and Figure 5 shows the high-level entry points into the Intranet information services and how various packages are configured to provide access to information and knowledge. The domains of knowledge which were derived for the ontology from the corporate process model developed for this project are customer, policy, compliance, scientific and species research, and location. These are the major navigation entry points. Over time, pointing to a particular object within the domains may open a conventional database, open a session with a person who has tacit knowledge of that object (i.e., compliance officers for an understanding of what comprises enforceable law) or show the axioms which make the information viable, that is, "you will only get good intelligence regarding poachers, if the relevant officer has a good relationship with the potential informant AND that informant respects the fairness of the law."

DISCUSSION

This action research project resulted in a high level knowledge map and Intranet portal design for the organization, developed by the researcher. The substantive component of this chapter, however, is the method of mapping and the resulting ontology, which contains contextualizing social elements. The basic ontology provides the foundation for designing an information repository, an Intranet knowledge portal structure, the beginnings of an organizational taxonomy, and a detailed set of issues which could be addressed by management decision.

Process modeling was used to arrive at the taxonomy and the relevant issues. This enabled a clear definition of the context within which the ontology could be developed and was most effective. Developing a process model has the advantage of capturing the most important activities in a clear and easy to understand format.

The formulation of each process within the model represented a "root definition" (Checkland & Scholes, 1990). The "CATWOE" was performed to establish

some base data about the overall process such as the customers, activities, transformation, worldview outputs, and environment of the overall process model. This assisted both the facilitator and the audience in focussing upon the context of the process and making the decisive components in the process present in the mind. Then a key process within the model was taken and formed the basis of the question: "What do you need to achieve success in the activity of X?" The information collected in the example was consistent, comprehensive, and rich. The formulation of question of "what causes success" in terms of the process is useful because it is very direct and reflects an activity which the staff perform and understand well.

The issues derived via brainstorming underscored the importance of problematic access to information or knowledge and are useful for showing where management can apply leverage to improve a situation. For example, staff continuity was highlighted in the process as the most important reason why uniform information and knowledge management solutions were required. When a single staff member develops a new policy, the knowledge is internalized and available on demand through personal memory: no external repository is required. But if that person leaves during policy development, the knowledge is gone. So some consistent form of management of explicit information during the preceding period of policy development must be introduced.

Moving from the data to the ontology modeling is the "design process" and so more of a "black art". This was done by examining the cognitive maps and abstracting or splitting the concepts as appropriate. Other concepts were derived from the documentation, using nouns as candidate objects for diagramming. This process arrived at an indicative UML class diagram, which is fairly easy to understand and can be used for further refinement. There are several things to be learned from the diagram:

- It raises knowledge objects which would not normally be visible (such as the quality of the relationships and trust) to the level where designer and possibly management attention is focussed. Contextual information becomes available to the designer at the object level within ontology, even though that information may never be a candidate for codification.

- It forms the basis for thesaurus/taxonomy and designing the Intranet storage and access paths.
- It could lead to electronic Web services later on, if required.

Finally, the methodology for deriving inputs for the ontology development must also be seen as itself part of a "reality creation process." Design ontologies reflect social knowledge of a domain which is depicted and stored in static form as an ontology diagram, and, in this case, forms the basis for Intranet portal design. Social knowledge develops through the workshop conversations and participation which facilitates the externalization and sharing of personal knowledge and the ways which individuals have of assessing and dealing with work situations. Discussion of this knowledge, placing it on the whiteboard or post-its, objectifies the knowledge, forming a new "common stock" which, (through nods, agreement, praise or other social signals which constitute a legitimation process) upgrades collective worldviews and generates validated, authorized organizational memory. The subsequent process of objectifying and legitimating the social knowledge as an ontology diagram is a further social ritual in the very creation of organizational reality.

The ontology diagram is both cause and effect of ongoing organizational learning. The degree to which personal and group memory are subject to ongoing learning and their exploitation depends upon a number of contingent factors, but one could assume that managers and other end-users who are aware of the learning processes can encourage and nurture them to develop a self-sustaining momentum of awareness, reflection, and sharing using an ontology diagram as a communications and boundary artefact. In terms of the KMS design and development process, the involvement of the end-user in this process and the resultant individual and collective learning can be considered to enhance both the development process and project ouctomes.

CONCLUSION

To return to the propositional and contextual elements required for Intranet and systems design defined previously, the work performed in this case study demonstrates:

- That an "ontology" approach, focussing upon deriving principles of causative action for people in social contexts, is revealing and enriching.
- That through the process of causal cognitive mapping in a workshop environment, the tacit elements (skills and relationships) which function as enablers of an effective work environment, can be identified and documented. This suggests that appropriate design solutions can then be developed.
- That it is possible to introduce "contextualizing objects" into ontology diagrams such as trust, values, or relationships.
- That through process modeling and soft systems analysis, a clear work context can be defined for the purposes of conveying understanding to the designer and providing a context for subsequent knowledge elicitation through cognitive mapping.
- That a representational convention like UML can be used to capture tacit information (in the form of classes), relationships (through associations, is-a-kind-of and part-of formalisms), and contextual information through the linking to process models and domains.
- The process of identifying and contextualizing issues pinpoints sensitivities in the current system, which will aid systems design into the future.

REFERENCES

Alavi, M., & Tiwana, A. (2002). Knowledge integration in virtual teams: The potential role of KMS. *Journal of the American Society for Information Science and Technology, 53*(12), 1029-1037.

Ambrosini, V., & Bowman, C. (2002). Mapping successful organizational routines. In A.S. Huff & M. Jenkins (Eds.), *Mapping strategic knowledge* (pp. 19-45). London: Sage Publications.

Baskerville, R. (2001). Conducting action research: High risk and high reward in theory and practice. In E. M. Trauth (Ed.), *Qualitative research in IS: Issues and trends* (pp. 192-217). Hershey, PA: Idea Group Publishing.

Bennett, S., McRobb, S., & Farmer, R. (1999). *Object-oriented systems analysis and design using UML.* Maidenhead: McGraw-Hill.

Berger, P.L., & Luckmann, T. (1967). *The social construction of reality - A treatise in the sociology of knowledge.* London: Penguin.

Berners-Lee, T. (1998). Semantic Web road map. Retrieved June 15, 2007, from http://www.w3.org/DesignIssues/Semantic.html

Boisot, M.H. (1998). *Knowledge assets—Securing competitive advantage in the information economy.* New York: Oxford University Press.

Checkland, P., & Scholes, J. (1990). *Soft systems methodology in action.* Chichester: John Wiley & Sons.

Collins, H. (2003). *Enterprise knowledge portals: Next generation portal solutions for dynamic information access, better decision making, and maximum results.* New York: AMACOM.

Davenport, T. (1997). *Information ecology: Mastering the information and technology environment.* Oxford: Oxford University Press.

Davenport, T., & Prusak, L. (1998). *Working knowledge: How organizations manage what they know.* Harvard Business School.

DTI. (2001). *Business in the information age.* International benchmarking report 2001. Retrieved June 15, 2007, from http://www.ukonlineforbusiness.gov.uk/main/resources/publication-htm/bench2001.htm

Ehn, P. (1992). Scandinavian design: On participation and skill. In P. Adler & T. Winograd (Eds.), *Usability.* New York: Oxford University Press.

Giddens, A. (1984). *The constitution of society: Outline of the theory of structuration.* Berkeley: University of California Press.

Gilchrist, A. (2003). Thesauri, taxonomies and ontologies; an etymological note. *Journal of Documentation, 59*(1), 7-18.

Gottschalk, P. (1999). Knowledge management in the professions: Lessons learned from Norwegian law firms. *Journal of Knowledge Management, 3*(3), 203-211.

Gruber, T.R. (1993). A translation approach to portable ontology specifications. *Knowledge Acquisition, 5*(2), 199-220.

Guarino, N. (1998, June 6-8). *Formal ontology in information systems.* Paper presented at the *Proceedings of FOIS'98*, Trento, Italy.

Hansen, M.T., Nohria, N., & Tierney, T. (1999). What's your strategy for managing knowledge? *Harvard Business Review, 77*(2), 106-116.

Huff, A.S., & Jenkins, M. (Eds.). (2002). *Mapping strategic knowledge.* London: Sage Publications.

Johnson, P., & Johnson, G. (2002). Facilitating group cognitive mapping of core competencies. In A.S. Huff & M. Jenkins (Eds.), *Mapping strategic knowledge* (pp. 220-236). London: Sage Publications.

Kemmis, S., & McTaggart. (2000). Participatory action research. In N. K. Denzin & Y. S. Lincoln (Eds.), *Handbook of qualitative research* (second ed., pp. 487-508). Thousand Oaks: Sage Publications.

Leonard-Barton, D. (1995). *Wellsprings of knowledge: Building and maintaining the sources of innovation.* Boston: Harvard Business School Press.

Mack, R., Ravin, Y., & Byrd, R. J. (2001). Knowledge portals and the emerging digital knowledge workplace. *IBM Systems Journal, 40*(4), 925-955.

Maedche, A., Staab, S., Stojanovic, N., Studer, R., & Sure, Y. (2003). SEmantic portAL: The SEAL approach. In D. Fensel, J. Hendler, H. Lieberman & W. Wahlster (Eds.), *Spinning the Semantic Web* (pp. 317-359). Cambridge, MA: The MIT Press.

Markus, M.L. (2001). Toward a theory of knowledge reuse: Types of knowledge reuse situations and factors in reuse success. *Journal of Management Information Systems, 18*(1), 57-93.

Masolo, C., Vieu, L., Bottazzi, E., Catenacci, C., Ferrario, R., Gangemi, A., et al. (2004, June 2-5). Social roles and their descriptions. Paper presented at the *Proceedings of the Ninth International Conference on the Principles of Knowledge Representation and Reasoning (KR2004)*, Whistler, BC, Canada.

McGuinness, D.L. (2003). Ontologies come of age. In D. Fensel, J. Hendler, H. Lieberman, & W. Wahlster (Eds.), *Spinning the semantic Web* (pp. 171-194). Cambridge, MA: The MIT Press.

Nissen, M., Kamel, M., & Sengupta, K. (2000). Integrated analysis and design of knowledge systems and processes. *Information Resources Management Journal, 13*(1), 24-43.

Object Management Group. (2006). *Business process modeling notation specification.* Retrieved August 24, 2007, from http://www.bpmn.org/

Rughase, O.G. (2002). Linking content to process. In A.S. Huff & M. Jenkins (Eds.), *Mapping strategic knowledge* (pp. 46-62). London: Sage Publications.

Schutz, A. (1972). *The phenomenology of the social world.* London: Heinemann Educational Books.

Simpson, J., & Weiner, E. (Eds.). (1989). T*he Oxford English Dictionary (2nd ed. Vol. X).* Oxford: Clarendon Press.

Vail, E.F. (1999). Knowledge mapping: Getting started with knowledge management. *Information Systems Management, 16*(4), 16-23.

von Krogh, G., & Roos, J. (1996). *Managing knowledge: Perspectives on cooperation and competition.* Thousand Oaks, CA: SAGE.

Wittgenstein, L. (1958). *Philosophical investigations.* Oxford: Basil Blackwell & Mott Ltd.

Chapter XIII
Modeling Semantic Business Process Models

Agnes Koschmider
Universität Karlsruhe (TH), Germany

Andreas Oberweis
Universität Karlsruhe (TH), Germany

ABSTRACT

Coupling of interorganizational business processes in electronic markets is a difficult and time-consuming task. In practice, business processes are geographically distributed, which makes it particularly difficult for business partners to coordinate their supply chains and customer relationship management with business units. By using formal description languages such as Petri Nets for modeling interorganizational business processes, purely syntactic composition problems of distributed business environments can be solved. However, the missing semantic representation of Petri Nets can hamper the interconnectivity of business processes. Usually, several business partners, even if they share similar demands, have their own specific vocabularies. By representing business processes with Petri Nets in combination with the Web ontology language (OWL), our approach provides flexibility, ease of integration, and a significant level of automation of loosely coupled business processes even if they do not share their respective vocabularies.

INTRODUCTION

Coupling of interorganizational business process models in electronic markets is a difficult and time-consuming task. The integration of different business partners into one single value creation chain demands enormous coordination activities. Business process models of different companies have to fit in another organizational environment and they have to complement each other. Furthermore, the rapid growth of electronic markets' activities demands flexibility and automation of involved systems in order to facilitate the interconnectivity of business process models and to reduce communication efforts.

By using Petri Nets (Reisig & Rozenberg, 1998) for modeling interorganizational business process models, syntactic composition problems of distributed business environments can be solved. Moreover, Petri Nets obey an operational semantics that facilitates composition, simulation, and validation of business process models. However, a missing semantic representation of Petri Net elements can hamper the interconnectivity of business process models, which ensures flexible process interface composition. When enterprises decide to interconnect business process models, synonyms, homonyms, or similarly labeled process elements have to be identified to avoid misunderstandings.

Semantic markup of business process models and automated reasoning is required in order to ensure consistent process interconnectivity and to reduce coupling efforts. An efficient approach for improving business process model interconnectivity can be provided by metadata-descriptions of the related process elements. In order to reduce negotiation efforts, these metadata-descriptions should be interpretable by machines. A necessary prerequisite for machine-interpretable metadata and (semi-) automated system cooperation is the availability of detailed knowledge about the underlying business process models. Furthermore, not only the syntax but also the application semantics of business process describing metadata must be considered. The syntax defines the structure of data and can be represented in XML notation. The Petri Net Markup Language (PNML) (Weber & Kindler, 2003) is a popular proposal for an XML-based interchange format for Petri Nets. Semantic Web languages such as the Resource Description Framework (RDF) (Powers, 2003) and the Web Ontology Language (OWL) (McGuinness & van Harmelen, 2004) were proposed to make it particularly easy to model information in a machine-interpretable form. OWL is syntactically layered on RDF. Therefore, the syntax of OWL is the syntax of RDF/XML. OWL may enable automation of a variety of tasks currently being performed "manually" by human agents.

Figure 1. Interorganizational business process

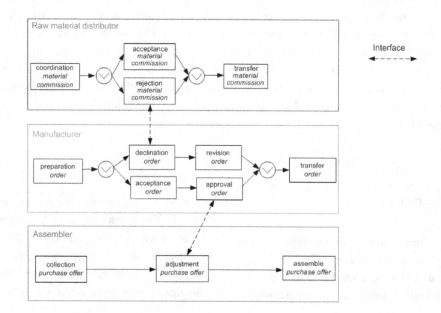

Figure 1 depicts a simplified interorganizational business process without using a specific modeling language. In short, this process represents three business processes of the application area of a raw material distributor, a manufacturer, and an assembler.

A possible interconnection of the subprocesses involved in this supply chain is highlighted by dotted arrows (named in the legend as interface). The interconnection of these business processes of different layers requires coordination time, coordination effort, and modeling experiences. Furthermore, the business partners are usually utilizing a different vocabulary. The partner on the first layer (raw material distributor) is using the term *material commission* in order to describe a commercial document used to request something, in contrast to the business partner on the second layer (manufacturer) that uses the term *order* and the one on the third layer (assembler) that uses the term *purchase order.*

To support automatic interconnectivity and business process coupling executed by machines, semantic representation of business units remains a challenge and has to be addressed by research. The aim of our approach is to provide a semantic description of process models represented with Petri Nets and to reduce efforts required to detect appropriate interfaces to support process interconnectivity. In summary, our objective is to provide flexibility, ease of integration, and a significant level of automation of loosely coupled business process models even if they do not share the respective vocabularies.

The structure of this chapter is as follows. In the next section we recall the main notions of Petri Nets. Thereafter, we will sketch the term ontology as being used in our application scenario and introduce a methodology in order to derive ontology based business process model descriptions. These so-called semantic business process models are then explained. Furthermore, we will elucidate a particular application scenario for semantic business process models. Especially we will introduce similarity measures which may help to solve ambiguity issues caused by the use of synonyms or homonyms for process element names and reasoning techniques to facilitate business

process interconnectivity. The development of a tool for modeling semantic business process models is described in the subsequent section. The final sections survey related work, discuss open problems, and give an outlook on future work.

MODELING BUSINESS PROCESS MODELS WITH PETRI NETS

Petri Nets are a widely accepted graphical language for the specification, simulation, and verification of information systems behavior. Moreover, they have been established in the context of workflow management to verify the correctness of workflow procedures.

Formally, a Petri Net is a directed bipartite graph with two sets of nodes (places and transitions) and a set of arcs (flow relation). Transitions are interpreted as dynamic elements and represent activities of a process. Conditions for the execution of activities are described by places. We will consider a Petri Net with P being the set of places, T being the set of transitions, F_r being the set of arcs connecting P-elements with T-elements, and F_w as arcs connecting T-elements and P-elements.

Numerous Petri Net variants have been introduced which can be subsumed in elementary or high-level Petri Nets. In elementary Petri Nets (place/transition nets), the flow of tokens representing anonymous objects defines the process flow. To describe objects with individual behavior, several variants of high-level Petri Nets have been proposed such as Predicate/Transitions Nets (Pr/T nets) (Genrich & Lautenbach, 1981) or XML Nets (Lenz & Oberweis, 2003).

In Predicate/Transition Nets, places represent relation schemes (predicates). A function assigns to each place a marking, which is a relation of the respective type. The set of all place markings at a given time describes a certain global system state. A transition represents an operation on the relations in its input/output places. If a transition occurs, tuples are removed from the relations in its input places and are inserted into the relations of its output places. A logical expression, which may be assigned to a transi-

Figure 2. Pr/T net representation of business processes (excerpt)

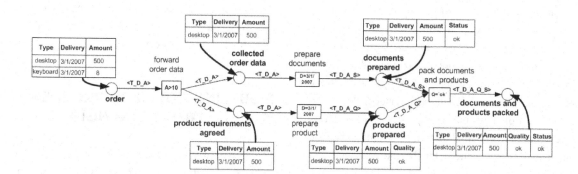

tion, makes it possible to specify certain conditions for the selection of tuples to be inserted or removed. When a transition fires, tupels are removed from the transition's input places and are inserted into the transition's output places according to the respective arc inscriptions. Figure 2 shows a (simplified) Pr/T Net description of a business process.

This business process performs order sending (where the order is described by its attributes Type, Delivery, and Amount). After receiving an order the forwarded order data will be collected and the product requirements will be agreed. If the documents are prepared and the quality of the products is "ok" (value of quality in relation to products prepared) then documents and products will be packed.

Petri Nets comprise an operational semantics for processes based on a formal interpretation of the net components and their dynamic behavior; however, interconnectivity between business partners requires that there is a common understanding of the real world meaning of places and transitions. Furthermore, in order to facilitate semantic interconnectivity between business process models, a (semi-) automated system cooperation is demanded. For this reason we describe an ontology based description for business process models. First, we introduce the term ontology in the following section.

ONTOLOGIES AND THE WEB ONTOLOGY LANGUAGE

An ontology (Baader, McGuinness, Nardi, & Patel-Schneider, 2003) defines the relevant concepts of its domain (the terminology), its properties, and instances (the world description). The following brief definition describes the term ontology as it is used in our scenario. An ontology O is defined by a tuple O as follows.

$$O := \left(C, H_c, P_c, H_p, I, A \right)$$

Concepts C are arranged in a subsumption hierarchy H_c. Concepts are defined by properties P_c (where properties can also be arranged in a hierarchy H_p). By instantiating concepts, each concept has a set of instances I. Additionally, an ontology might contain a set of axioms (denoted as A), which can be used to infer implicit knowledge from explicit knowledge. By standardizing the Web ontology language (OWL), the World Wide Web Consortium (W3C) laid the foundation for a wide-spread use of ontologies in business applications. OWL is syntactically layered on RDF; therefore, the syntax of OWL is the syntax of RDF/ XML (Beckett, 2004). The Web Ontology Language defines different properties to build an ontology such as object properties (link an individual to an individual),

Table 1. Example for OWL syntax

```
<owl:Class rdf:ID="Place">
   <rdfs:subClassOf rdf:resource="#PetriNet"/>
      <owl:Object property rdf:ID="transRef">
         <rdfs:domain rdf:resource="#Place"/>
         <rdfs:range rdf:resource=»#Transition»/>
      </owl:Object property>
   ...
</owl:Class>
```

datatype properties (link an individual to an XML Schema data type value or to an rdf literal), domains and ranges (properties link individuals from one domain to individuals from another domain), and datatypes and restriction types (Quantifier Restrictions, hasValue Restrictions and Cardinality Restrictions). Table 1 shows a simple example for OWL syntax. The concept *Place* is a subconcept of the concept *PetriNet* where *Place* has an Object property *transRef* with the domain *Place* and the range *Transition*.

OWL is given by three variants with an increasing degree of expressiveness: OWL Lite, OWL DL, and OWL Full. An ontology-based description of Petri Nets represents a foundation for an automatic or semi-automatic manipulation of business process models and supports the reasoning about data. This capability, particularly of OWL DL, will be required to realize an automatic assistant mechanism during process modelling; therefore, for our work, we will refer to OWL DL (description logic) in order to be able to use available off-the-shelf reasoning technologies. The sublanguage OWL Lite only uses some of the OWL language components, for example, concepts can only be defined in terms of named superconcepts (superconcepts cannot be arbitrary expressions), and only certain kinds of class restrictions can be used. OWL Full is not yet supported by reasoning software.

REALIZATION OF SEMANTIC BUSINESS PROCESS MODELS

A methodology for semantic business process models (ontology-based descriptions) and its realization are explained in this section.

Methodology

In order to define a methodology for creating an ontology, we refer to the steps as proposed in Noy and McGuiness (2001):

Step 1: Define concepts and properties of concepts of the application domain. Concepts represent a "group" where individuals belong. Concepts depend on the domain to be described by an ontology and may be, for instance, persons, resources, or objects.

Step 2: Classify concepts and properties in a concept hierarchy. The OWL specification distinguishes between object properties and datatype properties. Each object property is defined by a domain and a range that relate between instances of two concepts. Properties in an ontology express the relationships that may exist in the domain between concepts.

Step 3: Extend the defined concepts and properties with instances of the application domain. Each concept in the ontology is identified by an *identifier*. A concept has a set of *labels* that represent capable names for the concept.

Defining Concepts and Properties

Our approach is based on defining semantic metadata for business process models described with Petri Nets. This makes it particularly easy to automate the communication among process-implementing software components. Our starting point is a concise specification of Petri Net elements with the OWL elements *Concept*, together with the taxonomic construct

SubConceptOf and *Object-* and *Datatype Properties*. Every individual in the OWL world is a member of the concept *owl:Thing*. Thus each user-defined concept is implicitly a subconcept of *owl:Thing*.

The Petri Net structure comprises the elements places, transitions, arcs connecting places with transitions (F_r), and arcs connecting transitions with places (F_w). This structure is represented by the concepts:

- *Place* for all places in P,
- *Transition* for all transitions in T,
- *FromPlace* for all arcs in F_r,
- *ToPlace* for all arcs in F_w.

In order to express a coherency of nodes and arcs for Petri Nets, we introduce the object properties *hasNode* and *hasArc*. The object property *hasNode* is defined by the domain *PetriNet* and the range *Node* (with subclasses *Place* and *Transition* and the object property *hasArc* by the domain *PetriNet* and the range *Arc* with subclasses *FromPlace* and *ToPlace*). Figure 2 depicts the core concepts and properties of the Petri Net ontology.

The concepts *Place* and *Transition* have to be defined as disjoint concepts such that a single individual cannot be an instance of more than one of these two concepts. The disjointness of places and transitions can be expressed using the *owl:disjointWith* constructor.

Each arc concept (*FromPlace* and *ToPlace*) is identified by a pair of nodes being connected. Additionally, the property *hasNode* is defined by the domain *FromPlace* (with the range *Place*) and *ToPlace* (with the range *Transition*).

Table 2. owl: disjointWith

```
<owl:Class rdf:about="#Transition">
  <owl:disjointWith rdf:resource="#Place"/>
  <rdfs:subClassOf rdf:resource="#Node"/>
</owl:Class>
```

Figure 3. Core concepts of Petri Net ontology

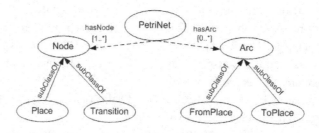

Figure 4. Object property hasNode

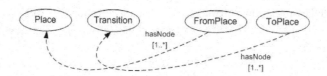

An arc connecting a transition to a place indicates an *Insert* operation, inserting, for example, attribute values into the transition's output place. An arc connecting a place to a transition indicates a *Delete* operation. Thus an object property *hasInscription* is introduced, which is defined by the domain *FromPlace* and *ToPlace* and the range *Delete* and *Insert*.

In Petri Net graphs a place follows a transition and vice versa. This is expressed via the object property *placeRef* (with domain *Transition* and range *Place*) or respectively *transRef* (with domain *Place* and range *Transition*).

A transition represents an operation on the relations in its input/output places. We express this property by assigning the object properties *hasCondition*, *hasOperation,* and *hasAttribute* with the domain *Transition* and the corresponding range.

The marking of a place in a Pr/T net is regarded as a set of tuples. Thus we introduce the concept *IndividualDataItem*. The tuples consist of attributes and values. To represent this structure of markings in our Petri Net Ontology we add to the concept *IndividualDataItem* the property *hasAttribute*. Values of Attributes are represented by the concept *Value*.

Important constructs in OWL are different restriction types, which are used to restrict the individuals that belong to a class. Restrictions in OWL fall into three main categories: quantifier restrictions (allValuesFrom, someValuesFrom), cardinality restrictions (minCardinality, maxCardinality, cardinality), and hasValue restrictions. Quantifier restrictions specify the exact number of relationships that an individual must participate in for a given property. In our Petri Net ontology, we denote that the concept *IndividualDataItem* has at least one attribute.

Quantifier restrictions consist of three parts:

1. A quantifier, which is either the existential quantifier ($\exists$), or the universal quantifier ($\forall$)
2. A property, along which the restriction holds
3. A filter that is a class description

For a given individual, the quantifier effectively puts constraints on the relationships in which the individual participates. This is done by specifying that at least one kind of relationship must exist or by specifying the only kinds of relationships that can exist. Existential restrictions describe the set of individuals that have at least one specific kind of relationship to individuals that are members of a specific class. In our Petri Net ontology, a restriction is defined that the object property *hasInscription* is defined either by all or some individuals from the concept *Attribute* (according to the respective arc inscriptions).

Classification of Concepts and Properties

In the next step, we classify all concepts and properties of the Petri Net ontology in a hierarchy. If software components of different business partners should interact, it must be known what is represented by a place, the meaning of objects contained in places, and their relationship to other objects.

Figure 5 depicts the Petri Net ontology. The Petri Net ontology comprises the concepts Place, Transition, FromPlace, ToPlace, Delete, Insert, LogicalConcept, IndividualDataItem, Condition, Operation, Attribute, and Value. For instance, the Object property *hasAttribute* is included in the concepts *LogicalConcept, IndividualDataItem, Delete,* and *Insert.*

Modeling of Instances

Our starting point was a concise specification of Petri Net elements with the OWL element *Concept*, the taxonomic constructor *SubConceptOf* and *Property,* and their modeling in OWL. In the following, we show the modeling of *Individuals* which is the third OWL element besides *Concepts* and *Properties*. Individuals or instances are specified by the modeler and depend on the modeling target. As an example, we show for the place *ORDER* of the business process in Figure 1 mapping individuals to OWL elements.

Figure 5. Petri Net ontology

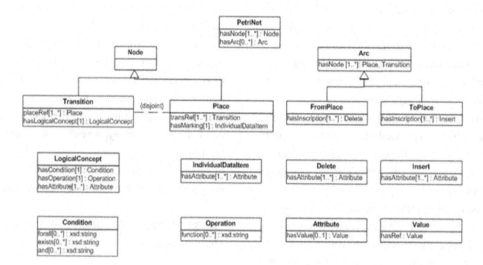

Figure 6. Mapping individuals to concepts and properties

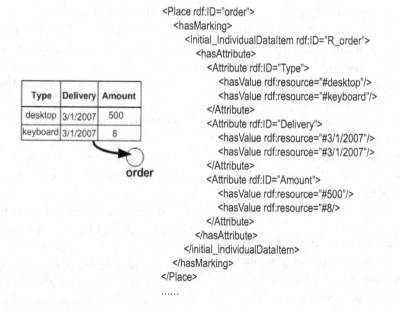

```
<Place rdf:ID="order">
  <hasMarking>
    <Initial_IndividualDataItem rdf:ID="R_order">
      <hasAttribute>
        <Attribute rdf:ID="Type">
          <hasValue rdf:resource="#desktop"/>
          <hasValue rdf:resource="#keyboard"/>
        </Attribute>
        <Attribute rdf:ID="Delivery">
          <hasValue rdf:resource="#3/1/2007"/>
          <hasValue rdf:resource="#3/1/2007"/>
        </Attribute>
        <Attribute rdf:ID="Amount">
          <hasValue rdf:resource="#500"/>
          <hasValue rdf:resource="#8/>
        </Attribute>
      </hasAttribute>
    </initial_individualDataItem>
  </hasMarking>
</Place>
......
```

APPLICATION SCENARIO

Figure 7 shows another Pr/T net representation of a business process. This business process performs hardware orders. After receiving an order, the checked orders will be sent to the invoicing and then the items will be packed.

When interconnecting the two processes (from Figures 2 and 7), specific business rules have to be considered in order to guarantee correct process composition. Usually, business process models are modeled according to specific business rules such as "if more than two persons travel together, then the third pays only half price."

These rules represent enterprise policies, knowledge, and expertise and thus have to be considered during process interconnectivity. Furthermore, in business relationships a commonly agreed vocabulary can usually not be postulated. Business rules and process element names may be described using different terms having the same meaning.

OWL itself does not provide any support for the specification of rules. The Semantic Web Rule Language (SWRL) (Horrocks, Patel-Schneider, Boley, Tabet, Grosof, & Dean, 2004a, 2004b), which maintains the flavor of OWL, extends the set of OWL axioms to include Horn-like rules of the form *if* (antecedent) … *then* (consequent). The combined adoption of semantic business process models and SWRL thus enables the realization of a rule-based interconnectivity of business processes, allowing reasoning support.

The ontology-based description of Petri Nets has to be extended with two Properties in order to support automatic rule inferencing. First we introduce a Property *isSelected* with the domain *Place* or *Transition* and the range *boolean* (true or false) that ensures only interconnectivity for the selected process element. The Property *initialElement* with the domain *PetriNet* and the range *Place* or *Transition* indicates the start element of a process. Besides this we also introduce the following SWRL predicates (expressed in natural language):

1. Value of the property *isSelected*(P- or T-element) must be true: the user chooses an element (P- or T-element; both named as *node1*) where the user has indicated that he or she wants to have an automatic interconnectivity of appropriately matching process elements (value of the property *isSelected*(*node1*) is true)

2. The property has a valid flow relation: a valid flow relationship ($F \subseteq (P \times T) \cup (T \times P)$) connects the selected *node1* and the first element (*node2*) of the process to be interconnected (named *net*).

Figure 7. Another Pr/T net representation of a business process (excerpt)

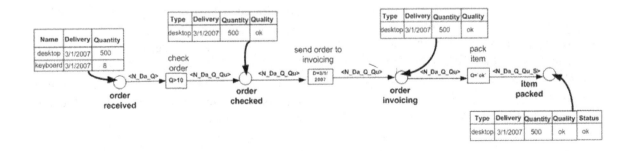

If these predicates are true, then all conditions in the IF part and all actions in the THEN part of the rule will be connected with AND operators. Additionally, specific SWRL predicates are inserted, which introduce the notion of order i.e. which action is performed before or after the other. (*beforeOrLast*, *afterOrFirst*).

The following example shows how a business rule will be transformed to SWRL syntax:

IF order is checked
THEN manufacture item AND pack item

isSelected(?node1,true) ∧ *initialElement(?net,?node2)* ∧

arcPossible(?node1,?net) ∧ *beforeOrLast(order_checked,?node2)*

∧ *afterOrFirst(manufacture_item,?node2)*

∧ *afterOrFirst(pack_item,?node2)* ⟶ *isPossible(?node1,?net)*

A commonly agreed vocabulary can usually not be postulated for rule description, for example, one user might denote the rule as given below and another one might denote it as given before.

IF customer order was verified
THEN initiate fabrication AND pack article

Therefore, the following shortly introduced similarity measures may help to overcome this problem (Ehrig, Koschmider, & Oberweis, 2007).

Intuitively, the degree of similarity between process models correlates positively with the number of used synonyms. Synonyms can be detected by a linguistic similarity measure that exploits all senses of a term as proposed by WordNet's (http://wordnet.princeton. edu/) synonym relationship. Typos in process element names can hamper correct calculation of linguistic similarity degrees. For instance, the terms (receive letter vs. recive leter) have a linguistic similarity of 0.0 due to spelling mistakes. Therefore we have extended an existing syntactic similarity measure for ontologies (Maedche & Staab, 2002) to support character string comparison.

Both similarity measures cannot support the

detection of homonyms. The syntactic and linguistic similarity for the terms (order vs. order) equals 1 because of identical pronounciation and character strings, but the terms may have different meanings (on the one hand an order may be a commercial document used to request someone to supply something, and on the other hand it may be a formal association of people with similar interests). A so-called context of process elements supports homonym detection by defining the set of all elements which influence the name's similarity. Furthermore, we assign to each context element weights in order to consider different influences of each context element.

To detect hyperonyms/hyponyms, we compute abstraction level similarities, which take into account the depth of terms in lexical reference systems such as WordNet.

Finally, we aggregate the four similarity measures syntactic, linguistic, structural similarity, and abstraction level-based similarity with particular weights to a combined similarity measure.

To include this semantic similarity in our reasoning process, we introduce a new predicate into SWRL denoted as *swrlb:semanticSimilarity*(?node1, ?node2), which evaluates to true if the semantic similarity of *node1* and *node2* is above a prespecified threshold.

IMPLEMENTATION

We have implemented a Petri Net editor called SemPeT (http://aifbserver.aifb.uni-karlsruhe.de/sempet/index.htm) that offers semantic business process models export, which employs the Jena Semantic Web Framework API Jena2 (HP). Users can model their Petri Net-based business process models in the graphical editor SemPeT. A screenshot of SemPeT is shown in Figure 8.

The extraction of ontological descriptions from business process models and the mapping to the Petri Net ontology is being carried out during the modeling process and is not visible to the modeler. The user can choose between several actions. The menu item

Import/Export offers export of the currently modeled business process to OWL and XML. In order to measure similarity between two business process models the user has to invoke the similarity measurement tool under the menu item Tools. Furthermore, this menu item offers a graphical user interface for a query language and a basic implementation of a recommendation system that are executed by KAON2 (http://kaon2.semanticweb.org/).

To store semantic business process models in Jena2 does not require any database management system. But, Jena2 supports relational database management systems such as MySQL, Oracle and PostgreSQL for persistent storage.

Currently, we are using the feasibility of semantic business process models for ontological reasoning to consider business rules in order to support users during process modeling and to decrease the amount of modeling time. For reasoning KAON2 supports a subset of OWL DL that makes reasoning decidable.

The integration of an ontology management system such as KAON2 makes it possible for business partners involved in business process interconnectivity to support (semi-) automatic parsing and reasoning about the data contained in Petri Nets.

RELATED WORK

To make data computer-interpretable has become ever more important since recent Web Services standards have paved the way for discovery and matching of semantically enriched data and services. Process execution languages such as BPEL4WS (Curbera et al., 2003) enable users to compose and orchestrate services to perform certain tasks. But these modeling languages do not yet support analysis methods to verify that business process models meet certain requirements.

In order to allow flexible automation and composition of semantic representations of Web services, OWL-S (OWL for Services) was proposed (Martin et al., 2004). Due to the lack of formal semantics in the OWL-S 1.0 specification, McIllraith and Narayanan use Petri Nets to test and verify the composition of Web services based on OWL-S (McIllraith & Narayanan, 2003). A lot of research is currently being done on automated provision and reasoning of Web Services (Cordoso & Sheth, 2002). Petri Nets can be used to concisely represent and analyze interorganizational business processes. Moreover, Petri Nets are suitable both for modeling business processes, which are to be implemented as Web services, and their coordination

Figure 8. Graphical user interface of SemPeT

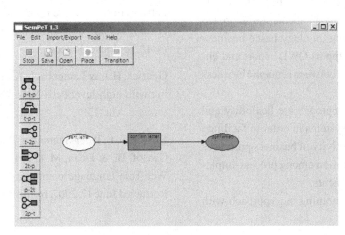

(Lenz & Oberweis, 2004).

To the best of our knowledge, there is no other approach that describes high-level Petri Nets in OWL. Gasevic and Devedzic (2004) propose a Petri Net ontology (for elementary Petri Nets) that should enable sharing Petri Nets on the Semantic Web and should make it possible to transform a specific XML-based Petri Net format into OWL. The aim of our work is to reuse and analyze business process models not primarily in the Semantic Web but in business environments. A domain ontology represents only a static structure of a domain; therefore, our Pr/T net Ontology contains, in contrast to Gasevic and Devedzic (2004), only static elements.

CONCLUSION AND OUTLOOK

The task to make business data computer-interpretable has become ever more important since recent Web Services standards have paved the way for discovery and matching of semantically enriched data and services. Furthermore, the rapid growth of data and communication technologies demands that companies focus on the content of data. Our approach provides concepts of semantic markup for Petri Nets. With this annotated semantics, one can define restrictions and reason about the process data contained in Petri Net components. Beyond the ontological representation of a Petri Net, we discussed the need of an ontology-based format for business process models that enable structured data to be interpreted unambiguously. Finally, we presented an implementation approach and a tool for representing ontology based business process models which support OWL export and enable to measure similarity between semantic business process models.

The benefits of our approach are flexibility and automation of involved systems in order to facilitate the semantic interconnectivity of business processes and to reduce communication among process-implementing software components.

Currently, we are combining our approach with

role- or document-based similarity methods in order to compute holistic similarities of business process models.

REFERENCES

Baader, F., McGuinness, D., Nardi, D., & Patel-Schneider, P. (2003). *The description logic handbook.* Cambridge.

Beckett, D. (2004). RDF/XML syntax specification, W3C Recommendation. Retrieved June 17, 2007, from *http://www.w3.org/TR/rdf-syntax-grammar/*

Cordoso, J., & Sheth, A. (2002). *Semantic e-Workflow composition* (Tech. Rep.). LSDIS Lab, Computer Science, University of Georgia.

Curbera, F., Goland, Y., Klein, J., Leymann, F., Roller, D., Thatte, S. et al. (2003). Business process execution language for Web services. *Retrieved June 17, 2007, from http://www.ibm.com/developerworks/library/ws-bpel/*

Ehrig, M., Koschmider, A., & Oberweis, A. (2007). Measuring similarity between semantic business process models. In J.F. Roddick & A. Hinze (Eds.), *Proceeding of the Fourth Asia-Pacific Conference on Conceptual Modeling, Vol. 67,* Australian Computer Science Communications, Ballarat, Australia (pp. 71-80).

Gasevic, D., Jovanovic, J., & Devedzic, V. (2004). Petrinet infrastructure for the semantic Web. In *Proceedings of the Symposium on Professional Practice in AI*, Toulouse, France.

Genrich, H.J., & Lautenbach, K. (1981). System modeling with high-level Petri Nets. *Theoretical computer science,* Vol. 13.

Horrocks, I., Patel-Schneider, P., Boley, H., Tabet, S., Grosof, B., & Dean, M. (2004). SWRL: A Semantic Web rule language combining OWL and RuleML. Retrieved June 17, 2007, from http://www.w3.org/Submission/2004/SUBM-SWRL-20040521/

Horrocks, I., Patel-Schneider, P.F., Boley, H., Tabet, S., Grosof, B., & Dean, M. (2004). Semantic Web rule language combining OWL and RuleML. W3C member submission. Retrieved June 17, 2007, from http://www.w3.org/Submission/SWRL/

HP. Jena 2 – a semantic Web framework. Retrieved June 17, 2007, from http://www.hpl.hp.com/semweb/jena.htm

Lenz, K., & Oberweis, A. (2003). Interorganizational business process management with XML nets. In H. Ehrig, W. Reisig, G. Rozenberg, & H. Weber (Eds.), *Petri Net technology for communication-based systems, advances in Petri Nets*, (Vol. 2472 of LNCS) (pp. 243-263). Springer-Verlag.

Lenz, K., & Oberweis, A. (2004). Workflow services: A Petri Net-based approach to Web services. In *Proceedings of International Symposium on Leveraging Applications of Formal Methods*, Paphos, Cyprus (pp. 35-42).

Maedche A., & Staab, S. (2002). Measuring similarity between ontologies. In *Proceedings of the European Conference on Knowledge Acquisition and Management, Lecture Notes in Computer Science* (pp. 251-263). Springer.

Martin, D., Paolucci, M., McIlraith, S., Burstein, M.,

McDermott, D., McGuinness, D. et al. (2004). Bringing semantics to Web services: The OWL-S approach. In *Proceedings of the First International Workshop on Semantic Web Services and Web Process Composition*, San Diego, CA (pp. 26-42).

McGuinness, D.L., & van Harmelen, F. (2004). OWL Web ontology language overview, W3C Recommendation. Retrieved June 17, 2007, from http://www.w3.org/TR/owl-features/

McIlraith, S., & Narayanan, S. (2003). Analysis and simulation of Web services. *Computer Networks: The International Journal of Computer and Telecommunications Networking, 42*(5), 675-693.

Noy, N.F., & McGuiness, D.L. (2001). *Ontology development 101: A guide to creating your first ontology* (Tech. Rep. KSL-01-05). Stanford Knowledge Systems Laboratory.

Powers, S. (2003). *Practical RDF* (1st ed.). Beijing; Köln: O'Reilly.

Reisig, W., & Rozenberg, G. (1998). *Lectures on Petri Nets I: Basic models. Lecture notes in computer science* (Vol. 1491). Berlin, Germany: Springer-Verlag.

Weber, M., & Kindler, E. (2003). The Petri Net markup language. In H. Ehrig (Ed.), *Petri Net technology for communication-based systems, advances in Petri Nets* (pp. 1-21). Berlin, Germany: Springer.

Section V
Applying Ontologies in a Business Context

Chapter XIV
Ontologies for Model–Driven Business Transformation

Juhnyoung Lee
IBM T. J. Watson Research Center, USA

ABSTRACT

Semantic markup languages such as RDF (resource description framework) and OWL (Web ontology language) are increasingly used to externalize metadata or ontology about business data, software, and services in a declarative form. Such externalized descriptions in ontological format are utilized for purposes ranging from search and retrieval to information integration and to business transformation. Ontology can significantly reduce the costs and improve the qualities of deploying, querying, integrating, and transforming enterprise systems. This chapter presents an innovative application of ontology to a model-driven approach to business analysis and transformation. The approach employs a daisy chain of business models for causality analyses. It links, by using semantic models, business processes and business components to IT solutions and capabilities at different phases of business transformation. The semantic models help infer causality of any business pain points and recommend appropriate solutions to fix business or IT shortfalls associated with the pain points in the process of business transformation. In addition, this chapter presents an enterprise-scale ontology management system which provides functionality, scalability, and performance demanded by enterprise applications such as the proposed model-driven business transformation. It describes the design and implementation of the management system which programmatically supports the ontology needs of business applications in a similar to that in which a database management system supports their data needs.

INTRODUCTION

Ontology is similar to a dictionary, taxonomy, or glossary, but with structure and formalism that enables computers to process its content. It consists of a set of concepts, axioms, and relations, and represents an area of knowledge. Unlike taxonomy or glossary, ontology allows to model arbitrary relations among concepts, also model logical properties and semantics of the relations such as symmetricity, transitivity, and inverse, and logically reason about the relations. Ontology is specified in a declarative form by using semantic markup languages such as RDF (W3C, 1999) and OWL (W3C, 2004). It provides a number of potential benefits in processing knowledge, including the separation of domain knowledge from operational knowledge, sharing of common understanding of subjects among humans and also among computer programs, and the reuse of domain knowledge. In general, ontology can be beneficial to any enterprise system dealing with multiple domain concepts that are interrelated and needs to use the concepts to describe the behavior or capabilities of its programs. Business application examples of ontology include business process integration by using Web services composition, information retrieval, and search systems for semantic-based search capabilities, video retrieval systems to annotate media with metadata, and business collaboration management using corporate social network to provide a common understanding to collaboration contexts and annotate them, to name a few.

Among the enterprise applications of ontology, this chapter focuses on its use in business transformation processes. Business transformation is a key executive management initiative that attempts to align the technology initiatives of a company closely with its business strategy and vision, and is achieved through efforts from both the business and IT sides of the company. However, the technology side of the company often emphasizes functions and capabilities, while the business side focuses on business impact and value. Because of this "business-IT gap" (McDavid, 2004), business transformation processes for IT and services are lengthy and costly. To address this problem, this chapter presents an innovative application of ontology to a model-driven approach to business analysis and transformation. This approach innovatively extends the model-driven business transformation (IBM, 2004; Lee, 2005) and utilizes semantic models that link business performance measures, business processes, and components with key IT enablers all the way down to the IT infrastructure. The ontological model

is used to infer both direct and indirect causalities of any business pain points and recommend appropriate solutions to fix the business or IT shortfalls associated with the business pain points.

In the second part of this chapter, we present an enterprise-scale ontology management system which provides functionality, scalability, and performance that enterprise applications such as the proposed model-driven business transformation would demand. In recent years, there has been a surge of interest in using ontological information for communicating knowledge among software systems. As a result, an increasing range of software systems need to engage in a variety of ontology management tasks, including the creation, storage, search, query, reuse, maintenance, and integration of ontological information. Recently, there have been efforts to externalize such ontology management burden from individual software systems and put them together in middleware known as an ontology management system. An ontology management system provides a mechanism to deal with ontological information at an appropriate level of abstraction. By using programming interfaces and query languages the ontology management system provides, application programs can manipulate and query ontologies without the need to know their details or to re-implement the semantics of standard ontology languages. Such a setting is analogous to the way a database management system allows applications to deal with data as tables and provides a query engine that can understand and optimize SQL queries. This chapter describes the design and implementation of the SnoBase ontology management system (Lee & Goodwin, 2006), which was developed at the IBM T.J. Watson Research Center.

The rest of this chapter is structured as follows: We introduce the model-driven business transformation and briefly describe how ontologies and semantic technologies can facilitate the business transformation process. Next, we present a semantic model for the proposed business transformation approach and then explain several qualitative business analyses helping business transformation. We then provide a schematic overview of the SnoBase ontology management system and describe the design of JOBC API with examples. The final sections present a model-driven approach to building an environment for the development and transformation of semantic applications and models and draw conclusions and outline future work.

MODEL-DRIVEN BUSINESS TRANSFORMATION

Among the emerging methods and the supporting technology for business transformation in the service-led economy is the *model-driven business transformation*. Briefly, the model-driven approach requires a model representation of business entities such as business processes, components, competencies, activities, resources, metrics, key performance indicators (KPI), and their relationships. Then, the model is utilized to identify opportunities for saving costs or improve business processes. Semantic models using ontology markup languages provide a useful representation of business models because they are not limited by types of relationships among business

entities. Also, the automatic reasoning capability of semantic models provides an effective method for analyzing business models for identifying cost-saving or process improvement opportunities. For example, business performance metrics naturally fit well with business activities and are traditionally represented that way. By using this relationship between business activities and metrics, and also the relationship between business components and business activities represented in a semantic model, a business analyst can infer a relationship between business components and metrics. This relationship can provides business insights into how the corporation can improve its performance metrics by addressing issues with the business components associated with the selected set of metrics. Then, by identifying, again in the semantic model, IT systems associated with the business components, the business analysts are able to suggest recommendations about IT system management to improve performance metrics.

More formally, the model-driven business transformation utilizes a multi-layer model approach to link business and IT semantics (Lee, 2005). The upper

Figure 1. Model-driven business transformation

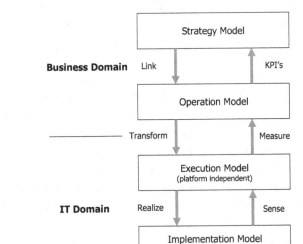

239

layers of the model represent business semantics in the terms familiar to business executives, business managers, and analysts such as key performance indicators, operational metrics, business processes, activities, and governance. The lower layers of the model represent IT architecture comprising a wide range of services implemented in IT infrastructure such as service-oriented architecture. The vision of this multi-layer model is to enable IT solutions to accurately reflect and be driven by business intent. Figure 1 illustrates the multi-layer model approach to business transformation.

The key to this multi-layer model is that the layers are linked in meaningful ways so that changes in one layer can ripple through other layers. The representation and enforcement of the semantics of the different layers and also of the connections between the layers is essential to the model-driven approach and also is an application area of the Semantic Web technology. This model-driven approach provides a convergence of the business and IT models using a multi-layer model, which tightly couples the business and IT models. In many ways, this vision is not new. Technologists have been working towards generalized business process integration and automation for many years. However, this approach is different from the typical technology-oriented business integration because it provides a top-down business perspective which enforces a business-orientation of business transformation.

Once equipped with end-to-end tools for the model design, connection, and transformation, this approach has the potential to reduce the time-to-value of business solution implementations. It would replace the manual creation of unstructured business documents and informal business models with a guided transformation of a structured multi-layer model. The IT solutions generated by this approach would accurately and precisely reflect the original business semantics and are directly deployable and executable in a service-oriented architecture. This model-driven business transformation approach is a significant step towards closing the infamous "business-IT gap" (McDavid, 2004), achieving maintainable alignment between business design and IT solutions.

Recent trends in business and software componentization and modeling would boost this model-driven approach as a prominent methodology for the service-led economy. In recent years, enterprises componentize into discrete services to achieve operational efficiency, flexibility, and to sharpen their focus. Also, the consulting industry increasingly utilizes sophisticated modeling techniques to understand and transform businesses. In the IT domain, software modeling technologies and methodologies such as the Object Management Group's universal modeling language (OMG, 2000) and model-driven architecture (OMG, 2001) are widely adopted and studied in both industry and academia. In addition, W3C's Web services (W3C, 2002) and related technologies accelerate the shift towards service-oriented architectures (W3C, 2001) which fit the model-driven business transformation approach. The trends in business and software componentization and modeling effectively converge to provide new layers of business understanding and responsiveness.

Traditionally, a model has been used to mean a physical representation of some thing in various contexts including studies of physics, mathematics, statistics, economics, geology, psychology, and computer science, to name a few. As we observe in examples such as the particle physics history, a good model capacitates the progress of the study, while a poor one limits it. A model often dominates the understanding and solution to the given problem in the domain. Additionally, the language used to specify a model often impacts on (either assists or limits) the thinking process with the model. The most important component of the model-driven business transformation approach is the model, for example, the representation of the semantics of business and IT resources. With the multiple layers in the model, another key component is the representation of the meaning of the links across different layers. It is crucial to this model-driven approach how we represent in a language and enforce the semantics of the layers and also of their links.

W3C's Semantic Web (W3C, 2001), which intends to create a universal medium for information exchange by giving semantics, in a manner understandable by machines, to the content of resources, provides an appropriate option to address this modeling requirement of the model-driven approach. The Semantic Web is comprised of the standards and tools of markup languages including XML (W3C, 1998), XML schema (W3C, 2001), RDF (W3C, 1999), RDF schema (W3C, 2004) and OWL (W3C, 2004). These semantic markup languages would be used to specify ontological representation of models including the business and IT models and their connections. The semantic markup languages would be used to specify the convergence of business and IT models, and, more importantly, their metamodels. The ontological representation of the metamodel of a constituent model enables reasoning about the instance model, which enables a dependency analysis to deduce unknown or implied relationships among entities within the instance model. The analysis would be extended across multiple layers of models. The semantic model-based dependency analysis would reveal which entity has an impact on which entities of the multiple layers of the model such as business components, business processes, key performance indicators, IT systems, software classes and objects, and so forth. This semantic model-based analysis can be applied to a model that provides an introspective view of the business within an enterprise. Also, it can be applied to a value network which yields an extrospective view of businesses in an ecosystem.

In addition to its use in the model-driven business transformation, the semantic model approach is also useful in business information and process integration. Suppose a business solution requires integrating a number of data sources (or application interfaces for process integration) which provide different but overlapping conceptual models. For information integration, we would start building a global conceptual model which is essentially a semantic model. Then, the data sources are defined as views into this global model, although there is no guarantee of completeness. A query to the data sources would be expressed in the global semantic model. The result set for the query would be constructed by finding all conjunctive queries over the views that are contained in the top-layer

query. A semantic model-based approach to process integration would require a similar set of steps over a set of overlapping application interfaces.

The model-driven business transformation approach proposes new business methods and the supporting technology by introducing a multi-layer model which couples business and IT models. It provides a top-down business perspective which enforces a business-orientated business transformation. It has the potential to provide a number of benefits over the traditional technology-oriented approach, including business-IT alignment, reason about business design and transformation, real-time visibility into business operation, improved business performance management, rapid and repeatable IT solution implementation, and adaptive IT solution implementation. The key to this model-driven approach is that the layers are linked in meaningful ways and that the semantics of the links are effectively represented and reasoned. Therefore, changes in one layer can accurately ripple through other layers. The semantic Web technology provides an appropriate option for this modeling requirement by enabling representation and enforcement of the semantics of the layers of the model. It poses a key enabling technology for the emerging service science, which will meld technology with an understanding of business processes and organization.

SEMANTIC MODELS FOR BUSINESS TRANSFORMATION

Figure 2 illustrates part of the high-level semantic model designed for the model-driven business transformation. The model was used in a research prototype system for business transformation referred to as *VIOLA* developed at the IBM T.J. Watson Research Center (Lee & Ivan, 2006). The model captures business entities (and their relationships) of an enterprise that are involved in creating or defining value. The business entities in the model include business components, business processes and activities, operational metrics, key performance indicators, and value drivers. In addition, the model represents their relationships to resources, services, messages, IT infrastructure, and solutions. Often, solutions refer to both IT and business capabilities to support certain business objectives and strategies or address business pain points.

It is important to note that each business entity in this model, such as business components, business processes, operational metrics, key performance indicators, value drivers and solutions, has its own (hierarchical or networked) structure with its own constituent elements; therefore, each forms a model in its own right. In that sense, our semantic model is a metamodel and we often call it a *daisy-chain of models*. It is the daisy-chain part that enables the causality analysis across business entities by discovering direct and indirect relationships among them through inference.

To allow the user to explore the rich information captured by this model, we define multiple views into the model referred to as *business maps*. Each business map shows various entities involved in running and

understanding of business and their relationships. Our business maps provide visual models which organize the above-mentioned business entities in a structured way. In addition, they provide user interfaces which allows the user to interactively navigate and explore the information space for an analysis purpose.

Figure 3 shows a screenshot of a business map in the VIOLA system that contains the component business map, the value driver tree, and the business activity tree. To build such a business map, we utilize industry standard taxonomies of business processes and metrics such as APQC process classification framework (APQC, 2004), and their relationship to value drivers and business components. Additionally, we allow the user to customize the industry standards to the needs of a specific enterprise, and import and export the enterprise-specific value driver trees and component business maps.

Figure 2. Semantic model for business transformation

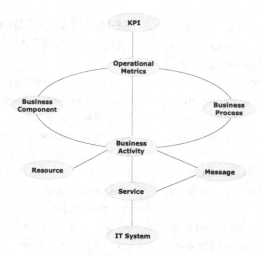

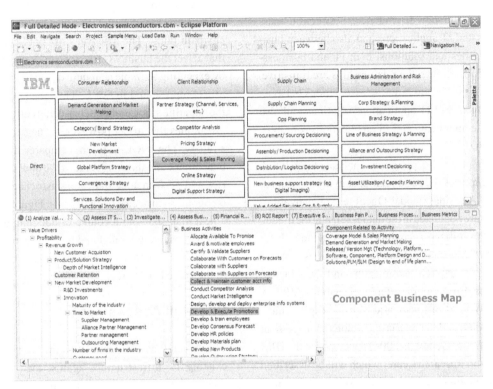

Figure 3. Business map views in VIOLA (permission provided by IBM)

SEMANTIC ANALYSES FOR BUSINESS TRANSFORMATION

The main advantage of the VIOLA semantic model is the enablement of various types of analyses that would allow the user to obtain interesting insights into the current state of a business and its possible business transformation opportunities. The VIOLA system is designed to provide the qualitative business analysis, among others, based on component business models, business process models, value driver models, and solution models. By linking them, VIOLA provides an end-to-end suite of business analysis capabilities, enabling business and value-oriented business trans-

formation. This section describes a few qualitative analysis capabilities of VIOLA.

Dependency Analysis

The dependency analysis allows the user to explore the business maps and understand the correlations and (direct and indirect) dependencies among business entities. For examples, this capability can interactively identify one or more business components associated with a particular value driver. Conversely, it can find one or more value drivers that are affected by the performance of a particular business component. The associations between value drivers and business components are discovered through their relationships with business processes and activities. Similarly, VIOLA can identify and show dependencies between business activities and IT applications and also between business activities and solutions, both IT and business-driven. Furthermore, the relationships are transitive, and so it is possible to infer the associations between value drivers and IT applications/solutions and also between components and IT applications/solutions, and so on.

To support the dependency analysis, the VIOLA system captures the basic relationship information in the VIOLA business model. Once the explicit relationship data are populated in the database using the model, the system utilizes a semantic query engine to infer implicit relationships among various business entities by using the explicit relationships and their logical properties. To provide the inference capability, VIOLA utilized W3C's OWL semantic Web markup language (W3C, 2004) and the SnoBase ontology management system (Lee & Goodwin, 2006) developed at the IBM T.J. Watson Research Center which will be described in the following sections. While OWL and SnoBase for VIOLA was a choice of convenience based on their immediate availability for the development, the semantic models used in VIOLA could be represented in knowledge model languages such as *topic map* (Topic Map, 2000), which is an ISO standard for the representation and interchange of knowledge, with an emphasis on the discoverability of information.

Heat Map Analysis

This analysis is an essential capability of component business modeling (CBM) (IBM, 2005) where the user discovers one or more "hot" components that are associated with one or more business strategies and/or pain points. In the traditional CBM analysis, this step was conducted manually by the analyst depending on his/her knowledge and expertise in the business domain. VIOLA automated the capability by taking performance values into account with the dependency analysis.

First, the system allows the user to explore the value driver tree to identify one or more value drivers that may be associated with a certain business strategy/pain point. The discovery of "hot" components that affect the business strategy can be accomplished by executing a simple semantic query to the business model represented in OWL. Then the system colors the identified hot components differently to distinguish ones that affect positively or negatively to the strategy. The VIOLA system compares the industry benchmark and the as-is value of the operational metrics and performance indicators associated with the components to decide on their color. Figure 3 displays a heat map showing a couple of hot components affecting positively (as denoted by the green color) to a value driver, customer retention, which is highlighted in the value driver tree.

Shortfall Assessment

The shortfall assessment allows the user to map the existing IT infrastructure against the "hot" components identified in the heat map analysis. It helps understand how the current IT infrastructure, such as applications and network capabilities, supports the business, especially for those hot components. The analysis requires collecting the information on the current IT infrastructure and representing it in a semantic business model in OWL. Then the mapping of IT applications and capabilities to the components becomes, again, an execution of a simple semantic query to the semantic model.

VIOLA visualizes the mapping on the CBM map by overlaying IT applications on components. Then, the user can visually identify possible IT shortfalls and classify them into several types. Typically, four types of opportunities tend to arise. First, a *gap* indicates that a hot component does not have any IT support. The enterprise may want to consider an IT investment to improve the component's performance and support the intended business transformation. Second, a *duplication* indicates that a component is supported by multiple IT applications, possibly, deployed over time. The business may want to consolidate the applications to improve performance and reduce cost in communication and maintenance overhead. Third, a *deficiency* indicates that the current application lacks key functionality or is poorly designed, and so incurs a project opportunity. Finally, an *over-extension* indicates that a system designed to support one business component is extended beyond its core capability to support others. Different definitions for the shortfall types may apply. With precise definitions of the shortfall types, the VIOLA system also automates the shortfall classification and recommends to the user the initially identified shortfalls.

It is important to note that an IT system can be involved with multiple situations. The value model of the VIOLA system takes that fact into account, with an optimized plan for implementation projects to maximize the investment. An integrated management approach such as project portfolio management ensures that the project opportunities are effectively taken into account, that the best use is made of available resources by applying them to the highest priority opportunities, that the projects are regularly assessed, and that management actions are taken to keep them aligned with objectives.

Solution Proposal

Once IT shortfalls are identified and classified, one or more solutions are proposed from solution catalogs which provide information on various IT and/or business solutions. The source of the solution catalogs are solution and service providers. The solutions may be prefabricated ones which can be deployed with relatively minor configuration and customization. Alternatively, the solutions can be designed for the specific IT shortfall and composed accordingly by using enabling technologies. Recently, more and more solutions are composed by using Web services (W3C, 2002) for their cost-effectiveness. The proposed solutions, prefabricated or composed, will address the shortfalls and support the intended business transformation. For example, the client's shortfall is a gap in a business component associated with, say, marketing. The user will want a CRM (Customer Relationship Management) solution that will replace the current manual work to improve the component's performance. If a duplication shortfall is identified, the user will propose an IT consolidation solution to fix it.

VIOLA allows the user to explore the solution space to identify one or more solutions that may address one or more shortfalls of interest. The discovery of solutions for supporting components associated with a shortfall can be automatically conducted by executing a semantic query that correlates solutions and components by using their relationships to business activities. In addition, VIOLA allows the user to manually correlate them, if desired. If there is no prefabricated solution available from existing solution catalogs to support a certain hot component and/or an IT shortfall, the VIOLA system helps the user start composing a new solution, by providing a link to a solution composer tool, such as IBM's WebSphere Business Modeler, which utilizes and supports service-oriented architecture.

SNOBASE ONTOLOGY MANAGEMENT SYSTEM

In recent years, an increasing range of business software systems need to engage in a variety of ontology management tasks, including the creation, storage, query, and integration of ontological information, and the needs turned into requirements for middleware known as ontology management systems. To make an ontology management system fit well into the current software development environment and reduce rather than increase the burden on software architects, programmers, and administrators, we synthesize concepts familiar to software developers with ideas from the semantic Web and ontology communities. The SnoBase system supports the ontology needs of applications in a similar way a database management system supports the data needs of applications: by design. For programmers, SnoBase provides a Java API

Figure 4. SnoBase ontology management system architecture

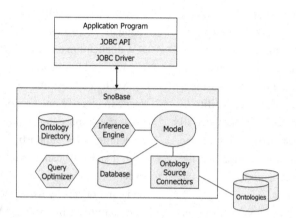

referred to as Java Ontology Base Connector (JOBC), which is the ontological equivalent of Java Data Base Connector (JDBC). JOBC provides a simple-to-use but powerful mechanism for application programmers to utilize ontologies without dealing with the details of ontological information. In addition, the ontology management system supports a number of query languages. At present, SnoBase supports a variant of SPARQL query language for RDF (W3C, 1999) as ontological equivalents of SQL of relational database systems.

One of challenges in the design of an industry-strength ontology management system is the versatility of application programming interfaces and query languages for supporting such diverse applications. This objective requires a careful design to simultaneously satisfy seemingly conflicting objectives such as being simple, easy-to-use, and easy-to-adopt for the developers. Another challenge in ontology management is to provide ontology-enhanced industrial applications with a system that is scalable (supporting thousands of simultaneous distributed users), available (running 365x24x7), fast, and reliable. These nonfunctional features are essential not only for the initial develop-

ment and maintenance of ontologies, but also during their deployment.

To provide a holistic management support for the entire lifecycle of ontological information, including ontology creation, storage, search, query, reuse, maintenance, and integration, an ontology management system needs to address a wide range of problems: ontology models, ontology base design, query languages, programming interfaces, query processing and optimization, federation of knowledge sources, caching and indexing, transaction support, distributed system support, and security support, to name a few. While some of these areas are new challenges for ontology management systems, some are familiar. There have been active studies, particularly in relation to traditional studies on knowledge representation, or recent studies on semantic Web standards. Our approach to the ontology management support is a pragmatic one, that is, we identify missing pieces in this picture, and engineer and synthesize them with prior work for providing a holistic management system for ontological information.

Figure 4 shows a schematic overview of the SnoBase ontology management system. Conceptually, the application programs interact with the JOBC API that provides high-level access to ontology resources and the ontology engine. The application program interacts with the JOBC API that provides an access to an implementation of the API via an ontology base driver. In this case, our driver is the SnoBase driver. In this section, we will describe the each component of the SnoBase ontology management system.

Java Ontology Base Connector

The SnoBase system provides a Java API referred to as Java Ontology Base Connector (JOBC), which is the ontological equivalent of the Java Data Base Connector (JDBC). The JOBC API follows the design patterns of JDBC, with several alterations. Just like JDBC, JOBC provides a connection-based interaction between applications and ontology sources. Also, JOBC provides JDBC-style, cursor-based result sets for representing query results. The similarity of JOBC to JDBC was a design decision to help application developers of SnoBase quickly learn the programming style of JOBC from their previous experience of the popular JDBC protocol. One difference between JOBC and JDBC is that JOBC allows connections to be made without reference to a particular base ontology. Such connections provide an access to default ontologies of the top-level definitions of XML-based ontology languages such as OWL, RDF, RDF Schema, and XML Schema. These definitions are required in order to process any ontological information.

SnoBase Driver

This component is an IBM driver for the JOBC interface that is equivalent to the IBM DB2 driver for JDBC. The SnoBase driver consists of Java classes that will provide an implementation of the JOBC API, and contains of a number of components: a local ontology directory, an inference engine, a working memory, a query optimizer, and a set of connectors, and other infrastructure needed to support ontology management.

Ontology Directory

This component provides the meta-level information about ontologies that are available to the SnoBase driver. By default, the ontology directory contains the references to the top-level definitions of OWL, RDF, RDF Schema, XML Schema, and similar definitions for the set of XML-based ontology languages supported. In addition, the ontology directory provides metadata such as deployment information and additional sources of ontology information. For each ontology source, the directory will need to store the URI, but may additionally store information about the contents of the ontology source to aid in query optimization.

Inference Engine

This component provides a mechanism for interpreting the semantics of an ontology language, represented as a set of language specific rules. The rules are used to answer queries, when the requested fact is not immediately available, but must be inferred from available facts. For example, if the application requests the childrenOf an individual, but the working memory only contains parentOf relations, the inference engine can use the inverse property statements about childrenOf and parentOf to identify the correct response. The details of this component, different approaches to implementing this component, and issues of the scalability and performance will be discussed in another section.

Query Language

Currently, the SnoBase system supports a variant of SPARQL Query Language for RDF as an ontological equivalent of SQL. SPARQL is a language and protocol supporting agent-to-agent query-answering dialogues using knowledge represented in RDF. It precisely specifies the semantic relations among a query, a query answer, and the ontology base(s) used to produce the answer. It also supports query-answering dialogues in which the answering agent may use automated reasoning methods to derive answers to queries. An SPARQL query contains a query pattern that is a collection of RDF sentences in which some literals and/or URIs have been replaced by variables. A query answer provides bindings of terms to some of these variables such that the conjunction of the answer sentences—produced by applying the bindings to the query pattern and considering the remaining variables in the query pattern to be existentially quantified—is entailed by a knowledge base (KB), called the answer KB. This design provides a simple but expressive query model. To make a query, a program simply describes the concept it is searching for, indicating with variables which aspects of matching concepts it is interested in receiving as part of a reply. This query model is similar to the concept of query-by-example, but with the advantage that the ontology language allows a richer method for describing the examples.

Query Optimizer

For applications that connect to large databases and/or ontologies, it will not be feasible to load the entire set of available information into working memory. Instead, the driver will query the ontology source for appropriate information as it is needed. In addition, the task of the query optimizer is to not only optimize the retrieval of information from ontology sources, but also coordinate queries that span multiple sources.

Ontology Source Connectors

These connectors provide a mechanism for reading, querying, and writing ontology information to persistent storage. The simplest connector is the file connector that is used to store information to the local file system. In addition, there will be connectors for storing ontological information in remote servers. Also, the connectors are used to implement caching of remote information to cache the definitions of the top-level ontology definitions OWL, RDF, RDF schema,

and XML schema to allow the system to work if the W3C Web site were inaccessible.

JAVA ONTOLOGY BASE CONNECTOR

As described earlier, we designed the JOBC API for SnoBase as an ontological equivalent of JDBC. The API is implemented using the abstract factory pattern (Grand, 1998). An abstract factory class defines methods to create an instance of each abstract class that represents a user interface widget. Concrete factories are concrete subclasses of an abstract factory that implements its methods to create instances of concrete widget classes for the same platform. The DataManager class provides a method that is used to construct a connection, based on the URI used to initiate the connection. There is a mechanism in the DataManager that uses the database type specified in the URI to identify and load the correct driver. This driver is then used to create a connection of the appropriate type. The connection then acts as a factory to produce objects, such as statements. The objects created implement interfaces defined in the JDBC package, but have implementations that are provided by the driver that is loaded. We follow a similar design pattern in the implementation of JOBC, with several alterations, as we previously described. The following code sample illustrates the use of JOBC.

In this example, the code first gets a connection. This connection is then used to create resources and a statement (john isA researcher). This statement is then asserted into the inference engine. The code then creates a simple query for the asserted fact and retrieves it from the working memory of the inference engine. More complex queries can be implemented using variables. For example, the following query requests all who are researchers.

The results of such a query are a set of triples that include the binding(s) of the variable(s) in the query. In this case, the variable X is bound to john. Using these basic APIs, SnoBase programmers can build

Figure 5. JOBC statement

```
/* We connect to an ontology resource. */
Connection connection = DriverManager.getConnection();
RDFResource john = connection.createRDFResource("John");
RDFProperty isA = connection.createRDFProperty("isA");
RDFClass researcher = connection.createRDFClass("researcher");

/* We assert a statement in inference engine: John isA researcher. */
Statement statement = connection.createStatement(John, isA, researcher);
connection.assert(statement);

/* We create a simple query. */
StatementCollection query = connection.createStatementCollection();
query.addStatement(statement);
ResultSet resultSet = connection.select(query);
```

Figure 6. JOBC query

```
/* We form a query: show me all who isA researcher. */
Variable X = connection.createVariable("?X");
Statement queryStatement = connection.createStatement(X, isA, researcher);

/* We create a simple query. */
query.addStatement(queryStatement);
resultSet = connection.select(query);
```

more complicated queries. For example, a query may contain multiple variables and multiple (query) statements. Also, note that SnoBase does not simply retrieve information previously stored for queries. Instead, by using an inference engine, it infers for answering facts that are not immediately available.

MODEL-DRIVEN APPROACH TO SEMANTIC TOOLKIT

Until now, we have focused on the description of the application programming interfaces, query languages, and inference engines of the SnoBase ontology management system. In this section, we will describe its environment for application and model development and transformation, which is equally important in the adoption of the semantic technology in the industry. The work presented in this section is a result from collaboration between the IBM T.J. Watson Research Center and the IBM China Research Lab.

Participating in a number of real-world applications by using the SnoBase ontology management system, we have learned that it is critical to provide a comprehensive development environment including supporting tools for the application developers. A pick-and-choose approach to the best of the breed tools from different environments does not always work well for the majority of the developers and often results in a longer learning curve for the developers. A comprehensive ontology development environment often means a tight integration of various tools for application development, ontology development, model import, and transformation, among others. Semantic markup languages such as W3C's RDF and OWL are based on the work in the logic and AI (artificial intelligence) communities, such as description logic and knowledge representation. The syntax of these languages is less intuitive to those trained for object-oriented programming and simple XML-based languages. This deficiency makes the job of subject matter experts and application developers difficult, and often affects negatively to the adoption of the semantic technology in the industry. An effective ontology application development environment should bridge this gap between the semantic markup languages and the object-oriented programmers by providing a tight and seamless integration.

Another consideration for the industry adoption of the semantic technology is the interoperability of the semantic markup languages with the well-established and widely-accepted industry standard modeling languages such as entity-relation (ER) modeling, XML schema, and unified modeling language (UML). The fact is that enterprises developed models in these languages for the past few decades and invested significantly to build systems around them. Despite all the advantages the semantic technology brings in, it is highly unlikely that the enterprises abandon the legacy systems and develop new systems around the semantic technology only. Rather, the users of the semantic technology in the industry would be interested in the interoperability of the modeling languages, and the reuse of the existing models and data with the semantic technology.

To address these practical requirements of the industry, we took an approach based on the model driven architecture (MDA), which enables developers and users to design, build, integrate, and manage applications throughout their lifecycle, while separating technology and business concerns (OMG, 2001). The Object Management Group's MDA specification provides means to organize and manage enterprise architectures supported by automated tools and services for both defining the models and facilitating transformations between different model types. It also provides an open, vendor-neutral approach against the challenge of interoperability. It facilitates efficient use of models in the software development process and reuse of best practices when creating families of systems.

For implementation, we utilized the eclipse modeling framework (EMF), which is IBM's open source MDA infrastructure for integration of modeling tools (Eclipse, 2004). A model specification described in various modeling languages including XML metadata interchange (XMI) language, XML Schema, and annotated Java source can be imported into EMF. Then EMF produces a set of Java classes for the model, a set of adapter classes that enable viewing and command-based editing of the model, and a basic editor. In its current implementation, EMF does not provide formal semantics definitions, inference, and the related model specifications. We are adding this capability to EMF for the comprehensive ontology application development environment and the dynamic application integration.

For adding the semantic model transformation capability to EMF, we utilized the OMG's specification of ontology definition metamodel (ODM) (Chang & Kendall, 2004), which provides metamodels of W3C's RDF and OWL in UML. By using EMF and ODM, we generated a foundational memory model, that is, Java classes, for the constructs of RDF and OWL.

This foundational memory model is referred to as EODM (eclipse ontology definition metamodel). By adding several necessary helper classes and methods to EODM, we can use it to create, edit, and navigate any models in RDF and OWL.

We also added an RDF/OWL parser to EODM, which can load RDF/OWL files into EODM and generate RDF/OWL files from EODM, that is, serialize EODM models to standard XML RDF/OWL files. The parser utilizes an XMI adaptor which enables the transformation between the RDF/OWL models and EMF Core (Ecore) models (Eclipse, 2004). The transformation is made possible by defining a mapping between RDF/OWL and the Ecore metamodel. The transformation opens a way to interoperability between RDF/OWL models and other EMF supported models, which currently include ones defined in XML Schema, UML, and annotated Java classes. The support of other models such as Entity Relationship models in EMF will be provided in the near future. By leveraging the RDF/OWL parser and the bidirectional transformation between the RDF/OWL models and the Ecore models, ontology application developers can develop ontologies using their favorite model building tools, import them into EMF, transform their models into OWL ontologies, enrich them with semantics, leverage their inference capability, and utilize the comprehensive development facility of Eclipse and EMF.

To be more specific, the EODM Ecore model is the core model that represents ontologies in memory. It is the intermediate model for imported and transformed legacy models, as well as the generated ontology, Java code, Java editor, and Java edit. The development environment allows its users to manipulate EODM Ecore models, enrich it with semantic specification, and generate Java code. A default set of mappings between metamodels of legacy models and OWL are developed in EMF. Eclipse plug-in developers can extend the mappings to handle other types of legacy models or other elements in legacy models specifying semantics. In the generated Java code, a small foot-print inference engine is shipped with the code and can be invoked by applications. The generated Java editor and Java edit provide ready-to-use visual tools to populate or manipulate instances of OWL models. The visual tools are actually copies of the standard methods of supporting application development in EMF.

CONCLUDING REMARKS

An increasing range of business software utilizes ontology that externalizes knowledge for a variety of purposes in a declarative way. In this chapter, we presented a semantic-based, model-driven business transformation as an emerging application domain of semantic models. While semantic technologies are actively applied to traditionally well-known areas such as information search and integration, their application to the areas of business transformation and services is still in its infancy. The presented approach is comprised of four modeling elements. First, *model-driven business transformation* provides a multilayer model linking business and IT semantics, and enables IT and services to accurately reflect and be driven by business value. The upper layers of model represent business semantics in the terms familiar to business executives, business managers, and analysts such as key performance indicators, operational metrics, business processes, activities, and governance. The lower layers of the model represent IT architecture comprising a wide range of services implemented in IT infrastructure such as service-oriented architecture. Second, *component business modeling* provides a strategic-level business view of an enterprise in a dashboard and enables business analyses based on business impacts. The CBM methodology enables a number of qualitative business analysis for identifying "hot" components and IT shortfalls that are associated with business pain points. Third, *value modeling* specifies multiple levels of key performance drivers, operational metrics, and value drivers, supports various quantitative business analyses including sensitivity analyses, and enables business optimization and risk assessment. Finally, *semantic business modeling* puts together business components, business activities, performance drivers, and IT by capturing their relationships. It formally represents meaning of business components, metrics, and their relationships and enables automated reasoning to identify dependencies and causality relationships across business entities. By using a research prototype, we demonstrated how ontologies and semantic technologies can help infer both direct and indirect causalities of any business pain points and recommend appropriate solutions to fix business or IT shortfalls in the process of business transformation.

In the second part of this chapter, we presented an enterprise-scale ontology management system which provides functionality, scalability, and performance that enterprise applications such as the proposed model-driven business transformation would demand. The primary objective of ontology management systems is to provide holistic control over management activities for ontological information by externalizing them from application programs. Ontology management systems provide ontology independence to applications in a similar way that database management systems provide data independence. One of the pragmatic challenges for ontology management system research is how to create missing component technology pieces and to engineer them with existing results from prior research work for providing a holistic management system. We described the design and implementation of the SnoBase ontology management system, which was developed at the IBM T.J. Watson Research Center. The programming interface of the SnoBase system provides a Java API, Java Ontology Base Connector, which is the ontological equivalent of JDBC. Similarly, this system supports a variant of SPARQL query language as our ontological equivalent of SQL.

REFERENCES

APQC. (2004). Process classification framework. Retrieved June 17, 2007, from http://www.apqc.org

Chang, D.T., & Kendall, E. (2004). Metamodels for RDF schema and OWL. Retrieved June 17, 2007, from http://www.sandsoft.com/edoc2004/ChangRDFS&OWLMDSW.pdf

Eclipse. (2004). Eclipse modeling framework. Retrieved June 17, 2007, from http://www.eclipse.org/emf/

Grand, M. (1998). A catalog of reusable design patterns illustrated with UML. *Patterns in Java* (Vol. 1). John Wiley & Sons.

IBM. (2004). Architecture of business. IBM Global Technology Outlook. Retrieved June 17, 2007, from http://www.ibm.com

IBM. (2005). Component business modeling. Retrieved June 17, 2007, from http://www-1.ibm.com/services/us/bcs/html/bcs_componentmodeling.html

Lee, J. (2005). Model-driven business transformation and semantic Web. *Communications of ACM, 48*(12).

Lee, J., & Ivan, A. (2006). Value-centric, model-driven business transformation. In *Proceedings of the IEEE Joint Conference on E-Commerce Technology and Enterprise Computing, E-Commerce and E-Services*.

Lee, J., & R. Goodwin, R. (2006). Ontology management for large-scale enterprise systems. *Journal of Electronic Commerce Research and Application, 5*(3).

McDavid, D. (2004). The business-IT gap: A key challenge (IBM Research Memo). Retrieved June 17, 2007, from http://www.almaden.ibm.com/coevolution/pdf/mcdavid.pdf

OMG. (2001) Model-driven architecture. Retrieved June 17, 2007, from http://www.omg.org/mda/

OMG. (2000). Universal modeling language. Retrieved June 17, 2007, from http://www.omg.org/uml/

Pan, Y., Xie, G., Ma, L., Yang, Y., Qiu, Z., & Lee, J. (2006). A model-driven system for ontology engineering. *Journal of Data Semantics VII*.

Topic Maps. (2000). Topic maps. Retrieved June 17, 2007, from http://www.topicmaps.org/

W3C. (1998). Extensible markup language. Retrieved June 17, 2007, from http://w3c.org/XML/

W3C. (1999). Resource description framework. Retrieved June 17, 2007, from http://www.w3.org/RDF/

W3C. (2001a). Semantic Web. Retrieved June 17, 2007, from http://www.w3.org/2001/sw/

W3C. (2001b). XML schema. Retrieved June 17, 2007, from http://w3c.org/XML/Schema

W3C. (2002). Web services. Retrieved June 17, 2007, from http://w3c.org/2002/ws/

W3C. (2003). Web services architecture. Retrieved June 17, 2007, from http://www.w3.org/TR/ws-arch/

W3C. (2004a). RDF vocabulary description language 1.0. Retrieved June 17, 2007, from http://www.w3.org/TR/rdf-schema/

W3C. (2004b). SPARQL query language for RDF. Retrieved June 17, 2007, from http://www.w3.org/TR/2004/WD-rdf-sparql-query-20041012/

W3C. (2004c). Web ontology language. Retrieved June 17, 2007, from http://www.w3.org/2004/OWL/

Chapter XV
Ontology as Information System Support for Supply Chain Management

Charu Chandra
University of Michigan-Dearborn, USA

ABSTRACT

Information is essential to integrating business processes. An information organization framework formalized as a reference model is proposed. It captures the specifics (e.g., dynamics and uncertainty) and functional requirements (e.g., information standardization and problem-orientation) of a supply chain (SC), assumed as a managerial, dynamic, complex, and open system. An information modeling formalism is presented that captures different aspects of SC information system support (ISS) as follows: (1) system taxonomy, tackling the problem of information standardization and unified presentation, (2) problem taxonomy, aiming to capture SC operational specifics, such as problem classification and modeling, (3) ontology, for representing problem specific knowledge in a computational language, and (4) ontology-driven information system, accumulating the above components in a collaborative environment, where SC members work on common problems. A SC-ISS reference model is introduced covering components of the above groupings. An industrial case study is presented.

INTRODUCTION

Supply chain (SC) has been traditionally described as a logistic network of manufacturing operations, distribution, and warehousing facilities utilized to effectively integrate plans and actions of suppliers, manufacturers, and distributors in procuring materials, transforming these into finished products, and distributing to customers while meeting required service level at minimal cost (Simcih-Levi, Kaminsky, & Simchi-Levi, 2003). SC is an alignment of firms bringing products or services to the market (Lambert,

Cooper, & Pagh, 1998). One of the ways to achieve SC is through information sharing. Many research works are devoted to what information to share. Li, Sikora, Shaw, and Tan (2006) contend that information to share across the SC relates to order, demand, inventory, and shipment. Lambert and Cooper (2000) identify customer service management, order fulfillment, and returns as key issues to be managed in the SC. Consequently, they propose sharing information for effective *supply chain management* (SCM).

The process of incorporating information pertaining to a new SC member into an existing SC information infrastructure is complex due to its dynamic and uncertain organization and operations. Considering the distributed structure and different, sometimes incompatible, information architectures across the SC, the necessity of information integration is critical (Chandra, Grabis, & Tumanyan, 2007).

A key issue in SCM is the integration of processes across its network for optimal product and service flow. Effective information organization and sharing facilitates this. Towards this end, a research direction proposing fundamental principles, framework, and implementation mechanisms for *information system support* (ISS) for SCM is enunciated.

The overall framework for research initiatives on "SC Information System Support" has four components:

1.   System taxonomy
2.   Problem Taxonomy
3.   Ontology
4.   Ontology-driven information system

This chapter is devoted to describing objectives of these components, their place in the overall framework, significance, and development methodologies. We also document accomplishments in implementing this framework and discuss plans for future research.

Our research so far has been mainly focused on studying the SC domain, a vision of its information support, and proposing approaches for its implementation. Principles borrowed from general system theory (GST) (Von Bertalanffy, 1968), biological

classification (McKelvey, 1982), and object-oriented *system design* are applied in understanding and designing SC complexity and building a hierarchy of characteristics, labeled system taxonomy (ST) (Chandra & Tumanyan, 2003, 2005b), which offers a domain independent system design. Organizational system theory principles are used in designing SC domain dependent architecture consisting of tasks and problems, labeled problem taxonomy (PT) (Chandra & Tumanyan, 2004b). Process modeling and object-oriented system design principles are applied in designing the PT. Ideas borrowed from knowledge management and artificial intelligence research help to conceptualize SC knowledge in content constructs called *ontologies* (Chandra & Tumanyan, 2004c). For this purpose, ontology engineering principles and methodologies have been developed (Chandra & Tumanyan, 2004a).

The focus of the current research is the ontology language specification development encompassing conceptual and formal representation notations (Chandra & Tumanyan, 2004a). Another direction currently being proposed is the development of a new paradigm in ISS, called *ontology-driven information system* (ODIS) (Chandra & Tumanyan, 2007a). In this regard, general ideas have been formulated but the implementation aspects are yet to be elaborated.

The future research is primarily aimed at reformulating theoretical foundations previously developed in our research. *Ontology editor*, a tool for ontology engineering is to be developed. The designed ontologies will be shared through Web servers. Ontology Web services will be designed to propagate ontologies in SC network. A collaboration example on solving a shared problem will be developed.

INFORMATION TO SUPPORT SYSTEM PROCESSES

To support system processes better, information should be compatible with the system's dynamics and be adaptable to its environment (Kampfner, 2002). Before information is designed to support system functions, the system model and its environment are designed, and then taking this model as a requirement, information support is organized. Depending on the methodology chosen for system modeling, different *information system architecture* (ISA) can be implemented and deployed. System theory can be applied in perceiving and modeling the nature of SC organization. The idea of modeling the system and its environment is to find required information to support processes and tasks, which are integral constituents of a system. Information is systematically organized and is explicit; otherwise it may not be correctly understood or adequately used. Since system is defined as a collection of clusters (or subsystems) and information support can be organized for clusters separately as well as for communication between them, the management of such system will become less complex and more feasible.

The fundamental knowledge necessary for successful development and management of SC system is to understand the impact various decision-making problems impose on the life of the whole system. Modeling these problems, designing knowledge used for deriving their solutions, and embedding it into information support infrastructure will provide the environment, where knowledgeable decision making is targeted at making SC streamlined and effectively managed. Various mechanisms have been studied for managing complex systems. Carlock and Fenton (2001) describe the emerging role of systems engineering in information intensive organizations by bringing together experts from relevant fields to model and address a set of problems involved in a complex system.

Various methods have been developed for modeling systems. IMAGE, an enterprise modeling and analysis framework (Delen, Benjamin, & Erraguntla, 1998), tries to overcome the problem of conventional methods, such as interdependence of system components and situations, and separate model development for each problem. It proposes the development of reusable enterprise models which can be secured by using the following sequence of developments: (1) a set of enterprise models, (2) generic models, and (3) specific models. This idea of generalization of problem models, thus achieving their reusability, seems quite appealing and is adopted for the research described in this chapter.

SC system model should reflect its organizational and operational specifics. SC organization structure is dynamic, wherein new members can be added while others removed. For this structure, various configurations, coordination schemas, and cooperation rules can be established. Operational uncertainty is another SC specific aspect. For instance, to meet the demand fluctuation, organizational units increase inventory levels, resulting in increased inventory-holding and operational costs.

Considering various SCM issues and based on available approaches for modeling a complex enterprise, we have developed a reference model for building SC system models and utilizing them in developing ISS. The main assumption made is that the SC is a complex, open, and organization system (Chandra & Tumanyan, 2004b). As a complex system, SC can be represented as a collection of interrelated subsystems, making SC a cohesive whole, yet providing the perspective of dealing with subsystems individually, thereby reducing the complexity and focusing on specific and more tangible subsystems. The openness is characterized by a high level interaction of SC with its environment. There are many issues that need to be considered when managing SC, for example, parts that are external to it and hence out of its immediate control, such as differences in legislation and culture where SC members operate, communication infrastructure, competition, and evolving organizational structure. The idea of organization system as one of the system facets is appealing. SCM involves a set of managerial issues covering operational, tactical, and strategic activities. Thinking about SC as an organization system brings out a picture of a complex system, where subsystems are identified to support managerial issues, linked to each other via whole-part, composition, aggregation, and association relationships.

A STRUCTURE OF INFORMATION SYSTEM SUPPORT FOR SUPPLY CHAIN

A structure of an ISS organization is proposed in Figure 1. It is based on the framework that *information system* organization can be viewed as successive layers of abstraction of information capture and representation. The purpose of this chapter is to propose a reference model that will offer a high-level analytical model of information representation at each level.

The significance of the proposed framework is the decomposition of ISS design process into separate subprocesses or levels and applying systematic mechanisms to each level. System modeling and based on it, *information modeling* is viewed as the main facilitator in making SC information resources to communicate with each other. Each level of the integrated model depicted in Figure 1 is concerned with specific aspects of SC domain, which are analyzed and designed by applying *system design* methodologies. The results are used as input for modeling information to represent

Figure 1. A structure of supply chain system modeling and representation integrated model (Chandra & Tumanyan, 2005a)

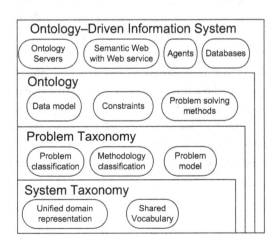

SC domain specific aspects. The result of *information modeling* of the preceding level is the input for the succeeding level.

The proposed framework is based on taxonomy and its applications to problems and problem-solving techniques, particularly when applied to *supply chain management*. According to the *American Heritage® Dictionary of the English Language* (4th ed., 2000), taxonomy is the classification of organisms in an ordered system that indicates natural relationships. It is the science, laws, or principles of classification. Further, it is an arrangement by which systems may be divided into some ordered groups or categories according to common characteristics (Chandra et al., 2007).

The first level, system taxonomy (ST), aims to standardize the information content and structure by providing common vocabulary and a hierarchy for its representation.

The second level, *problem taxonomy* (PT), is the system representation of SC problem domain that builds two constructs: problem classification (including a taxonomy of methods for problem solving), and problem model development, consisting of parameters necessary for dealing with the problem and solving it. It provides the overall framework under which problem-oriented *information system* components can be designed and implemented.

SC PT comprises classification of (a) SC problems, (b) classification of problem solving methodologies for SCM, and (c) variables necessary for modeling such problems. We explain this concept with the help of one of the fundamental problems in the SCM literature, the bullwhip effect. The most downstream SC unit observes an external demand, transmitted upstream as inventory replenishment orders from one unit to another. It has been observed that substantial information distortion, known as the bullwhip effect, and appearing as an order variance increase as one moves up the SC, may occur during this transmission.

The bullwhip effect is a prime example of problems encountered in a complex system, such as the SC. In these systems, problems are multifaceted with a primary problem and many related subproblems. According to Lee, Padmanabhan, and Whang (1997a), the bullwhip effect problem in a SC has several secondary problems, for example, order management, demand forecasting management, inventory management, and shipment tracking. Further, Lee, Padmanabhan, and Whang (1997b) discuss the managerial implications of bullwhip effect by stating that if following conditions hold: (1) demand is mean stationary and no signal processing is used; (2) lead time is zero; (3) fixed ordering cost is zero; and (4) no price variation occurs; therefore, the order variance increase does not occur. However, if some of these conditions are relaxed, the bullwhip effect may be observed. We discuss below some of the published techniques utilized in managing the bullwhip effect to highlight their classification.

Chen, Drezner, Ryan, and Simchi-Levi (2000) use the simple moving average forecasting technique to obtain forecasts and investigate the bullwhip effect according to lead-time and information sharing. Chen, Ryan, and Simchi-Levi (2000) and Xu, Dong, and Evers (2001) use the exponential smoothing forecasting technique. Chen, Ryan, et al. (2000) also show that if a smoothing parameter in exponential, smoothing is set in order to have equal forecasting accuracy for both exponential smoothing and moving average methods, then exponential smoothing gives larger order variance. Graves (1999) demonstrates the presence of the bullwhip effect, if external demand, which is the first order integrated moving average process, is forecasted using exponential smoothing with an optimally set smoothing parameter. Metters (1997) measures the impact of the bullwhip effect by comparing results obtained for highly variable and seasonal demand against the case with low demand variability and weak seasonality. Cachon (1999) proposes methods to reduce the bullwhip effect using balanced ordering.

Problem model taxonomy is a projection of ST and thus inherits system structure and vocabulary. A problem domain is presented at two levels, for example, generic and specific. Generic problem domain

taxonomy is a class of problems, such as "coordination of production activities" in a SC. It is a highly generic problem describing specific issues that comprises of several tasks, such as "scheduling of production" or "inventory replenishment". Specific problem domain taxonomy is represented by domain-dependent (or specialized) model(s). Splitting problem representation modeling into two parts enables developing generic and specific problem models. The case study: scheduling problem section demonstrates the application of problem model building at two levels.

The third level, *ontology*, extends problem models by providing rules and relationships of problem intrinsic properties. Ontology is also a construct for conceptualizing and representing problem solving methods, whose classification is provided in the previous PT level. The fourth level, ODIS, is a description of an architecture, where ontology is utilized during the development of three major IS components, namely gathering, management, and interfaces (Guarino, 1998) and drives their utilization in run-time.

The rest of the chapter is organized as follows. The next section describes SC system challenges in a dynamic and uncertain environment. The technical approach section presents a detailed list of requirements derived from SC specifics, as well as how these can be met. Particularly, standardization of information representation, problem orientation, and knowledge intensive process management are introduced, and methodologies are proposed for their implementation. The reference model section is devoted to formally representing the structure components identified in Figure 1 with formal mathematical models. The next section presents a vision of a SC ISS and its constituents: gathering, management, interface, and ontology, as well as how it will serve the problem on making the SC streamlined by integrating business processes. An industrial case study of applying the theoretical framework presented in the chapter is presented next. The chapter concludes with a summary of the research and its future direction.

SUPPLY CHAIN CHALLENGES AND ONTOLOGY

Various market forces are driving changes in SC. Some of these lead to dynamic organization structure, while others impact functional structure by creating uncertainty in operations. *Information system* infrastructures help attenuate negative effects of these changes by exchanging necessary information. On the other hand, customers require greater product variety, lower costs, and more flexibility from distributors and manufacturers. This trend leads to shortening product lead time, thus making accurate forecasting impossible for manufacturers and suppliers. In addition, fluctuating lead-time and demand uncertainty lead to operational uncertainty. To increase flexibility, manufacturers are configuring their SCs, thus increasing organization dynamics.

The performance of a SC is mainly affected by two factors: organizational structure, expressed by different configurations of SC, and operational collaboration among SC members, expressed by building highly coupled business processes and integrated decision support systems. These factors are reflected in the design of an ISS needed for effective SCM.

The first factor, organizational structure, is concerned with issues such as goal, administrative, product, process, project, and resource structures. Organizational structures contribute to the origination of requirements and specifications. Consequently, organization knowledge is captured and represented in IS. To support organizational functions, information support should be compatible with its structure. This is one of the most challenging issues of SC IS design, since structures change frequently and unexpectedly. The approach adopted in this chapter is based on modeling and building organizational knowledge, which is independent of specific IS solutions and is implemented through ontologies. An example of organization ontology is the goal structure. Whenever a new objective dictated by customer demand emerges, ontologies are redesigned. The shift in focus from low cost production to higher customer service level brings planning and operational changes. Various

activities are affected because of this shift; inventory management is one of them. The agent responsible for inventory replenishment is informed about this shift and makes sure that the available inventory level is compatible with the forecasted demand.

The approach proposed in this chapter suggests building a repository of organizational knowledge or ontology (Chandra & Tumanyan, 2007b). It is not linked to any particular IS implementation, but is rather an independent process that can be used in both development and run-time environments. Its usefulness is demonstrated in the example in the previous paragraph, where change to an objective brings about a change in decision on how to manage the inventory replenishment. It can be a new objective dictated by new customer demand or adding a new member to the SC. The existing IS infrastructure does not need to be revised rather it reflects changes in ontology and acts according to the new requirements.

The second factor in influencing changes in SC is collaboration. For SC members to work collaboratively, they must do more than merely cooperate. Working together, they have to decide on how capacities should be created throughout the SC, quantities of products stored and which policies to use for inventory replenishment, identify actions required when an event occurs, such as change in scheduling plans, or the temporary unavailability of some transportation resources.

Strategic, tactical, and operational plans must be developed collaboratively to achieve maximum efficiency and effectiveness. Problem ontology provides means to represent common problems and sharing common view to processes. It captures the meaning of the problem and represents it in a formal language. These are computational representations carrying knowledge about problems. Three main constituents of this knowledge have been identified:

1. Concepts, for example, setup cost, inventory holding cost
2. Relationships among concepts, for example, setup cost are related to the production of product P using resource R at time T

3. Problem solving methods that capture necessary knowledge for solving the problem, for example, step-by-step procedure that brings up a solution, such as check inventory level; if it is lower than L, place an order equal to O for replenishment

Before modeling knowledge, the meaning of these models must be understood. Sutcliffe (2000) identifies generic tasks that can be applied for designing specific models by reusing them as design templates. Similarly, in this chapter, organization and problem knowledge have been treated distinctly as being domain independent and dependent. Domain independent knowledge is a generic knowledge that captures features across domain elements. In contrast, domain dependent knowledge is problem specific. Classifying knowledge at two levels is with the aim of making designed ontologies reusable. Various specific solutions can be designed for modeling inventory management problems but there are common properties that are present in each model, such as "Forecasted demand" and "Inventory holding cost."

Problems are classified as clusters; for each cluster generic features are captured and represented with generic ontologies, while features describing members of each cluster are captured in problem specific ontologies. Generic ontologies can be used and reused independently of specific circumstances, but cannot be applied to solve specific problems. Domain dependent knowledge is designed for specific situations or problems by inheriting features described in generic ontology for the cluster for which the problem is a member.

Building ontologies is central to the overall ISS framework. Methodologies making it possible constitute other components of the proposed framework (ST and PT, ODIS is its implementation) elaborated in the next section.

TECHNICAL APPROACH

The application of ontology in *information modeling* proposed in this chapter is neither new nor unique (De-

vedzic, 2002; Fonseca, Egenhofer, Agouris, & Camara, 2002; Sugumaran & Storey, 2002). The missing aspect in these and other published research efforts, however, is the absence of a systematic approach for building ontologies which will start from understanding the system as a functional unity and modeling its information content. The advances proposed in the research effort described in this chapter are: (1) a systematic approach to information content organization based on ST principles which encompass the wholeness and interpretability of generated knowledge components, (2) integration of system workflow modeling with knowledge modeling in a holistic knowledge-based framework for supporting decision-making activities in the SC problem domain, and (3) the close integration of knowledge components with IS components, namely gathering, management, and interface.

In the process of searching an adequate ISS capable of making SC streamlined and effectively managed, we have identified a range of requirements needed to be taken into account and met with appropriate solutions. These are tabulated in Table 1 and used in an abbreviated manner throughout the rest of the chapter.

The four major elements depicted in Figure 1, namely (1) system taxonomy, (2) problem taxonomy, (3) ontology, and (4) ontology-driven information system, are the basis of methodologies for tackling these requirements and together they provide guidelines for building the SC information support reference model introduced in the "Information Support Reference Model" section. The research pertaining to these elements is elaborated in more detail in Chandra and Tumanyan (2003, 2004a, 2004b, 2004c, 2005b, 2006). This chapter amalgamates research findings from these cited works into a framework presented with a reference model.

System Taxonomy

To provide integration in SC, there should be a common understanding of terms and definitions, either syntactically or semantically (see requirement SSI). System is designed to meet the requirements UDR, SD, RK, and SSI described in Table 1 and is motivated by the following objectives (McCarthy & Ridgway, 2000):

- To introduce structure into a body of facts
- To build a unified and homogeneous view of the domain of interest

ST offers a generic approach for unifying information standardization and presentation, thus satisfying the requirement UDR. Its significance is in offering a syntactical layer, with which SC members can comply, thereby securing syntactical interoperability (requirement SSI). The process of building ST comprises methodologies from different fields of study: general system theory, biological classification, and object-orientation, which is the *system design* process (requirement SD). The result is a systematic representation of SC information: the ST. System approach ensures the wholeness of system and provides means for simplifying complex system (such as a SC) (Von Bertalanffy, 1968). Biological classification provides information-structuring mechanisms that allow gathering information into groupings and defining relationships among them (McKelvey, 1982). With object-oriented methodology, ST is represented using semantic diagrams. General system and SC system taxonomies are planned to be developed based on the proposed framework and methodology. The general ST decomposes system into seven interrelated components (Nadler, 1970) and defines their properties (for these components, see the information support reference model described in the "Information Support Reference Model" section). SC-ST inherits these properties as upper level groupings that need to be considered for specific aspects of SC domain. ST further decomposes general system components and defines domain and specific classes with their attributes and properties for them.

Problem Taxonomy

PT offers principles for systematically modeling SC problem domain. In this chapter, SC is considered a complex and organizational system consisting of

activities that need to be performed. PT is designed to meet the requirements KC, KR, OC, OM, GS, and RK described in Table 1 and consists of two major components, namely problem classification and problem model generation.

Building PT follows principles of axiomatic system design (Suh, 1998), thereby providing systematic principles for knowledge conceptualization (requirement KC). System functional domain is identified as functional requirements, classified (problem classification), and mapped to system physical domain represented by ST. As a result of linking functional domain to physical domain, problem models are generated. Since the physical domain representation (ST) is persistent for all problem models, the vocabulary, as well as the representation structure, is also standardized, thus satisfying the requirement KR. On the other hand, as shown in the "ontology" subsection, problem models are used for designing ontologies, thus committing to the requirement OC.

Problem classification development comprises two main constituents: (1) evaluation of SC functional domain complexity and proposing a structure that involves various types of relationships, such as generalization, isomorphism, whole-part, and association in building a SC problem hierarchy (problem classification), thus satisfying the requirement OM, and (2) for each species in problem classification, development of a set of subhierarchies, targeting to systematize the problem-solving methodology domain, using taxonomic classification principles.

Once the functional requirements (FR), problem classification, and design parameters (DP), ST, are modeled, the next step in PT design is the conceptualization process, which is the mapping process between functional and physical domains. During this process, the minimum set of DPs for fulfilling each FR is identified. The mapping process can be expressed algebraically as: $\{FRs\} = [A]\{DPs\}$, where $[A]$ is defined as a design matrix, every row of which defines one functional requirement through a set of DPs. Based on this matrix, three different types of design can be distinguished: uncoupled, decoupled, and coupled (Suh, 1998). Problem model is defined by a row in design matrix A and defines the participation of DPs in FRs. In case of uncoupled design, each problem in SC; FR, is presented by one class of concepts in DP. In case of decoupled design, SC problems do not depend on each other and can be handled separately, without considering other problems. Uncoupled or decoupled design is the target that each system designer should try to achieve, but unfortunately the SC is such a complex system that it is practically impossible to achieve this target. Coupled design assumes that problems have influence on each other. In this situation, problem models are designed in a way so as to minimize this influence, thus approaching the decoupled design. In coupled design, however, problems can be considered separately, while considering their links to other problems as part of the overall design.

Problem models are proposed to be designed at two levels, generic and specific (meeting the requirement GS). An example of this approach is the development of a generic model for a problem, such as for inventory management and specific models for each method that can be employed for addressing a specific inventory management policy. In generic model, properties relevant to all types of inventory models are projected, such as "inventory holding cost", or "forecasted demand". Problem model filters these variables from DP and assigns to the particular FR (inventory management). In specific models, variables specific to different methodologies can be incorporated. Whenever a new specific inventory management model is designed, it inherits features described in generic model, thus contributing to reusability of created problem models (requirement RK).

Ontology

Ontology is designed to meet requirements OC, SSI, DI, PI, OL, and is the third level and the most important aspect of overall ISS framework proposed in this chapter. It is built upon the problem model, turning it from an abstract representation of a problem into knowledge models by investigating the problem space, formulating rules, and committing characteristics to different interpretations employed by SC members. Ontology provides a common view of SC processes, thus ensuring shared understanding of common problems.

We have identified two types of knowledge that is potentially necessary for conceptualization and representation, namely organization and problem knowledge. This chapter addresses only the second type and provides formalism for its modeling (requirement OC).

Problem ontology development is a process where problems defined in the PT stage are studied to identify problem dynamics and property interpretation and formalizing them in a computational language (requirement OL). Problem dynamics assumes a set of states that SC system may possibly be in and a set of triggers causing changes to these states (Uschold, King, Moralee, & Zorgios, 1997). An example of a state is a situation where the service level is defined as 100%, implying that the level of available inventory is equal to or more than the demand. An example of a trigger is the event when the inventory level drops below a threshold and an order is to be placed affecting change in the inventory state.

Property interpretations are taxonomic linkages of various possible representations of same terms identified in ST. Different SC members can employ the property "Inventory level" by using different terms, such as "Inventory status", "Inv.", or something else. The idea of ontology interpretation function is to semantically map these terms, thus making possible the transparent usage of same properties regardless of their specific implementations and contributing to interoperability of SC members (requirement SSI) and the integration of data (requirement DI) and processes (requirement PI).

Ontology-Driven Information System (ODIS)

Traditionally, ISA can be divided into three layers or components (Guarino, 1998; Kerschberg & Weishar, 2000; Xu, 2000). These are:

Table 1. Requirements identified for building information support system

ISS requirement	Abbreviation	Brief description
Unified domain representation	UDR	Since SC members may have employed different information representation formalisms (vocabulary and database schemas), there is a need for a common, shared syntax of terms and definitions, as well as their structure.
Systematic principles of domain modeling and representation	SD	Models are not capable of capturing all features of the real world systems. Hence, systematic approaches are required to capture and represent the most important features.
Systematic principles for knowledge conceptualization	KC	System model needs to be explicitly represented. Conceptualization makes implicit knowledge explicit, thus making best use of it. Systematic principles are necessary to ensure adequate transformation.
Standardization of knowledge representation through ontologies	KR	Ontology has proven its worth in standardizing the conceptualized knowledge and is the accepted formalism for knowledge representation.
Organization and problem specific nature of ontology constructs	OC	Two main knowledge components identified in Chandra and Tumanyan (2004c) are adopted as domains for which ontologies should be designed.
Modularity and object nature of formed knowledge	OM	Complex systems cannot be designed without first decomposing them into components, and then designing these components independently, as well as in coordination with each other. Modularity is adopted as the method for managing complexity and uncertainly.
Generalization of generalizability of knowledge and correspondingly constructed ontologies	GS	Generalization is the fundamental principle of GST (Von Bertalanffy, 1968). Generalizing common features across domain issues helps provide reusability of created ontologies, thus reducing the extent of efforts in designing ontologies.
Reusability of created knowledge	RK	Over time, problems arising in SC need to be addressed and solved. Having explicit knowledge modules describing these problems will help reduce efforts in understanding the issue and resolving it.
Syntactic or semantic interoperability among ontologies	SSI	Interoperability among SC members can be accomplished in two ways. The first option is sharing same terms and definitions when describing a concept. This way (syntactic interoperability), there will be no ambiguity in understanding each other, but in practice it is difficult to implement; besides it doesn't provide enough flexibility. The second way is the semantic interoperability, which assumes that SC members have employed different terms in defining same concepts, but are committed to following a common ontology.
Integration of distributed data	DI	Data integration procedure reconciles the heterogeneous structure and content of multiple input data sources.

Table 1. continued

Integration of distributed processes	PI	SC members are disparate organizations, but are bound to work in close collaboration, hence their processes, activities, and tasks need to be synchronized to make the SC streamlined.
Machine readable format of delivered knowledge	OL	Interoperability can be accomplished either manually or automatically. Developed ontologies are consumable by software applications, which are viewed as independent intelligent software agents.
Integration of ontologies into ISS (ontology driven information system)	ODIS	This requirement is the cornerstone of the proposed overall framework. The knowledge modeled for system component is a part of information support, and its goal is to support functions of the particular component.

1. **Interface:** Users perceive the available information through browsing and making queries. This layer must support scalable organizing, browsing, and search.

2. **Management:** Responsible for integration and distribution of information and processing logic organization. Application programs belong to this layer.

3. **Gathering:** Responsible for collecting and storing information in a persistent way. Database systems and data repositories are these types of components.

ODIS extends the conventional perception of *information system* (IS) and envisions the utilization of its fourth component ontologies in the development and utilization of above components of ISA (Fonseca, Davis, & Camara, 2003; Guarino, 1998). Each of these components may use ontologies in their specific way. Ontology integration into the "gathering" component can be implemented in two ways: (1) by using syntax defined in ST, and (2) by creating an inference layer on top of the deployed databases that can semantically map local terminology to common ontology. Ontology represents domain knowledge that can be delivered to the management component in the form of explicit processing logic constructs. Ontology maps different forms and formats of information interpretation in a holistic environment, where queries could retrieve data from available resources, thus providing a common interface for members of a SC.

INFORMATION SUPPORT REFERENCE MODEL

The proposed information support reference model first introduced in Chandra and Tumanyan (2007b) and Chandra et al. (2007) and reproduced in Appendix A is developed for the first three levels of the component structure depicted in Figure 1 by identifying how they relate to each other. This model takes a broad view of its components, defining main concepts and leaving implementation aspects to ODIS development task, which is outside the scope of this chapter. The reference model is designed for SC domain but it can be generalized and applied to any other domain for its conceptualization and representation since it defines knowledge components at the higher, conceptual level. SC domain examples are brought only for illustrative purposes in the reference model.

SUPPLY CHAIN INFORMATION SYSTEM SUPPORT: A VISION

In subsection "Ontology-Driven Information System," while defining the traditional components of ISA, it was suggested that in a knowledge intensive organization such as a SC, ontology is the logical fourth component. The basis of this assertion in Chandra and Tumanyan (2006) was that it drives the other three components by delivering vocabulary and annotation to gathering processing logic and inference engine to management and semantics and structure to interface. These components and their role in ISA for ODIS as described in Chandra and Tumanyan (2006) are as follows:

1. *Management* component is implemented through software agents
2. *Interface* component is implemented with semantic Web and semantic Web services
3. *Ontology* component is the library and the ontology server that supports their capture, assembly, storage, and dissemination
4. *Gathering* component is the same as in traditional IS, but with taxonomic links with common ontologies

We discuss each of these components in the following subsections.

Interface-Semantic Web: An Environment for Supply Chain Collaboration

In Semantic Web, two aspects of information can be distinguished, for example, the description of things, or in other words the structure of the available resources or problem representations (Equation 11) and their content (Equation 21). In this chapter, we are concerned with the second aspect, leaving domain structure representation as a future research effort. The idea of resource standardization is partially covered in Chandra and Tumanyan (2004a) and is viewed to be implemented with extended RDF language. The problem content is captured and represented by ontologies, which are deployed on Semantic Web as XML documents.

The role of ontology in Web applications is limited to adding pointers from terms used in Web sites to common ontology (Berners-Lee, Hendler, & Lassila, 2001). The ontology is to be agreed upon, which means it is more a syntactical convention rather than semantic. The approach advocated in this chapter is to give a more proactive role to ontologies that serves as a common interface for knowledge searching, navigating, and browsing.

Ontologies as an interface component provide two functionalities implemented and deployed on the Semantic Web, namely (1) the structure of domain and (2) reasoning support. The domain can be organizational or problem, whose structure is represented by data model (Equation 24). The reasoning support provides query answering services as well as maps to other ontologies or term interpretations. Reasoning functions can be formally captured by Equation 25.

In order to create ontologies for SC applications, Semantic Web embellished with the service component, that is, Web service, is utilized. Web services provide mechanisms for finding ontologies (UDDI service), defining locations, where a particular ontology object is built up (WSDL service), and a message layout that defines a uniform way of passing XML encoded ontologies (SOAP service) (Bussler, Fensel, & Maedche, 2002).

Management-Software Agents: Supply Chain Collaborators

Software agents are the most effective technology for coping with SC system dynamics. Agents are interfaces through which SC members advertise their services, search for services provided by other SC members, accept requests by other agents, and deliver services. Ontologies are used for this purpose. Four main services provided by ontologies to agents build up the management component. They are: (1) communication language (Equation12), (2) data query engine (Equation25), (3) data representation structure (Equation10), and (4) problem solving methods (Equation23).

Ontologies provide a common vocabulary of terms and definitions for communication. As the data query engine, ontologies commit to data storage systems, linking terms and definitions identified in vocabulary with variables and values, and delivering ontology objects (these are ontology instances, described in Chandra and Tumanyan (2004c)) to software agents. Since agents are autonomous software, they require data to be structured to ensure their unambiguous consumption. Data representation structure is defined by problem models, which in turn are projections from ST.

Representing problem solving principles in knowledge design is a new application of ontology for this research effort and is still under development. The main idea is to separate the problem solving logic from software application and store it in ontologies.

Problem solving methods consist of concepts that present specific aspects of the problem dynamics for which the ontology is designed. For example, in determining when the order is to be placed, inventory replenishment algorithm assumes checking the inventory level periodically. If it is less than a predefined level, an order equal to a specified value is placed. This knowledge can be formalized using ontology calculus as follows:

$$Poss(do((L*AVG + z*STD) = s) > Il) \equiv MakeOrder(s - Il)$$

where s is the re-order level, L is the lead-time, AVG, STD are forecasted demand means and standard deviation, and z is the customer service indicator. If inventory level (IL) is less than the calculated reorder level, an order is placed (Order), which is equal to the difference of reorder and inventory levels.

Gathering-Databases with Ontological Links

As described in Chandra and Tumanyan (2004c), one of the challenges of SC IS organization is the integration of existing legacy systems. This is mostly related to the gathering component. Different database systems and interpretations of same concepts are some of the issues that ontology has to cope with. In order to make these different systems to work together and to understand each other's definitions, an additional layer is proposed to be implemented: ontology inference engine. Before a query accesses database tables, it is checked with the meaning of terms used in it. Chandra and Tumanyan (2004c) describe this process as ontological commitments, where abstract terms are linked with variables (Equation25). Ontology inference engine finds the terms used in specific database implementations and translates the query into another query, understandable by the particular system. For the simplest case, when there is only a common ontology, the inference engine has a flat structure, one engine for one database. For complex cases where there is more than one ontology, the engine may have a hierarchical structure implemented in a distributed environment, partly on an ontology server, and partly on a database system.

Ontology-Ontology Server: A Knowledge Repository

Ontology server is built to make use of ontologies via the Internet and provides an environment where ontologies are captured, assembled, and stored (Chandra & Tumanyan, 2004c). In order to understand the idea of ontology server on a SC domain, we have to clearly distinguish two notions: SC ontology and organization and problem ontologies. The former is a specification of conceptualization of a SC system and offers a set of rules on the structure of data models and axioms. The computational implementation of SC ontology is performed on a XSD schema, which provides the format and representation of organization and problem ontologies. The scenario of having a common ontology is a simplified version of ontology server construction, where a common vocabulary is adopted. In cases where SC members have developed different ontologies, they must be clustered and integrated in ontology server. For this purpose, taxonomy of terms and definitions can be constructed to link different interpretations of same terms and definitions.

CASE STUDY: SCHEDULING PROBLEM

This case study described in Chandra and Tumanyan (2007b) and presented in this section in an abbreviated form is about steel processing and shipment (SPS), a multistage manufacturing process in a SC environment. The automobile SC depicted in Figure 2 consists of several raw material suppliers and a stamping plant which transports steel to produce assembly components. The stamping plant is comprised of blanking, pressing, and assembly departments. The blanking department cuts the raw steel into rectangular pieces. The pressing department stamps the blanks into parts. Welding and other operations are

performed on stamped parts at the metal assembly department. There is substantial setup time involved in various processes.

Ontology Development for Steel Shipment and Processing Supply Chain

The ontology development framework for *information modeling* described in an earlier section is applied to the scheduling problem in SPS-SC. We briefly describe its implementation.

The general ST development concepts discussed in Chandra and Tumanyan (2003, 2005b) are applied in representing the above problem. ST is a hierarchy of concepts inherent to a SC system. This taxonomy defines the vocabulary and relationships between these concepts, thereby ensuring homogeneity and compatibility of problem models projected from ST.

Problem model development starts with studying the generic problem, that is, activities coordination of SC members and its information needs. An analysis of the SPS-SC reveals a list of parameters necessary for addressing the coordination issue by incorporating it into decision modeling systems and finding solu-

Figure 2. Steel processing and shipment supply chain (Chandra & Tumanyan, 2007b)

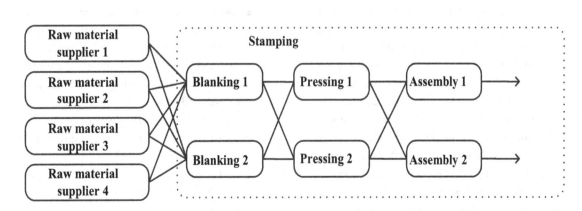

tions for optimal problem solving. Coordination is a generic problem whose subclasses are more specific problems, such as delivery scheduling and inventory control. A data model is designed for the coordination problem and for one of the specific issues, that is, inventory control.

The parameters considered are translated into terms and definitions identified in ST. The process of this transformation is finding classes where the above characteristics reside and projecting these onto a new hierarchy, that is, the problem model. The transformed inventory problem structure constitutes the data model component (M_w) of ontology (Equation 24 in the *ontology reference model*) and is projected from ST. Things (T_w) are concepts in the form of classes and class properties. Subsumption relationships (R_w) are links between classes. For details, please see Chandra and Tumanyan (2007b).

Ontology model development is a two-dimensional process. One dimension is concerned with the development aspects and the other with ontology constituents. Development aspects are capture, assembly, store, and usage. Ontology constituents are data model, axiom, and algorithm. For this case study, ontology constituent algorithm is not considered. However, model and axiom constituents are discussed below for each development aspect.

- **Capture:** The data model is captured by inheriting the data structure from the problem model and adding ontological commitments – I, Equation 25 in the ontology reference model, for connecting data sources and transforming abstract characteristics into variables with real values. Formulation of rules is performed with formal analysis of both problem domains: coordination and inventory control. Seventeen rules are identified, and corresponding axioms – C, Equation 22 in the ontology reference model, are formulated. Axioms relate problem-specific characteristics with IF – THEN relationships, such as "If a product is assigned to a resource, then all materials should be available." A more complex example of an axiom is "If a product

is ordered, and its resource is busy with another product without an order, then the resource load is switched." Some axioms declare assertions that should be considered when modeling the problem, for example, "Each product should have demand, internal or external."

- **Assemble:** A sample from the list of axioms formulated as XML files is presented in Figure 3, which is a formal representation of situations and conditions that can exist in the SC domain under study. These have been identified by domain experts. The first service-level axiom describes the condition where "Service Level" is 100%, only when the inventory level is always higher than demand.

  Ontological commitments are implemented as a software application that connects the problem model to a database system. The data model is implemented as an XML data file following specifications identified in an XSD schema with SC as the domain.

- **Store:** The coordination problem ontology is incorporated in the ontology server, which is implemented as a Web portal. SC problems are classified in a hierarchy to make their search and navigation easier. For each problem, various policies are arranged in taxonomy and deployed on the Web portal. For each policy implementation, ontologies are designed and posted on the Web portal database. There are three ontology components for the inventory control problem, data model, rules, and algorithms, which may be extracted and displayed on a screen. A user can choose any of them and the screen will present their content. The data model is represented as an XML file. For axioms and algorithms, extended style sheet language (XSL) translators are developed for representing XML data structures with HTML format. Any of the ontology components can be browsed or downloaded from the knowledge portal.

- **Use:** The data model and axioms can be found in the Web portal. These can be viewed and downloaded. Developed ontologies are URL-

Figure 3. Ontology axioms for SC scheduling problem (Chandra & Tumanyan, 2007b)

```
<SupplyChain>
  <Axioms>

    <Rule Number="2" Name="Product Resouce assignment">
      <Argument Name="P" Description="Product"/>
      <Argument Name="R" Description="Resource"/>
      <Body>FOR EACH P EXIST R</Body>
    </Rule>
    <Rule Number="3" Name="Changing transportation type">
      <Argument Name="TT" Description="Transportation ti
      <Argument Name="DD" Description="Data of delivery
      <Argument Name="DT" Description="Delivery time
      <Argument Name="T" Description="Transportation type"/>
      <Body>IF DT&lt;DD+TT THEN Change(T)</Body>
    </Rule>
    <Rule Number="4" Name="Process Production Unit correspondance/">
      <Argument Name="R" Description="Resource"/>
      <Argument Name="PU" Description="Production Unit"/
      <Body>FOR EACH R EXIST PU</Body>
    </Rule>
    <Rule Number="5" Name="Resource utilization should be less then its capacity">
      <Argument Name="R_U" Description="Resource utilization"/>
      <Argument Name="R_C" Description="Resource capacity"/>
      <Body>R_U&gt;=R_C</Body>
    </Rule>
    <Rule Number="6" Name="Processes can start when resource and materials are available">
      <Argument Name="R" Description="Resource"/>
      <Argument Name="M" Description="Material"/>
      <Argument Name="Pr" Description="Process"/>
      <Body>For each Pr exist all R, M</Body>
    </Rule>
    <Rule Number="7" Name="If a product is waiting for a resource, the latter's utilization is not 0">
      <Argument Name="P" Description="Product"/>
      <Argument Name="R" Description="Resource"/>
      <Argument Name="Pr" Description="Process"/>
      <Body>For each Pr exist all R, M</Body>
    </Rule>
  </Axioms>
</SupplyChain>
```

> This rule states that there cannot be orphan products. For each a production unit is to be assigned.

> This rule is a constraint stating utilization cannot be more than the capacity.

> This rule states the condition when utilization of a resource is not zero.

addressable XML data structures. These can be accessed automatically or manually. The automatic mode assumes the existence of software agents that can operate autonomously or semi-autonomously by searching and finding necessary knowledge and communicating with each other by exchanging messages. The manual mode requires a human operator navigating the Web portal, finding the necessary problem representation ontology, and downloading it manually into the local hard drive. The two components of ontology (the third, algorithm, component, is not implemented) can be accessed and retrieved independently of each other.

Object model is an instance of the ontology model. When the ontology is downloaded, it collects data using ontological commitments, fills the XML data model structure with content, and delivers it to system users. If the same ontology is accessed another time, the object model can be different from the prior access since SC members can update data in real-time.

CONCLUSION

Information support adequacy to underlying tasks and problems in a system is becoming an increasingly important factor in successfully managing SC business processes. Contemporary information support solutions are focusing on software and database development while paying less attention to the system and business process modeling. In ISS development, we advocate the necessity of systematic approaches aiming to analyze the domain of interest and conceptualize the knowledge required for managing the particular domain. Towards this end, an integrated structure modeling and representation model is introduced that consists of methodologies for analyzing and modeling the SC system at domain independent and domain dependent levels, capturing and representing knowledge relevant to system models, and integrating this knowledge into ISS solutions.

The proposed structure delineates ISS design stages and for each one (except the final one) a reference model is introduced. This model takes a broader view of ISS components and defines their concepts. The main thrust of this chapter is the mathematical formulation of system components that has to be studied and modeled. Following the structure, physical and functional domains of a system are designed and mapped through generating problem models, which are enriched with problem solving knowledge and describing problem properties, and conceptualizing them with ontologies.

Ontologies are viewed as constructs that facilitate interoperability among SC members, thus making the SC streamlined. The goal of the proposed reference model is the development of SC ontology as a fourth component in the ISA. Although it is considered as a separate component, its main function is to drive the other three components, gathering, management, and interface, thus making information system ontology-driven. Ontology delivers vocabulary and annotations to gathering, processing logic and inference engine to management, and semantics to interface.

This chapter shows that the ISS design is a fertile area of research with challenging problems. The body of this research is enriched with ideas on *information modeling* in the form of ontology and its embeddedness into ISA components introduced in this chapter. These ideas engender several directions that can be elaborated further, particularly specification for ontology language, workflow modeling methodologies, intelligent software agents, Semantic Web applications, and integration of heterogeneous disparate information systems, among others.

REFERENCES

American Heritage® Dictionary (2000). Taxonomy. *American Heritage® Dictionary of the English Language 4th ed.*

Berners-Lee, T., Hendler, J., & Lassila, O. (2001). The semantic Web. *Scientific American, 284*(5), 34-43.

Bussler, C., Fensel, D., & Maedche, A. (2002). A conceptual architecture for Semantic Web services. *SIGMOD Rec.*, 31(4), 24-29.

Cachon, G.P. (1999). Managing supply chain demand variability with scheduled ordering policies. *Management Science, 45*(6), 843-856.

Carlock, P.G., & Fenton, R.E. (2001). System of systems (SoS) enterprise systems engineering for information-intensive organizations. *Systems Engineering, 4*(4), 242-261.

Chandra, C., Grabis, J., & Tumanyan, A. (2007, June). Problem taxonomy: A step towards effective information sharing in supply chain management [Special issue on knowledge and information technology management in the 21st century manufacturing]. *International Journal of Production Research, 45*(11), 2507-2544.

Chandra, C., & Tumanyan, A. (2003). Supply chain system taxonomy: Development and application. In *Proceedings of the 12th Annual Industrial Engineering Research Conference*, Portland, OR.

Chandra, C., & Tumanyan, A. (2004a). Supply chain system analysis and modeling using ontology engineering. In *Americas Conference on Information Systems*, New York.

Chandra, C., & Tumanyan, A. (2004b). Information modeling to manage supply chain: Problems taxonomy. In *Proceedings of the 13th Annual Industrial Engineering Research Conference*, Houston, TX.

Chandra, C., & Tumanyan, A. (2004c). Ontology driven knowledge design and development for supply chain management. In *Proceedings of the 13th Annual Industrial Engineering Research Conference*, Houston, TX.

Chandra, C., & Tumanyan, A. (2005a). Research commentary: Information system support for supply chain. In *Proceedings of Fourteenth Annual Industrial Engineering Research Conference*, Atlanta, GA.

Chandra, C., & Tumanyan, A. (2005b). Supply chain system taxonomy: A framework and methodology. *Human Systems Management Journal, 24*, 245-258.

Chandra, C., & Tumanyan, A. (2007a). Ontology-driven information system for supply chain management. In R. Sherman, R. Kishore, & R. Ramesh (Eds.), *Ontologies: A handbook of principles, concepts and applications in information systems* (pp. 697-726). Boston: Springer.

Chandra, C., & Tumanyan, A. (2007b). Organization and problem ontology for supply chain information support system. *Data and Knowledge Engineering, 61*(2), 263-280.

Chen, F., Drezner, Z., Ryan, J.K., & Simchi-Levi, D. (2000). Quantifying the bullwhip effect in a simple supply chain: The impact of forecasting, lead times, and information. *Management Science, 46*(3), 436-443.

Chen, F., Ryan, J.K., & Simchi-Levi, D. (2000). Impact of exponential smoothing forecasts on the bullwhip effect. *Naval Research Logistics, 47*(4), 269-286.

Delen, D., Benjamin, P.C., & Erraguntla, M. (1998). Integrated modeling and analysis generator environment (IMAGE): A decision support tool. In *Winter Simulation Conference* (pp. 1401-1408).

Devedzic, V. (2002). Understanding ontological engineering. *Communications of the ACM, 45*(4), 136-144.

Fonseca, F., Davis, C., & Câmara, G. (2003). Bridging ontologies and conceptual schemas in geographic information integration. *GeoInformatics, 7*(4), 355-375.

Fonseca, F.T., Egenhofer, M.J., Agouris, P., & Câmara, G. (2002). Using ontologies for integrated geographic information systems. *Transactions in GIS, 6*(3), 231-257.

Graves, S.C. (1999). A single-item inventory model for a nonstationary demand process. *Manufacturing and Service Operations Management, 1*(1), 50-61.

Guarino, N. (1998). Formal ontology and information systems. In *Proceedings of FOIS'98* (pp. 3-15). Amsterdam: IOS Press.

Kampfner, R. (2002). *Adaptive systems view of organizational functions* (Tech. Rep.). Dearborn, MI: University of Michigan – Dearborn.

Kerschberg, L., & Weishar, D.J. (2000). Conceptual models and architectures for advanced information systems. *Applied Intelligence, 13*, 149-164.

Klir, G.J. (1984). *Architecture of systems problems solving*. New York: Plenium Press.

Lambert, D.M. & Cooper, M.C. (2000). Issues in supply chain management. *Industrial Marketing Management, 29*, 65-83.

Lambert, D.M., Cooper, M.C., & Pagh, J.D. (1998). Supply chain management: Implementation issues and research opportunities. *The International Journal of Logistics Management, 9*(2), 1-19.

Lee, H.L., Padmanabhan, V., & Whang, S. (1997a). The bullwhip effect in supply chains. *Sloan Management Review, 38*(3), 93-102.

Lee, H.L., Padmanabhan, V., & Whang, S. (1997b). Information distortion in a supply chain: The bullwhip effect. *Management Science, 43*(4), 546-558.

Li, J., Sikora, R., Shaw, M.J., & Tan, G.W. (2006). A strategic analysis of interorganizational information sharing. *Decision Support Systems, 42*, 251-266.

McCarthy, I., & Ridgway, K. (2000). Cladistics: A taxonomy for manufacturing organizations. *Integrated Manufacturing Systems, 11*(1), 16-29.

McKelvey, B. (1982). *Organizational systematics taxonomy, evolution, classification*. Berkeley: University of California Press.

Metters, R. (1997). Quantifying the bullwhip effect in supply chains. *Journal of Operations Management, 15*(2), 89-100.

Nadler, G. (1970). *Work design: A system concept*. Homewood, IL: Richard D. Irwin, Inc.

Simchi-Levi, D., Kaminsky, D., & Simchi-Levi, E. (2003). *Designing and managing the supply chain: Concepts, strategies and case studies*. New York: McGraw-Hill Irwin.

Sugumaran, V., & Storey, V.C. (2002). Ontologies for conceptual modeling: Their creation, use, and management. *Data and Knowledge Engineering, 42*(3), 251-271.

Suh, N.P. (1998). Aiomatic design theory for systems. *Research in Engineering Design, 10*, 189-209.

Sutcliffe, A. (2000). Domain analysis for software reuse. *The Journal of Systems and Software, 50*, 175-199.

Uschold, M., King, M., Moralee, S., & Zorgios, Y. (1997). *The enterprise ontology*. Edinburgh, UK: The University of Edinburgh.

Von Bertalanffy, L. (1968). *General system theory*. New York: George Braziller.

Xu, L.D. (2000). The contribution of system science to information system research. *Systems Research and Behavioral Science, 17*, 105-116.

Xu, K., Dong, Y., & Evers, P.T. (2001). Towards better coordination of the supply chain. *Transportation Research Part E: Logistics and Transportation Review, 37*(1), 35-54.

APPENDIX A

Notations Related to System Taxonomy

S – System

T – Thing symbolizing the elements of a system

R – Relationships among things of a system defined on T

Notations Related to General Problem Representation

GP – Generic problem model

at_i^1 – Attribute

At_i – Set of instances of at_i attribute

vv_i – Variable assigned to attribute at_i for generic problems

VV_i – Set of possible values for variable vv_i

ww_i – Observation channels for vv_i

WW_i – Set of possible states of observation channels ww_i

Notations Related to Specific Problem Representation

Ob – Object model

b_i – Backdrop

B_i – Set of backdrop b_i states

SP – Specific problem model

v_i – Variable assigned to attribute at_i for specific problems

V_i – Set of possible values for variable v_i

w_i – Observation channel for backdrop b_i

W_i – Set of possible states of observation channels w_i

o_i – Observation channel for attributes at_i

$\tilde{O}$ – Relationship between object system and problem system

W – Class instances of S for SC domain (general representation of W_i)

Notations Common for Specific and General Problem Representations

$\hat{E}$ – Relationship between specific and generic systems

e_i – Relationship between V_i, VV_i

k_j^2 – Relationship between W_j, WW_j

S_w – Specific system for SC domain (an instance of S)

T_w – Things specific to SC domain (an instance of T)

R_w – Set of relationships held on T_w

Notations for Ontology

M – Data model for SC domain

I – Ontological commitments. Functions interpreting characteristics into variables

V – Set of variables (General representation of V_i)

B_w, B_C, B_H – Observation channels for defining variables, constraints, and algorithms, respectively

J – Set of Interpretation functions I

M_w – Data model for SC problem

C – Constraints on data

O – Ontology model

A – Set of axioms

H – Algorithm or heuristics

G – Set of equations

System Taxonomy Reference Model

The proposed ST considers SC as a whole, which consists of parts. However, the whole is more than the collection of parts. Having complex non-linear relationships, these parts build a whole, which can be described with two attributes: 1) system parts, things T, and 2) their relationships R. Klir (1984) represents a system, S, as:

$$S = (T, R) \tag{1}$$

Thing (T) consists of seven components (Nadler, 1970):

$$I, O, E, A, F, M, P \qquad (2)$$

where, I= input, O=output, E=environment, A=agent, F=function, M=mechanism, and P=process. These components comprise all system elements and each element in the system can be assigned to one of them. A component can be described either by naming its elements or by specifying properties of these elements. Thus, component-containing element I is written as

$$I = \{i_1, i_2, \ldots, i_n\} \qquad (3)$$

The component I can be represented also as consisting of all elements i that has properties $I_1, I_2, \ldots$

$$I = \{i : i\_has\_properties\_ I_1, I_2\} \qquad (4)$$

Each element can be a characteristic or a set of other elements. Thing (T) of system in general consists of a subset of a Cartesian product of seven system components described earlier:

$$T \subseteq (I \times O \times E \times A \times F \times M \times P) \qquad (5)$$

Two types of relationships among things can be identified, viz., horizontal and vertical. The horizontal relationship between input and output sets that can be written as $R(I, O)$, is a subset of the Cartesian product and is defined as follows:

$$R(I, O) \subseteq \{(i, o) : (i, o) \in I \times O\} \qquad (6)$$

where i, o are elements of I, O, and are related to each other. This is a binary relation, but in most cases more than two elements participate in these horizontal relationships.

The vertical relationship is of composition, or aggregation, or association type, where one component is designed to present an element of another component in more detail with a set of elements. Vertical relation-

ship is a predecessor - successor type of relationship and can be formally presented as:

$$R(X, Y) = \{(x, y) : y \in \{Y\} \wedge x = \{X\} \wedge \forall x \mapsto y\} \qquad (7)$$

where, R is a relationship between components X and Y, x and y being their elements. In each relationship there is only one y, which is an element of a set Y (predecessor). x is a set of attributes of component X (successor). And each x is designed to describe the element y.

The process of decomposing seven system components is proposed to be implemented using classification schemas borrowed from biological sciences (McCarthy and Ridgway, 2000; and McKelvey, 1982). The upper seven components are big families, inside which smaller families can be identified based on a set of similar features. An example of a big family can be the package[c] "Output", comprising all types, viz., products and services offered by a SC. The package "Product" is a family, which is a type of output and comprises information about the list of products and their properties. SC species are classes, such as "Product demand", which is associated with the "Product" family and contains characteristics, such as "Demand type", "Period", "Quantity", and so forth. During the problem model design when problems are mapped to ST hierarchy, groupings are captured at the species level, for example, when designing a model for inventory management, the atomic construct is considered the class "Product demand". All properties describing the product demand are projected from ST into problem model. Later, in the process of ontology design, some characteristics can be pruned to make it concise.

Problem Domain Reference Model

In PT reference model, we redefine the system definition in reference to the problem domain. This redefinition does not contradict concepts described in ST, but complements it with new meanings. Things and relationships in a system can be represented as

$$T = \{T_w \mid w \in W\} \qquad (8)$$

$$R = \{R_w \mid w \in W\} \qquad (9)$$

where, W is a set of system instances denoting all possible SC system situations or states, such as various SC configurations, coordination schemas, cooperation variants, and so forth.

Following system representation adopted convention; a problem can be represented as

$$S_w = (T_w, R_w) \qquad (10)$$

$$S = \{S_w \mid w \in W\} \qquad (11)$$

Conceptually, each problem in SC can be considered as a thing T that has the same complex structure as its predecessor. Problems in SC can be introduced as a combination of two formalisms, viz., problem object model *Ob* and problem representation formal model, which consists of two components: generic *GP* and specific *SP* problem representations. Object model is a structure of terms projected from ST, such as "Demand" and "Order size". Problem solving tools need variables to operate with, such as "Demand = 100" and "Order size = 12". Formal problem model extends the object model with this information. Other two elements in Equation 12 represent relationships between generic and specific models and between object and problem models.

$$T_w = (Ob, GP, SP, \hat{E}, \tilde{O}) \qquad (12)$$

Object model *Ob* is an abstract structure of characteristics at_i relevant to the problem. Seven system components identified for ST with their further decomposition correspond to object model *Ob*, are applied to the entire SC domain. Problem object model is a projection from ST, filtered to problem specific characteristics. The set of possible characteristic's interpretation is denoted by At_i and can be collected through studying observation channels b_j. The set of interpretations aims to provide a layer for semantic in-

teroperability (linking specific terminology employed by a SC member to the terms identified in ST) among different interpretations of system characteristics. Particularly, it can be used for building semantic annotations. Observation channels are situations, circumstances, processes, narrative descriptions, or any other sources where the problem can be investigated. The set of possible observation channels are denoted by B_j.

$$Ob = (\{(at_i, At_i) \mid i \in N_n\}, \{(b_j, B_j) \mid j \in N_m\}) \qquad (13)$$

Object model is a structure of abstract names, while problem-solving tools need concrete variables with values to operate with. For this purpose, problem variables are defined and mapped to object model characteristics, thus ensuring syntactic interoperability between various system components or problems.

To better serve the needs of problem solving tools and provide reusability of problem models, the information representing their content is captured at different levels of abstractions. Particularly, it is proposed to have two representation levels: generic and specific. For solving each problem, various methodologies can be applied. Correspondingly, various problem models can be designed. The problem generic representation tries to capture features that are same across all (or most of) possible methods. Generic problem representation formalisms consist of a set of variables generic to problem vv_i that may have a set of values VV_i. Generic problem variables are collected through studying problem generic states ww_j, WW_j.

$$GP = (\{(vv_i, VV_i) \mid i \in N_n\}, \{(ww_j, WW_j) \mid j \in N_m\}) \qquad (14)$$

Problem specific representation captures problem specific information for its utilization by a particular method. Specific problem representations are less reusable than generic models and complement (or prune) those by adding new, method specific variables (or removing superfluous variables in case of pruning). Specific variables v_i may have a set of values denoted by V_i through studying problem specific states w_j, W_j.

$$SP = (\{(v_i, V_i) \mid i \in N_n\}, \{(w_j, W_j) \mid j \in N_m\}) \quad (15)$$

Specific problem representation contains variables related to a set of abstractions (one for each variable), expressing the relationships between specific and general problem systems. It can be called an abstraction channel, which formally can be represented as:

$$\hat{E} = (\{(VV_i, V_i, e_i) \mid i \in N_n\}, \{(WW_j, W_j, e_j) \mid j \in N_m\}) \quad (16)$$

The abstraction channel $\hat{E}$ maps specific and generic problems, defining what is inherited, what is morphed, and what is pruned.

The relationship between the object system and the problem system (Equation17) is expressed by a model consisting of individual observations channels o_i for mapping each attribute in At_i to a variable in V_i, identified for the system state w_j, through studying the observation channel B_j. N_n and N_m are the number of properties selected for the particular problem and the number of observation channels, respectively.

$$\tilde{O} = (\{(At_i, V_i, o_i) \mid i \in N_n\}, \{(B_j, W_j, w_j) \mid j \in N_m\}) \quad (17)$$

As in the case of ST, in problem domain, relationships can be classified into two types: vertical and horizontal with the difference that in this case only those relationships are considered, which are relevant to the particular problem. The vertical relationships are for building domain structure. The horizontal ones are for linking outputs of some problems with inputs of others.

$$R_w = (RV_w, RH_w) \quad (18)$$

In vertical relationship RV_w, one component is designed to present an element of another component in more detail with a set of elements. Vertical relationship can be formally presented as:

$$RV_{w1,3}(T_{w1}, T_{w2}) = \begin{cases} (x, y) : y \in \{T_{w1}\} \wedge x = \\ \{T_{w2}\} \wedge \forall x \mapsto y \mid w1, w2 \in W \end{cases} \quad (19)$$

A relation between input and output sets that can be written as RH_w, is a subset of the Cartesian product of elements of two components and is defined as follows:

$$RH_{w1,2}(T_{w1}, T_{w2}) = \begin{cases} (x, y) : (x, y) \in \\ \{T_{w1} \times T_{w2}\} \mid w1, w2 \in W \end{cases} \quad (20)$$

Problem domain reference model defines its components, but fails in providing methodologies of how these components can be implemented. As in the case of building ST, principles borrowed from biological classification can also be applied. As a development tool, object-oriented modeling is found very useful. Both methodology and implementation aspects are out of scope of this chapter.

Ontology Reference Model

Ontologies are intended to conceptualize and represent knowledge about each problem identified at PT level. **Ontology reference model** should comprise data necessary for dealing with the problem and rules that relate data elements to each other. Formally, ontology can be represented as:

$$O = (M, C, H) \quad (21)$$

where, O is the target ontology, M is the problem or process data model, C is a set of axioms formalizing constraints placed on entities, H is a set of axioms formally representing problem behavior.

Constraints can be identified by studying situations where problems occur. More is the number of situations (observation channels), more are the chances that all possible constraints are studied.

$$C = (C \rightarrow V \cup B_C) \quad (22)$$

where, B_C is the set of observation channels (Guarino, 1998), through which constraint C is assigned to variable V. Algorithms capture the conceptualized knowledge related to problem solving methods. Observation channels B_H are required for defining algorithm H, which utilizes data model M to solve the problem.

$$H = (H \rightarrow M \cup B_H) \tag{23}$$

Problem data model consists of problem representation and its commitments to existing IS infrastructures. Data model can be formally represented as:

$$M_w = (S_w, I) \tag{24}$$

where, S_w is a problem representation and I are ontological commitments that link ontology vocabulary with the terminology adopted and used by existing IS.

$$I = (V \rightarrow T_w \cup B_w) \tag{25}$$

Problem model S_w is an abstract representation of a problem domain: a meta-model. Ontological commitments are utilized for developing a data model out of

this meta-model. These commitments are interfaces between abstract problem representation and their interpretations across the SC network.

ENDNOTES

[1]   The index i here and afterwards signifies the ith attribute in the set of attributes.

[2]   The index j signifies the jth relationship between general WW_j and specific W_j system states as well as between B_j and W_j.

[3]   Hereafter, terminology used for providing examples is borrowed from the object-oriented system design topic, since for implementing the reference model this methodology has been utilized.

Chapter XVI
Matching Dynamic Demands of Mobile Users with Dynamic Service Offers

Bernhard Holtkamp
Fraunhofer Institute for Software and Systems Engineering, Germany

Norbert Weißenberg
Fraunhofer Institute for Software and Systems Engineering, Germany

Manfred Wojciechowski
Fraunhofer Institute for Software and Systems Engineering, Germany

Rüdiger Gartmann
University of Münster, Germany

ABSTRACT

This chapter describes the use of ontologies for personalized situation-aware information and service supply of mobile users in different application domains. A modular application ontology, composed of upper-level ontologies such as location and time ontologies and of domain-specific ontologies, acts as a semantic reference model for a compatible description of user demands and service offers in a service-oriented information-logistical platform. The authors point out that the practical deployment of the platform proved the viability of the conceptual approach and exhibited the need for a more performant implementation of inference engines in mobile multi-user scenarios. Furthermore, the authors hope that understanding the underlying concepts and domain-specific application constraints will help researchers and practitioners building more sophisticated applications not only in the domains tackled in this chapter but also transferring the concepts to other domains.

INTRODUCTION

Regarding the trend towards ubiquitous computing and ambient intelligence, modern information systems basically have to support mobile users. As a first step towards fulfilling dynamic demands of mobile users, the concept of context-awareness has been introduced to enable filtering of information based on user-specific context information.

To cope with user acceptance, we abstract from context information and use a situation model. Situations are easy to understand for a user and can be derived from a set of context information, including location and time and even user profile information and other sources. They are named cognitive abstractions of context. When such situations are linked with user goals (e.g., get food when hungry), it is evident that different situations imply the need for different information and services to help a user in achieving his goals. User profiles are used for describing personal data, preferences, and interests of individual users, from which user goals can be derived.

Furthermore, we observe a growing demand to cope with dynamic service offers. Service-oriented architectures mainly integrate Web-based services from different providers. One consequence is the need to cope with unavailability of services, for example, due to broken connections or limited scopes of service validity. To enable an automatic replacement of services, that is, service roaming, service profiles are used that provide for a matching with user profiles and context information.

To enable matching of dynamic user demand and service offers on a semantic level, we use semantic technologies. This includes the development of a description model for service semantics and a semantic registry able to cope with such descriptions. The service ontology is modular, based on other ontology modules covering general concepts, situations, and the application domains. As demands from a large number of users are to be matched dynamically with service descriptions provided by a large number of service providers, the application ontology acts as a semantic reference system.

In the following, we start with the discussion of the conceptual background of our approach, followed by an outline of sample application scenarios. In the main part, we discuss the construction and use of the application ontology as a basis for a semantic matching of demand and offers and give an overview of the system architecture supporting this process. A brief summary of practical experiences gained from the deployment of the system as a mobile tourist guide follows. The chapter closes with a look at future trends.

BACKGROUND

Following Dey (2001, p. 5), "context is any information useful to characterize the situation of an entity. An entity is a person, place, or object considered relevant to the interaction between a user and an application, including the user and application themselves." Context-aware applications are able to adapt their functionality based on existing context information towards the user's environment. This includes filtering and provision of information and services being of interest to the user in his specific context, thus making applications more proactive and reducing the need for explicit user interactions. This property is of value especially for mobile applications due to the restricted interaction capabilities of mobile devices. Mobility always has a location aspect that is an important part of almost any context-aware application. In this way, mobile computing and context-awareness are good supplementations in order to provide users with the right information anywhere and anytime.

Research on context-aware applications started in the beginning of the 1990s. One of the first applications was the Active Badge System (Want, Hopper, Falcao, & Gibbons, 1992) from Olivetti Research Lab. It allowed users to locate people in the office and to redirect incoming calls to the closest phone. This system was later in operation at Olivetti STL, Xerox EuroParc, MIT Media Lab, and Xerox PARC.

The Conference Assistant (Dey, Salber, Abowd, & Futakawa, 1999) was developed at the Georgia Institute of Technology. Its aim was to assist conference attendants. Based on user profiles including a list of research interests, the Conference Assistant displays the timetable with events highlighted that are of interest for the user. When entering a room, the Conference Assistant gives information on the presenter and shows the presentation material. The user can then make notes during the presentation, which are recorded together with additional context information, for example, the time, author, and content information useful for later retrieval.

Another type of popular context-aware applications is location-based tourist guides. There are quite a number of examples available from the mid 1990s. The Cyberguide project (Long et al., 1996) from Georgia Tech was aimed at providing information to a tourist based on his position and orientation. The user could see his position on a map. Selecting points on the map the user could get more information about his environment. A similar guide has been developed by the University of Lancaster and tested between 1996 and 1999 for visitors of the City of Lancaster (Davies, Mitchell, Cheverest, & Blair, 1998). Based on location and user preference, the visitor could get information about points of interest in the region.

Both these tourist guides were restricted to location information. The COMPASS2008 project, which has been realized based on the information-logistical service platform described in this chapter, also aims at assisting tourists in providing suitable information and services dynamically in each situation. In contrast to the previous projects, the COMPASS2008 application is not restricted to the location of the user as a context dimension. Another context dimension is time. Dependent on the current time, different time aspects are inferred, for example, activity of the user, eating time, opening hours of shops, and so forth. In addition, parts of the user profile and even external sources like event calendars are used as context dimensions. Based on the complex context model, a set of situations is derived to provide the basis for a personalized situation-aware filtering of information and services for a user.

Most of the above described applications are prototypes developed in research labs and the academic

world. There are not many complex context-aware commercial solutions. However, there are several location-based services offered by mobile communication providers and service providers. Examples are route planning services, city guides, hotel and shopping guides, and location services for nearby gas stations. Most of the commercial and academic applications only use a few context dimensions, mostly location, time, and identity.

APPLICATION SCENARIOS

In this section we describe and analyze scenarios from different application domains, namely tourism and emergency management, regarding their requirements on dynamic information and service supply, ontology support, and relevant context information and user profile data.

Tourism

One application domain for ontology-based service provision is guidance for tourists. Since the behavior of tourists is not predictable and depends on various influencing factors such as personal moods, personal interests, and so forth, an intelligent system should be able to conclude the user's current needs. Furthermore, information relevant for tourists is provided by many different sources.

To be able to decide what information could be relevant for a tourist, it is crucial to detect in which kind of situation the user currently is in. Context information and user profile information are the basis for that decision. For instance, a user standing in front of a sports stadium in which a sports event is about to start could be there accidentally, could intend to see the event, or could look for tickets. If the user profile indicates no interest in this kind of event, the first option is probably correct, otherwise the user profile could indicate whether the user has a ticket for that event. This information would either lead to provision of, for example, a navigation service to the right entrance and further information about the event (e.g., starting lists), or the system would offer an online booking service.

The COMPASS system (Weißenberg, Voisard, & Gartmann, 2006) being based in the technical infrastructure described in this chapter has recently shown in a field test in Beijing that situation detection is applicable to tourist guide systems and that this is a basis for an intelligent selection of appropriate services, which unburdens the user from searching for desired services among huge offers.

Emergency Response Support

Support for emergency response is a very demanding task. Emergency cases are always different and unpredictable, information needs depend on various parameters, and response times are always critical. A precise efficient demand-specific filtering of information from a huge information offer is needed.

The information needed highly depends on the kind of emergency and a precise recognition of the emergency case is crucial for information selection. Typically, not all relevant parameters are known initially. For instance, fighting a fire in a chemical plant is influenced by the chemical substances stored or processed here. Thus, information about the emergency case is completed gradually, and the system has to refine the provided information accordingly.

An ontology-based service selection, based on situation information such as the type of emergency and context data, is very effective to meet the mentioned requirements. An actual example is the MONA system, the Mobile Emergency Assistant (Holtkamp, Weißenberg, & Speckmann, 2005), developed for the Duisburg fire brigades. This system is fed information about the emergency, such as the location and situation (fire in different levels of escalations, car accident, rescue of jammed persons, and so forth). It has access to all internal information sources of the fire brigades and can additionally access external Web services such as geospatial mapping services to get further information if necessary. That leads to an improved information supply for the officers-in-charge and leads to a more efficient mission processing.

APPLICATION ONTOLOGY

As a basis for semantic matching of dynamic offers with dynamic requests in all scenarios and as a base data model, we use a modular extensible application ontology for the description of both demands and offers. In a first step, the ontology structure is explained. Then dynamic aspects of the ontology are discussed in more detail, such as changes in user profiles, contexts or service sets, and service roaming. Finally, we have a closer look at the implementation side, including performance issues.

Ontology Structure

Following Guarino (1998), an ontology can be structured into different kinds of subontologies as depicted by Figure 1:

- The *upper ontology* is limited to generic and abstract concepts, independent of, and thus addressing a broad range of, application domains. It covers reusable dimensions like location, time, and content, which may be refined in other ontologies.
- *Domain ontologies* specify concepts of different application domains and scenarios (e.g., tourism, emergency) and may refine concepts from the upper ontologies. For new application scenarios, mainly new domain ontologies are needed.
- *Task ontologies* code knowledge about the usage of domain ontologies, that is, they characterize computational aspects. They make generic use of domain ontologies, that is, they are independent of special domain ontologies.
- The *application ontology* at the lowest level integrates all other ontologies for the application.

Upper Ontologies

Ontology design has to keep in mind for what the ontology is used. In our case, it is intended for dynamic personalized service provision to a huge amount of concurrent users in scenarios as defined above, that

Figure 1. Modular ontology architecture

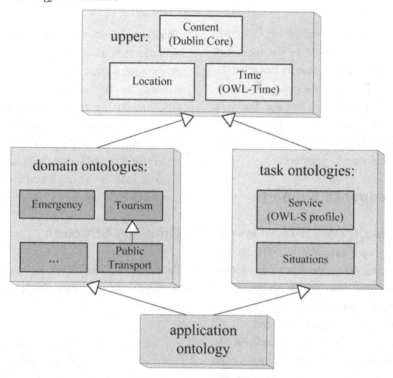

is, for information logistics. Existing upper or top-level ontologies like OpenCyc (Cycorp, 2002) and SUMO (Niles & Pease, 2001) are too large for our scenarios. Hence, we took a more pragmatic approach, concentrating on the main aspects of time, location, and content, which are seen as the main dimensions of information logistics (Deiters, Löffeler, & Pfennigschmidt, 2003).

Location Ontology

For mobile applications, the location aspect is of utmost importance and the use of ontologies for this purpose has been long-praised. Fonseca, Egenhofer, Davis, & Borges (2000) summarize several such approaches.

Our location ontology, however, is not a complete geo ontology, but pragmatically provides basic concepts which may be refined in (geo) domain ontologies. There are two layers: the logical or *cognitive* location concepts and their lower-level *geographic extent*, both inheriting from the root concept *Location*. The root concept of the logical layer is *LocationName*, having subconcepts like *Country, Region,* and *AdministrativeArea,* the latter having subconcepts like *State* and *City*. Multiple inheritance is used to model entities such as *Municipalities*, being a city and a state. A tourism ontology might add concepts like *POI* (point of interest), *Hotel, Shop,* and *Restaurant,* and an emergency ontology might add concepts like *Plant* and its various parts. Instances of the higher-level concepts (i.e., the known locations) are mapped to lower-level concept *GeographicExtent*, having subconcepts like *Point, Box,* and *Polygon*. For example, a *Restaurant* instance is mapped to a *Polygon* instance having some set of points with coordinates (e.g., by using spatial extensions of a database). Using geographic relationships like containment and overlapping at the lower level, corresponding relationship for the higher-level instances can be inferred.

Time Ontology

To define temporal aspects of services and situations, a time ontology is needed. Our time ontology is structured similarly to the location ontology: both have an abstract and a physical layer. The lower physical layer is a subset of OWL-Time (Hobbs & Pustejovsky, 2003), consisting of the *TemporalEntity* subconcepts *Instant* and *Interval*, together with basic relationships (*after, before)*. The additional abstract layer with root concept *PeriodicInterval* is mapped to the lower layer by timestamp patterns, which play the role of coordinates. It has subconcepts like *Yearly* and *Daily.* For example, *Yearly* is instantiated by *January*, representing the month occurring every year periodically, not a concrete month as in the lower layer. Instantiations of *Daily* concepts may even be personalized, depending on a user's context (e.g., *Sunrise*) and preferences (e.g., *Lunchtime, Dinnertime,* and *Morning*), or may be object-dependent (e.g., *TradingHours* of a shop). The personalized time *abstraction* method accesses the user profile and yields a set of known logical time concepts for a user for the current time. While the lower level of our time ontology is based on OWL-Time, the higher level is a simplification of concept *CalendarDescription*, found in some versions of OWL-Time. In the OpenCyc upper ontology it is called *RegularlyRepeatedEvent*.

Content Ontology

For the content dimension, Qualified Dublin Core (Kokkelink & Schwänzl, 2002) is often used, which is mainly a refinement of Dublin Core (DCMI, 2004),

providing access to information and services at document metadata level.

Domain and Task Ontologies

The modular application ontology is open for different domain ontologies to be added, to support different scenarios. For example, a tourism ontology has different kinds of POIs, restaurants, hotels, and the like, and may use an ontology of public transport. The domain ontologies are mainly used as value pool for different properties in all other ontologies.

There is no separate *user profile ontology*, but it consists of different domain ontologies covering the interests and preferences of users in the application domain. The profile values stemming from a separate system (e.g., from LDAP) are interpreted using the knowledge of domain ontologies. Additional rules may be meaningful when some profile attributes are to be inferred by others.

Also task ontologies can be added when needed. The main task ontologies in our case are the service ontology and the situation ontology.

Service Ontology

Service (and information) advertisements and demands are described independently by different user groups (i.e., service provider and user), not knowing exactly the needs of each other. The most flexible way to match demands against offers is to use semantic technologies, that is, ontologies and inference. The *ServiceProfile* is a subconcept of concept *Content* having Qualified Dublin Core properties. Thus, services are special content, having content properties and additionally service-specific properties. Registered services are facts connected by their properties to instances or concepts of other ontologies, which serve as dimensions. The top level ontologies *Location* and *Time* as well as all domain and task ontologies are used as value space for different service properties. This results in a star schema, in which service properties are characterized by subprofiles, which again are characterized by their properties. For example, the *geoRegion* of a specific service may be characterized by a location instance, which itself is characterized by a set of properties and the cost aspect may be characterized by a cost subprofile.

A simplified sample service ontology of this construction is sketched by Figure 2, which is both a relational schema and an ontology, since shadowed boxes indicate the root concepts of subontologies used for a dimension. Only some sample properties are shown here.

Service retrieval is supported by different multivalued classification properties. The values are concepts from different domain or task ontologies. Such rather orthogonal classifications together already cover much of the semantics of a service:

- **General classifications** using a service type taxonomy (property *type*), a product taxonomy (for *products* related to the service), and concepts from other domain ontologies used as service subjects (property *subject*).

- **QoS classifications** summarize nonfunctional quality of service aspects, for example, characterizing of main factors of service cost, quality, security, and possible device restrictions in the case of locally installed services (running on PDAs or home gateways).

- **Context** aspects support restricting a service to a multidimensional context and even to detected situations. This includes location and time properties for service validity (service accessibility, that is, *geoRegion*, *upTime*) and service coverage (for its result, that is, *coveredRegion*, *coveredEpoch*). An example is to find services callable *now* (validity is actual context) but delivering information (coverage) for a restaurant or event to visit this evening.

- **Contacts** and **clientele** summarize relational contact data of different parties involved in the service, like service provider and call center, as well as the clientele (for multiclientele ability).

Figure 2. Modular service ontology schema

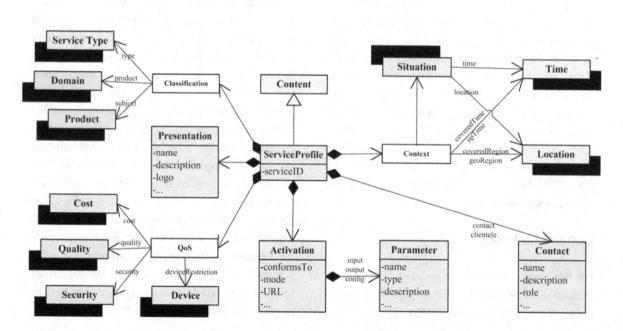

For *presentation and activation* of retrieved services, the following aspects are specified (not necessarily in an ontology but relational, since these aspects are seldom needed for service retrieval):

- **Presentation** covers all information needed to display retrieved service at the user's front-end, and includes multilingual information such as a service name or description and possibly icons. For use of services by programs, this aspect is not relevant.
- **Activation** provides all information needed to call the service, such as an *URI*, the communication standard used (property *conformsTo*), the *mode* (active, passive, etc.) and the parameters. Since we currently do not use a process model for the service, our grounding is simple.
- **Parameter** describes each input, output, and configuration parameter of the services, for example, its name, type, and a brief description, to be used for GUI generation and parameter marshaling.

The service ontology is influenced by standards like OWL-S (Martin et al., 2004), a Web service ontology submitted to the W3C, but we focus on the service profile. However, OWL-S is not the only approach towards Web service ontologies. The Web Service Modeling Ontology (WSMO) has also been submitted to W3C and a third approach is Semantic Web Services Ontology (SWSO). There is a migration process for these approaches. However, they focus on the process model, while their service profile is only basic. In contrast, the service ontology presented here focuses on the service profile, since it is used for demand-based service retrieval primarily.

Situation Ontology

Situation detection requires a modular ontology with subontologies for all context dimensions, all combined in the situation ontology. Thus, the situation ontology extensively depends on its dimension ontologies. It consists of a hierarchy of situation profile concepts, instantiated to characterize different situations. Situations are described by semantic situation profiles, being named sets of characteristic features of situations. Situation descriptions instantiate these concepts by defining a semantic classification of an aggregate of abstracted user context, user profile, and related information and can be inferred from these. At a given time, a user may be in zero, one, or many situation known by the system.

Ontology Usage

The application ontology is used as follows: Whenever an event occurs that might influence the service set of a user, the set is recalculated by situation detection and service matching (and possibly service roaming). These significant events include:

- **Context changes**: Our application scenarios are mobile, thus location changes occur often. We have developed an algorithm to detect significant location changes based on geographic extents of logical location concepts used in service registrations. This algorithm runs on mobile devices. Any user's GPS locations are only transmitted by his phone or PDA to the context server when a *significant* change has occurred and a new significance specification is returned. The same mechanism can be applied to other context dimensions as well. In this way, frequent context changes of mobile users lead only occasionally to service set recalculations. In a field trial in Beijing discussed in this chapter, only 86 significant context changes were produced by 15 users in approximately 4 hours in total.
- **User profile changes**: Whenever a user entered or modified his user profile, an event is fired, causing the system to react by calculating new situations and an appropriate new service set.
- **Service set changes**: Whenever a new service is provided to the public or whenever a service is changed or removed, an event is fired, causing service set recalculation.

- **Ontology changes:** Our inference engine is RDBMS-based (i.e., inference is directly executed in the relational database management system), thus ontology changes are controlled by the database and valid for the next semantic query, which is triggered.

Situation Detection

Situation detection occurs when context sensors report *significant* context changes. The abstraction and aggregation mechanisms of all dimensions are used to obtain a set of instances of the higher-level situation concepts. For example, not only the location and time may characterize a situation but also whether an action takes place at that location and time, by consulting for example a social event directory service or weather service. The resulting situation request profile is then semantically matched to all situation profiles known to the system, leading to a (possibly empty) set of situations fulfilling the request profile. A user may be in any of these situations or may be interested in being in this situation. For example, if a user is in a filled stadium, situation *Watching Competition* is detected. If it is personal lunchtime, the additional situation *Eating in Stadium* provides corresponding service offers. Only well-defined situations can be detected. If a user is in a situation not known by the system, he will only get situation-independent support.

Service Matching

The service selection process is a semantic matching of an implicitly dynamically constructed service request profile against the profiles of all known services found in the semantic registry. The request profile uses the matching situations determined previously. User profile and context are also used in the request profile, for example, to select only services matching the user's interests at the current location. Some user preferences are mapped to service types or service subjects, which requires fine-grained taxonomies of these kinds, being related to the preferences hierarchy. Other preferences are used for a personalized instantiation of time ontology concepts like *Morning* and *Lunchtime*, which are used to infer situations. The matching evaluates different types of semantic relationships for all profile properties, like subclass, instance, and containment relationships. Different matching strategies can be realized by defining different semantics when using our *ModelAccess* component described below. For example, for a class-valued property (e.g., property *type* or *subject* in our service ontology), it can be defined whether it matches with subclasses, with superclasses, or with both, and to what semantic distance.

Service Roaming

Mostly, services are defined for a certain scope, which could be a geographical area they cover or certain timeframes or situations for which they are useful. Obviously, a service scope can be described based on restrictions defined on context attributes. Service matching regards the actual user context and adds it to the service request profile in order to select only services which scope covers this context. Based on context-specific service selection, service roaming aims at providing certain service functionality to a user constantly during changing contexts. Whenever the actual user context leaves the scope of the used service, a new service instance with similar functionality but with a scope fitting to the new context has to be found and invoked transparently for the user. An example is a service offering parking information for a certain city. Such a service could, for example, be used in a navigation application. If a user leaves one city and enters another, the navigation application is automatically disconnected from the currently used service and connected to the one covering the area of the new city.

Implementation Aspects

Currently, our extensible ontology comprises about 300 concepts with 1900 properties and 900 instances (among them the registered services and locations), divided into several top-level, domain, and task ontologies. It is completely stored in relational database tables, combined with relational data and accessed from all subsystems by our *ModelAccess* component. Multi-user access is controlled by a sophisticated RDBMS. We have done extensive load testing of the new architecture, which proved to scale well with the number of users (concurrent threads), the size of the ontology, and the size of the answer set. The numbers can be summarized as follows: With 100, 000 registered service profiles and about the same number of related entities as above retrieval times of about a second are achieved on a 3.2 GHz, 2 GB RAM PC, of course depending on the complexity of the query.

SYSTEM ARCHITECTURE

To support scenarios like those described, we have developed an information-logistical semantic service platform. We give a gross outline of the system architecture and the interoperation of its subsystems for semantic matching of user demands and registered offers.

Use of Profiles

All subsystems use profiles for describing entities in their interface methods. A profile is a structured set of properties covering different dimensions and characterizing an entity. Each property has a type (range) and may have several values. Samples are user profiles, service profiles, situation profiles, location profiles, and device profiles. They may be used for characterizing offers and also for describing an actual demand of such entities, and are thus a basis for semantic matching of both.

Profiles may be interpreted either directly or semantically. In a semantic profile, the range and values of the attributes are semantic categories stemming from an ontology, which forms background knowledge for interpreting the syntactic (e.g., relational) data. The ontology can also be used to guide the process of creating or modifying profile properties (e.g., to offer allowed value for properties), and to assure consistency of stored profile properties with the ontology.

Gross Architecture

The information-logistical semantic service platform provides basic functionalities needed for intelligent demand-specific selection and provision of information and services. The key technologies used and combined by the platform are the following:

*   **Personalization** is used for the selection of services and information according to a user's profile, preferences, interest, and other user-related information, and for the adaptation of filtered information to the user's needs.
*   **Context and situation awareness:** Context information includes any relevant information about the user's state and his environment including the derived situations. It can be used to retrieve the information needed at the location and time or in the situation the user currently is in.
*   **Open infrastructure:** The service platform uses and builds on top of existing open and distributed service infrastructures. This enables the dynamic use and selection of already existing information and services.
*   **Mobile computing:** A mobile device provides users with information and services everywhere. This allows further integration of the platform in the user's daily life and work processes. The restricted communication and interaction capability of mobile devices, as well as communication costs, reliability, and security aspects have to be considered when selecting suitable presentation forms and delivery strategies.
*   **Information-logistical evaluation:** All described key technologies are combined by application-specific evaluation knowledge. The evaluation component of the platform controls the appropriate selection and presentation of services and information. This may even include business processes, being out of scope for this chapter.

Main Components

The logical architecture defines overall system functionality as a cooperation of different subsystems providing specialized tasks related to the key technologies. The subsystems are application-independent and can also be used stand-alone. They all build on services and models of the core layer. As sketched, the platform developed consists of the following main components:

ModelAccess

Inference engines are not yet as mature as relational database systems. Especially, they are not as fast and only some of them support multi-threading, which is a prerequisite for having a large number of concurrent users. Therefore, we developed a *ModelAccess* component with integrated basic and pragmatic inference support. The principle idea of *ModelAccess* is the generation and execution of *closed* structured query language (SQL) queries from semantic profiles based on ontologies that map the original semantics. The generation is based on an extensible set of registered parameterized SQL parts. Predefined parts for standard relationships like *subtype, instanceOf, partOf, geoContains* exist, and rules or characteristics for new kinds of relationships can be stored as user-defined SQL parts. The parts are selected and composed based on stored semantic metadata of table properties. The *closed* queries generated only need simple transactions handled by the RDBMS automatically. The *ModelAccess* component was built with the main design goals to support dynamic online multi-user access to semantic data, to support efficient retrieval on voluminous persistent semantic data, and to combine relational concepts with semantic features by an abstract model access layer and runtime-engine used within all subsystems of the service platform.

Most inference engines and ontology design tools today enable to store ontologies in an RDBMS. For example, Protégé provides to store ontologies as Protégé database and others even offers to use database

tables during inference (which often makes inference slower, and is intended for large ontologies that cannot completely be kept in main memory). However, *ModelAccess* is not the first inference engine using a relational database directly for inference. In Das, Chong, Eadon, and Srinivasan (2004), an approach is described to implement inference on top of an Oracle RDBMS. Semantic queries are formulated using SQL with additional operators, based on a general schema for storing concepts, properties and relationships. Due to performance reasons they perform an initial materialization of all OWL axioms (e.g., subproperties and transitivity of properties) after loading the ontology, followed by individual inferences for each semantic query. The differences to our approach are: they need initial materialization of, for example, transitivity (computing the transitive closure) to get meaningful performance and directly work on SQL level, while we use transitive discriminates (no transitive closure) and add semantic profiles and SQL generation as an optional abstraction level. In Chong, Das, Eadon, and Srinivasan (2005), the same authors describe a similar approach to realize inference based on resource description framework (RDF). Performance is optimized by providing indexed materialized views on the two tables of their normalized schema, which *results* in a table design similar to ours. Chong et al. (2005) conclude, "a promising storage representation is *partial* normalization" (2005, p.12).

Service Subsystem

This subsystem is responsible for selecting content and services. It is an open service infrastructure and provides functionality for management and provision of services. This includes the semantic description of services by definable ontology schemas, as described above. The semantic *ServiceRegistry* (implemented by *ModelAccess*) provides dynamic ad hoc integration of services of different kinds from third party providers. It allows for retrieval of registered services and customized service offers. The *ServiceFacade* supports use of services of any kind, provides basic

Figure 3. Gross architecture of the semantic service platform

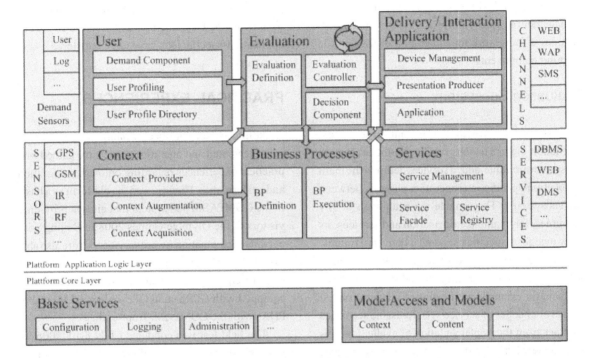

mechanisms for controlling access rights and billing, and enables service roaming. Not only passive services are supported, but also subscribing active services which may fire events.

Context Subsystem

This subsystem provides functionality for definition and provision of application-specific context models, which are a machine readable representation of the part of the world relevant for an application, based on a context meta model. Normally, this model includes the user and other items like locations and relations between these objects. The subsystem provides functionality for detection and provision of context information for any entity. This includes ad hoc integration, management, selection, and use of distributed context sensors, the derivation of related

context information and the detection of situations (to enable situation-awareness). The subsystem follows a layered component architecture that separates the different aspects of context detection, integration, refinement, model management and operation, and context information access.

User Subsystem

This subsystem defines the infrastructure for the personalization of any application, used for centralized management and provision of user information. This includes the provision of user data (relatively static user information like the user's name and gender), user preferences (like preferred language or modality), and user interests (in specific topics). Complex application-specific user model can be defined. Securing privacy of such information is important here. In the current version of the subsystem a lightweight directory access protocol (LDAP) server is used as the basis for management and provision of user information. It also includes a framework for integration of user profile learning components.

Evaluation Subsystem

This subsystem provides information-logistical evaluation logic. The jobs residing in the evaluation subsystem are value-added services defining the main application-specific interoperation patterns between the subsystems. They enable the evaluation of any resources, for example, information and services, its relevance for a specific user, and a delivery strategy. The subsystem executes in cooperation with the other subsystems, thus delegating special evaluation jobs to them, for example, notification of relevant context events or changes of service sets. Reusable scenarios abstract from the implementation of evaluation jobs within the other subsystems. The current implementation of the job model is based on a Boolean ECA-paradigm: events can be subscribed from the other subsystems. The condition is a Boolean expression on events that lead to the action part defining a coordinated execution of functionality using the other subsystems.

Instantiation for Application Scenarios

All application scenarios described above have common requirements on a supporting platform, namely information-logistical support by dynamic information and service supply, based on registered offers, relevant context information, and user profile data. These are the objective of the semantic service platform.

Instantiation of the platform for a new application possibly added to the set of already existing applications (ability to clientele processing) begins with extending the data models (namely ontologies). Each subsystem can be instantiated by configuration and by describing its application-dependent behavior using a domain-specific language. Then the platform component's application programming interfaces (APIs) are used by the new application, and services as well as application-specific jobs have to be registered.

PRACTICAL EXPERIENCES

As the information-logistical semantic service platform is implemented and operational, we have gained first practical experiences regarding ontology integration and performance. Having used the platform as a basis in the COMPASS2008 system that aims at providing visitors of the Olympic Games 2008 in Beijing with personalized situation-aware services, we are also able to include experiences from a recently performed field test in Beijing. During that field test the users were equipped with GPRS- und GPS-enhanced MDA Pro PDAs with the COMPASS front-end.

The field test was conducted July 8-10, 2006, in Beijing. To enable testing of the COMPASS system under real-life conditions, we defined a test scenario for Beijing. This scenario aims at covering the most common situations visitors (especially Western foreigners) experience when visiting Beijing. Regarding the resources available in the project we had to restrict the test to a part of Beijing, for example, to limit the content needed.

The test users represented Beijing Olympic visitors, that is, they acted in the role "tourist". For the field test we had foreign users from the U.S. Korea, Japan, and Italy as well as Chinese, thus representing native and non-native English speakers. Of the 15 users, 12 were male and 3 were female. Their average age was about 26 years. Approximately 40% of the users had experience in the use of PDAs and/or smartphones. The foreign users mostly had only little knowledge of the Chinese language and were to some extent familiar with Beijing. Six foreigners were in Beijing for one month or less.

In the next step, the test users were sent out to perform the test. Each user had to fulfil 16 tasks, some of them repeatedly, for example, find restaurant/coffee shop, order a drink, plan the day, pay, communicate destination to taxi driver, buy an item, and find restrooms. A COMPASS2008 team member accompanied each test user to assure a proper conduction of the different tasks.

Situation-aware service provision was considered useful by most subjects. No test person criticized it, and most people even desired to improve the feature. From the COMPASS system perspective we obtained the following results regarding the quality of the situation awareness feature: recall 95.8% (correct situation identified, only relevant services offered), precision 51.0% (only correct situation identified, redundant services offered). The recall value looks quite satisfying for the first deployment in the field. An analysis of the reason for wrong situation identifications turned out that deviation of the GPS signal led to mismatches of a user's position and the geographical locations of points-of-interest.

During the field test, the semantic service platform was integrated into the Internet infrastructure of a Chinese Internet service provider. It was fully available with no problems in providing its functionality. Even though there was a problem in the context subsystem leading to an unnecessarily high number of context change events, there was no visible delay in providing the user with situation-specific services.

A problem faced was the unreliable and imprecise location detection of a user through GPS. Even when a user did not move, the GPS detector reported a position change of more than 30 meters. Another problem was the unreliability and limited performance of data communication using general packet radio service (GPRS) in China. Beside these problems, the technical performance of our platform during the field test was satisfying.

FUTURE TRENDS

Currently we observe a convergence of communication and information infrastructures towards Internet-based systems. This convergence eases the integration of information flows into applications. This trend is backed by service-oriented architectures where system components communicate via the Internet, residing at arbitrary locations. Consequently, information overflow of users will intensify. Customer satisfaction can only be achieved when an intelligent information supply is provided, taking care of individual user needs.

A broader adoption of semantic registries and situation-aware demand description as standards enables a guided use of offered services and service-specific contents in individual user contexts. This leads to higher acceptance on the user side and at the same time enables the forming of value chains on the business side, as service providers can establish networks where each provider covers a specific service offer that seamlessly integrates with others.

In summary, user profiles, context-awareness, and semantic service descriptions provide the basis for a demand-driven personalized information and service logistics using multistage value chains.

CONCLUSIONS

In this chapter, we tried to point out that ontologies and their evaluation are well suited to define a semantic reference system accessed by large heterogeneous user groups. In the COMPASS2008 project, an application ontology for Beijing Olympics tourists has been developed. On this basis a dynamic semantic matching of user demands derived from user profiles and context-driven situation detection with semantically described service offers is performed. The COMPASS pilot system proved the applicability of these concepts for situation-aware semantic Web applications in a field test in Beijing.

Although the results from the field test are satisfying, the entire development was not as smooth as it might seem. We had to solve problems on all levels, including nonsynchronized funding on the Chinese and German sides, content procurement, and system integration or technical problems when setting up the field test. Some of these problems are intrinsic to international projects with multiple partners; others are more specific, like the restricted access to digital maps in China or the impreciseness of GPS in a mega city like Beijing. The cooperative atmosphere within the consortium, however, was a major success factor. A more detailed discussion of the problems sketched above is beyond the scope of this contribution. Here we focused on ontology related issues.

The COMPASS system provides for user-individual demand description and situation-aware service filtering in the context of the Olympic Games 2008 in Beijing. The MONA prototype deploys the same technologies for situation-specific information and service provision in emergency cases, supporting emergency response teams on the spot. Here, situation awareness is used for a more precise content selection.

The insights gained from the deployment of semantic Web technologies show that they are very powerful and helpful for the development of adequate models. On the implementation side, however, mass applications are still a critical issue as the performance of inference engines falls short compared with relational database technology. Hence, for larger applications we recommend use of ontology development tools for the conceptual phase and transferring the result in the implementation phase to a database solution.

ACKNOWLEDGMENTS

COMPASS/FLAME2008 was developed in the context of the project "Personalized Web Services on Internet III for the Olympic Games 2008 in Beijing", October, 2002 – September, 2006, supported by the German Ministry of Education and Research (BMBF Grant No. 01AK055) and the Chinese Ministry of Science and Technology (MOST).

REFERENCES

Chong, E.I., Das, S., Eadon, G., & Srinivasan, J. (2005). An efficient SQL-based RDF querying scheme. In *Proc. 31st VLDB Conf* (pp. 1216-1227). Trondheim, Norway.

Cycorp, Inc. (2002). OpenCyc selected vocabulary and upper ontology. Retrieved June 19, 2007, from *http://www.cyc.com/cycdoc/vocab/vocab-toc.html*

Das S., Chong, E.I., Eadon, G., & Srinivasan, J. (2004). Supporting ontology-based semantic matching in RDBMS. In *Proc. 30th VLDB Conference* (pp 1054-1065). San Francisco, CA: Morgan Kaufmann.

Davies, N., Mitchell, K., Cheverest, K., & Blair, G. (1998). Developing a context sensitive tourist guide. In *First Workshop on Human Computer Interaction with Mobile Devices* (GIST Tech. Rep. G98-1) (pp 17-24).

Deiters, W., Löffeler, T., & Pfennigschmidt, S. (2003). *The information logistics approach toward a user demand-driven information supply.* In D. Spinellis (Ed.), *Cross-media service delivery* (pp. 37-48). Boston, MA.

Dey, A. (2001). Understanding and using context. *Personal and Ubiquitous Computing Journal, 5*(1), 4-7.

Dey, A., Salber, D., Abowd, G.D., Futakawa, M. (1999). The conference assistant: Combining context-awareness with wearable computing. In *3rd International Symposium on Wearable Computer,* San Francisco, CA, (pp. 21-28).

Dublin Core Metadata Initiative (DCMI). (2004). Dublin core metadata element set, reference description. Retrieved June 19, 2007, from *http://dublincore.org/documents/dces/*

Fonseca, F., Egenhofer, M., Davis, C., & Borges, K. (2000). Ontologies and knowledge sharing in urban GIS. *Computer, Environment and Urban Systems, 24*(3), 251-272.

Guarino, N. (1998). Formal ontology and information systems. In *Proc. FOIS'98* (pp. 3-15). Trento, Italy: IOS Press.

Hobbs, J., & Pustejovsky, J. (2003). Annotating and reasoning about time and events. In *Proc. AAAI*

Spring Symposium on Logical Formalization of Commonsense Reasoning (pp. 74-82). Menlo Park, CA: AAAI Press.

Holtkamp, B., Weißenberg, N., & Speckmann, H. (2005). MONA – A situation-aware decision support system for emergency situations. In *Proc 19th Int. Conf. EnvironInfo - Informatics for Environmental Protection,* Brno, Czech Republic (pp. 186-190).

Kokkelink, S., & Schwänzl R. (2002). Expressing qualified Dublin core in RDF/XML. Retrieved June 19, 2007, from *http://dublincore.org/documents/dcq-rdf-xml/*

Long, S., Kooper, R., Abowd, G. D., & Atkeson, C. G. (1996). Rapid prototyping of mobile context-aware applications: The cyberguide case study. In *2nd ACM International Conference on Mobile Computing and Networking* (pp 97-107).

Martin, D. (Ed.) (2004). OWL-S: Semantic markup for Web services (W3C Member Submission). Retrieved June 19, 2007, from *http://www.w3.org/Submission/OWL-S*

Niles, I., & Pease, A. (2001). Towards a standard upper ontology. In *Proc FOIS'01* (pp 2-9). Ogunquit, ME.

Weißenberg, N., Voisard, A., & Gartmann, R. (2006). An ontology-based approach to personalized situation-aware mobile service supply. *Springer GeoInformatica, 10*(1), 55-90.

Want, R., Hopper, A., Falcao, V., & Gibbons, J. (1992). The active badge location system. *ACM Transactions on Information Systems, 10*(1), 91-102.

Chapter XVII
Knowledge Management Support for Enterprise Distributed Systems

Yun-Heh Chen-Burger
The University of Edinburgh, UK

Yannis Kalfoglou
University of Southampton, UK

ABSTRACT

Explosion of information and increasing demands on semantic processing Web applications have pushed software systems to their limits. To address this problem, we propose a semantic-based formal framework (ADP) that makes use of promising technologies to enable knowledge generation and retrieval. We argue that this approach is cost-effective, as it reuses and builds on existing knowledge and structure. It is also a good starting point for creating an Organizational Memory and providing Knowledge Management functions.

BACKGROUND

The era we are living in is characterized by an unprecedented explosion of information that is digitized and available to large audiences through online, distributed, and open-ended environments. Presented with it are also opportunities to exploit and benefit from it. Organizations have to quickly adapt to this new phenomenon. Software applications, database and expert systems designed and run by a closed group of software and knowledge engineers who had centralized control over the lifecycle of IT artefacts seem to be outdated. Moreover, the distributed nature of IT systems has experienced a dramatic explosion with the arrival and revolutionary use of the Internet and its associated technologies—hypertext and XML-based

documents, online databases, terminological repositories, Web services, and blogs—which continually
challenge the traditional roles of IT in our society.

One promising approach for IT system architects
is to use intelligent knowledge management (KM)
methods to cope with this expanding nature of distributed systems in a global scale. At the cornerstone
of most of these tools lies the buzzwords of *semantics
technologies* that are deployed in the Semantic Web
(SW). Semantic technology is a broad term coined
recently in the business domain to refer to technologies
ranging from ontologies and information extraction
on the SW to ebXML schemata and service-oriented
architecture based systems. This term enables synergies in distributed systems that automate semantic
(meaning) interoperability between processes and
services.

The successful blending of semantic technologies
with the traditional KM systems starts from a fundamental part of any business: *process*. For more than
10 years, the values of process-oriented approaches,
such as BPR (business process reengineering) and BPI
(business process improvement) are well-recognized.
Today, it is one of the fundamental steps to radically
improving organizational performance. Processes
are treated as tangible entities that can be formally
captured, analyzed, incrementally, and radically
modified to change organizational behaviors and
achieve goals. Recent KM that have taken process-
oriented approaches are exemplified in Schreiber, de
Hoog, Akkermans, Anjewierden, Shadbolt, and Van
de Velde (1999) and Abecker, Bernardi, Hinkelmann,
Kuhn, and Sintek (1998).

KM is no longer just about identifying and storing
knowledge, but also about providing efficient ways to
retrieve, disseminates, and use knowledge to achieve
goals. It embeds "KM processes" as a part of normal
business practices, so no more than necessary efforts
need to be spent to benefit from KM. Furthermore,
KM as a discipline can benefit from process-oriented
approaches. KM tasks can be described in learnable
processes that can be compared with business processes, analyzed and improved upon. In addition, in
KM, the human is the central issue—they are the key

knowledge creators, holders, and users; organizational
memories (OM) are often the main tool to hold and
provide information central to an organization. In this
chapter, we therefore examine the roles played by human, OM, and business processes in an organization
and how they relate to each other. We also speculate
that formal logical methods, such as the proposed semantic-based Actor, Data and Process-oriented (ADP)
framework, can interface these fundamental organizational components to help improve the utilization
of an OM, thus leading to organizational performance
enhancements. We start our exploration of KM support
for enterprise distributed systems by focussing on a
core component of many enterprises: the OM.

ORGANIZATIONAL MEMORIES

We witness a shift in the decision support literature
from data-oriented processing systems to ones integrated with human intellect and organizational processes
(Carlsson & Turban, 2002). These have been studied
in the context of KM and OM to provide means for
easy access and retrieval of information for users. In
parallel, we see recognition that the goals of KM will
be most effectively realized through actions connected
to normal day-to-day business processes (Breuker &
Van de Velde, 1994). This makes it easier to demonstrate value-added contributions to an organization,
which is better than isolated KM efforts (Abecker et
al., 1998). An ideal OM could assist in effective decision-making, which means information regarding the
organization could be made easily accessible.

However, there is little support to help create an
OM. It is difficult to identify the right information to
include. This process is time-consuming, manual, and
error-prone, given the diversity, quality, and quantity of
resources to be analyzed for reliability and relevance.
Semi-automatic methods *do* exist, but these are bound
to individual technologies. It is always the user who
has to initiate search in the OM. But this requires the
user to be able to formulate a query, with or without
automated help; the OM system must be able to correctly parse this query, retrieve relevant information

according to predefined mechanisms, and present it back to the user.

Several issues are identified in field surveys (Dieng, Corby, Goboin, & Ribiere, 1999) and systems (Abecker et al., 1998). It is a multifaceted problem because it is not only concerned with the quality and elicitation of resources, or the difficulties in engaging the user in technical tasks, but is also related to the usage of these resources. They may be (a) used by other systems for different purposes, (b) "unspecified" or "ambiguous" and need to be interpreted or composed by other (external) resources, and (c) once these resources are identified and used, they act as a qualitative measure for the OM. That is, if OM users are not satisfied with the quality of information presented to them, it is unlikely that they will return.

One way to tackle this problem is to identify the purpose of an OM project early on (Dieng et al., 1999): what are the users' needs and what will the OM be used for. Most techniques and methods are taken from requirements analysis and elicitation research. However, one should be cautious when using requirement engineering techniques. Zave and Jackson (1997) reported that vague and imprecise requirements are difficult to formalize and convert to specifications and further refinements are necessary.

This problem has led some OM designers to build their systems around existing workflow process engines, for example, the *KnowMore* OM (Abecker et al., 1998). We are sceptical of this approach, as it requires familiarization and the existence of robust workflow processes, supported by intensive modeling to link the two systems. We therefore propose an ontology based approach for seeding OMs.

SEEDING ORGANIZATIONAL MEMORIES USING ONTOLOGY NETWORK ANALYSIS

Since it is common that ontologies are used in organizations—for semantic interoperability and reuse—one could also use them for other purposes. Ontology network analysis (ONA) (Alani, Kalfoglou, O'Hara, &

Shadbolt, 2002) applies information network analysis methods to a populated ontology to uncover trends and object characteristics, such as shortest paths, object clusters, semantic similarity, object importance, and/or popularity. Similar methods have also been explored for information retrieval purposes. ONA uses these methods to analyze the network of instances and relationships in a knowledge base, guided by ontology. There are many types of networks that can be studied (Alani, Dasmahapatra, O'Hara, & Shadbolt, 2003). The advantage of studying ontologies is that the relations therein have semantics that provide rich sources of information over and above connectivity or simple subsumption. This semantic information can be used to enable "raw'" results to be refined on a relatively principled basis. An example ONA application is described in another section of this chapter.

ONA methods can be harnessed by selecting a set of focused resources to feature in a new OM based on existing populated ontologies. The fact that this method is automatic takes some of the burden of OM development from its users and managers and allows quality content to be put in place prior to use, thereby increasing the likelihood of early take-up by its users. Being automatic, ONA is not entirely foolproof. Points of interests may not be spotted, especially if the ontology is incomplete or fails to cover some important aspects in the domain; however, by extracting information from ontologies currently in use, ONA suggests an initial reliable set of interesting concepts and relations. Certain assumptions must be made to support the use of ONA, but as the OM develops, such assumptions are relaxed, and the OM begins to be populated by its users.

During the seeding exercise, the ONA technique is used to carry out network measures to an ontology to determine popular entities in the domain. Such entities can be either classes or instances, and *popularity* is (a) defined in terms of the number of instances particular classes have (class popularity), and the number and type of relation paths between an entity and other entities (instance popularity), and (b) regarded as a proxy for importance. The working assumption is that important objects will have a stronger presence in a representation of the domain, and will have a lot of key relationships with many other entities (i.e., they will act as "hubs" in the domain).[1]

ONTOLOGY NETWORK ANALYSIS ALGORITHM

Given a first pass ONA of an ontology, given the most popular entities, an OM developer can exploit user feedback to hone the analysis. Two ways of doing this are:

- Important instances can be selected—these instances may have been counted as "popular" under the first pass analysis or not, as the case may be, and hence could be manually selected as important instances independently of the governing assumption that popularity = importance—and the ONA performed once more, this time measuring not the quantity of relations between all entities, but measuring the quantity of relations between the selected instances and other entities.

- Relations can be weighted according to their importance and the weights transferred from entity to entity along the relation-connection. Hence one relation (e.g., *co-author-with*) might be weighted more highly than another more common one (e.g., *shares-office-with*), whose relevance to the domain in question is not as high. In that case, the effect when performing an ONA is to privilege the entities that enter into the highly-weighted relations as against those that do not. There are two classes of ways of differentially weighting relations.

  ○ First, relations could be differentially weighted automatically on similar lines to the selection of important entities, viz., the relations most often filled with values in the knowledge base will be weighted higher than others.

  ○ Alternatively, the weights can be fixed manually. This has the advantage of be-

ing sensitive to user understanding of the domain and the disadvantage of being a complex and difficult process that could be time-consuming, especially if there are a lot of relations about. Of course, as with entity-selection, an initial cut using automatically-created weights could be run past a user who might suggest adjustments; this might be the cheapest method of getting the best of both worlds.

The spreading activation algorithm underpinning ONA also identifies nodes similar to a specific node. This is the premise underlying our hypothesis. It could be argued that our analysis is not a qualitative one, but a quantitative one. However, Cooper (1997) argues that quality can be measured in two ways, in terms of popularity or importance. Our analysis yields concepts that are the most popular in the network and since the network is about an ontology that *by default* represents important concepts, then these concepts are also important.

To operate our hypothesis, we assume that (a) ontologies will be available in the organization in which we want to deploy an OM, and (b) these will be populated. These assumptions are strong and indeed are ongoing research issues in the knowledge engineering community. However, we should accept and anticipate that ontologies are popular in organizational settings nowadays: in the form of database repositories, SW data formatted in resource description framework schema (RDF/RDFS), and Web ontology language (OWL) ontologies.

USING ONTOLOGY NETWORK ANALYSIS IN ORGANIZATIONAL MEMORIES

Using ontologies as the foundation for an OM is not a unique idea, but the use of ONA to provide initial information for populating the OM is novel. We should also mention that using an ontology at the start of an OM's lifecycle allows us to provide support to users in formulating their queries from an early stage. Normally, users have to formulate initial queries unaided since there is no prior information available as no retrievals have been made yet. In applying ONA, we support users in formulating queries by providing them with ontological information regarding the starting node for initiating an ONA-based search. This information is readily available in existing slots in the ontology (e.g., documentation slots).

In Figure 1 we depict a high-level diagram of an OM. This is not meant to be a reference architecture for OMs. This figure emphasizes the dual role of ONA and the supportive role ontologies play in our scenario. On the left-hand side of the figure we have users of an organization performing their regular tasks.

In the center we have an OM which is composed, at this abstract level, by two interfaces to users and OM developers, a port to external resources, and internal resources existing in the organization's repositories. The latter could have several forms, ranging from tacit knowledge possessed by experts to explicit knowledge expressed formally in knowledge bases or digital discussion spaces. In the center of our abstract OM lie the ontologies that underpin the entire OM. These are either existing resources or are constructed (semi-) automatically with the aid of knowledge acquisition, retrieval, and modeling techniques. The focus, though, is on the use of ONA: the two rectangular boxes denoting "ONA" are placed between the ontologies and OM interfaces to users and developers.

Figure 1. Supporting initial seeding of an OM: Pushing knowledge into the OM and pulling it out—using ontology network analysis and business process analysis techniques

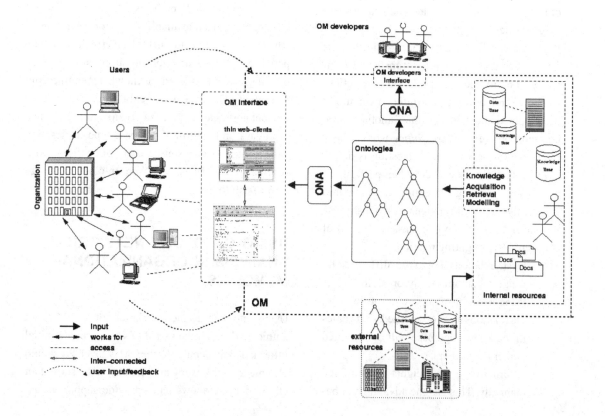

The generality of ONA makes it possible to use it for pushing knowledge to users but also as an aid for the OM's developers. They could apply ONA to the organization's ontologies in order to identify which concepts should be presented to certain types of users. For instance, assuming that there is a workflow engine in the organization, and developers are looking for ways of linking the OM to it, they could either engage in modeling exercises such as those reported in (Abecker et al., 1998), or they could use ONA to help them identify concepts from the underlying ontologies and map them onto workflow processes. The developers can then use these concepts found used in the workflow processes as a starting node for his/her next round of ONA analysis. This could reveal further node linkages, thus saving development time and allowing developers to deal with ontologies that they are not familiar with.

We also include two curly dotted arcs in Figure 1 linking users with the OM. These denote users' feedback and input. This is a very important element of an OM architecture, as OMs can be improved over time by user feedback and inputs. In our abstract architecture, we implemented light-weight feedback mechanisms, like thin Web-clients, accessible through Web browsers, as a means for eliciting feedback on an OM's resources (see Figure 2). Finally, the OM interface to its users is light-weight and accessible from distributed clients on the Web. We have developed two kinds of interfaces: a dedicated OM interface, where the user can state preferences in selecting the appropriate node to search for related information, or there could be a customized rendering of information into a user's Web browser. The latter is extracted automatically after applying ONA to the underlying ontology, whereas the former requires user input to tune the search criteria.

LIMITATIONS

We identified potential caveats to using ONA to bootstrap OMs and categorize them in three areas:

a. **Information overload:** A progressive and query-based interaction with the OM from initial set-up acts as a safeguard against unwanted information overload. However, progressive interaction means that the initial set-up suffers from cold-start syndrome—not enough information will be available; query-based interaction requires expertise and domain familiarization from the users to get the most out of an OM.

b. **Context-awareness:** This has been recognized as the Achilles' heel for OMs. One proposed remedy, advocated by proponents of marrying workflow processes and OMs, seems to work well only in settings where workflow processes are either existing, or are relatively easy to identify and model.

c. **Domain-independence:** This is a desired feature for OMs. But, the proposed ONA approach is not specific to any kind of ontology, or indeed to any ontology at all! This makes it possible to apply ONA to more than one ontology as are likely to exist in large organizations.

The ONA-based solution we proposed above addresses the problem of setting up a comprehensive OM in a bid to attract high usage rates. However, in a dynamic and ever-changing organizational context, we are faced with a number of challenges related to the capturing of the right types of (business) requirements. In the next section we elaborate on how we assist the appropriate capturing of organizational requirements with the use of a novel business process approach that is geared towards supporting an OM, thus extending and complementing our ONA based method for seeding the initial OM.

A CASE STUDY: ONTOCOPI

An example application is to use ONA to identify communities of practice (CoP) within organizations. One such tool is ONTOlogy-based community of practice identifier (ONTOCOPI) (O'Hara et al., 2002).

ONTOCOPI's algorithm combines and improves ideas from previous work on similarity measures, such as shortest path measures (Rada, Mili, Becknell, & Blettner, 1989), multi-path traversal (Paice, 1991), and constrained spreading activation methods (Cohen & Kjeldsen, 1987). Its algorithm makes use of the ontology to make decisions about which relationships to select and how they should be valued. Ontological axioms can also be consulted in the relationship selection process.

Relationships in ontologies are described formally. They stand as proxies to informal ones—the types of relationships found in CoPs. One may infer that two people who co-author a paper are likely to be members of the same CoP. If two CoP members share no formal relationships, then any vector addition of formal relations can also stand proxy for informal

ones. For instance, if A co-authored a paper with B, who works on a project with C, then it may be inferred that A and C, are likely to be members of the same CoP. Total accuracy, however, is impossible for an informal and rapidly-evolving social group like a CoP. Furthermore, the aim of ONTOCOPI is to *support* CoP identification, an expensive operation in its own right (Wenger, 1999). A certain measure of indeterminacy is inevitable.

ONTOCOPI cannot identify relationships that are not represented: if two people in the same CoP have no formal relationship recorded in the ontology, and no chain of formal relations link them, then their comembership cannot be found. ONTOCOPI also can't distinguish *between* CoPs. If someone is a *broker*, that is, a person who functions in two separate CoPs, then ONTOCOPI will tend to select the union of the two

Figure 2. ONTOCOPI: Ontology based communities of practice identifier

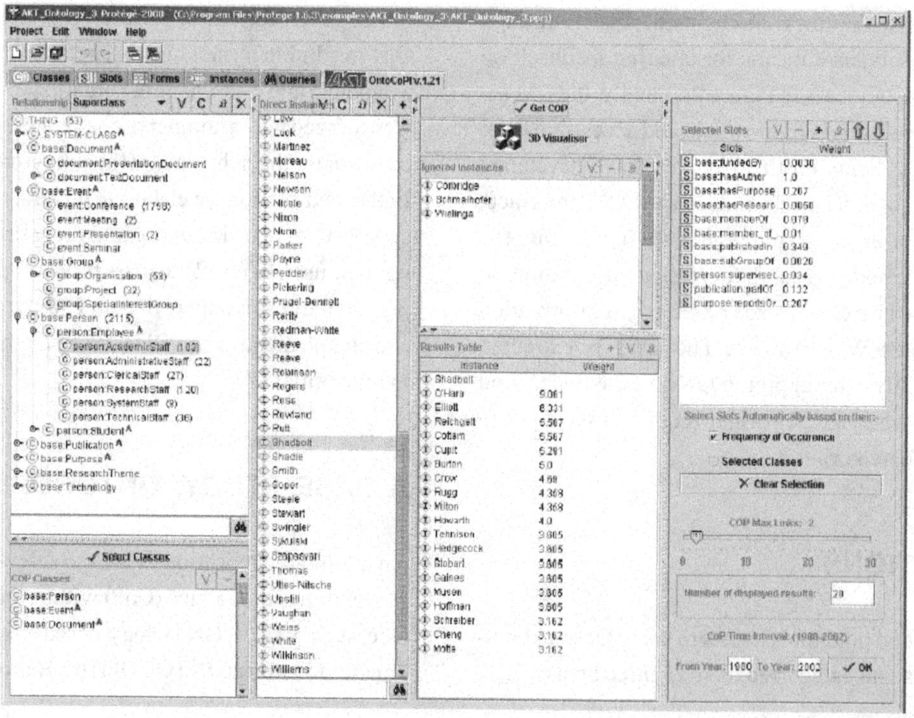

CoPs. ONTOCOPI, however, does support CoP identification, a resource-heavy task that may be alleviated to some extent by assumptions that formal connections can approximate informal relationships.

Figure 2 shows an ONTOCOPI'S interface. The panel on the far left shows the class hierarchy of the ontology. The panel next to it shows the instances of a selected class. From this panel, an instance can be selected to be the "center" of the CoP (the relations radiating out from this individual are used for CoP identification). The panels on the right set the relation weights and parameter values (e.g., the number of links the algorithm will spread to). Clicking the "Get COP" button will run the algorithm. The center right top panel displays the current calculations and center right bottom displays the weights that have been transferred to other instances, in descending order of weight (the main output of ONTOCOPI). In this diagram, the CoP of *Shadbolt* has been investigated, and ONTOCOPI has suggested, in descending order of preference, *O'Hara*, *Elliott, Reichgelt, Cottam, Cupit, Burton* and *Crow*, then the *Intelligence, Agents, Multimedia Group* of which *Shadbolt* is a member, then *Rugg*.

Ordering and relative weights are important. *O'Hara* scores 13.5; this is meaningless except in the context of a search. Here, 13.5 is good, twice the score of the next candidate. However, the user may be suspicious of the ordering of *Tennison*, who scores 2.0, and *Motta*, who scores 1.5. These figures have no absolute interpretation (except in terms of the algorithm); it is therefore for the users to interpret them according to their own understanding of the structure of their CoP.

Weights can be created based on frequency or manually assigned. In this example, the weights were calculated automatically, with the most frequently used relation getting weight 1; those not used getting 0; anything in between is allocated accordingly. A second run might adjust the weights manually, perhaps giving some less used but important relations higher weights.

The algorithm initializes instance weights to 1. It then applies a breadth-first search, following the relations, transferring the weights of the relation and

instance to the next nodes. It continues until time out from the start node. Instances accumulate weights according to the numbers of relations from the starting node; the longer the path, the smaller the weight transferred. The weightier the relation, the larger the weight transferred. Therefore a short distance, or a significant connection, with the base instance will tend to push an instance up the batting order. In this example, since *O'Hara* has written many papers with *Shadbolt*—many individual relations with a heavy weighted node—it has increased *O'Hara's* score, and other nodes connected to it.

THE ACTOR, DATA, AND PROCESS-ORIENTED (ADP) APPROACH

To support today's knowledge economy, an appropriately designed OM must closely support organizational operations and its business aims. To address these needs, we combine the use of the ONA method with methods that capture and analyze two other important aspects of an organization—the human and operational aspects.

In our approach, we examine an organizational context in three different dimensions: *the data* that the (virtual) organization operates upon, *the actors* that operate within the organization, and *the processes* that the organization carries out. These three dimensions are the cornerstones of any organization and are closely interconnected with each other. We show how these important aspects of an organization can be used seamlessly in different modeling and analytical methods to help support an OM.

The ONA approach we presented in the previous section dealt mostly with *the data* aspect. In the following two sections we will introduce the other two aspects: *actor* and *process*. First, we describe a role-odeling method that suitably captures the *actor* aspect of a (virtual) organization and then a rich business process modeling method that captures the *process* aspect of an organization.

A ROLE-AWARE SUPPORT FOR OM

RACD Role Modeling as part of role activity and communication diagram (RACD) (Chen-Burger et al., 2000) was firstly introduced and used to capture U.S. Air Force operations, and roles of their personnel in connection with their operations in U.S. DARPA-funded Air Operations Enterprise Modeling (AOEM) project. Similar role modeling methods are organizational charts that are commonly used to illustrate organizational structures. Such methods, however, are typically informal that does not support formal reasoning tasks. They also do not capture sufficient information for KM tasks. RACD Role Models are formal descriptions that describe KM-related data: the different types of roles and relationships between them are formally defined in an underlying ontology. A Role Model depicts roles that different personnel may play within one or more organizations while interacting with other roles. It also indicates the formal, informal, and operational relationships between the different types of roles. Figure 3 illustrates an example role model that depicts personnel's roles in U.S. Air Force Operations. Typically, such roles span across different organizations.

This role model enables one to describe the typical organizational *hierarchical relationship* between roles, such as "has authority over." It also enables one to capture *functional relationships* such as "provides data to" and "collaborates with." Broadly speaking, there are two types of influence relationships between different roles: formal and informal (Schreiber et al., 1999). Formal influences are explicitly described in an organizational context, such as "has authority over," "audit" or "give advice to." Informal influences, on the other hand, are not explicitly described, as some roles support other roles in their tasks that they have implicit influence over them. For example, the "supports" relationships between secretaries and their bosses and colleagues are informal influences.

Figure 3. A high-level RACD role model that depicts the roles personnel play in U.S. Air operations that span across different organizations (a screen capture of KBST-EM)

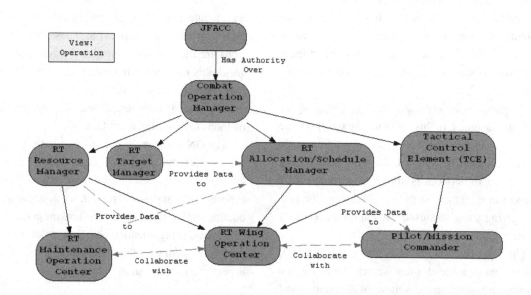

Hierarchical relationships (denoted in solid links) normally have a direct correspondence with organizational charts. *Functional relationships* (denoted in dashed links) describe the functional roles that a role plays while interacting with others. Functional relationships also give detailed insights into how the different roles relate with, support, command, monitor, and/or constraint each other. This is invaluable for KM tasks, as it captures knowledge flows and the functions of these flows. For instance, if a KM task is to assess how a certain knowledge item was used, one can relate this knowledge item to its provider and then by following the different role-relationships, one can discover how the knowledge item may be used by the different knowledge users.

In RACD models, two types of roles are described: *abstract* and *concrete* roles. *Abstract roles* are performed by a collective group of actors such as an organization or its subdivisions. *Concrete roles* can be mapped to an individual actor (whether that is a human or a piece of software). An abstract role can be decomposed to more detailed ones. For instance, Figure 3 provides a higher-level view on personnel roles and their relations. However, these abstract roles may consist of smaller ones: for example, "RT (Real-Time) Wing Operation Center" may consist of several smaller and more detailed roles that support each other. The ability of being able to compose and decompose roles enables one to gain a concise view of organizational structures—which is invaluable, especially in the context of a virtual organization where roles, their functions and interactions between them are complex. It also allows one to gain a detailed understanding of responsibilities of individual actors and how they support each other given certain tasks. By doing so, one gains in-depth comprehension of an organization and may thus improve organizational efficiency. In addition, such organizational role modeling methods may be used to provide a direct input when capturing organizational processes, which will be discussed in the following session.

A RICH PROCESS SUPPORT FOR OM

Process models are commonly used to describe and analyse an organization's operations. Popular process models are IDEF3, UML's activity diagram and Petri Net. When a process model is developed with an organization's context in mind, a process model can be used instrumentally to achieve organizational goals—an aim for methods such as BPR and BPI. When used with a close integration and good understanding of the actor and data aspects of an organization, a process model can act as an integrated part of an OM life cycle. Fundamental business process modeling language (FBPML) is equipped to meet with such requirements (Chen-Burger & Stader, 2003). It is described in a rich three-layered objective-process-application modeling framework that is fully aware of an organization's environment. It is suitable to be used in business contexts, but is also applicable to other more generic process modeling needs. FBPML is goal-directed. That is to say that those corresponding long- and short-term business objectives are explicitly encoded in their processes and business rules are closely linked to these processes.

In our proposed ADP-based approach, the process modeling method acts as a glue to interact with the *actor* and *data* aspects (the ONA method described before deals with the data aspect) within an organizational context. FBPML is ontology based, which means that each data item that a process manipulates is defined in an ontology. It also supplies a formal data language, FBPML-DL, which describes the domain concepts (including instances, classes, and axioms) that processes operate upon. The formal process representation of FBPML, FBPML-PL (process language) takes in FBPML-DL constructs as part of its description and provides them to the *Workflow Engine* for interpretation and execution. Figure 4 provides a conceptual overview of how a FBPML workflow engine works in practice. This figure shows how a user can directly conduct the workflow engine's behaviors by providing initial process descriptions. It also shows how a user can create workflow system behaviors in real-time and in a flexible manner by dynamically interact with the workflow engine. This ability consequently enables us to carry out more flexible and adaptive KM processes later on.

THE WORKFLOW ENGINE

The workflow engine has two components: a *process manager* for handling the execution of the workflow and a *meta-interpreter* for reading and understanding the descriptions of processes and data. Equipped with an appropriate workflow algorithm, the workflow engine periodically retrieves new events that occur dynamically and identifies processes that have been specified in the process model which are relevant to these events. It examines the truth value of the triggers of each of those retrieved processes. It then creates a process instance for each of those processes and put it in the *Process Agenda,* that is, if all of the corresponding triggers are found to be true.

The workflow engine also looks for discrepancies between process instances in the Process Agenda. One example conflict is when one process wishes to delete data while another needs it (as its preconditions) for its execution. In this case, individually, each process will have its triggers and preconditions satisfied prior to execution. However, when examined together, their execution goals conflict with each other. Once culprit processes are found, the conflict is explained and resolution suggestions are given to the user (Chen-Burger & Robertson, 2005).

The Process Agenda stores a list of all process instances that are waiting to be executed. However, process instances that are in conflict with other instances are reported to the user and left in the agenda until the conflicts are resolved. For this, a time-out mechanism has been put in place to prevent indefinite waits in the agenda, thus also preventing the agenda to store expired/irrelevant old process instances indefinitely. Once a list of "clear" process instances are ready to

be executed, they are added to the Process Execution queue and are executed instantly.

USING PROCESS MODEL FOR ADP-BASED KM ANALYSIS

From the simplified overview depicted in Figure 4, one gets an insight into how the FBPML workflow engine works and also the fact that it takes at least two elements as main inputs: the data and process descriptions. This is where an ontological method such as ONA can tap into a process modeling method and make a direct influence into how processes may be carried out—which produces significant impact in KM tasks. For example, in the scenario mentioned before, where interesting knowledge items, for example, certain instances in a populated ontology, have been identified via the ONA powered algorithm. The user is interested to find out information about these knowledge items, in particular, regarding their relations with organizational processes. Example queries in this scenario therefore are: "Who has created these knowledge items?," "What process has created them?," "When are they being modified?," "How are they being used?," "Who are using them?," "Where are they being stored," "How are they being stored," "What are the frequencies that those knowledge items are being used and in what context," "How critical are those knowledge items—for example, to which task and to whom?" and, ultimately, "What are the impacts of those knowledge items to the organization?" A carefully combined actor, data/ontological, and process based approach can provide good approximate answers to most of these questions with minimum effort required.

For example, our proposed ADP approach will work as follows: as FBPML is embedded with a formal description of a data language, interesting knowledge items may be formulated using FBPML-DL. These will have been identified with ONA, and thus will already be in a formal representation format. A FBPML model will therefore take such FBPML-DL constructions as part of its process description

Figure 4. A conceptual overview of the FBPML workflow engine

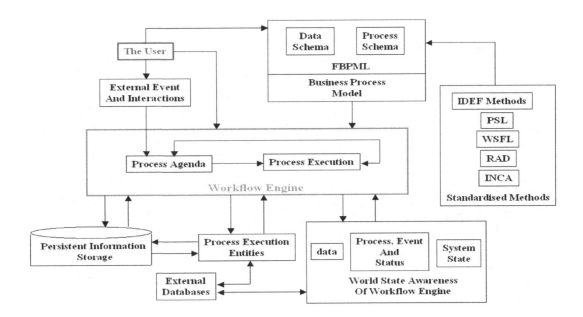

that is used as a basis for searching. For instance, based on FBPML-DL constructs, typical automated actions, such as *Create*, *Update*, *Monitor*, *Query*, and so forth, are formulated. Therefore, one can perform a relatively easy pattern-matching algorithm on the different process descriptions to work out the processes that generate, use, refer to, and audit those knowledge items. In addition, it is common practice in process modeling methods that relevant business analysis are carried out, such as identification of *critical processes* in an organization and the frequencies of a process. One may therefore derive approximate answers for such knowledge items based on information that he or she already knows about the processes that operate upon them. For instance, for a knowledge item/piece of information that is the main or only input for a critical process, he or she may derive that this piece of knowledge or information is also of critical importance. Another example is when a knowledge item or a piece of information is only used (e.g., referred to) by very few and low-frequency processes, it is straightforward

to derive that this knowledge item/information is not used frequently.

In this way, we can now infer new knowledge about the data base upon existing knowledge about processes that is of minimum effort. In addition, as FBPML allows its users to define new process constructs. To identify such novel processes, we need to search for the relevant FBPML-DL constructs within all FBPML process descriptions. However, to understand the semantics of such process components, we will need to look into the description and definitions of its underlying computational module.

ACTOR-RELATED QUERIES

We have so far answered the above proposed process-related queries. Some of the above queries, however, are relevant to the "who" questions and their answers are not provided yet. To answer these "who" questions, we need to ask how the RACD role models fit with the

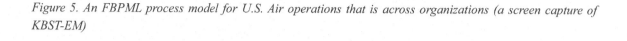

Figure 5. An FBPML process model for U.S. Air operations that is across organizations (a screen capture of KBST-EM)

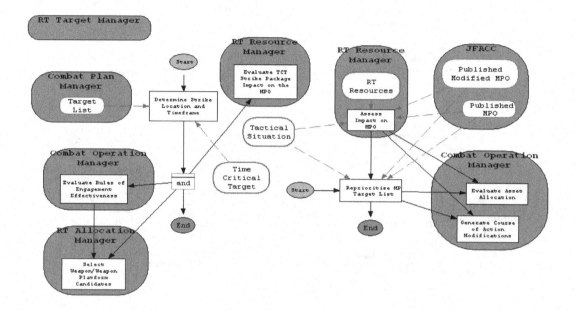

FBPML model, so that we can provide suitable answers with it. FBPML processes are grouped and describes in terms of actor roles. Each process is labelled with the corresponding "actor" that carries out the task. In this way, it is possible to see all of the processes that an actor carries out. It is also easy to see how the different actors collaborate with each other through sharing a larger process model.

Figure 5 shows an example FBPML process model (that is a screen capture of KBST-EM) for the same domain of U.S. Air Force operations. This figure shows the two operations of the RT (real-time) Target Manager. These are the two operations (indicated in squared boxes) that are outside of any rounded outer squares. However, in the same diagram it also encompasses different roles that other personnel play (indicated in the rounded outer squares) and their corresponding processes (indicated in squares) that they perform.

The links between the different processes indicate the directional control and data flows between them. Note that this diagram also indicates the data types that a role stores (denoted in small rounded boxes). Figure 6 gives another example model that describes the two main processes of RT Wing Operation Center: launch and monitor aircrafts (indicated by their headings "Process:"). While interacting with other roles, note the document MPO (published and modified) are used in operations in the two provided process models and by several personnel as input of their activities. In conjunction with process knowledge, we can now answer most of the above "who" questions.

By seeking out the relevant processing components in a process model, we could now identify the actors who carried out these tasks. For example, if it is a "creation" type of task that the actor performs, then this actor is the one who has created the knowl-

Figure 6. A FBPML process model for RT wing operation center (a screen capture of KBST-EM)

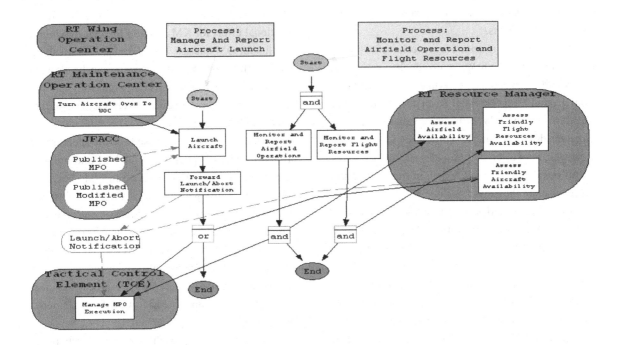

edge/information item in the data store. Similarly, if it is a "reference" type of task, we may say that the corresponding actor is using that piece of information or knowledge as a part of their work. If it is the same actor who creates, updates, uses, and monitors the same information, one may say that this is the main actor that creates, maintains, and uses that piece of information or knowledge. In this way, one can get good quality initial answers.

Use of the combined ADP formal approach requires minimum additional effort and it is reliable for as long as the domain knowledge captured is as accurate and complete as possible. However, this approach is not entirely infallible. One possible problem resides in the fact that informal processes are often not recorded in a formal (business) process model. In the example of the creation type of processes above, it is possible that they may be performed by separate key-in person-

nel and not by the knowledge creators themselves. However, in this case, one still gets the first line of defence—it helps to identify the first person to talk to in order to find out who is the original knowledge creator (a piece of information that may be indicated in the electronic or paper-based record that is not part of the formal system).

SOCIAL AND MANAGERIAL IMPLICATIONS

The KM approach proposed is an incremental one. This separates it from other more radical approaches where much existing practices, including organizational structures, are subject to changes. Such methods are therefore more likely to attract staff resistances. Our approach, instead, re-uses existing knowledge and tools to derive new knowledge. In this way, less resistance should be met. Due to less disruption in existing work, it is also easier for the staff to contribute towards KM projects.

In addition, due to selective reuse, benefits for the KM project can be quicker realized when compared with another project that needs to create information from ground level. This will be an attractive feature for the management. When business value creation is a direct result of deploying KM processes and appropriate rewards are offered, it provides strong incentives for all personnel involved, which in turn boosts the success rate of the project.

One issue of KM is human resources management—to make sure that knowledge is distributed appropriately and stable within the organization. One way to do this is to map the actual personnel to the RACD role model for knowledge distribution analysis. When it is identified that a person performs several roles in an organization, the information may become saturated. It is therefore important to identify such information overload and capture critical knowledge through KM processes, thereby reserve/distribute important knowledge within the organization.

FUTURE TRENDS AND CONCLUSION

In this Knowledge Era we are living in, an organization's economical growth heavily depends upon the wealth of its knowledge and how well it taps into it. It is therefore critical that KM tasks are carried out efficiently and effectively to its advantages, especially when a large OM is present. Perfect KM solutions that entirely unlock knowledge from information, however, are not available yet. The increasingly high demand for immediate usable knowledge stemmed from information explosion will continue to inspire new and specialized KM related technologies to be included in systems of a variety types of applications for many years to come.

To address these demands, our combined ADP analytical and inference framework provides rich support for KM tasks in the context of OM. Its main advantages are to make use of existing reliable methods and their known properties, thereby minimizing additional effort for KM tasks so to elicit maximum benefits for OM queries. Based on the ADP method, good quality approximate answers can be derived with minimal effort when compared with another approach where brand new answers must be sought and compiled from raw data.

Furthermore, the ONA-based OM architecture we proposed makes it possible to analyze and propose content for the initial seeding of an OM. This is a powerful incentive and tool for OM engineers, as they can effectively tackle the cold-start syndrome that haunts most of these systems in their initial set up. The ONA-based approach coupled with the modeling flexibility of an ADP approach provides an interesting and holistic ontology-based business process support geared towards comprehensive OM for distributed enterprises.

However, these approaches are not entirely infallible, as not all organizational aspects can be captured explicitly. This is a common challenge when trying to provide a complete set of KM and OM support. When facing the trade-offs between utilizing knowledge for gains and bearing the cost of capturing and maintaining it at the first place, a balance is often struck. To compensate for the information gap caused by informality, one must employ common sense and domain specific knowledge when searching for the true answers to queries. Another useful approach to combat missing information is to employ iterative and adaptive KM life cycles, thus improve the underlying three ADP models based on query demands. Hence, the quality of KM and answers to queries can be improved incrementally through time.

ACKNOWLEDGMENT

This work is supported under the Advanced Knowledge Technologies (AKT IRC) project, UK EPSRC GR/N15764/01. The views and conclusions contained herein are those of the authors and should not be interpreted as necessarily representing official policies or endorsements, either expressed or implied, of the EPSRC or any other member of the AKT IRC.

REFERENCES

Abecker, A., Bernardi, A., Hinkelmann, K., Kuhn, O., & Sintek, M. (1998). Toward a technology for organizational memories. *IEEE Intelligent Systems, 13*(3), 40-48.

Alani, H., Dasmahapatra, S., O'Hara, K., & Shadbolt, N. (2003 March/April). Identifying communities of practice through ontology network analysis. *IEEE Intelligent Systems*, 2-9.

Alani, H., Kalfoglou, Y., O'Hara, K., & Shadbolt, N. (2002). Initiating organizational memories using ontology-based network analysis as a bootstrapping tool. *BCS-SGAI Expert Update, 5*(3), 43-46.

Breuker, J., & Van de Velde,W. (1994). *The commonKADS library for expertise modeling.* Netherlands: IOS Press.

Carlsson, C., & Turban, E. (2002). DSS: Directions for the next decade. *Decision Support Systems, 33,* 105-110.

Chen-Burger, Y-H., & Robertson., D. (2005). *Automating business modeling: A guide to using logic to represent informal methods and support reasoning.* Book Series of Advanced Information and Knowledge Processing. Springer.

Chen-Burger, Y-H., Robertson, D., & Stader, Y. (2000). *A modeling support framework for enterprise knowledge capturing, sharing and reusing.* In Proceedings of the International Conference on Applications of Prolog, Tokyo Japan.

Chen-Burger, Y-H., & Stader, Y. (2003). *Formal support for adaptive workflow systems in a distributed environment.* In L. Fischer (Ed.), *Workflow handbook* (pp. 93-118). Future Strategies Inc.

Cohen, P., & Kjeldsen, R. (1987). Information retrieval by constraint spreading activation in semantic networks. *Information processing and management, 23*(4), 255-268.

Cooper, W.S. (1997). On selecting a measure of retrieval effectiveness. In K.S. Jones, & P. Willet., (ed.) *Readings in Information Retrieval.* Morgan Kaufmann.

Dieng, R., Corby, O., Giboin, A., & Ribiere, M. (1999). Methods and tools for corporate knowledge management. *International Journal of Human-Computer Studies (IJHCS), 51,* 567-598.

Paice, C.D. (1991). A thesaural model of information retrieval. *Information processing and management, 27*(5), 433-447.

Rada, R., Mili, H., Bicknell, E., & Blettner, M. (1989). Development and application of a metric on semantic nets. *IEEE Transactions on systems, management, and cybernetics, 19*(1), 17-30.

Schreiber, G., de Hoog, R., Akkermans, H., Anjewierden, A., Shadbolt, N., Van de Velde, W. et al. (Eds.). (1999). *Knowledge engineering and management: The commonKADS methodology.* MIT Press.

Wenger, E. (1999). Communities of practice: The key to knowledge strategy. In E.L. Lesser, M.A. Fontaine & J.A. Slusher (Eds.), *Knowledge and Communities* (pp. 3-20). Butterworth-Heinemann.

Zave, P., & Jackson, M. (1997). Four dark corners of requirements engineering. *ACM Transactions on Software Engineering and Methodology, 6*(1), 1-30.

ENDNOTE

[1] One doubtless common circumstance where this assumption will *not* be reliable would be where an ontology is pieced together from legacy datasets. In such a case, the most popular entities are likely to be those represented in detail elsewhere for other purposes whose importance may not carry over into the current application.

Chapter XVIII
Modeling Strategic Partnerships Using the E³value Ontology:
A Field Study in the Banking Industry

Carol Kort
Vrije Universiteit Amsterdam, The Netherlands

Jaap Gordijn
Vrije Universiteit Amsterdam, The Netherlands

ABSTRACT

The banking industry is subject to a wave of consolidation taking the form of mergers but also the formation of strategic partnerships. In this chapter, we present how such a partnership can be assessed using the e³value ontology. This ontology allows us to model networks of enterprises and partnerships, exchanging things of economic with each other. To adequately model strategic partnerships, the e³value ontology has been extended to represent investment arrangements and outsourcing constructs. All this is explained using an industry-strength case banking study.

INTRODUCTION

Companies increasingly form networked value constellations to jointly satisfy a complex need. Well known examples are Cisco Systems (Tapscott, Ticoll, & Lowy, 2000) and Dell Computers (Magretta, 1998). In a value constellation, a series of enterprises and final customers coproduce things of economic value using network technology such as the Internet to coordinate this process. By doing so, they exploit each other's core competencies to a maximum extent and enterprises can concentrate on and develop their own core competencies themselves.

Obviously, forming a constellation requires coordination and communication to facilitate coworking between the various enterprises of which the constellation exists. One of the problems is that every enterprise speaks another language, thereby creating misunderstandings and barriers to proper communication. Such misunderstanding happens at all levels: information systems of various enterprise that are not very well interconnected, business processes that can not easily interoperate over enterprise borders, and even the constellation itself in terms of the participating enterprises and the services and products these enterprises transfer between each other.

One approach to address the misunderstanding is to use ontologies. According to Gruber (1995), ontology can be defined as "an explicit specification of a conceptualization." The term "ontology" is borrowed from philosophy, here an ontology is a systematic account of existence. In the realm of information systems and artificial intelligence (AI), ontology has a somewhat different interpretation: "an ontology is what a community of practice believes to exist." This is close to the opinion of Quine (1961), who says that an ontology specifies things that we must assume to exist in order for our theories to be true. What people believe to exist, we call a "conceptualization". It represents an abstract, simplified view on the world. Modern definitions of ontology, for example, Borst, Akkermans, and Top (1997), emphasize that there must be an agreement on the conceptualization that is specified: "An ontology is a formal specification of a shared conceptualization." This notion of shared conceptualization is important to us because we aim at a shared understanding of a constellation by enterprises involved.

Ontologies can be developed at various abstraction levels. For instance, recent Web standards such as OWL (e.g., http://www.w3.org/2004/OWL/) or Web services such as BPEL4WS (Andrews et al., 2003) provide ontological foundations for the communication *between information systems* of individual enterprises. Approaches like ebXML (see http://www.ebxml.org) focus on ontologies to enhance *cross-organizational business process* integration. And finally ontologies such as BMO (Osterwalder, Pigneur, & Tucci, 2005), REA (McCarthy, 1982) and *e³value* (Gordijn & Akkermans, 2003) aim at the shared understanding of the *business value level*: what do enterprises offer each other of economic value.

In this chapter, we focus on the use of these business *value* ontologies, and more specifically on the *e³value* ontology. This ontology understands a value constellation as a set of enterprises that transfer things of economic value with each other. It features an ontology editor (see http://www.e3value.com/ for a free download) that allows for a graphical representation of a constellation and supports various kinds of reasoning about the constellation.

One specific issue in *e³value* is how to represent partnerships. There is a specific construct for doing so, but a question is whether this construct is sufficient for representing advanced partnering issues. In this chapter, we use an industrial strength case study in the realm of banking to assess *e³value*'s capabilities with respect to the modeling of partnerships.

This chapter is organized as follows. In the second section we briefly introduce the *e³value* ontology and in the third section we introduce "partnership" as conceptual artefact in business sciences and discuss, in the fourth section, whether the *e³value* ontology can represent partnership. We explain this by using our case study in the banking industry. In the fifth section, we report on our experiences while using the *e³value* ontology in this industry. In the sixth section, we present some final observations.

THE *E³VALUE* ONTOLOGY

The *e³value* ontology provides modeling constructs for representing and analyzing a network of enterprises exchanging things of economic value with each other. The ontology itself has been expressed as a UML class diagram, Prolog code, and RDF/S (see http://www.w3c.org/RDF). A graphical *e³value* ontology editor as well as analysis tool is available for download (see http://www.e3value.com) (Gordijn & Akkermans, 2003).

We briefly introduce the *e³value* modeling concepts below with an example (Figure 1). For a more detailed explanation, see Gordijn and Akkermans (2003).

- Actor: An actor is perceived by his/her environment as an economically independent entity.

Figure 1. Educational e³value example

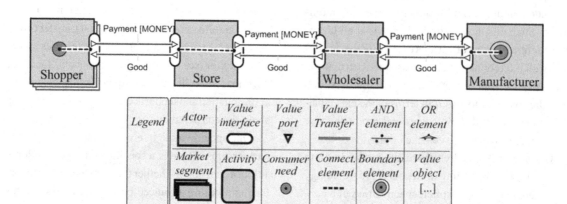

The Store, Wholesaler, and Manufacturer are all examples of actors.

- Value Object: Actors exchange value objects (e.g., Money). A value object is a service, a good, money, or even an experience, which is of economic value for at least one of the actors.

- Value Port: An actor uses a value port to provide or request value objects to or from other actors.

- Value Interface: Actors have one or more value interfaces, grouping value ports, and showing economic reciprocity. Actors are only willing to offer objects to someone else if they receive adequate compensation in return. Either all ports in a value interface each precisely exchange one value object, or none at all.

- Value Transfer: A value transfer is used to connect two value ports with each other. It represents one or more potential trades of value objects. In the example, transfers of a Good or a Payment are both examples of value transfers.

- Value Transaction: A value transaction groups value transfers that all should happen, or none at all. In most cases, value transactions can be

derived from how value transfers connect ports in interfaces.

- Market Segment: A market segment breaks actors into segments of actors that assign economic value to objects equally. This construct is often used to model that there is a large group of end-consumers who value objects equally. The Shopper is a market segment consisting of a number of individual shoppers.

- Value Activity: An actor performs one or more value activities. These are assumed to yield a profit.

- Dependency Path: A dependency path is used to reason about the number of value exchanges in an *e³value* model. A path consists of consumer needs, connections, dependency elements, and dependency boundaries. A consumer need is satisfied by exchanging value objects (via one or more interfaces). A connection relates a consumer need to an interface, or relates various interfaces of a same actor. A path can take complex forms, using AND/OR dependency elements taken from UCM scenarios (Buhr, 1998). A dependency boundary represents that we do not consider any more value exchanges on the path. In the example, by following the path we can see that to satisfy the need of the Shopper, the Manufacturer has to provide Goods.

Given an *e³value* model, attributed with numbers (e.g., the number of consumer needs per timeframe and the valuation of objects exchanged), net value sheets (NVF) can be generated (for a free software tool see http://www.e3value.com/). Such sheets show the net cash flow for each actor involved and are a first indication whether the model at hand can be commercially successful for each actor. Additionally, a series of *e³value* models can be constructed, modeling how a value model evolves over time. Each value model represents, then, a snapshot at a specific point in time (say on a yearly basis). For such a series, accepted calculations such as discounted net present cash flow (DNPC) (Horngren & Foster, 1987) can be done to assess economic sustainability on a per actor basis.

STRATEGIC PARTNERSHIPS

According to Yoshino and Rangan (1995), a strategic partnership has at least three characteristics: (1) although the partnering companies jointly pursue certain agreed upon goals, they remain *independent*, (2) the partnering companies *share the benefits* of the agreement and *control* over the performance, and (3) the agreement covers *one or more key strategic areas* of both partnering companies." This explicitly excludes mergers, acquisitions, and joint venture (JV) subsidiaries of multinational companies (MNCs), because there is no shared control in these constructions, and also they result in one company only. Also, licensing, franchising, cross-licensing, and arm's-length contracts are excluded from this definition as these constructions also don't involve shared control, there is no long-term mutual dependence, nor are there any continuing contributions of technology or products. Various classifications of strategic partnerships in literature by Yoshino and Rangan (1995), Todeva and Knoke (2005), and Porter (1985, 1986) have been reviewed resulting in four dimensions of strategic partnerships, usable to construct a conceptual model of a strategic partnership.

The first partnership dimension is the *legal form* of a strategic partnership, which refers to the formal control mechanism used in order to secure the relationship between the partnering organizations.

A *contractual agreement* is used to formally document the operational activities covered by the partnership in terms of who does what, and how. As such, a contractual agreement influences the division of value activities among the partners, which can already be captured in an *e³value* model using the existing modeling constructs.

Through an *equity investment,* an organization acquires a share of the control over the total activities of its partner, giving the investing organization more leverage in the partnership. Equity investments directly influence the value network of the partnership because the organization also acquires the right to a share of the total profit the partner generates. However, this influence on the value network of a partnership is not on the level of the value activities covered in the partnership. Therefore, an equity investment cannot yet be modeled using existing *e³value* modeling constructs.

A *joint venture* is a new legal entity, jointly established by the partnering organizations, that performs the activities covered by the partnership. As such, the activities of the partnership are legally separated from the existing activities of the partnering organizations. The partners each account for a share of the equity investment needed to establish the new organization, and this division influences both the measure of control each partner has over the partnership, as well as the share of the profits of the partnership each partner gets. Thus, a joint venture structure also influences the value network of the partnership to the partners, but this influence cannot be captured in a value activity, and thus this influence cannot yet be modeled using existing modeling constructs.

The second partnership dimension is the *nature of the activities of a partnership*. The nature of the partnership activities can match one of the value chain activities as distinguished by (Porter, 1985) and can thus be considered either a *primary* activity or a *support* activity of the partnering organizations, in which case the nature of activities dimension influences the partnership on the level of value activities, which can be captured in an *e³value* model using the existing constructs. Two kinds of activities however cannot be mapped onto a value chain activity: *sourcing agreement* and *standards setting*.

A *sourcing agreement* covers the arrangement in which one company out-sources part of its operational activities to another organization that is better equipped to perform them efficiently. The charges connected to the out-sourcing should be less than the operational expenses would be for the out-sourcing company to perform the activities. From the perspective of the customer, the out-sourcing company acts as a front office and the in-sourcing organization as a back office. As the out-sourcing organization still offers the product/service resulting from the out-sourced activities to the client, it technically also performs a value activity for the client that results in the offering of the product/service. For the out-sourcing organization, the sourcing agreement influences the internal structure of the respective value activities: the front-office value activity is based on the reselling of a product/service and thus has a relatively small margin compared to the actual (or back office) value activity related to the same product/service. This influence on *internal structure* of a value activity cannot yet be captured using existing *e³value* constructs.

Standards setting covers the arrangement whereby organizations in an industry join forces in order to develop a process or system and enforce this as a standard onto the entire industry.

An industry standard can also be commercially exploited by the organizations behind it, in which case the use of the standard is often put under a license and other organizations have to pay in order to obtain this license and implement the standard. The commercial exploitation of a standard therefore does influence the value network of the partnership to the partners involved, and it does so through a licensing structure. The *e³value* constructs that have

been introduced in this chapter are not sufficient to capture this licensing structure, but constructs to do so have been developed by Tan, Thoen, and Gordijn (2004). These constructs will therefore not be further elaborated on in this chapter.

The third partnership dimension is the *configuration of the activities* in the partnership, which depends on the way the partnering companies each contribute to the activities that are covered by the partnership.

The *activities* of the partnership can be *divided* among the partners; each activity is performed by one of the partners only, as each activity is the specialization of one of the partners only. This division of value activities among the partners can be captured using existing *e³value* constructs.

The partners can also *jointly perform* at least one of the activities. In this case, the partnering organizations' joint contributions improve the way the activities are performed, while they both retain (shared) control over the performance. As a value activity is a collection of operational activities, the partners will jointly contribute to any value activity that contains a jointly performed operational activity. Not all operational activities in a Y partnership have to be jointly performed, and therefore it is important to be able to capture this difference between value activities that contain jointly performed operational activities and those that do not. Using the current *e³value* constructs, it is not possible to attribute one value activity to two separate actors. It is possible to combine two actors into one virtual actor, but doing this abstracts away from the way the value activities that are not jointly performed are divided among the partners.

The fourth partnership dimension is the *supply chain relationship* between the partners, which depends on their respective positions in the industry supply chain. (Porter, 1985) introduced the concept "supply chain", which provides a means to analyze the competitive position of an organization relative to the other organizations in its industry. A supply chain links an organization to its suppliers, channels, and customers. An organization can be a peer, a supplier, a distributor (channel), or a customer to its partner. The configuration of the supply chain determines the profit margin that is available to each of the participants and the organizations in a partnership will try to optimize and consolidate these margins. The power an organization has in the negotiations with its partners respect depends on the uniqueness and scarcity of the activities it performs and needs, and the transaction costs that are associated with these activities. As such, the influence of the supply chain relationships on the value network of a partnership depends on the characteristics of the value activities performed by the partners, and this influence can thus be captured using existing *e³value* constructs.

BRINGING PARTNERING-SPECIFIC MODELING CONSTRUCTS INTO E³VALUE

Four partnering concepts can not be represented using existing *e³value* constructs: *equity investment, joint venture, jointly performed value activity,* and *sourcing agreement*. In this paragraph, for each of these concepts a construct is defined that can be added to the *e³value* construct set.

Representing Equity Investments

A modeling construct representing an *equity investment* should capture the value structure of an equity investment in a reciprocal value transaction. The proposed construct models the equity relationship as a value transaction consisting of two reciprocal value transfers between two *actors* (and not between value interfaces as is normally the case in *e³value*). The investing organization receives *dividend*, and in order ensure economic reciprocity it offers the holding of a *certain percentage of shares*. The modeling construct defined to capture the value structure of an equity investment is shown below and highlighted in red.

Representing Joint Ventures

The modeling construct representing a *joint venture* should capture the *value structure* of a joint venture in a *reciprocal value transaction* consisting of four value transfers (two reciprocal transfers per enterprise in the joint venture). The proposed construct therefore reflects that the partners each account for a share of the equity investment needed to establish the

Figure 2. An equity investment by actor 1 in actor 2

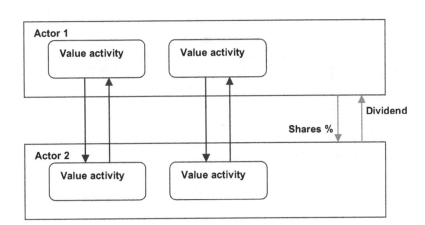

new organization and that the total profits of the joint venture are divided among the partners according to this investment ratio. The joint venture construct thus contains the equity investment construct. Furthermore the construct reflects that all of the shares of the joint venture are accounted for by the partnering organiza-

tions, and that all activities covered by the partnership are attributed to the joint venture. The modeling construct defined to capture the value structure of a joint venture is shown below and highlighted in red.

A Y partnership is characterized by the fact that the partners jointly perform at least one of the value

Figure 3. A joint venture by actor 1 and actor 2

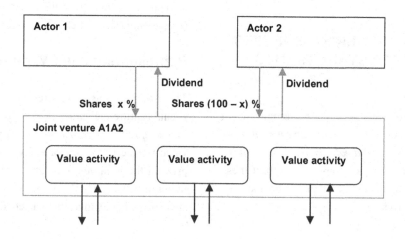

Figure 4. A Y partnership between actor 1 and actor 2 with one jointly performed value activity

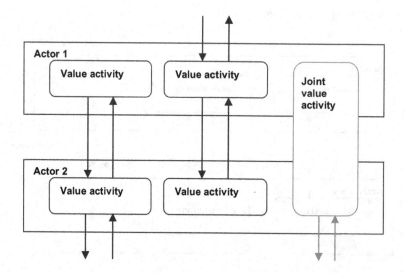

Figure 5. A sourcing arrangement between actor 1 (outsourcer) and actor 2 (insourcer)

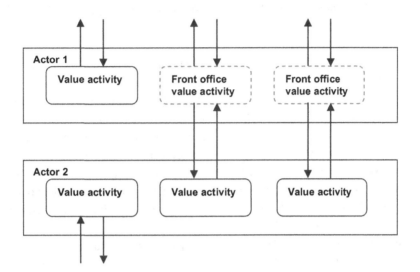

activities. The modeling construct should therefore reflect the assignment of one value activity to multiple actors. The modeling construct defined to capture a joint value activity is shown below and highlighted in red.

The modeling construct for a sourcing agreement should reflect that for the outsourcing organization the value activity related to the product/service is reduced to a front-office value activity, not based on the actual operational activities associated with the product/service but on the reselling of the product/service, with a resulting relatively small margin. The modeling construct defined to capture a front office value activity is chosen to be similar to the construct for a normal value activity, only drawn with dashed lines instead of solid lines in order to reflect the fact that the activity is not based on the actual operational activities producing the offered product/service and the resulting small value margin. The construct is shown below and highlighted in red.

CASE STUDY: EVALUATING THE PARTNERSHIP BETWEEN BANK X AND BANK Y

Context

In order to evaluate whether the extensions to the *e³value* ontology are of use for understanding strategic partnerships, a case study has been conducted at a bank, referred to as Bank X. One of the strengths of Bank X is its global network, as it has a local presence in many countries around the world. As a result, many multinational corporations turn to Bank X seeking regional or even global banking solutions that will cover their banking needs in all countries in which they conduct business. There are several countries in which Bank X does not have a direct presence, but which it does want to be able to include in its offering of regional and global solutions because there is a clear request for banking services in those countries by its corporate clients. In order to include these countries in its global network, Bank X has several strategic partnerships with other banks. A partner bank is usually one of the top three local banks in a country in which Bank X has no presence.

The *e³value* ontology, including the new partnering-specific constructs, has been applied to one of these network partnerships of Bank X; the partnership with Bank Y. For Bank X, establishing its own operations in the country would be highly inefficient as the costs would far outweigh the revenues. Through the partnership, Bank X obtains financial services in the country at a much smaller cost, even relative to the as a result also smaller revenues. For Bank Y, the partnership enables it to optimize the use of its scale of its operations: the extra client volume from Bank X reduces the unit costs resulting in a revenue increase. Also, Bank Y obtains the revenues from the activities it performs for Bank X.

Constructing an *E³value* Model for the Partnership Between Bank X and Bank Y

The actors in the partnership are: *Bank X*, *Bank Y*, and a *market segment* consisting of *corporate clients of Bank X*. In addition to these actors, the *money market* has to be included in the model as an *environmental actor* to be able to model how the banks actually make money; banks invest the balances of their clients in the money market and receive a percentage on top of the invested amounts in return (see Figure 6). The value activities of an environmental actor are not relevant to the value model.

The billing records of the partnership have been reviewed in order to determine which products are included in the partnership. Four main product groups were distinguished: payment products, cash management products, reporting, and balance management.

Figure 6. A first version of the value model of the XY partnership

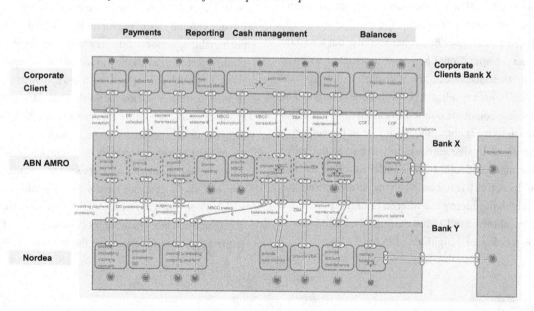

Also, the billing records were used to derive the value activities, the value transfers and the value objects transferred. The value activities of the corporate client market segment reflect the needs of the corporate client with respect to banking services. The value activities of Bank X reflect the products and services it *provides* for the corporate clients. The partnership specific construct that models a sourcing agreement should thus be included in the model in order to be able to show that the actual operational activities related to these services are performed by Bank Y, and the value activities at Bank X are *front office value activities*. The value activities of Bank Y reflect the products and services it *produces* for Bank X.

The value objects and value transfers have been identified as a logical consequence of the value activities performed by the actors. The resulting value model can be seen in Figure 6.

The value models have been presented to the stakeholders at Bank X as a PowerPoint slide (Figure 6). In order to make the contents of the model more insightful the *actors* are highlighted by placing colored textboxes displaying the actor name next to the actor construction. Furthermore, in order to make the various value activities that are identified in the model more insightful they are grouped in the four main product groups, which are highlighted above the value model in a colored text box.

In this first value model, the constructs have been conceptualized as prescribed in Gordijn (2003) and also all constructs that need to be part of a value model according to Gordijn have been included. In a number of feedback sessions the banking stakeholders could comment on the value model. Their comments were incorporated in next versions of the value model, ultimately leading to a final version. In The feedback on the first and consecutive versions of the value model, leading to the final value model, will be discussed here to illustrate the changes made to the *e³value* ontology in order to accommodate the banking stakeholders.

Feedback by Bank X on the *E³value* Model

Before the actual presentation of the *e³value* model to the executive decision makers of Bank X, the first version of the model has been reviewed for its fit for purpose, namely taking a decision about participating in the partnership or not. The following feedback was obtained on the use of the *e³value* ontology:

- Feedback 1. The models were considered very intricate and not easily understandable, because the many value activities made the model too complex. The advice was to reduce the number of value activities modeled by logically grouping value activities, whereby each group should include value activities that are based upon the same type of operational activities; value activities that can thus be thought of as quite similar.

- Feedback 2. With respect to the concepts included in the value model, the value objects themselves were considered irrelevant. Also the value interfaces, value ports, connect elements, AND elements, OR elements, and start and stop nodes in the model were considered distractions, as it was considered not particularly important how value exchanges are triggered and where the money flow starts.

- Feedback 3. The value transactions as included in the model were considered distracting and unnecessarily complex; rather the value model would only show the actual money flows.

- Feedback 4. The most interesting part of the model was considered to be the net value of each value activity, which can be calculated by taking the ingoing money flow of a value activity and reducing this amount with the outgoing money flow of the value activity. The first version of the value model does not include these numbers; it only quantifies and labels the value flows themselves, reflecting revenues generated on a monthly basis. In fact, these labels of the value exchanges were also considered to be distracting, adding to the complexity of the model.

- Feedback 5. The profitability of the actors was considered one of the most important insights of the value model, and should be more prominently included in the value model. In this first preliminary value model, the profitability for each actor has been placed in the upper left corner on the actor constructs. The profitability sheets clearly state the profitability for each actor involved and also provide insight in the value structure behind these profitabilities, but the Bank X stakeholders did not want to review the profitability sheets as they were considered too cumbersome.

- Feedback 6. The stakeholders were asked to place even more emphasis on the value activities, relative to the actors. The actors, which are modeled as a solid rectangle, were now seen as too much of a fixed partitioning of the value activities, while the value activities are only

tied to the value model in this configuration of the partnership, and hence the partitioning of the value activities can be altered.

- Feedback 7. The partnership has mainly qualitative value for Bank X. As mentioned in the paragraph on the value of the partnership, the partnership is mostly intended to retain business and to be able offer regional solutions to clients, not to generate revenue. The request, therefore, also was to incorporate these quantitative aspects in the value model in some way.

Modified *E³value* Model of the Partnership Between Bank X and Bank Y

A modified version of the value model incorporates all changes that have been made as a result of the feedback obtained by the Bank X stakeholders. The changes made will consequently be explained. Note

Figure 7. The final version of the value model of the XY partnership

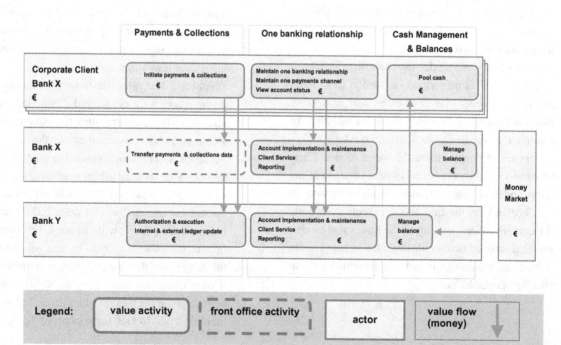

that the number of the change made corresponds to the number of the feedback obtained.

- Change 1. The number of value activities was drastically reduced. In the first model also, four main groups of value activities were distinguished. It turned out that, for all groups, the activities belonging to a group could be merged into one value activity. The final version of the value model shows only three groups, as the groups cash management and balances were also merged. Furthermore, the group reporting was merged into the group one banking relationship, which will be fully introduced discussing Change 7.
- Change 2. Value objects, value transactions, value interfaces, value ports, connect elements, AND elements, OR elements, and start and stop nodes have all been left out of the value model.
- Change 3. The value transactions were left out of the model, and the money flows between the actors were clearly indicated, represented by solid green arrows (green has been chosen for the arrows as this color is associated with money).
- Change 4. The net values of the value activities are prominently included on the value activity constructs, indicated in the model by a euro sign. The money flows themselves are not labeled with the amounts being exchanged as this was considered irrelevant relative to the net values of the value activities.
- Change 5. The profitability of the actors is prominently included on the actor constructs, indicated by a euro sign underneath the actor name.
- Change 6. The value activities were considered one of the most interesting and relevant parts of the value model and not necessarily permanently tied an actor. In the final version of the value model; therefore, the actor constructs are more transparent relative to the value constructs, and have a pale color. The value activities, on the

other hand, are highlighted using a bright color. In order to emphasize the nature of the *front office value activity* construct, front office value activities have the same color as the normal value activities, but more transparent.
- Change 7. The one banking partnership value activities incorporate some of the qualitative value of the partnership to the client; the fact that they have to maintain only one banking relationship, with Bank X, while still obtaining the activities from Bank Y. The clients actually pay an account maintenance fee to Bank X and this could be seen as the fee Bank X requests for its service of offering the partnership to its client. Also, the operational activities related to reporting, client service, and the actual account maintenance are part of these value activities.

The Financial Analysis of the Value Model of the XY Partnership

In order to evaluate the value proposition of the partnership for Bank X, a financial analysis of the value model of the partnership was conducted, using the billing records of the partnership as input. These billing records, covering two consecutive months worth of data, were obtained in the form of two large excel files. For each of the months covered by the billing records, the respective value flows from the corporate client to Bank X and from Bank X to Bank Y with respect to *payments & collections* and *one banking relationship* were calculated using excel pivot tables in which all subproducts were systematically selected and the *sums* of the related revenues were totaled. Next, the related average yearly value flows from the corporate client to Bank X and from Bank X to Bank Y could be derived. Net Value sheets for each actor were created in Excel (Figure 8) in order to total the incoming and outgoing money flows and obtain the resulting profitability of the partnership for each of the actors involved. One of the reasoning capabilities of the *e³value* ontology is to derive such sheets automatically.

The result of the financial analysis has been placed in a diagram (Figure 9), in order to offset the profit-

Figure 8. Example net value sheet for the actor bank x

value activities	incoming money flow	outgoing money flow	net value
transfer payments & collections data			
account implementation & maintenance, client service, reporting			
manage balance			
			Total

Figure 9. The value division of the partnership between bank x and bank y

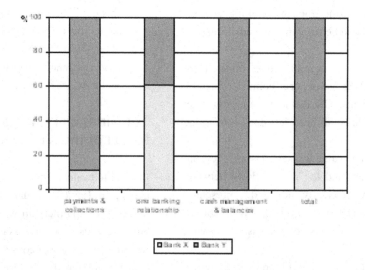

ability of Bank X and Bank Y against one another.

With respect to *payments & collections*, the relatively small share of value captured by Bank X is partly the logical consequence of the *front office value activity* at Bank X with respect to *payments & collections*. This construction is a direct result of the nature of the partnership and can therefore not be changed. Would Bank X be able to maintain a normal value activity with respect to *payments & collections*, there would be no need for a partnership with Bank Y in the first place. However, Bank X still captures some value with respect to payments and collections because

it offers partnership clients the use of centralized billing. Through centralized billing, the Bank Y bills Bank X for the performed financial services and Bank X in its turn bills the respective clients. The benefit for the partnership client is that, for all its banking services, its only contact is with Bank X. Corporate clients do prefer to keep their banking relationships to a minimum, as this allows them to conduct their finances more efficiently and as a result to save costs. Centralized billing thus allows Bank X to capture revenue through the application of a surcharge on the services performed by Bank Y, charging a little more for certain financial services to its clients than it has to pay to Bank Y, in exchange for the added service. The relatively small share of value captured by Bank X with respect to payments and collections is also the result of the fact that only 23% of the partnership clients uses centralized billing. This can be seen in Figure 6 also; one money flow goes from the corporate client, through Bank X, to Bank Y, and one goes directly from the corporate client to Bank Y. The direct money flow constitutes 77% of the value.

The qualitative value of the partnership to the client was incorporated in the model through the *one banking relationship* value activities, because the Bank X stakeholders considered these partnership aspects to be the added value of the partnership to the corporate client. However, this fact is not reflected in the related value captured by Bank X, which represents only 10% of total partnership value.

With respect to *cash management & balances*, Bank Y captures 100% of the value, which constitutes 37% of the total partnership value. Bank Y thus captures a relatively large share of partnership value because of the balances of the Bank X corporate clients it has in its books. None of the corporate clients that make use of the partnership are subscribed to the automatic balance transfer service Bank X has, while this service would allow for an automatic periodical transfer of balances from a client's Bank Y account to its Bank X account in order to optimize balances at Bank X.

After performing the financial analysis of the value model and evaluating the revenue configuration of the partnership, it could be concluded that the value proposition of the partnership for Bank X can be significantly improved, given that the following recommendations are put into action:

Bank X should promote and stimulate the use of centralized billing among the corporate clients (increasing payment and collection revenues up to 77%).

Bank X should investigate the corporate clients' willingness to pay with respect to the one banking relationship and increase account maintenance fees accordingly (currently only 10% of partnership value)

Bank X should promote and stimulate the use of automated balance transfer among the corporate clients (increasing partnership revenue up to 37%)

FINAL OBSERVATIONS

We conclude this chapter with some final observations made while applying the *e³value* ontology in a banking setting to discuss strategic partnerships.

- **The *e³value* ontology and its models should first be seen as an analysis tool.** Because of the small quantitative value generated by Bank X relative to the value generated by Bank Y, the concern was that the value model did not support the bank X stakeholders in the "selling" of the partnership to Bank X upper management: they feared the small quantitative value might distract away from the fact that the partnership has a substantial qualitative value for Bank X. However, the value model itself should not be considered as a marketing tool that can be used to sell the partnership. Rather, it should be considered as an *analysis tool* that provides insight in the partnership, and has allowed us to perceive which changes can be made that increase the quantitative profitability of the partnership for Bank X. As a result of studying the value model, a better understanding of the quantitative aspects of the partnership might enable the Bank X stakeholders to "sell" the partnership more convincingly, but not necessarily by showing the model to upper management.

- **The *e³value* ontology and its models should focuses on cash flow.** Bank X pointed out that the value shows an incomplete picture of the partnership, as it does not include those aspects of the partnership that might not be related to actual money transactions, but are still of (qualitative) *value* to Bank X. However, one should not expect a value model to offer a complete picture of all facets of the partnership, including all kinds of value. The value model only captures the value that is influenced by the *money*-based transactions among the actors in the partnership. This is a purposefully limited perspective on a partnership, as qualitative factors still should (ultimately) result in cash flow. In other words: the *e³value* ontology assumes that ultimately only sustainable net cash flow matters.

- **No inclusion of operational costs in the *e³value* ontology.** The fact that the operational costs are not included in the model was also difficult to accept by the Bank X stakeholders, in the sense that it seemed unclear how much of the value identified could realistically be considered value. However, especially in the context of banking, this feature of the value model seems to be particularly appropriate: typically for banking products the costs are not easily relatable to the activities performed. Activity based costing, a popular accounting method that does exactly that, is therefore very difficult to apply on the revenues and expenses of a bank. Also it was explained that in a value model the operational costs are not included yet, but that one should actually view the value model as a first step of a thorough analysis. In order to completely analyze the partnership according to the *e³value* ontology, a process model of the partnership would have to be constructed as a next step in which operational expenses are reviewed.

- **The front office value activity extension is useful.** The *front office value activity construct* proved to have a significant added value to the value model as it sets the respective "front office" value activity clearly apart from the other value activities. As mentioned above, one of the biggest concerns of the Bank X stakeholders was the relatively small value captured by Bank X in the partnership compared to the value captured by Bank Y, as they feared that this might negatively influence the image of the partnership. The *front office value activity construct* helped to emphasize the fact that the difference in values captured by Bank X and Bank Y respectively is a logical consequence of

the partnership nature. The construct supports the model in conveying the fact that an actor who performs a front office value activity will logically capture less value than the actor that performs the related normal value activity. The way the *front office value activity construct* is modeled, dashed lines instead of the solid lines used for normal value activities, and a more transparent shade of the color used for normal value activities, also reflects the thin nature of a front office value activity with respect to revenues captured. Therefore, in addition to explaining the revenue structure when discussing the model, this structure could also be clearly identified in the model, significantly increasing the expressive power of the model. Presenting the final value model to other Bank X stakeholders that had not been involved in the research process, the front office value activity really helped the people in visualizing the revenue structure of the partnership, and therefore they were able to understand the results of the financial analysis behind the value model and accept the related conclusions.

REFERENCES

Andrews, T., Curbera, F., Dholakia, H., Goland, Y., Klein, J., Leymann, F. et al. (2003). *Business process execution language for Web services version 1.1* (Tech. Rep.). BEA Systems, IBM, Microsoft, SAP, Siebel.

Borst, W.N., Akkermans, J.M., & Top, J.L. (1997). Engineering ontologies. *International Journal of Human-Computer Studies, 46,* 365-406.

Buhr, R.J.A. (1998). Use case maps as architectural entities for complex systems. *IEEE Transactions on Software Engineering, 24*(12), 1131-1155.

Gordijn, J., & Akkermans, H. (2003). Value based requirements engineering: Exploring innovative e-commerce idea. *Requirements Engineering Journal, 8*(2), 114-134.

Gruber, T.R. (1995). Towards principles for the design of ontologies used for knowledge sharing. *International Journal of Human-Computer Studies, 43,* 907-928

Horngren, C.T., & Foster, G. (1987). *Cost accounting: A managerial emphasis* (6th ed.). Englewood Cliffs, NJ: Prentice-Hall.

Magretta, J. (1998). The power of virtual integration: An interview with Dell computer's Michael Dell. *Harvard Business Review, 76*(2), 72-84.

McCarthy, W.E. (1982). The REA accounting model: A generalized framework for accounting systems in a shared data environment. *Accounting Review, 57*(3), 554-578.

Osterwalder, A., Pigneur, Y., & Tucci, C.L., (2005). Clarifying business models: Origins, present, and future of the concept. *Communications of the Association for Information Systems (CAIS), 16*(1), 1-25. Retrieved June 22, 2007, from http://cais.isworld.org/contents.asp/

Porter, M.E. (1985). *Competitive advantage: Creating and sustaining superior performance.* Boston: Harvard Business School Press.

Porter, M.E., & Fuller, M.B. (1986). Coalitions and global strategy. In M.E. Porter (Ed.), *Competition in global industries* (pp. 315-343). Boston: Harvard Business School Press.

Quine, W.V.O. (1961). *From a logical point of view. Nine logico-philosophical essays.* Cambridge, MA: Harvard University Press.

Tan, Y.H., Thoen, W., & Gordijn, J. (2004). Modeling controls for value exchanges in virtual organizations. In *LNCS 2995, Trust Management, Proceedings of the 2nd International Conference on Trust Management* (pp. 236-250). Oxford, UK: Springer Verlag.

Todeva, E., & Knoke, D. (2005). Strategic alliances and models of collaborations. *Management Decision, 1*(43), 123-148

Tapscott, D., Ticoll, D., & Lowy, A. (2000). *Digital capital - harnessing the power of business Webs.* London: Nicholas Brealy Publishing.

Yoshino, M.Y., & Rangan, U.S. (1995). *Strategic alliances.* Boston: Harvard Business School Press.

Chapter XIX
Towards Adaptive Business Networks:
Business Partner Management with Ontologies

Peter Weiß
Universität Karlsruhe (TH), Germany

ABSTRACT

This chapter proposes a new approach for business partner management with ontologies in large business communities. The often postulated adaptiveness and intelligence of new collaborative structures, foremost collaborative networks, require new approaches to deal with the increasing difficulty in handling the resulting complexity of relational ties in communities and business networks. With a growing number of business entities involved in the system, the network management starts to lose overview and control concerning the entities in the pool of partners. Then it seems asked too much establishing, promoting, and maintaining relational ties on a personal basis. A possible solution seems to be support through adequate services of the information and communication technology (ICT) infrastructure. Ontologies offer support for communication processes and complex interactions of business entities in collaborative spaces.

INTRODUCTION

New business patterns are characterized by diminishing geographical and time boundaries, globalization of the labor market, increased connectivity, extended or virtual enterprises, new forms of customer management, and individualized marketing (Lengrand & Chatrie, 2000). Beyond doubt, the relevance of networked cooperations in business can be expected to increase strongly in future. Delic and Dayal (2003) discuss and describe future enterprises that will transform themselves into better forms by becoming "more intelligent". In this connection the authors refer to the capability of a business entity to exploit emerging business opportunities and to adapt its operations to changing market conditions. Intelligence in this sense requires the ability of a business entity to sense its environment, to understand the situation, and to adapt its business objectives and behavior accordingly. Delic and Dayal (2002) argue that in near future enterprises will form strategic partnerships with other enterprises "to create dynamic business ecosystems", that will be self-managed, self-configured, and self-optimized. Self-organization is a popular concept that is currently raising considerable interest among researcher from different background (Martin-Flatin, Sventek, & Geihs, 2006). However, there is still considerable controversy regarding how self-managing systems are to be defined and how they can be engineered. Biological and sociological phenomena often serve as inspirations and guidelines for the design of systems. Adaptation can be identified as a key behavior derived from the behavior of natural systems. Both systems natural and business systems share the same ultimate objective: to survive in an evolving environment and changing circumstances (Delic & Dayal, 2002).

Thus the question arises: how far are future dynamic business ecosystems from real business reality? Actually, new efficiencies can be mainly achieved through the automation of core business processes and the exploitation of collaborative knowledge. In this connection, popular concepts are customer relationship management (CRM), enterprise resource planning (ERP), enterprise application integration (EAI), and enterprise knowledge management (EKM). In essence, they encompass enterprise activities that strive for improving efficiency or injecting intelligence into operations (Delic & Dayal, 2002). This requires the availability of standardized interfaces for integrating proprietary information systems from both internal perspective and external perspective to realise the flexible integration of respective business partners, suppliers, and customers into the enterprise's own operations. Consequently, enterprise's borders are blurring, turning into fuzzy and dynamic borders (Picot, Reichwald, & Wigand, 2003). Today, many research endeavors noticeably gravitate around the realization and problems related to the implementation of the concepts mentioned above. The common denominator and underlying problem of many business

endeavors can be subsumed in the right combination of two extremes: self vs. extrinsic organization or more general evolution vs. organization. The vision sets clear targets for this research endeavor. After having motivated the background of our research, the following actual needs and aims of the research are further elicited. One strand to be specifically looked into relates to problems associated with the interplay and interdependency of concepts as ERP, CRM, EKM (see Figure 1). This has been the subject of many past and ongoing research projects (Camarinha-Matos, 2002; Camarinha-Matos, 2004; Camarinha-Matos & Afsarmanesh, 2003; Camarinha-Matos, Afsarmanesh, & Ollus, 2006). The holistic view on an enterprise's operations through integrating information flows and respective applications and systems can be envisioned to be the foundation of any required business intelligence.

Many of these new paradigms are currently being broadly discussed by academia. Industry has commenced with the design and engineering of new software concepts, architectures, and solutions. The newly emerging concepts and architectures based on the new paradigm "service-orientation" as, for example, SOA (service oriented architecture) strive to overcome actual limits of traditional solutions for managing and controlling networked systems (Newcomer & Lomow, 2005; Martin-Flatin et al., 2006). However, problems related to the technical integration of heterogeneous enterprise information systems are not subject hereafter. Although it has to be underlined that any research endeavor addressing electronic networks is likely more or less intertwined and dependent on ICT technology.

In the following, it is focused on the implementation of described abilities and the prior motivated behavior of dynamic business ecosystems, namely evolution and organization. Self-organization serves as inspiration and guideline. The selection of business partners is to be seen as key to success for the realization of dynamic business ecosystems in the near future; therefore, business relationships need to be perceived increasingly as intangible assets of an enterprise that need special care. Namely, they have

Figure 1. Partnership relationship management in the intelligent enterprise (Delic & Dayal, 2002)

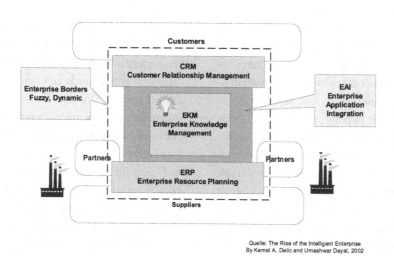

Quelle: The Rise of the Intelligent Enterprise
By Kemal A. Delic and Umeshwar Dayal, 2002

to be maintained continuously through an adequate management. Thus, the areas under investigation are relational ties and enabling organizational structures and cultures in the light of aspired intelligence and ability of systems to self-organize.

The goal is to ease the fast and easy docking and quick formation of network entities or new business partners. Evaluation criteria applied in the discovery and selection process have been identified as a main study area. Prior criterion to be applied in connection with selection of business partners is offered business value and ability to complement knowledge, skills, and competencies of the network. The aim is to enhance quality and to add value to existing or new products and/or services. As already been pointed out besides these "harder" facts, however, in particular "softer" aspects need to flow into the decision making process.

The proposed ontology-based framework for partner integration aims at developing and supporting trust building mechanisms. Trust building is, beyond any question, a complex issue that offers and necessitates different research perspectives and therefore has been subject of many investigations through different scientific disciplines (Weiß, 2005, p. 81). However, trust building evidently depends on the quality and intensity of communication and information exchange in a collaborative environment. This could be shown by empirical studies (see, e.g., Jung, 1999, p. 180; Bienert, 2002, p. 102). An ontology-based methodology is outlined that facilitates harmonization and parallelizing of different cultures. In this way, a breeding environment comes into existence from which relational ties and organizational structures are likely to emerge. Moreover, the required characteristic and ability to self-organize are facilitated through self-reference and an initiated learning curve. In this way, a kind of "fingerprint" represents network entities by describing their cooperation ability and requirements. In a process of self-reflection and self-reference, relational structures and cultures are then supposed to emerge.

First, the chapter introduces briefly the visionary scenario of dynamic business ecosystems. Next, actual developments, trends, and requirements are discussed and then the applied methodology for enterprise modeling is described. After that, the implementation of the demonstrator is depicted using KAON tool set and infrastructure (see http://kaon.semanticweb.org/). The goal is to achieve the aspired proof of concept and to demonstrate its practicability. The chapter presents an ontology-based approach for dynamic integration of business partners on demand. Ontology-Based Business Partner Relationship Management Methodology (ODAMY), an ontology-based methodology, is introduced to support dynamics and evolution of business networks to adapt to environmental changes.

BACKGROUND

In the past, the network perspective has proven fruitful in a wide range of social and behavioral science disciplines. Today, the network perspective noticeably impacts other research disciplines, namely informatics, economics, engineering, law, and so forth. The network concepts are conceived increasingly as fundamental components for research activities in the field of virtual organization (Camarinha-Matos, 2002, 2004; Camarinha-Matos & Afsarmanesh, 2003; Camarinha-Matos et al., 2006; Krystek, Redel, & Reppegather, 1997; Picot et al., 2003; Sydow, 1992; Ritter, 1998; Weiß, 2005).

The Scenario of Dynamic Business Ecosystems

Since 1993, many concepts emerged dealing with the enormous impact of ICT on businesses. Collaborative business nowadays impacts nearly every sector of our economy and has turned to be an important strategy and task on the daily agenda of decision makers in industry. ICT is seen as enabler and key driver of today's newly emerging organizational shapes and new ways to organize business collaboration. Companies strive for better interoperability and easier integration of their ICT systems with the aim to leverage "business intelligence" and to boost competitiveness by reducing time to market and increasing flexibility through business alliances. Before requirements of existing business to business (b2b) integration concepts are described, the process of dynamic formation of new business partners needs to be shortly depicted. In Figure 2 the typical lifecycle of a virtual organization is shown.

ODAMY (Weiß, 2005) strives for supporting the process of discovery, formation, agreement, and operation within the illustrated lifecycle. Further, it is required to scrutinize the integration process itself that notably discovers and selects business partners from an open-ended collection of prequalified partners.

Figure 2. ODAMY supporting the life-cycle and self-formation of virtual enterprises (Weiß, 2005)

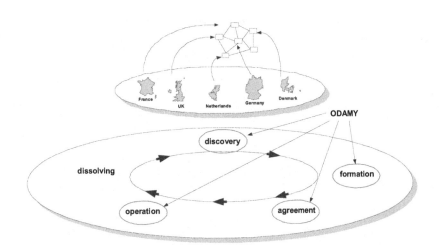

The business partners have agreed to form a pool of potential members to converge to virtual organizations. How potential members of the pool are selected from the universe of modules will be looked into later on. The breeding environment originates from this pool of independent enterprises, which have generally expressed their interest to cooperate. From this pool, virtual corporations come into being (Franke & Hickmann, 1999). In Figure 3 the partner integration process is depicted. Business partners are selected from an open-ended collection of prequalified partners to a pool of potential business partners.

The communication and interaction of business entities in a collaborative space seems to be an appropriate way to allow harmonizing and parallelizing individual cultures and organizational structures at an early stage of (pre-) selection. In Figure 4, it is therefore investigated how the communication and interaction of business entities can be supported and started at an early stage in the life-cycle of dynamic business ecosystems. Dynamic business ecosystems can be subsumed under the term organizational networks. Networks rely per se on the personal ties between its members. They are essential for the emergence of relational ties within a collaborative and innovation environment. Obviously, the increasing dynamics in the interaction of business partners combined with the shortening life-cycle of cooperations contradict the nature and actual needs of business relationships regarding trust and commitment. Both concepts occur over a longer time period and necessitate stable relationships. Once trust is established, it reduces opportunistic behavior. This is substantiated by existing organization theories as, for example, transaction cost, principal-agent, and property-rights (Picot et al., 2003, p. 45; Sydow, 1992, p. 130).

Current b2b integration concepts are focused merely on technical needs and aspects as definition of interfaces for information exchange, remote invocation of applications, or formalization of business transactions and processes as well as business semantics (Weiß & Stucky, 2004). Most influential initiatives to be mentioned here are EDI[1]-based and/or XML[2]-based (Weiß, 2005).

On top is the organizational layer, the first conceptual layer depicted in Figure 4. At this level, strategic aspects such as alignment of goals, risks, organizational structure, and network culture are dealt with. The next conceptual layer is the process layer that interacts with the first layer. At this level, the focal point is business processes, which need to be described, analyzed, modeled, simulated, run, and

Figure 3. Dynamic formation of new partners and partner fit (partly based on Saabeel, Verduijn, Hagdorn, & Kumar, 2002; Source: Weiß, 2005)

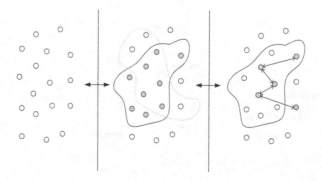

Figure 4. Three layer architecture of adaptive business networks (Weiß, 2005)

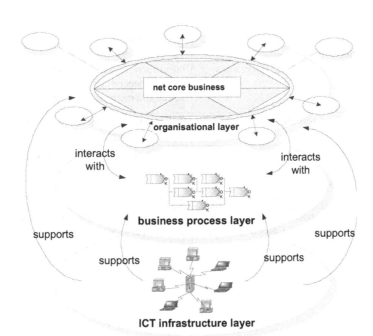

monitored. At last, the underlying ICT infrastructure layer is supporting the higher layers. In this connection, semantics are discussed to better interlink the distinct layers. An ontology-based model is developed with the aim to achieve the aspired interaction and communication between the organizational and ICT infrastructure layer. This model represents in a formal and machine-processable form the above mentioned decision and selection criteria applied in the selection process. Furthermore, the aggregated collaborative information concerning business partners and collaborative behavior supports services of the ICT infrastructure, namely discovery and matchmaking. The relevant information to assess the strategic fit is stored as "fingerprint" of a business entity with the aim of supplying the underlying infrastructure with strategic selection criteria in machine-processable form ("ICT infrastructure layer"). The goal is to support the self-formation of virtual enterprises within dynamic business ecosystems as motivated in the previous sections. The work can be partly related to the discovery, matching, and selection of Web service descriptions (Field & Hoffner, 2003) as postulated by newly emerging approaches to self-managed systems and services. Information is stored in publicly accessible electronic service directories. Exiting examples are e-business standards such as UDDI or ebXML.

Table 1 reflects and summarizes the central ideas and key aspects pointed out. Further they underline the actual needs and derived measures in the direction of adaptive business networks with ontologies.

Communication and Ontology

During the last years, ontologies have been increasingly seen as a key technology for enabling semantics-driven knowledge processing. Semantics and, consequently, the concept of ontologies are seen to overcome exist-

Table 1. Towards adaptive business networks with ontologies

Actual need	Derived measure
Partner searching and fitting in dynamic networked organizations is a time-consuming and difficult process.	The process has to be supported through the ICT infrastructure layer. Despite the fact that the quality of linkages depends on personal ties, ontologies help to search and merge information from diverse communities.
Achieving adaptive business networks through dynamic and flexible extension is a challenge.	To apply the network concept of latent and evident business relationships.
Especially organizations striving for loosely coupled, project-oriented cooperations are challenged by the selection of appropriate business partners.	Initiate a continuous learning process that harmonizes and parallelizes goals, culture, and structure.
Means for capturing knowledge about the business behavior to support automatic trust building are currently not provided.	Collaborative information needs to be assessed and delivered in structured, machine-readable form. Apply an empirical model that allows analyzing, configuring, and describing business relationships according to actual needs.

ing barriers and problems related to interoperability of business applications and transactions by many authors. Ontology is a shared conceptual model established by a community of interest and provides a framework for sharing precise meaning of symbols exchanged in the course of communication (Maedche, 2002). Many applications benefit from semantically-enriched information, for example, knowledge management or e-business, to name just a few. It is widely accepted that next-generation knowledge management systems will rely on conceptual models in the form of ontologies in order to precisely define the meaning.

The evolving Semantic Web[3] promises automated information access based on machine-processable semantics of data and heuristics that use these meta data. Within this "new Web," the explicit representation of the semantics of data, accompanied with domain theories (i.e., ontologies), will enable a Web that provides a qualitatively new level of service. It will weave an incredibly large network of human knowledge and will complement it with machine processability. Various automated services will help the user achieve goals by accessing and providing information in machine understandable form. This process may ultimately create extremely knowledgeable systems with various specialized reasoning services systems that can support us in nearly all aspects of life and that will become as necessary to us as access to electric power.

An ontology defines the terms used to describe and represent an area of knowledge. It represents the semantics of business objects and enables the use of semantics through ICT applications and machine agents. Thus, ontologies are used primarily by people, databases, and applications that need to share domain information. Domain is perceived as a specific subject area of knowledge, like manufacturing, automotive, finance, medicine, chemistry, and so forth. In this sense, ontologies are seen as critical for applications that need to search or merge information from diverse communities. Ontologies include computer-usable definitions of basic concepts in the domain and the relationships among them.[4] Ontology is one of the fundamental theoretical concepts that build the semantic Web technology stack. Typically the following concepts are applied: classes, relationships, and properties. Classes represent general things, relationships describe how things are related to each other, and properties are attributes to describe things.

The Semantic Web builds on a technology stack with different layers to describe above concepts. The static part of the Semantic Web is Unicode, the URI[5], namespaces (NS) syntax, and XML[6] which serves as a basis. RDF[7] allows making simple assertions about Web resources or any other entity that can be named. RDF Schema[8] extends RDF with the concepts of class and property hierarchies that enable the creation of simple ontologies. On the next higher level, the ontology layer encompasses OWL[9] which is a family of richer ontology languages that augment RDF schema. The simplest language is OWL Lite, a limited version of OWL Full that enables simple and efficient implementation. Lastly, OWL DL[10] is a simpler subset for which reasoning is known to be decidable so that complete reasoners can be constructed on this basis, even if less efficient than OWL Lite reasoners. OWL Full is the full ontology language which is in theory undecidable, but in practice useful reasoners can be constructed (Oberle, Volz, Staab, & Motik, 2003; Weiß, 2005). Current research is gravitating around the next higher level, the logic layer. It strives for the provision of an interoperable language for describing the sets of deductions one can make from a collection of data (Volz, 2004). A given domain ontology now allows us to make connections and new facts can be derived about it. Further layers to be looked into are proof and trust that all together form the technology stack and in the future will make the vision of the Semantic Web possibly come true. The standardization process has currently reached the ontology layer.

KAON Infrastructure

KAON[11] is an open-source ontology management infrastructure targeted for business applications. It includes a comprehensive tool suite allowing easy ontology creation and management and provides a framework for building ontology-based applications. An important focus of KAON is scalable and efficient reasoning with ontologies.

The KAON language (KAON, 2004) (the so-called "ontology-instance (OI) models") supports frequently occurring patterns of logical axioms such as the specification of algebraic characteristics of relations, for example, symmetry, inverse, transitivity, and constraints on the cardinality of relations. The extension also brought several nonlogical features like modularization, strict separation of ontologies and instances, and support for spanning objects. The change in ontology language went along with a complete redesign of the KAON API and the development of new user-level tools, for example, the KAON Portal and KAON OI-modeler ontology editor.

In KAON ontologies consist of concepts, properties, and instances grouped in reusable units called OI-models (ontology-instance models). The division between concepts and instances is not strict—an entity can be interpreted as a concept, as well as an instance, depending on the view of the observer. An OI-model may include other OI-models, thus having immediate access to all definitions from the included model (KAON, 2003).

An OI-model represents a self contained unit of structured information that may be reused. An OI-model consists of entities and may include a set of other OI-models. A mathematical definition of the conceptual modeling language can be found in Motik et al. (2003), and Maedche (2002, p. 18). For the modeling of the domain ontology, the OI-Modeler of the KAON infrastructure is used. OI-Modeler is a tool for ontology creation and maintenance. The goal of the tool is to allow scalability for editing large ontologies, as well as to incorporate some usability issues related to ontology management. As a guide for the modeling, the KAON OI-Modeler User's Guide is recommended (see KAON, 2002).

KAON currently is working on a parallel support for the recently standardized Web ontology language (OWL). KAON contributed to the development of the OWL API[12] and investigated how efficient reasoning support for OWL can be provided. The basic strategy behind this research endeavor is to rely on (deductive) database-techniques to support efficient reasoning with instances. KAON maintains two ontology languages in parallel, since the expressivity of OWL is not needed in many applications. State-of-the-art ontology tools do not support the semi-automatic acquisition of complex logical axioms such as expressible in OWL (for more detailed information and further development see http://kaon.semanticweb.org/).

RESULTS/RESEARCH

In this section, the results yielded from our research are presented. The investigation and analysis of existing virtual business networks revealed that "partner fit" is crucial for the success of business networks. A methodology is presented using ontologies to implement an efficient business partner relationship management in the before motivated scenario of dynamic business ecosystems. In order to enable consistent behaviors among the participants in virtual organizations and to allow complex interactions such as negotiation and mediation, greater levels of semantic content need to be made explicit and formally represented. Consequently, the envisaged solution has to provide a means for capturing knowledge about the business behaviors to support trust building. However, our investigations have revealed that currently no appropriate proven methodologies can be found supporting the dynamic on demand integration of network entities to set up and configure an inter-firm value creation chain. Actually, many efforts are being undertaken concentrating on the dynamic and flexible integration and coupling of existing ICT systems in business networks.

It has been argued that organizational structures with the asked abilities to self-manage, self-configure, and self-optimize require besides the necessary culture, "semantic-informed self-organizing structures" (Camarinha-Matos & Afsarmanesch, 2003, p. 8). Culture and structure are constituted in the collaboration and innovation environment. This collaborative space provides the above mentioned "breeding environment" for relational ties to emerge between agents (e.g., units, actors, etc.). From a network perspective, linkages and related relational processes and structures are subject of analysis. The status of relational ties is either latent (passive) or evident (active) (Weiß, 2005, p. 210). If made evident in a specific context given, they offer the channels for transfer or "flow" of resources (either

material or nonmaterial). The framework allows to analyze and to conceptualize structures in form of models as lasting patterns of emerging relationships among agents. Again the conditions and environment catalysing the emergence of relational processes and structures in the context of collaboration and innovation processes are looked into. The goal is to analyze related interactions at the level of individuals, teams (or groups), organizations, networks, and communities.

The goal is to help business entities to exchange information concerning business partners in a dynamic networked environment as described above. It is envisioned to describe relevant information in a formal and machine-processable way, so that human and machine agents, respectively, can be supported to find the right business partners that match their own requirements (Field & Hoffner, 2003). This research work has been realized between 2003 and 2005, dealing with the need to deliver concrete criteria to be assessed and stored in business partner profiles. The profiles represent information required to discover, select and integrate business partners preferably dynamic, on demand into emerging or existing value chains. The approach chosen combines concepts and methods of business engineering, empirical research, and applied informatics. The basic idea of the proposed method is to introduce the concept of "strategic partner fit". Partner fit encompasses the assessed similarity of strategy, culture, and structure. It allows breaking down the preferred collaborative culture of network companies being rather abstract into concrete dimensions and criteria to be obtained and fed into the (pre-)selection process (Weiß, 2005; Weiß & Stucky, 2004).

In the previous section, important elements and characteristics were been pointed out. Based on the described scenario of future digital business ecosystems, the following research objectives can be derived. The future exploitation and enormous business potential of new forms of organizations is jeopardized by missing holistic approaches taking into consideration all three layers of organizations (see Figure 4). The envisaged solution to integrate business partners on demand or initiate and form a collaborative network quickly if the demand occurs has to respond to the requirements of existing b2b integration concepts. Solutions to the scenarios and problems as depicted above can be likely seen as extensions to b2b integration technology architectures with a component that manages the formation of virtual enterprises.

That component may use the existing b2b integration technology components and add its functionality on top of it (Bussler, 2003). A proper solution is to deliver the information required for the strategic planning, formation and finally operation of business collaborations (Bussler, 2003). A holistic approach has to respond to the needs on the three different layers as depicted in Figure 4. The suggested distinction of three layers allows a precise discussion of the goals and focus of b2b integration concepts. Today, we observe that most approaches address merely one or two of the layers but in most cases not a holistic approach.

In summary, Figure 5 depicts the overall research approach. The configuration of the business relationship takes place primarily on the organizational layer. To involve the ICT infrastructure collaborative data

has to be represented in machine-processable form. This can be realized using ontologies for the structuring and modeling of the business partner profiles (BPP). Profiles are a prominent concept, for example, used by Web services to store service descriptions. Therefore, this is seen as an appropriate way to approach the problem at hand. BPP are conceived to bridge the existing barrier between the organizational and ICT infrastructure layer. Through the application of ontologies, collaborative services as, for example, for discovery and/or matching of BPP, can be used to support the self-reference and emergence of collaborative structure and cultures. Especially zones of trust can be established through filtering of collaborative information and an intensified interaction and information exchange of business entities in forefront of concrete business endeavors.

The domain ontology is developed on the basis of a domain model encompassing dimensions to be considered from both an inter- and intra-organizational perspective. The dimensions allow the proper

Figure 5. Business partner relationship management with ontologies: overview of research objectives

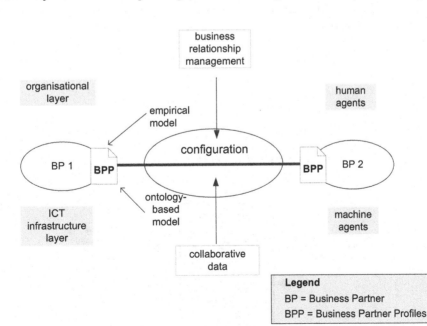

management of a company's business relationships. The domain model represents an empirical model that measures the similarity of cooperation preferences of business partners expressed as partner fit. The methodology relies on methods and applications that are oriented basically towards applied approaches in social network analysis. Social network analysis is seen as an important area and flows in our research methodology. The area has shown of growing popularity and interest for researchers as it provides the substrate and proved measures to investigate and model the behavior of networks (Scott, 2000; Weiß, 2005; Wasserman & Faust, 1994).

Later on in this chapter the empirical model is introduced and explained. It lays the theoretical and practical foundation to measure the similarity of business partner profiles. The profiles represent factors with aggregated values that are computed according to specific rules. How these values are assessed, represented, and computed is explained later on in more detail. The chosen approach follows the idea to represent each business entity entering the system through an instance of the BPP. BPP is structured according to the introduced dimensions of the empirical model. In this way, the relational culture and network structure is assessed and stored for each network entity. The degree of similarity of business partner profiles is subsumed through the concept "partner fit".

This is realized by means of a measurement based on strategic fit criteria. The criteria applied are based on an empirical model and are explained later on in more detail. The integration on demand of new partners in such a network is in practice a difficult and time consuming task which runs contrary to the basic idea of flexibility and anticipated fast reactions for virtual organizations. There is an obvious need to construct complex data structures to express the complexity of business related information. Besides, there is a need to be able to access these complex data structures and extract the relevant information from them within a specification of requirements (Field & Hoffner, 2003) (see Figure 6).

The aim is to develop an ontology-based approach that allows the flexible docking and integration of business partners on demand. Besides the technical information to be described, our work takes in particular focus on the "softer" aspects of business integration covering information concerning the behavior of business partners and the criteria allowing the configuration and management of business relationships. As already pointed out, this tends to become an important capability as companies will need to stay competitive and to run their business successfully in the future. Based on the previous analysis and discussion the objectives of our research can be further specified as follows:

Figure 6. Describing smart companies formally (Weiß & Maedche, 2003)

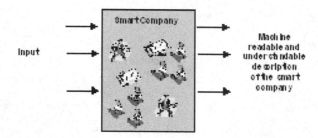

- Develop a smart organization ontology (describing relevant criteria dimensions for "smart companies")
- Define metadata for "smart companies" on the basis of the common ontology and collect the distributed descriptions in a centralized portal
- Provide ontology-based querying, ranking, matching, and tracking functionality
- Provide decision support criteria for business partner relationship management.

Measurement

Although, given the fact that business reality is too complex to be described by means of an empirical model, a theoretical model however enables to investigate systems by simplifying a deeper understanding of key drivers and determinants, a methodology often applied in socio-economic research approaches. The applied methodology aims to compare identified networks and cooperations against a continuum framework build on simplified, idealized network types. These ideal types span a continuum of virtuality.

The degree of virtuality is measured as already mentioned in different dimensions. The dimensions are the substrate that has been condensed from a profound assessment of state-of-the-art scientific literature. The complete empirical model encompasses both an internal and an external perspective to analyze relational ties between business partners. The internal perspective comprises various dimensions and relevant aspects for the configuration of business relationships. The dimensions applied are the degree of alignment of common with individual business goals, information exchange performance among entities, degree of transparency, congruency of perceived network, and individual success, interaction frequency, type of coupling, and so forth (Weiß, 2005). The external perspective offers seven dimensions of analysis: flexibility, time-horizon, trust level, type of market, integration

Figure 7. Seven dimensions to measure network typology (Weiß, 2002, 2005)

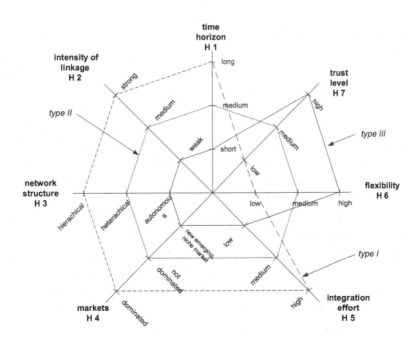

effort, intensity of linkage, and network structure. The empirical model strives for finding common culture and structures through existing similarities as well as the matching of assessed values. In this way, the approach elaborates a classification of business entities and building classes of similar entities (Weiß, 2005). The full-fledged model and approach with description of all dimensions is explained in detail in Weiß.

The empirical model is applied to measure the strategic fit of network companies to create the aforementioned fingerprint of a business partner. The main criteria for the measurement are the network typology on basis of the assessed virtuality degree (seven dimensions of the external perspective) (see Figure 7). Additionally, the created fingerprint of a network company contains information regarding technology degree (usage and experiences with ICT technologies) and related indicators as transparency, interaction frequency, and cooperation requirements. Performance indicators may be used to describe past performances. The information is assessed by using an online questionnaire. Figure 6 depicts the empirical model and its seven dimensions of the external perspective as basis for the modeling of the reference ontology. The reference ontology is modeled using OI-modeler as ontology editor.

Ontology Structure of the Business Partner Profiles

The empirical model is in a next step transferred into an ontology-based model that represents the data structure of the business partner profile. The approach transforms the metrics of the empirical model into concepts of the ontology based model. In Figure 8, the mapping of the dimensions of the empirical model to the concepts of the ontology-based model are displayed. The arrows highlight the concepts network company and its subconcepts strategic fit and typology as elements of both models. The ontology is instantiated (the concrete description of a company is generated) and used to generate smart company descriptions (e.g., including competencies, financial figures, ratings, used ICT technologies, etc.). The

resulting company profile is machine readable and understandable (see Figure 5). The goal is to transfer implicit knowledge from the strategic layer (Figure 4) into explicit domain knowledge processable by the supporting ICT infrastructure layer.

As described in the previous section, for the modeling, the Semantic Web technology stack was applied. The Figure 9 shows an excerpt of the business partner profile represented in RDF(S). Again the concepts network company and strategic fit are highlighted. The information of the business partners is stored in RDF. Now that the meta data contained in the BPP has been explained, it is next looked at for clarification at some concrete examples. In this way, the underlying principles of the approach chosen are pointed out.

Example

The values of the variables before stored are aggregated to factors as, for example, trust level according to predefined rules that are as well stored in the ontology-based model. The questionnaire is as well-modeled as ontology structure with the subconcepts questions, answers, and code. The latter concept contains the respective rules how the answers of respondents that are stored as values of variables are to be aggregated to qualitative values (*low, medium, high*). To determine the degree of similarity of two different profiles the relative distances of values are computed. In order to achieve best possible results the stored original values of respondents are applied.

Figure 10 depicts the reference ontology. The company profiles are assessed using a Web-based questionnaire. The profiles are stored as instances of the reference ontology. Figure 9 shows a contact person "Hubert" with contact details. "Hubert" is working for a network company EBV-Elektronik has a function "others." The strategic fit of the company is *medium* with regard to the defined criteria. The ICT infrastructure is heterogeneous. The goal binding with the virtual organizations is medium. The company intends to cooperate in the long term with business partners.

Figure 8. Business partner profiles (Weiß, 2005)

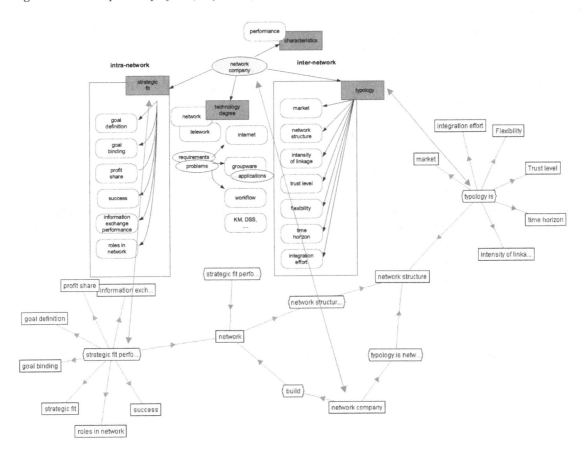

Figure 9. Business partner profiles (Weiß, 2005)

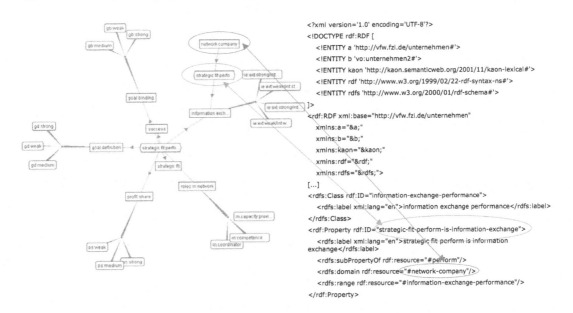

The fingerprint of a network company is produced using a formal explicit ontology-based model structuring criteria for measuring strategic partner fit. In this way, the underlying ICT infrastructure is capable for example to infer that a network company "has" a typology based on "time horizon", "integration effort", "intensity of linkage", and so forth (Maedche & Weiß, 2002; Weiß & Trunko, 2002). In Figure 10, an excerpt of the fingerprints of two network companies are shown and compared. Company "a", for example, is looking for a cooperation with medium time horizon, whereas the network company "b" prefers to cooperate in the long-term. The companies share the same conceptual model; therefore, the values are comparable. A matchmaking environment of a b2b integration technology architecture can process this information and may have discovered and selected business partners 'b.' The information exchange performance (IEP) of both companies is "strong", the preferred network structure is "heterarchical" and the trust-level is "average", intensity of linkage rated as "medium" (see Figure 11).

Discovery and Matchmaking

Network companies are able to search for potential business partners using the query user interface of the demonstrator. As an advantage of using an explicit information model in form of an ontology based model, ODAMY is able to use semantic discovery to identify the best fitting partners based on the selected search criteria and applied weightings. The use of ontology brings service provider and service requestor to a common conceptual space and supports to realize semantic matching of collaborative information stored in the BPP.

Figure 10. Reference ontology (Weiß & Maedche, 2003)

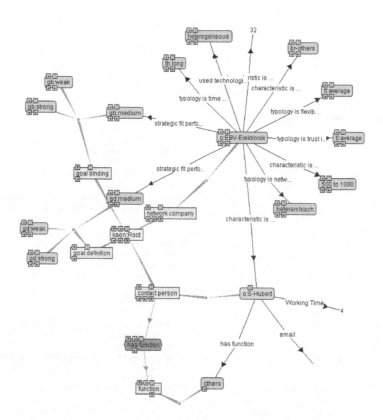

Figure 11. Excerpt ODAMY fingerprint of network company (Weiß, 2005)

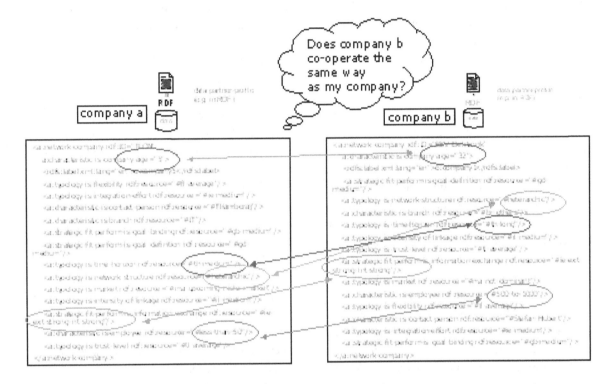

Currently, we are investigating the application of different available semantic discovery mechanisms. Especially the matchmaking module still requires specifically further investigations and research efforts; however, researchers of different disciplines, especially those working in the fields of SOA, electronic markets, as well as Web services and business process modeling and management, are currently looking into the possibilities to determine the degree of similarity of applied meta models. Therefore, it can be likely taken for granted that soon a variety of approaches and solutions will emerge and will add enhanced functionalities to an adequate matchmaking environment. A matchmaking engine is where advertisements are directed to and stored, and where search queries are sent. The task is to search for an existing offer or offers that match each received search query.

A central element of a matchmaking environment is the aspect of symmetry (Field & Hoffner, 2003). Both sides send a profile that contains relevant data concerning description of the own entity and requirements that the other party must satisfy. According to Field and Hoffner (2003), the customization of a related service of the ICT infrastructure results from coupling the availability of information from both parties with the ability to dynamically update some service properties.

In the current version of the demonstrator, the similarity of profiles A and B is measured as sum of the distances measured of the normed values a_i and b_i of a specific theme i. For each query, themes can be selected from the list of available concepts that can be queried. Each theme i can be weighted in the range of one to five to enrich the query with the individual preferences of the searching entity. The computation of similarity of profiles is described in detail in (Weiß, 2005, p. 242). Related work of interest is the current developments in the field of semantic Web services and matchmaking on electronic markets (Veit, 2003).

Implementation

ODAMY is implemented using KAON infrastructure (KAON, 2003). The demonstrator is available and is currently being evaluated using available use cases. A user model was developed defining roles and assigning required tasks to provide guidance for the end-user. The user model foresees the role of an information broker who is responsible for the maintenance of the system and the ontology engineering. The end-user is a network company who has to register to create a fingerprint to be stored in the directory. The information broker and the network company use the query interface to search for best fitting partners based on the chosen criteria and possible weightings to express the importance for each criterion. By this means, the network company of highest strategic partner fit can

be discovered and selected from the pool of entities. Figure 12 displays the architecture of the developed demonstrator. The main modules are OI-Modeler (ontology editor), KAON Portal and the developed Enterprise Portal (user interface). The Enterprise Portal has been implemented with JSP (Java Server Pages). It embodies the user interface and the imaginary gate to enter the business community.

Figure 13 lists the options for the business entity entering the network. In this connection, two roles are foreseen: the administrator and the user. The user has to register before he is allowed to enter the collaborative space. The registration module encompasses the assessment of the cooperation requirements and preferences of a business entity by means of a standardized questionnaire. The results of the assessment are stored in a business partner profile that is created at the end of the registration process and stored in RDF. Having registered in the system, the offered functionality now is to search by key words or through a predefined query interface for matching BPP. The query module offers to prepare and sent queries using simple key word search based on the KAON query module (discovery) or using

Figure 12. Architecture of the enterprise portal (Weiß, 2005)

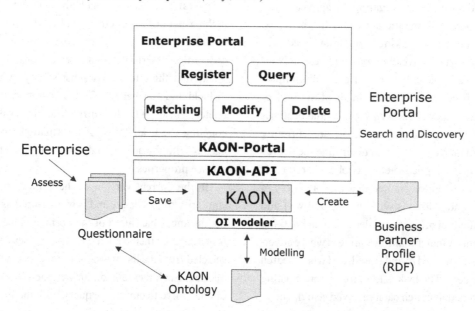

a predefined query form (matchmaking). The interface lists the available concepts of the ontology. The user selects from the list appropriate concepts and builds a query; thereby, standardized weightings are applied to each concept permit to personalize the query. In this way, it expresses the individual preferences of the user. After having sent the query, the degree of similarity is then determined by matching the set of selected values from the individual profile with respective set of values of BPPs that are registered and stored in the collaborative repository. Further modules of the enterprise portal in place are Matching, Modify, and Delete. The module Matching offers basic elements and functionality of a matchmaking environment. The matchmaking environment supports queries with a set of values (multidimensional), as aforementioned, in order to allocate profiles with best fit against the set of predefined values. The modules Modify and Delete allow the user to modify and maintain the values of his profile. The module Delete offers to delete the profile, and, consequently, to leave the business community. In the case that a business partner erases his profile, this means he withdraws his membership and is required to leave the network.

CONCLUSION AND OUTLOOK

One of the challenging tasks analyzing business networks is to propose the clearest possible view of network characteristics. The concept of network suggests the existence of nodes, which interplay in different patterns according to the network structure. In the future, networks will be likely characterized by the ability to self-organize their shape and to adapt rapidly to changes in their direct environment as, for example, the change of market conditions or new developments in technology. In this chapter, we presented ODAMY to implement an efficient partner relationship management in dynamic business eco-systems. The methodology intends to extent existing b2b integration technology architectures. ODAMY transforms the metrics of an empirical model into concepts of an ontology based model. KAON tool set and infrastructure is used to implement and demonstrate its functionality. In the future we will have to pay further attention to how to integrate ODAMY in the concrete working process. Future research activities will concentrate on its extension by using a decentralized model for the fingerprints.

Figure 13. Screenshot of the enterprise portal and options (Weiß, 2005)

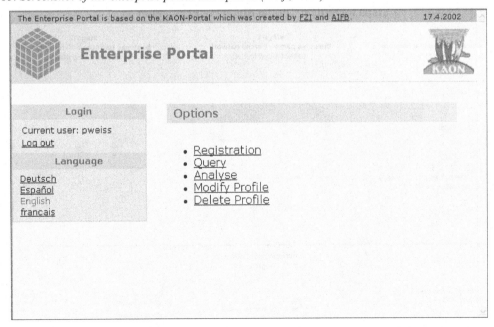

The described research focused on dynamic integration of business partners in the light of emerging digital business ecosystems. The work followed the approach to assess decision criteria in order to support the self-formation and self-organization of adaptive business networks. A centralized approach with a shared explicit data model for the business partner profiles as fingerprints was explained. The profiles are based on an ontology-based model which has been developed on basis of an empirical model encompassing important dimensions for the configuration and analysis of business relationships. In Figure 14, the future and emerging trends are discussed.

Figure 14 illustrates the three stages towards a digital business ecosystem are illustrated. The research presented addresses foremost the scenario at stage one. At this stage, a centralized model for the business partner profiles is applied. The business partners that can be accessed through the ICT infrastructure are limited to the information stored and accessible through the registry in form of an Enterprise Portal of the domain network. Related work can be found in the area of business registries for Web services as, for example, UDDI and ebXML.

Current research gravitates around the realization of the scenario shown at stage two and three. At these stages, a decentralized model is developed. BPPs are no longer stored centrally in an information portal. The profiles are stored decentralized but are created on the basis of a shared conceptual model in the form of a domain ontology. Business partners maintain latent business relationships solely within the boundaries of the business network they have registered to. The boundaries of this network are defined by the number of registered users. At stage three, the approach strives for an advanced decentralized model that allows to contact and query business partners not limited to the boundaries of the defined network. The information desired for the discovery and selection of business partners is likely to be retrieved beforehand through machines in form of agents or Web crawlers.

To dissolve the boundaries drawn at stage one, the functionality of the demonstrator has to be expanded. Information retrieval techniques are likely seen to

Figure 14. Steps towards a digital business ecosystem (Weiß, 2005)

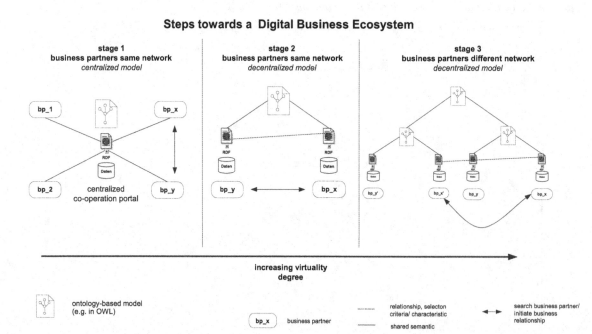

have potential to fulfil the imposed requirements at the next, upper stages. However, this is the subject of ongoing research and is currently being investigated. The semantics of the data in the profiles has to be made explicit and has to be stored in a machine-processable form. The described approach fulfils the needs of the described scenario but has to be further elaborated and developed. Especially, the retrieval of collaborative information and data stored in the BPPs poses interesting questions for future research endeavors. Future developments in adaptive business networks will be driven and dominated by current paradigms of service oriented architecture (SOA) and technologies related to Web services. The further flexibility and interoperability of the underlying ICT infrastructure (see Figure 4) is expected to have a tremendous impact on the ways business is conducted. Semantics and related technologies are expected to be of growing importance and are an important enabler for the scenario described above. Enterprise modeling has to respond to these developments through the development and take up of appropriate technologies, methods, and tools. The research presented has highlighted important characteristics and has shown possible ways forward for the development of adaptive business networks.

REFERENCES

Bienert, M. (2002). *Organization und Netzwerk: Organizationsgestaltung durch Annäherung an Charakteristika der idealtypischen Organizationsform Netzwerk*. Wiesbaden: Dt. Univ.-Verlag.

Bozsak, E., Ehrig, M., Handschuh, S., Hotho, A., Maedche, A., & Motik, B., et al. (2002). *KAON: Towards a large scale semantic Web* (Tech. Rep.). Institute AIFB, University of Karlsruhe (TH). Retrieved June 23, 2007, from http://kaon.semanticweb.org/

Bussler, C. (2003). *B2B integration*. Springer.

Camarinha-Matos, L.M. (2002). Collaborative business ecosystems and virtual enterprises. In *IFIP TC5/WG5.5, Proceedings 3rd Working Conference on Infrastructures for Virtual Enterprises (PRO-VE02)*. Kluwer Academic Publishers.

Camarinha-Matos, L.M. (2004). Virtual enterprises and collaborative networks. In *IFIP TC5/WG5.5, Proceedings PRO-VE'04 Proceedings, 5th IFIP Working Conference on Virtual Enterprises*.

Camarinha-Matos, L.M., & Afsarmanesh, H. (2003). Processes and foundations for virtual organizations. In *IFIP TC5/WG5.5, Proceedings PRO-VE'03 Proceedings, 4th IFIP Working Conference on Virtual Enterprises*.

Camarinha-Matos, L.M., Afsarmanesh, H., & Ollus, M. (2006). Network-centric collaboration and supporting frameworks. In *IFIP TC5/WG5.5, Proceedings PRO-VE'06 Proceedings, 7th IFIP Working Conference on Virtual Enterprises*.

Delic, K.A., & Dayal U. (2002, December). The rise of the intelligent enterprise. Mother nature knows best - how engineered organizations of the future will resemble natural-born systems. *ACM Ubiquity, 3*(45).

Delic, K.A., & Dayal U. (2003, Spring). The rise of the intelligent enterprise. *Virtual Strategist. A Journal of Strategy & Business Transformation, 5*. Retrieved June 23, 2007, from http://www.acm.org/ubiquity

Field, S., & Hoffner, Y. (2003). Web services and matchmaking. *International Journal Networking and Virtual Organization, 2*(1), 16-32.

Franke, U., & Hickmann, B. (1999, September 23-24). Is the net-broker an entrepreneur? What role does the net-broker play in virtual Webs and virtual corporations? *eJOV—The Journal for the Domain, 1*(1), 120-139.

Jung, S. (1999). In H.H. Bauer & C. Homburg (Eds.), *Das management von geschäftsbeziehungen: Ein Ansatz auf transaktionstheoretischer, sozialpsychologischer und spieltheoretischer basis*. Wiesbaden: Gabler Verlag.

KAON (2002, November). OI-modeler user's guide. Retrieved June 23, 2007, from http://kaon.semanticweb.org

KAON (2003, February). The Karlsruhe ontology and semantic Web framework. Developer's guide for

KAON 1.2.5. Retrieved June 23, 2007, from http://wim.fzi.de or http://kaon.semanticweb.org

KAON (2004, January). KAON 1.2.5 Developer's Guide. Retrieved June 23, 2007, from http://kaon.semanticweb.org

Krystek, U., Redel, W., & Reppegather, S. (1997). *Grundzüge virtueller organizationen: Elemente und erfolgsfaktoren, chancen und risiken.* Wiesbaden: Gabler Verlag.

Lengrand, L., & Chatrie, I. (2000). *Business networks and the knowledge-driven economy.* An empirical study carried out in Europe and Canada commissioned by the DG Enterprise.

Maedche, A. (2002). Fakultät für Wirtschaftswissenschaften der Universität Karlsruhe (TH) [Ontology learning for the semantic Web]. Dissertation, Kluwer.

Maedche, A., Motik, B., Stojanovic, L., Studer, R., & Volz, R. (2001). *Ontologies for enterprise knowledge management* (Tech. Rep.). FZI - Research Center for Information Technology at the University of Karlsruhe, Haid-und-Neu-Str. 10-14, 76131 Karlsruhe, Germany, Institute AIFB, University of Karlsruhe, 76128 Karlsruhe, Germany. Was: Studer et al. (2001)

Maedche, A., & Weiß, P. (2002, May). Towards ontology-based smart organizations. In *PRO-VE' 02, Conference Proceedings, 3rd IFIP Working Conference on Infrastructures for Virtual Enterprises, 2* (pp. 201-208). Sesimbra, Portugal.

Martin-Flatin, J.-P., Sventek, J., & Geihs, K. (2006, March). Self-managed systems and services. *Communications of the ACM, 49*(3).

Oberle, D., Volz, R., Staab, S., & Motik, B. (2003). An extensible ontology software environment (Tech. Rep. and Handbook). Institute AIFB, University of Karlsruhe (TH). Retrieved June 23, 2007, from http://kaon.semanticweb.org/

Motik, B., Maedche, A., & Volz, R. (2003). A conceptual modeling approach for semantics-driven enterprise applications (Tech. Rep.). FZI Research Center for Information Technologies at the University of Karlsruhe, Karlsruhe, Germany.

Newcomer, E., & Lomow, G. (2005). *Understanding SOA with Web services.* Addison-Wesley.

Österle, H., Fleisch, E., & Alt, R. (Eds.). (2002). *Business networking in der Praxis.* Springer Verlag.

Picot, A., Reichwald, R., & Wigand, R.T. (2003). *Die grenzenlose unternehmung.* 5. Auflage: Gabler Verlag.

Ritter, T. (1998). Innovationserfolg durch netzwerkkompetenz: Effektives management von unternehmensnetzwerken. Wiesbaden, Fakultät für Wirtschaftswissenschaften der Universität Fridericiana zu Karlsruhe, Dissertation, Juli 1998.

Saabeel, W., Verduijn, T.M., Hagdorn, L., & Kumar, K. (2002). *A model of virtual organization: A structure and processs perspective.* eJOV 4 (2002) 1, Electronic Journal of Organizational Virtualness. Retrieved June 23, 2007, from http://www.virtual-organization.net/

Scott, J. (2000). *Social network analysis* (2nd ed.). London: SAGE Publications Ltd.

Sydow, J. (1992). *Strategische netzwerke: Evolution und organisation.* Wiesbaden: Gabler Verlag.

Veit, D. (2003). *Matchmaking in electronic markets: An agent-based approach towards matchmaking in electronic environments.* Springer Verlag.

Volz, R. (2004). Fakultät für Wirtschaftswissenschaften der Universität Karlsruhe (TH) [Web ontology reasoning with logic databases]. Dissertation.

Wasserman, S., & Faust, K. (1994). *Social network analysis: Methods and applications.* Cambridge, UK: Cambridge University Press.

Weiß, P. (2002, October). Set up and management of SME business networks, eBusiness, and eWork. In *e2002 Proceedings,* Prague, Czech Republic (p. 16).

Weiß, P. (2005). Management von Geschäftsbeziehungen in virtuellen Organizationsstrukturen.

Genehmigte dssertation Universität Karlsruhe (TH), Dr. Hut-Verlag, München, 2005.

Weiß, P., & Maedche, A. (2003, October 30). Towards adaptive ontology-based business networks. In *PRO-VE'03 Proceedings, 4th IFIP Working Conference on Virtual Enterprises* (pp. 297-304), Lugano, Switzerland.

Weiß, P., & Stucky, W. (2004, August 22-27). ODAMY extending b2b integration technology architecture. In L.M. Camarinha-Matos (Ed.), *Virtual enterprises and collaborative networks*. Toulouse, France: Kluwer Academic Publishers. 5th Working Conference on Virtual Enterprises (PRO-VE'04) at 18th IFIP World Computer Congress (pp. 43-50).

Weiß, P., & Trunko, R. (2002, May). Smart organization metrics – partner fit. In *PRO-VE' 02, Conference Proceedings, 3rd IFIP Working Conference on Infrastructures for Virtual Enterprises,* Sesimbra, Portugal (p. 2).

ENDNOTES

[1]   EDI = Electronic Data Interchange. Retrieved 14 March 2007

[2]   XML = Extensible Markup Language; see http://www.w3.org/XML/. Retrieved 14 March 2007.

[3]   "Semantic Web is a web of data"; for further information please visit http://www.w3.org/2001/sw/. Retrieved 14 March 2007.

[4]   What is an ontology? See http://www.w3.org/TR/2004/REC-webont-req-20040210/#onto-def; retrieved 01 February 2007.

[5]   URI = Uniform Resource Identifier. Retrieved 14 March 2007.

[6]   Extensible Markup Language; see http://www.w3.org/XML/. Retrieved 14 March 2007.

[7]   RDF = Resource Description Framework; see http://www.w3.org/RDF/. Retrieved 14 March 2007.

[8]   For further information please visit: http://www.w3.org/TR/2004/REC-owl-features-20040210/#ref-rdf-schema; retrieved 01 February 2007.

[9]   OWL = Ontology Web Language; see http://www.w3.org/2004/OWL/. Retrieved 14 March 2007.

[10]   DL = Description Logic.

[11]   See http://kaon.semanticweb.org/, Retrieved 14 March 2007.

[12]   API = Application Programming Interface.

Section VI
Ontology Management

Chapter XX
POVOO:
Process Oriented Views on Ontologies Supporting Business Interaction

Eva Gahleitner
voestalpine IT GmbH, Austria

Wolfram Wöß
Johannes Kepler University Linz, Austria

ABSTRACT

Ontologies still lack in including and considering the dynamic aspects of business processes. Therefore, existing ontology-based information systems provide only static information which does not suit the actual working context of a user. In this project we extend information retrieval techniques with ontologies through a process oriented view on ontologies (POVOO). The purpose is to satisfy a user with information that depends on the current process the user is working on. Due to a context aware approach, it is possible to adapt the information to the user's current working situation dynamically. We introduce a methodology for generating views on ontologies and we illustrate how an application can use them to query highly specialized knowledge bases.

INTRODUCTION

Ontologies are widely used in the area of computer science, but did not really step into the area of commercial business engineering. Semantic enrichment has an important impact in the business process area to gain a representation of the knowledge which is nowadays implicitly defined in single processes or a business process chain. In this context the emphasis is on machine-based interpretation of processes and, ultimately, autonomous operation. This is equally important to reach the global goal of autonomous business interaction. Context aware systems which are able to interpret business processes automatically based on the semantics they represent, are a prerequisite for this challenge.

Whereas in the field of information retrieval (IR) ontologies emerged as a major support for improving the recall and precision of search mechanisms, they only play a subordinate role in process modeling. Within business process modeling, ontologies are used to represent explicit formal specifications of the terms in the entire process management domain and relationships among them. Nevertheless, in daily work business processes are often the starting point for software development and define requirements for software systems. Research and industry have addressed the alignment of business processes and information technology (IT) only marginally. This leads to separate modeling areas: one for information management and retrieval and one for business engineering.

Ontology-based query techniques suffer from a number of disadvantages which have major impacts on their usage in business process modeling:

- Ontologies provide a single monolithic structure; splitting them up into small units is hardly possible.
- Ontologies do not consider dynamic aspects. A process is typically characterized by a dynamic sequence of events and operations. The need for knowledge may change according to these different process events and operations. For example, a technician who designs a new car engine needs information which is different from the information a worker at the assembly line or a car dealer requires for the customers.
- As the size of the ontology raises, so does the complexity of its structure and therefore the complexity for a user to find the right concepts (highly specialized ontologies in medicine like UMLS (2006).
- The context in which a user (an employee in a department, a user of a software application, etc.) works determines the user's view on the available knowledge. Much work has already been done in the field of context-based ontologies for certain users or user groups, but little for particular views on knowledge in the context

of business processes (Abecker, Metzas, Legal, Ntioudis, & Papavassiliou, 2001).

- One structure does not fit all: information can not easily be categorized within a single (tree) structure, so that users will always find what they are looking for. This is due to the multidimensional nature of the information. Any piece of information can be categorized according to one or more facets. Such a multi-faceted categorization better reflects the different viewpoints one can have on a single piece of information.

In this work we introduce our approach to integrating views on ontologies in the information retrieval process with specific consideration on business processes. The acronym POVOO stands for process oriented views on ontologies. The purpose of POVOO is to satisfy a user with information that depends on the current process the user is working in. We propose a context aware solution which considers a user's working process and the corresponding information required by a user during certain tasks in this process. For example, when office workers are working on a specific task, they are working in a certain context, thus only specific information is necessary to get the work done. Working contexts differ according to the required information and the involved people. This characteristic of work is exploited in the IR mechanism of our approach where views on ontologies represent the working contexts. In this way the system can search and present relevant information in the current context.

For highly specialized knowledge bases which can be found, for example, in medicine or biology, we assume that the information itself, which is relevant to execute a certain task (the documents in a knowledge base), stays the same, whereas the relationships, the various specialization and generalizations, the integration of various concepts in a new one, the ordering of the concepts, and so forth, may differ depending on the user or the actual business process step. We therefore emphasize an approach which uses ontologies not only as simple vocabulary to define a lingua franca in business process engineering but rather as a way to structure the knowledge for particular processes. Within POVOO we develop a methodology for generating views on ontologies (which we call *ontology views*) and we demonstrate how applications can use them to query ontology-based knowledge bases.

A Grid infrastructure is the underlying technological basis, which is implemented using the semantic data integration middleware G-SDAM (Austrian Grid, 2006). This is important to be able to build up interorganizational cooperations as well as virtual organizations with seamless data interchange facilities and subsequently to enable enterprise and application over-spanning business processes.

The remainder of the chapter is organized as follows: The second section overviews related work concerning ontologies in IR and process modeling, view based search, and process oriented ontologies. The third section describes the characteristics of highly specialized knowledge bases, presents POVOO's three ontology levels, and the concept of ontology views. The fourth section gives an explanation of our query mechanisms and how ontologies are connected with process modeling techniques. In the fifth section, we show how POVOO accomplish autonomous business interaction in a grid environment. Finally, the sixth section describes further research and concludes the chapter.

RELATED WORK

A business process defines the sequence of activities and the kind of resources (machine or human) which a process or an activity needs for its execution (Workflow Management, 1999). For years, organizations have used Workflow Management Systems (WfMS) to describe and execute their business processes (Georgakopoulos, Hornick, & Sheth, 1995). Underlying these WfMS are different workflow methods and languages with many different meta models. In recent years various (business) process modeling techniques have been introduced; starting from the well-known Petri Nets (Petri, 1962) or high-level Petri nets (Brauer, Reisig, & Rozenberg, 1987), over UML activity diagrams (UML,

2006) and object behavior diagrams (Bichler, Preuner, & Schrefl, 1997) to more enterprise and business related techniques such as event-driven process chains (EPC) (Staud, 2001), UML profile for enterprise distributed object computing (EDOC) (UML, 2006) or the business process modeling language (BPML, 2006).

All these techniques have in common that they describe the *behavior* of a system. By contrast, ontologies describe the *knowledge* of the system. Ontology is an explicit specification of a conceptualization (Gruber, 1993)—it captures the knowledge of a certain domain. But ontologies are not limited to the description of domain knowledge. They can also be used to define problem-solving knowledge (so-called task knowledge or task ontologies). In business engineering task ontologies create an ordering over sets of tasks and subtasks and are therefore defined as hierarchically ordered task ontologies (Benjamins, Nunes de Barros, & Valente, 1996; Pease, 1998; Tate, 1998). In these approaches ontologies are simply used as a common vocabulary for processes and tasks.

Upcoming standards of the semantic Web provide a set of concepts that can be used to annotate processes in a way machines can analyze (METEOR-S, 2006; Martin, Burstein, Hobbs, Lassila, McDermott, & McIlraith, et al., 2004; Battle, Bernstein, Boley, Grosof, Gruninger, & Hull, et al., 2005; Lausen, Polleres, & Roman, 2005). These concepts are summarized in an ontology which then so-called semantic Web services can use for describing their functional behavior, for example, input and output parameters, preconditions and effects, description of the quality of service, and so forth. Most of these concepts can be applied to business processes as well (Drumm, Lemcke, & Namiri, 2006). The advantage of these semantic Web approaches is their ability to describe the data structure as well as the dynamic behavior of an enterprise. The main focus of semantic Web service standards relies on better supporting business to business interaction on a technical level. They provide descriptions as to what a service does and how it interacts with others. But semantic Web standards lack a holistic view on business processes which common business modeling languages already support, which is shown in the fourth section.

In contrast to business engineering methods, information engineers have already used ontologies for a long time. For example, in information retrieval (IR), ontologies have been applied to improve recall and precision (Mönch, 2003). Their main advantage relies in their ability to organize information into hierarchically ordered concept taxonomies and to define attributes and relationships between these concepts (cf. the ontology language OWL (Dean & Schreiber, 2004)). Two approaches are used in IR: query expansion and conceptual distance measures. The former expands the user query by adding terms semantically related to those used in the original user's query and therefore documents that do not necessarily contain the queried terms may be retrieved (Guarino, Masolo, & Vetere, 1999). The latter uses a conceptual distance measure to calculate the similarity between terms in a query and terms in a document (Khan, 2000).

An extension to these IR methods is the concept of view-based or multi-facet search methods (Pollitt, 1998; Mäkelä, Hyvönen, & Sidoroff, 2005). Here the idea is to organize the terminological keywords of the underlying knowledge base into various hierarchies which help the user to better formulate queries. For example, the keywords of a knowledge base can be ordered according to different aspects, for example, "Time" or "Place". Such hierarchies are often called facets or views. The facets provide complementary views on the content along different dimensions.

However, existing multifacet search tools use simple subclass-taxonomies (Pollitt, Ellis, & Smith, 1994). They do not consider various relations between the concepts of an ontology (they are built for database querying). The Ontogator (Hyvönen, Saarela, & Viljamen, 2003) approach combines the usage benefits of multi-facet search with the answer quality benefits of ontology-based search. But Ontogator does not support automatic querying; the users have to define the queries on their own.

VIEWS ON ONTOLOGIES

Ontologies describe those parts of knowledge which are interesting for a certain domain. If a user likes to tailor ontologies to specific aspects of the phenomena of interest (e.g., to implement a certain application) the user has to create different versions of the same ontology. Ontology versioning is a well-nown research area in the field of ontology engineering (Klein, Fensel, Kiryakov, & Ognyanov, 2002). Unfortunately, these approaches only take care of the changes in the ontology *itself*, they do not deal with different *views* somebody may have when working with the ontology within a given process. In that case the ontology does *not* change, only the parts which are relevant to a certain user query change.

In general, views create virtual schemas and resource descriptions reflecting only the users' (applications') conception of a specific application domain. In other words, a view is a dynamic data set, virtually computed or collated from data in a knowledge base. There is a large body of work on views for the relational data model. For example, the commonly used structured query language (SQL), see SQL (2006), serves as a view definition language. By contrast, in the semantic Web ontology views have been regarded only marginally until now. One known adoption is the use of scopes within topic maps (Luckeneder, Steiner, & Wöß, 2001; Topic Maps, 2006). Currently, there are only two semantic Web view languages for ontologies, both of them are built upon RQL query language and are aimed at RDF(S) data models: RDF view language (RVL) (Magkanaraki, Tannen, Christophides, & Plexousakis, 2003) and the ontology view language proposed by Volz, Oberle, and Studer (2003).

3-Level Architecture of Ontologies

Views (also called facets) provide complementary views on the content along different dimensions. They are widely used by database management systems (DBMS). A prominent role in DBMS plays the ANSI 3-schema architecture (Tsichritzis & Klug, 1978) that describes the different views on a database. In the center of the 3-schema architecture is the logical schema, which represents a complete business-oriented view on the information model. The underlying physical schema reflects the physical representation of data according to the requirements of the database. The external schema on top of the architecture represents specific views on the logical schema from the perspective of an individual application.

The 3-schema architecture has a great impact on the concept of data independence. Data independence is the capacity to change physically or logically the schema at one level of a database system without having to change the schema at the next higher level. Only the mapping between the different levels has to be changed. Hence, application programs referring to the higher-level schema need not be changed.

This ANSI reference model can be adapted to the area of ontologies (Figure 1). The ontology concepts and their interrelationships, which are described according to the terms and principles of the domain (the semantic), represent the logical schema. We call this level the *semantic level*. The physical schema represents the syntactic specification of the ontology (e.g., built-in constructs given in RDF(S) or OWL); the *syntactic level*. The external schema is a mapping between the ontology schema and the schema the application is using. In the simplest case this is just a subset of the concepts, attributes, and relations of the ontology. For more complex applications, views are arranged in the

way how the ontology concepts and relationships are viewed by an agent (human or software agent). More precisely, creating such a view over some data on the semantic Web essentially consists of the creation of virtual metadata schemas and descriptions consistent with the agent's perception of those data. We call this level the *application level*.

Whereas the semantic and syntactic level is discussed in the semantic Web, views on ontologies are only marginally regarded. Establishing ontology views offers a number of important advantages:

1. The application level has a major impact on the usability of existing ontology based knowledge systems. Ontology views provide logical independence between the data (the semantics) and the application which uses them. A system's ontology could be changed without having to change external schemas and applications.

2. Ontology views provide a way to change the application context when the domain should remain unchanged. For example, ontology change management could be based on views where each view represents a major change in

Figure 1. Ontologies and ontology views analogous to the ANSI 3-level architecture

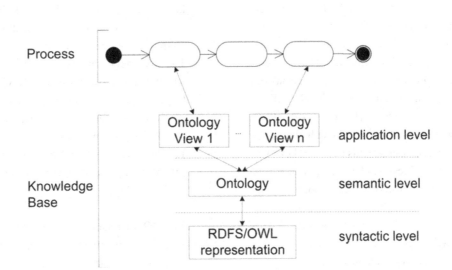

the knowledge model. Different versions of the same ontology can be specified as different views on that ontology. These is especially important for domain ontologies which already reached a very standardized and fixed state and which only have to be marginally adopted for specific applications. Additionally, working with views makes maintenance of ontologies easier when changes are only done on the application level.

3. Another advantage of ontology views is that they describe information according to different contexts. This characteristic can be used to align ontology management systems with process oriented approaches. The kind of working process and its different conditions and dependencies between the single process steps have a major influence on the kind of information a worker requires. This information is described through various ontology views (cf. Figure 1). The ontology views are based on the underlying ontology of the system (of the semantic level).

4. Like in DBMS, views can be used to restrict access to parts of the ontology. Hence, the knowledge base designer is able to control how much information different users can see in the ontology.

Specialized Domain Ontologies

Views on ontologies can only be built for relatively static and constant processes (Volz et al., 2003). Such processes can be found, for example, in medicine (e.g., diagnostic processes in medicine have a common structure). Ontologies belonging to specialized fields of long academic and professional tradition show a high degree of stability (Hyvönen et al., 2003). Although disciplines such as medicine or biology have experienced drastic changes, this does not, however, mean that these novelties completely invalidate earlier conceptual organizations. An ontology about oncology may be affected by scientific advances but it is much less likely that it will be reformed in its totality. This relies on the high level of international consensus that some of these disciplines demonstrate.

Another feature of specialized field ontologies is the high granularity of their content. For example, UMLS (UMLS, 2006) provides a content base with highly specialized terms and documents. Additionally, the sources used for constructing specialized domain ontologies are well structured. Proof-reading and controlled communication lead to a high formality of the sources. This high level of granularity makes it easier to split up knowledge in small, coherent knowledge pieces.

These properties (stability, high granularity, and formality) make specialized domain ontologies a reliable resource for the retrieval of information, as well as a more effective one than its counterparts of nonrestricted fields and those used for common language. In other domains which are not that structured and well defined, the building of views on ontologies and the alignment of views to processes may lead to modeling problems (DynamOnt, 2007).

Specialized field ontologies play a major role in the GRID environment illustrated in the fifth section (Austrian Grid, 2006).

Creating Ontology Views in POVOO

Existing approaches in view based ontology management (Hyvönen et al., 2003) have a number of disadvantages:

- Views are only built on taxonomies: the multi-faceted search just regards concept hierarchies (*subclass_of* or *part_of* relationships) not the entire semantic relationships of an ontology.
- The taxonomies are built on hierarchy rules which tell how to construct the taxonomies. In the mentioned approaches, the taxonomies are built on simple Java applications and are therefore hard to maintain.
- The graphical user interfaces (GUIs) are not suitable for large ontologies with various views on the ontology.

In POVOO, we regard ontology views not only as a set of simple taxonomies. In our approach a view consists of various concepts, attributes and relationships which themselves build an ontology. The querying is therefore not restricted to a set of hierarchical ordered concepts but considers the entire semantic dependencies of concepts.

In general, views are built in two ways: (1) by explicitly defining the structure or (2) by composing the structure implicitly as the result set of a query. Based on these modeling conventions, in POVOO, views on ontologies are created in two ways:

- Manually by using an editor: this editor allows the integration of different classification schemas into the ontology as well as various relationships between the concepts. The editor will be integrated in the Protégé ontology editor framework (Protégé, 2007).
- With the help of semantic Web querying languages, for example, RDQL (RDF Query Language) (Seabourne, 2004) and OWL-QL (OWL Query Language) (Fikes, Hayes, & Horrocks, 2003).

The connection of process modeling and ontology views disburdens the user from choosing the right facets in the querying process. POVOO automatically identifies the necessary ontology views for the given process step, expands the user query, and displays the result set according to this view. For example, when searching for medical reports one gets an anatomical ordering during the anamnesis process, whereas the same reports are relevant in a temporal ordering when preparing a surgery. Due to traceability reasons a user can always switch to a non-view-based search. The result set is then presented according to the underlying ontology of the information system.

INTEGRATING PROCESS MODELS AND ONTOLOGIES

When integrating structural and behavioral system aspects into an information system it is necessary to know (a) which processes should be performed, (b) who is responsible for certain tasks, (c) which kind of information is needed, and (d) which resources are used or produced by the business process.

These different viewpoints are regarded in various business process engineering models. For example, architecture of integrated information systems (ARIS) (Scheer, 1992), a well-known method in the German speaking part of Europe for analyzing processes distinguishes between a workflow model, functions, data, and data flows as well as organizational units.

In addition, ADONIS follows a very similar approach (ADONIS, 2006). It assumes that a company can be characterized via four parameters: products, business processes, organizational units, and information technology (cf. Figure 2). A company has to decide which kind of products or services they want to offer and how they can realize them (that means they have to design the business process). The products/services are developed in a business process by human resources who play a specific role in the organization. Information technology supports the execution of the business processes by providing appropriate tools to the employees and supporting the users in getting the right information at the right time. For years, organizations used workflow management systems (WfMS) to describe and execute business processes. Examples for WfMS are SAP Business Workflow (SAP, 2006), or IvyGrid (IvyGrid, 2006).

Figure 2. Four parameters of a company (ADONIS, 2006)

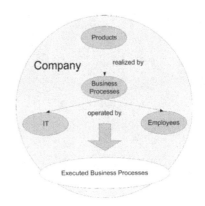

POVOO maintains the mentioned four viewpoints and connects them with the help of ontology views. In POVOO ontologies are used to represent the information model of a company's knowledge base. The information model (the ontology) is the central model for which various ontology views are built in order to connect all other models together (cf. Figure 3). The workflow or process models are based on existing process modeling languages. Analogously, this is true for the management and resource models.

In the first phase of our work we will place emphasis on the integration of ontologies and workflow models; in later stages we will also integrate the used resources (e.g., lexicons) and the responsibilities of the users in the process (their position in the organization). Ontology views are strongly affected by existing authentication and authorization structures within an organization. The ontology designer has to control how much information is presented to the users and which resources they are allowed to use.

POVOO Querying Mechanisms

With POVOO a user has the opportunity to search for relevant information in two ways. First, by using a simple keyword based search mechanism, and second, with the help of views on ontologies. The search mechanism then regards the certain role a user is playing when acting in a process. For example, in a medical environment a user may be a surgeon, an internist, a nursery, and so forth, who plays a certain role in the process. In the first phase of a process one may need more generic information including only generic knowledge bases, whereas in subsequent process steps one may need a more specialized view on the ontology, including more specialized knowledge bases.

Figure 4 shows a possible scenario where different views provide different result sets for the same user query within a business process. The views are built on the same ontology. Within a view the structure of

Figure 3. Ontology views for integrating information, business process, organizational unit, and resource model

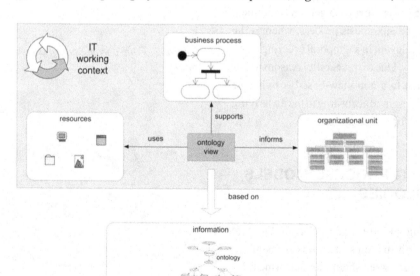

Figure 4. View-based query process in POVOO

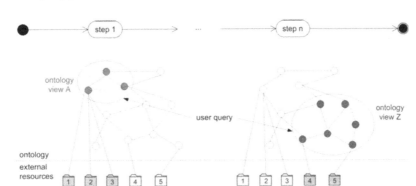

the ontology may be changed, for example, a new or existing concept is added or deleted, or the relationships between concepts are changed.

In the example on the left side in Figure 4, ontology view A is used to create the result set of a user query. Due to the modeled structure for the specific working context of step 1 only the documents 1, 2, and 3 are presented as result set to the user. By contrast, the query result set based on the view on the right side contains documents 4 and 5. Documents 1 to 3 are not regarded in the current working process step n.

For a better understanding of the presented query result, the result entries are organized according to the structure of the current ontology view. Additionally, for traceability reasons the user can at any time switch to the underlying ontology.

Connecting Ontologies with Process Modeling Techniques

In order to connect ontologies with process modeling techniques, we rely on existing process modeling languages described in the second section. It is more efficient to use established de facto standards instead of introducing another new process modeling language, which then may be perfectly suitable for aligning process models with ontologies, but which has no acceptance and no support in existing management tools.

Figure 5 shows the connection between processes and ontology views. In Figure 5, a certain business process represented with the modeling language EPC (event-driven process chains) is connected with an ontology view. EPC is an important aspect of the ARIS model and connects all other views. It describes the dynamics of the business process. Therefore, it is possible to identify a user's role, the triggering event of a certain process step (in EPC this is modeled by using "functions") and the generated events. If the user acts in this specific role for this specific function the querying mechanisms are based on the given ontology view.

In the shown example event e1 causes a resource (e.g., a user) to perform function f1. The resource acts in the specific role r1. Given these facts, the Information Retrieval (IR) system now knows that for f1 and r1 ontology view z has to be used to create a specific result set. According to the results of function f1 event e2, e3 or e4 is produced.

The IR mechanism of POVOO is independent of the granularity of the modeled business processes (for example, when a business process is ordered into task and subtasks within a task ontologies). Ontology views can be aligned to tasks at any hierarchical level in the task ontology. POVOO only has to know which kind of task should currently be supported and which role a user plays within this task.

Figure 5. Example connection EPC with views

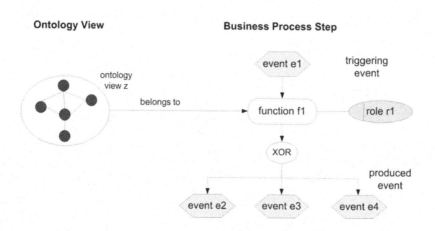

POVOO uses XML to link ontology views with process models. EPC diagrams can be represented in the vendor neutral XML based exchange format event driven process chain markup language (EPML) (Mendling & Nüttgens, 2002). EPML provides standardized tags for the main EPC elements. Ontology views are modeled with the Web ontology language OWL, which is itself an XML format (Dean , & Schreiber, 2004).

BUSINESS INTERACTION: THE NEW OLD CHALLENGE

Business interaction, one of the most important consequences of business process management, does not only mean to use a framework which allows to share and reuse data in the form of business-to-business communication having been the main challenge for the last two decades. In order to reach the global goal of autonomous business interaction beside electronic data interchange (EDI), in most cases realized as point to point communication, also business processes concerning *two dimensions* have to be considered.

First, business processes within the boundaries of an enterprise and second, business processes across application and enterprise boundaries.

The efficient realization of this challenge requires a homogeneous communication platform which is able to integrate heterogeneous applications and data structures, regardless if they are part of one or several enterprises. For this purpose, POVOO uses a Grid infrastructure as underlying technology. The key advantages of using Grid technology in this context is on the pragmatic side that it is based on standards and on the innovative side that it allows to establish virtual organizations covering business processes and their data flows within a homogenous environment.

Focusing on the data interchange problem we developed Grid semantic data access middleware (G-SDAM) (Austrian Grid, 2006), which allows a user to integrate multiple data sources providing data stored in various different ways (relational databases, file systems, locally available external resources such as FTP-repositories, remote mount points, etc.). G-SDAM, for example, can be used in combination with Globus (Globus, 2006) in order to allow Grid nodes to access G-SDAM data sources (Blöchl, Langegger,

Gruberz, & Wöß, 2006). Because data sources need not necessarily to be also Grid nodes, G-SDAM can also be used to bridge those other data sources into the Grid.

For the registration of a local data node (LDN) at a global repository node (GRN), local data schemas (e.g., relational schema, ontologies, directory metadata, etc.) are mapped to a global common ontology database featuring various domain and subontologies for all application domains that become relevant in a G-SDAM overlay. A global data structure (GDS) and a global ontology, respectively, are needed to map and to associate the LDS and the GDS allows the mapping or transformation of data from two or more LDNs. All participating LDN declare mapping rules and possibly also transformation rules corresponding to the GDS. Hence, queries to be executed are formulated in SPARQL according to this global ontology. G-SDAM selects all relevant data sources, generates local schema-specific queries, transforms local results to global instances, and supplies a reference to the merged result set on the GRN to the query client.

In the POVOO scenario virtual organizations can be established as business processes over several enterprise applications or over multiple enterprises. In any case a single unit (application or enterprise) is represented by an ontology view which is set equivalent to a domain ontology in G-SDAM (cf. Figure 6). Hence, in G-SDAM a POVOO's ontology view is implemented as LDN. In order to build up a virtual inter-organizational business process those LDNs have to be registered at the GRN. Consequently, G-SDAM as underlying communication infrastructure provides seamless data interchange mechanisms which are the prerequisite for efficient business integration purposes.

Figure 7 shows an exemplary scenario with different data sources providing environmental data. Solid lines show links between Grid nodes; dot-dashed lines show links from the GRN to LDNs. A scientist at a workstation which is part of the Grid (bottom of Figure 7) is able to compose a query to fetch, for example, all available air temperature and humidity records for a specific location for a specific time period. The

Figure 6. Virtual inter-organizational business process enabled by G-SDAM

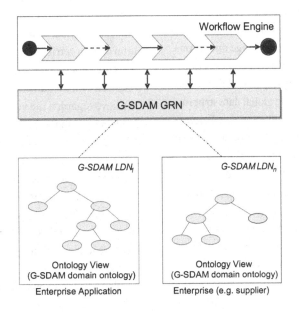

Figure 7. Environmental data integration with the G-SDAM Grid data middleware

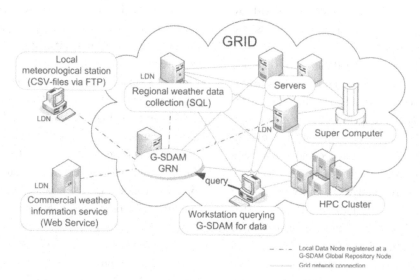

result set of this query is collected from data sources which are spread over different organizational units represented by LDNs.

G-SDAM as Grid data middleware therefore fulfills one of the main requirements of cooperative applications and companies. To allow the specification of workflows based on G-SDAM, different applications which are part of a business process are represented by a LDN (cf. Figure 6). A workflow in this context is a sequence of two or more data interchange operations. Data of a specific application is retrieved by a query operation. The result set of the query is transformed according to the specification of the global data structure (GDS) which has a semantic mediation role between the source and the destination application both acting as *step n* and *step n+1* of a specific workflow.

For further development it is planned to extend G-SDAM with a workflow engine as a direct link to POVOO. Consequently, this is an important step to machine-based interpretation of processes and, ultimately, autonomous operation in order to reach the global goal of autonomous business interaction.

CONCLUSION AND FURTHER RESEARCH

Context aware systems pose a major challenge for existing business and information engineering methods. In this chapter a new approach to integrate ontology-based information systems with business process engineering have been introduced. We have shown how process oriented views on ontologies can improve the information retrieval process by considering a user's working process and the corresponding information required by a user during certain tasks in this process. We have regarded the various viewpoints on business models (information model, resources, organizational units, and business processes) and how they affect the retrieval mechanism. Thus, POVOO better supports the users in querying information.

Throughout the use of commonly accepted modeling standards for ontology and business engineering we have made sure that our model can be realized with existing management tools. Furthermore, we have illustrated how ontology views make maintenance of ontology based knowledge bases easier.

Nevertheless, we have argued that views on ontologies can only be built for relatively static and constant processes which can be found, for example, in medicine. Additionally, the used ontologies must reach a high degree of stability.

A Grid infrastructure is the underlying technological basis, which is implemented using the semantic data integration middleware G-SDAM. This is important to be able to build up inter-organizational cooperations as well as virtual organizations with seamless data interchange facilities and subsequently to enable enterprise and application over-spanning business processes.

Further work will focus on the development of a workflow engine which is the missing link between POVOO and G-SDAM. Moreover, the extension with context awareness features is expected as optimization towards automatically interpretable business processes.

REFERENCES

Abecker, A., Metzas, G., Legal, M., Ntioudis, S., & Papavassiliou, G. (2001). Business-process oriented delivery of knowledge through domain ontologies. In *Proceedings of 2nd International Workshop on Theory and Applications of Knowledge Management*, Munich, Germany.

ADONIS©. *The business process management tool.* (2007) BOC Information Technologies Consulting GmbH. Retrieved June 24, 2007, from http://www.boc-eu.com/

Austrian Grid. (2006). Project funded by the bm:bwk (Federal Ministry for Education, Science and Culture). Austria. Retrieved June 24, 2007, from http://www.austriangrid.at/

Battle, S., Bernstein, A., Boley, H., Grosof, B., Gruninger, M., & Hull, R. et al. (2005). *SWSF -Semantic Web Services Framework.* W3C Member Submission 9. Retrieved June 24, 2007, from http://www.w3.org/Submission/SWSF/

Benjamins, V.R., Nunes de Barros, L., & Valente, A. (1996). Constructing planners through problem-solving methods. In *Proceedings of the 10th Banff Knowledge Acquisition for Knowledge-Based Systems Workshop,* Banff, Canada.

Bichler, P., Preuner, G., & Schrefl, M. (1997). Workflow transparency. Advanced Information Systems Engineering. In *Proceedings of the 9th International Conference on Advanced Information Systems Engineering,* Barcelona, Spain.

Blöchl, M., Langegger A., Gruber G., & Wöß, W. (2006). G-SDAM – seamless semantic data interchange for grid computing. In *Proceedings of the 1st Austrian Grid Symposium, OCG Österreichische Computer Gesellschaft* (Vol. 210), Austria.

Brauer, W., Reisig, W., & Rozenberg, G. (1987). Petri Nets: Central models and their properties. *Advances in Petri Nets. Lecture Notes in Computer Science, 254,* 338-358.

Business Process Management Initiative (2007). *Business Process Modeling Language (BPML).* Retrieved June 24, 2007, from http://www.bpmi.org/BPML.htm

Dean, M., & Schreiber, G. (Eds.) (2004). *Web Ontology Language OWL.* W3C Recommendation. Retrieved June 24, 2007, from http://www.w3.org/TR/owl-ref/

Drumm, C., Lemcke, J., & Namiri, K. (2006). Integrating semantic Web services and business process management: A real use case. In *Proceedings of the Workshop on Semantics for Business Process Management. 3rd European Semantic Web Conference 2006,* Budva, Montenegro.

DynamOnt. (2007). *DynamOnt: Methodology for dynamic ontology creation.* Project funded by the Austrian Federal Ministry bm:vit (FIT-IT Semantic Systems programme). Retrieved June 24, 2007, from http://dynamont.factlink.net/

Fikes, R., Hayes, P., & Horrocks, I. (2003). *OWL-QL – A language for deductive query answering on the semantic Web.* Knowledge Systems Laboratory. CA: Stanford University.

Georgakopoulos, D., Hornick, M., & Sheth, A. (1995). An overview of workflow management: From process modeling to workflow automation infrastructure. *International Journal of Distributed and Parallel Databases, 3*(2), 119-153.

Globus ©. Project page. Retrieved June 24, 2007, from http://www.globus.org

Gruber, T.R. (1993). A translation approach to portable ontology specifications. *International Journal of Knowledge Acquisition, 5*(2), 199-220.

Guarino, N., Masolo, C., & Vetere, G. (1999). Ontoseek: Content-based access to the Web. *International Journal of IEEE Intelligent Systems, 14*(3), 70-80.

Hyvönen, E., Saarela, S., & Viljanen, K. (2003). Ontogator, combining view- and ontology based search with semantic browsing. In *Proceedings of the International SEPIA Conference,* Helsinki, Finland.

IvyGrid ©. Project page. Retrieved June 24, 2007, from http://www.workflowdownload.com/workflow/ivygrid.htm

Khan, L. (2000). *Ontology-based information selection.* Doctoral dissertation, Department of Computer Science, University of Southern California.

Klein, M., Fensel, D., Kiryakov, A., & Ognyanov, D. (2002). Ontology, versioning and change detection on the Web. In *Proceedings of the 13th International Conference on Knowledge Engineering and Knowledge Management,* Siguenza, Spain.

Luckeneder, T., Steiner, K., & Wöß, W. (2001). Integration of topic maps and databases: Towards efficient knowledge representation and directory services. In *Proceedings of the 12th International Conference on Database and Expert Systems Applications,* Munich, Germany.

Magkanaraki, A., Tannen, V., Christophides, V., & Plexousakis, D. (2003). Viewing the semantic Web through RVL lenses. In *Proceedings of the 2nd International Semantic Web Conference,* Sanibel Island, U.S.

Mäkelä, E., Hyvönen, E., & Sidoroff, T. (2005). View-based user interfaces for information retrieval on the semantic Web. In *Proceedings of the 4th International Semantic Web Conference*, Galway, Ireland.

Martin, D., Burstein, M., Hobbs, J., Lassila, O., McDermott, D., & McIlraith, S, et al. (2004).OWL-S: Semantic Markup for Web Services. W3C Member Submission. Retrieved June 24, 2007, from http://www.w3.org/Submission/OWL-S/

Mendling, J., & Nüttgens, M. (2004). Exchanging EPC business process models with EPML. In *Proceedings of the 1st GI Workshop XML4BPM - XML Interchange Formats for Business Process Management,* Marburg, Germany.

METEOR-S. *Semantic Web services and processes.* Project at the LSDIS Lab, University of Georgia. Retrieved June 24, 2007, from http://lsdis.cs.uga.edu/projects/meteor-s/

Mönch, E. (2003). SemanticMinerTM: Ein integratives Ontologie-basiertes Knowledge Retrieval System. In *Proceedings of Workshop Ontologie-basiertes Wissensmanagement. 2. Konferenz Professionelles Wissensmanagement - Erfahrungen und Visionen,* Swiss.

OML: Object Management Group. *UML - unified modeling language.* Retrieved June 24, 2007, from http://www.uml.org/

Pease, A. (1998). The warplan: A method independent plan schema. In *Proceedings of the AI Planning System 1998, Workshop on Knowledge Engineering and Acquisition for Planning* (Tech. Rep. WS-98-03). Menlo Park, CA: The AAAI Press.

Petri, C.A. (1962). *Kommunikation mit Automaten.* Doctoral dissertation, Institut für Instrumentelle Mathematik, Bonn, Germany.

Pollitt, A.S. (1998). The key role of classification and indexing in view-based searching. *International Journal of International Cataloguing and Bibliographic Control, 27*(2), 37-40.

Pollitt, A.S., Ellis, G.P., & Smith, M.P. (1994). HIBROWSE for bibliographic database. *International Journal of Information Science, 20*(6), 413-426.

Protégé ©. (2007) *Project page.* Retrieved June 24, 2007, from http://protege.semanticweb.org

SAP (2007) *SAP Business Workflow: Project page.* Retrieved June 24, 2007, from http://www.sap.com/platform/netweaver/index.epx

Scheer, A.W. (1992). Architektur integrierter Informationssysteme. Berlin/Heidelberg, Germany: Springer Verlag.

Seabourne, A. (2004). *RDQL - A Query Language for RDF.* W3C Member Submission. Retrieved June 24, 2007, from http://www.w3.org/Submission/2004/SUBM-RDQL-20040109/

SQL (2007). *SQL - Structured Query Language.* Retrieved June 24, 2007, from http://www.sql.org/

Staud, J. (2001) *Geschäftsprozessanalyse: Ereignisgesteuerte Prozessketten und objektorientierte Geschäftsprozessmodellierung für Betriebswirtschaftliche Standardsoftware.* Berlin, Germany: Springer Verlag.

Tate, A. (1998). Roots of SPAR - shared planning and activity representation. *International Journal of The Knowledge Engineering Review, 13*(1), 121-128.

Tsichritzis, D., & Klug, A. (1978). The ansi/x3/sparc/dbms framework. Report of the Study Group on Database Management Systems. *International Journal of Information Systems, 3*(3), 173-191.

UMLS (2007) *UMLS – unified medical lnguage system.* Retrieved June 24, 2007, from http://www.nlm.nih.gov/research/umls/

Volz, R., Oberle, D., & Studer, R. (2003). Views for light-weight Web ontologies. In *Proceedings of the ACM Symposium on Applied Computing,* New York.

Workflow management coalition, terminology & glossary. (1999). Document Number WFMC-TC-1011, Document Status - Issue 3.0. Retrieved June 24, 2007, from http://www.wfmc.org/standards/docs/TC-1011_term_glossary_v3.pdf

Lausen, H., Polleres, A., & Roman, D. (Eds.) (2005). *WSMO - Web service modeling ontology.* W3C Member Submission 3. Retrieved June 24, 2007, from http://www.w3.org/Submission/WSMO/

Topicmaps.org (2000) *XML topic maps (XTM) 1.0.* TopicMaps. Org. Specification. Retrieved June 24, 2007, from from http://www.topicmaps.org

Chapter XXI
Ontology–Based Partner Selection in Business Interaction

Jingshan Huang
University of South Carolina, USA

Jiangbo Dang
Siemens Corporate Research, USA

Michael N. Huhns
University of South Carolina, USA

ABSTRACT

Traditional businesses are finding great advantages from the incorporation of e-business capabilities, especially for participation in the global economy, which is inherently open and dynamic. This imposes a requirement that businesses must coordinate with each other if they are to be most efficient and successful. To aid in this coordination and achieve seamless and autonomic interoperation, e-business partners are chosen to be represented by service agents. However, before agents are able to coordinate well with each other, they need to understand each others' service descriptions. Ontologies developed by service providers to describe their service can render help. Unfortunately, due to the heterogeneity implicit in independently designed ontologies, distributed e-businesses will encounter semantic mismatches and misunderstandings. We introduce a compatibility vector system, created upon a schema-based ontology-merging algorithm, to determine and maintain ontology compatibility, which can be used as a basis for businesses to select candidate partners with which to interoperate.

INTRODUCTION

Because of its potential to provide new opportunities and unparalleled efficiencies, e-business is increas-ingly being utilized by enterprises. Broadly speaking, e-business can be regarded as any business process that relies on an automated information system, which typically incorporates Web-based technologies. The

Web-based technologies within e-business enable companies to link their internal and external data processing systems in more efficient and flexible ways, so that they can be more agile and responsive to their customers.

E-business is usually conducted using the dynamic environment of the Internet and the World-Wide Web. Therefore, to introduce agents into e-business, that is, to represent services or business partners by agents, might increase the extent to which the data process is automated. This possible advantage results from agents' autonomy and proactiveness.

It has been discovered that exposing formerly internal activities to external business collaborators can yield increased value. Although there is value in accessing the service provided by a single agent through a semantically well-founded interface, greater value is derived through enabling a flexible composition of e-businesses, which not only creates new services, but also potentially adds value to existing ones (Singh & Huhns, 2005). As the first step of communication and integration of e-business activities, mutual understanding of semantics among services plays an important role in the composition process.

An ontology serves as a declarative model for the knowledge and capabilities possessed by an agent or of interest to an agent. It forms the foundation upon which machine-understandable service descriptions can be obtained and, as a result, it makes automatic coordination among agents possible. By providing a more comprehensible and formal semantics, the use of and reference to ontologies can help the functionalities and behaviors of agents to be described, advertised, discovered, and composed by others. Eventually, these agents would be able to interoperate with each other, even though they have not been designed to do so.

However, because it is impractical to force all agents to adopt a global ontology that describes every concept that is or might be included as part of their services, ontologies from different agents typically have heterogeneous semantics. Due to this basic characteristic, agents need to reconcile ontologies and form a mutual understanding when they interact with each other. Only via this means will agents be able to comprehend and/or integrate the information from different sources and enhance process interoperability thereafter.

In this chapter, we focus on an important but mostly neglected research topic—how to select suitable business partners with which to interact. More compatible ontologies are likely to yield better understanding among the partners. In this sense, ontology compatibility is used as a basis for businesses to select candidate partners. Based on this insight, we design a compatibility vector system built upon an ontology-merging algorithm to measure and maintain ontology compatibility.

RELATED WORK

Related Work in Ontology Matching

The need for automatic or semi-automatic mapping, matching, and merging of ontologies from different sources has prompted considerable research, such as GLUE (Doan et al., 2003), PROMPT (Noy & Musen, 2000), Cupid (Madhavan, Bernstein, & Rahm, 2001), COMA (Do & Rahm, 2002), Similarity Flooding (Melnik, Garcia-Molina, & Rahm, 2002), S-Match (Giunchiglia, Shvaiko, & Yatskevich, 2005), and Puzzle (Huang, Zavala, Mendoza, & Huhns, 2005). Here we briefly describe these systems. The more detailed information about their comparisons can be found in our other publications about ontology-matching algorithms, http://www.cse.sc.edu/~huang27/paper/JPCC.pdf, for example.

PROMPT is a tool that uses linguistic similarity matches between concepts for initiating the merging or alignment process and then uses the underlying ontological structures of the Protégé-2000 environment to inform a set of heuristics for identifying further matches between the ontologies. PROMPT has good performance in terms of precision and recall. However, user intervention is required, which is not always available in many applications.

Similarity Flooding utilizes a hybrid matching technique based on a measure of similarity spreading from similar nodes to their adjacent neighbors. Before a fix-point is reached, alignments between nodes are refined iteratively. This algorithm considers only simple linguistic similarity between node names, ignoring node properties and internode relationships.

Cupid combines linguistic and structural schema-matching techniques, as well as the help of a precompiled dictionary. But it can only work with a tree-structured ontology instead of a more general graph-structured one. As a result, there are many limitations to its application because a tree cannot represent multiple inheritance, an important characteristic in ontologies.

COMA provides an extensible library of matching algorithms, a framework for combining results, and an evaluation platform. According to their evaluation, COMA is performing well in terms of precision, recall, and other measures. Although it is a composite schema-matching tool, COMA does not integrate reasoning and machine learning techniques.

S-Match is a modular system into which individual components can be plugged and unplugged. The core of the system is the computation of relations. Five possible relations are defined between nodes: equivalence, more general, less general, mismatch, and overlapping. Giunchiglia et al. (2005) claim that S-Match outperforms Cupid, COMA, and Similarity Flooding in measurements of precision, recall, overall, and F-measure. However, like Cupid, S-Match uses a tree-structured ontology.

GLUE introduces well-founded notions of semantic similarity, applies multiple machine learning strategies, and can find not only one-to-one mappings, but also complex mappings. However, it depends heavily on the availability of instance data. Therefore, it is not practical for cases where there is an insufficient number of instances or no instance at all.

Related Work in Ontology Application in E-Service

The application of ontologies in e-service environments has been studied widely. In Honavar et al. (2001), the authors describe several challenges in information extraction and knowledge acquisition from heterogeneous, distributed, autonomously operated, and dynamic data sources when scientific discovery is carried out in data-rich domains. They outline the key elements of algorithmic and systems solutions for computer-assisted scientific discovery in such domains, including ontology-assisted approaches to customizable data integration and information extraction from heterogeneous and distributed data sources. Ontology-driven approaches to exploratory data analysis from alternative ontological perspectives are also discussed.

An ontology-based information retrieval model for the Semantic Web is presented in Song, Zhang, Xiao, Li, and Xu (2005). The authors generate an ontology through translating and integrating domain ontologies. The terms defined in the ontology are used as metadata to markup the Web's content; these semantic markups are semantic index terms for information retrieval. The equivalent classes of semantic index terms are obtained by using a description logic reasoner. It is claimed that the logical views of documents and user information needs, generated in terms of the equivalent classes of semantic index terms, can represent documents and user information needs well, so the performance of information retrieval can be improved when a suitable ranking function is chosen.

Tijerino, Embley, Lonsdale, Ding, and Nagy (2005) introduce an approach, TANGO, to generate ontologies based on table analysis. TANGO aims to understand a table's structure and conceptual content, discover the constraints that hold between concepts extracted from the table, match the recognized concepts with ones from a more general specification of related concepts, and merge the resulting structure with other similar knowledge representations. The authors claim that TANGO is a formalized method of processing the format and content of tables that can serve to incrementally build a relevant reusable conceptual ontology.

Related Work in Quality of Service

Quality of service (QoS) is becoming a significant factor with the widespread deployment of Web services. By QoS, we refer to the nonfunctional properties of services, such as reliability, availability, and security. Ontology quality consists of many aspects, of which the compatibility is one of the most important, because better compatibility leads directly to better understanding, which is critical during business interactions. Notice that the quality of services themselves is a separate research topic that will not be covered in this chapter.

Bilgin and Singh (2004 proposes a Service Query and Manipulation Language (SWSQL) to maintain QoS-attribute ontologies and to publish, rate, and select services by their functionality as well as QoS properties. Based on SWSQL, they extend the universal description, discovery, and integration (UDDI) registry to a service repository by combing a relational database and an attribute ontology.

Zhou, Chia, and Lee (2004) provide a DAML-QoS ontology as a complement to a DAML-S ontology in which multiple QoS profiles can be attached to one service profile. In addition, they present a matchmaking algorithm for QoS properties.

One widely used QoS attribute is user rating, but it is subjective to the perception of an end user and is limited by the lack of an objective representation of performance history. Kalepu, Krishnaswamy, and Loke (2004) introduce reputation, a composition of user rating, compliance, and verity as a more viable QoS attribute. Ontologies are applied to QoS-aware service selection, execution, and composition. A selected ontology itself can adopt some QoS measures to facilitate mutual ontology understanding as discussed in this chapter.

EXAMPLE SCENARIO AND OUR SOLUTION

A Running Example

An example scenario of the business interaction within an e-business environment can be envisioned as follows. E-business partners are represented by service agents, then:

1. A number of agents form an e-business community (EBC) within which services provided by different agents might be integrated and have the ability to render a more complete and functional service. This integration requires the mutual understanding of the individual ontology underlying each agent.

2. The agents outside this EBC can request help from the community and make use of its services, either the original ones or the integrated one. This request requires not only an understanding of the related ontologies, but also the ability to choose suitable agent(s), especially under the situations where resources are limited.

Consider the travel business as an example. Many Web sites provide services for this business area, for example, Expedia.com, Orbitz.com, and Hotels.com. When a customer makes travel plan, it is very possible that, for some specific dates, one Web site would provide a flight ticket with the lowest price, while another Web site would have the best offer in car rentals, and a third Web site would offer the cheapest hotel reservations. Therefore, it is preferable for the services from all these Web sites to be integrated to render the best vacation package for each customer. On the other hand, some customers might be interested in one service alone, only to buy a flight ticket, for example. In this case, these customers would find it beneficial if there is an agent gathering and comparing information from all related Web sites. In either case, the mutual understanding among agents representing different Web sites is necessary.

Two major problems need to be solved. First, during the formation of an EBC, how can it be ensured that all agents within the community have no problem in understanding each other's ontology? Second, an agent seeking coordination from outside this community would like to choose those agents that understand its ontology best. How can it ensure this selection is a correct one?

SOLUTION OVERVIEW

We design an ontology compatibility vector system to tackle the above challenges. This vector system is built upon an ontology-merging algorithm. Our main idea is: along with the formation of an EBC, we create a center ontology by merging all original ones; then the distances (dissimilarities) from original ontologies to this center are suitably encoded in the compatibility vectors stored in the center. Based on the information contained in the vectors, partners are supposed to understand the ontology from each other without trouble, and the partner from outside this community will have no difficulty in choosing candidate partners that have ontologies with good compatibilities. In addition, these vectors can be adjusted efficiently and dynamically during the period in which the EBC is formed. In the following sections, we will first briefly introduce our algorithm in merging ontologies and then we present the compatibility vector system in detail.

A SCHEMA-BASED ONTOLOGY-MERGING ALGORITHM

Our goal is to develop a methodology for constructing a merged ontology from two original ones. This methodology can then be applied iteratively to merge all original ontologies within an EBC. Our methodology extends the ontology-merging algorithm presented in Huang et al. (2005) and is summarized next.

Top-Level Procedure

The ontology merging is carried out at the schema level. Internally we represent an ontology using a directed acyclic graph $G(V, E)$, where V is a set of ontology concepts (nodes), and E is a set of edges between two concepts, that is, $E = \{(u, v) \mid u, v \in V$ and u is a super-Class of $v\}$. In addition, we assume that all ontologies share "Thing" as a common built-in root. In order to merge two ontologies, G_1 and G_2, we try to relocate each concept from one ontology into the other one. We adopt a breadth-first order to traverse G_1 and pick up a concept C as the target to be relocated into G_2. Consequently, at least one member of C's parent set $Parent(C)$ in the original graph G_1 has already been put into the suitable place in the destination graph G_2 before the relocation of C itself. The following pseudo-code describes this top-level procedure, whose time complexity is $O(n^2)$, with n the number of concepts in the resultant merged ontology.

Input: Ontologies G_1 and G_2
Output: Merged Ontology G_2

```
begin
        new location of G₁'s root = G₂'s root
        for each node C (except for the root) in G₁
                Parent(C) = C's parent set in G₁
                for each member pᵢ in Parent(C)
                        pⱼ = new location of pᵢ in G₂
                        relocate(C, pⱼ)
                end for
        end for
end
```
Top-Level Procedure - merge(G_1, G_2)

Relocate Function

The *relocate* function in the top-level procedure is used to relocate C into a subgraph rooted by p_j. The main idea is: try to find the relationship between C and p_j's direct child(ren) in the following descending priorities:

equivalentClass, superClass, and subClass. Because equivalentClass has most significant and accurate information, it is straightforward that equivalentClass has been assigned the highest priority. For superClass and subClass, since we adopt a top-down procedure to relocate concepts, the former has been given a higher priority than the latter. If we cannot find any of these three relationships, the only option for us is to let C be another direct child of p_j.

Extensions to Puzzle

In this chapter, two extensions have been applied to Puzzle system. The purpose is to increase the performance of this ontology-merging algorithm.

1.   Enriched Contextual Matching

relocation value $= w_{linguistic} \times v_{linguistic} + w_{contextual} \times v_{contextual}$.   (1)

In Huang et al. (2005), Equation (1) is used to figure out the likelihood of correctly relocating a concept. $v_{contextual}$, calculated based on a concept's contextual feature, considers a concept's properties and its *subClassOf* relationship. We enrich the contextual matching by including a concept's other relationships, such as *disjointWith*, *partOf*, and *contains*, and so forth. By taking into account more relationships, we gain more complete semantics of concepts of interest.

2.   Weight Learning through Artificial Neural Networks

In Huang et al. (2005), different weights for the linguistic matching and the contextual matching, that is, $w_{linguistic}$ and $w_{contextual}$, are specified by a developer based on trial-and-error. Here we apply an artificial neural network (ANN) technique to learn these weights. For simplicity, we rewrite $w_{linguistic}$ as w_1, $w_{contextual}$ as w_2, $v_{linguistic}$ as v_1, and $v_{contextual}$ as v_2. Our learning problem is designed as follows.

- Task T: match two ontologies
- Performance measure P: *Precision* and *Recall* with regard to manual matching
- Training experience E: a set of equivalent concept pairs by manual matching
- Target function V: a pair of concepts $\rightarrow \Re$
- Target function representation:

$$\hat{V}(b) = \sum_{i=1}^{2} (w_i v_i)$$

In this learning problem, the hypothesis space is a two-dimensional space consisting of w_1 and w_2. For every weight vector $\vec{w}$ in our hypothesis space, our learning objective is to find the vector that best fits the training examples. We adopt gradient descent (delta rule) as our training rule, and our searching strategy within the hypothesis space is to find the hypothesis, for example, weight vector, that minimizes the training error with regard to all training examples. The training error E and the weight update rule are given in Equations (2) and (3), respectively.

$$E(\vec{w}) \equiv \frac{1}{2} \sum_{d \in D} [\, t_r - o_d) + (t_c - o_d]^{\,2}.$$ (2)

$$\Delta w_i \equiv h \sum_{d \in D} [\, t_r - o_d) + (t_c - o_d]\, v_{id}.$$ (3)

D is the set of training examples; o_d is the output of the network for a specific training example d; h is the learning rate; and v_{id} is the v_i value for d. t_r and t_c are explained here. We have a matrix M recording the relocation values for pairwise concepts, one from G_1, the other from G_2. A given pair of manually matched concepts corresponds to a cell $[i, j]$ in M, and t_r and t_c are the maximum value for row i and column j in M, respectively.

COMPATIBILITY VECTOR SYSTEM

We first create a center ontology, then we calculate the concept distance from original ontologies to this center. Finally, compatibility vectors are created and stored in the center. Notice that this whole process is carried out incrementally, along with the joining of partners into an EBC.

Center Ontology and Concept Distance

1. Formation of a Center

As mentioned before, the center is generated by merging all original ontologies, step by step, as each new partner joins an EBC. At the beginning, when there is only one partner, its ontology is regarded as the center. When new partners join the community, the new ontologies are merged with the current center. The resultant merged ontology is the newly obtained center.

2. Concept Distance Calculation

Being the result of merging original ontologies, the center contains information from all sources. With respect to whether or not a specific original ontology, O_i, understands each concept in the center, there are two situations. The first one is that for one specific concept in the center, O_i can understand it, but possibly with less accurate and/or complete information. The second situation is that O_i is not able to recognize that concept at all. In either case, the concept distance is represented by the amount of information missing, that is, the number of relationships not known in O_i. Equation (4) formalizes the concept distance d.

Figure 1. Graphical representations for O_1 and center$_1$

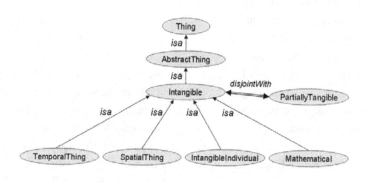

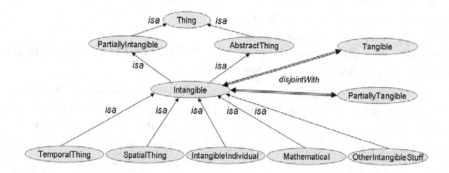

$$d = \sum_{i=1}^{2} (w_i n_i), \qquad (4)$$

where n_1 is the number of *sub/superClassOf* relationships not known in O_i, n_2 is the number of other relationships not known; w_i's are corresponding weights, and $w_1 + w_2 = 1$. Notice that w_i's could be specified by users, or learned through an ANN similar to the one in the sub-section of "Extensions to Puzzle."

Consider the ontologies in Figure 1. For O_1 on the top, concept "Intangible" has one *subClassOf* ("AbstractThing"); four *superClassOf* ("TemporalThing," "SpatialThing," "Mathematical," and "IntangibleIndividual"); and one *disjointWith* ("PartiallyTangible"). For merged *center* on the bottom (note that center is built incrementally, therefore, we have different *center_i*'s), the concept "Intangible" has more information from other ontologies: one more *subClassOf* ("PartiallyIntangible"); one more *disjointWith* ("Tangible"); and one more *superClassOf* ("OtherIntangibleStuff"). Thus, the concept distance from "Intangible" in O_1 to "Intangible" in *center_i* is $w_1 \times 2 + w_2 \times 1$. Notice that one "isa" link in Figure

1 corresponds to a pair of relationships. That is, if C_1 "isa" C_2, then C_1 has a *subClassOf* relationship with C_2, and C_2 has a *superClassOf* relationship with C_1. Also notice that Equation (4) is suitable for both situations, that is, independent of whether or not the original ontology recognizes that concept. For example, if in O_1 there is no concept "Intangible," then the distance becomes $w_1 \times 7 + w_2 \times 2$.

Compatibility Vectors

Inside the center, there is a set of compatibility vectors, one for each original ontology. A compatibility vector consists of a set of dimensions, each corresponding to one concept in the center; therefore, all compatibility vectors have identical number of dimensions, that is, equal to the number of the concepts in the center. Each dimension has three subdimensions. The first subdimension tells us whether or not the original ontology understands this concept; the second subdimension records the concept name in the original ontology if the latter does recognize that concept; and the third subdimension encodes the distance from the concept

Figure 2. Compatibility vectors

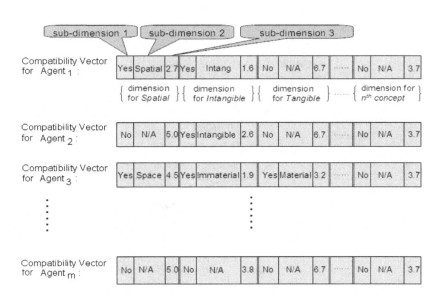

of the original ontology to the concept of the center. An example of compatibility vectors is shown in Figure 2.

For the first concept in the center, "Spatial," *Agent₁* knows it as "Spatial" and has a concept distance of 2.7; *Agent₃* also understands this concept, but with a different name, "Space," and a bigger concept distance of 4.5; neither *Agent₂* nor *Agentₘ* recognizes concept "Spatial," therefore, they have the same concept distance, 5.0.

Dynamically Adjusting Vectors

As mentioned before, when there is only one partner, its compatibility is perfect. In the compatibility vectors stored in the center, each concept distance has a value of zero. However, with the adding of new partners into this EBC, the compatibilities for existing partners might be changed, because newly joined partners could contain ontologies with more accurate and/or complete information.

An example is shown in Figure 3, demonstrating the process of dynamic distance adjustment. After *ontology₁* and *ontology₂* are merged to generate *center₁*, the distance between these two original ontologies and the merged one, *center₁*, is calculated and stored in the compatibility vectors of *center₁*. Upon the joining of *ontology₃* and the generation of *center₂*, the compatibility vector for *center₁* in *center₂* is calculated and integrated with the compatibility vectors for *ontology₁* and *ontology₂* in *center₁*; then we generate the compatibility vectors for *ontology₁* and *ontology₂* in *center₂*. This is explained in detail next.

For example, we have compatibility vectors in both *center₁* and *center₂*. Now we want to update the compatibility vectors in *center₂*. Originally there are

Figure 3. Dynamic adjustment of compatibility vectors

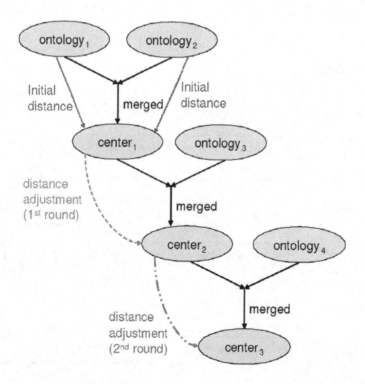

two compatibility vectors in $center_2$: one for $ontology_3$, and the other for $center_1$. The former will remain the same as is, while the latter will be replaced by several new vectors, the number of which is determined by the number of the vectors in $center_1$ (two in our example).

Remember that $center_1$ has one vector for each agent when $center_1$ is generated. Each vector in $center_1$ will be integrated with the vector for $center_1$ in $center_2$, therefore creating a new vector correspondingly in $center_2$. The following procedure describes the generation of such a new vector.

Input:

- compatibility vector v for $center_1$ in $center_2$
- compatibility vector u for $partner_i$ in $center_1$

Output:

- compatibility vector w for $partner_i$ in $center_2$

```
begin
    for each dimension d in v
        yn = d's first subdimension's value
        nm = d's second subdimension's value
        dis = d's third subdimension's value
        create a new dimension nd in w
        if yn = "Yes"
            find in u the dimension od for concept nm
            yn_old = od's first subdimension's value
            nm_old = od's second subdimension's value
            dis_old = od's third subdimension's value
            nd's first subdimension = yn_old
            nd's second subdimension = nm_old
            nd's third subdimension = dis + dis_old
        else (yn = "No")
            nd's first subdimension = yn
            nd's second subdimension = nm
            nd's third subdimension = dis
        end if
    end for
end
```

Pseudocode for New Vector Generation

It is not difficult to figure out that the time complexity for the above procedure is $O(nlogn)$, because there are n dimensions in each vector, requiring n steps for the loop. Within each loop, all steps take constant time, except for the one finding some dimension in u. Suppose in u the dimensions are indexed by the concept names, then a binary search is able to locate a specific dimension within $O(logn)$.

Figure 4 exemplifies how the above pseudocode works. There are two source vectors, u and v, and we traverse the second one, one dimension each time.

1. The values for the first dimension are "Yes," "Intangible," and "2.3." We then find the dimension for "Intangible" in u, and obtain "Yes," "Intang," and "1.6." Finally we calculate the values for the new dimension in the resultant vector w, which are "Yes," "Intang," and "3.9" (the result of 1.6 + 2.3).

2. The values for the second dimension are "Yes," "Tangible," and "1.7." After we obtain the values for dimension "Tangible" in u, that is, "No," "N/A," and "6.7," we figure out the values for the new dimension in w are "No," "N/A," and "8.4" (the result of 6.7 + 1.7).

3. The values for the third dimension are "No," "N/A," and "5.9." We simply copy these three values into the new dimension in w.

4. This continues until we finish the traverse of all dimensions in v.

Utilities of Compatibility Vectors

1. Ontology Understanding Within the EBC

The center maintains the compatibility vectors for all original ontologies; in addition, the vectors themselves contain such information as whether or not

Figure 4. Example of new vector generation

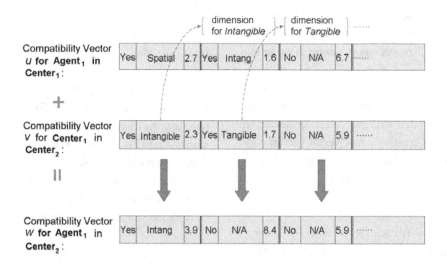

an original ontology understands a specific concept, what is the concept name in the original ontology, and so on. Therefore, if two partners would like to try to understand each other's ontology, they can simply refer to the center and obtain the corresponding compatibility vectors. By this means, compatibility vectors help partners in their mutual understanding of ontological concepts.

2. Partner Selection from Outside the EBC

When a partner from outside this EBC requests for partner(s) to coordinate with, it would like to choose those that understand its ontology best. The requesting partner first compares its own ontology with the center, and then searches in the compatibility vectors to find all partners understanding the concept of its interest. If there is more than one candidate, the coordination request will be sent to those with good compatibilities, that is, with low concept distances. Because the compatibility vectors are stored and maintained by the center, the partners have no way to modify or

manipulate the vectors. In this sense, the selection of partner(s) is objective and without bias.

Features of Compatibility Vectors

1. Correctness of Compatibility Vectors: A Precise Approach

In this section, we prove that our approach obtains correct compatibilities for partners. To record and maintain the proper compatibility of each partner inside an EBC, the key is to obtain a correct center by which to evaluate the distance from the center to each original ontology, and thereby acquire the corresponding compatibility vector. When a new partner joins the EBC, instead of communicating with each existing partner, it only talks with the center. Therefore, if we can prove that the newly merged ontology is a correct new center, the correctness of compatibility vectors is guaranteed.

First, we point out that according to the merging algorithm in the section of "A Schema-Based Ontology-Merging Algorithm," each time we merge two ontologies, the resultant one will contain all information from both original ones. Next, we introduce *Lemma* 1 and *Theorem* 1.

Lemma 1. When we merge two ontologies, A and B, using the algorithm in the section of "A Schema-Based Ontology-Merging Algorithm," the result is the same regardless of whether we merge A into B or merge B into A.

Proof by induction:
- Base Case: Both A and B contain two concepts, that is, besides one common built-in root, "Thing," A contains C_1 and B contains C_2.
  If we merge A into B according to the top-level merging procedure, "Thing" in A is considered equivalent with "Thing" in B; then C_1 is compared with all the direct children of the root in B, in this case C_2, to determine where to put C_1 in B. This is based on the relocate function inside the top-level merging procedure. On the contrary, if we merge B into A, "Thing" in B is considered equivalent with "Thing" in A; then C_2 is compared with C_1 to determine where to put C_2 in A. Obviously, we obtain the same merged ontology in both cases.
- Induction: Assume that Lemma 1 holds for all cases where the numbers of concepts contained in A and B are less than (i+1) and (j+1), respectively. Now consider the case where A and B contain (i+1) and (j+1) concepts, respectively. Suppose the superClass set of the $(i+1)^{\text{th}}$ concept in A, C_{i+1}, is $P_A(C_{i+1})$, and suppose the location of $P_A(C_{i+1})$ in merged ontology M is $P_M(C_{i+1})$. The position of C_{i+1} in M is determined by the relationships between C_{i+1} and all the direct children of $P_M(C_{i+1})$. From the inductive hypothesis we know that $P_M(C_{i+1})$ is identical no matter whether we merge A into B or merge B into A. Therefore, the position of C_{i+1} in M will also be the same in both situations. That is, C_{i+1}, the $(i+1)^{\text{th}}$ concept in A, will be put into the same position in M in both merging orders. Similarly,

the $(j+1)^{\text{th}}$ concept in B will also be put into the same position in M in both merging orders. Therefore, in the case where A and B contain (i+1) and (j+1) concepts, respectively, we still have the same resultant ontology regardless of the merging order taken.

Theorem 1. The final result of merging a number of ontologies is identical no matter in which order the original ontologies are merged using the algorithm in the section of "A Schema-Based Ontology-Merging Algorithm."

Proof by induction:
- Base Case: There are two ontologies to be merged.
  According to Lemma 1, when we merge two ontologies A and B, the result is the same no matter whether we merge A into B, or merge B into A.
- Induction: Assume that Theorem 1 holds for all cases where the number of ontologies to be merged is less than (n+1). Now consider the case where we merge (n+1) ontologies.
  Let the indexes of these ontologies be: 1, 2, ..., (n+1). Consider two arbitrary orders by which we merge these (n+1) ontologies: *order₁* and *order₂*. Suppose the last indexes in *order₁* and *order₂* are i and j, respectively.
  - If i equals j, then the first (n) indexes in *order₁* and *order₂* are the same, just in different orders. We merge the first (n) ontologies to get Merged$_n$. According to the inductive hypothesis, Merged$_n$ in *order₁* is identical with Merged$_n$ in *order₂*. Then we merge Merged$_n$ with the last ontology in both *order₁* and *order₂*, and we will get the same result.
  - If i does not equal j, we mutate the first (n) indexes in *order₁* and make the nᵗʰ index be j; then mutate the first (n) indexes in *order₂* and make the nᵗʰ index be i. Now the first (n-1) indexes in *order₁* and *order₂*

are in common (possibly in different orders), and the last two are (j, i) and (i, j), respectively. Notice that this kind of mutation will not affect the merging result of the first (n) ontologies according to our inductive hypothesis. We then merge the first (n-1) ontologies to get $Merged_{n-1}$. According to the hypothesis, $Merged_{n-1}$ in $order_1$ is identical with $Merged_{n-1}$ in $order_2$. Finally we merge $Merged_{n-1}$ with the last two ontologies in both $order_1$ and $order_2$, and we will get the same result.

2. Complexity of Compatibility Vectors: An Efficient Approach

- The time complexity of establishing an EBC, along with the achievement of a mutual understanding of ontological concepts, is on the order of $O(mn^2)$, with n the number of the concepts in the center, and m the number of original ontologies. The process of creating an EBC is the one to generate a merged center. For the ontology merging, $O(mn^2)$ is needed, because we need to merge m ontologies, and each merging procedure takes time $O(n^2)$ as described in the section of "A Schema-Based Ontology-Merging Algorithm."

- In order to dynamically update the compatibility vectors during the formation of an EBC, extra time will be spent. According to the previous analysis in the subsection of "Dynamically Adjusting Vectors," $O(nlogn)$ is needed for updating one partner, so the extra time for all partners is $O(mnlogn)$. Therefore, the total time complexity of establishing an EBC becomes $O(mn^2 + mnlogn)$, which is still on the order of $O(mn^2)$.

- For partner selection, the time complexity is $O(n^2)$, because we only need to compare the ontology from the requesting partner with the center.

Comparison to Other Vector-Based Approaches

Vector-based approach is widely adopted in ontology matching and text classification area. Some well known systems are summarized in the following.

In Soh (2002) and Soh (2003), description vectors are introduced and adopted in the conceptual learning during ontology matching. A description vector consists of a list of word-frequency pairs. For each word found in all the experience cases describing the same concept, the agent manages to find the word's frequency, and therefore learns the different significance of the words that describe an ontology concept. The vector fields are then fed into an inductive learner that parses the input vectors into a decision tree, which deterministically allocates each example into a semantically unique branch. Finally, these branches are traversed to arrive at a set of rules.

Lacher and Groh (2001) employ machine learning techniques for text categorization. Their methodology is to calculate a representative feature vector for each concept node in an ontology and then to measure similarity of two of those class vectors by a simple cosine measure. The representative feature vector for one concept node is calculated as a modified Rocchio centroid vector. By this means, the representative vector for a concept node represents an average of all documents assigned to that concept node. The feature vectors are extracted from the documents and weighted. That is, a word-count feature vector is created and the features are weighted with a TF/IDF weighting scheme (Term Frequency/Inverse Document Frequency). In essence, vectors are computed from the instance data.

Williams (2004) tackles the issue of sharing meaning in a multiagent system through ontology learning. The author describes how agents learn representations of their own ontologies using a machine learning algorithm and then seek to locate and/or translate semantic concepts by using examples of their concepts to query each other. In this chapter, a semantic concept comprises a group of semantic objects that define each token, that is, word and HTML tag from the Web page, as a boolean feature. The entire collection of Web pages that were categorized by a user's bookmark hierarchy is tokenized to find a vocabulary of unique tokens. This vocabulary is then used to represent a Web page by a vector of ones and zeroes corresponding to the presence or absence of a token in a Web page.

Our compatibility vector system is quite different from the systems mentioned above.

- Our system is based on ontology schemas (structures) alone, aiming to avoid the difficulty in getting enough/good quality instance data from real-world ontologies. Ontology schemas usually have a lot more varieties than instance data; we are therefore dealing with a more challenging problem than those algorithms that make use of instances as well.

- Our focus is on the comparison between original ontologies and the merged center ontology. By considering both concept names and concept relationships, we aim to include more complete semantics for concepts of interest.

- The information contained in our vector system is in great details. This will facilitate the mutual understanding among agents, by simply referring to the center ontology for the corresponding vectors.

EXPERIMENT RESULTS

Test Ontologies

We take ten *real-world* ontologies, created and maintained by professionals, as our test ontologies:

1. terror: http://www.mindswap.org/2003/owl/swint/terrorism
2. travel: http://opales.ina.fr/public/eon2003/Travel-OilEdExportRDFS.rdfs
3. tour: http://homepages.cwi.nl/_troncy/DOE/eon2003/Tourism-OilEdExportRDFS.rdfs
4. space: http://212.119.9.180/Ontologies/0.3/space.owl
5. priv: http://www.daml.org/services/owl-s/security/privacy.owl
6. ops: http://moguntia.ucd.ie/owl/Operations.owl
7. obj: http://www.flacp.fujitsulabs.com/tce/ontologies/2004/03/object.owl
8. swap: http://svn.mindswap.org/pychinko/pychinko/allogtests/mindswapRealized.rdf
9. mgm: http://ontologies.isx.com/onts/2005/02/isxbusinessmgmtont.owl
10. gfo: http://www.onto-med.de/ontologies/gfo.owl

These ten ontologies are all in "Business" domain, specified by OWL. Their characteristics are summarized in Table 1.

Table 1. Characteristics of test ontologies

Features	terror	travel	tour	space	priv	ops	obj	swap	mgm	gfo
Max Depth of Ontology	5	7	6	8	5	8	8	7	9	11
Number of Concepts	27	51	53	90	26	91	38	61	72	127
Number of Relationships	41	47	48	158	38	139	70	87	109	162
super/subClassOf Relationships	29	36	33	115	31	110	57	64	75	117
Percentage of *super/subClassOf*	70%	77%	68%	73%	81%	79%	82%	73%	69%	72%

Experiments on Merging Algorithm

We randomly pick up an order to merge these 10 ontologies, and we compare the results from our merging algorithm with those from a manual matching by three ontology experts. We then evaluate on both *Precision* and *Recall* measures and plot the results in Figure 5. "Precision 1" and "Recall 1" are for the original algorithm in Huang et al. (2005); they range from 73% to 83%, and 66% to 81%, respectively. "Precision 2" and "Recall 2" are for the extended version in this chapter, range from 80% to 88%, and 75% to 86%, respectively. After the extensions discussed in the subsection of "Extensions to Puzzle," *Precision* and *Recall* have an average increase of 6.9% and 8.3%, respectively.

Experiments on Compatibility Vectors

We first fix one original ontology (randomly chosen) as the one from the coordination-requesting partner, and then simulate an EBC out of the remaining nine ontologies. In our first setting, the requesting ontology interacts with a randomly chosen ontology; while in our second setting, this interaction always happens with the ontology with the best compatibility, according to concept distances calculated. We switch the fixed ontology from the first one to the tenth one, calculate the average values of *Precision* and *Recall* for all settings, and then plot the results in Figure 6. It is clear that, after adopting our compatibility vectors, both measures have been improved. Therefore, in cases where sufficient resources are not available and only a certain number of partners can be chosen for coordination, our approach increases the efficiency by choosing suitable partners.

CONCLUSION

E-business is having a significant impact on the evolution of the Internet. In order to meet the new demands of highly dynamic environments and open e-markets,

Figure 5. Ontology merging results

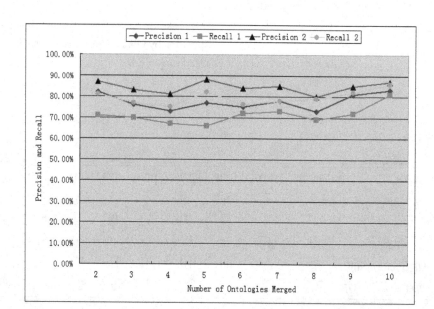

Figure 6. Utility of vectors

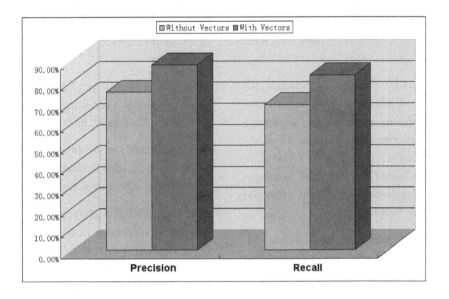

there has been a growing need for e-businesses to coordinate their activities. The first step towards this coordination is for e-business partners to understand each other's service description. Although using ontologies can aid in this understanding, independently designed ontologies usually have heterogeneous semantics, resulting in each partner having its own unique semantics. To tackle this emerging challenge, we present an ontology compatibility vector system as a method to evaluate and maintain ontology compatibilities, thereby handling the problem of how to choose partners with good compatibilities. We not only prove that our approach is both precise and efficient, but also show promising results experimentally.

Some future work is envisioned here: (1) how to handle the vulnerability issue inherent in the centralized solution that our current approach uses, (2) how to update compatibility vectors when existing partners modify their corresponding ontologies, (3) what kind of mechanism is suitable if we simultaneously consider qualities of both ontologies and services, and (4) we plan to design a graphical user interface (GUI) for our algorithm, and we believe that such a front-end would make it easier for a practitioner to use.

ACKNOWLEDGMENT

Thanks to Ning Yang for her effort in helping with the preparation for the final version of this chapter.

REFERENCES

Bilgin, A., & Singh, M. (2004, July). A daml-based repository for qos-aware semantic Web service selection. In *Proceedings of IEEE International Conference on Web Services (ICWS 04)*, San Diego, CA.

Do, H., & Rahm, E. (2002). Coma – a system for flexible combination of schema matching approaches. In *Proceedings of the Twenty-eighth VLDB Conference*, Hong Kong, China.

Doan, A., Madhavan, J., Dhamankar, R., Domingos, P., & Halevy, A. (2003). Learning to match ontologies on the semantic Web. *The VLDB Journal, 12*(4), 303-319. New York, NY: Springer-Verlag.

Giunchiglia, F., Shvaiko, P., & Yatskevich, M. (2005, November). Semantic schemamatching. In *Proceedings of the Thirteenth International Conference on Cooperative Information Systems (CoopIS 05)*, Agia Napa, Cyprus.

Honavar, V., Andorf, C., Caragea, D., Silvescu, A., Reinoso-Castillo, J., & Dobbs, D. (2001, August). Ontology-driven information extraction and knowledge acquisition from heterogeneous, distributed biological data sources. In *Proceedings of the IJCAI-2001 Workshop on Knowledge Discovery from Heterogeneous, Distributed, Autonomous, Dynamic Data and Knowledge Sources*, Seattle, WA.

Huang, J., Zavala, R., Mendoza, B., & Huhns, M. (2005, September). Ontology reconciling agent ontologies for Web service applications. In *Proceedings of Multiagent System Technologies: Third German Conference (MATES 05)*, Berlin, Germany.

Kalepu, S., Krishnaswamy, S., & Loke, S. (2004, July). Reputation = f(user ranking, compliance, verity). In *Proceedings of IEEE International Conference on Web Services (ICWS 04)*, San Diego, CA.

Lacher, M., & Groh, G. (2001, May). Facilitating the exchange of explicit knowledge through ontology mappings. In *Proceedings of 14ᵗʰ International FLAIRS Conference*, Key West, FL.

Madhavan, J., Bernstein, P., & Rahm, E. (2001). Generic schema matching with cupid. In *Proceedings of the Twenty-seventh VLDB Conference*, Roma, Italy.

Melnik, S., Garcia-Molina, H., & Rahm, E. (2002). Similarity flooding: A versatile graph matching algorithm and its application to schema matching. In *Proceedings of the Eighteenth International Conference on Data Engineering (ICDE 02)*, San Jose, CA.

Noy, N., & Musen, M. (2000). Prompt: Algorithm and tool for automated ontology merging and alignment. In *Proceedings of the 17ᵗʰ National Conference on Artificial Intelligence (AAAI 00)*. Menlo Park, CA: AAAI Press.

Singh, M., & Huhns, M. (Eds.). (2005). *Service-oriented computing - semantics, processes, agents* (1ˢᵗ ed.). Wiley, Chichester, England: England Press.

Soh, L.-K. (2002, July). Multiagent distributed ontology learning. In *Working Notes of the second AAMAS OAS Workshop*, Bologna, Italy.

Soh, L.-K. (2003). Collaborative understanding of distributed ontologies in a multiagent framework: Design and experiments. In *Proceedings of the Third International Workshop on Ontologies in Agent Systems (OAS 03)*, Melbourne, Australia.

Song, J., Zhang, W., Xiao, W., Li, G., & Xu, Z. (2005, March). Ontology-based information retrieval model for the semantic Web. In *Proceedings of IEEE International Conference on e-Technology, e-Commerce and e-Service (EEE 05)*, Hong Kong, China.

Tijerino, Y., Embley, D., Lonsdale, D., Ding, Y., & Nagy, G. (2005). Towards ontology generation from tables. *World Wide Web: Internet and Web Information Systems*, 8(3), 261-285.

Williams, A. (2004). Learning to share meaning in a multiagent system. *Autonomous Agents and Multi-Agent Systems*, 8(2), 165-193. The Netherlands: Kluwer Academic Publishers.

Zhou, C., Chia, L., & Lee, B. (2004, July). Daml-qos ontology for Web services. In *Proceedings of IEEE International Conference on Web Services (ICWS 04)*, San Diego, CA.

Chapter XXII
A Language and Algorithm for Automatic Merging of Ontologies

Alma-Delia Cuevas-Rasgado
Instituto Politécnico Nacional, Mexico

Adolfo Guzman-Arenas
Instituto Politécnico Nacional, Mexico

ABSTRACT

Ontologies are becoming important repositories of information useful for business transactions and operations since they are amenable to knowledge processing using artificial intelligence techniques. They offer the potential of amassing large contents of relevant information, but until now the fusion or merging of ontologies, needed for knowledge buildup and its exploitation by machine, was done manually or through computer-aided ontology editors. Thus, attaining large ontologies was expensive and slow. This chapter offers a new, automatic method of joining two ontologies to obtain a third one. The method works well in spite of inconsistencies, redundancies, and different granularity of information.

INTRODUCTION

Computers are no longer isolated devices but they are important to the world-wide network that interchanges knowledge for business transactions. Nowadays, using the Internet to get data, information, and knowledge is a business need.

Most of the important information resources that businessmen require are available through the Internet. Here, machines face the problem of heterogeneous sources. The computer has a hard time finding whether two data representations refer to the same object (a *bill* can be a bank tender or an invoice)[1] because there are no suitable standards in knowledge representation. This chapter addresses this need of businesses and academia.

When businessmen demand answers that require access to several Internet data sources, they have to manually or mentally merge the acquired information in a reasonable way. It would be nice if a computer program helped in this very useful but tedious task. This chapter solves this problem, which has important implications (see the section on "Commercial Areas Ready to Exploit OM").

The Problem to Solve[2]

To merge two data sources in such a way that its common knowledge could be represented and more easily used in further tasks.

Computers represent the information in files, databases, text documents, lists, and so forth. Computer merging of information in databases or in semistructured data, has its own challenges, and will not be addressed here. Merging information stored in documents is done manually, since the computer does not "understand" what a document says. If the information is stored in spreadsheets, merging can be done by a computer-aided person who understands the contents of different cells and their units. Information can also be stored in ontologies and thus be subject to merging. So far, merging of ontologies has been done manually (see the section on "Ontology Merging") using an ontology editor.

Ontology

An ontology is a data structure where information is stored as nodes (representing concepts such as `hammer`, `printer`, `document`, appearing in this chapter in `Courier font`) and relations (representing restrictions among nodes, such as cuts, transcribes, or hair color, appearing in this chapter in Arial Narrow font, as in (`hammer` cuts `wood`), (`printer` transcribes `document`), Figure 9. Usually, the information it stores is "high level" and it is known as *knowledge*. For working purposes, we further restrict this defini-

tion to those data structures compliant with ontology merging (OM) notation (*quo vide*).

Ontologies are useful when arbitrary relations need to be represented; one has more freedom to represent different types of concepts.

Current notations to represent ontologies are DAML+OIL (Connoly et al., 2001), RDF (Manola & Miller, 2004; Asunción & Suárez, 2004) and OWL (Bechnofer et al., 2004). These languages are a notable accomplishment, but some lack certain features:

- A relation can not be a concept. For instance, if color is a relation, it is difficult to relate color to other concepts (such as shape) by using other relations.
- Partitions (subsets with additional properties, see the section on "Contributions of OM Notation") can not be represented.

This chapter offers the *OM notation* to represent ontologies that solves above problems and better represents the semantics involved.

Ontology Merging

Realizing the importance of the problem to solve, different scientists have approached it. Previous works incudes CYC (Lenat & Guha, 1989), whose goal was to represent common sense knowledge in a gigantic hand-built ontology. CYC does not do merging. Prompt (Noy & Musen, 2000), Chimaera (McGuinness, Fikes, Rice, & Wilder, 2000), OntoMerge (Stumme & Maedche, 2001) and ISI (Loom) rely on the user to solve the most important problems found in the process, and are considered non automatic methods. FCA-Merge (Dou, McDermott, & Qi, 2002) and IF-Map (Kalfoglou & Schorlemmer, 2002) require consistent ontologies that are expressed in a formal notation employed in Formal Concept Analysis (Ganter, Stumme, & Wille, 2005) which limits their use. Hcone (Kotis, Vouros, & Stergiou, 2006) uses WordNet and a formal approach to ontology merging. Cuevas-Rasgado (2006) mentions additional previous works.

Our solution to the above problem is the *OM algorithm,* which performs the fusion in a robust[3] consistent,[4] complete,[5] and automatic[6] manner. When compared with fusion done by hand and with current computer-assisted methods, OM does "very good" ($\approx$ 96%, Table 1), but manual methods may achieve 100% accuracy, depending on the user or expert that makes the correct choices, solves contradictions, and eliminates redundancies. OM also fused some ontologies expressed in current ontology languages, hand-translated to OM notation. The results are good (100%, Table 1) but care should be exercised: the ontologies merged contain only shallow information,[9] most are merely a taxonomy.

The section on "OM Notation" explains the OM notation, and the section on "OM Algorithm for Automatic Merging of Ontologies" the OM algorithm. The chapter concludes with examples.

Increased Yield Through Better Processing the Web Resources

This chapter describes important contributions towards the task of obtaining more benefits from Web resources: (1) the OM notation, (2) the OM algorithm, which automatically merges two ontologies, (3) a mapping algorithm among ontologies, called COM (see the section on "The Comparison Function COM"), that finds similarity among concepts belonging to different ontologies, and (4) the use and exploitation of a theory that measures the *confusion* (see the section on "Confusion") in using a symbolic value instead of another (the intended value). This theory solves some inconsistencies arising during the union of ontologies and lets the process proceed further.

In addition to being useful for businesses, ontology merging is an Artificial Intelligence (AI) tool that could harvest the knowledge (in a given area, say, oil production) available in the Web from documents in English and other natural languages, and (if they were translated to our ontology format)[7] automatically produce a new ontology that captures the (total, joint) knowledge available in all these documents. How? By joining consecutively ontology after ontology from those documents. See the section on "Suggestions for Further Work" for uses of this joint knowledge.

Issues, Problems, and Trends

One of the hard problems keeping AI people busy is how to provide the computer with a "deep" or "semantic" understanding of the information it is processing. In order to give it, for instance, the ability to answer complex, nontrivial queries about the information it has. One way is to construct a large ontology, understandable (processable) by machine, where mechanical reasoning could be achieved. Initially, a 10-year project (Lenat & Guha, 1989) was going to build by hand the common sense ontology. As time passed, numerous groups hand-crafted their own ontologies. People wondered how to map a concept from one of these ontologies to the closest concept in another ontology, and Guzman and Olivares (2004) were the first to solve this. OM uses and has improved their COM algorithm. See the section on "The Comparison Function COM". Inspired in COM, Cuevas-Rasgado (2006) reflected that automatic ontology merging was possible and desirable. This chapter presents her work. Until now, merging of ontologies was accomplished with the help of a user that resolved differences and made important decisions.

The trend is now clear: keep improving the merging algorithms, giving them access to "semantic sources of knowledge" (see the section, "Discussion"), and to knowledge previously processed (see the section on "Suggestions for Further Work"), in order to continue adding pieces of knowledge to growing ontology, which could be one day "the ontology of knowledge," much as Wikipedia is now the encyclopedia of knowledge.

Knowledge Support for OM

OM uses some built-in knowledge resources, which help to detect contradictions, find synonyms, and the like. These are:

1. Stop words (in, the, for, this, those, it, and, or...) are ignored form word phrases;

2. It takes into account words that change the meaning of a relation (without, except…);

3. Hierarchies (simplified ontologies, merely trees of concepts where each node is a concept or, if it is a set, its descendants must form a partition of it) represent a taxonomy of related terms, and are used to measure confusion (See the section on "Confusion"), and later can be used for synonym detection. Guzman and Levachkine (2004) explain how to build these hierarchies.

Future additions include using a stemmer, to find the root of words (love, lover, lovingly…), reliance on linguistic resources such as WordNet, use of a dictionary to find synonyms, homonyms, and so forth. The result of previous fusions could also be part of the built-in knowledge base for OM.

OM NOTATION

OM Notation represents ontologies through a structural design with XML-like labels, identifying the concepts and their relations. See Figure 1.

The label of each concept (such as thing) comes after <concept>; the language of the concept's definition (such as English) goes between <language> and </language>; the definition of the concept (such as concrete_object, physical_object) goes between <word> and </word>; the relations of the concept (such as eats) go between <relation> and </relation>. The description of a concept ends in </concept>. Nested concepts (such as physical_object within thing) indicate that physical_object is subordinate (or hyponym) of thing, the precise meaning of this subordination is indicated by <subset> thing </subset> (physical_object ⊂ thing)

Figure 1. Representation of an ontology in OM notation

```
<concept>thing
        <language> English <word>thing, something, object, entity </word> </Language>
        <concept>physical_object
                <language> English <word> concrete_object, physical_object</word> </Language>
                <subset>thing </subset>
                <concept>plant
                        <language> English <word>plant, tree</word> </Language>
                        <subset> physical_object </subset>
                        <concept>fruit
                                <language> English<word>fruit, citric</word> </Language>
                        </concept>
                </concept>
                <concept> human being,
                        <language> English
                        <subset>physical_object </subset>
                        <word> person, people, human being</word></Language>
                        <relation>eats=tropical_fruit, citrus</relation>
                        <relation>Partition=age {0<age<=1 : baby; 1<age<=10 : child;10<age<=17 : puberty; 17<age<=29 :
                        young; 29<age<=59 : mature; age>59 : old;}</relation>
                </concept>
        </concept>
        <concept>abstract_object
                <language> English <word>imaginary object, abstract thing</word> </Language>
                <subset> thing </subset>
                <concept>soul
                        <language> English <word>soul, spirit</word> </Language>
                        <subset> abstract_object </subset>
                </concept>
        </concept>
</concept>
```

The relations expressed by nesting are called implicit relations. Currently, they are member of, part of, subset (represented in this chapter as ⊂), and part* ("one of my domain elements is part of one of my codomain elements," as in country part* continent). The other relations, such as eats, are called explicit. These are known elsewhere as properties or attributes of the concept. Cuevas-Resgado (2006) gives a complete description of the OM notation

In OM Notation, a relation can be n-ary; a relation relates nodes (concepts); a relation can be a concept (a node), too. For example, the Zebra concept has a Color relation that connects to two elements White and Black. Relations can be considered as properties or characteristics of the node or concept where they are defined. Nested concepts imply subordinate relations (see the caption of Figure 1).

Contributions of OM Notation

Most important are:

a.   Ability to represent partitions. A *partition* of a set is a collection of subsets such that any two of them are mutually exclusive, and all are collectively exhaustive. OM can represent partitions, while current ontology languages (DAML, RDF, OWL) can not. For instance, not only male _ person and female _ person are subsets of person, they are a partition of person. Alternatively, the gender of a person will tell us to which of the partitions male _ person or female _ person the person belongs.

b.   A concept also can be a relation. Often, ontologies are represented as a graph $O = (C, R)$ consisting of two *disjoint* sets: C (nodes, or concepts) and R (edges, or relations).[8] Two disadvantages of this visually oriented approach are: all the relations are binary and a concept can not be a relation. In OM, it is possible[9] to add relations *to a relation*, to provide more semantics. For example, one can say Mary Washington mother of George Washington to indicate that Mary is Washington's mother, but mother_of

can be a concept that contains more information, for instance, related to child_of by the relation inverse.[10]

c.   OM's graphs are hypergraphs, since relations are n-ary.

OM ALGORITHM FOR AUTOMATIC MERGING OF ONTOLOGIES

This algorithm fuses two ontologies A and B, building a third ontology $C = A \cup B$ containing the information in A, plus the information in B not contained in A, without repetitions (redundancies) or contradictions.

The information in B not contained in A can be: (1) new nodes, for instance B contains information about dinosaurs, which A lacks; (2) new relations, for instance, B knows that Gabriel García Márquez wrote *The Colonel has Nobody to write to him*, in addition to *One Hundred Years of Loneliness*, already known to A; (3) improved or more precise relations, for instance A knows that Abraham Lincoln was born in United States, while B knows that Lincoln was born in Kentucky; (4) new synonyms in B for current nodes in A enrich C; and (5) relations can be better defined in B, for instance B has a better description of lend money to than A. Thus, the addition of B to A is "carefully done" by OM.

OM proceeds and Cuevas-Rasgado (2006) gives more details:

1.   **C ← A**. Ontology A is copied into C.
2.   **Search in B each concept C_c of C**.[11] This step describes the *deep copy* of a concept.[12] At the start of the search, concept C_c is the root of ontology C. Then, C_c will be each of the descendants of C_c, and so on, so that each of the nodes of ontology C will be visited by C_c.[13] For each C_c, COM looks for the concept that best resembles C_c in B, such concept is called the *most similar concept* in B to C_c, or *cms*. Two cases exist:

a.   If **C_c has a most similar concept** *cms* in B, then:

i. Relations that are synonyms (see the section on "Knowledge Support for OM") are enriched. To enrich a concept C_C is to add to its definition the new words that are in the definition of *cms,* when C_C and *cms* are synonyms. [14]

ii. New relations (including partitions) that *cms* has in *B*, are added to C_C.

1. For each added relation, concepts related by that relation and not present in *C* are copied to *C*. Example: if *cms* color red and concept red is not in *C*, it is copied to *C*, together with its ascendants who are not present in *C*.

   In this step we copy partitions of C_C, if they exist, since they are relations, too.

iii. Inconsistencies between the relations of C_C and those of *cms* are detected.

1. If it is possible, by using confusion (see the section on "Confusion"), to resolve the inconsistency, the correct concepts are added to *C*. For instance, in Contribution g, ontology *A* says AcmeCorp incorporated_in Maryland and *B* says AcmeCorp incorporated_in USA. Since *incorporated_in* can only have a single value, a contradiction is detected and solved, thus AcmeCorp incorporated_in Maryland is added to C_C.

2. When the inconsistency can not be solved, OM rejects the contradicting information in *B*, and C_C keeps the original relation coming from *A*. [21]

iv. Concepts that are descendants of *cms* not present in *C* are copied to *C*, in a superficial manner. [11]

b. **C_C can not find in B a good resemblance**. That is, *B* contains no object *cms* resembling C_C.

i. Take the next descendant of C_C, which will become the new C_C.

ii. Go to step 2 until all the nodes of *C* are visited (including the new nodes that were being superficially added by OM).

The Comparison Function COM

Four cases are used to find *cms* = COM(C_C, *B*), the most similar concept in ontology *B* to the concept C_C in ontology *C*. Guzman and Olivares (2004) explain COM in detail.

CASE A. A concept C_B having a definition similar to the definition of C_C is found in *B*, and the parent[o] of C_B has a definition matching the definition of the parent[15] of C_C. In this case, COM returns *cms* = C_B. See figure 2.

CASE B. C_C does not find a similar concept in *B* matching C_C, but the parent (let us call it P_C) of C_C finds a match with a node P_B in *B*. Then, we search for a son (or grandson, or nephew) of P_B having most of its relations match (using COM) with those of C_C. If such candidate has also descendants, do they coincide with the descendants of C_C? The best candidate becomes *cms*. If no candidate is good enough, COM returns *cms* = "son of P_B" (meaning that C_C must be some son of node P_B, unknown to *B*). In this case, OM will try to merge P_B with P_C.

CASE C. C_C finds a match C_B in *B*, but the parents P_C and P_B (of C_C and C_B) do not match. COM verifies if most of the relations of C_C correspond to those in the candidate, and if most of the descendants of C_C match those of the candidate C_B. That being the case, it returns the C_B with the best match as *cms*. If only some properties of C_C and C_B match,

COM returns cms = "probably C_B." OM treats this (arbitrarily) as a match between C_C and C_B.[16] If few or no properties of any candidate match, COM returns "no match" (Figure 3).

CASE D. C_C does not find a match in B, and neither its parent P_C does. COM returns "no match."

Confusion

I ask for a *European car*, and I get a *German car*. Is there an error? Now, I ask for a *German car*, and a *European car* comes. Can we measure this error? Can we systematize or organize these values? Hierarchies of symbolic values allow measuring the similarity between these values, and the error when one is used instead of another (the intended or real value). This measurement is accomplished by the theory of confusion (Guzman & Levachkine, 2004) and the function *conf*, which is used by OM to solve some inconsistencies.

Confusion, contradiction, or inconsistency arise when a concept in A has a relation that is incompatible, contradicts or negates other relation of the same concept in B. For instance, Earth in A has shape flat; and in B Earth has the relation shape round. Contradiction arises from two relations: in our example, the shapes are not the same, are inconsistent since shape can only have a single value.

Because OM must copy concepts keeping the semantics of the sources in the result, and both semantics are incompatible, a contradiction is detected. It is not possible to keep both meanings because they are inconsistent.[17] To solve some of these inconsistencies, OM uses the theory of confusion.

Function CONF(r,s), called the *absolute confusion*, computes the confusion that occurs when object r is used instead of object s, as follows:

CONF(r, r) = CONF(r, s) = 0 when s is some ascendant of r;

CONF(r, s) = 1 + CONF$(r,$ father_of$(s))$ otherwise.

CONF is the number of descending links when one travels from r (the used value) to s (the intended or real

value), in the hierarchy to which r and s belong.

Absolute confusion CONF returns an integer between 0 and h, where h is the height of the hierarchy (Figure 4). CONF is granularity-dependant, since its value changes merely by adding nodes between the root of the hierarchy and s. To make it insensitive to this, we normalize it by dividing into h, the height of the hierarchy, thus:

Definition.
conf(r, s), the confusion when using r instead of s, is:
conf(r, s) = CONF$(r, $ s$) / h$

conf returns a number between 0 and 1.
Example: conf(Hydrology, river) = 0.2 (Figure 4).

OM uses conf, whereas Guzman and Levachkine (2004) describe CONF. Confusion is not a distance. In general, conf $(a, b) \neq$ conf(b, a). conf(r, s) is domain-dependant, as reflected by the hierarchy used to compute it.

Besides *confusion,* there are many forms to measure similarity or likeness between qualitative values r and s. For instance, seeing how far apart in Wordnet (wordnet.princeton.edu/) are the synsets where r and s lie, or comparing their definitions (or glosses) in a dictionary. OM uses confusion due to its asymmetry, but it could easily adapt or add some other similarity functions. A complete discussion of similarity is in Guzman and Levachkine (2004).

Contributions of the OM (Ontology Merging) Algorithm:

a. *It is totally automatic*, requiring no human intervention.

b. *It handles partitions* as well as subsets (explained in "Contributions of OM Notation").

c. *It handles concepts in an ontology that are described "shallowly"* by just a word, a word phrase or a set of them (see footnote 9).

d. *Relations among nodes can also be concepts*, as explained in "Contributions of OM Notation."

e.   With the help of COM, OM takes into account:

1.   *Synonyms.* Example: If *A* contains boat ("boat", "ship") ⊂ vessel, and *B* contains dinghy ("skipper", "boat") ⊂ vessel, then *C* will contain boat ("boat", "ship", "skipper") ⊂ vessel. Other example: In figure 2, method in *A* matches procedure in *B* and the parent (of method) technique in *A* matches the parent of procedure in *B*. Thus, this is case A of COM. Other example is found in part c of example 3; see Figure 9.

2.   *Homonyms.* If *A* contains fly ⊂ insect ⊂ animal and *B* contains fly ⊂ navigate, then *C* will contain fly ⊂ insect ⊂ animal and fly ⊂ navigate, that is, OM recognizes (Case C of COM) two different concepts with the same name. Another example: if *A* contains the concept printer ⊂ company and *B* contains printer ⊂ computer peripheral, then *C* will contain both: printer ⊂ company and printer ⊂ computer peripheral, that is, OM recognizes

both concepts as different, although they have the same name printer (Figure 11).

3.   *Synonyms when considering their properties.* If *A* has maize ("maize") ⊂ cereal, color yellow, size 1cm, contains hydrocarbons and *B* has corn ("corn") ⊂ cereal, color yellow, size 0.5inch, contains carbohydrates, then case B of COM will correctly identify maize and corn as synonyms, and thus will contain maize ("maize", "corn") ⊂ cereal, color yellow, size 1cm (0.5inch), contains hydrocarbons ("hydrocarbon", "carbohydrates"). That is, corn and maize have many properties equal or similar (by recursive use of COM). See Figure 3.

4.   *New knowledge.* If one ontology knows nothing about dinosaurs, and the other has some concepts about them, then *C* will contain each ontology's unique knowledge, appropriately referring to knowledge common to both ontologies, such as "legs" or "fly."

5.   *Other cases* where the knowledge in each ontology is properly taken into account

Figure 2. Case A of COM

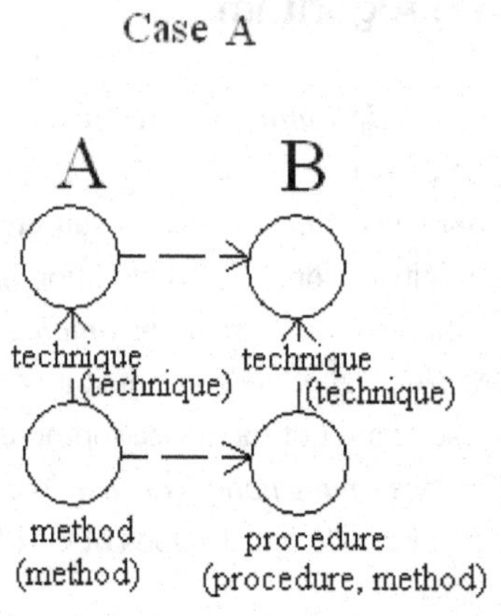

Case A

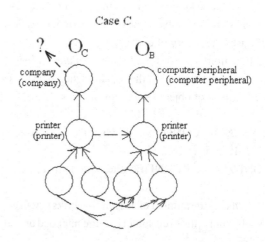

Figure 3. Case C of COM

are discussed in "Using OM. Examples," and by Cuevas-Rasgado (2006).

f. *OM avoids placement of redundant relations.* If *A* contains lemon ⊂ fruit, and *B* contains lemon ⊂ citric ⊂ fruit, then the resulting merged ontology *C* will contain lemon ⊂ citric ⊂ fruit, finding that *A*'s knowledge (lemon ⊂ fruit) is redundant.

g. *The OM algorithm detects inconsistencies* (contradictions) in the knowledge in *A* vs. the knowledge in *B*, using inconsistency measurements (Jimenez, n.d.) and confusion. An example where inconsistency is detected and solved is: Let *A* contain AcmeCorp incorporated_in Maryland and incorporated _ in arity 1; let *B* contain AcmeCorp incorporated_in USA. OM detects an (apparent) inconsistency between Maryland and USA (two different concepts), which is solved by conf because Maryland is part of USA, conf(Maryland, USA)=0. Then, OM stores in *C* AcmeCorp incorporated_in Maryland (but it does not store in *C* AcmeCorp incorporated_in USA). Nevertheless, when trying to merge *A* with *D* which contains AcmeCorp incorporated_in France, OM will detect a contradiction, since the confusion between Maryland and France is large, and incorporated_in is single-valued. Unable to solve this contradiction, OM keeps in *C* the knowledge coming from *A*.[20]

h. *Expunging redundant values.* If *A* contains George_Washington visited (Paris, Africa, Madrid, Maryland) and *B* contains George_Washington visited (France, Morocco, Spain, USA, Argentina), then OM uses confusion to prune *C* to contain George_Washington visited (Paris, Morocco, Madrid, Maryland, Argentina). *Warning:* In the presence of symbolic values (places visited, in the example) at different hierarchy levels, selecting the most specific values may work, but there are other cases where the more general values are preferred. More knowledge is needed for OM to always solve correctly this case. See the section on "Suggestions for Further Work."

i. Cuevas-Rasgado (2006) provides *other heuristics* and rules that fortify OM.

Commercial Areas Ready to Exploit OM

OM enables the automatic development of larger and better ontologies. Also, with OM it is possible (but see footnote 7) to generate on-demand ontologies, tailored to the application needs.

Ontology merging is at its infancy (see the section on "Suggestions for Further Work"). Its promise is the automatic acquisition of relevant knowledge. How can this help a business?

*   Discovery of new markets. A glass factory in Indonesia may discover that their small glasses could be used in Mexico to drink tequila.
*   Market trends. How many newspaper job ads demand a manufacturing engineer? How many require persons speaking Cantonese? (now done through text mining).
*   Business intelligence. Mexico has large oil deposits in semifractured strata. How are other nations exploiting similar beds? (now done through word search of documents).
*   Product improvement. Japanese consumers pay dearly for a fruit similar to a prickly pear, but without seeds. Can Jalisco adapt its prickly pears to this market?
*   Electronic commerce.
*   Public relations monitoring. What is New Yorkers' perception about the occupation of Irak? And Australian citizens' perception? (now done through polls).

Additional areas where OM can be productively used are: [18]

Semantic Web: Crawlers need to understand[19] large amounts of Web-available information. Central to this understanding is the assimilation of new information in ways consistent with already acquired knowledge. Use: to answer non-trivial

Figure 4. Solving contradictions. conf(river, Hidrology)= 0 whereas conf(Hidrology, river)= 0.2

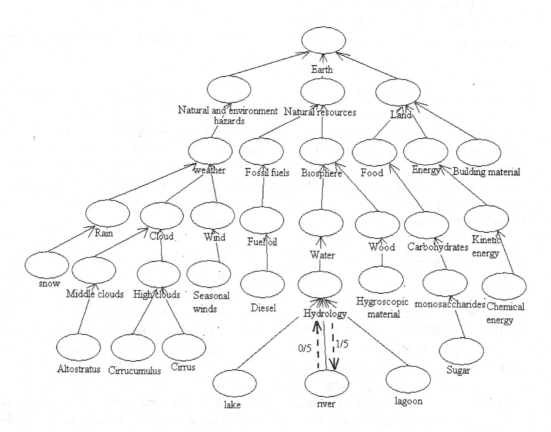

questions (see "Suggestions for Further Work") needing multiple Web sources.

Electronic Commerce: Agent *A* can enrich its ontology (in order to acquire synonyms for its products, to facilitate finding new customers, suppliers or uses of its products) by joining its ontology with suitable ontologies *B*, *C*, ... Such "enriched agent" will understand better the queries and needs from other agents (or human beings) that may acquire products from *A*.

Virtual learning: Virtual book *A* in International Finance can merge its ontology with the ontol-ogy of another virtual book dealing with the same or near-by topic. The enriched ontology will be better suited for students learning from *A*. Also, *A* can join its ontology with a "pre-decessor" ontology from other book dealing with Economics. This helps students to refresh previous concepts.

USING OM: EXAMPLES

Figures 5 and 6 show only relevant parts of large ontologies *A*, *B* and *C*.

Figure 5. Ontology A has deeper knowledge about `hammer` *than ontology B*

```
<concept>tool
        <Language>english<word>tool</word> </Language>
        <subset>thing </subset>
        <concept>hammer
                <Language>english<word>hammer</word> </Language>
                <subset>tool </subset>
                <concept>carpenter hammer
                        <Language>english<word>carpenter hammer</word> </Language>
                        <subset>hammer </subset>
                </concept>
                <concept>blacksmith hammer
                        <Language>english<word>blacksmith hammer</word></Language>
                        <member>hammer </member>
                </concept>
        </concept>
        <concept>nail
                <Language>english<word>nail </word></Language>
                <subset> tool</subset>
        </concept>
</concept>
```

Example 1: Ontology Merging in spite of the Generality or Specificity of Contents

Here we merge two ontologies of businesses that sell tools for handcrafts.

Ontology *A* describes `hammer` with two sons: `carpenter hammer` and `blacksmith hammer` (Figure 5). Ontology *B* (Figure 6) contains a more general description of `hammer`. During the merging

of *A* and *B*, OM detects that COM matches `hammer` in *A*, and its two sons, with the (unique) `hammer` in *B* (Figure 6).

Figure 7 presents concepts of *A* that have matched with those of *B* and vice versa. *A*'s `hammer` has matched with *B*'s `hammer`. When OM complements the words and properties of `hammer`, it copies the brothers of *B*'s `hammer` to *C*, but before that copying, it searches each of these brothers in *A*.

Figure 6. Ontology B has concepts screw and saw, inexistent in A

```
<concept>tool
        <Language>english<word>tool</word> </Language>
        <subset>thing </subset>
        <concept>hammer
                <Language>english<word>hammer</word> </Language>
                <subset>tool </subset>
        </concept>
        <concept>screw
                <Language>english<word>screw</word></Language>
                <subset> tool</subset>
        </concept>
        <concept>saw
                <Language>english<word>saw </word></Language>
                <subset> tool</subset>
        </concept>
</concept>
```

Figure 7. Mapping between A and B. Hammer, carpenter hammer, blacksmith hammer and nail from A match with hammer in B (dotted lines). Heavy lines identify matches from B into A

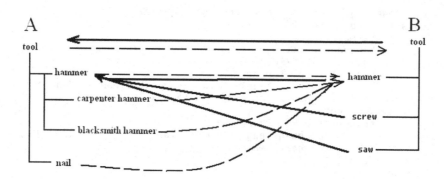

Figure 8. Result C for example 1. Here, C is symmetric: A ∪ B = B ∪ A. In the presence of contradictions, such symmetry may not hold (Cuevas, 2006; footnote 20)

```
<concept>tool
        <Language>english<word>tool</word> </Language>
        <subset>thing </subset>
        <concept>hammer
                <Language>english<word>hammer</word> </Language>
                <subset>tool </subset>
                <concept>carpenter hammer
                        <Language>english<word>carpenter hammer</word> </Language>
                        <subset>hammer </subset>
                </concept>
                <concept>blacksmith hammer
                        <Language>english<word>blacksmith hammer</word> </Language>
                        <subset>hammer </subset>
                </concept>
        </concept>
        <concept>nail
                <Language>english<word>nail </word></Language>
                <subset> tool</subset>
        </concept>
        <concept>screw
                <Language>english<word>screw</word></Language>
                <subset> tool</subset>
        </concept>
        <concept>saw
                <Language>english<word>saw </word></Language>
                <subset> tool</subset>
        </concept>
</concept>
```

For screw in *B*, even when COM answers hammer (from *A*) as the most similar concept in *A* (because the parents of screw and hammer coincide), OM compares their names: "hammer" and "screw". Being different, it considers screw as a new son of tool in *A*, and it copies screw into the merged result as a new node. The same happens to concept saw in *B*, and to carpenter hammer, blacksmith hammer, and nail in *A* (which are found by COM to be similar to hammer in *B*): they all go to *C*, Figure 8.

Example 2: Merging Ontologies with Mutually Inconsistent Knowledge

Differences in *A* and *B*'s knowledge arise from repetitions, reference to the same facts through diverse words, different level of details, type of description, and contradictions. For instance, *B* contains: veteran John Nash Sr. was born in Bluefield, while *A* contains: mathematician John Forbes Nash was born in West Virginia. Both ontologies duplicate some information (Nash's birthplace), different expressions (veteran / mathematician), different level of details (Bluefield / West Virginia), and contradictions (John Nash Sr. / John Forbes Nash). A person will have in her mind a consistent combination of information: John Nash Sr. and John Forbes Nash are not the same person, or perhaps they *are* the same. If she knows them she may deduce that one is the son of the other. We solve these problems everyday via *common sense knowledge* and previously acquired information. This is not so easy for computers, since they lack everyday's knowledge and usually they don't use, as OM, a previous knowledge base (See "Knowledge Support for OM"). Also, OM deals with inconsistency by measuring (step 2.a.iii of its algorithm) conf(Bluefield, West Virginia). [20]

Example 3: Joining Partitions, Synonym Identification

Numbers in Figure 9 match those below, for easy identification.

1. Copying new partitions. *B* has one partition: printing technology. *A* has two partitions: types and methods of image creation. Thus, printing technology is added to *C* (thin lines in Figure 9).

2. Copying concepts. procedure in *B* is copied to *C*, because it is not found in *A*. Its ascendant (not shown in Figure 9) is also copied to *C*.

3. Change into a (full) concept. Synonym identification. Adding more semantics. Relation method in *A* is copied to *C*; then, procedure in *B* is identified as a synonym of method, so method in *C* changes to procedure. In addition, procedure is a concept in *B* (it was just a phrase in *A*)[9], so it becomes a full concept in *C*. Finally, new semantics is added to procedure in *C* by adding to its definition print striking to the paper with small pieces from *B*.

Example 4: Numbers in Figure 10 Match Those Below

4. Removing redundant relations. In *A*, liquid inkjet printer ⊂ printer, whereas in *B* liquid inkjet printer ⊂ non-impact printer ⊂ printer. Adding both to *C* would make liquid inkjet printer to have two ascendants: printer and non-impact printer. OM detects the redundancy liquid inkjet printer ⊂ printer and expunges it from *C*, to keep only liquid inkjet printer ⊂ non-impact printer ⊂ printer.

5. Comparing relations (Figure 10). The relations method in *B* and its method is in *A* are considered to be the same, because connectors and, or, its, and so forth, are ignored (see the section on "Knowledge Support for OM").

Example 5: Homonyms

Concepts printer in *A* (Figure 11) and in *B* have the same syntax, but different semantics. OM finds them different, as explained in Example 1.

Figure 9. Relations method in A and procedure in B are synonyms, thus both of their definitions are added to node procedure in C

```
     <concept>printer
            <language>english <word>printer </word></language>
            <subset> computer peripheral</subset>
            <relation>transcribes = document </relation>
            <relation>physical route = paper </relation>
            <relation>Partition=types {*: monochrome printer ,color printer}</relation>
  A         <relation>partition=methods of image creation {laser:toner printer ;
                    liquid:liquid inkjet printer; solid: solid ink printer;
                     impact :impact printer}</relation>
            <concept>impact printer
                  <language>english <word>impact printer </word></language>
                  <subset>printer</subset>
                  <relation>method =forcible impact to tranfer ink to the media </relation>
            </concept>
<concept>printer
            <language>english <word>printer</word></language>
            <subset> computer peripheral</subset>
            <relation>utility = display information printed in paper </relation>
            <relation>partition=Printing technology{*: impact printer,non-impact printer}</relation>
            <concept>impact printer
  B               <language>english <word>impact printer</word></language>
                  <subset> printer</subset>
                  <relation>procedure= print striking to the paper with small pieces </relation>
            </concept>
            ***
<concept>procedure
            <Language>english<word>procedure, method</word></Language>
            <subset>technique</subset>
</concept>

<concept>printer
            <Language>english<word>printer</word></Language>
            <relation>transcribes = document</relation>
            <relation>physical route = paper</relation>
            <relation>utilidad = presentar informacion impresa en papel</relation>
  C         <subset>computer peripheral</subset>
            <relation>Partition=types {*: monochrome printer ,color printer}</relation>
            <relation>Partition=methods of image creation {laser:toner printer ;
                  liquid:liquid inkjet printer; solid: solid ink printer;
                  impact :impact printer}</relation>        ①
            <relation>Partition= Printing technology {*: impact printer,non-impact printer}</relation>
            <concept>impact printer
                  <Language>english<word>impact printer</word></Language>
                  <relation>procedure =forcible impact to tranfer ink to the media ,
                        print striking to the paper with small pieces</relation>  ③
                  <subset>printer</subset>
            </concept>
            ***
<concept>procedure    ②
            <Language>english<word>procedure, method</word></Language>
            <subset>technique</subset>
</concept>
```

Figure 10. Relations method in A and its method is in B are the same, so they are merged in a single relation method in C (label 5)

```
        <concept>printer
              <language>english <word>printer </word></language>
              <subset> computer peripheral</subset>
              ...
   A    <concept>liquid inkjet printer
                    <language>english <word>liquid inkjet printer </word></language>
                    <subset>printer</subset>
                    <relation>method = spill towards the paper very small amounts of red </relation>
                    <relation>partition=methods to inject red{*:thermal method, piezoelectric method }</relation>
              </concept>
        <concept>printer
              <language>english <word>printer</word></language>
              <subset> computer peripheral</subset>
              <relation>utility = display information printed in paper </relation>
              <relation>partition=Printing technology{*: impact printer,non-impact printer}</relation>
              ...
              <concept>non-impact printer
                    <language>english <word>non-impact printer</word></language>
   B                <subset> printer</subset>
                    <concept>liquid inkjet printer
                          <language>english <word>liquid inkjet printer </word></language>
                          <relation>its method is = inkjet printers spray very small,
                                    precise amounts of ink onto the media </relation>
                          <subset> non-impact printer</subset>
                    </concept>
        <concept>printer
              <Language>english<word>printer</word></Language>
              ...
              <concept>non-impact printer
                    <Language>english<word>non-impact printer</word></Language>
                    <subset>printer</subset>                                           (4)
                    <concept>liquid inkjet printer
   C                      <language>english <word>liquid inkjet printer </word></language>
                          <subset>non-impact printer</subset>
                          <relation>method = spill towards the paper very small amounts of red,    (5)
                                    inkjet printers spray very small,
                                    precise amounts of ink onto the media </relation>
                          <relation>methods to inject red{*:thermal method, piezoelectric method }</relation>
                    </concept>
```

Figure 11. Concepts printer in A and in B are found not to be the same, they both go to C (not shown) as two different concepts with the same name

```
        <concept> company
              <Language>english<word>company</word></Language>
   A    <concept> printer
                    <Language>english<word>company</word></Language>
                    <relation>operation = company that provides commercial printing services </relation>

        <concept> computer peripheral
              <Language>english<word>computer peripheral</word></Language>
   B    <concept> printer
                    <Language>english<word>printer</word></Language>
                    <relation>transcribes = document </relation>
```

Example 6: Promotion of Subsets to Partitions

Figures 12 and 13. In *A*, Etnolinguistic group of Oaxaca has subsets zoque set, ixcateco set, huave set and mixteco set, whereas in *B*, the same concept Etnolinguistic group of Oaxaca has a partition with the same elements that *A* has a subsets. Therefore, OM adds to *C* the partition from *B*. (A small error: OM fails to remove those elements as subsets from Etnolinguistic group of Oaxaca in *C*).

Example 7: Unsuccessful Promotion of Subset to Partition

It is not always possible to organize subsets into partitions. Figure 14 shows concept stem in *A* matching with stem in *B*. Thus, the partition Color belonging to stem in *B* is considered for copying to *C*. This partition has two elements: Gray and Green, which are searched in *A*. OM finds that Gray and Green are not descendants of stem in *A*.[21] OM finds them in Color in *A* (not shown in Figure 14), but they have

Figure 12. The partition Etnolinguistic in B is not in A, but before adding it to C, OM verifies that each of its elements (zoque set, ixcateco set...) are brothers in A and that no additional brother appears in A. These elements are all descendants of Etnolinguistic group of Oaxaca (thus, they are brothers) and no additional brother appears in A. Therefore, the partition Etnolinguistic from B is copied to concept Etnolinguistic group of Oaxaca in the resulting ontology C. Sizes of complete ontologies: A = 234 nodes; B = 117

```
<concept> Etnolinguistic  group of Mexico
        <Language>English<word> Etnolinguistic   group of Mexico</word></Language>
        <subset> Etnolinguistic   group </subset>
        <concept> Etnolinguistic   group of Oaxaca
            <Language>Ingles<word> Etnolinguistic   group of Oaxaca </word></Language>
            <subset> Etnolinguistic   group of Mexico</subset>
            <concept> zoque set
                    <Language>English<word> zoque set</word></Language>
                    <subset> Etnolinguistic   group of Oaxaca</subset>
            </concept>
            <concept> ixcateco set
                    <Language>English<word> ixcateco set</word></Language>
                    <subset> Etnolinguistic   group of Oaxaca</subset>
            </concept>
            <concept> huave set
                    <Language>English<word> huave set</word></Language>
                    <subset> Etnolinguistic   group of Oaxaca</subset>
            </concept>
            <concept> mixteco set
                    <Language>English<word> mixteco set</word></Language>
                    <subset> Etnolinguistic   group of Oaxaca</subset>
            </concept>

<concept> Etnolinguistic  group of Oaxaca
        <Language>Ingles<word> Etnolinguistic group   de Oaxaca</word></Language>
        <subset> Etnolinguistic   group of Mexico</subset>
        <relation>Partition = Etnolinguistic  {
                *zoque set, ixcateco set, huave set, mixteco set }
        </relation>
```

A

B

Figure 13. The result C shows the partition Etnolinguistic added to the concept Etnolinguistic group of Oaxaca

```
<concept> Etnolinguistic  group of Mexico
        <Language>English<word> Etnolinguistic  group of Mexico</word></Language>
        <subset> Etnolinguistic  group </subset>
        <concept> Etnolinguistic  group of Oaxaca
                <Language>Ingles<word> Etnolinguistic  group of Oaxaca </word></Language>
                <subset> Etnolinguistic  group of Mexico</subset>
                <relation>Partition = Etnolinguistic  {
                        *:zoque set, ixcateco set, huave set, mixteco set }
                </relation>
                <concept> zoque set
                        <Language>English<word> zoque set</word></Language>
                        <subset> Etnolinguistic  group of Oaxaca</subset>
                </concept>
                <concept> ixcateco set
                        <Language>English<word> ixcateco set</word></Language>
                        <subset> Etnolinguistic  group of Oaxaca</subset>
                </concept>
                <concept> huave set
                        <Language>English<word> huave set</word></Language>
                        <subset> Etnolinguistic  group of Oaxaca</subset>
                </concept>
                <concept> mixteco set
                        <Language>English<word> mixteco set</word></Language>
                        <subset> Etnolinguistic  group of Oaxaca</subset>
                </concept>
```

C

Figure 14. B has a partition Color, while A does not have it

```
<concept>stem
        <Language>English<word>stem </word></Language>
        <part>poppy </part>
        <relation>ramification = little graft </relation>
        <relation>forms = erect </relation>
        <relation>consists of = central ribbing </relation>
        <relation>forms = fine </relation>
</concept>
<concept>stem
        <Language>English<word>stem </word></Language>
        <part>poppy </part>
        <relation>Partition = Color {*:Gray, Green} </relation>
        <relation>it has = vein </relation>
        <relation>forms = smooth </relation>
</concept>
```

A

B

Figure 15. The resulting ontology C for example 7. Stem is partitioned into Green (that is, green stem) and Gray (that is, gray stem) while color still has as subsets gray, green, white and red

```
<concept>stem
        <Language>English<word>stem </word></Language>
        <part>poppy </part>
        <relation>ramification = little graft </relation>
        <relation>forms = erect,fine,smooth </relation>
        <relation>consists of = central ribbing </relation>
        <relation>Partition = Color {*:Gray, Green} </relation>
        <relation>it has = vein </relation>
</concept>
...
<concept>Color
        <Language>English<word>Color </word></Language>
        <subset>Cosa </subset>
        <concept>gray
                <Language>Spanish<word>gray </word></Language>
                <subset>Color </subset>
        </concept>
        <concept>green
                <Language>English<word>green </word></Language>
                <subset>Color </subset>
        </concept>
        <concept>white
                <Language>English<word>white </word></Language>
                <subset>Color </subset>
        </concept>
        <concept>red
                <Language>English<word>red </word></Language>
                <subset>Color </subset>
        </concept>
</concept>
```

C

two additional brothers: white and red. Thus, they are not added to C (Figure 15) as a partition of Color, but as a partition of stem.

ADDITIONAL EXAMPLES FOR REAL-WORLD CASES

OM has been applied by Cuevas-Rasgado (2006) to ontologies derived from Web documents (see Appendix), including:

- Geographic zones: two different documents about Oaxaca
- Animals and flowers: two description of turtles, two of poppies
- Biographies: two about Benito Juárez, two about Newton
- Description of tools and products
- Novels: portions of *100 Years of Loneliness* (two different texts)

From these documents, ontologies were manually written in OM notation, obtaining two ontologies for

Table 1. Performance of OM in some real-world examples

Table 1. Performance of OM in some real-world examples. How to read the table: Row *Neurotransmitter-Schizophrenia* says that OM merged the two ontologies in 2 seconds. 79 relations in B and 51 in A produced 127 relations in C, but the correct result (obtained by hand) contains 129 relations. OM missed 2 of 129 relations. *For concepts*, OM merged 56 concepts from B and 26 from A, producing 77 concepts in C, while the correct result contains 79 concepts. OM missed 2 of 79 concepts. The error is computed as (relations + concepts wrongly copied in the C produced by OM) / (relations + concepts in the correct C) = (2 + 2)/(129 + 79) = 4/208 = 0.019. Similarly, efficiency = 100 * (relations + concepts correctly copied to the C produced by OM) / (relations + concepts in the correct C) = 100*(127 +77)/208 = 98%

ONTOLOGIES	TIME	RELATIONS	CONCEPTS	ERR	% Effic
Turtles	4 sec.	6(B) ∪ 8(A) = 10(C). All were correctly copied..	35(B) ∪ 29(A) = 35(C). All nodes were correctly copied.	0	100
Martillo (Hammer)	6 sec.	30(B) ∪ 8(A) = 36(C). All were correctly copied.	33(B) ∪ 24(A) = 51(C). All nodes were correctly copied.	0	100
Amapola (Poppy)	14 sec.	20(B) ∪ 21(A) =37(C). All were correctly copied.	35(B) ∪ 34(A) = 58(C). All nodes were correctly copied.	0	100
100 Años de Soledad	10min.	283(B) ∪ 231(A) =420. * 432 (-12 from 432). 12 out of 432 relations were incorrectly omitted from C.	126 (B) ∪90 (A)=141 (C). * 149 (-8, 149). 8 out of 149 concepts were incorrectly omitted.	0.034	96
Oaxaca	5 min.	43(B) ∪ 61(A) =96(C). All relations were correctly copied	117(B) ∪ 234(A) =309(C). * 310 (- 1, 310). 1 out of 310 concepts were incorrectly omitted.	0.002	99.7
Neurotransmitter-Schizophrenia	2 sec.	79(B) ∪ 51(A) =127(C). * 129 (-2 from 129). 2 out of 129 relations were incorrectly omitted	56 (B) ∪26 (A)=77 (C). * 79 (- 2, 79). 2 out of 79 concepts were incorrectly omitted	0.019	98
Inconsistent Ontologies	1 sec.	3(B) ∪ 4(A) = 7(C). * 2 (C 1). 1 of 2 inconsistencies was solved	5(B) ∪ 6(A) = 9(C). * 5 (C 5). 5 inconsistencies were not solved.	0	100
Tourism of Acapulco	20 sec.	60(B) ∪ 64(A) =131(C). All were correctly copied	61(B) ∪ 65(A) = 124(C). All nodes were correctly copied.	0	100
Multimedia	10 sec.	7(B) ∪ 6(A) = 10(C). All were correctly copied	8(B) ∪ 7(A) = 11(C). All concepts were correctly copied.	0	100

each animal, flower, and so forth. Each pair of ontologies was merged (automatically) by OM. Validation of results (more at the section entitled "Discussion") has been made by comparing against a person's results, yielding Table 1.

CONCLUSION

As the world becomes a global village, businesses that do not adopt tools for automatic harvesting of knowledge disseminated through the Web will be at a disadvantage. Unfortunately, until now there were only tools that partially met this need. The emergence of OM provides new support.

OM is an automatic, robust algorithm that fuses the knowledge from two ontologies into a third one, solving some inconsistencies and avoiding redundancies.

The examples shown, as well as others (Cuevas-Rasgado, 2006), illustrate the power of OM: in spite of joining very general or very specific ontologies, it generally does a good job. This is because OM not only compares words, but it also takes into account the semantics or context of each node in the source ontologies for copying or modifying new properties and concepts into the resulting ontology. It also uses its base knowledge (see the section on "Knowledge Support for OM").

DISCUSSION

Syntactic vs. semantic analysis. OM builds data structures (in OM notation) from data structures, and thus uses limited knowledge (its in-built knowledge, plus the knowledge in A, plus the knowledge in B) and it exploits "only" syntactic facts. OM does not pretend to find "the truth"[22] among two inconsistent relations, but as more knowledge (more syntactic facts) come into its built-in knowledge, it will do a better job. In fact, when compared with the fusion done by a person imbedded with semantic knowledge, OM already does a reasonable job (Table 1), despite its "limited methodology" and its use of "only syntactic analysis."

OM is automatic. Human intervention takes place outside OM (see the section on "Additional Examples for Real-World Cases"). OM will produce consistent (no redundancies, no contradictions) and complete (no concepts missing in the fusion) ontologies if it were to achieve 100% accuracy (that is, the accuracy of a person that does the merging by hand). This is the goal of OM. How well does OM achieve its goal? About 96% (see Table 1). The section on "Suggestions for Further Work" explain how to improve further its performance.

VERIFICATION OF RESULTS

How can we be sure that OM (or some other merger tool) did a good job? We check (as in Table 1) for wrong, missing, misplaced, or additional (but wrong) relations and nodes in OM's result, against the result manually obtained by a person. At times, the person uses previous knowledge to build nodes or relations in the result that are impossible to be added by OM with the information available to it. The person may add Dog eats meat, among nodes Dog and meat, but neither A nor B say this. We do not count these as mistakes, but we mark them as "areas where more knowledge should produce *this* result." Another verification method could use the editor-reasoner when built, in order to pose questions to the resulting ontology, and check its answers against the answers from a person. These are subjective methods, but probably there could never be (for this purpose) an objective method, where a person's opinion is absent.[23]

REAL WORLD EXAMPLES AND CHALLENGES

Until now, ontology merging was a machine-aided activity, so few real world problems were tackled. OM is the first automated tool for ontology merging, but it has not yet tackled commercially interesting problems. The examples in the chapter come from ontologies obtained from documents found in the Web. But the largest ontology produced by OM (that for a portion of One Hundred Years of Loneliness, Table 1) has only 561 concepts (420 relations + 141 nodes). Larger experiments need to be carried out.

Issues, problems and trends are touched upon in that section.

SUGGESTIONS FOR FURTHER WORK

- Commercial applications appearing in the section on "Commercial Areas Ready to Exploit OM."

- As more knowledge is fused by OM, it could be kept and used as its built-in knowledge (explained in "Knowledge Support for OM"), to improve its accuracy.
- OM could resort to external knowledge sources—some are mentioned in "Knowledge Support for OM." These will help to eradicate some of the arbitrary decisions that current OM makes:
    o Uncertain handling of Case C, footnote 16
    o Preferring its own knowledge, footnote 20
    o Expunging redundant values, contribution h
    o Mistake in Example 6
- Another improvement may come from adding more similarity measures, see "Confusion."

Needed extensions to OM are:

- Handling of time. When young, Juárez was a law student; later he became Governor of Oaxaca, then President of the Supreme Court, then President of Mexico; at that time he fought against Emperor Maximiliam of Habsburg…
- Representing and merging disjunctions. Ann bought (a `candy` or an `ice cream`).
- How to represent (and merge) beliefs.
- How to represent conditionals and in general logic restrictions *in a way that OM can analyze*, check (for mutual inconsistency, say), improve, and change them. They should not be *opaque* to OM machinery.

Tools external to OM that will extend OM's applicability:

- A parser that transforms a document into a data structure using OM notation. A difficult task (footnote 7).
- A deductive machinery (a *reasoner*) that answers complex questions posed to the ontology perhaps as graphs, to avoid using a natural language interface.

- Those in footnote 7.

With these, the goal of attaining a large knowledge ontology (see the section on "Increased Yield Through Better Processing the Web Resources"), ready to answer difficult questions, could be achieved—building it incrementally by a tool, not by hand. Let us call this extended tool OM*. And what could be its use? Well, we could add it to our system software, perhaps as a part of the operating system. In the same manner as current word processors check for spelling and grammar, OM* would check documents or data bases for factual or semantic mistakes (assertions not agreeing with OM*'s knowledge), tagging for instance sentences or rows in a data base such as "Abraham Lincoln was born in Japan," "The applicant's age is 27, and he has been working in his previous job for 25 years," or "the shoe has hepatitis." In addition to *common sense knowledge,* OM* will provide *real world knowledge* to the computer. This sounds like exaggerations and wild thoughts, so we shall stop here and concentrate instead in the construction of missing parts of OM*.

ACKNOWLEDGMENT

We acknowledge support from CONACYT Grant 43377.

REFERENCES

Asunción, P., & Suárez, M. (2004). Evaluation of RDF[S] and DAML+OIL import/export services within ontology platforms. *Lecture Notes in Artificial Intelligence, 2972*, 109-118.

Bechnofer, S., van Harmelen, F., Hendler, J., Horrocks, I., McGuinness, D., Patel-Schneider, P. et al. (2004, February 10). *OWL Web ontology language* (reference). W3C Recommendation. Retrieved June 26, 2007, from http://www.w3.org/TR/2004/REC-owl-ref-20040210/

Connolly, D., van Harmelen, F., Horrocks, I., Mc-Guinnes, D., Patel-Schneider, P., & Stein, L. (2001, March). *DAML+OIL reference description*. W3C Note, December, 18, 2001. Retrieved June 26, 2007, from from http://www.w3.org/TR/2001/NOTE-daml+oil-reference-20011218

Cuevas-Rasgado, A.A. (2006). *Merging of ontologies using semantic properties*. Unpublished doctoral dissertation (in Spanish), CIC-IPN, Mexico. Retrieved June 26, 2007, from http://148.204.20.100:8080/bib-liodigital/ShowObject.jsp?idobject=34274&idreposit orio=2&type=recipiente

Dou, D., McDermott, D., & Qi, P. (2002). Ontology translation by ontology merging and automated reasoning. In *Proceedings of EKAW Workshop on Ontologies for Multi-Agent Systems* (pp. 73-94).

Ganter, B., Stumme, G., & Wille, R. (2005). *Formal concept analysis: Foundations and applications* (1st ed.). New York, NY: Springer

Guzman, A., & Levachkine, S. (2004). Hierarchies measuring qualitative variables. *Lecture Notes in Computer Science (LNCS)*, *2945*, 262-274.

Guzman, A., & Olivares, J. (2004). Finding the most similar concepts in two different ontologies. *Lecture Notes in Artificial Intelligence (LNAI)*, *2972*, 129-138.

Jimenez, A. (n.d.). *Quantifying inconsistencies in sentences (facts) with symbolic values*. Ph. D. thesis. CIC-IPN, Mexico.

Kalfoglou, Y., & Schorlemmer, M. (2002). Information-flow-based ontology mapping. In *Proceedings of the 1st International Conference on Ontologies, Databases, and Applicatio of Semantics* (pp. 1132-1151).

Kotis, K., Vouros, G., & Stergiou. K. (2006). Towards automatic of domain ontologies: The HCONE-merge approach. *Elsevier's Journal of Web Semantic, 4*(1), 60-79. Retrieved June 26, 2007, from http://authors.elsevier.com/sd/article/S1570826805000259

Lenat, D., & Guha. R. (1989). *Building large knowledge-based systems*. Addison-Wesley.

Loom. (1986). Retrieved June 26, 2007, from http://www.isi.edu/isd/LOOM/LOOM-HOME.html

Manola, F., & Miller, E. (2004). *RDF primer*. W3C Recommendation. Retrieved June 26, 2007, from http://www.w3.org/TR/2004/REC-rdf-primer-20040210/

McGuinness, D., Fikes, R., Rice, J., & Wilder, S. (2000). The chimaera ontology environment knowledge. In *Proceedings of the Eighth International Conference on Conceptual Structures Logical, Linguistic, and Computational Issues* (pp. 1123-1124). Darmstadt, Germany.

Noy, N., & A. Musen, M. (2000). PROMPT: Algoritm and tool for automated ontology merging and alignment. In *Proceedings of the Seventeenth National Conference on Artificial Intelligence (AAAI-2000)* (pp. 450-455). *Austin, TX.*

Stumme, G. & Maedche, A. (2001, September) Ontology merging for federated ontologies on the semantic web. In *Proceedings of the International Workshop for Foundations of Models for Information Integration (FMII-2001)* (pp. 16-18). Viterbo, Italy.

ENDNOTES

[1]   An easy task for a person who uses *context* and previous knowledge.

[2]   Other important problems (question-answering, reasoning, the handling of time, how to represent beliefs, and so forth; see "Suggestions for Further Work") are outside the scope of this chapter.

[3]   OM forges ahead and does not fall into loops.

[4]   Without contradictions.

[5]   The result contains *all* available knowledge from the sources, avoiding redundancies.

[6]   Without user intervention.

[7]   A Ph.D. Thesis in progress by Paola Neri seeks to make such translation.

[8]   Some representations are even more restrictive: an ontology has to be a *tree*. In these, a concept could not have two parents: Mexico could not be both a *nation* and an *emerging market*.

9   A relation may be a (full) concept or just a name, a label, a "shallow" relation. Same applies to concepts.

10 Another example: the relation to light (that is, to illuminate) may also be a concept, if one wishes to add more properties to this action. A different concept that can also be represented is light (that is, an electromagnetic radiation). OM does not consider them equivalent, even if somebody gave them the same name. OM has machinery to identify homonyms (contribution e.2).

11 Ontology *C* is incrementally constructed, starting from ontology *A* (step 1). In step 2, OM first adds to *C* nodes in a "superficial" manner (only the label, description, and implicit relations are copied), later in that step 2 these nodes will be completed and "deeply" copied. See footnote 12.

12 *Deep copying.* OM finishes copying a node already superficially copied, adding to it its explicit relations. These new relations link to other concepts, which could already be in *C*. If they are not, they are now superficially copied, and later they, in turn, will be deeply copied.

13 Ontology *C* is searched *depth-first*. A branch of the tree is traveled until the deepest descendant is reached, before OM considers another branch. Since the OM notation uses trees, OM finds easy to do these travels.

14 For instance, in *A* we find impact printer method uses force... (Figure 9) and in *B* we find impact printer procedure uses print striking to the paper and C_c = impact printer in *A* has a most similar concept *cms* = impact printer in *B*, and

method and procedure are found by OM to be synonyms. Then all the words in the definition of procedure in *B* are copied into the definition of method in *C* (Figure 9).

15 Or grandparent, or great-grand parent.

16 This may be a mistake. More information is needed if OM were always to make the right decision. More at "Suggestions for Further Work."

17 In *C*= *A* $\cup$ *B*, OM assumes *A*, *B*, *C* to be self-consistent. But mutual inconsistency can arise when joining *A* and *B*.

18 Progress will be slow until better tools appear (like OM*) and businesses become aware of them.

19 To *understand x* means: to process, exploit, make intelligent inferences about *x*. Pragmatically, a program *understands* some text, information, or situation when such program can productively use it to advance in its goals and objectives.

20 As last resort, if *B*'s new knowledge is inconsistent with *A*'s knowledge, *A* refuses to acquire this new knowledge.

21 If Gray and Green were the only descendants of its ascendant (Color), the partition would be added to Color.

22 How can a program that diagnoses EKG anomalies be checked: (1) by comparing its results against experts' diagnosis (subjective method), and (2) by checking reality, for example, an autopsy of the person will show his heart's ailments (objective method). But the purpose of OM is not to find out what is true in the real world; its purpose is to build a consistent *C* from *A*, *B* and its previous knowledge.

APPENDIX

- **Ontologies about Benito Juarez:** Retrieved June 26, 2007, from http://es.wikipedia.org/wiki/Benito_Ju%C3%A1rez (2003) and http://www.artehistoria.com/historia/personajes/6496.htm (2001)
- **Ontologies about cien años de soledad:** Retrieved June 26, 2007, from http://html.rincondelvago.com/cien-anos-de-soledad_gabriel-garcia-marquez_22.html (n.d.) and http://www.monografias.com/trabajos10/ciso/ciso.shtml (2002)
- **Ontologies about Newton:** Retrieved June 26, 2007, from http://es.wikipedia.org/wiki/Isaac_Newton (2003) and http://thales.cica.es/rd/Recursos/rd97/Biografias/03-1-b-newton.html (n.d.)
- **Ontologies about Oaxaca:** Retrieved June 26, 2007, from http: www.oaxaca-mio.com/atrac_turisticos/infooaxaca.htm (2001) and http: www.elbalero.gob.mx/explora/html/oaxaca/geografia.html (1999)
- **Ontologies about poppy:** Retrieved June 26, 2007, from http://es.wikipedia.org/wiki/Amapola (2003) and http://www.buscajalisco.com/bj/salud/herbolaria.php?id=1 (n.d.)
- **Ontologies about tools and products:** Retrieved June 26, 2007, from http://sumesa.com/ (n.d.)
- **Ontologies about turtles:** Retrieved June 26, 2007, from www.damisela.com/zoo/rep/tortugas/index.htm (1999) and http://www.foyel.com/cartillas/37/tortugas_en_extincion.html (n.d.)

About the Contributors

Peter Rittgen received an MSc in computer science and computational linguistics from the University Koblenz-Landau, Germany, and a PhD in economics and business administration from Frankfurt University, Germany. He is currently a senior lecturer at the School of Business and Informatics of the University College of Borås, Sweden. He has been doing research on business processes and the development of information systems since 1997 and has published many articles in these areas.

Artur Caetano is an information systems lecturer at the Instituto Superior Técnico, Technical University of Lisbon, Portugal, and a PhD candidate at the same university on the topic of business process modeling with separation of concerns. He holds a master's degree in computer engineering and information systems from the Technical University of Lisbon, and his education consists of a background in computer science and software engineering. He has worked on several international projects concerning enterprise architecture and enterprise-distributed object computing. His PhD research work focuses the development of a role-based framework for enterprise modeling.

Abraham Carmeli is a faculty member of the Graduate School of Business Administration at Bar-Ilan University. He received a PhD from the University of Haifa. His current research interests include complementarities and fit, top management teams, organizational identification, learning from failures, interpersonal relationships, and individual behaviors at work.

Werner Ceusters studied medicine, neuropsychiatry, informatics, and knowledge engineering in Belgium. Since April 2006, he has been health sciences professor and coordinator of bioinformatics for the Health Science Faculties at the University at Buffalo, New York, and director of the Ontology Research Group of the New York State Center of Excellence in Bioinformatics and Life Sciences, Buffalo, New York.

Charu Chandra is an associate professor of industrial and manufacturing systems engineering at the University of Michigan-Dearborn. He is involved in research in supply chain management and enterprise integration issues in large complex systems. Specifically, his research focuses on studying complex systems with the aim of developing cooperative models to represent coordination and integration in an enterprise. He has published several books, papers in leading archival research journals, book chapters and conference proceedings in the areas of supply chain management, enterprise modeling, information systems support, inventory management, and group technology. He teaches courses in information technology, operations research and supply chain management. His PhD and master's degrees are in industrial engineering and operations research from the Arizona State University and the University of Minnesota, respectively. He is a member of Institute of Industrial Engineers,

Institute of Operations Research and Management Sciences, Decision Sciences Institute, Production and Operations Management Society, and American Association of Artificial Intelligence. He serves on the editorial board of *OMEGA-The International Journal of Management Science* as associate editor with editorial responsibilities for supply chain management track papers. He is also a member of the editorial board of the *International Journal of Procurement Management.*

Yun-Heh Chen-Burger is a senior researcher in AIAI, Informatics, University of Edinburgh, UK. She received a PhD from the same university. Her research interests are knowledge and workflow management in the Semantic Web and Grid. She has recently published a book, *Automating Business Modeling* (Springer), that details how knowledge technologies may be used in a business context to help capture, reason, and automate business operations. Her paper "Formal Support for Adaptive Workflow Systems in a Distributed Environment" was published in the *Workflow Handbook 2003*, which is one of the most influential workflow management books in the field. She serves as a regular reviewer for paper publishing in eight international journals and book proposals for two large publishing houses, Springer and John Wiley. She is research active and has served as a member of program committee for 16 conferences and workshops, held a workshop and worked as a session chair for a conference and workshop. She has over 50 publications in leading journals, books, conferences, and workshops. As a part of her normal work, she leads and participates in commercial projects where she transfers her technical knowledge to realistic life-size problems.

After graduating with a first class BSc (Hons) in psychology and statistics from the University of Sydney, **Anne Cregan** worked for 12 years in IT programming and design, project management, business analysis, process modeling, and consulting prior to enrolling in a PhD program in semantic technologies at UNSW. Cregan is one of a select number of post-graduate research students sponsored by the National Information and Communication Technology Center of Excellence, Australia, whose aim is to attract researchers of the highest calibre to produce world-leading research in Australia. Anne is involved in work efforts led by the World Wide Web Consortium (W3C), ISO, and Standards Australia in the area of semantic technologies.

Alma Delia Cuevas-Rasgado has been a university professor at the Department of Systems and Computation of the Instituto Tecnológico de Oaxaca since 1992. She obtained a PhD in computer science from the Centro de Investigación en Computación, Instituto Politécnico Nacional, Mexico. Her recent work (her doctoral thesis) involves fusing ontologies without losing information in the process. She forms part of a group of scientists from Mexico and other countries that apply ontologies to Semantic Web problems and the intelligent recovery of information in data bases.

Jiangbo Dang is a research scientist at Siemens Corporate Research, Princeton, New Jersey. His research interests include multiagent systems, service-oriented computing, business process modeling and management, and knowledge management. He has a PhD in computer science from the University of South Carolina. He also had worked at People's Bank of China as a system engineer after he earned a bachelor's degree from the University of Science and Technology of China.

Stéphane Faulkner is an associate professor in technologies and information systems at the University of Namur (FUNDP). Dr. Faulkner is also invited professor with the Universitary Faculties St. Louis of Brussels. His interests of research evolve around requirements engineering and the development of precise (formal) modeling notations, systematic methods, and tool support for the development of multi-agent systems, database, and information systems. His publications include more than 40 international refereed journals or periodicals and proceedings papers.

Olov Forsgren received a PhD in informatics from Umeå University, Sweden. Forsgren is the Sjuhärad distinguished professor at the University College of Borås and has 20 years research experience from Umeå University, Mid-Sweden University and Örebro University. He has also been a visiting professor at the University of Southern California, Berkeley University, California and Southern Methodist University in Dallas, Texas. He has been the scientific principal investigator responsible for a number of successful pioneering national and international research projects on information systems development in collaboration with multiple academic and industrial research partners.

Ariel Frank has been a member of the Department of Computer Science, Faculty of Exact Sciences, Bar-Ilan University, Israel, since 1984. He has served as deputy chairperson of his department for 15 years. He received his undergraduate, master's, and PhD degrees in computer science from Bar-Ilan University (Israel), Weizmann Institute (Israel), and SUNY at Stony Brook (USA), respectively. Frank's main areas of interest are Internet resources discovery (IRD), including search engines (SE) and digital libraries (DL), distance/distributed education (DE), multimedia (MM), and distributed systems (DS). Frank has served as chairperson and directorate member of the Israeli UNIX User Association (AMIX) for close to a decade. He has served as chair and committee member of numerous conferences and workshops, including a dozen such UNIX events, and as organizing chair of Bar-Ilan International Symposium on Foundations of AI (BISFAI) series of conferences.

Eva Gahleitner received an MSc in business informatics from the Johannes Kepler University of Linz (JKU) in 2001. From 2001 to 2006, she was a scientific research member at the "Institute for Applied Knowledge Processing (FAW)." In 2005 she received a PhD in Semantic Web and ontology management from the Johannes Kepler University. Since 2006, she has worked for Voestalpine Information Technology in Linz where she is responsible for collaborative software solutions. Her research interests are Semantic Web applications, ontology learning, semantic search, and social software.

Aldo Gangemi is senior researcher at the Institute for Cognitive Sciences and Technology (http://www.istc.cnr.it) at the Italian National Research Council (http://www.cnr.it). He is cofounder of the Laboratory for Applied Ontology (http://www.loa-cnr.it), a leading research unit in the areas of conceptual modeling, formal ontology, and ontology engineering. His research topics include knowledge engineering, the Semantic Web, NLP, and business modeling, with about 90 publications on international refereed journals, books and conferences. He has been working in many national and EU projects, spanning from the pioneering biomedical ontology project GALEN (1992) to the current largest ontology engineering project NeOn (http://www.neon-project.com). He is currently coordinating the workpackage on collaborative aspects of ontology design in NeOn, and an Italian project on the use of semantic technologies in organizational intranets. He is reviewer for the EU and Italian governmental agencies and consultant for Italian and international organizations.

Rüdiger Gartmann studied business computer science at the University of Essen, where he received his diploma in 2000. Since 2000 he has been a research assistant at Fraunhofer ISST Dortmund. His interests are in Web service technology, in particular within the geospatial domain, where he conducts several projects. He is also working in the FLAME2008 and COMPASS2008 projects. His research focuses on roaming concepts for mobile services. At end of 2006, he changed to the University of Münster to complete his PhD.

Roy Gelbard is a faculty member of the information systems program at the Graduate School of Business Administration, Bar-Ilan University. He received a PhD and an MSc in information systems from Tel-Aviv University. He holds also degrees in biology and philosophy. His work involves data and knowledge representation, data mining, software engineering, and software project management.

Göran Goldkuhl, professor of information systems development at Linköping University and professor of informatics at Jönköping International Business School, received a PhD from Stockholm University in 1980. He is the director of the Swedish research network VITS, consisting of more than 40 researchers at eight Swedish universities. He is currently developing a family of theories which all are founded on socio-instrumental pragmatism: workpractice theory, business action theory, and information systems actability theory. He has a great interest in interpretive, qualitative, and pragmatic research methods and he has contributed to the development of multi-grounded theory (a modified version of grounded theory). He is editor-in-chief for the open journal *Systems, Signs & Actions* (www.sysiac.org).

Jaap Gordijn (gordijn@cs.vu.nl) is an associate professor of e-business at the Faculty of Exact Sciences of the Free University, Amsterdam. His research interest concentrates on innovative e-business applications. He is a key developer of, and has internationally published on, the e^3-*value* e-business modeling methodology, addressing the integration of strategic e-business decision making with ICT requirements and systems engineering. Before joining the Free University, he was a member of Cisco's Internet Business Solution Group and senior manager of the e-business group at Deloitte & Touche. As such, he was involved in rolling out e-business applications in the banking, insurance, and digital content industries.

Adolfo Guzman-Arenas is a computer science professor at Centro de Investigación en Computación, Instituto Politécnico Nacional, Mexico City, of which he was founding director. He holds a BSc in electronics from ES-IME-IPN, and a PhD from MIT; he is an ACM fellow and received the National Prize in Science and Technology (Mexico). He is a member of the Academia de Ingeniería and the Academia Nacional de Ciencias (México). He was awarded (2006) the Premio Nacional a la Excelencia "Jaime Torres Bodet." His work is in semantic information processing and AI techniques, often mixed with distributed information systems.

Bernhard Holtkamp is with Fraunhofer ISST since 1992. For more than 10 years he was head of the information management department. Now he is manager strategic project development and deputy director of SIGSIT (Sino-German Joint Laboratory of Software Integration Technologies). He was also project manager of the institute's China related projects FLAME2008, COMPASS2008, and VAS CHINA. Dr. Holtkamp got his diploma and PhD in computer science from the University of Dortmund in 1982 and 1985, respectively. He was then with the University of Dortmund and worked as a research professor at the Naval Postgraduate School in Monterey, California, before he joined Fraunhofer.

Jingshan Huang earned a PhD in computer science from Computer Science and Engineering Department at the University of South Carolina. Dr. Huang is a member of IEEE, AAAI, SIAM, and a review board member of *Journal of Open Research on Information Systems (JORIS)*. He has served as a program committee member for several international conferences and is a technical paper reviewer for many journals and conferences. Dr. Huang's research interests include ontology matching/aligning, ontology quality, semantic integration, Web services, and service-oriented computing.

Michael N. Huhns is the NCR professor of computer science and engineering and director of the Center for Information Technology at the University of South Carolina. His degrees in electrical engineering are from the University of Michigan (BS) and the University of Southern California (MS and PhD). He is the author of six books and more than 200 papers in machine intelligence, including the recently coauthored textbook *Service-Oriented Computing: Semantics, Processes, Agents*. He serves on the editorial boards for eight journals, is a senior member of the ACM, and is a fellow of the IEEE.

Paul Jackson has been an IT industry practitioner for over twenty years. He has managed development of large software systems in diverse application areas in Australia and Germany. He has consulted to industry and public service organizations in strategic IS planning, IS-business alignment, and systems development. He joined Edith Cowan University in June 2002 as a lecturer in the School of MIS. He has a PhD in information systems development and his particular research interest is investigating knowledge and information management in projects from philosophical, social and cognitive perspectives to improve outcomes.

Ivan J. Jureta currently pursues PhD studies at the Information Management Research Unit, University of Namur, under the supervision of Stéphane Faulkner. In 2005, he received an MSc in management from Université de Louvain and a CEMS MSc in International Management from the London School of Economics and Political Science and Université de Louvain. His PhD research focuses on the specification and analysis of adaptive and open service-oriented systems.

Yannis Kalfoglou is a senior research fellow, School of Electronics and Computer Science, the University of Southampton. He received a PhD in AI from the University of Edinburgh, UK. He is working on the AKT (Advanced Knowledge Technologies) project. He was the principle investigator of an industrial project funded by Hewlett Packard, CROSI, which explored application of ontology mapping to industry. He is working on Semantic Web technologies, in particular, semantic interoperability and integration. Dr Kalfoglou has published over 49 works in leading journals, conferences, and specialized workshops in the areas of the Semantic Web, artificial intelligence, and knowledge engineering. He has served as member of various program and editorial committees for international journals and conferences, and refereed national projects for the Greek government. He organized a prestigious Dagstuhl seminar on semantic interoperability and integration. He is currently a member of the steering committee of the Ontology Alignment Evaluation Initiative (OAEI), a large international dissemination effort for ontology mapping technology.

Manuel Kolp is an associate professor in computer science at the Université catholique de Louvain, Belgium where he is head of the Information Systems Research Unit and coordinator of the Center of Excellence in Management and Information Technology. Dr. Kolp is also invited professor with the University of Brussels and the Universitary Faculties St. Louis of Brussels. His research work deals with agent architectures for ERP II systems. He was previously adjunct professor at the University of Toronto. He has been involved in the organization of international conferences such as CAiSE 2002 or VLDB 2004 and is cochair of workshops like AOIS. His publications include more than 50 refereed journals or periodicals and proceedings papers as well as three books.

Carol Kort obtained an MSc from the Free University Amsterdam in information sciences. Her MSc project was carried out in banking industry, to assess whether the e^3-value e-business modeling methodology is of use for reasoning about strategic partnerships.

Agnes Koschmider is a doctoral student/scientific coworker at the Institute of Applied Informatics and Formal Description Methods at University of Karlsruhe. Her primary research interests are user assistance systems for business process modeling and ontology based business processes. Koschmider studied economics with a main focus on information technology and information management. She graduated in 2003 at the Johann Wolfgang Goethe-University in Frankfurt/Main. She has been a member of several program committees in the area of business process management. She is an elected member of the executive committee of the Gesellschaft für Informatik.

Juhnyoung Lee is a research staff member at the IBM T.J. Watson Research Center in New York. He is currently working in the Business Informatics Group. He finished his PhD at the Department of Computer Science in the University of Virginia at Charlottesville in 1994. He received a BS and MS in computer science from Seoul National University in 1985 and 1987, respectively. Since joining IBM Research in 1997, he has worked on e-commerce intelligence, electronic marketplaces, decision support systems, semantic Web technologies, and ontology management systems. Before joining IBM, he was a researcher at Los Alamos National Lab in New Mexico and at Lexis-Nexis in Ohio. His current research interests include service science, engineering and management, business and IT modeling, cost and value estimation, model-driven business transformation, and Semantic Web.

Mikael Lind, associate professor, is with the University College of Borås and Linköping University, Sweden. He is the leader of the Informatics Department at the School of Business and Informatics in Borås. He is also associated to the research network VITS in Sweden. His current research interests are business process management, e-services, method engineering, codesign of business and IT, design and evaluation of business process oriented information systems, and research methods for information systems development. His research is mainly characterized by empirically driven theory and method development. He is involved in several action-research projects in different settings focusing business processes and information systems. He is associate editor for the open journal *Systems, Signs & Actions* (www.sysiac.org).

Rodrigo Magalhães is the academic director of Kuwait Maastricht Business School and invited associate professor at Instituto Superior Técnico of Lisbon. He holds a PhD in information systems from the London School of Economics, an MBA from Sheffield University, and an MA from Leeds Metropolitan University, UK. He is also lecturer in postgraduate programs at the Portuguese Catholic University (UCP) and at the Instituto Superior de Ciências do Trabalho e da Empresa (ISCTE) in Lisbon. He has been involved in consultancy projects in information systems and organization areas for over 20 years and has several books and publications on organizational change, knowledge management, organization learning, information systems management, business process management, and e-learning.

Fabio Massacci received an MEng in 1993 and a PhD in computer science and engineering at University of Rome "La Sapienza" in 1998. He visited Cambridge University in 1996-1997. He joined University of Siena as assistant professor in 1999 and was visiting researcher at IRIT Toulouse in 2000. In 2001 he joined the University of Trento as associate professor. In 2001 he received the Intelligenza Artificiale award, a young researchers career award from the Italian Association for Artificial Intelligence. He is member of AAAI, ACM, IEEE Computer society, and is a chartered engineer. His research interests are in automated reasoning at the crossroads between artificial intelligence and computer security. He has worked on automated deduction for modal and dynamic logics and their application to access control.

John Mylopoulos received a BEng from Brown University in 1966 and a PhD from Princeton in 1970, the year he joined the faculty of the University of Toronto. His research interests include requirements engineering, conceptual modeling, data semantics, and knowledge management. Mylopoulos is the recipient of the first-ever Outstanding Services Award given by the Canadian AI Society, a corecipient of the Best Paper Award of the 1994 International Conference on Software Engineering, a fellow of the American Association for AI, and the elected president of the VLDB Endowment (1997-2003). He is co-editor of the *Requirements Engineering Journal*. He has also contributed to the organization of major international conferences, including program cochair of the International Joint Conference of AI (1991), general chair of the Entity-Relationship conference (1994), program chair of the International IEEE Symposium of Requirements Engineering (1997), and general chair of the VLDB Conference (2004).

Andreas Oberweis received a Diploma in industrial engineering from the University of Karlsruhe in 1984 and a PhD in computer science from the University of Mannheim in 1990. From 1985 to 1995 he was a research assistant at the Universities of Darmstadt, Mannheim and Karlsruhe. In 1995 he received a Habilitation degree in applied computer science from the University of Karlsruhe. From 1995 to 2003 he was a full professor for information systems at Goethe-University in Frankfurt/Main. Since 2003 he has been a professor for applied informatics at the University of Karlsruhe. Since 2004 he has also been a director at the Research Center for Information Technologies (FZI) Karlsruhe.

H. Sofía Pinto (INESC-ALGOS researcher) is an assistant professor at the Department of Computer Science and Engineering of Instituto Superior Tecnico (IST) and a senior researcher at the Algos Group, INESC-ID. She holds a PhD in computer science/AI from IST. She has been an invited researcher at the Ontology Group at FI-Universidad Politécnica de Madrid, at the Knowledge Management Group of the AIFB Institute of the Karlsruhe University, and at the Semantic Web Group at Koblenz-Landau University. She has worked mainly in knowledge representation fields. She has published over 60 research papers on ontologies and other areas. She leads a research group on Ontologies and Semantic Web topics, Algos-Ontol. She has participated in several national and European projects.

Valentina Presutti is a research fellow at the Laboratory for Applied Ontology (http://www.loa-cnr.it) of the Institute for Cognitive Sciences and Technology (http://www.istc.cnr.it) at the Italian National Research Council (http://www.cnr.it). She received a PhD in computer science at the University of Bologna. Her research interests include ontology-driven software engineering, ontology engineering, and Semantic Web. She is currently working under the EU-funded ontology engineering project NeOn (http://www.neon-project.com).

Christophe Roche is a professor at the University of Savoie (France) and the director of the "Condillac" Research Group in Knowledge Engineering. He has been giving lectures on knowledge representation, logic, object-oriented languages, and ontology in Chambéry and in Paris since 1990. Roche previously worked in private research institutes in artificial intelligence for several years and was professor of AI at Neuchâtel University (Switzerland). His main works are about Aristotelian ontology and terminology for content management systems. He has published about 50 publications and he is currently involved in several European and industrial projects in knowledge economy.

Barry Smith is Julian Park distinguished professor of philosophy in the University at Buffalo (New York) and director of the Institute for Formal Ontology and Medical Information Science in Saarbrücken, Germany.

Smith's current research focus is ontology and its applications in biomedicine and biomedical informatics, where he is working on projects relating to biomedical terminologies and electronic health records.

Marcus Spies, born in 1956, is a professor of KM and enterprise computing at Munich University. He is currently on leave to the Digital Enterprise Research Institute (DERI), where he is a leading contributor to EU projects on service oriented computing and semantic services, especially in the financial services sector. Spies was research staff member and senior consultant at IBM for 14 years, were he authored a patent in language modeling for speech recognition. He originally graduated in cognitive science, earning a PhD in habilitation at Berlin Technical University. Spies has published over 50 publications in different areas related to statistical and semantic modeling. He is a member of IEEE and serves as program chair of the 2007 IEEE Enterprise Distributed Object Conference (EDOC) in Annapolis.

Dov Te'eni is a professor of information systems in the Faculty of Management at Tel-Aviv University, Israel. He is also the chairman of Meital – Israel's Higher Education E-Learning Center. Te'eni studies several related areas of information systems: human-computer interaction, computer support for communication, knowledge management, systems design, and non-profit organizations. His research usually combines model building, laboratory experiments, and development of prototypes like Spider and kMail. Te'eni is co-author of a new book on human-computer interaction for organizations published in 2007 by Wiley. He has published in journals such as *Management Science, MISQ, Organization Science, Communications of the ACM,* and in more specific journals of HCI such as *IJHCS, Behavior and Information Technology, Computers in Human Behavior,* and *IEEE Transactions.* Dov serves as Senior Editor for *MIS Quarterly* and associate editor for *Journal of AIS, Information and Organizations,* and *Internet Research.* He is conference co-chair of ICIS2008 (International Conference on Information Systems) to be held in Paris.

José Tribolet is a full professor of computer engineering and IT at Instituto Superior Técnico, Technical University of Lisbon, Portugal. He holds a PhD in electrical and computer engineering from the Massachusetts Institute of Technology. He was a visiting fellow at the Center for Coordination Sciences in MIT's Sloan School of Management (1998). He leads of the Organizational Engineering Center (CEO) at the Institute for Systems and Computer Engineering (INESC), a private sector, contract-based research organization, which he founded in 1980. He has been involved in several research and consultancy projects concerning organizational engineering, including organizing the ACM SAC Organizational Engineering special track.

Ray Webster has a PhD in educational research and has almost 25 years of experience in professional involvement in learning and teaching in many forms (FT, PT, industry, professional), at various levels (school, FE, UG, PG, professional) and in several countries (England, Malaysia, Australia). He has taught on Post Graduate Certificate in Education courses and has assessed students on teaching practice. His current and recent research is investigating student learning profiles and their impact on learning environment design.

Hadas Weinberger is an assistant professor of information systems in the Department of Instructional Technology at Holon Institute of Technology. She received a PhD from the Department of Information Science at Bar-Ilan University (2005), Israel, and an MLS (1996) from the Hebrew University of Jerusalem, Israel. Her research involves several related areas of information systems: knowledge management and organizational memory, ontology design and evaluation, information retrieval, and Web technologies. She participated in a research for the Ministry of Science of the Israeli government (1995), in the area of information architecture and digital library. She was visiting doctoral student at the Institute of Information Systems research at the University of Koblenz-Landau (2003). She has published in important national and international conferences and workshops of the IS community (ECIS 2000; E-CSCW 2001; ECIS 2003; MKWI 2006).

Peter Weiß is a research associate at the University of Karlsruhe (TH) in Germany. He is project manager at the Institute of Applied Informatics and Formal Description Methods (AIFB). He joined the research group of Dr. Wolffried Stucky in 2004. He received a PhD in applied informatics from the University of Karlsruhe (TH) in 2005. Prior to joining AIFB, he was leading the international relations office at the FZI Research Center for Information Technologies in Karlsruhe, Germany. His educational and professional background include a diploma degree in Business Engineering from the University of Karlsruhe (TH) (1999) and a certificate of apprenticeship as Industrial Clerk (1992) from a leading manufacturer of diesel engines and drive systems in Germany.

Norbert Weißenberg received his diploma in computer science from the University of Dortmund in 1985. Then he was a research assistant at the Information Science Department of that university where he worked on different projects on the development of a performance modeling and evaluation tool. Since 1992 he has been a researcher at Fraunhofer ISST Dortmund. He was involved in many projects and in particular on projects FLAME2008 and its successor COMPASS2008. He is the author of the ModelAccess component. His current interests are ontologies, semantic service descriptions, and semantic matching in the context of information logistics.

Manfred Wojciechowski has been a research scientist at Fraunhofer ISST since 1996 when he received his diploma in computer science from the University of Dortmund. Currently he is a group leader responsible for the development of an information logistical service platform. In 2004 he was a representative of Fraunhofer ISST in Beijing, working as an Assistant Director of SIGSIT in Beijing. There he was working on context awareness and software integration within the COMPASS2008 project. At the same time he was busy in building networks towards other European R&D teams in China. His areas of expertise include multimedia, database design, software architectures, Internet, information logistical applications, and context awareness.

Wolfram Wöß received an MSc in computer science from the Johannes Kepler University of Linz (JKU) in 1993 and joined the "Institute for Applied Knowledge Processing (FAW)." In 1996 he received a PhD. Between 1990 and 1993 he gained industrial experiences in an Austrian medium-sized company. In 2002 he got his professorship (habilitation) in applied computer science. Wöß is now vice head of the FAW institute. His research and teaching work covers topics in the field of advanced information systems, e-business and process management, Grid-computing, accessibility, context and semantic awareness, and Web semantics. Wöß has published in scientific journals and conference proceedings on these topics. He is also member of numerous program committees and program chair of the International Conference on Warehousing and Knowledge Discovery (DaWaK, 2003 and 2004) as well as chair of the International Workshop Web Semantics (WebS) in 2003-2007. During his work at the FAW, he managed industrial as well as national funded projects in the areas of computer integrated manufacturing, process management, medical information systems and advanced information systems.

Marielba Zacarias is a lecturer of information systems, software engineering and data base systems at the Algarve University, Faro, Portugal. She holds an MSc in IS from Simón Bolívar University of Venezuela and has background education on computer sciences. She has a professional experience of over 20 year in the IS field, both as a developer and project manager. Currently, she is a PhD candidate at the Instituto Superior Técnico, Technical University of Lisbon, Portugal. Her research work focuses the development of a conceptual framework to enable the dynamic alignment between individuals and organizations, and she has written six scientific papers on this topic.

Nicola Zannone received an MS in computer science at the University of Verona in 2003. He is currently a PhD student in the Department of Information and Communication Technology at the University of Trento. He visited the Center for Secure Information Systems at George Mason University in 2005 and the IBM Zurich Research Laboratory in 2006. He received the IBM PhD Fellowship Award for the 2006-2007 Academic Year. His research interests include computer security and formal verification. He is mostly interested in security requirements engineering, and, in particular, in the application of formal analysis techniques to the design of socio-technical systems.

Index